ERIC CLAPTON
DAY BY DAY

ERIC CLAPTON
DAY BY DAY

The Later Years, 1983-2013

MARC ROBERTY

An Imprint of Hal Leonard Corporation

Published in 2013 by Backbeat Books
An Imprint of Hal Leonard Corporation
7777 West Bluemound Road
Milwaukee, WI 53213

Trade Book Division Editorial Offices
33 Plymouth St., Montclair, NJ 07042

Every reasonable effort has been made to contact copyright holders and secure permissions. Omissions can be remedied in future editions.

All images are from the author's collection unless otherwise noted.

Photo credits can be found on pages 413–414, which constitute an extension of this copyright page.

Book design by Kristina Rolander

Book production by March Tenth, Inc.

Printed in the United States of America

Library of Congress Cataloging-in-Publication Data is available upon request.

ISBN 978-1-61713-053-3

www.backbeatbooks.com

CONTENTS

There are many people I need to thank for their help with this massive project: Mal Barker, Nigel Carroll, Rita DeVries, Michael Eaton, Tony Edser, Barry Fisch, Boris Jaeggi, Cecil Offley, Mike Sawin, Stephanie Lynne Thorburn, Larry Yelen, Steve Weintraub, Linda Wnek, and Andy Zwick.

I would like to thank the following, whom I have interviewed and spoken with for this project over the years: Jon Astley, Terry Britten, Gary Brooker, Jeff Beck, Anina Capaldi, Nigel Carroll, Oscar Castro-Neves, Gustavo Celis, Eric Clapton, Alan Darby, Stuart Epps, Vic Flick, Joe Hadlock, Tom Hambridge, George Harrsion, Cory Hart, Aaron Hurwitz, Andy Jackson, Glyn Johns, Mike Kappus, Jim Keltner, David Leaf, Albert Lee, Bill Levenson, Marcy Levy, Mark Linett, David Mackay, Doug McClement, Peter Moore, Mike Moran, Peter Moshay, Yoni Nameri, Michael Omartian, Bob Pritt, Jimmy Rip, Bub Roberts, John Robinson, Maggie Ryder, Mike Sanchez, Paul Stewart, Dave Swift, Stephen Taylor, John Taylor, Russ Titelman, and Bobby Whitlock.

A big thank you to the following photographers, who have been so generous in allowing me to use their amazing photos: Simon Bell, Gustavo Celis, Paul Cook, Rita DeVries, Joe Hadlock, Chikahiko Inden, John Peck, Mike Sawin, and Lynda Vollmer.

All of these photos remain the copyright of all the named photographers and cannot be reproduced without permission from the individual photographers.

As in volume 1, I would like to especially thank Karen Daws for all her help and patience during the last few years.

This second volume starts in 1983, in many ways a new start for Eric with a new band and new album. You could argue that Eric's most creative and exciting period can be found in the first volume, but that would be a little short-sighted. Those years were very much development years with Eric searching for his voice. The next three decades would offer fans many surprises and some of his most successful and memorable music.

At the time of this writing it appears that Eric will be retiring from lengthy tours and any live appearances after he reaches the age of seventy. As a music fan I hope that he will continue to make music, but equally I appreciate that he certainly deserves his retirement after providing so much pleasure to so many people over the last fifty years.

Whatever happens, I hope that these two volumes will provide the reader with new information and hopefully inspire them to look into some previously unexplored Eric Clapton music.

ERIC CLAPTON
DAY BY DAY

1983

By 1983 Eric Clapton was enjoying lengthy periods of sobriety and spending most of his spare time fly-fishing. What he was not doing was writing songs. The year would turn out to be a dryspell for him in terms of writing. With a new album in the can ready for release, Eric flew out to Los Angeles on 10 January to start rehearsing for a month-long tour of the U.S. The new band consisted of Donald "Duck" Dunn on bass, Roger Hawkins on drums, Albert Lee on guitar—all of whom had been on the *Money and Cigarettes* album sessions—and the welcome return of Chris Stainton on keyboards.

Eric had come to know Ry Cooder during the sessions for *Money and Cigarettes* in 1982. He liked Ry and had long admired his style of playing. Ry seemed an obvious choice to be the support act for Eric on the 1983 U.S. tour. As Eric was now hardly drinking, certainly not on the road, anyway, his performances were a lot tighter than those on the tours between 1980 and 1982. That said, his guitar tone was lacking fire and passion, but at least he was much more out front, confident, and getting favorable reviews.

As the new album was called *Money and Cigarettes* the marketing men thought it would make sense to have a big cigarette company come on board and promote the tour. After some negotiations the U.S. tour ended up being sponsored by Camel cigarettes, which caused a certain amount of controversy. The American Lung Association felt that Eric was neglecting his social responsibilities as a famous person by encouraging people to buy cigarettes. Clearly they were a little misguided, as the advertising was obviously aimed at encouraging existing smokers

to change brands. Ironically for Camel, Eric is seen with a pack of Rothmans on the front cover of the album. Actually, the cover is one of Eric's best, offering a Dali-meets-Magritte image with a melting Strat on an ironing board.

Roger Hawkins, the well-respected Muscle Shoals drummer, decided to quit the tour after only a couple of weeks as he was finding touring a little too hard. He had been off the road for ten years since playing with Traffic. He admitted that he hated the traveling, and this, coupled with the fact that he was not able to bring his family along, spurred his decision to return to Muscle Shoals. Jamie Oldaker, who had been Eric's drummer in the seventies, stepped in and played on the remainder of the tour. Surprisingly, Ry Cooder only jammed with Eric once on the tour, in Philadelphia on an encore of "Crossroads." They sounded great together, so it is surprising that they didn't get together more on the tour.

Later in the year Eric celebrated his twentieth anniversary as a recording artist in style. He decided to play a couple of high-profile shows at the prestigious Royal Albert Hall in London along with some of his famous mates. The presence of Jeff Beck and Jimmy Page in the lineup certainly made headlines as this would be the first time all three of the Yardbirds' guitarists would be on the same stage since 1966 when they had all jammed together with John Mayall. As well as celebrating his twentieth anniversary, the shows would be played for charity. The first night was for Action Research for Multiple Sclerosis, which was a charity that Ronnie Lane was trying to help establish in England as he was an MS victim. The second night would benefit the Prince's Trust, the first of several events that Eric would participate in for that charity.

At first the idea was for all the musicians to loosely jam on standards, but things developed into a more formal format. All the musicians were really involved in the whole process, and a great sense of camaraderie prevailed over the rehearsals for the Royal Albert Hall shows. The rehearsals took place at Glyn Johns's Warnham Lodge Farm in East Sussex in September. The only disappointment was the absence of Rod Stewart, who was of course lead singer in the Faces with Ronnie Lane. He had flown in to London a few days before the first show at the Royal Albert Hall declaring to all who would listen that he was in town to help and support his old friend. He never showed, and Eric went apoplectic, especially as Rod was spotted skulking out of the country with a mystery blonde a few days later while avoiding the press and offering no excuse for his no-show. In fact Rod was very unpopular with most of the musicians at the show and several admitted that they would have walked off if he had turned up. Ronnie recalled: "The first I heard about Rod playing was when I read it in the papers. That was also the last I heard about it!" He was very disappointed that Rod let him down.

The anger towards Rod Stewart extended on to the U.S. portion of the ARMS Tour where instructions were given to security to eject the tartan legend should he dare show his face. One welcome surprise guest at the New York shows was Ronnie Wood, who had been the guitarist in the Faces.

MONEY AND CIGARETTES U.S. TOUR 1983 (First leg)

BAND LINEUP:
Eric Clapton: guitar, vocals
Roger Hawkins: drums (until 15 February)
Jamie Oldaker: drums (from 17 February)
Chris Stainton: keyboards
Donald "Duck" Dunn: bass
Albert Lee: guitar, vocals

SUPPORT LINEUP:
Ry Cooder: vocals, guitar
John Hiatt: guitar
Steve Douglas: saxophone
Jim Dickinson: keyboards

Jim Keltner: drums
Bobby King: backing vocals
Willie Green: backing vocals

FEBRUARY 1983

1 February 1983, Paramount Theater, Seattle, Washington (with Ry Cooder)

SETLIST: After Midnight / I Shot The Sheriff / Crazy Country Hop / Pretty Girl / Slow Down Linda / Lay Down Sally / Wonderful Tonight / Sweet Little Lisa / Key To The Highway / Tulsa Time / Nobody Knows You When You're Down And Out / I've Got A Rock 'N' Roll Heart / Crosscut Saw / Cocaine / Blues Power / That's All Right / Have You Ever Loved A Woman / Ramblin' On My Mind / Let It Rain / Layla / Further On Up The Road

2 February 1983, Paramount Theater, Seattle, Washington (with Ry Cooder)

SETLIST: After Midnight / I Shot The Sheriff / Crazy Country Hop / Crosscut Saw / Slow Down Linda / Pretty Girl / Sweet Little Lisa / Key To The Highway / Tulsa Time / I've Got A Rock 'N' Roll Heart / Wonderful Tonight / Cocaine / Blues Power / That's All Right / Have You Ever Loved A Woman / Ramblin' On My Mind / Let It Rain / Layla / Further On Up The Road

3 February 1983, Memorial Coliseum, Portland, Oregon (with Ry Cooder)

SETLIST: After Midnight / I Shot The Sheriff / Worried Life Blues / Crazy Country Hop / Crosscut Saw / Slow Down Linda / Sweet Little Lisa / Key To The Highway / Tulsa Time / I've Got A Rock 'N' Roll Heart / Wonderful Tonight / Blues Power / That's All Right / Have You Ever Loved A Woman / Ramblin' On My Mind / Let It Rain / Cocaine / Layla / Further On Up The Road

6 February 1983, Memorial Auditorium, Sacramento, California (with Ry Cooder)

SETLIST: After Midnight / I Shot The Sheriff / Worried Life Blues / Crazy Country Hop / Crosscut Saw / Slow Down Linda / Sweet Little Lisa / Key To The Highway / Tulsa Time / I've Got A Rock 'N' Roll Heart / Wonderful Tonight / Blues Power / That's All Right / Have You Ever

Loved A Woman / Ramblin' On My Mind / Let It Rain / Cocaine / Layla / Further On Up The Road

7 February 1983, Cow Palace, San Francisco, California (with Ry Cooder)

SETLIST: After Midnight / I Shot The Sheriff / Worried Life Blues / Crazy Country Hop / Crosscut Saw / Slow Down Linda / Sweet Little Lisa / Key To The Highway / Tulsa Time / I've Got A Rock 'N' Roll Heart / Wonderful Tonight / Blues Power / Have You Ever Loved A Woman / Ramblin' On My Mind / Let It Rain / Cocaine / Layla / Further On Up The Road

8 February 1983, Universal Amphitheatre, Los Angeles, California (with Ry Cooder)

SETLIST: After Midnight / I Shot The Sheriff / Worried Life Blues / Crazy Country Hop / Crosscut Saw / Slow Down Linda / Sweet Little Lisa / Key To The Highway / Tulsa Time / I've Got A Rock 'N' Roll Heart / Wonderful Tonight / Blues Power / That's All Right / Have You Ever Loved A Woman / Ramblin' On My Mind / Let It Rain / Cocaine / Layla / Further On Up The Road

9 February 1983, Long Beach Arena, Long Beach, California (with Ry Cooder)

SETLIST: After Midnight / I Shot The Sheriff / Worried Life Blues / Crazy Country Hop / Slow Down Linda / Sweet Little Lisa / Key To The Highway / I've Got A Rock 'N' Roll Heart / Wonderful Tonight / Blues Power / That's All Right / Have You Ever Loved A Woman / Ramblin' On My Mind / Let It Rain / Cocaine / Layla / Further On Up The Road

11 February 1983, Veterans Memorial Coliseum, Phoenix, Arizona (with Ry Cooder)

SETLIST: After Midnight / I Shot The Sheriff / Worried Life Blues / Key To The Highway / Tulsa Time / I've Got A Rock 'N' Roll Heart / Wonderful Tonight / Blues Power / That's All Right / Have You Ever Loved A Woman / Ramblin' On My Mind / Let It Rain / Cocaine / Layla / Further On Up The Road

13 February 1983, Frank Erwin Center, Austin, Texas (with Ry Cooder)

SETLIST: After Midnight / I Shot The Sheriff / Worried Life Blues / Slow Down Linda / Lay Down Sally / Sweet Little Lisa / Key To The Highway / Tulsa Time / I've Got A Rock 'N' Roll Heart / Wonderful Tonight / Blues Power / That's All Right / Have You Ever Loved A Woman / Ramblin' On My Mind / Let It Rain / Layla / Cocaine / Further On Up The Road

14 February 1983, Summit, Houston, Texas (with Ry Cooder)

SETLIST: After Midnight / I Shot The Sheriff / Worried Life Blues / Slow Down Linda / Lay Down Sally / Sweet Little Lisa / Key To The Highway / Tulsa Time / I've Got A Rock 'N' Roll Heart / Wonderful Tonight / Blues Power / That's All Right / Ramblin' On My Mind / Have You Ever Loved A Woman / Let It Rain / Layla / Cocaine / Further On Up The Road

15 February 1983, Reunion Arena, Dallas, Texas (with Ry Cooder) (last show with Roger Hawkins)

SETLIST: After Midnight / I Shot The Sheriff / Worried Life Blues / Slow Down Linda / Lay Down Sally / Sweet Little Lisa / Key To The Highway / Tulsa Time / I've Got A Rock 'N' Roll Heart / Wonderful Tonight / Blues Power / That's All Right / Ramblin' On My Mind / Have You Ever Loved A Woman / Let It Rain / Layla / Cocaine / Further On Up The Road

17 February 1983, Mid-South Coliseum, Memphis, Tennessee (with Ry Cooder) (drummer Jamie Oldaker joins the band as replacement for Roger Hawkins)

SETLIST: After Midnight / I Shot The Sheriff / Worried Life Blues / Slow Down Linda / Lay Down Sally / Let It Rain / Sweet Little Lisa / Key To The Highway / Tulsa Time / I've Got A Rock 'N' Roll Heart / Wonderful Tonight / Blues Power / That's All Right / Have You Ever Loved A Woman / Ramblin' On My Mind / Layla / Cocaine / Further On Up The Road

18 February 1983, Kiel Auditorium, St. Louis, Missouri (with Ry Cooder)

SETLIST: After Midnight / I Shot The Sheriff / Worried Life Blues / Slow Down Linda / Lay Down Sally / Let It Rain / Sweet Little Lisa / Key To The Highway / Tulsa Time / I've Got A Rock 'N' Roll Heart / Wonderful Tonight

/ Blues Power / That's All Right / Have You Ever Loved A Woman / Ramblin' On My Mind / Layla / Cocaine / Further On Up The Road

19 February 1983, Hara Arena, Dayton, Ohio (with Ry Cooder)

SETLIST: After Midnight / I Shot The Sheriff / Worried Life Blues / Slow Down Linda / Lay Down Sally / Let It Rain / Sweet Little Lisa / Key To The Highway / Tulsa Time / I've Got A Rock 'N' Roll Heart / Wonderful Tonight / Blues Power / That's All Right / Have You Ever Loved A Woman / Ramblin' On My Mind / Layla / Cocaine / Further On Up The Road

21 February 1983, Spectrum, Philadelphia, Pennsylvania (with Ry Cooder)

SETLIST: After Midnight / I Shot The Sheriff / Worried Life Blues / Slow Down Linda / Lay Down Sally / Let It Rain / Pink Bedroom / Key To The Highway / Tulsa Time / I've Got A Rock 'N' Roll Heart / Wonderful Tonight / Blues Power / That's All Right / Have You Ever Loved A Woman / Ramblin' On My Mind / Cocaine / Layla / Crossroads[1]

[1] with Ry Cooder on guitar and vocals

22 February 1983, Brendan Byrne Arena, East Rutherford, New Jersey (with Ry Cooder)

SETLIST: After Midnight / I Shot The Sheriff / Worried Life Blues / Slow Down Linda / Lay Down Sally / Let It Rain / Pink Bedroom / Key To The Highway / Tulsa Time / I've Got A Rock 'N' Roll Heart / Wonderful Tonight / Blues Power / That's All Right / Have You Ever Loved A Woman / Ramblin' On My Mind / Cocaine / Layla / Further On Up The Road

25 February 1983, Omni, Atlanta, Georgia (with Ry Cooder)

SETLIST: After Midnight / I Shot The Sheriff / Worried Life Blues / Slow Down Linda / Lay Down Sally / Let It Rain / Sweet Little Lisa / Key To The Highway / Tulsa Time / I've Got A Rock 'N' Roll Heart / Wonderful Tonight / Blues Power / That's All Right / Have You Ever Loved A Woman / Ramblin' On My Mind / Cocaine / Layla / Further On Up The Road

26 February 1983, Louisville Gardens, Louisville, Kentucky (with Ry Cooder)

SETLIST: After Midnight / I Shot The Sheriff / Worried Life Blues / Slow Down Linda / Lay Down Sally / Let It Rain / Pink Bedroom / Key To The Highway / Tulsa Time / I've Got A Rock 'N' Roll Heart / Wonderful Tonight / Blues Power / That's All Right / Have You Ever Loved A Woman / Ramblin' On My Mind / Cocaine / Layla / Further On Up The Road

28 February 1983, Capital Centre, Largo, Washington, D.C. (with Ry Cooder)

SETLIST: After Midnight / I Shot The Sheriff / Worried Life Blues / Slow Down Linda / Lay Down Sally / Let It Rain / Pink Bedroom / Key To The Highway / Tulsa Time / I've Got A Rock 'N' Roll Heart / Wonderful Tonight / Blues Power / That's All Right / Have You Ever Loved A Woman / Ramblin' On My Mind / Cocaine / Layla / Further On Up The Road

MARCH 1983

1 March 1983, Centrum, Worcester, Massachusetts (with Ry Cooder)

SETLIST: After Midnight / I Shot The Sheriff / Worried Life Blues / Slow Down Linda / Lay Down Sally / Let It Rain / Key To The Highway / Tulsa Time / I've Got A Rock 'N' Roll Heart / Wonderful Tonight / Blues Power / That's All Right / Have You Ever Loved A Woman / Ramblin' On My Mind / Cocaine / Layla / Further On Up The Road

2 March 1983, Hershey Park Arena, Hershey, Pennsylvania (with Ry Cooder)

SETLIST: After Midnight / I Shot The Sheriff / Worried Life Blues / Slow Down Linda / Lay Down Sally / Let It Rain / Sweet Little Lisa / Key To The Highway / Tulsa Time / I've Got A Rock 'N' Roll Heart / Wonderful Tonight / Blues Power / That's All Right / Have You Ever Loved A Woman / Ramblin' On My Mind / Cocaine / Layla / Further On Up The Road

3 March 1983, Civic Arena, Pittsburgh, Pennsylvania (with Ry Cooder)

SETLIST: not known

4 March 1983, Eric returns to England

MONEY AND CIGARETTES UK / EUROPEAN TOUR 1983

BAND LINEUP:
Eric Clapton: guitar, vocals
Jamie Oldaker: drums
Chris Stainton: keyboards
Donald "Duck" Dunn: bass
Albert Lee: guitar, vocals

APRIL 1983

3 April 1983–6 April 1983, rehearsals at Easyhire, London

8 April 1983, Playhouse, Edinburgh, Scotland

SETLIST: Tulsa Time / I Shot The Sheriff / Worried Life Blues / Ain't Going Down / Let It Rain / Double Trouble / Pink Bedroom / Key To The Highway / After Midnight / The Shape You're In / Wonderful Tonight / Blues Power / Ramblin' On My Mind / Have You Ever Loved A Woman / Cocaine / Layla / Crossroads

9 April 1983, Playhouse, Edinburgh, Scotland

SETLIST: Tulsa Time / I Shot The Sheriff / Lay Down Sally / Worried Life Blues / Let It Rain / Ain't Going Down / Double Trouble / Key To The Highway / After Midnight / The Shape You're In / Wonderful Tonight / Blues Power / Ramblin' On My Mind / Have You Ever Loved A Woman / Cocaine / Layla / Further On Up The Road

11 April 1983, City Hall, Newcastle-Upon-Tyne

SETLIST: Tulsa Time / I Shot The Sheriff / I've Got A Rock 'N' Roll Heart / Worried Life Blues / Ain't Going Down / Let It Rain / Double Trouble / Sweet Little Lisa / Key To The Highway / After Midnight / The Shape You're In / Wonderful Tonight / Blues Power / Ramblin' On My Mind / Have You Ever Loved A Woman / Cocaine / Layla / Further On Up The Road

12 April 1983, Empire, Liverpool

SETLIST: Tulsa Time / I Shot The Sheriff / Lay Down Sally / Worried Life Blues / Ain't Going Down / Let It Rain / Double Trouble / Pink Bedroom / Key To The Highway / After Midnight / The Shape You're In / Wonderful Tonight / Blues Power / Ramblin' On My Mind / That's All Right / Have You Ever Loved A Woman / Cocaine / Layla / Further On Up The Road

14 April 1983, National Stadium, Dublin, Ireland

SETLIST: Tulsa Time / I Shot The Sheriff / Lay Down Sally / Worried Life Blues / Ain't Going Down / Let It Rain / Double Trouble / Sweet Little Lisa / Key To The Highway / After Midnight / The Shape You're In / Wonderful Tonight / Blues Power / Ramblin' On My Mind / Have You Ever Loved A Woman / Cocaine / Layla / Further On Up The Road

15 April 1983, National Stadium, Dublin, Ireland

SETLIST: Tulsa Time / I Shot The Sheriff / Lay Down Sally / Worried Life Blues / Let It Rain / Double Trouble / Sweet Little Lisa / After Midnight / The Shape You're In / Wonderful Tonight / Blues Power / Ramblin' On My Mind / Have You Ever Loved A Woman / Cocaine / Layla / Further On Up The Road

16 April 1983, National Stadium, Dublin, Ireland

SETLIST: Tulsa Time / I Shot The Sheriff / Lay Down Sally / Worried Life Blues / Let It Rain / Double Trouble / Sweet Little Lisa / After Midnight / The Shape You're In / Wonderful Tonight / Blues Power / Ramblin' On My Mind / Have You Ever Loved A Woman / Cocaine / Layla / Further On Up The Road

19 April 1983, Eric and band fly to Bremen, Germany, for start of European tour

20 April 1983, Stadthalle, Bremen, Germany

SETLIST: Tulsa Time / I Shot The Sheriff / Lay Down Sally / Worried Life Blues / Let It Rain / Double Trouble / Sweet Little Lisa / After Midnight / The Shape You're In / Wonderful Tonight / Blues Power / Ramblin' On My Mind / Have You Ever Loved A Woman / Cocaine / Layla / Further On Up The Road

21 April 1983, Grugahalle, Essen, Germany

SETLIST: Tulsa Time / I Shot The Sheriff / Lay Down Sally / Worried Life Blues / Let It Rain / Double Trouble / Sweet Little Lisa / Key To The Highway / The Shape You're In / Wonderful Tonight / Blues Power / Ramblin' On My Mind / Have You Ever Loved A Woman / Cocaine / Layla / Further On Up The Road

23 April 1983, Ahoy Hall, Rotterdam, Netherlands

SETLIST: Tulsa Time / I Shot The Sheriff / Lay Down Sally / Worried Life Blues / Let It Rain / Double Trouble / Sweet Little Lisa / Key To The Highway / After Midnight / The Shape You're In / Wonderful Tonight / Blues Power / Ramblin' On My Mind / Have You Ever Loved A Woman / Cocaine / Layla / Further On Up The Road / Crossroads

24 April 1983, Chapiteau De Pantin, Paris, France

SETLIST: Tulsa Time / I Shot The Sheriff / Lay Down Sally / Worried Life Blues / Let It Rain / Double Trouble / Sweet Little Lisa / Key To The Highway / After Midnight / The Shape You're In / Wonderful Tonight / Blues Power / Ramblin' On My Mind / Have You Ever Loved A Woman / Cocaine / Layla / Further On Up The Road / Crossroads

26 April 1983, Sporthalle, Köln, Germany

SETLIST: Tulsa Time / I Shot The Sheriff / Lay Down Sally / Worried Life Blues / Let It Rain / Double Trouble / Sweet Little Lisa / Key To The Highway / After Midnight / The Shape You're In / Wonderful Tonight / Blues Power / Ramblin' On My Mind / Have You Ever Loved A Woman / Cocaine / Layla / Further On Up The Road

27 April 1983, Festhalle, Frankfurt, Germany

SETLIST: Tulsa Time / I Shot The Sheriff / Lay Down Sally / Worried Life Blues / Let It Rain / Double Trouble / Sweet Little Lisa / Key To The Highway / After Midnight / The Shape You're In / Wonderful Tonight / Blues Power / Ramblin' On My Mind / Have You Ever Loved A Woman / Cocaine / Layla / Further On Up The Road

29 April 1983, Rhein-Neckar-Halle, Heidelberg, Germany

SETLIST: Tulsa Time / I Shot The Sheriff / Lay Down Sally / Worried Life Blues / Let It Rain / Double Trouble / Sweet Little Lisa / Key To The Highway / After Midnight / The Shape You're In / Wonderful Tonight / Blues Power / That's All Right / Have You Ever Loved A Woman / Ramblin' On My Mind / Cocaine / Layla / Further On Up The Road

30 April 1983, St. Jakob Sportshalle, Basel, Switzerland

SETLIST: Tulsa Time / I Shot The Sheriff / Worried Life Blues / Lay Down Sally / Let It Rain / Double Trouble / Sweet Little Lisa / Key To The Highway / Wonderful Tonight / The Shape You're In / After Midnight / Blues Power / That's All Right / Have You Ever Loved A Woman / Ramblin' On My Mind / Cocaine / Layla / Further On Up The Road

> "In 1983 Eric had his concert in Basel and invited me after the show to the hotel and next morning for breakfast at the hotel, during our breakfast Eric got the telephone call from Pattie [Boyd] that Muddy Waters died that night. Eric was shocked and tears were running down his face. By coincidence there was an exhibition of musical instruments at the Hilton, but still closed in the morning. I asked the manager to open up the door. Eric, the manager, and myself entered in the room, which was full of instruments. Eric took an acoustic guitar and started playing the blues because he was so sad about the death of Muddy."
>
> —BORIS JAEGGI
> (friend of Eric's)

MAY 1983

2 May 1983, Palaeur, Rome, Italy

SETLIST: Tulsa Time / I Shot The Sheriff / Worried Life Blues / Lay Down Sally / Let It Rain / Double Trouble / Sweet Little Lisa / Key To The Highway / After Midnight / The Shape You're In / Wonderful Tonight / Blues Power / That's All Right / Have You Ever Loved A Woman / Ramblin' On My Mind / Cocaine / Layla / Crossroads / Further On Up The Road

3 May 1983, Palasport di Genova, Genova, Italy

SETLIST: Tulsa Time / I Shot The Sheriff / Worried Life Blues / Lay Down Sally / Let It Rain / Double Trouble / Sweet Little Lisa / Key To The Highway / After Midnight / The Shape You're In / Wonderful Tonight / Blues Power / Honey Bee / Have You Ever Loved A Woman / Ramblin' On My Mind / Cocaine / Layla / Further On Up The Road / Crossroads

Eric Clapton at the Hammersmith Odeon in May 1983.

5 May 1983, Palais Des Sports, Toulouse, France

SETLIST: not known

7 May 1983, Palacio Municipal De Deportes, Barcelona, Spain

SETLIST: not known

8 May 1983, Velódromo de Anoeta, San Sebastián, Spain

SETLIST: Tulsa Time / I Shot The Sheriff / Worried Life Blues / Lay Down Sally / Let It Rain / Double Trouble / Sweet Little Lisa / Key To The Highway / After Midnight / The Shape You're In / Wonderful Tonight / Blues Power / Ramblin' On My Mind / Have You Ever Loved A Woman / Cocaine / Layla / Further On Up The Road

9 May 1983, Eric and band fly back to England

13 May 1983, Cornwall Coliseum, St. Austell, Cornwall

SETLIST: not known

14 May 1983, Arts Centre, Poole, Dorset

SETLIST: Tulsa Time / I Shot The Sheriff / Worried Life Blues / Lay Down Sally / Double Trouble / Sweet Little Lisa / Key To The Highway / After Midnight / The Shape

You're In / Wonderful Tonight / Blues Power / Standing Around Crying / Have You Ever Loved A Woman / Ramblin' On My Mind / Cocaine / Layla / Further On Up The Road

16 May 1983, Hammersmith Odeon Theatre, London

SETLIST: Tulsa Time / I Shot The Sheriff / Worried Life Blues / Lay Down Sally / Let It Rain / Double Trouble / Sweet Little Lisa / Key To The Highway / After Midnight / The Shape You're In / Wonderful Tonight / Blues Power / Honey Bee / Have You Ever Loved A Woman / Ramblin' On My Mind / Cocaine / Layla / Further On Up The Road

17 May 1983, Hammersmith Odeon Theatre, London

SETLIST: Tulsa Time / I Shot The Sheriff / Worried Life Blues / Lay Down Sally / Let It Rain / Double Trouble / Sweet Little Lisa / Key To The Highway / After Midnight / The Shape You're In / Wonderful Tonight / Blues Power / Honey Bee / Have You Ever Loved A Woman / Ramblin' On My Mind / Cocaine / Layla / Further On Up The Road

18 May 1983, Hammersmith Odeon Theatre, London

SETLIST: Tulsa Time / I Shot The Sheriff / Worried Life Blues / Lay Down Sally / Let It Rain / Double Trouble / Sweet Little Lisa / Key To The Highway / After Midnight / The Shape You're In / Wonderful Tonight / Blues Power / That's All Right / Have You Ever Loved A Woman / Ramblin' On My Mind / Cocaine / Layla / Further On Up The Road

19 May 1983, Hammersmith Odeon Theatre, London

SETLIST: Tulsa Time / I Shot The Sheriff / Worried Life Blues / Lay Down Sally / Let It Rain / Double Trouble / Sweet Little Lisa / Key To The Highway / After Midnight / The Shape You're In / Wonderful Tonight / Blues Power / Ramblin' On My Mind / Have You Ever Loved A Woman / Cocaine / Layla / Further On Up The Road

21 May 1983, Apollo Theatre, Manchester

SETLIST: Tulsa Time / I Shot The Sheriff / Worried Life Blues / Lay Down Sally / Let It Rain / Double Trouble / Sweet Little Lisa / Key To The Highway / After Midnight / The Shape You're In / Wonderful Tonight / Blues Power /

Ramblin' On My Mind / Have You Ever Loved A Woman / Cocaine / Layla / Further On Up The Road

22 May 1983, De Montford Hall, Leicester, Leicestershire

SETLIST: Tulsa Time / I Shot The Sheriff / Worried Life Blues / Lay Down Sally / Let It Rain / Double Trouble / Sweet Little Lisa / Key To The Highway / After Midnight / The Shape You're In / Wonderful Tonight / Blues Power / That's All Right / Ramblin' On My Mind / Have You Ever Loved A Woman / Cocaine / Layla / Further On Up The Road

23 May 1983, Civic Hall, Guildford, Surrey (amazing hometown gig with special guests joining in the fun. The biggest surprise was the appearance of the elusive Jimmy Page who had been out of the public eye for several years since the death of Led Zeppelin drummer John Bonham. It was wonderful to see him on a live stage again. The next time fans would see Jimmy would be at the ARMS and Prince's Trust shows at the Royal Albert Hall in September)

SETLIST: Tulsa Time / I Shot The Sheriff / Worried Life Blues / Lay Down Sally / Let It Rain / Double Trouble / Sweet Little Lisa / The Shape You're In / Wonderful Tonight / Blues Power / Sad Sad Day / Have You Ever Loved A Woman / Ramblin' On My Mind / Layla / Further On Up The Road[1,2] / Cocaine[1,2] / Roll Over Beethoven[1,2,3] / You Win Again[1,2,3,4] / Matchbox[1,2,3,4] / Goodnight Irene[1,2,3,4]

[1]with Jimmy Page on guitar
[2]with Phil Collins on drums
[3]with Chas Hodges and Dave Peacock on vocals
[4]with Paul Brady on acoustic guitar and vocals

JUNE 1983

SAVE THE CHILDREN BENEFIT

5 June 1983, New Victoria Theatre, London (Save The Children Benefit Concert with Chas and Dave with Eric guesting)

SETLIST: Tulsa Time / Stormy Monday / Further On Up The Road / Goodnight Irene / Roll Over Beethoven

MONEY AND CIGARETTES U.S. TOUR 1983 (Second leg)

24 June 1983, rehearsals in Toronto, Ontario, Canada

25 June 1983, Kingswood Music Theater, Toronto, Ontario, Canada (with the Blasters)

SETLIST: not known

27 June 1983, Pine Knob Pavilion, Detroit, Michigan (with the Blasters)

SETLIST: Tulsa Time / I Shot The Sheriff / Worried Life Blues / Lay Down Sally / Let It Rain / Double Trouble / Sweet Little Lisa / Key To The Highway / After Midnight / The Shape You're In / Wonderful Tonight / Blues Power / Standing Around Crying / Have You Ever Loved A Woman / Cocaine / Layla / Further On Up The Road

28 June 1983, Pine Knob Pavilion, Detroit, Michigan (with the Blasters)

SETLIST: Tulsa Time / I Shot The Sheriff / Worried Life Blues / Lay Down Sally / Let It Rain / Double Trouble / Sweet Little Lisa / Key To The Highway / After Midnight / The Shape You're In / Wonderful Tonight / Blues Power / Standing Around Crying / Have You Ever Loved A Woman / Cocaine / Layla / Further On Up The Road

29 June 1983, Pine Knob Pavilion, Detroit, Michigan (with the Blasters) (this one gets off to a bad start with Jamie Oldaker knocking himself out cold during the intro into "Tulsa Time," delaying the show. Once he regains consciousness they restart the show. The setlist was shortened this night dropping "After Midnight" and "The Shape You're In" to keep from going past the venue's curfew.)

SETLIST: Tulsa Time / I Shot The Sheriff / Worried Life Blues / Lay Down Sally / Let It Rain / Double Trouble / Sweet Little Lisa / Key To The Highway / Wonderful Tonight / Blues Power / Standing Around Crying / Have

You Ever Loved A Woman / Cocaine / Layla / Further On Up The Road

JULY 1983

1 July 1983, Performing Arts Center, Saratoga Springs, New York (with the Blasters)

SETLIST: Tulsa Time / I Shot The Sheriff / Worried Life Blues / Lay Down Sally / Let It Rain / Double Trouble / Sweet Little Lisa / Key To The Highway / The Shape You're In / Wonderful Tonight / Blues Power / Long Distance Call / Have You Ever Loved A Woman / Ramblin' On My Mind / Cocaine / Layla / Further On Up The Road

2 July 1983, Jones Beach Amphitheater, Jones Beach, Long Island, New York (with the Blasters)

SETLIST: Tulsa Time / I Shot The Sheriff / Worried Life Blues / Lay Down Sally / Let It Rain / Double Trouble / Sweet Little Lisa / Key To The Highway / The Shape You're In / Wonderful Tonight / Blues Power / Have You Ever Loved A Woman / Ramblin' On My Mind / Cocaine / Layla / Further On Up The Road

3 July 1983, Jones Beach Amphitheater, Jones Beach, Long Island, New York (with the Blasters)

SETLIST: not known

5 July 1983, Merriweather Post Pavilion, Columbia, Maryland (with the Blasters)

SETLIST: not known

7 July 1983, Blossom Music Center, Cleveland, Ohio (with the Blasters)

SETLIST: not known

9 July 1983, Civic Center Arena, St. Paul, Minnesota (with the Blasters)

SETLIST: not known

10 July 1983, Summerfest, Milwaukee, Wisconsin (with the Blasters)

SETLIST: Tulsa Time / I Shot The Sheriff / Worried Life Blues / Lay Down Sally / Let It Rain / Double Trouble / Sweet Little Lisa / Blow Wind Blow / The Shape You're In / Wonderful Tonight / Blues Power / Long Distance Call / Have You Ever Loved A Woman / Ramblin' On My Mind / Cocaine / Layla / Further On Up The Road

11 July 1983, Poplar Creek Music Theater, Hoffman Estates, Chicago, Illinois (with the Blasters)

SETLIST: Tulsa Time / I Shot The Sheriff / Worried Life Blues / Lay Down Sally / Let It Rain / Double Trouble / Sweet Little Lisa / Blow Wind Blow / The Shape You're In / Wonderful Tonight / Blues Power / Sad Sad Day / Have You Ever Loved A Woman / Ramblin' On My Mind / Cocaine / Layla / Further On Up The Road

11 July 1983, Checker Board Lounge, Chicago (after his Poplar Creek show, Eric visits the Checker Board Lounge and jams with Buddy Guy)

13 July 1983, Timberwolf Amphitheater at Kings Island, Cincinnati, Ohio (with the Blasters)

SETLIST: not known

14 July 1983, Wings Stadium, Kalamazoo, Michigan (with the Blasters)

SETLIST: not known

16 July 1983, Red Rocks Amphitheatre, Denver, Colorado (with the Blasters)

SETLIST: Tulsa Time / I Shot The Sheriff / Worried Life Blues / Lay Down Sally / Let It Rain / Double Trouble / Sweet Little Lisa / Key To The Highway / The Shape In You're In / Wonderful Tonight / Blues Power / Sad Sad Day / Have You Ever Loved A Woman / Ramblin' On My Mind / Cocaine / Layla / Further On Up The Road

17 July 1983, Red Rocks Amphitheatre, Denver, Colorado (with the Blasters)

SETLIST: Tulsa Time / I Shot The Sheriff / Worried Life Blues / Lay Down Sally / Let It Rain / Double Trouble / Sweet Little Lisa / Key To The Highway / The Shape You're In / Wonderful Tonight / Blues Power / That's All

Right / Have You Ever Loved A Woman / Ramblin' On My Mind / Cocaine / Layla / Further On Up The Road[1]

[1]with the Blasters

SEPTEMBER 1983

ARMS / PRINCE'S TRUST CONCERTS 1983

BAND LINEUP:
Eric Clapton: guitar, vocals
Jeff Beck: guitar
Jimmy Page: guitar
Andy Fairweather Low: guitar, vocals
Steve Winwood: keyboards, Minimoog, vocals
Chris Stainton: keyboards
James Hooker: keyboards
Tony Hymas: keyboards
Bill Wyman: bass
Fernando Saunders: bass
Charlie Watts: drums
Kenney Jones: drums
Simon Phillips: drums
Ray Cooper: percussion
Ronnie Lane: vocals

For these shows Eric's amp was a '57 blonde Fender Twin. His guitars were "Blackie," a Gibson Explorer, a Martin acoustic, and a couple of sunburst Fender Stratocasters.

10 September 1983–18 September 1983, rehearsals at Warnham Lodge Farm, Warnham, West Sussex

ARMS BENEFIT CONCERT 1983

20 September 1983, Royal Albert Hall, London

AT
The Royal Albert Hall to celebrate twenty years as a recording artist.

ERIC CLAPTON
will be appearing in concert with

JIMMY PAGE, BILL WYMAN, CHARLIE WATTS, JEFF BECK, STEVE WINWOOD, KENNEY JONES, ANDY FAIRWEATHER LOW,
and more...

Tickets £35, £20, £12.50, £8.50 from Royal Albert Hall Box Office, Keith Prowse Shops, HMV Oxford Street & usual agents and instant credit card reservations on 01-836 2184 (plus booking fee where applicable)
ON
Tuesday 20 September in aid of ARMS–Action Research into Multiple Sclerosis
AND
Wednesday 21 September in aid of The Prince's Trust
In the gracious presence of Their Royal Highnesses The Prince and Princess of Wales

Advert for the ARMS and Prince's Trust concerts at the Royal Albert Hall on 20 and 21 September 1983.

SETLIST:

Everybody Oughta Make A Change available on Videoform's *ARMS Concert* VHS video released July 1984 / audio broadcast on Westwood One's *Superstars in Concert*

Eric Clapton: vocals, slide guitar
Andy Fairweather Low: guitar
Steve Winwood: keyboards
Chris Stainton: piano
Charlie Watts: drums
Kenny Jones: drums
Bill Wyman: bass
Ray Cooper: bass

Lay Down Sally available on Videoform's *Arms Concert* VHS video released July 1984 / audio broadcast on Westwood *One's Superstars in Concert*

Eric Clapton: vocals, guitar
Andy Fairweather Low: guitar
Steve Winwood: keyboards
Chris Stainton: piano
Charlie Watts: drums
Kenny Jones: drums
Bill Wyman: bass
Ray Cooper: percussion

Wonderful Tonight video unreleased / audio broadcast on Westwood One's *Superstars in Concert*

Eric Clapton: vocals, guitar
Andy Fairweather Low: guitar
Steve Winwood: keyboards
Chris Stainton: piano
Charlie Watts: drums
Kenny Jones: drums
Bill Wyman: bass
Ray Cooper: percussion

Ramblin' On My Mind / Have You Ever Loved A Woman available on Videoform's *ARMS Concert* VHS video released July 1984

Eric Clapton: vocals, guitar
Andy Fairweather Low: guitar
Steve Winwood: keyboards

```
Chris Stainton: piano
Charlie Watts: drums
Kenny Jones: drums
Bill Wyman: bass
Ray Cooper: percussion
```

Rita Mae available on Videoform's *ARMS Concert* VHS video released July 1984

```
Eric Clapton: vocals, guitar
Andy Fairweather Low: guitar
Steve Winwood: keyboards
Chris Stainton: piano
Charlie Watts: drums
Kenny Jones: drums
Bill Wyman: bass
Ray Cooper: percussion
```

Cocaine available on Videoform's *Arms Concert* VHS video released July 1984 / audio broadcast on Westood One's *Superstars in Concert*

```
Eric Clapton: vocals, guitar
Andy Fairweather Low: guitar
Steve Winwood: keyboards
Chris Stainton: piano
Charlie Watts: drums
Kenny Jones: drums
Bill Wyman: bass
Ray Cooper: percussion
```

Man Smart Woman Smarter available on Videoform's *ARMS Concert* VHS video released July 1984 / audio broadcast on Westwood One's *Superstars in Concert*

```
Eric Clapton: slide guitar, vocals
Andy Fairweather Low: vocals, guitar
Chris Stainton: piano
Charlie Watts: drums
Kenny Jones: drums
Bill Wyman: bass
Ray Cooper: percussion
```

Hound Dog unreleased

```
Steve Winwood: Minimoog, vocals
Eric Clapton: guitar
Andy Fairweather Low: guitar
Fernando Saunders: bass
James Hooker: keyboards
Chris Stainton: piano
Charlie Watts: drums
Kenny Jones: drums
Ray Cooper: percussion
```

The Best I Can unreleased

```
Steve Winwood: keyboards, vocals
Eric Clapton: guitar
Andy Fairweather Low: guitar
Fernando Saunders: bass
```

```
James Hooker: keyboards
Chris Stainton: piano
Charlie Watts: drums
Kenny Jones: drums
Ray Cooper: percussion
```

Roadrunner available on Videoform's *ARMS Concert* VHS video released July 1984 / audio broadcast on Westwood One's *Superstars in Concert*

```
Steve Winwood: Minimoog, vocals
Eric Clapton: guitar
Andy Fairweather Low: guitar
Fernando Saunders: bass
James Hooker: keyboards
Chris Stainton: piano
Charlie Watts: drums
Kenny Jones: drums
Ray Cooper: percussion
```

Slowdown Sundown available on Videoform's *ARMS Concert* VHS video released July 1984 / audio broadcast on Westwood One's *Superstars in Concert*

```
Steve Winwood: mandolin, Minimoog, vocals
Eric Clapton: guitar
Andy Fairweather Low: guitar
Fernando Saunders: bass
James Hooker: keyboards
Chris Stainton: piano
Charlie Watts: drums
Kenny Jones: drums
Ray Cooper: percussion
```

Take Me To The River available on Videoform's *ARMS Concert* VHS video released July 1984 / audio broadcast on Westwood One's *Superstars in Concert*

```
Steve Winwood: vocals
Eric Clapton: guitar
Andy Fairweather Low: guitar
Fernando Saunders: bass
James Hooker: keyboards
Chris Stainton: piano
Charlie Watts: drums
Kenny Jones: drums
Ray Cooper: percussion
```

Gimme Some Lovin' available on Videoform's *ARMS Concert* VHS video released July 1984 / audio broadcast on Westwood One's *Superstars in Concert*

```
Steve Winwood: keyboards, vocals
Eric Clapton: guitar
Andy Fairweather Low: guitar, backing vocals
Fernando Saunders: bass, backing vocals
Charlie Watts: drums
Kenny Jones: drums
Ray Cooper: percussion
```

Star Cycle available on Videoform's *ARMS Concert* VHS video released July 1984 / audio broadcast on Westwood One's *Superstars in Concert*

Jeff Beck: guitar
Fernando Sanders: bass
Tony Hymas: keyboards
Simon Phillips: drums

The Pump available on Videoform's *ARMS Concert* VHS video released July 1984 / audio broadcast on Westwood One's *Superstars in Concert*

Jeff Beck: guitar
Fernando Sanders: bass
Tony Hymas: keyboards
Simon Phillips: drums

Goodbye Pork Hat available on Videoform's *ARMS Concert* VHS video released July 1984 / audio broadcast on Westwood One's *Superstars in Concert*

Jeff Beck: guitar
Fernando Sanders: bass
Tony Hymas: keyboards
Simon Phillips: drums

Led Boots video unreleased / audio broadcast on Westwood One's *Superstars in Concert*

Jeff Beck: guitar
Fernando Sanders: bass
Tony Hymas: keyboards
Simon Phillips: drums

People Get Ready video unreleased / audio broadcast on Westwood One's *Superstars in Concert*

Jeff Beck: guitar
Fernando Sanders: bass
Tony Hymas: keyboards
Simon Phillips: drums

Hi Ho Silver Lining available on Videoform's *ARMS Concert* VHS video released July 1984 / audio broadcast on Westwood One's *Superstars in Concert*

Jeff Beck: guitar, vocals
Fernando Sanders: bass
Tony Hymas: keyboards
Simon Phillips: drums
Steve Winwood: vocals
Andy Fairweather Low: vocals

Prelude available on Videoform's *ARMS Concert* VHS video released July 1984 / audio broadcast on Westwood One's *Superstars in Concert*

Jimmy Page: guitar
Steve Winwood: keyboards
Chris Stainton: keyboards
James Hooker: Royal Albert Hall organ

Fernado Saunders: bass
Simon Phillips: drums
Ray Cooper: percussion

Who's To Blame available on Videoform's *ARMS Concert* VHS video released July 1984 / audio broadcast on Westwood One's *Superstars in Concert*

Jimmy Page: guitar
Steve Winwood: vocals
Andy Fairweather Low: guitar
Fernado Saunders: bass
Simon Phillips: drums
Ray Cooper: drums

City Sirens available on Videoform's *ARMS Concert* VHS video released July 1984 / audio broadcast on Westwood One's *Superstars in Concert*

Jimmy Page: guitar
Steve Winwood: vocals
Andy Fairweather Low: guitar
Chris Stainton: keyboards
James Hooker: keyboards
Fernado Saunders: bass
Simon Phillips: drums
Ray Cooper: percussion

Stairway To Heaven available on Videoform's *ARMS Concert* VHS video released July 1984

Jimmy Page: guitar
Chris Stainton: keyboards
Fernando Saunders: bass
Simon Phillips: drums

Tulsa Time available on Videoform's *ARMS Concert* VHS video released July 1984 / audio broadcast on Westwood One's *Superstars in Concert*

Eric Clapton: vocals, slide guitar
Jeff Beck: guitar
Jimmy Page: guitar
Andy Fairweather Low: guitar, vocals
Steve Winwood: mandolin, vocals
Chris Stainton: piano
James Hooker: keyboards
Charlie Watts: drums
Kenny Jones: drums
Bill Wyman: bass
Ray Cooper: percussion

Wee Wee Baby unreleased

Eric Clapton: vocals, guitar
Jeff Beck: guitar
Jimmy Page: guitar
Andy Fairweather Low: guitar, vocals
Steve Winwood: keyboards, vocals
Chris Stainton: piano
James Hooker: keyboards

Charlie Watts: drums
Kenny Jones: drums
Bill Wyman: bass
Ray Cooper: percussion

Layla available on Videoform's *ARMS Concert* VHS video released July 1984 / audio broadcast on Westwood One's *Superstars in Concert*

Eric Clapton: vocals, guitar
Jeff Beck: guitar
Jimmy Page: guitar
Andy Fairweather Low: guitar, vocals
Steve Winwood: keyboards, vocals
Chris Stainton: piano
James Hooker: keyboards
Charlie Watts: drums
Kenny Jones: drums
Bill Wyman: bass
Ray Cooper: percussion

Bomber's Moon audio broadcast on Westwood One's *Superstars in Concert*

Ronnie Lane: vocals
Eric Clapton: vocals, acoustic guitar
Jeff Beck: acoustic guitar
Jimmy Page: guitar
Andy Fairweather Low: vocals
Steve Winwood: mandolin, vocals
Chris Stainton: piano
James Hooker: keyboards
Charlie Watts: drums
Kenny Jones: drums
Bill Wyman: bass
Ray Cooper: percussion

Goodnight Irene available on Videoform's *ARMS Concert* VHS video released July 1984 / audio broadcast on Westwood One's *Superstars in Concert*

Ronnie Lane: vocals
Eric Clapton: vocals, acoustic guitar
Jeff Beck: acoustic guitar
Jimmy Page: guitar
Andy Fairweather Low: vocals
Steve Winwood: mandolin, vocals
Chris Stainton: piano
James Hooker: keyboards
Charlie Watts: drums
Kenny Jones: drums
Bill Wyman: bass
Ray Cooper: percussion
Producer: Glyn Johns
Engineers: Mick McKenna / Charles McPherson
Recorded by: Rolling Stones Mobile Studio
Video directed by: Stanley Dorfman

PRINCE'S TRUST CONCERT 1983

21 September 1983, Royal Albert Hall, London

"Stew [Ian Stewart from the Rolling Stones] had invited me to do this concert at a party at Jeff Beck's country home. It was to be for Ronnie Lane and the Action Research Into Multiple Sclerosis, a condition to which he unfortunately had become a victim.

It had been outlined that the three former Yardbirds would be playing separate sets and maybe play together at the end of the evening. Steve Winwood was also to perform. I agreed enthusiastically to commit to the show. It was only the following day that it dawned on me that I was the only one not to have a solo career with the exception of the *Death Wish II* soundtrack which made putting a set together for this event an interesting and challenging experience.

The opening number was 'Prelude,' a rearranged Chopin prelude in E minor, performed specifically to employ the house built-in Victorian pipe organ into the set. It was played magnificently by American James Horner. 'City Sirens' and 'Who's To Blame' from the *Death Wish II* album had Steve Winwood graciously supplying vocals.

The set culminated in an instrumental version of 'Stairway to Heaven'—the first time I had performed this on my own. Simon Phillips threw me a wink and surprised me with a double bass drum pattern to great effect."

—JIMMY PAGE
(from his website)

Prince's Trust concert at the Royal Albert Hall on 21 September 1983. L to R: Andy Fairweather Low, Jimmy Page, Eric Clapton, Bill Wyman, Ray Cooper, Jeff Beck.

SETLIST:

Everybody Oughta Make A Change unreleased

Lay Down Sally unreleased

Ramblin' On My Mind / Have You Ever Loved A Woman unreleased

Rita Mae unreleased

Cocaine unreleased

Man Smart Woman Smarter unreleased

The Best I Can unreleased

Roadrunner unreleased

Slowdown Sundown unreleased

Take Me To The River unreleased

Gimme Some Lovin' unreleased

Star Cycle unreleased

The Pump unreleased

Goodbye Pork Hat unreleased

Led Boots unreleased

People Get Ready unreleased

Hi Ho Silver Lining unreleased

Prelude unreleased

Who's To Blame unreleased

City Sirens unreleased

Stairway To Heaven unreleased

Wee Wee Baby unreleased

Layla unreleased

Goodnight Irene unreleased

Producer: Glyn Johns
Engineers: Mick McKenna / Charles McPherson
Recorded by: Rolling Stones Mobile Studio

> **"**The gig itself was dominated by the consummate playing of Eric Clapton who, despite an unassuming style, showed he could nevertheless still play the blues with a depth of feeling that transcended the showbiz nature of the gala event.**"**
> —*SOUNDS*
> 1 October 1983

ARMS U.S. TOUR 1983

BAND LINEUP:
Eric Clapton: guitar, vocals
Jeff Beck: guitar
Jimmy Page: guitar
Andy Fairweather Low: guitar, vocals
Ronnie Wood: guitar (Madison Square Garden only)
Joe Cocker: vocals
Chris Stainton: keyboards
James Hooker: keyboards
Jan Hammer: keyboards
Bill Wyman: bass
Fernando Saunders: bass
Charlie Watts: drums
Kenney Jones: drums
Simon Phillips: drums
Ray Cooper: percussion
Ronnie Lane: vocals

NOVEMBER 1983

23 November 1983, Tango's, Greenville Avenue, Dallas, Texas (on a night off from rehearsals, Eric, Bill Wyman, and Kenny Jones check out a gig by the Marcia Ball Band at this newly opened club)

28 November 1983, Reunion Arena, Dallas, Texas

ERIC CLAPTON SETLIST: Everybody Oughta Make A Change / Lay Down Sally / Wonderful Tonight / Rita Mae / Sad Sad Day / Have You Ever Loved A Woman / Ramblin' On My Mind / Cocaine / Man Smart Woman Smarter

JOE COCKER, ERIC CLAPTON SETLIST: Don't Talk To Me / Watching The River Flow / Worried Life Blues / You Are So Beautiful / Seven Days / Feelin' Alright

JEFF BECK SETLIST: Star Cycle / Pump / Blue Wind / People Get Ready / Going Down Slow

JIMMY PAGE, PAUL ROGERS SETLIST: Prelude / Who's To Blame / City Sirens / Boogie Mama / Midnight Moonlight

JIMMY PAGE, ERIC CLAPTON, JEFF BECK SETLIST: Stairway To Heaven

ALL-STAR SETLIST: Layla / With A Little Help From My Friends

ALL-STARS WITH RONNIE LANE SETLIST: Goodnight Irene

29 November 1983, Reunion Arena, Dallas, Texas

ERIC CLAPTON SETLIST: Everybody Oughta Make A Change / Lay Down Sally / Wonderful Tonight / Rita Mae / Sad Sad Day / Have You Ever Loved A Woman / Ramblin' On My Mind / Cocaine

JOE COCKER, ERIC CLAPTON SETLIST: Don't Talk To Me / Watching The River Flow / Worried Life Blues / You Are So Beautiful / Seven Days / Feelin' Alright

JEFF BECK SETLIST: Star Cycle / Pump / Definitely Maybe / Blue Wind / People Get Ready / Going Down Slow

JIMMY PAGE, PAUL ROGERS SETLIST: Prelude / Who's To Blame / City Sirens / Boogie Mama / Midnight Moonlight

JIMMY PAGE, ERIC CLAPTON, JEFF BECK SETLIST: Stairway To Heaven

ALL-STAR SETLIST: Layla / With A Little Help From My Friends

ALL-STARS WITH RONNIE LANE SETLIST: Goodnight Irene

29 November 1983, Tango's, Greenville Avenue, Dallas, Texas (after the ARMS show at the Reunion Arena, Eric and Bill Wyman and others go and jam with Lonnie Mack)

DECEMBER 1983

1 December 1983, Cow Palace, San Francisco, California

ERIC CLAPTON SETLIST: Everybody Oughta Make A Change / Lay Down Sally / Wonderful Tonight / Rita Mae / Sad Sad Day / Have You Ever Loved A Woman / Ramblin' On My Mind / Cocaine

JOE COCKER, ERIC CLAPTON SETLIST: Don't Talk To Me / Watching The River Flow / Worried Life Blues / You Are So Beautiful / Feelin' Alright / Seven Days

JEFF BECK SETLIST: Star Cycle / The Pump / Definitely Maybe / Blue Wind / People Get Ready / Going Down Slow

JIMMY PAGE, PAUL ROGERS SETLIST: Prelude / Who's To Blame / City Sirens / Boogie Mama / Midnight Moonlight

JIMMY PAGE, ERIC CLAPTON, JEFF BECK SETLIST: Stairway To Heaven

ALL-STAR SETLIST: Layla / With A Little Help From My Friends

Jimmy Page, Eric Clapton, and Jeff Beck together on stage during the U.S. ARMS shows in December 1983.

ALL-STARS WITH RONNIE LANE SETLIST: Goodnight Irene

2 December 1983, Cow Palace, San Francisco, California

ERIC CLAPTON SETLIST: Everybody Oughta Make A Change / Lay Down Sally / Wonderful Tonight / Rita Mae / Ramblin' On My Mind / Have You Ever Loved A Woman / Cocaine

JOE COCKER, ERIC CLAPTON SETLIST: Don't Talk To Me / Watching The River Flow / Worried Life Blues / You Are So Beautiful / Seven Days / Feelin' Alright

JEFF BECK SETLIST: Star Cycle / The Pump / Definitely Maybe / Blue Wind / People Get Ready / Going Down Slow

JIMMY PAGE, PAUL ROGERS SETLIST: Prelude / Who's To Blame / City Sirens / Boogie Mama / Midnight Moonlight

JIMMY PAGE, ERIC CLAPTON, JEFF BECK SETLIST: Stairway To Heaven

ALL-STAR SETLIST: Layla / With A Little Help From My Friends

ALL-STARS WITH RONNIE LANE SETLIST: Goodnight Irene

3 December 1983, Cow Palace, San Francisco, California

ERIC CLAPTON SETLIST: Everybody Oughta Make A Change / Lay Down Sally / Wonderful Tonight / Rita Mae / Ramblin' On My Mind / Have You Ever Loved A Woman / Cocaine

JOE COCKER, ERIC CLAPTON SETLIST: Don't Talk To Me / Watching The River Flow / Worried Life Blues / You Are So Beautiful / Feelin' Alright / Seven Days

JEFF BECK SETLIST: Star Cycle / The Pump / Definitely Maybe / Blue Wind / People Get Ready / Going Down Slow

JIMMY PAGE, PAUL ROGERS SETLIST: Prelude / Who's To Blame / City Sirens / Boogie Mama / Midnight Moonlight

JIMMY PAGE, ERIC CLAPTON, JEFF BECK SETLIST: Stairway To Heaven

ALL-STAR SETLIST: Layla / With A Little Help From My Friends

Jimmy Page, Joe Cocker, Eric Clapton, and Jeff Beck together on stage during the U.S. ARMS shows in December 1983.

ALL-STARS WITH RONNIE LANE SETLIST: Goodnight Irene

5 December 1983, Forum, Los Angeles, California

ERIC CLAPTON SETLIST: Everybody Oughta Make A Change / Lay Down Sally / Wonderful Tonight / Rita Mae / Ramblin' On My Mind / Have You Ever Loved A Woman / Cocaine

JOE COCKER, ERIC CLAPTON SETLIST: Don't Talk To Me / Watching The River Flow / Worried Life Blues / You Are So Beautiful / Feelin' Alright / Seven Days

JEFF BECK SETLIST: Star Cycle / The Pump / Definitely Maybe / Blue Wind / People Get Ready / Going Down Slow

JIMMY PAGE, PAUL ROGERS SETLIST: Prelude / Who's To Blame / City Sirens / Boogie Mama / Midnight Moonlight

JIMMY PAGE, ERIC CLAPTON, JEFF BECK SETLIST: Stairway To Heaven

ALL-STAR SETLIST: Layla / With A Little Help From My Friends

ALL-STARS WITH RONNIE LANE SETLIST: Goodnight Irene

> ❝Judging by Monday night's show, the spirit that fired these musicians initially has not been diminished at all. Those men on stage shared in [Ronnie] Lane's struggle and many had faced their mortality already. The common bond and unfettered affection for each other led to a combination of talents that did nothing less than reinforce the unifying, inspirational spirit of rock 'n' roll at its best.❞
>
> **—L.A. LIFE DAILY NEWS**
> (December 1983)

6 December 1983, Forum, Los Angeles, California

ERIC CLAPTON SETLIST: Everybody Oughta Make A Change / Lay Down Sally / Wonderful Tonight / Rita

Mae / Ramblin' On My Mind / Have You Ever Loved A Woman / Cocaine

JOE COCKER, ERIC CLAPTON SETLIST: Don't Talk To Me / Watching The River Flow / Worried Life Blues / You Are So Beautiful / Feelin' Alright / Seven Days

JEFF BECK SETLIST: Star Cycle / The Pump / Definitely Maybe / Blue Wind / People Get Ready / Going Down Slow

JIMMY PAGE, PAUL ROGERS SETLIST: Prelude / Who's To Blame / City Sirens / Boogie Mama / Midnight Moonlight

JIMMY PAGE, ERIC CLAPTON, JEFF BECK SETLIST: Stairway To Heaven

ALL-STAR SETLIST: Layla / With A Little Help From My Friends

ALL-STARS WITH RONNIE LANE SETLIST: April Fool / Goodnight Irene

8 December 1983, Madison Square Garden, New York City

ERIC CLAPTON SETLIST: Everybody Oughta Make A Change / Lay Down Sally / Wonderful Tonight / Rita Mae / That's All Right / Have You Ever Loved A Woman / Ramblin' On My Mind / Cocaine[1]
[1]with Ronnie Wood

JOE COCKER, ERIC CLAPTON, RONNIE WOOD SETLIST: Don't Talk To Me / Watching The River Flow / Worried Life Blues / You Are So Beautiful / Seven Days / Feelin' Alright

JEFF BECK SETLIST: Star Cycle / The Pump / Definitely Maybe / Blue Wind / People Get Ready / Going Down Slow

JIMMY PAGE, ERIC CLAPTON, JEFF BECK SETLIST: Prelude / Who's To Blame / City Sirens / Boogie Mama / Midnight Moonlight

JIMMY PAGE, ERIC CLAPTON, JEFF BECK SETLIST: Stairway To Heaven

ALL-STAR SETLIST: Layla / With A Little Help From My Friends

ALL-STARS WITH RONNIE LANE SETLIST: April Fool / Goodnight Irene

9 December 1983, Madison Square Garden, New York City

ERIC CLAPTON SETLIST: Everybody Oughta Make A Change / Lay Down Sally / Wonderful Tonight / Rita Mae / Sad Sad Day / Have You Ever Loved A Woman / Ramblin' On My Mind / Cocaine[1]
[1]with Ronnie Wood

JOE COCKER, ERIC CLAPTON, RONNIE WOOD SETLIST: Don't Talk To Me / Watching The River Flow / Worried Life Blues / You Are So Beautiful / Seven Days / Feelin' Alright

JEFF BECK SETLIST: Star Cycle / The Pump / Definitely Maybe / Blue Wind / People Get Ready / Going Down Slow

JIMMY PAGE, PAUL ROGERS SETLIST: Prelude / Who's To Blame / City Sirens / Boogie Mama / Midnight Moonlight

JIMMY PAGE, ERIC CLAPTON, JEFF BECK SETLIST: Stairway To Heaven

ALL-STAR SETLIST: Layla / With A Little Help From My Friends

ALL-STARS WITH RONNIE LANE SETLIST: April Fool / Goodnight Irene

RECORDING SESSIONS 1983
ERIC CLAPTON GUEST SESSION
REVOLUTION STUDIOS
11 Church Road, Cheadle Hulme, Cheshire

Session for Corey Hart

JENNY FEY (Corey Hart) *First Offense* LP EMI America 2401861 released June 1984 / *First Offense* CD EMI America CDP 7 46077 2 released 1991

Corey Hart: vocals, backing vocals
Eric Clapton: Dobro
Gary Tibbs: bass
Paul Burgess: drums
Richie Close: piano
Andy Barnett: guitar

Producers: Jo   n Astley / Phil Chapman
Engineer: Andy Macpherson

The album was originally released in Canada in November 1983 but did not get a wider release until June 1984.

> **"**I am forever grateful for the guidance and immense talent of my two UK producers Jon and Phil. One afternoon while Jon and I strolled the park with his two young daughters near their home in Twickenham, he casually turned to me and said: 'I thought of ringing up Eric to come play on "Jenny Fey."' Eric?? 'Eric who?' I asked confused. Jon replied with his cheeky soft grin: 'Eric Clapton, playing on Dobro perhaps.' Holy shit, miracles!
>
> The experience of watching Mr. Clapton record his Dobro will always remain one of my true career highlights. He played so gracefully you could hear his deep breathing through the open mic. As if he was living through the song, becoming a part of the song's soul through the process. When he finished he came into the studio for a playback listen. He looked towards me, as I was kind of sheepishly hiding in the corner trying not to get in the way. He gently expressed words I shall never forget: 'What a very pretty song you wrote there, Corey.' Thank you, Mr. Eric Clapton.**"**
>
> **—COREY HART**
> (from his website)

> **"**I asked Eric if he could bring a slide Dobro over. It was in G and everything worked out great. The Jenny Fey overdub was recorded at Revolution Studio Manchester and Andy Mac was the engineer.**"**
>
> **—JON ASTLEY**

ERIC CLAPTON GUEST SESSION

THE BILLIARD ROOM STUDIOS
Roger Waters's home recording studios, Barnes, London
Session for Roger Waters

AUGUST 1983

4:30 A.M. (APPARENTLY THEY WERE TRAVELLING ABROAD) unreleased

4:33 A.M. (RUNNING SHOES) unreleased

4:37 A.M. (ARABS WITH KNIVES AND WEST GERMAN SKIES) unreleased

4:39 A.M. (FOR THE FIRST TIME TODAY, PART 2) unreleased

4:41 A.M. (SEXUAL REVOLUTION) unreleased

4:47 A.M. (THE REMAINS OF OUR LOVE) unreleased

4:50 A.M. (GO FISHING) unreleased

4:56 A.M. (FOR THE FIRST TIME TODAY, PART 1) unreleased

4:58 A.M. (DUNROAMIN, DUNCARIN, DUNLIVIN) unreleased

5:01 A.M. (THE PROS AND CONS OF HITCH HIKING) unreleased

5:06 A.M. (EVERY STRANGER'S EYES) unreleased

5:11 A.M. (THE MOMENT OF CLARITY) unreleased

THE PROS AND CONS OF HITCH HIKING CD US Columbia CK 39290 / UK *Harvest* CDP 7 46029 2 released April 1984

Roger Waters: vocals, rhythm guitar, bass
Eric Clapton: lead guitar
Andy Bown: Hammond B3 organ, 12-string guitar
Ray Cooper: percussion
Michael Kamen: piano
Andy Newmark: drums
David Sanborn: saxophone
Raphael Ravenscroft: horns
Kevin Flanagan: horns
Vic Sullivan: horns
Madeline Bell: backing vocals
Katie Kissoon: backing vocals
Doreen Chanter: backing vocals

Producers: Roger Waters / Michael Kamen
Engineer: Andy Jackson

> **"**Eric's session was done at Roger's—The Billiard Room. Called that by the way as most of the space in there was taken up by a snooker table. Used a Strat and a smallish Fender amp, may well have been 'Blackie' but I wouldn't put money on that. I think it was done in one stint, as an overdub session, over a few days.**"**
>
> **—ANDY JACKSON**
> (engineer

OLYMPIC STUDIOS
117 Church Road, London
Session for Christine
McVie

SEPTEMBER 1983

THE CHALLENGE (Christine McVie / Todd Sharp) *Christine McVie* LP
Warner Bros. 1-25059 released January 1984 / CD Warner Bros. 9 25059-2
released 1997

Christine McVie: vocals, keyboards
Eric Clapton: lead guitar
Todd Sharpe: guitar
Lindsey Buckingham: backing vocals
George Hawkins: bass
Steve Ferrone: drums
Ray Cooper: percussion

Producer: Russ Titelman
Engineer: David Richards

2

1984

Eric had slowly started to write new material for his next album. One of the first, "Same Old Blues," was about Eric's life on the road away from home. After returning from a short tour around Europe and the Middle East in February, Eric rented a cottage in Wales by himself and took along some recording equipment so that he could write more songs in seclusion. The trip was successful inasmuch as he was able to write some memorable songs, many of which have stood the test of time. These would be recorded for the *Behind The Sun* album in April.

A large portion of the year was spent touring with Roger Waters for his *Pros And Cons Of Hitch Hiking* album, on which Eric had played back in August of 1983. Eric's manager, Roger Forrester, advised Eric against joining the tour as he felt Eric's name was too big for him to just be a sideman in Waters's band. He also felt that Eric should concentrate on his solo career. In reality, this was something Eric needed to do. He was fed up with being the lead man and enjoyed the idea of being the guitarist in a band with no responsibilities. Sadly, the fun element soon faded away as Eric found the highly controlled environment of the stage show to be too boring for him with no opportunity to improvise. There were click tracks to play to with cues and it simply was too formulaic for Eric, who could not wait for the tour to end.

The shows were very much in the vein of Pink Floyd with extravagant visuals and elaborate lighting. Each concert was visually stunning with amazing crystal clear audio. Even when bored, Eric played spectacularly and it was interesting for his fans to hear

another side of him. All things considered, it turned out to be a very worthwhile exercise.

ERIC CLAPTON EUROPEAN / MIDDLE EASTERN TOUR 1984

BAND LINEUP:
Eric Clapton: guitar, vocals
Albert Lee: guitar, vocals
Jamie Oldaker: drums
Donald "Duck" Dunn: bass
Chris Stainton: keyboards

JANUARY 1984

15 January–18 January 1984, rehearsals at Shepperton Studios, Shepperton, Middlesex

19 January 1984, travel to Zurich

20 January 1984, Hallenstadion, Zürich, Switzerland

SETLIST: Everybody Oughta Make A Change / Motherless Children / I Shot The Sheriff / The Sky Is Crying / Badge / The Shape You're In / Same Old Blues / Rita Mae / Blow Wind Blow / Wonderful Tonight / Let It Rain / Key To The Highway / Sweet Little Lisa / Double Trouble / Tulsa Time / Bottle Of Red Wine / Standing Around Crying / Have You Ever Loved A Woman / Ramblin' On My Mind / Cocaine / Layla / Further On Up The Road

21 January 1984, Hallenstadion, Zürich, Switzerland

SETLIST: Everybody Oughta Make A Change / Motherless Children / I Shot The Sheriff / The Sky Is Crying / Badge / The Shape You're In / Same Old Blues / Rita Mae / Let It Rain / Key To The Highway / Sweet Little Lisa / Double Trouble / Blues Power / Bottle Of Red Wine / Honey Bee / Have You Ever Loved A Woman / Ramblin' On My Mind / Cocaine / Layla / Further On Up The Road

22 January 1984, travel to Milan

23 January 1984, Teatro Tenda, Milan, Italy

SETLIST: Everybody Oughta Make A Change / Motherless Children / I Shot The Sheriff / The Sky Is Crying / Badge / The Shape You're In / Same Old Blues / Rita Mae / Blow Wind Blow / Wonderful Tonight / Let It Rain / Key To The Highway / Sweet Little Lisa / Double Trouble / Tulsa Time / Bottle Of Red Wine / Have You Ever Loved A Woman / Cocaine / Layla / Further On Up The Road

24 January 1984, Teatro Tenda, Milan, Italy

SETLIST: Everybody Oughta Make A Change / Motherless Children / I Shot The Sheriff / The Sky Is Crying / Badge / The Shape You're In / Same Old Blues / Rita Mae / Blow Wind Blow / Wonderful Tonight / Let It Rain / Key To The Highway / Sweet Little Lisa / Double Trouble / Tulsa Time / Bottle Of Red Wine / Cocaine / Layla / Further On Up The Road

25 January 1984, travel to Belgrade

26 January 1984, Beogradski Sajam Hala, Belgrade, Serbia, Yugoslavia

SETLIST: Everybody Oughta Make A Change / Motherless Children / I Shot The Sheriff / The Sky Is Crying / Badge / The Shape You're In / Same Old Blues / Rita Mae / Blow Wind Blow / Wonderful Tonight / Let It Rain / Key To The Highway / Sweet Little Lisa / Double Trouble / Tulsa Time / Bottle Of Red Wine / Cocaine / Layla / Further On Up The Road

27 January 1984, fly to Athens

28 January 1984, Sporting of Athens, Athens, Greece

SETLIST: Everybody Oughta Make A Change / Motherless Children / I Shot The Sheriff / The Sky Is Crying / Badge / The Shape You're In / Same Old Blues / Rita Mae / Blow Wind Blow / Wonderful Tonight / Let It Rain / Key To The Highway / Sweet Little Lisa / Double Trouble / Tulsa Time / Bottle Of Red Wine / Cocaine / Layla / Further On Up The Road

29 January 1984, Sporting of Athens, Athens, Greece

SETLIST: Everybody Oughta Make A Change / Motherless Children / I Shot The Sheriff / The Sky Is Crying / Badge / The Shape You're In / Same Old Blues / Rita Mae / Blow Wind Blow / Wonderful Tonight / Let It Rain / Key To The Highway / Sweet Little Lisa / Double Trouble / Tulsa Time / Bottle Of Red Wine / Cocaine / Layla / Further On Up The Road

30 January 1984, day off

31 January 1984, travel to Cairo

FEBRUARY 1984

1 February 1984, day off

2 February 1984, American University, Cairo, Egypt (according to Nigel Carroll: "My 1984 Tour Diary shows Feb 2, American University Cairo. We flew to Cairo but the show was canceled, it was actually canceled before we went, but Eric wanted to visit Egypt so the band and management flew there, and the crew went direct to Israel from Athens.")

3 February 1984, travel to Jerusalem

4 February 1984, day off

5 February 1984, Binyanei Ha'Ooma, Jerusalem, Israel

SETLIST: not known

6 February 1984, Binyanei Ha'Ooma, Jerusalem, Israel

SETLIST: Everybody Oughta Make A Change / Motherless Children / I Shot The Sheriff / The Sky Is Crying / Badge / The Shape You're In / Same Old Blues / Blues Power / Blow Wind Blow / Wonderful Tonight / Let It Rain / Key To The Highway / Sweet Little Lisa / Double Trouble / Tulsa Time / Bottle Of Red Wine / Cocaine / Layla / Further On Up The Road

7 February 1984, return to London, England

ROGER WATERS'S
THE PROS AND CONS OF HITCH HIKING
EUROPEAN TOUR 1984

BAND LINEUP:

Roger Waters: bass, vocals

Eric Clapton: guitar, vocals

Mel Collins: saxophone

Michael Kamen: keyboards

Andy Newmark: Drums

Tim Renwick: guitar, bass

Chris Stainton: keyboards, bass

Doreen Chanter: backing vocals

Katie Kissoon: backing vocals

Advert for Eric Clapton and Roger Waters at Earls Court for The Pros and Cons Of Hitch Hiking *Tour, 21- 22 June 1984.*

MAY 1984

21 May 1984–31 May 1984, rehearsals at Roger Waters's house

JUNE 1984

1 June 1984–2 June 1984, rehearsals at Roger Waters's house

3 June 1984, day off

4 June 1984–10 June 1984, rehearsals move from Roger's house to Bassingbourn Barracks, Royston, Hertfordshire

11 June 1984–14 June 1984, days off

15 June 1984, depart for Stockhom

16 June 1984, Johanneshovs Isstadion, Stockholm, Sweden

FIRST SET: Set The Controls For The Heart Of The Sun / Money / If / Welcome To The Machine / Have A Cigar / Wish You Were Here / Pigs On The Wing, Part 1 / In The Flesh / Nobody Home / Hey You / The Gunner's Dream

SECOND SET: 4:30 A.M. (Apparently They Were Traveling Abroad) / 4:33 A.M. (Running Shoes) / 4:37 A.M. (Arabs With Knives And West German Skies) / 4:39 P.M. (For The First Time Today, Part 2) / 4:41 A.M. (Sexual Revolution) / 4:47 A.M. (The Remains Of Our Love) / 4:50 A.M. (Go Fishing) / 4:56 A.M. (For The First Time Today, Part 1) / 4:58 A.M. (Dunroamin Duncarin Dunlivin) / 5:01 A.M. (The Pros and Cons of Hitch Hiking) / 5:06 A.M. (Every Stranger's Eyes) / 5:11 A.M. (The Moment Of Clarity) / Brain Damage / Eclipse

Eric Clapton on The Pros and Cons Of Hitch Hiking *Tour, Johanneshovs Isstadion, Stockholm, Sweden, 16 June 1984.*

17 June 1984, Johanneshovs Isstadion, Stockholm, Sweden

FIRST SET: Set The Controls For The Heart Of The Sun / Money / If / Welcome To The Machine / Have A Cigar / Wish You Were Here / Pigs On The Wing, Part 1 / In The Flesh / Nobody Home / Hey You / The Gunner's Dream

SECOND SET: 4:30 A.M. (Apparently They Were Traveling Abroad) / 4:33 A.M. (Running Shoes) / 4:37 A.M. (Arabs With Knives And West German Skies) / 4:39 P.M. (For The First Time Today, Part 2) / 4:41 A.M.

(Sexual Revolution) / 4:47 A.M. (The Remains Of Our Love) / 4:50 A.M. (Go Fishing) / 4:56 A.M. (For The First Time Today, Part 1) / 4:58 A.M. (Dunroamin Duncarin Dunlivin) / 5:01 A.M. (The Pros and Cons of Hitch Hiking) / 5:06 A.M. (Every Stranger's Eyes) / 5:11 A.M. (The Moment Of Clarity) / Brain Damage / Eclipse

19 June 1984, Sportpaleis Ahoy, Rotterdam, Netherlands

FIRST SET: Set The Controls For The Heart Of The Sun / Money / If / Welcome To The Machine / Have A Cigar / Wish You Were Here / Pigs On The Wing, Part 1 / In The Flesh / Nobody Home / Hey You / The Gunner's Dream

SECOND SET: 4:30 A.M. (Apparently They Were Traveling Abroad) / 4:33 A.M. (Running Shoes) / 4:37 A.M. (Arabs With Knives And West German Skies) / 4:39 P.M. (For The First Time Today, Part 2) / 4:41 A.M. (Sexual Revolution) / 4:47 A.M. (The Remains Of Our Love) / 4:50 A.M. (Go Fishing) / 4:56 A.M. (For The First Time Today, Part 1) / 4:58 A.M. (Dunroamin Duncarin Dunlivin) / 5:01 A.M. (The Pros and Cons of Hitch Hiking) / 5:06 A.M. (Every Stranger's Eyes) / 5:11 A.M. (The Moment Of Clarity) / Brain Damage / Eclipse

21 June 1984, Earls Court Arena, London

FIRST SET: Set The Controls For The Heart Of The Sun / Money / If / Welcome To The Machine / Have A Cigar / Wish You Were Here / Pigs On The Wing, Part 1 / In The Flesh / Nobody Home / Hey You / The Gunner's Dream

SECOND SET: 4:30 A.M. (Apparently They Were Traveling Abroad) / 4:33 A.M. (Running Shoes) / 4:37 A.M. (Arabs With Knives And West German Skies) / 4:39 P.M. (For The First Time Today, Part 2) / 4:41 A.M. (Sexual Revolution) / 4:47 A.M. (The Remains Of Our Love) / 4:50 A.M. (Go Fishing) / 4:56 A.M. (For The First Time Today, Part 1) / 4:58 A.M. (Dunroamin Duncarin Dunlivin) / 5:01 A.M. (The Pros and Cons of Hitch Hiking) / 5:06 A.M. (Every Stranger's Eyes) / 5:11 A.M. (The Moment Of Clarity) / Brain Damage / Eclipse

Eric Clapton and Roger Waters at Earls Court on The Pros and Cons Of Hitch Hiking *Tour, 21 June 1984.*

22 June 1984, Earls Court Arena, London

FIRST SET: Set The Controls For The Heart Of The Sun / Money / If / Welcome To The Machine / Have A Cigar / Wish You Were Here / Pigs On The Wing, Part 1 / In The Flesh / Nobody Home / Hey You / The Gunner's Dream

SECOND SET: 4:30 A.M. (Apparently They Were Traveling Abroad) / 4:33 A.M. (Running Shoes) / 4:37 A.M. (Arabs With Knives And West German Skies) / 4:39 P.M. (For The First Time Today, Part 2) / 4:41 A.M. (Sexual Revolution) / 4:47 A.M. (The Remains Of Our Love) / 4:50 A.M. (Go Fishing) / 4:56 A.M. (For The First Time Today, Part 1) / 4:58 A.M. (Dunroamin Duncarin Dunlivin) / 5:01 A.M. (The Pros and Cons of Hitch Hiking) / 5:06 A.M. (Every Stranger's Eyes) / 5:11 A.M. (The Moment Of Clarity) / Brain Damage / Eclipse

26 June 1984, National Exhibition Centre, Birmingham

FIRST SET: Set The Controls For The Heart Of The Sun / Money / If / Welcome To The Machine / Have A Cigar / Wish You Were Here / Pigs On The Wing, Part 1 / In The Flesh / Nobody Home / Hey You / The Gunner's Dream

SECOND SET: 4:30 A.M. (Apparently They Were Traveling Abroad) / 4:33 A.M. (Running Shoes) / 4:37 A.M. (Arabs With Knives And West German Skies) / 4:39 P.M. (For The First Time Today, Part 2) / 4:41 A.M. (Sexual Revolution) / 4:47 A.M. (The Remains Of Our Love) / 4:50 A.M. (Go Fishing) / 4:56 A.M. (For The First

Time Today, Part 1) / 4:58 A.M. (Dunroamin Duncarin Dunlivin) / 5:01 A.M. (The Pros and Cons of Hitch Hiking) / 5:06 A.M. (Every Stranger's Eyes) / 5:11 A.M. (The Moment Of Clarity) / Brain Damage / Eclipse

27 June 1984, National Exhibition Centre, Birmingham

FIRST SET: Set The Controls For The Heart Of The Sun / Money / If / Welcome To The Machine / Have A Cigar / Wish You Were Here / Pigs On The Wing, Part 1 / In The Flesh / Nobody Home / Hey You / The Gunner's Dream

SECOND SET: 4:30 A.M. (Apparently They Were Traveling Abroad) / 4:33 A.M. (Running Shoes) / 4:37 A.M. (Arabs With Knives And West German Skies) / 4:39 P.M. (For The First Time Today, Part 2) / 4:41 A.M. (Sexual Revolution) / 4:47 A.M. (The Remains Of Our Love) / 4:50 A.M. (Go Fishing) / 4:56 A.M. (For The First Time Today, Part 1) / 4:58 A.M. (Dunroamin Duncarin Dunlivin) / 5:01 A.M. (The Pros and Cons of Hitch Hiking) / 5:06 A.M. (Every Stranger's Eyes) / 5:11 A.M. (The Moment Of Clarity) / Brain Damage / Eclipse

29 June 1984, Westfalenhalle, Dortmund, Germany (canceled)

JULY 1984

1 July 1984, Festhalle, Frankfurst, Germany (canceled)

3 July 1984, Hallenstadion, Zürich, Switzerland

FIRST SET: Set The Controls For The Heart Of The Sun / Money / If / Welcome To The Machine / Have A Cigar / Wish You Were Here / Pigs On The Wing, Part 1 / In The Flesh / Nobody Home / Hey You / The Gunner's Dream

SECOND SET: 4:30 A.M. (Apparently They Were Traveling Abroad) / 4:33 A.M. (Running Shoes) / 4:37 A.M. (Arabs With Knives And West German Skies) / 4:39 P.M. (For The First Time Today, Part 2) / 4:41 A.M. (Sexual Revolution) / 4:47 A.M. (The Remains Of Our Love) / 4:50 A.M. (Go Fishing) / 4:56 A.M. (For The First Time Today, Part 1) / 4:58 A.M. (Dunroamin Duncarin Dunlivin) / 5:01 A.M. (The Pros and Cons of Hitch Hiking) / 5:06 A.M. (Every Stranger's Eyes) / 5:11 A.M. (The Moment Of Clarity) / Brain Damage / Eclipse

4 July 1984, Hallenstadion, Zürich, Switzerland (canceled)

6 July 1984, Palais Omnisports de Bercy, Paris, France (last show of European tour)

FIRST SET: Set The Controls For The Heart Of The Sun / Money / If / Welcome To The Machine / Have A Cigar / Wish You Were Here / Pigs On The Wing, Part 1 / In The Flesh / Nobody Home / Hey You / The Gunner's Dream

SECOND SET: 4:30 A.M. (Apparently They Were Traveling Abroad) / 4:33 A.M. (Running Shoes) / 4:37 A.M. (Arabs With Knives And West German Skies) / 4:39 P.M. (For The First Time Today, Part 2) / 4:41 A.M. (Sexual Revolution) / 4:47 A.M. (The Remains Of Our Love) / 4:50 A.M. (Go Fishing) / 4:56 A.M. (For The First Time Today, Part 1) / 4:58 A.M. (Dunroamin Duncarin Dunlivin) / 5:01 A.M. (The Pros and Cons of Hitch Hiking) / 5:06 A.M. (Every Stranger's Eyes) / 5:11 A.M. (The Moment Of Clarity) / Brain Damage / Eclipse

7 July 1984, Palais Omnisports de Bercy, Paris, France (canceled)

BOB DYLAN, WEMBLEY STADIUM 1984

7 July 1984, Wembley Stadium, Wembley, London (Eric joins Bob Dylan along with other special guests)

The complete show is recorded and six numbers from this concert will make the *Real Live* album in December 1984. This was the only stadium tour Dylan ever undertook. None of the tracks with Eric have been released officially.

Just before "Leopard-Skin Pill-Box Hat" Bob Dylan states in his inimitable style: "I wanna bring somebody out. We played together before, we played on some shows. We go back a long way, good friends. Eric Clapton! I know you'll welcome him. There's too many guitar players up here. I may just sing the first verse and leave."

SETLIST:

Leopard-Skin Pill-Box Hat (Bob Dylan) unreleased
Bob Dylan: guitar, vocals

Eric Clapton: guitar
Mick Taylor: guitar
Carlos Santana: guitar
Chrissie Hynde: harmonica, backing vocals
Colin Allen: drums
Greg Sutton: bass
Ian MacLagan: keyboards

It's All Over Now Baby Blue (Bob Dylan) unreleased

Bob Dylan: guitar, vocals
Eric Clapton: guitar
Mick Taylor: guitar
Carlos Santana: guitar
Van Morrison: acoustic guitar, vocals
Chrissie Hynde: backing vocals
Colin Allen: drums
Greg Sutton: bass
Ian MacLagan: keyboards

Tombstone Blues (Bob Dylan) unreleased

Bob Dylan: guitar, vocals
Eric Clapton: guitar
Mick Taylor: guitar
Carlos Santana: guitar
Colin Allen: drums
Greg Sutton: bass
Ian MacLagan: keyboards

Señor (Bob Dylan) unreleased

Bob Dylan: guitar, vocals
Eric Clapton: guitar
Mick Taylor: guitar
Carlos Santana: guitar
Colin Allen: drums
Greg Sutton: bass
Ian MacLagan: keyboards

The Times They Are A-Changin' (Bob Dylan) unreleased

Bob Dylan: guitar, vocals
Eric Clapton: guitar
Mick Taylor: guitar
Carlos Santana: guitar
Chrissie Hynde: backing vocals
Colin Allen: drums
Greg Sutton: bass
Ian MacLagan: keyboards

Blowin' In The Wind (Bob Dylan) unreleased

Bob Dylan: guitar, vocals
Eric Clapton: guitar
Mick Taylor: guitar
Carlos Santana: guitar
Chrissie Hynde: backing vocals
Colin Allen: drums
Greg Sutton: bass
Ian MacLagan: keyboards

Knockin' On Heaven's Door (Bob Dylan) unreleased

Bob Dylan: guitar, vocals
Eric Clapton: guitar
Mick Taylor: guitar
Carlos Santana: guitar
Chrissie Hynde: backing vocals
Colin Allen: drums
Greg Sutton: bass
Ian MacLagan: keyboards
Producer: Glyn Johns
Engineer: not known
Recorded by: not known

ROGER WATERS'S *THE PROS AND CONS OF HITCH HIKING* U.S. / CANADA TOUR 1984

17 July 1984, Civic Center, Hartford, Connecticut

FIRST SET: Set The Controls For The Heart Of The Sun / Money / If / Welcome To The Machine / Have A Cigar / Wish You Were Here / Pigs On The Wing, Part 1 / In The Flesh / Nobody Home / Hey You / The Gunner's Dream

SECOND SET: 4:30 A.M. (Apparently They Were Traveling Abroad) / 4:33 A.M. (Running Shoes) / 4:37 A.M. (Arabs With Knives And West German Skies) / 4:39 P.M. (For The First Time Today, Part 2) / 4:41 A.M. (Sexual Revolution) / 4:47 A.M. (The Remains Of Our Love) / 4:50 A.M. (Go Fishing) / 4:56 A.M. (For The First Time Today, Part 1) / 4:58 A.M. (Dunroamin Duncarin Dunlivin) / 5:01 A.M. (The Pros and Cons of Hitch Hiking) / 5:06 A.M. (Every Stranger's Eyes) / 5:11 A.M. (The Moment Of Clarity) / Brain Damage / Eclipse

18 July 1984, Civic Center, Hartford, Connecticut

FIRST SET: Set The Controls For The Heart Of The Sun / Money / If / Welcome To The Machine / Have A Cigar / Wish You Were Here / Pigs On The Wing, Part 1 / In The Flesh / Nobody Home / Hey You / The Gunner's Dream

SECOND SET: 4:30 A.M. (Apparently They Were Traveling Abroad) / 4:33 A.M. (Running Shoes) / 4:37 A.M. (Arabs With Knives And West German Skies) / 4:39 P.M. (For The First Time Today, Part 2) / 4:41 A.M. (Sexual Revolution) / 4:47 A.M. (The Remains Of Our Love) / 4:50 A.M. (Go Fishing) / 4:56 A.M. (For The First

Time Today, Part 1) / 4:58 A.M. (Dunroamin Duncarin Dunlivin) / 5:01 A.M. (The Pros and Cons of Hitch Hiking) / 5:06 A.M. (Every Stranger's Eyes) / 5:11 A.M. (The Moment Of Clarity) / Brain Damage / Eclipse

20 July 1984, Brendan Byrne Arena, East Rutherford, New Jersey

FIRST SET: Set The Controls For The Heart Of The Sun / Money / If / Welcome To The Machine / Have A Cigar / Wish You Were Here / Pigs On The Wing, Part 1 / In The Flesh / Nobody Home / Hey You / The Gunner's Dream

SECOND SET: 4:30 A.M. (Apparently They Were Traveling Abroad) / 4:33 A.M. (Running Shoes) / 4:37 A.M. (Arabs With Knives And West German Skies) / 4:39 P.M. (For The First Time Today, Part 2) / 4:41 A.M. (Sexual Revolution) / 4:47 A.M. (The Remains Of Our Love) / 4:50 A.M. (Go Fishing) / 4:56 A.M. (For The First Time Today, Part 1) / 4:58 A.M. (Dunroamin Duncarin Dunlivin) / 5:01 A.M. (The Pros and Cons of Hitch Hiking) / 5:06 A.M. (Every Stranger's Eyes) / 5:11 A.M. (The Moment Of Clarity) / Brain Damage / Eclipse

21 July 1984, Brendan Byrne Arena, East Rutherford, New Jersey

FIRST SET: Set The Controls For The Heart Of The Sun / Money / If / Welcome To The Machine / Have A Cigar / Wish You Were Here / Pigs On The Wing, Part 1 / In The Flesh / Nobody Home / Hey You / The Gunner's Dream

SECOND SET: 4:30 A.M. (Apparently They Were Traveling Abroad) / 4:33 A.M. (Running Shoes) / 4:37 A.M. (Arabs With Knives And West German Skies) / 4:39 P.M. (For The First Time Today, Part 2) / 4:41 A.M. (Sexual Revolution) / 4:47 A.M. (The Remains Of Our Love) / 4:50 A.M. (Go Fishing) / 4:56 A.M. (For The First Time Today, Part 1) / 4:58 A.M. (Dunroamin Duncarin Dunlivin) / 5:01 A.M. (The Pros and Cons of Hitch Hiking) / 5:06 A.M. (Every Stranger's Eyes) / 5:11 A.M. (The Moment Of Clarity) / Brain Damage / Eclipse

22 July 1984, Brendan Byrne Arena, East Rutherford, New Jersey

FIRST SET: Set The Controls For The Heart Of The Sun / Money / If / Welcome To The Machine / Have A Cigar /

Wish You Were Here / Pigs On The Wing, Part 1 / In The Flesh / Nobody Home / Hey You / The Gunner's Dream

SECOND SET: 4:30 A.M. (Apparently They Were Traveling Abroad) / 4:33 A.M. (Running Shoes) / 4:37 A.M. (Arabs With Knives And West German Skies) / 4:39 P.M. (For The First Time Today, Part 2) / 4:41 A.M. (Sexual Revolution) / 4:47 A.M. (The Remains Of Our Love) / 4:50 A.M. (Go Fishing) / 4:56 A.M. (For The First Time Today, Part 1) / 4:58 A.M. (Dunroamin Duncarin Dunlivin) / 5:01 A.M. (The Pros and Cons of Hitch Hiking) / 5:06 A.M. (Every Stranger's Eyes) / 5:11 A.M. (The Moment Of Clarity) / Brain Damage / Eclipse

24 July 1984, Spectrum, Philadelphia, Pennsylvania

FIRST SET: Set The Controls For The Heart Of The Sun / Money / If / Welcome To The Machine / Have A Cigar / Wish You Were Here / Pigs On The Wing, Part 1 / In The Flesh / Nobody Home / Hey You / The Gunner's Dream

SECOND SET: 4:30 A.M. (Apparently They Were Traveling Abroad) / 4:33 A.M. (Running Shoes) / 4:37 A.M. (Arabs With Knives And West German Skies) / 4:39 P.M. (For The First Time Today, Part 2) / 4:41 A.M. (Sexual Revolution) / 4:47 A.M. (The Remains Of Our Love) / 4:50 A.M. (Go Fishing) / 4:56 A.M. (For The First Time Today, Part 1) / 4:58 A.M. (Dunroamin Duncarin Dunlivin) / 5:01 A.M. (The Pros and Cons of Hitch Hiking) / 5:06 A.M. (Every Stranger's Eyes) / 5:11 A.M. (The Moment Of Clarity) / Brain Damage / Eclipse

26 July 1984, Rosemont Horizon, Rosemont, Illinois

FIRST SET: Set The Controls For The Heart Of The Sun / Money / If / Welcome To The Machine / Have A Cigar / Wish You Were Here / Pigs On The Wing, Part 1 / In The Flesh / Nobody Home / Hey You / The Gunner's Dream

SECOND SET: 4:30 A.M. (Apparently They Were Traveling Abroad) / 4:33 A.M. (Running Shoes) / 4:37 A.M. (Arabs With Knives And West German Skies) / 4:39 P.M. (For The First Time Today, Part 2) / 4:41 A.M. (Sexual Revolution) / 4:47 A.M. (The Remains Of Our Love) / 4:50 A.M. (Go Fishing) / 4:56 A.M. (For The First Time Today, Part 1) / 4:58 A.M. (Dunroamin Duncarin Dunlivin) / 5:01 A.M. (The Pros and Cons of Hitch

Hiking) / 5:06 A.M. (Every Stranger's Eyes) / 5:11 A.M. (The Moment Of Clarity) / Brain Damage / Eclipse

26 July 1984, Checkerboard Lounge, Chicago (after his show with Roger Waters, Eric joins Buddy Guy on stage)

Buddy Guy and Eric Clapton jam at Chicago's Checkerboard Lounge, 26 July 1984.

28 July 1984, Maple Leaf Gardens, Toronto, Ontario, Canada

FIRST SET: Set The Controls For The Heart Of The Sun / Money / If / Welcome To The Machine / Have A Cigar / Wish You Were Here / Pigs On The Wing, Part 1 / In The Flesh / Nobody Home / Hey You / The Gunner's Dream

SECOND SET: 4:30 A.M. (Apparently They Were Traveling Abroad) / 4:33 A.M. (Running Shoes) / 4:37 A.M. (Arabs With Knives And West German Skies) / 4:39 P.M. (For The First Time Today, Part 2) / 4:41 A.M. (Sexual Revolution) / 4:47 A.M. (The Remains Of Our Love) / 4:50 A.M. (Go Fishing) / 4:56 A.M. (For The First Time Today, Part 1) / 4:58 A.M. (Dunroamin Duncarin Dunlivin) / 5:01 A.M. (The Pros and Cons of Hitch Hiking) / 5:06 A.M. (Every Stranger's Eyes) / 5:11 A.M. (The Moment Of Clarity) / Brain Damage / Eclipse

29 July 1984, Maple Leaf Gardens, Toronto, Ontario, Canada

FIRST SET: Set The Controls For The Heart Of The Sun / Money / If / Welcome To The Machine / Have A Cigar / Wish You Were Here / Pigs On The Wing, Part 1 / In The Flesh / Nobody Home / Hey You / The Gunner's Dream

SECOND SET: 4:30 A.M. (Apparently They Were Traveling Abroad) / 4:33 A.M. (Running Shoes) / 4:37 A.M. (Arabs With Knives And West German Skies) / 4:39 P.M. (For The First Time Today, Part 2) / 4:41 A.M. (Sexual Revolution) / 4:47 A.M. (The Remains Of Our Love) / 4:50 A.M. (Go Fishing) / 4:56 A.M. (For The First Time Today, Part 1) / 4:58 A.M. (Dunroamin Duncarin Dunlivin) / 5:01 A.M. (The Pros and Cons of Hitch Hiking) / 5:06 A.M. (Every Stranger's Eyes) / 5:11 A.M. (The Moment Of Clarity) / Brain Damage / Eclipse

31 July 1984, Forum, Montreal, Quebec, Canada

FIRST SET: Set The Controls For The Heart Of The Sun / Money / If / Welcome To The Machine / Have A Cigar / Wish You Were Here / Pigs On The Wing, Part 1 / In The Flesh / Nobody Home / Hey You / The Gunner's Dream

SECOND SET: 4:30 A.M. (Apparently They Were Traveling Abroad) / 4:33 A.M. (Running Shoes) / 4:37 A.M. (Arabs With Knives And West German Skies) / 4:39 P.M. (For The First Time Today, Part 2) / 4:41 A.M. (Sexual Revolution) / 4:47 A.M. (The Remains Of Our Love) / 4:50 A.M. (Go Fishing) / 4:56 A.M. (For The First Time Today, Part 1) / 4:58 A.M. (Dunroamin Duncarin Dunlivin) / 5:01 A.M. (The Pros and Cons of Hitch Hiking) / 5:06 A.M. (Every Stranger's Eyes) / 5:11 A.M. (The Moment Of Clarity) / Brain Damage / Eclipse

AUGUST 1984

PHIL COLLINS WEDDING RECEPTION 1984

4 August 1984, Old Croft, Christmas Hill, Shalford, Guildford (Eric jams with Phil Collins, Mike Rutherford, Robert Plant, Peter Gabriel, Phil Carson, and others)

Robert Plant is at the mic singing, Phil Collins is on drums, and Eric is on the far right on guitar.

SEPTEMBER 1984

TRANCAS JAM 1984

18 September 1984, Trancas Club, Malibu, California (Eric jams with Leon Russell and Jesse Ed Davis)

AUSTRALIAN TOUR 1984

BAND LINEUP:
Eric Clapton: guitar, vocals
Donald "Duck" Dunn: bass
Chris Stainton: keyboards
Peter Robinson: synthesizer
Jamie Oldaker: drums
Marcy Levy: backing vocals
Shaun Murphy: backing vocals

OCTOBER 1984

1 October 1984–31 October 1984, rehearsals

NOVEMBER 1984

1 November 1984–2 November 1984, rehearsals

3 November 1984–7 November 1984, days off

8 November 1984, travel to Sydney, Australia

10 November 1984, arrive in Sydney, Australia

11 November 1984, day off

12 November 1984, rehearsals in Sydney

13 November 1984, Hordern Pavilion, Sydney, Australia (with Renee Geyer)

Advert for Eric Clapton Australian Tour 1984.

SETLIST: Everybody Oughta Make A Change / Motherless Children / I Shot The Sheriff / Same Old Blues / Tangled In Love / She's Waiting / Someone Else Is Steppin' In / Tulsa Time / Badge / Love Side / Wonderful Tonight / Let It Rain / That's All Right / Have You Ever Loved A Woman / Ramblin' On My Mind / Cocaine / Layla / Knock On Wood / You Don't Know Like I Know

14 November 1984, Hordern Pavilion, Sydney, Australia (with Renee Geyer)

15 November 1984–16 November 1984, days off

17 November 1984, Festival Hall, Brisbane, Australia (with Renee Geyer)

18 November 1984–19 November 1984, days off

20 November 1984, Hordern Pavilion, Sydney, Australia (with Renee Geyer)

21 November 1984, Hordern Pavilion, Sydney, Australia (with Renee Geyer)

22 November 1984, day off

23 November 1984, Sports and Entertainment Center, Melbourne, Australia (with Renee Geyer)

SETLIST: Everybody Oughta Make A Change / Motherless Children / I Shot The Sheriff / Same Old Blues / Tangled In Love / She's Waiting / Someone Else Is Steppin' In / Tulsa Time / Badge / Love Side / Wonderful Tonight / Let It Rain / That's All Right / Have You Ever Loved A Woman / Ramblin' On My Mind / Cocaine / Layla / Knock On Wood / You Don't Know Like I Know

24 November 1984, Sports and Entertainment Center, Melbourne, Australia (with Renee Geyer)

SETLIST: Everybody Oughta Make A Change / Motherless Children / I Shot The Sheriff / Same Old Blues / Tangled In Love / She's Waiting / Someone Else Is Steppin' In / Tulsa Time / Badge / Love Side / Wonderful Tonight / Let It Rain / That's All Right / Have You Ever Loved A Woman / Ramblin' On My Mind / Cocaine / Layla / Knock On Wood / You Don't Know Like I Know

25 November 1984, Sports and Entertainment Center, Melbourne, Australia (with Renee Geyer)

26 November 1984–27 November 1984, days off

28 November 1984, Entertainment Center, Perth, Australia (with Renee Geyer)

> **"**Angry at being woken up at ungodly hours because of the renovations taking place at the Sheraton Hotel in Perth, Ritchie Blackmore, lead guitarist with antique rockers Deep Purple, led an impromptu jam session at 1:30 a.m. But not for long. Although protests from other guests failed to move the group from their vigilante performance, fellow guitar expert Eric Clapton wasn't having any of it. With the music at window-shaking levels, his minder, Alphie, shouldered his way into the Deep Purple room and warned: 'If I have to come back here there's going to be a stoush.' Such was Alphie's stature that silence reigned supreme.**"**
>
> **—THE TELEGRAPH**

29 November 1984, day off
30 November 1984, fly to Hong Kong

DECEMBER 1984

1 December 1984, day off

2 December 1984, Hong Kong Coliseum, Hong Kong

3 December 1984, day off

4 December 1984, fly home

RECORDING SESSIONS 1984

ROCK CITY STUDIOS
Shepperton Studio Centre, Studios Road, Shepperton, Middlesex
Session for *The Hit* soundtrack

JANUARY 1984

THE HIT (Eric Clapton / Roger Waters) only available on the DVD of the film

Eric Clapton: guitar
Roger Waters: synth

Lasting no more than a minute and a half, this instrumental piece, which plays over the introduction in the film, would not be out of place in Roger Waters's *Pros And Cons Of Hitch Hicking* album.

FRIAR PARK STUDIOS
Henley on Thames
Session for *Water* soundtrack

AUGUST 1984

FREEDOM (Eric Clapton) *Water* soundtrack

Eric Clapton: guitar
Billy Connolly: vocals
Drums: not known
Bass: not known
Keyboards: Chris Stainton
Percussion: Ray Cooper

> **"**I was the resident composer on Water's and Eric's track which was negotiated by Denis O'Brien, who managed George Harrison at the time and was exec producer on *Water*.
>
> There were a number of songs in the movie, most were done at my own studio or George's but due to availability and time constraints, Eric and Eddie Grant supplied the already completed tracks.
>
> I took Eric's track and remixed it with Richard at my place but have no idea who played on it or indeed where it was initially recorded. When we recorded the film sequence at Shepperton, myself and Jon Lord were the keyboard players, Ringo and Ray Cooper were drums/percussion, Chris Stainton was on bass, and Eric and George were on guitars.**"**
>
> **—MIKE MORAN**

AIR STUDIOS
Waterworks Estate, Montserrat, West Indies
Sessions for *Behind The Sun*

MARCH 1984–APRIL 1984

Air Studios in Montserrat, owned by George Martin, better known as the man who produced the Beatles, was opened in 1979. He owned a holiday home on the island called Olveston House and any visiting musician using the studio would stay at the property. Eric's label, Warner Bros., were cutting loose several of their acts who they felt were not producing enough commercial material and had low sales. Eric, aware that he could be a possible casualty of these cuts, decided to hire Phil Collins as the producer for the sessions for his new album. As well as being friends with Eric since the late seventies, Phil had already released two hugely successful solo albums and it was clear he had the magic touch required to produce a commercial record.

SHE'S WAITING (Eric Clapton / John Robinson) A-side single Duck W8954 UK-only, released June 1985 / *Behind The Sun* LP UK Duck W925166-1, US Warner Bros. 925166 released March 1985 / *Behind The Sun* remastered CD released September 2000

Eric Clapton: guitar, vocals
Donald "Duck" Dunn: bass
Jamie Oldaker: drums
Peter Robinson: synthesizer
Chris Stainton: synthesizer, Hammond B3 organ
Ray Cooper: percussion
Phil Collins: Simmons and snare drum
Marcy Levy: backing vocals
Shaun Murphy: backing vocals

HEAVEN IS ONE STEP AWAY (Eric Clapton) 12-inch single B-side to "Forever Man" UK Duck W9069T released March 1985 / *Crossroads* box set Polydor 835 261-2 released April 1988

Eric Clapton: guitar, vocals
Donald "Duck" Dunn: bass
Jamie Oldaker: drums
Peter Robinson: synthesizer
Chris Stainton: synthesizer, Hammond B3 organ
Ray Cooper: percussion
Phil Collins: Simmons and snare drum
Marcy Levy: backing vocals
Shaun Murphy: backing vocals

SAME OLD BLUES (Eric Clapton) *Behind The Sun* LP UK Duck W925166-1, US Warner Bros. 925166 released March 1985 / *Behind The Sun* remastered CD released September 2000

Eric Clapton: guitar, vocals
Donald "Duck" Dunn: bass
Jamie Oldaker: drums
Peter Robinson: synthesizer
Chris Stainton: synthesizer, Hammond B3 organ
Ray Cooper: percussion
Phil Collins: Simmons and snare drum
Marcy Levy: backing vocals
Shaun Murphy: backing vocals

ONE JUMP AHEAD OF THE STORM (Eric Clapton) unreleased

Eric Clapton: guitar, vocals
Donald "Duck" Dunn: bass
Jamie Oldaker: drums
Peter Robinson: synthesizer
Chris Stainton: synthesizer, Hammond B3 organ
Ray Cooper: percussion
Phil Collins: Simmons and snare drum
Marcy Levy: backing vocals
Shaun Murphy: backing vocals

JAILBAIT (Eric Clapton) single B-side to "She's Waiting" Duck W8954 UK only, released June 1985

Eric Clapton: guitar, vocals
Donald "Duck" Dunn: bass
Jamie Oldaker: drums
Peter Robinson: synthesizer
Chris Stainton: synthesizer, Hammond B3 organ
Ray Cooper: percussion
Phil Collins: Simmons and snare drum
Marcy Levy: backing vocals
Shaun Murphy: backing vocals

YOU DON'T KNOW LIKE I KNOW (Isacc Hayes / David Porter) A-side single Duck 7-29113 released in Australia only to coincide with November 1984 tour

Eric Clapton: guitar, vocals
Donald "Duck" Dunn: bass
Jamie Oldaker: drums
Peter Robinson: synthesizer
Chris Stainton: piano, synthesizer
Phil Collins: backing vocals

KNOCK ON WOOD (Eddie Floyd / Steve Cropper) single B-side to "You Don't Know Like I Know" Duck 7-29113 released in Australia only to coincide with tour in November 1984 / *Behind The Sun* LP UK Duck W925166-1, US Warner Bros. 925166 released March 1985 / *Behind The Sun* remastered CD released September 2000

Eric Clapton: guitar, vocals
Donald "Duck" Dunn: bass
Jamie Oldaker: drums
Peter Robinson: synthesizer
Chris Stainton: piano, synthesizer
Phil Collins: backing vocals

TANGLED IN LOVE (Marcella Levy / Richard Feldman) *Behind The Sun* LP UK Duck W925166-1, US Warner Bros. 925166 released March 1985 / Behind The Sun remastered CD released September 2000

Eric Clapton: guitar, vocals
Donald "Duck" Dunn: bass
Jamie Oldaker: drums
Peter Robinson: synthesizer
Chris Stainton: synthesizer, Hammond B3 organ
Ray Cooper: percussion
Phil Collins: Simmons and snare drum
Marcy Levy: backing vocals
Shaun Murphy: backing vocals

TOO BAD (Eric Clapton) single B-side to "Forever Man" UK Duck W9069, US Duck 29081 released March 1985 / 12-inch single B-side to "Forever Man" UK Duck W9069T released March 1985 / *Crossroads* box set Polydor 835 261-2 released April 1988

Eric Clapton: guitar, vocals
Donald "Duck" Dunn: bass
Chris Stainton: keyboards
Phil Collins: drums

NEVER MAKE YOU CRY (Eric Clapton / Phil Collins) *Behind The Sun* LP UK Duck W925166-1, US Warner Bros. 925166 released March 1985 / *Behind The Sun* remastered CD released September 2000

Eric Clapton: guitar, Roland guitar synth, vocals
Donald "Duck" Dunn: bass
Jamie Oldaker: drums, backing vocals
Peter Robinson: synthesizer
Chris Stainton: Fender Rhodes
Ray Cooper: percussion
Phil Collins: shaker, vocals
Marcy Levy: backing vocals

JUST LIKE A PRISONER (Eric Clapton) *Behind The Sun* LP UK Duck W925166-1, US Warner Bros. 925166 released March 1985 / *Behind The Sun* remastered CD released September 2000

Eric Clapton: guitar, vocals
Donald "Duck" Dunn: bass
Jamie Oldaker: drums (left)
Peter Robinson: synthesizer
Chris Stainton: synthesizer
Phil Collins: drums (right)

IT ALL DEPENDS (Eric Clapton) *Behind The Sun* LP UK Duck W925166-1, US Warner Bros. 925166 released March 1985 / *Behind The Sun* remastered CD released September 2000

Eric Clapton: guitar, vocals
Donald "Duck" Dunn: bass
Jamie Oldaker: drums
Peter Robinson: synthesizer
Chris Stainton: synthesizer
Ray Cooper: bongos
Phil Collins: shaker
Marcy Levy: backing vocals
Shaun Murphy: backing vocals

Producer: Phil Collins / Eric Clapton ("Heaven Is One Step Away")
Engineer: Nick Launay

"I wrote a song with Richard Feldman called 'Tangled In Love.' Jamie Oldaker who was still in Eric's band got the song to Eric. Eric loved it. The album was being produced by Phil Collins and I was invited to come down to Montserrat where they were recording. I was told to 'bring a friend' to help sing some background vocals so I brought a great singer friend of mine named Shaun Murphy. We flew down to Montserrat, sang on many songs on the album and were asked to be in the band again which we both agreed to and ended up touring with Eric for about a year."

—MARCY LEVY
(from her website, US marcella-detroit.com)

"Eric's last couple of albums were a little bland production-wise, so when Eric asked me to produce him, I thought it would be a great idea to shake up his music and make it stand out."

— PHIL COLLINS

AIR STUDIOS
Waterworks Estate, Montserrat, West Indies
Sessions for Stephen Bishop's *Bowling In Paris*

APRIL 1984

HALL LIGHT (Stephen Bishop) *Bowling In Paris* LP Atlantic 81970-1 released 1989 / *Bowling In Paris* CD Atlantic 7 81970-2 released 1989

Stephen Bishop: vocals, acoustic guitar
Eric Clapton: guitar
Phil Collins: drums
Sting: bass, harmony vocal
Michael Omartian: piano, organ

Producer: Phil Collins
Engineer: Nick Launay

"After we'd recorded one song, Stephen, as an afterthought, went in to add some electric guitar. He went back into the studio, picked up my special guitar ['Blackie'], and began playing it—very brutally. This felt, to me, as if someone had taken a dagger and plunged it into my arm and was twisting it. I screamed, ran into the studio, and grabbed it off him. I believe that guitar has got some of me in it. So to see someone else pick it up and abuse it was unbearable."

—ERIC CLAPTON
(as told to Ray Coleman in his *Survivor* Clapton biography)

LION SHARE STUDIOS
8255 Beverly Boulevard, Los Angeles, California
and
AMIGO STUDIOS
Cumpston Avenue, North Hollywood, California
Sessions for *Behind The Sun*

SEPTEMBER 1984

HALL LIGHT (Stephen Bishop) *Bowling In Paris* LP Atlantic 81970-1 released 1989 / *Bowling In Paris* CD Atlantic 7 81970-2 released 1989

Stephen Bishop: vocals, acoustic guitar
Eric Clapton: guitar
Phil Collins: drums
Sting: bass, harmony vocal
Michael Omartian: piano, organ

Producer: Phil Collins
Engineer: Nick Launay

LION SHARE STUDIOS
8255 Beverly Boulevard, Los Angeles, California

and

AMIGO STUDIOS
Cumpston Avenue, North Hollywood, California
Sessions for *Behind The Sun*

SEPTEMBER 1984

FOREVER MAN (Jerry Williams) A-side single UK Duck W9069, US Duck 29081 released March 1985 / B-side to 12-inch "Forever Man" single UK Duck W9069T released March 1985 / *Behind The Sun* LP UK Duck W925166-1, US Warner Bros. 925166 released March 1985 / Behind The Sun remastered CD released September 2000

Eric Clapton: guitars, vocals, backing vocals
Jeff Porcaro: drums
Nathan East: bass
Steve Lukather: rhythm guitar
Michael Omartian: synthesizers
Lenny Castro: congas
Ted Templeman: timbales
Marcy Levy: backing vocals

SEE WHAT LOVE CAN DO (Jerry Williams) *Behind The Sun* LP UK Duck W925166-1, US Warner Bros. 925166 released March 1985 / *Behind The Sun* remastered CD released September 2000

Eric Clapton: guitar, vocals
Jeff Porcaro: drums
Nathan East: bass
Steve Lukather: rhythm guitar
Michael Omartian: synthesizers
Lenny Castro: congas
Jerry Williams: backing vocals
Marcy Levy: backing vocals

SOMETHING'S HAPPENING (Jerry Williams) *Behind The Sun* LP UK Duck W925166-1, US Warner Bros. 925166 released March 1985 / *Behind The Sun* remastered CD released September 2000

Eric Clapton: guitar, vocals
John Robinson: drums
Nathan East: bass, backing vocals
Greg Phillinganes: synthesizer, backing vocals
James Newton Howard: synthesizer
Lindsey Buckingham: rhythm guitar
Jerry Williams: backing vocals

LOVING YOUR LOVIN' (Jerry Williams) *Wayne's World* CD soundtrack Reprise 7599-26805-2 released February 1992

Eric Clapton: guitar, vocals
John Robinson: drums
Nathan East: bass, backing vocals
Greg Phillinganes: keyboards, backing vocals
Michael Omartian: synthesizer

Marcy Levy: backing vocals

Producers: Ted Templeman / Lenny Waronker
Engineer: Lee Hershberg

> **"**I believe the tracks were cut at Lionshare and overdubs and mixing were done at Amigo. I did some overdubs and mixed three songs at Amigo.**"**
>
> —MARK LINETT

> **"**Eric came in with a Pignose little amp. Nathan was on bass. I think Greg Philliganes was on keys. We recorded two songs.**"**
>
> —JOHN ROBINSON

> **"**It would be during 1984. I played on a the song 'Forever Man' along with a couple of other tracks. I am trying to remember whether we did these particular tracks at one time or if it was over a couple of days. There was always so much going on. I was a staff A&R man and producer at Warner Bros. during that time. Eric was totally cool and relaxed and we didn't do a lot of takes on the songs. It came together rather quickly. I can't remember who else was on the session, but Ted Templeman was producing and Lenny Waronker was at the sessions.**"**
>
> —MICHAEL OMARTIAN

ERIC CLAPTON GUEST SESSION

BRITANNIA STUDIOS
Cahuenga Boulevard, Hollywood, California
Session with JJ Cale

18 SEPTEMBER 1984

ROLL ON (JJ Cale) *Roll On* CD Rounder released February 2009

JJ Cale: vocals, guitar
Eric Clapton: guitar
Christine Lakeland: acoustic guitar
Jim Keltner: drums
Mark Leonard: bass
Glen Dee: piano
Steve Ripley: acoustic guitar
John "Juke" Logan: harmonica

Producer: JJ Cale
Engineer: Ed Barton

Eric dropped by at a session for JJ Cale during down time from recording more material for his own *Behind The Sun* album. Around six tracks were recorded and only one has been released to date, "Roll On," which can be found on the album of the same name released in February 2009. During those sessions, Eric, along with JJ Cale and Jerry Williams, went by to see a show by Leon Russell, who was playing at Trancas in Malibu. Eric ended up on stage with Leon and Jesse Ed Davis for an hour or so. Bob Britt, who was in Leon's band that night, told me, "That jam was in Malibu at a club called Trancas. I was playing there with Leon Russell. Jesse would often come out and sit in with us when we were on the West Coast. That was the second night of a two-night stand, and Eric came out along with JJ Cale and Jerry Lynn Williams. I believe Eric was working on *Behind The Sun* at the time. A fun night."

> **"**Cale remembers this more as Eric stopping in during sessions in L.A. for a day or two and playing on more like four to six songs. This was prior to my managing Cale so I don't have specifics. There was a Britannia Studios in L.A. and that's where this 'Roll On' was done.**"**
> —**MIKE KAPPUS**
> (JJ Cale's manager)

3

1985

This was another year of transition for Eric. Building on his new-found inspiration, a rejuvenated Eric played his ass off during the massive *Behind The Sun* Tour. He was sober and healthy and that was reflected in his music.

Eric's main guitars for his 1985 world tour were "Blackie," a sunburst Fender Stratocaster, and a custom light blue metallic Stratocaster, which was made for him by Roger Giffin and used exclusively for slide work.

Effects board containing a Jim Dunlop Crybaby re-issue pedal, a Bradshaw foot controller, and a Roland 700 synthesizer bank were used. The rack was controlled by a pedal board consisting of an Ibanez Harmonics / Delay, a DBX 160 compressor, a Roland SDE-3000 delay, a Tri Stereo Chorus [Dyno-My-Piano], a Boss CE-1 chorus, and a Boss Heavy Metal pedal. Eric Clapton switched from Music Man amps to Marshall 800 series heads (50 watts) during this time. The amp settings were: presence 3; bass and middle 1 o'clock; treble 8; and volume just under 9. The strings he used were Ernie Balls .010-.046. He also used a Dean Markely head with Marshall cabinets.

Rehearsals took place at the Brixton Academy in January and February. MTV filmed some of the rehearsals to run alongside an exclusive interview filmed at the same time.

BEHIND THE SUN UK / EUROPEAN TOUR 1985

FEBRUARY 1985

BAND LINEUP:
Eric Clapton: guitar, vocals
Donald "Duck" Dunn: bass
Tim Renwick: guitar
Chris Stainton: keyboards
Jamie Oldaker: drums
Shaun Murphy: backing vocals

11 February 1985–12 February 1985, filming of "Forever Man" video directed by ex-10CC members Kevin Godley and Lol Crème

> **"**Recently we did Eric Clapton's 'Forever Man' single. Now he's a classic rock figure and purist, in a sense. His LP is exactly what people want him to do. So we tried to show him in a new light but retaining his more mystic overtones. We shot him in a 'live' situation but showing a profusion of cameras.**"**
> **—KEVIN GODLEY**
> (*Record Mirror,* 6 July 1985)

13 February 1985–25 February 1985, Brixton Academy, Brixton, London (rehearsals for forthcoming tour)

26 February 1985, day off

27 February 1985, Playhouse, Edinburgh, Scotland

SETLIST: Everybody Oughta Make A Change / Motherless Children / I Shot The Sheriff / Same Old Blues / Blues Power / Tangled In Love / Someone Else Is Steppin' In / Just Like A Prisoner / Something Is Wrong With My Baby / Badge / Behind The Sun / Wonderful Tonight / Let It Rain / That's All Right / Have You Ever Loved A Woman / Ramblin' On My Mind / Cocaine / Layla / Knock On Wood / Further On Up The Road

28 February 1985, Playhouse, Edinburgh, Scotland

SETLIST: Everybody Oughta Make A Change / Motherless Children / I Shot The Sheriff / Same Old Blues / Blues Power / Tangled In Love / Someone Else Is Steppin' In / Just Like A Prisoner / Tulsa Time / Something Is Wrong With My Baby / Badge / Behind The Sun / Wonderful Tonight / Let It Rain / That's All Right / Have You Ever Loved A Woman / Ramblin' On My Mind / Cocaine / Layla / Knock On Wood / Further On Up The Road

MARCH 1985

1 March 1985, National Exhibition Centre, Birmingham, Midlands

SETLIST: Everybody Oughta Make A Change / Motherless Children / I Shot The Sheriff / Same Old Blues / Blues Power / Tangled In Love / Someone Else Is Steppin' In / Just Like A Prisoner / Tulsa Time / Something Is Wrong With My Baby / Badge / Behind The Sun / Wonderful Tonight / Let It Rain / That's All Right / Have You Ever Loved A Woman / Ramblin' On My Mind / Cocaine / Layla / Knock On Wood / Further On Up The Road

2 March 1985, National Exhibition Centre, Birmingham, Midlands

SETLIST: Everybody Oughta Make A Change / Motherless Children / I Shot The Sheriff / Same Old Blues / Blues Power / Tangled In Love / Someone Else Is Steppin' In / Tulsa Time / Lay Down Sally / Something Is Wrong With My Baby / Badge / Behind The Sun / Wonderful Tonight / Let It Rain / That's All Right / Have You Ever Loved A Woman / Ramblin' On My Mind / Cocaine / Layla / Knock On Wood / Further On Up The Road

3 March 1985, day off

4 March 1985, Wembley Arena, London

SETLIST: Everybody Oughta Make A Change / Motherless Children / I Shot The Sheriff / Same Old Blues / Blues Power / Tangled In Love / Someone Else Is Steppin' In / Tulsa Time / Lay Down Sally / Something Is Wrong With My Baby / Badge / Behind The Sun / Wonderful Tonight / Let It Rain / That's All Right / Have You Ever Loved A Woman / Ramblin' On My Mind / Cocaine / Layla / Knock On Wood / Further On Up The Road

Advert for additional dates for UK 1985 tour.

5 March 1985, Wembley Arena, London

SETLIST: Everybody Oughta Make A Change / Motherless Children / I Shot The Sheriff / Same Old Blues / Blues Power / Tangled In Love / Someone Else Is Steppin' In / Tulsa Time / Lay Down Sally / Something Is Wrong With My Baby / Badge / Behind The Sun / Wonderful Tonight / Let It Rain / That's All Right / Have You Ever Loved A Woman / Cocaine / Layla / Knock On Wood / Further On Up The Road[1]

[1] with Dan Akroyd on vocals, harmonica

6 March 1985–7 March 1985, days off

8 March 1985, fly to Finland

9 March 1985, Icehall, Helsinki, Finland

SETLIST: Everybody Oughta Make A Change / Motherless Children / I Shot The Sheriff / Same Old Blues / Blues Power / Tangled In Love / Someone Else Is Steppin' In / Tulsa Time / Lay Down Sally / Something Is Wrong With My Baby / Badge / Behind The Sun / Wonderful Tonight / Let It Rain / That's All Right / Have You Ever Loved A Woman / Ramblin' On My Mind / Cocaine / Layla / Knock On Wood/ Further On Up The Road

10 March 1985, travel to Sweden

11 March 1985, Scandinavium, Gothenburg, Sweden

SETLIST: Everybody Oughta Make A Change / Motherless Children / I Shot The Sheriff / Same Old Blues / Blues Power / Tangled In Love / Someone Else Is Steppin' In / Tulsa Time / Lay Down Sally / Something Is Wrong With My Baby / Badge / Behind The Sun / Wonderful Tonight / Let It Rain / That's All Right / Have You Ever Loved A Woman / Ramblin' On My Mind / Cocaine / Layla / Knock On Wood / Further On Up The Road

12 March 1985, Valbyhallen, Copenhagen, Denmark

SETLIST: Everybody Oughta Make A Change / Motherless Children / I Shot The Sheriff / Same Old Blues / Blues Power / Tangled In Love / Someone Else Is Steppin' In / Tulsa Time / Lay Down Sally / Something Is Wrong With My Baby / Badge / Behind The Sun / Wonderful Tonight / Let It Rain / That's All Right / Have You Ever Loved A Woman / Ramblin' On My Mind / Cocaine / Layla / Knock On Wood / Further On Up The Road

13 March 1985, travel to Norway

14 March 1985, Drammenshallen, Oslo, Norway

SETLIST: Everybody Oughta Make A Change / Motherless Children / I Shot The Sheriff / Same Old Blues / Blues Power / Tangled In Love / Someone Else Is Steppin' In / Tulsa Time / Lay Down Sally / Something Is Wrong With My Baby / Badge / Behind The Sun / Wonderful Tonight / Let It Rain / That's All Right / Have You Ever Loved A Woman / Ramblin' On My Mind / Cocaine / Layla / Knock On Wood / Further On Up The Road

15 March 1985, Isstadion, Stockholm, Sweden

SETLIST: Everybody Oughta Make A Change / Motherless Children / I Shot The Sheriff / Same Old Blues / Blues Power / Tangled In Love / Someone Else Is Steppin' In / Tulsa Time / Lay Down Sally / Something Is Wrong With My Baby / Badge / Behind The Sun / Wonderful Tonight / Let It Rain / That's All Right / Have You Ever Loved A Woman / Ramblin' On My Mind / Cocaine / Layla / Knock On Wood / Further On Up The Road

BEHIND THE SUN U.S. TOUR 1985 (First leg)

BAND LINEUP:
Eric Clapton: guitar, Roland guitar synthesizer, vocals
Donald "Duck" Dunn: bass
Tim Renwick: guitar
Chris Stainton: keyboards
Jamie Oldaker: drums
Marcy Levy: backing vocals
Shaun Murphy: backing vocals

APRIL 1985

5 April 1985–8 April 1985, rehearsals in Dallas

9 April 1985, Convention Center, Dallas, Texas (with Graham Parker and the Shot)

SETLIST: not known

10 April 1985, Summit, Houston, Texas (with Graham Parker and the Shot)

SETLIST: not known

11 April 1985, South Park Meadows, Austin, Texas (with Graham Parker and the Shot)

SETLIST: not known

12 April 1985, day off

13 April 1985, Civic Center, Pensacola, Florida (with Graham Parker and the Shot)

Eric playing a Roland G-505 synthesizer guitar for "Never Make You Cry" which was later dropped for the second leg of the tour.

SETLIST: Tulsa Time / Motherless Children / I Shot The Sheriff / Same Old Blues / Blues Power / Tangled In Love / Behind The Sun / Wonderful Tonight / Someone Else Is Steppin' In / Never Make You Cry / She's Waiting / Something Is Wrong With My Baby / Lay Down Sally /

Badge / Let It Rain / Double Trouble / Cocaine / Layla / Knock On Wood / Further On Up The Road

14 April 1985, day off

15 April 1985, Civic Center, Lakeland, Florida (with Graham Parker and the Shot)

SETLIST: Tulsa Time / Motherless Children / I Shot The Sheriff / Same Old Blues / Blues Power / Tangled In Love / Behind The Sun / Wonderful Tonight / Someone Else Is Steppin' In / Never Make You Cry / She's Waiting / Something Is Wrong With My Baby / Lay Down Sally / Badge / Let It Rain / Double Trouble / Cocaine / Layla / Knock On Wood / Further On Up The Road[1]

[1] with George Terry on guitar

16 April 1985, James L. Knight Center, Miami, Florida (with Graham Parker and the Shot)

SETLIST: Tulsa Time / Motherless Children / I Shot The Sheriff / Same Old Blues / Blues Power / Tangled In Love / Behind The Sun / Wonderful Tonight / Someone Else Is Steppin' In / Never Make You Cry / She's Waiting / Something Is Wrong With My Baby / Lay Down Sally / Badge / Let It Rain / Double Trouble / Cocaine / Layla / Knock On Wood / Further On Up The Road

17 April 1985, day off

18 April 1985, Duke University, Durham, North Carolina (with Graham Parker and the Shot)

SETLIST: Tulsa Time / Motherless Children / I Shot The Sheriff / Same Old Blues / Blues Power / Tangled In Love / Behind The Sun / Wonderful Tonight / Someone Else Is Steppin' In / Never Make You Cry / She's Waiting / Something Is Wrong With My Baby / Lay Down Sally / Badge / Let It Rain / Double Trouble / Cocaine / Layla / Knock On Wood / Further On Up The Road

19 April 1985, Civic Center, Savannah, Georgia (with Graham Parker and the Shot)

SETLIST: Tulsa Time / Motherless Children / I Shot The Sheriff / Same Old Blues / Blues Power / Tangled In Love / Behind The Sun / Wonderful Tonight / Someone Else Is Steppin' In / Never Make You Cry / She's Waiting / Something Is Wrong With My Baby / Lay Down Sally /

20 April 1985, The Omni, Atlanta, Georgia (with Graham Parker and the Shot)

SETLIST: Tulsa Time / Motherless Children / I Shot The Sheriff / Same Old Blues / Blues Power / Tangled In Love / Behind The Sun / Wonderful Tonight / Someone Else Is Steppin' In / Never Make You Cry / She's Waiting / Something Is Wrong With My Baby / Lay Down Sally / Badge / Let It Rain / Double Trouble / Cocaine / Layla / Forever Man / Further On Up The Road

21 April 1985, day off

22 April 1985, Coliseum, Richmond, Virginia (with Graham Parker and the Shot)

King Biscuit Flower record the show and an edited version is later broadcast in the U.S.

SETLIST: Tulsa Time[1] / Motherless Children / I Shot The Sheriff[1] / Same Old Blues[1] / Blues Power[1] / Tangled In Love[1] / Behind The Sun[1] / Wonderful Tonight[1] / Someone Else Is Steppin' In / Never Make You Cry / She's Waiting[1] / Something Is Wrong With My Baby / Lay Down Sally / Badge[1] / Let It Rain[1] / Double Trouble / Cocaine / Layla[1] / Forever Man[1] / Further On Up The Road

[1] broadcast on various *King Biscuit Flower Hour* syndicated radio shows

23 April 1985, Civic Center, Baltimore, Maryland (with Graham Parker and the Shot)

SETLIST: not known

24 April 1985, day off

25 April 1985, Brendan Byrne Arena, East Rutherford, New Jersey (with Graham Parker and the Shot)

SETLIST: not known

26 April 1985, Nassau Veterans Memorial Coliseum, Uniondale, New Jersey (with Graham Parker and the Shot)

SETLIST: Tulsa Time / Motherless Children / I Shot The Sheriff / Same Old Blues / Blues Power / Tangled In Love / Behind The Sun /Wonderful Tonight / Someone Else Is Steppin' In / Never Make You Cry / She's Waiting

/ Something Is Wrong With My Baby / Lay Down Sally / Badge / Let It Rain / Double Trouble / Cocaine / Layla / Forever Man / Further On Up The Road

27 April 1985, day off

28 April 1985, Civic Center, Providence, Rhode Island (with Graham Parker and the the Shot)

SETLIST: Tulsa Time / Motherless Children / I Shot The Sheriff / Same Old Blues / Blues Power / Tangled In Love / Behind The Sun / Wonderful Tonight / Someone Else Is Steppin' In / Never Make You Cry / She's Waiting / Something Is Wrong With My Baby / Lay Down Sally[1] / Badge / Let It Rain / Double Trouble / Cocaine / Layla / Forever Man

[1] with Dick Sims on keyboards

29 April 1985, Spectrum, Philadelphia, Pennsylvania (with Graham Parker and the Shot)

SETLIST: Tulsa Time / Motherless Children / I Shot The Sheriff / Same Old Blues / Blues Power / Tangled In Love / Behind The Sun / Wonderful Tonight / Someone Else Is Steppin' In / Never Make You Cry / She's Waiting / Something Is Wrong With My Baby / Lay Down Sally / Badge / Let It Rain / Double Trouble / Cocaine / Layla / Forever Man / Further On Up The Road

30 April 1985, day off

MAY 1985

1 May 1985, Civic Center, Hartford, Connecticut (with Graham Parker and the Shot)

This show is filmed and recorded for video release. Filmed in 35mm and directed by Jim Yukich.

SETLIST:

Tulsa Time (Danny Flowers) *Live 85* VHS video Channel 5 CFV 05922 released 1986

Motherless Children (traditional) *Live 85* VHS video Channel 5 CFV 05922 released 1986

I Shot The Sheriff (Bob Marley) *Live 85* VHS video Channel 5 CFV 05922 released 1986

Same Old Blues (Eric Clapton) *Live 85* VHS video Channel 5 CFV 05922 released 1986

Blues Power (Eric Clapton / Leon Russell) *Live 85* VHS video Channel 5 CFV 05922 released 1986

Tangled In Love (Marcy Levy / Richard Feldman) *Live 85* VHS video Channel 5 CFV 05922 released 1986

Behind The Sun (Eric Clapton) unreleased

Wonderful Tonight (Eric Clapton) *Live 85* VHS video Channel 5 CFV 05922 released 1986

Someone Else Is Steppin' In (Denise LaSalle) unreleased

Never Make You Cry (Eric Clapton / Phil Collins) unreleased

She's Waiting (Eric Clapton / Peter Robinson) *Live 85* VHS video Channel 5 CFV 05922 released 1986

Something Is Wrong With My Baby (Isaac Hayes / David Porter) unreleased

Lay Down Sally (Eric Clapton / Marcy Levy / George Terry) *Live 85* VHS video Channel 5 CFV 05922 released 1986

Badge (Eric Clapton / George Harrison) *Live 85* VHS video Channel 5 CFV 05922 released 1986

Let It Rain (Eric Clapton / Delaney Bramlett) *Live 85* VHS video Channel 5 CFV 05922 released 1986

Double Trouble (Otis Rush, arranged by Eric Clapton) unreleased

Cocaine (JJ Cale) *Live 85* VHS video Channel 5 CFV 05922 released 1986

Layla (Eric Clapton / Jim Gordon) *Live 85* VHS video Channel 5 CFV 05922 released 1986

Forever Man (Jerry Williams) *Live 85* VHS video Channel 5 CFV 05922 released 1986

Further On Up The Road (Don D. Robey / Joe Medwich Veasey) unreleased

2 May 1985, Cumberland County Civic Center, Portland, Maine (with Graham Parker and the Shot)

SETLIST: Tulsa Time / Motherless Children / I Shot The Sheriff / Same Old Blues / Blues Power / Tangled In Love / Behind The Sun / Wonderful Tonight / Someone Else Is Steppin' In / Never Make You Cry / She's Waiting / Something Is Wrong With My Baby / Lay Down Sally / Badge / Let It Rain / Double Trouble / Cocaine / Layla / Forever Man / Further On Up The Road

3 May 1985, Forum, Montreal, Quebec, Canada (with Graham Parker and the Shot)

SETLIST: Tulsa Time / Motherless Children / I Shot The Sheriff / Same Old Blues / Blues Power / Tangled In Love / Behind The Sun / Wonderful Tonight / Someone Else Is Steppin' In / Never Make You Cry / She's Waiting / Something Is Wrong With My Baby / Lay Down Sally / Badge / Let It Rain / Double Trouble / Cocaine / Layla / Forever Man / Further On Up The Road

4 May 1985–7 May 1985, days off

LATE NIGHT WITH DAVID LETTERMAN 1985

8 May 1985, Late Night With David Letterman TV show, NBC Studios, New York City (Eric is interviewed by David Letterman. He joins the house band to play all the interlude music leading in and out to all the commercial breaks. Playing Cream's classic "White Room" inspired him to include it in his set for the second part of the Behind The Sun Tour)

BAND LINEUP:
Eric Clapton: guitar
Paul Shaffer: keyboards
Will Lee: bass
Steve Jordan: drums

SETLIST: Late Night With David Letteman Theme / Layla / Lay Down Sally / White Room / Forever Man / Further On Up The Road / Same Old Blues / Knock On Wood / End Theme

BEHIND THE SUN U.S. TOUR 1985 (Second leg)

JUNE 1985

BAND LINEUP:
Eric Clapton: guitar, vocals
Donald "Duck" Dunn: bass
Tim Renwick: guitar
Chris Stainton: keyboards
Jamie Oldaker: drums
Marcy Levy: backing vocals
Shaun Murphy: backing vocals

17 June 1985–20 June 1985, rehearsals in Toronto, Ontario, Canada

21 June 1985, Kingswood Music Theater, Toronto, Ontario, Canada (with Graham Parker and the Shot)

SETLIST: Tulsa Time / Motherless Children / I Shot The Sheriff / Same Old Blues / Tangled In Love / White Room / Someone Else Is Steppin' In / Wonderful Tonight / She's Waiting / Something Is Wrong With My Baby / Badge / Let It Rain / Double Trouble / Cocaine / Layla / Further On Up The Road

22 June 1985, Blossom Music Center, Cleveland, Ohio (with Graham Parker and the Shot)

SETLIST: Tulsa Time / Motherless Children / I Shot The Sheriff / Same Old Blues / Tangled In Love / White Room / Someone Else Is Steppin' In / Wonderful Tonight / She's Waiting / Something Is Wrong With My Baby / Badge / Let It Rain / Double Trouble / Cocaine / Layla / Further On Up The Road

23 June 1985, Finger Lakes Performing Arts Center, Canandaigua, New York (with Graham Parker and the Shot)

SETLIST: Tulsa Time / Motherless Children / I Shot The Sheriff / Same Old Blues / Tangled In Love / White Room / Someone Else Is Steppin' In / Wonderful Tonight / She's Waiting / Something Is Wrong With My Baby / Badge / Let It Rain / Double Trouble / Cocaine / Layla / Further On Up The Road

24 June 1985, day off

25 June 1985, Performing Arts Center, Saratoga Springs, New York (with Graham Parker and the Shot)

SETLIST: Tulsa Time / Motherless Children / I Shot The Sheriff / Same Old Blues / Tangled In Love / White Room / Someone Else Is Steppin' In / Wonderful Tonight / She's Waiting / She Loves You / Badge / Let It Rain / Double Trouble / Cocaine / Layla / Forever Man / Further On Up The Road

26 June 1985, Centrum, Worcester, Massachusetts (with Graham Parker and the Shot)

SETLIST: Tulsa Time / Motherless Children / I Shot The Sheriff / Same Old Blues / Tangled In Love / White Room / Someone Else Is Steppin' In / Wonderful Tonight / She's Waiting / She Loves You / Badge / Let It Rain / Double Trouble / Cocaine / Layla / Forever Man / Further On Up The Road

27 June 1985, Merriweather Post Pavilion, Columbia, Maryland (with Graham Parker and the Shot)

SETLIST: not known

28 June 1985, Garden State Arts Center, Holmdel, New Jersey (with Graham Parker and the Shot)

SETLIST: Tulsa Time / Motherless Children / I Shot The Sheriff / Same Old Blues / Tangled In Love / White Room / Someone Else Is Steppin' In / Wonderful Tonight / She's Waiting / She Loves You / Badge / Let It Rain / Double Trouble / Cocaine / Layla / Further On Up The Road

29 June 1985, day off
30 June 1985, Summerfest, Henry Maier Festival Grounds, Milwaukee, Wisconsin (with Graham Parker and the Shot)

SETLIST: not known

JULY 1985

1 July 1985, Lousiville Gardens, Louisville, Kentucky (with Graham Parker and the Shot)

SETLIST: not known

2 July 1985, Pine Knob Pavilion, Detroit, Michigan (with Graham Parker and the Shot)

SETLIST: not known

3 July 1985, Pine Knob Pavilion, Detroit, Michigan (with Graham Parker and the Shot)

SETLIST: not known

4 July 1985, day off

5 July 1985, Poplar Creek Music Theater, Hoffman Estates, Illinois (with Graham Parker and the Shot)

SETLIST: Tulsa Time / Motherless Children / I Shot The Sheriff / Same Old Blues / Tangled In Love / White Room / Someone Else Is Steppin' In / Wonderful Tonight / She's Waiting / She Loves You / Badge / Let It Rain / Double Trouble / Cocaine / Layla / Forever Man / Further On Up The Road

5 July 1985, Legends, Chicago, Illinois (Eric jams with Buddy Guy after the gig at the Poplar Creek Music Theater)
6 July 1985, Sports Arena, Indianapolis, Indiana (with Graham Parker and the Shot)

SETLIST: Tulsa Time / Motherless Children / I Shot The Sheriff / Same Old Blues / Tangled In Love / White Room / Someone Else Is Steppin' In / Wonderful Tonight / She's Waiting / She Loves You / Badge / Let It Rain / Double Trouble / Cocaine / Layla / Forever Man / Further On Up The Road

7 July 1985, Riverbend Music Theater, Cincinnati, Ohio (with Graham Parker and the Shot)

SETLIST: Tulsa Time / Motherless Children / I Shot The Sheriff / Same Old Blues / Tangled In Love / White Room / Someone Else Is Steppin' In / Wonderful Tonight / She's Waiting / She Loves You / Badge / Let It Rain / Double Trouble / Cocaine / Layla / Forever Man / Further On Up The Road

8 July 1985, day off
9 July 1985, Sandstone Amphitheater, Bonner Springs, Kansas (with Graham Parker and the Shot)

SETLIST: Tulsa Time / Motherless Children / I Shot The Sheriff / Same Old Blues / Tangled In Love / White Room / Someone Else Is Steppin' In / Wonderful Tonight / She's Waiting / She Loves You / Badge / Let It Rain / Double Trouble / Cocaine / Layla / Forever Man / Further On Up The Road

10 July 1985, day off
11 July 1985, Red Rocks Amphitheater, Denver, Colorado (with Graham Parker and the Shot)

Advert for Eric at Red Rocks, Denver, 11 July 1985.

SETLIST: Tulsa Time / Motherless Children / I Shot The Sheriff / Same Old Blues / Tangled In Love / White Room / Someone Else Is Steppin' In / Wonderful Tonight / She's Waiting / She Loves You / Badge / Let It Rain / Double Trouble / Cocaine / Layla / Forever Man / Further On Up The Road

12 July 1985, day off

LIVE AID 1985

13 July 1985, JFK Stadium, Philadelphia, Pennsylvania (Live Aid concert)

Advert for Live Aid, 13 July 1985.

SETLIST: White Room / She's Waiting / Layla / We Are The World

All four songs are available on Rhino's 4DVD *Live Aid* box set.

Phil Collins had flown over on the Concorde to make the show in the U.S. after playing at the Wembley Stadium Live Aid show. He doubled up on drums with Eric's band for their three-song set. Later on, Eric played guitar with all the artists of the day at JFK Stadium on "We Are The World," the final number of the concert.

Early in the summer of 1985, Eric received a phone call from Pete Townshend asking if he would be available to play at a huge charity concert being organized by Bob Geldof to raise money for the famine victims in Africa. The event was called "Live Aid" and two main concerts were organized to play simultaneously in London and Philadelphia on 13 July 1985. Everything was broadcast live on television and radio across the world. Eric was halfway through a U.S. tour but agreed to play. As a result he had to cancel his show in Las Vegas the night before Live Aid as well as reshuffling some dates in Denver. Eric recalls that it was a very warm day and both he and Donald Dunn almost passed out due to the intense heat.

When Eric and the band walked on stage that afternoon, Eric could hear Lee, his guitar tech, going apoplectic with the stage manager as the wrong guitar amps had been delivered. This naturally unnerved Eric and the band. But the presence of his old mentor Ahmet Ertegun, who was side stage smiling reassuringly at Eric, put his mind at ease.

The curtains across the wide stage were pulled back as Eric and his band hit the first notes of the Cream classic "White Room." As he moved up to the microphone to sing the first line he got an electric shock off it, giving him another reason to be unnerved.

While Eric may have been uneasy during the event, there is no doubt that it did wonders for his career. Not only did it remind people how great he was, it also gave him many new fans who were unaware of his illustrious past.

14 July 1985, Red Rocks Amphitheater, Denver, Colorado (with Graham Parker and the Shot)

SETLIST: Tulsa Time / Motherless Children / I Shot The Sheriff / Same Old Blues / Tangled In Love / White Room / Someone Else Is Steppin' In / Wonderful Tonight / She's Waiting / She Loves You / Badge / Let It Rain / Double Trouble / Cocaine / Layla / Forever Man / Further On Up The Road

15 July 1985–16 July 1985, days off

17 July 1985, Universal Amphitheater, Los Angeles, California (with Graham Parker and the Shot)

SETLIST: Tulsa Time / Motherless Children / I Shot The Sheriff / Same Old Blues / Tangled In Love / White Room / Someone Else Is Steppin' In / Wonderful Tonight / She's Waiting / She Loves You / Badge / Let It Rain / Double Trouble / Cocaine / Layla / Forever Man / Further On Up The Road

18 July 1985, Universal Amphitheater, Los Angeles, California (with Graham Parker and the Shot)

SETLIST: Tulsa Time / Motherless Children / I Shot The Sheriff / Same Old Blues / Tangled In Love / White Room / Someone Else Is Steppin' In / Wonderful Tonight / She's Waiting / She Loves You / Badge / Let It Rain / Double Trouble / Cocaine / Layla / Forever Man / Further On Up The Road

19 July 1985, Universal Amphitheater, Los Angeles, California (with Graham Parker and the Shot)

SETLIST: Tulsa Time / Motherless Children / I Shot The Sheriff / Same Old Blues / Tangled In Love / White Room / Someone Else Is Steppin' In / Wonderful Tonight / She's Waiting / She Loves You / Badge / Let It Rain / Double Trouble / Cocaine / Layla / Forever Man / Further On Up The Road[1]

[1]with Sergio Pastora on percussion

20 July 1985, day off

21 July 1985, Compton Terrace, Phoenix, Arizona (with Graham Parker and the Shot)

SETLIST: Tulsa Time / Motherless Children / I Shot The Sheriff / Same Old Blues / Tangled In Love / White Room / Someone Else Is Steppin' In / Wonderful Tonight / She's Waiting / She Loves You / Badge / Let It Rain / Double Trouble / Cocaine / Layla / Forever Man / Further On Up The Road

22 July 1985, Pacific Amphitheatre, Costa Mesa, California (with Graham Parker and the Shot)

SETLIST: Tulsa Time / Motherless Children / I Shot The Sheriff / Same Old Blues / Tangled In Love / White Room / Someone Else Is Steppin' In / Wonderful Tonight / She's Waiting / She Loves You / Badge / Let It Rain / Double Trouble / Cocaine / Layla / Forever Man / Further On Up The Road

23 July 1985, Concord Pavilion, Concord, California (with Graham Parker and the Shot)

SETLIST: Tulsa Time / Motherless Children / I Shot The Sheriff / Same Old Blues / Tangled In Love / White Room / Someone Else Is Steppin' In / Wonderful Tonight / She's Waiting / She Loves You / Badge / Let It Rain / Double Trouble / Cocaine / Layla / Forever Man / Further On Up The Road[1]

[1]with Carlos Santana on guitar

24 July 1985, Concord Pavilion, Concord, California (with Graham Parker and the Shot)

SETLIST: Tulsa Time / Motherless Children / I Shot The Sheriff / Same Old Blues / Tangled In Love / White Room / Someone Else Is Steppin' In / Wonderful Tonight / She's Waiting / She Loves You / Badge / Let It Rain / Double Trouble / Cocaine / Layla / Forever Man / Further On Up The Road

25 July 1985, day off

26 July 1985, Center Coliseum, Seattle, Washington (with Graham Parker and the Shot)

SETLIST: Tulsa Time / Motherless Children / I Shot The Sheriff / Same Old Blues / Tangled In Love / White Room / Someone Else Is Steppin' In / Wonderful Tonight / She's Waiting / She Loves You / Badge / Let It Rain / Double Trouble / Cocaine / Layla / Knock On Wood[1] / You Don't Know Like I Know[1]

[1]with Lionel Richie

27 July 1985, Pacific National Exhibition Coliseum, Vancouver, British Columbia, Canada (with Graham Parker and the Shot)

SETLIST: Tulsa Time / Motherless Children / I Shot The Sheriff / Same Old Blues / Tangled In Love / White Room / Someone Else Is Steppin' In / Wonderful Tonight / She's Waiting / She Loves You / Badge / Let It Rain / Double Trouble / Cocaine / Layla / Forever Man / Further On Up The Road

OCTOBER 1985

BEHIND THE SUN
JAPAN TOUR 1985

BAND LINEUP:
Eric Clapton: guitar, vocals
Tim Renwick: guitar
Jamie Oldaker: drums
Donald "Duck" Dunn: bass
Chris Stainton: keyboards
Laura Creamer: backing vocals
Shaun Murphy: backing vocals

2 October 1985–4 October 1985, rehearsals in Tokyo
5 October 1985, Yoyogi Olympic Pool, Tokyo, Japan

SETLIST: Tulsa Time / Motherless Children / I Shot The Sheriff / Same Old Blues / Tangled In Love / White Room / You Got Me Hummin' / Wonderful Tonight / She's Waiting / Lay Down Sally / Badge / Let It Rain / Double Trouble / Cocaine / Layla / Forever Man / Further On Up The Road

6 October 1985, Yoyogi Olympic Pool, Tokyo, Japan

SETLIST: Tulsa Time / Motherless Children / I Shot The Sheriff / Same Old Blues / Tangled In Love / White Room / You Got Me Hummin' / Wonderful Tonight / She's Waiting / Lay Down Sally / Badge / Let It Rain / Double Trouble / Cocaine / Layla / Forever Man / Further On Up The Road

7 October 1985, Koseinenkin Kaikan Dai, Osaka, Japan

SETLIST: Tulsa Time / Motherless Children / I Shot The Sheriff / Same Old Blues / Tangled In Love / White Room / You Got Me Hummin' / Wonderful Tonight / She's Waiting / Lay Down Sally / Badge / Let It Rain / Double Trouble / Cocaine / Layla / Forever Man / Further On Up The Road

9 October 1985, Shimin Kaikan, Nagoya, Japan

SETLIST: Tulsa Time / Motherless Children / I Shot The Sheriff / Same Old Blues / Tangled In Love / White Room / You Got Me Hummin' / Wonderful Tonight / She's Waiting / Lay Down Sally / Badge / Let It Rain / Double Trouble / Cocaine / Layla / Forever Man / Further On Up The Road

10 October 1985, Festival Hall, Osaka, Japan

SETLIST: Tulsa Time / Motherless Children / I Shot The Sheriff / Same Old Blues / Tangled In Love / White Room / You Got Me Hummin' / Wonderful Tonight / She's Waiting / Lay Down Sally / Badge / Let It Rain / Double Trouble / Cocaine / Layla / Forever Man / Further On Up The Road

11 October 1985, Sun Paresu Hall, Fukuoka, Japan

SETLIST: Tulsa Time / Motherless Children / I Shot The Sheriff / Same Old Blues / Tangled In Love / White Room / You Got Me Hummin' / Wonderful Tonight / She's Waiting / Lay Down Sally / Badge / Let It Rain / Double Trouble / Cocaine / Layla / Forever Man / Further On Up The Road

BEHIND THE SUN
ALASKA TOUR 1985

14 October 1985, George Sullivan Arena, Anchorage, Alaska

SETLIST: Tulsa Time / Motherless Children / I Shot The Sheriff / Same Old Blues / Tangled In Love / White Room / You Got Me Hummin' / Wonderful Tonight / She's Waiting / Lay Down Sally / Badge / Let It Rain / Double Trouble / Cocaine / Layla / Forever Man / Further On Up The Road

HOMETOWN SHOW IN GUILDFORD 1985

20 October 1985, Civic Hall, Guildford, Surrey

Eric's hometown gigs were always special and guaranteed that some of his friends would drop by for a jam. This show saw Carl Perkins, Gary Brooker, and Phil Collins coming out in the encores.

SETLIST: Tulsa Time / Motherless Children / I Shot The Sheriff / Same Old Blues / Tangled In Love / White Room / Hungry For Love / Wonderful Tonight / She's Waiting / Lay Down Sally / Badge / Let It Rain / Double Trouble / Cocaine / Layla / Knock On Wood[1, 3] / You Don't Know Like I Know[1, 3] / Matchbox[1, 2, 3] / Blue Suede Shoes[1, 2, 3] / Goodnight Irene[1, 2, 3]

[1] with Phil Collins on drums
[2] with Carl Perkins on guitar and vocals
[3] with Gary Brooker on keyboards

BLUE SUEDE SHOES: A ROCKABILLY SESSION 1985

21 October 1985, Limehouse Television Studios, Canary Wharf, London

Filming for *Blue Suede Shoes: A Rockabilly Session*. Fantastic concert that seems to have slipped from people's memory. The legendary Carl Perkins is surrounded by his friends in this television special with George Harrsion, Ringo Starr, Eric Clapton, Dave Edmunds, Rosanne Cash, Earl Slick, Lee Rocker, Slim Jim Phantom, Geraint Watkins, Mickey Gee, Greg Perkins, David Charles, and John David. Eric plays some exceptional solos and both the CD and DVD are well worth having in any collection.

SETLIST:

Matchbox (Carl Perkins) *Blue Suede Shoes: A Rockabilly Session* CD Snapper SDPCD 206 SDVD514 / DVD Snapper released June 2006

Carl Perkins: vocals, guitar
Eric Clapton: vocals, guitar
Ringo Starr: drums
Dave Edmunds: guitar
Micky Gee: guitar
John David: bass
Geraint Watkins: piano

Mean Woman Blues (Claude Demetrius) *Blue Suede Shoes: A Rockabilly Session* CD Snapper SDPCD 206 released June 2006 / DVD Snapper SDVD514

Carl Perkins: vocals, guitar
Eric Clapton: vocals, guitar
David Charles: drums

Dave Edmunds: guitar
Micky Gee: guitar
John David: bass
Geraint Watkins: piano

MEDLEY: That's All Right Mama (Arthur Crudup) / **Blue Moon of Kentucky** (Monroe) / **Night Train To Memphis** (Owen Bradley) / **Glad All Over** (Bennett) / **Whole Lotta Shakin' Goin' On** (Dave Williams / James Fay Hall) *Blue Suede Shoes: A Rockabilly Session* CD Snapper SDPCD 206 released June 2006 / DVD Snapper SDVD514

Gone Gone Gone (Carl Perkins) *Blue Suede Shoes: A Rockabilly Session* CD Snapper SDPCD 206 released June 2006 / DVD Snapper SDVD514

Blue Suede Shoes (Carl Perkins) *Blue Suede Shoes: A Rockabilly Session* CD Snapper SDPCD 206 released June 2006 / DVD Snapper SDVD514

Blue Suede Shoes (Carl Perkins) (reprise) *Blue Suede Shoes: A Rockabilly Session* CD Snapper SDPCD 206 released June 2006 / DVD Snapper SDVD514

Carl Perkins: vocals, guitar
George Harrison: vocals, guitar
Ringo Starr: vocals, drums
Eric Clapton: vocals, guitar
Dave Edmunds: vocals, guitar
Geraint Watkins: piano
Mickey Gee: guitar
David Charles: drums
John David: bass
Roseanne Cash: vocals
Slim Jim Phantom: drums
Lee Rocker: double bass
Earl Slick: guitar
Greg Perkins: bass
Producer: Dave Edmunds

BEHIND THE SUN SWISS / ITALIAN TOUR 1985

BAND LINEUP:
Eric Clapton: guitar, vocals
Tim Renwick: guitar
Jamie Oldaker: drums
Donald "Duck" Dunn: bass
Chris Stainton: keyboards
Laura Creamer: backing vocals
Shaun Murphy: backing vocals

23 October 1985, Halle des Fêtes, Lausanne, Switzerland

SETLIST: Tulsa Time / Motherless Children / I Shot The Sheriff / Same Old Blues / Tangled In Love / White Room / You Got Me Hummin' / Wonderful Tonight / She's Waiting / Lay Down Sally / Badge / Let It Rain / Double Trouble / Cocaine / Layla / Forever Man / Further On Up The Road

24 October 1985, Hallenstadion, Zürich, Switzerland

SETLIST: Tulsa Time / Motherless Children / I Shot The Sheriff / Same Old Blues / Tangled In Love / White Room / You Got Me Hummin' / Wonderful Tonight / She's Waiting / Lay Down Sally / Badge / Let It Rain / Double Trouble / Cocaine / Layla / Forever Man / Further On Up The Road

27 October 1985, Teatro Tenda, Milano, Italy

SETLIST: Tulsa Time / Motherless Children / I Shot The Sheriff / Same Old Blues / Tangled In Love / White Room / You Got Me Hummin' / Wonderful Tonight / She's Waiting / Lay Down Sally / Badge / Let It Rain / Double Trouble / Cocaine / Layla / Forever Man / Further On Up The Road

28 October 1985, Teatro Tenda, Milano, Italy

SETLIST: Tulsa Time / Motherless Children / I Shot The Sheriff / Same Old Blues / Tangled In Love / White Room / You Got Me Hummin' / Hold Me Now / Wonderful Tonight / She's Waiting / Lay Down Sally / Badge / Let It Rain / Double Trouble / Cocaine / Layla / Forever Man / Further On Up The Road

29 October 1985, Palasport, Turin, Italy

SETLIST: Tulsa Time / Motherless Children / I Shot The Sheriff / Same Old Blues / Tangled In Love / White Room / You Got Me Hummin' / Wonderful Tonight / She's Waiting / Lay Down Sally / Badge / Let It Rain / Double Trouble / Cocaine / Layla / Forever Man / Further On Up The Road

31 October 1985, Palamaggiò, Caserta, Italy

SETLIST: Tulsa Time / Motherless Children / I Shot The Sheriff / Same Old Blues / Tangled In Love / White Room / You Got Me Hummin' / Wonderful Tonight / She's

Waiting / Lay Down Sally / Badge / Let It Rain / Double Trouble / Cocaine / Layla / Forever Man / Further On Up The Road

NOVEMBER 1985

1 November 1985, Palaeur, Rome, Italy

SETLIST: not known

2 November 1985, Palasport, Génova, Italy

SETLIST: not known

4 November 1985, Teatro Tenda, Bologna, Italy

SETLIST: Tulsa Time / Motherless Children / I Shot The Sheriff / Same Old Blues / Tangled In Love / White Room / You Got Me Hummin' / Wonderful Tonight / She's Waiting / Lay Down Sally / Badge / Let It Rain / Double Trouble / Cocaine / Layla / Forever Man / Further On Up The Road

5 November 1985, Palasport, Florence, Italy

SETLIST: not known

6 November 1985, Palasport, Padova, Italy

SETLIST: Tulsa Time / Motherless Children / I Shot The Sheriff / Same Old Blues / Tangled In Love / White Room / You Got Me Hummin' / Wonderful Tonight / She's Waiting / Lay Down Sally / Badge / Let It Rain / Double Trouble / Cocaine / Layla / Forever Man / Further On Up The Road

DECEMBER 1985

3 December 1985, Dingwalls, Camden, London (Eric jams with Buddy Guy and Junior Wells)

6 December 1985, Teatro Tenda Lampugnano, Milan, Italy (Eric makes a surprise guest appearance with Sting)

BAND LINEUP:
Sting: guitar, vocals
Branford Marsalis: soprano and tenor saxophones
Kenny Kirkland: piano, keyboards
Darryl Jones: bass
Omar Hakim: drums
Janice Pendarvis: backing vocals
Dolette McDonald: backing vocals
Eric Clapton: guitar[1]

[1] borrowed Fender Telecaster

SETLIST: Down So Long / Tea In The Sahara / Every Breath You Take / Need Your Love So Bad

PIER END RESTORATION BAND 1985

12 December 1985, Dickens Pub, Southend

BAND LINEUP:
Gary Brooker: vocals, keyboards
Eric Clapton: guitar, vocals
Mickey Jupp: guitar, vocals
Dave Bronze: bass
Henry Spinetti: drums
Ronnie Cary: saxophone

SETLIST: Roberta / Be My Guest / Smokey Joe's Café / Willie And The Hand Jive / Sweet Little Rock 'N' Roller / Good Golly Miss Molly / Walking To New Orleans / No Money Down / Little Egypt / Sea Cruise / Memphis Tennessee / Promised Land / Too Much Monkey Business / Sweet Memories / Hey Bo Diddley / You Can't Judge A Book / Blue Monday / Piano Boogie / So Many Roads / Shotgun / Roll Over Beethoven / Move On Down The Line / Ubangi Stomp /Bonie Moronie / Little Queenie / Stay / Young Blood / Let's Stick Together / Money / Long Tall Sally

13 December 1985, Parrot Inn, Forest Green, Surrey

Eric joins Gary Brooker and most of the Pier End band for an evening of rock and roll covers.

DIRE STRAITS CHRISTMAS CONCERTS 1985

19 December 1985, Hammersmith Odeon, London (Eric sits in with Dire Straits)

SETLIST: Two Young Lovers / Cocaine / Solid Rock / Further On Up The Road

22 December 1985, Hammersmith Odeon, London (Eric sits in with Dire Straits)

SETLIST: Two Young Lovers / Cocaine / Solid Rock / Further On Up The Road

GARY BROOKER CHRISTMAS CONCERT 1985

23 December 1985, Village Hall, Dunsfold, Surrey (Eric joins Gary Brooker and friends)

RECORDING SESSIONS 1985

ERIC CLAPTON GUEST SESSION

JACOBS STUDIOS
Ridgway House, Runwick Lane, Farnham, Surrey
Session for Gary Brooker

JANUARY 1985

ECHOES IN THE NIGHT (Gary Brooker / Matthew Fisher / Keith Reid)
Echoes In The Night US LP Mercury 824 652-1 M-1, UK Mercury MERL68
released 1985

Gary Brooker: vocals, keyboards
Eric Clapton: guitar
Tim Renwick: guitar
Matthew Fisher: keyboards
Matt Lettly: drums

John Giblin: bass
Linda Page: backing vocals
Jannette Sewell: backing vocals
Shola Phillips: backing vocals

Producers: Matthew Fisher / Gary Brooker
Engineer: Terry Barnham

THE WOODLANDS SOUND STUDIOS
Wood Lane, London
and
EEL PIE STUDIOS
The Boathouse, Ranelagh Drive, Twickenham
Session for the *Edge Of Darkness* soundtrack

MAY 1985–JUNE 1985

Michael Kamen took Eric to see *Brazil*, Terry Gilliam's fantasy sci-fi film, in February 1985. Michael had scored the music and shortly after seeing the movie, Eric asked him if he would like to collaborate with him on the soundtrack for a BBC series called *Edge Of Darkness*. Michael was thrilled at the prospect of working with Eric and the two set about working on their first collaborative project. Together they composed the theme as well as the full soundtrack for the complete series. Other than the short intro music for the film *The Hit*, this was Eric's first real foray into film score writing. He would subsequently work on the *Lethal Weapon* soundtracks among many others.

It is worth noting that on the 2009 release of the BBC DVD of the series, there is a music-only audio option that isolates the Eric Clapton / Michael Kamen BAFTA-winning score.

EDGE OF DARKNESS (Eric Clapton / Michael Kamen) 12-inch mini-album BBC Records 12RSL 178 / CD released November 1985

SHOOT OUT (Eric Clapton / Michael Kamen) 12-inch mini-album BBC Records 12RSL 178 / CD released November 1985

OBITUARY (Eric Clapton / Michael Kamen) 12-inch mini-album BBC Records 12RSL 178 / CD released November 1985

ESCAPE FROM NORTHMOOR (Eric Clapton / Michael Kamen) 12-inch mini-album BBC Records 12RSL 178 / CD released November 1985

OXFORD CIRCUS (Eric Clapton / Michael Kamen) 12-inch mini-album BBC Records 12RSL 178 / CD released November 1985

NORTHMOOR (Eric Clapton / Michael Kamen) 12-inch mini-album BBC Records 12RSL 178 / CD released November 1985

Producer: Michael Wearing
Engineer: Andy Jackson

> **"**Eric played to picture, which would be pretty normal practice. It would be mono as it was fo r TV and that's all there was in that day. One trivial detail I remember is that the bit that sounds like wah wah guitar is not a wah wah but me doing it on the desk EQ.**"**
>
> —ANDY JACKSON
> (engineer)

> **"**Because Eric Clapton asked me to make the music to *Edge of Darkness,* I began working on that. I bought a Kurzweil, twenty thousand pounds of Kurzweil. I mean, the whole instrument is about eight thousand dollars now. Kurzweil is this, basically, it's the first digital sampling keyboard. It was the first and the best of them in my eyes. It preserved the feel of a piano. It had a major sample of a piano, fantastic for that time, in 1982. That was unbelievable, that you could plug something in and it would sound like a piano as close as that.**"**
>
> —MICHAEL KAMEN
> (from an interview in *MacAddict*)

ERIC CLAPTON GUEST SESSION
BEAR CREEK RECORDING STUDIOS
6213 Maltby Road, Woodinville, Washington
Guitar overdub for Lionel Richie

26 JULY 1985

Eric and Lionel Richie during sessions for "Tonight Will Be Alright" at Bear Creek Recording Studios on 26 July 1985.

TONIGHT WILL BE ALRIGHT (Lionel Richie) *Dancing On The Ceiling* remastered CD Motown 3746361582 released May 2003

Lionel Richie: vocals, keyboards
Eric Clapton: guitar solo
Carlos Rios: guitar
Greg Phillinganes: keyboards
Joseph Chemay: bass
Paul Leim: drums
Paulinho Da Costa: percussion
Michael Boddicker: synthesizer
Deborah Thomas: backing vocals
Julia Waters: backing vocals
Maxine Waters: backing vocals
Richard Marx: backing vocals

Producer: Lionel Richie
Engineer: Fred Law

❝I remember it well. Eric and Richie talked at the recording of 'We are the World' and decided to do something together. They decided that Seattle would be the best place to meet since they would be in town at the same time and I think it was the last stop on Clapton's U.S. tour. I heard that Richie joined Clapton for a song at his show. A day was booked at Bear Creek, I think the day before the show and Richie's producer and engineer showed up. They were wonderful people and we had a good visit while we waited. The session was canceled a little later because Eric needed some emergency dental work and it was booked for the next night after the concert. It was pretty late—probably around 11:00 or 12:00—when they showed up. They were a little surprised that it was about a half-hour drive from the show location in Seattle out to our studio in the country. Both Eric and Richie were wonderful and gracious and immediately disarmed any nervous feelings on the part of our staff by complimenting our facility and thanking us for our time. I think Clapton said, 'Wow. I wish I had a place like this.' We put up their two-inch tapes, and even though everyone was a little tired, went to work. We were surprised that Clapton didn't bring an amp, and we didn't have a suitable amp in the studio. Had I known that he needed an amp I could have had one of several friends bring an array of great vintage amps out. I went across the pasture to our farmhouse where we lived and got a Fender Champ amp from my ten-year-old son's room. In the positive spirit of the session Clapton said, 'That'll work just fine.' It was great to hear Clapton licks in our studio. I asked Richie how they decided to come to Bear

Creek Studio. He said that they were working at Oceanway in Hollywood and when they asked where to record in Seattle an engineer said, 'You've got to go to Bear Creek.' So the session went well with a great vibe of mutual respect. Everyone involved was professional and wonderful to work with. We got a great snapshot of the two of them in the control room. Richie invited me to drop in to Oceanway if I was ever in L.A. and I did the next month when I was down there for an AES [Audio Engineering Society] convention. It was a great night and we got our first platinum record. It was a high point of our forty years in the recording biz. What an honor to work with those two. My son Ryan, whose amp Clapton used, is now running the studio and just got his first platinum record for producing the Lumineers.❞

—JOE HADLOCK
(Bear Creek producer and engineer)

ERIC CLAPTON GUEST SESSION
UTOPIA STUDIOS
Utopia Village, 7 Chalcot Road, London
Session for Paul Brady

NOVEMBER 1985

DEEP IN YOUR HEART (Paul Brady) *Back To The Centre* CD Mercury 826 809-2 released 1986

Paul Brady: vocals, keyboards, acoustic guitar
Eric Clapton: guitar
Phil Palmer: guitar
Ole Romo: drums
Mitt Garmon: harmonica
Betsy Cook: keyboards
Ian Maidman: bass, percussion

Producer: Ian Maidman
Engineer: John Lee

4

1986

Nineteen eighty-six was another busy year for Eric. First off there was a change of band to arguably a leaner and meaner one, made up of the guys who would soon record *August,* his new album. The band consisted of Phil Collins on drums, Nathan East on bass, and Greg Phillinganes on keyboards. This represented a much more commercial sound for him. The other change this year was a brand new guitar especially developed in consultation with Eric, the Fender Eric Clapton Signature Stratocaster. "Blackie" was wearing out, especially the neck, and it was time to look at getting a new guitar with all the latest electronics. Eric explained: "Dan Smith . . . who was head of Fender at the time, asked me if I'd be interested in putting out a guitar with my name on it and specifying the way I would want it. When he asked me what my favorite guitar was, I said 'Blackie' was it, so if they could make copies of that, especially the neck shape—I wouldn't want any changes made except for optional sound, to fatten it up. You've got one volume and two tone knobs. The second tone is the compression sound. The more you turn it clockwise, the fatter the sound gets. The colors I asked for were Ferrari red, 7-Up green, and charcoal gray."

The initial prototype guitar's neck was a one-piece maple construction with 22 frets and a small headstock. The frets were positioned to allow the action to be set very low without creating a buzz. It was a softer V-neck than "Blackie" which Eric preferred. The body had a white single-ply pickguard and the original prototype had a 14db boost but Eric wanted more. Fender then created a new prototype with three Fender Gold Lace Sensor pickups (neck, middle, bridge) and this time the circuit had a 25db boost in the midrange at around 500 Hz. This was the Fender Eric Clapton Signature Stratocaster model that went into production. At Eric's request the first models were only available in three colors, Ferrari red, 7-Up green, and charcoal gray. And you could buy one! Over the years adjustments to the specs and colors were made, some specifically for Eric and not the commercial editions.

In February, Eric participated in Ian Stewart's memorial concert at the intimate 100 Club in London's Oxford Street which saw him play with the Rolling Stones alongside Jeff Beck, Pete Townshend, and others. It was the musical send-off that Ian would have loved.

Scandinavia had the privilege of having the world premiere of Eric's new four-piece band with shows in Norway and Denmark. Fans and critics received the shows very warmly. Eric then played the prestigious Montreux Jazz Festival for the first time. The Montreux festival had always been known for the amazing musical jams that took place and this year proved no different. On 9 July, Otis Rush was headlining and Eric joined him for four numbers. Other than the obvious treat of seeing Eric with Otis Rush, the highlight of the evening had to be the incredible guitar tone Eric had on his new Ferrari-red Signature Strat. It just cut through the air like the Les Paul sound he had achieved in his live Bluesbreakers days. Luckily, the event was captured on video and audio.

FEBRUARY 1986

IAN STEWART MEMORIAL CONCERT

An amazing concert for family and friends of Ian Stewart took place at the very intimate 100 Club in London's Oxford Street. L to R: Mick Jagger, Keith Richards, Eric Clapton.

At the 100 Club. L to R: Keith Richards, Pete Townshend, Eric Clapton.

23 February 1986, 100 Club, Oxford Street, London

Eric greatly admired Ian Stewart and participated in a memorial jam session with the Rolling Stones and friends. The memorial concert honored Ian "Stu" Stewart, the original "Sixth Stone" and pianist for the Rolling Stones. Ian had died of a heart attack on 12 December 1985 and the Rolling Stones organized this jam session at the 100 Club in London. In attendance were a very small audience who were limited to close friends and family members. Ian's band, Rocket 88, opened the show followed by the Stones and friends who played for just over an hour.

The songs were not recorded.

BAND LINEUP:
Mick Jagger: vocals
Keith Richards: guitar
Ron Wood: guitar
Charlie Watts: drums
Bill Wyman: bass
Simon Kirke: drums
Eric Clapton: guitar
Jeff Beck: guitar
Pete Townshend: guitar
Colin Golding: bass
Jack Bruce: bass

SETLIST:

Route 66 (with Simon Kirke)

Down The Road A Piece (with Eric Clapton, Pete Townshend, Simon Kirke)

Hoochie Coochie Man (with Eric Clapton, Pete Townshend, Simon Kirke)

Key To The Highway (with Eric Clapton, Simon Kirke)

Confessin' The Blues (with Simon Kirke)

Mannish Boy (with Simon Kirke)

Bye Bye Johnny (with Eric Clapton, Jeff Beck)

Harlem Shuffle (with Jeff Beck, Pete Townshend)

Little Red Rooster (with Jeff Beck, Pete Townshend)

Down In The Bottom (with Eric Clapton, Jeff Beck, Pete Townshend)

Dust My Broom (with the Rolling Stones)

Little Queenie (with Eric Clapton, Jack Bruce)

JUNE 1986

PRINCE'S TRUST CONCERT 10th BIRTHDAY PARTY 1986

20 June 1986, Wembley Arena, London (10th Birthday Party of the Prince's Trust)

At the time this was quite an extraordinary concert with all the top artists of the day playing for charity in the presence of Prince Charles and Princess Diana at a sold-out Wembley Arena. The event was filmed and recorded.

BAND LINEUP:

Eric Clapton: guitar, vocals
Midge Ure: guitar, vocals
Mark Knopfler: guitar, vocals
Bryan Adams: guitar, vocals
Paul McCartney: guitar, vocals
Joan Armatrading: guitar, vocals
Rick Parfitt: guitar
Francis Rossi: guitar
Ray Cooper: percussion
Elton John: piano
David Bowie: vocals
Mick Jagger: vocals
Paul Young: vocals
George Michael: vocals
Sting: vocals
Rod Stewart: vocals
Mark King: bass
John Illsley: bass
Howard Jones: keyboards, vocals
Vicki Brown: backing vocals
Samantha Brown: backing vocals
Jimmy Chambers: backing vocals
George Chandler: backing vocals
Jimmy Helms: backing vocals

SETLIST:

Better Be Good To Me (Tina Turner) *Recorded Highlights Of The Prince's Trust 10th Anniversary Birthday Party* CD A&M 396925-2 released 1987, also available on VHS video

Tearing Us Apart (Tina Turner, Eric Clapton) *Recorded Highlights Of The Prince's Trust 10th Anniversary Birthday Party* CD A&M 396925-2 released 1987, also available on VHS video

Call Of The Wild (Midge Ure) *Recorded Highlights Of The Prince's Trust 10th Anniversary Birthday Party* CD A&M 396925-2 released 1987 / also available on VHS video

Money For Nothing (Mark Knopfler, Sting) *Recorded Highlights Of The Prince's Trust 10th Anniversary Birthday Party* CD A&M 396925-2 released 1987, also available on VHS video

Everytime You Go Away (Paul Young) *Recorded Highlights Of The Prince's Trust 10th Anniversary Birthday Party* CD A&M 396925-2 released 1987, also available on VHS video

Reach Out (Joan Armatrading) *Recorded Highlights Of The Prince's Trust 10th Anniversary Birthday Party* CD A&M 396925-2 released 1987, also available on VHS video

No One Is To Blame (Howard Jones) *Recorded Highlights Of The Prince's Trust 10th Anniversary Birthday Party* CD A&M 396925-2 released 1987, also available on VHS video

Sailing (Rod Stewart) *Recorded Highlights Of The Prince's Trust 10th Anniversary Birthday Party* CD A&M 396925-2 released 1987

I'm Still Standing (Elton John) *Recorded Highlights Of The Prince's Trust 10th Anniversary Birthday Party* CD A&M 396925-2 released 1987

Everytime You Go Away (Paul Young, George Michael) only available on VHS video

I Saw Her Standing There (Paul McCartney) only available on VHS video

Long Tall Sally (Paul McCartney) *Recorded Highlights Of The Prince's Trust 10th Anniversary Birthday Party* CD A&M 396925-2 released 1987

Dancing In The Street (David Bowie, Mick Jagger) unreleased

Get Back (Paul McCartney, everyone) *Recorded Highlights Of The Prince's Trust 10th Anniversary Birthday Party* CD A&M 396925-2 released 1987

Producer: Andrew Sheehan
Engineer: Barry Sage
Recorded by: Pumacrest Mobile Unit

JULY 1986

SCANDINAVIAN / EUROPEAN TOUR 1986

BAND LINEUP:
Eric Clapton: guitar, vocals
Phil Collins: drums, vocals
Nathan East: bass
Greg Phillinganes: keyboards

3 July 1986, Kalvoyafestivalen, Kalvoya, Sandvika, Barum Kommune, Norway

SETLIST: Crossroads / White Room / I Shot The Sheriff / Wanna Make Love To You / Run / Forever Man / Same Old Blues / Miss You / Tearing Us Apart / Holy Mother / Behind The Mask / Badge / Let It Rain / In The Air Tonight / Cocaine / Layla / Sunshine Of Your Love / Further On Up The Road

4 July 1986, Roskilde Festival, Roskilde, Denmark

SETLIST: Crossroads / White Room / I Shot The Sheriff / Wanna Make Love To You / Run / After Midnight / Same Old Blues / Miss You / Tearing Us Apart / Holy Mother / Behind The Mask / Badge / Let It Rain / In The Air Tonight / Cocaine / Layla / Sunshine Of Your Love / Further On Up The Road

MONTREUX JAM WITH OTIS RUSH 1986

9 July 1986, Le Casino, Montreux, Switzerland (Eric jams with Otis Rush. The tone on his new Fender is spectacular. Luckily the show is filmed and recorded)

SETLIST:

Crosscut Saw (R.G. Ford) *Otis Rush And Friends Live At Montreux 1986* CD/DVD Eagle Rock released December 2008

Otis Rush: vocals, guitar
Eric Clapton: guitar
Professor Eddie Lusk: keyboards
Anthony Palmer: guitar
Fred Barnes: bass
Eddie Turner: drums

Double Trouble (Otis Rush) *Otis Rush And Friends Live At Montreux 1986* CD/DVD Eagle Rock released December 2008

Otis Rush: vocals, guitar
Eric Clapton: guitar
Professor Eddie Lusk: keyboards
Anthony Palmer: guitar
Fred Barnes: bass
Eddie Turner: drums

All Your Love (Willie Dixon / Otis Rush) *Otis Rush And Friends Live At Montreux 1986* CD/DVD Eagle Rock released December 2008

Otis Rush: vocals, guitar
Eric Clapton: guitar

Professor Eddie Lusk: keyboards
Anthony Palmer: guitar
Fred Barnes: bass
Eddie Turner: drums

Everyday I Have The Blues (Memphis Slim) *Otis Rush And Friends Live At Montreux 1986* CD/DVD Eagle Rock released December 2008

Otis Rush: vocals, guitar
Eric Clapton: guitar
Luther Allison: guitar, vocals
Professor Eddie Lusk: keyboards
Anthony Palmer: guitar
Fred Barnes: bass
Eddie Turner: drums
Executive Producer: Claude Nobs

10 July 1986, Le Casino, Montreux, Switzerland

SETLIST:

Crossroads (Robert Johnson) *Eric Clapton Live At Montreux 1986* DVD Eagle Rock released September 2006

White Room (Jack Bruce / Pete Brown) *Eric Clapton Live At Montreux 1986* DVD Eagle Rock released September 2006

I Shot The Sheriff (Bob Marley) *Eric Clapton Live At Montreux 1986* DVD Eagle Rock released September 2006

Wanna Make Love To You (Jerry Williams) *Eric Clapton Live At Montreux 1986* DVD Eagle Rock released September 2006

Run (Lamont Dozier) unreleased

Miss You (Eric Clapton / Bobby Columby / Greg Phillinganes) *Eric Clapton Live At Montreux 1986* DVD Eagle Rock released September 2006

Same Old Blues (Eric Clapton) *Eric Clapton Live At Montreux 1986* DVD Eagle Rock released September 2006

Tearing Us Apart (Eric Clapton / Greg Phillinganes) *Eric Clapton Live At Montreux 1986* Eagle Rock DVD released September 2006

Holy Mother (Eric Clapton / Stephen Bishop) *Eric Clapton Live At Montreux 1986* DVD Eagle Rock released September 2006

Behind The Mask (Chris Mosdell / Ryuichi Sakamoto / Michael Jackson) *Eric Clapton Live At Montreux 1986* DVD Eagle Rock released September 2006

Badge (Eric Clapton / George Harrison) *Eric Clapton Live At Montreux 1986* DVD Eagle Rock released September 2006

Let It Rain (Eric Clapton / Delaney Bramlett) *Eric Clapton Live At Montreux 1986* DVD Eagle Rock released September 2006

In The Air Tonight (Phil Collins) *Eric Clapton Live At Montreux 1986* DVD Eagle Rock released September 2006

Cocaine (JJ Cale) *Eric Clapton Live At Montreux 1986* DVD Eagle Rock released September 2006

Layla (Eric Clapton / Jim Gordon) *Eric Clapton Live At Montreux 1986* DVD Eagle Rock released September 2006

Sunshine Of Your Love (Jack Bruce / Pete Brown / Eric Clapton) *Eric Clapton Live At Montreux 1986* DVD Eagle Rock released September 2006

Further On Up The Road (Joe Medwick Veasey / Don Robey) *Eric Clapton Live At Montreux 1986* DVD Eagle Rock released September 2006

Ramblin' On My Mind[1] (Robert Johnson) unreleased (not filmed, only audio recorded)

Have You Ever Loved A Woman[1] (Billy Myles) unreleased (not filmed, only audio recorded)

[1] with Robert Cray on guitar

Executive producer: Claude Nobs

One of Eric's favorite concerts, and rightly so. The show was filmed and recorded and was also broadcast live on radio including two extra encores. On the night of the show, however, the camera crew assumed that the show had finished as the band had played their planned encore, so they packed up and left. After fifteen minutes the band returned to the stage, much to everyone's surprise. Eric introduced a special guest and out walked Robert Cray. They played "Ramblin' On My Mind" and "Have You Ever Loved A Woman."

12 July 1986, La Pinède Gould, Juan-Les-Pins, Antibes, France

Eric looking relaxed in the afternoon sunshine during a soundcheck at La Pinède Gould, Juan-Les-Pins, Antibes, France, on 12 July 1986. Note the Ferrari red Strat.

SETLIST: Crossroads / White Room / I Shot The Sheriff / Wanna Make Love To You / Run / Miss You / Same Old Blues / Tearing Us Apart / Holy Mother / Behind The Mask / Badge / Let It Rain / In The Air Tonight / Cocaine / Layla / Sunshine Of Your Love

14 July 1986, National Exhibition Centre, Birmingham

The show is recorded but nothing is released from this performance. Only the 15th July show is filmed.

SETLIST: Crossroads / White Room / I Shot The Sheriff / Wanna Make Love To You / Run / Miss You / Same Old Blues / Tearing Us Apart / Holy Mother / Behind The Mask / Badge / Let It Rain / In The Air Tonight / Cocaine / Layla / Sunshine Of Your Love / Further On Up The Road

15 July 1986, National Exhibition Centre, Birmingham

SETLIST:

Crossroads (Robert Johnson) *Behind The Mask / Grand Illusion* UK Special Limited Edition 4-track 2-disc gatefold picture sleeve vinyl single Warners Bros. W8461F. The second single has live recordings of "Crossroads" and "White Room," released 1987 / *Eric Clapton & Friends Live 1986* CD Eagle Vision EREDV 355 released 2003

White Room (Jack Bruce / Pete Brown) *Behind The Mask / Grand illusion* UK Special Limited Edition 4-track 2-disc gatefold picture sleeve vinyl single Warners Bros. W8461F. The second single has live recordings of "Crossroads" and

"White Room," released 1987 / *Eric Clapton & Friends Live 1986* CD Eagle Vision EREDV 355 released 2003

I Shot The Sheriff (Bob Marley) unreleased

Wanna Make Love To You (Jerry Williams) unreleased

Run (Lamont Dozier) *Eric Clapton & Friends Live 1986* CD Eagle Vision EREDV 355 released 2003

Miss You (Eric Clapton / Bobby Columby / Greg Phillinganes) *Eric Clapton & Friends Live 1986* CD Eagle Vision EREDV 355 released 2003

Same Old Blues (Eric Clapton) unreleased

Tearing Us Apart (Eric Clapton / Greg Phillinganes) *Eric Clapton & Friends Live 1986* CD Eagle Vision EREDV 355 released 2003

Holy Mother (Eric Clapton / Stephen Bishop) *Eric Clapton & Friends Live 1986* CD Eagle Vision EREDV 355 released 2003

Behind The Mask (Chris Mosdell / Ryuichi Sakamoto / Michael Jackson) unreleased

Badge (Eric Clapton / George Harrison) unreleased

Let It Rain (Eric Clapton / Delaney Bramlett) unreleased

In The Air Tonight (Phil Collins) *Eric Clapton & Friends Live 1986* CD Eagle Vision EREDV 355 released 2003

Cocaine (JJ Cale) unreleased

Layla (Eric Clapton / Jim Gordon) *Eric Clapton & Friends Live 1986* CD Eagle Vision EREDV 355 released 2003

Sunshine Of Your Love (Jack Bruce / Pete Brown / Eric Clapton) *Eric Clapton & Friends Live 1986* CD Eagle Vision EREDV 355 released 2003

Further On Up The Road[1] (Joe Medwick Veasey / Don Robey) unreleased

[1] with Robert Cray on guitar

AUGUST 1986

JAM WITH PRINCE

14 August 1986, Kensington Roof Gardens, Derry Street, Kensington, London (Eric joins Prince for a lengthy version of "I Can't Get Next To You")

CHARITY CONCERT

15 August 1986 Finchley Cricket Club, East End Road, London (Eric joins Stan Webb and Chicken Shack for some blues after the cricket games are over)

VIDEO SHOOT

16 August 1986, Ronnie Scott's Club, Soho, London (film session for "Tearing Us Apart" video)

Eric and the band are at Ronnie Scott's to film a video for "Tearing Us Apart." As Tina Turner is unavailable, a lookalike model is brought in. In between takes, the band jam on some soul classics.

SETLIST: Tearing Us Apart, Take 1 / Tearing Us Apart, Take 2 / Jam / Tearing Us Apart, Take 3 / Take A Chance / Behind The Mask / Tearing Us Apart, Take 4 / Signed, Sealed, Delivered / Easy Lover / Tearing Us Apart, Take 5 / Everytime You Go Away / September / Controversy / 1999 / Billy Jean / On Broadway

OCTOBER 1986

CHUCK BERRY'S 60th BIRTHDAY CONCERT 1986

10 October 1986–14 October 1986, Berry Park, St. Charles County, Wentzville, Missouri

A big concert was planned to celebrate the 60th birthday of the notoriously belligerent Chuck Berry and the whole event was to be filmed by Taylor Hackford. Keith Richards took on the unenviable role of musical director. Rehearsals took place between 10 October and 14 October at Chuck's home, Berry Park. Chuck is notoriously cheap when it comes to sourcing backing musicians. As this event was going to be filmed and recorded, Keith Richards got together a top-notch backing band consisting of Johnnie Johnson on piano, Joey Spampinato (from the obscenely talented NRBQ) on bass, Bobby Keys on saxophone, Chuck Leavell on organ, and Steve Jordan on drums. The rehearsals were filmed and clips were included in both the film and expanded DVD release. There are some hilarious scenes such as Chuck trying to teach Keith how to play "Carol." Eric and Chuck can be seen in an acapella version of "It Don't Take But A Few Minutes." A highlight has to be a near ten-minute guitar jam with the band with Chuck, Eric, and Keith on a stage inside Berry Park.

15 October 1986, Fox Theatre, St. Louis, Missouri

A full dress rehearsal was arranged at the venue the day prior to the main event. Things did not go well, with Chuck refusing to sing giving the excuse that he needed to save his voice for the following day's concert. Instead, the ever precocious Berry decided to play instrumentally only which of course rendered the dress rehearsal useless. After Keith begged him one last time, Berry reluctantly agreed to whisper the lyrics to a handful of songs. Keith deserved a medal for his patience and utter professionalism when most people would have decked Berry, rock and roll legend or not.

Eric plays three takes of "Wee Wee Hours," singing lead and playing guitar. The second take breaks down after ten seconds. He comes back later for a fourth take, which is then followed by several jams with some stunning guitar work.

16 October 1986, Fox Theatre, St. Louis, Missouri (Show 1)

Rock and roll legend Chuck Berry and guitarist Eric Clapton raise their hands together at Berry's 60th Birthday Concert at the Fox Theatre, St. Louis, Missouri, on 16 October 1986.

Two shows were scheduled in front of a live audience. What was supposed to be a concise 70-minute show overran by five hours! The audience were not familiar with film shoots where lengthy interruptions are the norm and thus grew impatient. The crew needed to reload film, check camera angles, etc. As a result many people left early. Eric was on the following numbers this night:

Wee Wee Hours (Chuck Berry) *Hail Hail Rock 'N' Roll* CD MCA 6217 / 4DVD edition Image Entertainment ID3156THDVD released 2006

Chuck Berry: guitar
Eric Clapton: guitar, vocals
Keith Richards: guitar
Johnnie Johnson: piano
Joey Spampinato: bass
Chuck Leavell: organ
Steve Jordan: drums

Eric's Blues (unknown blues jam) unreleased

Eric Clapton: guitar
Keith Richards: guitar
Johnnie Johnson: piano
Joey Spampinato: bass
Chuck Leavell: organ
Steve Jordan: drums

Rock 'N' Roll Music (Chuck Berry) unreleased

Etta James: vocals
Chuck Berry: guitar
Eric Clapton: guitar
Keith Richards: guitar
Robert Cray: guitar
Johnnie Johnson: piano
Joey Spampinato: bass
Bobby Keys: saxophone
Chuck Leavell: organ
Steve Jordan: drums

17 October 1986, Fox Theatre, St. Louis, Missouri (Show 2)

As the first show overran, the second show actually took place just after midnight in the early hours of 17 October. Eric played on the following songs:

Wee Wee Hours (Chuck Berry) unreleased

Chuck Berry: guitar
Eric Clapton: guitar, vocals
Keith Richards: guitar
Johnnie Johnson: piano
Joey Spampinato: bass
Chuck Leavell: organ
Steve Jordan: drums

Rock 'N' Roll Music (Chuck Berry) *Hail Hail Rock 'N' Roll*
CD MCA 6217 / 4DVD edition Image Entertainment
ID3156TH DVD released 2006

Etta James: vocals
Chuck Berry: guitar
Eric Clapton: guitar
Keith Richards: guitar
Robert Cray: guitar
Johnnie Johnson: piano
Joey Spampinato: bass
Bobby Keys: saxophone
Chuck Leavell: organ
Steve Jordan: organ

Hoochie Coochie Man (Willie Dixon) unreleased

Etta James: vocals
Chuck Berry: guitar
Eric Clapton: guitar
Robert Cray: guitar
Johnnie Johnson: piano
Joey Spampinato: bass
Bobby Keys: saxophone
Chuck Leavell: organ
Steve Jordan: drums

Jam unreleased

Chuck Berry: guitar, vocals
Eric Clapton: guitar
Keith Richards: guitar, vocals
Robert Cray: guitar
Joe Walsh: guitar
Johnnie Johnson: piano
Joey Spampinato: bass
Bobby Keys: saxophone
Chuck Leavell: organ
Steve Jordan: drums

School Days (Chuck Berry) 4DVD edition Image
Entertainment ID3156TH released 2006

Chuck Berry: guitar, vocals
Eric Clapton: guitar
Keith Richards: guitar, vocals
Robert Cray: guitar
Joe Walsh: guitar
Johnnie Johnson: piano
Joey Spampinato: bass
Bobby Keys: saxophone
Chuck Leavell: organ
Steve Jordan: drums
Etta James: vocals
Ingrid Berry: vocals
Julian Lennon: vocals

Producer: Keith Richards
Engineer: Bridget Daly
Recorded by: Remote Recording Services

> **"**I was very pleased with my performance. In fact, having done very little rehearsing, there was little for me to do there except sit and kick my heels. By the time I got to play, I was very frustrated and it showed when I attacked the guitar.**"**
> —ERIC CLAPTON

JAM WITH LIONEL RICHIE 1986

27 October 1986, Madison Square Garden, New York City (guest appearance with Lionel Richie)

NIGHTLIFE 1986

29 October 1986, Nightlife, Unitel Video Studio, New York City

As well as being interviewed, Eric played a few numbers with the house band which included Lou Marini and Billy Preston.

SETLIST: It's In The Way That You Use It / Miss You / I Shot The Sheriff (only part is broadcast)

NOVEMBER 1986

JAM WITH ROBERT CRAY 1986

8 November 1986, Mean Fiddler, 22-28 High Street, Harlesden, London (guest appearance with Robert Cray)

BAND LINEUP:
Robert Cray: guitar, vocals
Eric Clapton: guitar
Robert Cousins: bass
David Olsen: drums
Peter Boe: keyboards

> **"**It's a lovely band to play with. You can play along and not have to learn anything or there's no awkward chords that are going to come up. It's pretty straightforward, and with a great feeling. It's great to play with Robert anytime.**"**
>
> **—ERIC CLAPTON**

SETLIST: Smoking Gun / Playing In The Dirt / The Last Time / Bad Influence / Phone Booth

A soundboard recording was made at the show, and the May 1987 *Guitar Player* magazine gave away a free flexi-disc featuring "Phone Booth" from the soundboard tape.

U.S. CLUB TOUR 1986

BAND LINEUP:
Eric Clapton: guitar, vocals
Greg Phillinganes: keyboards
Nathan East: bass
Steve Ferrone: drums

20 November 1986, Metro, Boston, Massachusetts

SETLIST: Crossroads / White Room / I Shot The Sheriff / Wanna Make Love To You / It's In The Way That You Use It / Run / Miss You / Same Old Blues / Tearing Us Apart / Holy Mother / Badge / Let It Rain / Cocaine / Layla / Sunshine Of Your Love

21 November 1986, Metro, Boston, Massachusetts

SETLIST: Crossroads / White Room / I Shot The Sheriff / Wanna Make Love To You / It's In The Way That You Use It / Run / Miss You / Same Old Blues / Tearing Us Apart / Holy Mother / Badge / Let It Rain / Cocaine / Layla / Sunshine Of Your Love

23 November 1986, Ritz, New York City

SETLIST: Crossroads / White Room / I Shot The Sheriff / Wanna Make Love To You / It's In The Way That You Use It / Run / Miss You / Same Old Blues / Tearing Us Apart / Holy Mother / Badge / Let It Rain / Cocaine[1] / Layla[1] / Sunshine Of Your Love / Further On Up The Road

[1]with Keith Richards on guitar

24 November 1986, Ritz, New York City

SETLIST: Crossroads / White Room / I Shot The Sheriff / Wanna Make Love To You / It's In The Way That You Use It / Run / Miss You / Same Old Blues / Tearing Us Apart / Holy Mother / Badge / Let It Rain / Cocaine / Layla / Sunshine Of Your Love

DECEMBER 1986

23 December 1986, Village Hall, Dunsfold, Surrey (charity show with Gary Brooker)

RECORDING SESSIONS 1986
ERIC CLAPTON GUEST SESSION
AUDIO INTERNATIONAL STUDIOS
18 Rodmarton Street, London
Session for Liona Boyd

FEBRUARY 1986

An obscure session for Eric but a worthy one where both he and Michael Kamen carry on in the *Edge Of Darkness* soundtrack style with some beautifully haunting guitar work. David Gilmour and Yo Yo Ma also guest on the album.

LABYRINTH (Michael Kamen) *Persona* CD CBS MK 42120 released 1986
Liona Boyd: acoustic guitar
Eric Clapton: electric guitar
Dean Garcia: bass
Michael Kamen: Kurzwell drums, piano, percussion

Producer: Liona Boyd
Engineer: Andrew Jackson

SUNSET SOUND RECORDING STUDIO
6650 Sunset Boulevard, Los Angeles, California

Session for *August*

APRIL 1986–MAY 1986

RUN (Lamont Dozier) *August* LP Duck WX71 925 476-1 / CD 925476-2 released August 1986

Eric Clapton: guitar, vocals
Phil Collins: drums
Nathan East: bass
Greg Phillinganes: keyboards
Michael Brecker: saxophone
Randy Brecker: trumpet
Dave Bargerone: trombone
John Faddis: trumpet

TEARING US APART (Eric Clapton / Greg Phillinganes) *August* LP Duck WX71 925 476-1 / CD 925476-2 released August 1986

Eric Clapton: guitar, vocals
Phil Collins: drums
Nathan East: bass
Greg Phillinganes: keyboards
Tina Turner: vocal

BAD INFLUENCE (Robert Cray / Michael Vannice) *August* LP Duck WX71 925 476-1 / CD 925476-2 released August 1986

Eric Clapton: guitar, vocals
Phil Collins: drums
Nathan East: bass
Greg Phillinganes: keyboards
Michael Brecker: saxophone
Randy Brecker: trumpet
Dave Bargerone: trombone
John Faddis: trumpet

WALK AWAY (Richard Feldman / Marcy Levy / Eric Clapton / Greg Phillinganes) *August* LP Duck WX71 925 476-1 / CD 925476-2 released August 1986

Eric Clapton: guitar, vocals
Phil Collins: drums
Nathan East: bass
Greg Phillinganes: keyboards
Richard Feldman: keyboards

HUNG UP ON YOUR LOVE (Lamont Dozier) Eric Clapton / Greg Phillinganes) *August* LP Duck WX71 925 476-1 / CD 925476-2 released August 1986

Eric Clapton: guitar, vocals
Phil Collins: drums
Nathan East: bass
Greg Phillinganes: keyboards
Michael Brecker: saxophone
Randy Brecker: trumpet
Dave Bargerone: trombone
John Faddis: trumpet

TAKE A CHANCE (Eric Clapton / Nathan East / Greg Phillinganes) *August* LP Duck WX71 925 476-1 / CD 925476-2 released August 1986

Eric Clapton: guitar, vocals
Phil Collins: drums
Nathan East: bass
Greg Phillinganes: keyboards
Michael Brecker: saxophone
Randy Brecker: trumpet
Dave Bargerone: trombone

Jon Faddis: trumpet
Tessa Niles: backing vocals
Katie Kissoon: backing vocals

HOLD ON (Eric Clapton / Phil Collins) *August* LP Duck WX71 925 476-1 / CD 925476-2 released August 1986

Eric Clapton: guitar, vocals
Phil Collins: drums
Nathan East: bass
Greg Phillinganes: keyboards
Tina Turner: vocals

MISS YOU (Eric Clapton / Bobby Columby / Greg Phillinganes) *August* LP Duck WX71 925 476-1 / CD 925476-2 released August 1986

Eric Clapton: guitar, vocals
Phil Collins: drums
Nathan East: bass
Greg Phillinganes: keyboards
Michael Brecker: saxophone
Randy Brecker: trumpet
Dave Bargerone: trombone
Jon Faddis: trumpet

HOLY MOTHER (Stephen Bishop / Eric Clapton) *August* LP Duck WX71 925 476-1 / CD 925476-2 released August 1986

Eric Clapton: guitar, vocals
Phil Collins: drums
Nathan East: bass
Greg Phillinganes: keyboards
Tessa Niles: backing vocals
Katie Kisson: backing vocals

BEHIND THE MASK (Chris Mosdell / Ryuichi Sakamoto / Michael Jackson) *August* LP Duck WX71 925 476-1 / CD 925476-2 released August 1986

Eric Clapton: guitar, vocals
Phil Collins: drums
Nathan East: bass
Greg Phillinganes: keyboards
Tessa Niles: backing vocals
Katie Kissoon: backing vocals

GRAND ILLUSION (Bob Farrell / Dave Robbins / Wesly Stephenson) *August* LP Duck WX71 925 476-1 / CD 925476-2 released August 1986

Eric Clapton: guitar, vocals
Phil Collins: drums
Nathan East: bass
Greg Philinganes: keyboards

WANNA MAKE LOVE TO YOU (Jerry Williams) *Crossroads* box set Polydor released 1988

Eric Clapton: guitar, vocals
Phil Collins: drums
Nathan East: bass
Greg Phillinganes: keyboards
Tessa Niles: backing vocals
Katie Kissoon: backing vocals

LADY OF VERONA (Eric Clapton) unreleased

WALKING THE WHITE LINE unreleased

Producer: Tom Dowd (associate)
Engineers: Magic Moreno / Peter Hefter / Paul Gommersall

> "People will say that *Behind The Sun* and *August* are Phil Collins records. Fine—if that's all they can hear, they are not listening properly. I'm in there with as much as I've got, but not in a competative way. If I did, it would be a mess. It works pretty good for me to allow people to be themselves rather than trying to lay down the law."
>
> **—ERIC CLAPTON**

ERIC CLAPTON GUEST SESSION

FARMYARD STUDIOS
Little Chalfont, Buckinghamshire
Session for Bob Geldof

AUGUST 1986

LOVE LIKE A ROCKET (Bob Geldof / Raymond Doom) *Deep In The Heart Of Nowhere* CD Mercury 830 607-2 released November 1986

AUGUST WAS A HEAVY MONTH (Bob Geldof) *Deep In The Heart Of Nowhere* CD Mercury 830 607-2 released November 1986

THE BEAT OF THE NIGHT (Bob Geldof) *Deep In The Heart Of Nowhere* CD Mercury 830 607-2 released November 1986

GOOD BOYS IN THE WRONG (Bob Geldof) *Deep In The Heart Of Nowhere* CD Mercury 830 607-2 released November 1986

Bob Geldof: vocals
Eric Clapton: guitar
Rupert Hine: programmed keyboards, drums, bass

Producer: Rupert Hine
Engineer: Stephen Taylor

> "I never thought I would be any good to Bob Geldof. But playing with him was great! He was so good to work with. He gave me complete carte blanche. Normally I would find someone saying, What do you think? and I would say, 'Well, maybe I could do it better,' then they'd go, 'Okay go ahead.' Bob said, 'No, you can't. Don't do it again. Keep what you've done, that's fine.' So I did a lot of work in a very shot amount of time, because he was wise enough to catch me on my first and second takes, which is usually when I'm best. But I always think I can do better, and I blow it. He knew better than that, which is great. I think it is a good album."
>
> **—ERIC CLAPTON**

> "Farmyard was owned by drummer Trevor Morais and was run by him and his partner, producer Rupert Hine. Rupert produced the album. I remember that Eric did his overdubs on his own. On many tracks the keys, bass, and drums [programmed] were handled by Rupert, and acoustic guitar was played by Bob."
>
> **—STEPEN TAYLOR**

ERIC CLAPTON GUEST SESSION

THE FACTORY SOUND
Toftees, Church Road, Woldingham, Surrey
Session for *The Bunburys*

14 AUGUST 1986

FIGHT (THE GOOD FIGHT) (Barry Gibb / Robin Gibb / Maurice Gibb / David English) UK 7" single Island Records LBW 2 released 1986 / 1988 *Summer Olympics—One Moment In Time* CD Arista 209 247 released 1988 / 12" single Arista 611 810 released 1988 / *Bunbury Tails* CD Polydor 515 784-2 released 1992

Eric Clapton: guitar, vocals
Laurence Cottle: bass
Duncan Mackay: keyboards
Barry Gibb: vocals
Robin Gibb: vocals
Maurice Gibb: vocals
David English: additional vocals
Ian Botham: additional vocals
Maurice Gibb: programmed drum machine

Producers: David Mackay / Barry Gibb
Engineer: David Mackay

> "I co-produced one track only for Eric, a co-production with Barry Gibb. The song is called 'Fight.' The Bee Gees wrote it for a TV series called *The Bunburys*. It was recorded about eighteen or so years ago at my studio called the Factory Sound in Woldingham, Surrey. Present were myself and the three Bee Gees, plus keyboard player Duncar MacKay and Laurence Cottle on bass. Guitars and lead vocals were of course Eric and backing vocals were Barry, Robin, and Maurice, and Maurice programmed the drums."
>
> **—DAVID MACKAY**
> (producer)

> "David English invented *The Bunburys* as a cartoon and he put out books first of all. And then he thought about music to go with it. He's an old friend of Barry Gibb's and those two started writing. Barry wrote a song for me to do called 'Fight.' That will be on the new *Bunburys* album. Elton's on it, as is George Harrison. It's all been held up for one reason or another. I don't know what record label it is going to be on."
>
> **—ERIC CLAPTON**

The album was eventually released in 1992 and has become a highly collectable item.

ERIC CLAPTON GUEST SESSION

TOWN HOUSE STUDIOS
150 Goldhawk Road, London
Session for Bob Dylan

27 AUGUST 1986–28 AUGUST 1986

THE USUAL (John Hiatt) Take 1 unreleased
THE USUAL (John Hiatt) Take 2 unreleased
THE USUAL (John Hiatt) Take 3 unreleased
THE USUAL (John Hiatt) Take 4 unreleased
THE USUAL (John Hiatt) Take 5 unreleased
RIDE THIS TRAIN (Bob Dylan) unreleased
HAD A DREAM ABOUT YOU, BABY (Bob Dylan) Take 1 unreleased

HAD A DREAM ABOUT YOU, BABY (Bob Dylan) Take 2 unreleased
HAD A DREAM ABOUT YOU, BABY (Bob Dylan) Take 3 unreleased
HAD A DREAM ABOUT YOU, BABY (Bob Dylan) Take 4 unreleased
HAD A DREAM ABOUT YOU, BABY (Bob Dylan) Take 5 unreleased
OLD FIVE AND DIMER (LIKE ME) (Billy Joe Shaver) Take 1 unreleased
OLD FIVE AND DIMER (LIKE ME) (Billy Joe Shaver) Take 2 unreleased
OLD FIVE AND DIMER (LIKE ME) (Billy Joe Shaver) Take 3 unreleased
HAD A DREAM ABOUT YOU, BABY (Bob Dylan) Take 6 unreleased
HAD A DREAM ABOUT YOU, BABY (Bob Dylan) Take 7 unreleased
TO FALL IN LOVE WITH YOU (Bob Dylan) unreleased
NIGHT AFTER NIGHT (Bob Dylan) Take 1 unreleased
NIGHT AFTER NIGHT (Bob Dylan) Take 2 unreleased
HAD A DREAM ABOUT YOU, BABY (Bob Dylan) Take 8 unreleased
HAD A DREAM ABOUT YOU, BABY (Bob Dylan) Take 9 unreleased

Bob Dylan: vocals, guitar (Fender Telecaster)
Eric Clapton: guitar (Fender Stratocaster Signature Series)
Ron Wood: bass
Henry Spinetti: drums

Producer: Beau Hill
Engineer: Beau Hill

The above songs are the only ones in which Eric participated due to his busy scheduling. Overdubs and remixing were done later in Los Angeles with no involvement from Eric.

"The Usual" and "Night After Night" with overdubs including horns and a remixed "Had A Dream About You, Baby" appear on the *Hearts of Fire* soundtrack CBS 460001 2. Another mix of "Had A Dream About You, Baby" with some echo on the vocals is released on the *Down In The Groove* CD CBS460267 2.

> "Bob came into London looking to get a band together. He seemed to be flying pretty blind. He knew he had to get some music for his film *[Hearts Of Fire]* and it was so early on in the stage of the game that he did not know what he wanted to sound like—what the part entailed in the film.
>
> He called me to help out and I got involved, but was pretty tightly scheduled to do other things as well, so I could only do two or three days and then I had to move on. Basically, I just played rhythm parts and a little bit of lead. I would have liked to get more involved, but at the time I was really busy and could not commit myself to more than that."
>
> **—ERIC CLAPTON**

"Dylan rang Eric, he said, 'I'm in town, I need a drummer, can you suggest anybody?' Eric said, 'Oh yeah I know just the guys, so Eric suggested me for this session. On this session was Ron Wood on bass, Eric on guitar, me on drums. I went in, set up the drums, all of a sudden Bob arrived, he had real dark glasses on, he couldn't see through them. I went up and said, 'Hi Bob, my name's Henry, I'm playing drums.' He just looked at my hand, he didn't appear to be that friendly. I just thought 'okay.' Eric came in, then Ron, the next amazing thing was Bob picked up a Telecaster and near this amp was a bass amp, he plugged into it and put a microphone right in front of him and started to play. Of course, I'm behind Bob in a booth with glass doors, so I thought 'I suppose I'd better join in then.' I join in, everybody joins in, and that's one tune. He starts again, that sounds ok, and he starts again."

—HENRY SPINETTI
(from an interview with Mike Dolbear)

AIR STUDIOS
214 Oxford Street, London
Session for *The Color Of Money* soundtrack

SEPTEMBER 1986

IT'S MY LIFE BABY (Don Robey / Ferdinand Washington) unreleased

Eric Clapton: guitar, vocals
Mike Sanchez: piano
Ian Jennings: bass
Andy Silvester: guitar
John Spinetto: drums
Ricky Cool: tenor saxophone
John Wallace: baritone saxophone

Producer: Tom Dowd
Engineers: John Jacobs / Steve Chase

"I would like to get into the studio with the Big Town Playboys again and make a blues album. That probably will come after my next solo album, which I think I am going to do as a commercial venture again. Pretty much like *August*—not perhaps as commercial as *August* was set out to be."

—ERIC CLAPTON

AIR STUDIOS
214 Oxford Street, London
Session for *The Color Of Money* soundtrack

SEPTEMBER 1986

IT'S IN THE WAY THAT YOU USE IT (originally "The Gift") (Eric Clapton / Robbie Robertson) *The Color Of Money* LP MCA 6189 released 1986 / *August* LP US Duck 925 476-2 / UK Duck 9362-47762-2 released November 1986

Eric Clapton: guitar, vocals
Gary Brooker: keyboards, vocals
Laurence Cottle: bass
Richard Cottle: synthesizer
Henry Spinetti: drums

Producer: Tom Dowd
Engineers: John Jacobs / Steve Chase

This song reunited Eric with Robbie Robertson after a long separation. Robbie and Martin Scorsese were friends and that's how Eric got involved in the soundtrack for the film. Robbie was looking for a particular style of lyrics from Eric to suit the mood of the film. But whatever he presented to Robbie just wasn't what was needed. So Eric asked Robbie to write the lyrics and he would handle the music.

"I preferred the Bobby Bland song, which you didn't get to hear hardly at all, and it didn't get on to the soundtrack album. That was the better of the two tracks for me."

—ERIC CLAPTON

ERIC CLAPTON GUEST SESSION

MAYFAIR STUDIOS
11a Sharpleshall Street, Primrose Hill, London
Session for Tina Turner

SEPTEMBER 1986

"Dylan rang Eric, he said, 'I'm in town, I need a drummer, can you suggest anybody?' Eric said, 'Oh yeah I know just the guys, so Eric suggested me for this session. On this session was Ron Wood on bass, Eric on guitar, me on drums. I went in, set up the drums, all of a sudden Bob arrived, he had real dark glasses on, he couldn't see through them. I went up and said, 'Hi Bob, my name's Henry, I'm playing drums.' He just looked at my hand, he didn't appear to be that friendly. I just thought 'okay.' Eric came in, then Ron, the next amazing thing was Bob picked up a Telecaster and near this amp was a bass amp, he plugged into it and put a microphone right in front of him and started to play. Of course, I'm behind Bob in a booth with glass doors, so I thought 'I suppose I'd better join in then.' I join in, everybody joins in, and that's one tune. He starts again, that sounds ok, and he starts again."

—HENRY SPINETTI
(from an interview with Mike Dolbear)

AIR STUDIOS
214 Oxford Street, London
Session for *The Color Of Money* soundtrack

SEPTEMBER 1986

IT'S MY LIFE BABY (Don Robey / Ferdinand Washington) unreleased

Eric Clapton: guitar, vocals
Mike Sanchez: piano
Ian Jennings: bass
Andy Silvester: guitar
John Spinetto: drums
Ricky Cool: tenor saxophone
John Wallace: baritone saxophone

Producer: Tom Dowd
Engineers: John Jacobs / Steve Chase

"I would like to get into the studio with the Big Town Playboys again and make a blues album. That probably will come after my next solo album, which I think I am going to do as a commercial venture again. Pretty much like *August*—not perhaps as commercial as *August* was set out to be."

—ERIC CLAPTON

AIR STUDIOS
214 Oxford Street, London
Session for *The Color Of Money* soundtrack

SEPTEMBER 1986

IT'S IN THE WAY THAT YOU USE IT (originally "The Gift") (Eric Clapton / Robbie Robertson) *The Color Of Money* LP MCA 6189 released 1986 / *August* LP US Duck 925 476-2 / UK Duck 9362-47762-2 released November 1986

Eric Clapton: guitar, vocals
Gary Brooker: keyboards, vocals
Laurence Cottle: bass
Richard Cottle: synthesizer
Henry Spinetti: drums

Producer: Tom Dowd
Engineers: John Jacobs / Steve Chase

This song reunited Eric with Robbie Robertson after a long separation. Robbie and Martin Scorsese were friends and that's how Eric got involved in the soundtrack for the film. Robbie was looking for a particular style of lyrics from Eric to suit the mood of the film. But whatever he presented to Robbie just wasn't what was needed. So Eric asked Robbie to write the lyrics and he would handle the music.

"I preferred the Bobby Bland song, which you didn't get to hear hardly at all, and it didn't get on to the soundtrack album. That was the better of the two tracks for me."

—ERIC CLAPTON

ERIC CLAPTON GUEST SESSION

MAYFAIR STUDIOS
11a Sharpleshall Street, Primrose Hill, London
Session for Tina Turner

SEPTEMBER 1986

"We did that session at Air Studios, Oxford Circus, London. The producer was none other than the legendary Tom Dowd. I believe it must have been at the end of summer 1986, most possibly September into October. The session lasted the whole day and I recall we recorded around four songs but the main one was Bobby Bland's 'It's My Life Baby.' Now my memory is not working when I think of what other tracks we recorded. I do recall we had some time left in the studio and Eric let us record some tracks by ourselves with Tom Dowd. I think Tom enjoyed what we were doing and made some judgment over what our band was about but . . . oh lawd, I can't remember what he said.

We first met Eric at one of Gary Brooker's little charity events at Gary's local village hall in Dunsfold, Surrey, mid to late summer of 1986. Gary had become a 'fan' of the Big Town Playboys a year before when we started a regular appearance at a pub/live venue called the Dickens in his original hometown of Southend. Gary did for a while try and become our manager but I believe all he needed to do was to introduce us to some of his old pals in the business.

We performed as the first band of the evening at Dunsfold Village Hall and then we were followed by the main band which consisted of Gary Brooker, Andy Fairweather Low, Eric Clapton, Henry Spinetti, Dave Bronze, Frank Mead, and I'm not sure who else.

Eric at the time was still enjoying a drink or two and he was really happy and laid back. When we started the evening he watched every second of our show and I could tell he enjoyed it very much. After the audience left at the end of the evening Eric sat and chatted to me just smiling the whole time. I suggested we jam a while and Eric called Lee Dickson to get his black Strat out again and so we had a jam around some blues.

We finished off and left the village hall. Later that week we got a call from Roger Forrester asking us to do the session at Air Studios which was coming up a few days later. After that session we headed home and then a week or so later Roger called us again asking if we could be the support for Eric at a bunch of Albert Hall shows and a month of European touring. Those shows kicked off at the start of 1987. It was a fabulous experience for all of us in the band.

We have always been focused on powerful but authentic rhythm & blues music from the late 40s and early 50s, the stuff that later in the 50s became known as rock 'n' roll and I believe we were one of the first bands in the UK or Europe to actually feature those styles. We played a real piano instead of something electric, our guitarist played vintage Fender guitars and amps, sometimes used a Gibson semi, a real double bass instead of bass guitar, a vintage drum kit instead of a basic rock drummer's kit, sometimes we even used those old vintage Shure microphones to sing in. We also wore old style suits, baggy trousers, slicked our hair back. My mentor in the band was the guitarist Andy Silvester who taught us a lot of what we learnt. Andy was much older than the rest of us and had been involved all his life in music. He was bassist in Blue Horizon artists Chicken Shack during their hits "I'd Rather Go Blind" and "Tears In The Wind" so Andy was very much involved in the late 60s British blues boom alongside his mates Peter Green's Fleetwood Mac. Andy later went on to join stadium filling blues rock band Savoy Brown, then California-based Big Whakoo, then back in the UK with Steve Gibbons Band and finally Robert Plant's original Honeydrippers which is where Andy moved from bass to guitar and formed the Big Town Playboys with me during the summer of 1984. I started with rockabilly music but Andy taught us so much about the blues that we fell straight into it. We were listening to T-Bone Walker, Pee Wee Crayton, Amos Milburn, Joe Liggins, Wynonie Harris, etc., all the forgotten greats from the black rhythm & blues charts of the late 40s–early 50s, as well as classic Chicago blues, New Orleans, and West Coast artists of that period and it helped make us sound very authentic.

We looked and sounded the part and a lot of the musicians who started their careers in the 60s and 70s and saw us perform in the mid 80s really fell in love with what we were doing because for a lot of them it was something they would have maybe done as well.

Just like Gary Brooker fell in love with our thing, so did Eric who we supported at countless RAH shows ('87, '90, and '93) and European tour ('87), Andy Fairweather Low who later joined Big Town Playboys for eighteen months in the mid '90s between his stints with Eric; Mike Rutherford who still involves me in big parties in Surrey every now and then; Jeff Beck who we've toured and recorded with ('93 Sony Music, Crazy Legs, Jeff Beck and the Big Town Playboys); Robert Plant who was a friend and supporter since my first band when I left high school (it was Robert who introduced me to Andy Silvester and got our ball rolling with the BTPs and involved the BTPs as his band at a huge televised charity event at the NEC Birmingham in 1985 called Heartbeat, Mick Fleetwood who brought us to the U.S. to perform on TV and toured with us as our star drummer; Rick Vito from Fleetwood Mac who even recorded one of my songs, 'Hungry Man,' on his solo album. I need to get my memory back on all of this and excatly who we performed and made friends with!"

—MIKE SANCHEZ
(Big town Playboys)

WHAT YOU GET IS WHAT YOU SEE (Extended Rock Mix) (Terry Britten / Graham Lyle) 12" single Capitol 20 1620 6 released 1986

Tina Turner: vocals
Eric Clapton: guitar
Terry Britten: guitar, bass, drum progamming
Nick Glennie Smith: keyboards
Graham Lyle: mandolin

Producer: Terry Britten
Engineer: John Hudson

> **"**Eric's guitar was only used on the 12-inch mix. . . . Recorded at Mayfair Studios in Primrose Hill. Sadly no longer there. I remember him saying he hadn't played on anything in the key of F. It was a great day for me being that close and seeing him play. Wonderful.**"**
>
> **—TERRY BRITTEN**

> **"**Terry Britten got so excited recording one of his heroes that he recorded it an octave lower than it was supposed to be.**"**
>
> **—TINA TURNER**

TOWN HOUSE
150 Goldhawk Road, London
Sessions for *Lethal Weapon* soundtrack

8 DECEMBER 1986–16 DECEMBER 1986

MEET MARTIN RIGGS *Lethal Weapon* soundtrack CD Bacchus Media Group Inc. released 2002

THE JUMPER / ROG & RIGGS CONFRONTATION *Lethal Weapon* soundtrack CD Bacchus Media Group Inc. released 2002

ROGER *Lethal Weapon* soundtrack CD Bacchus Media Group Inc. released 2002

COKE DEAL *Lethal Weapon* soundtrack CD Bacchus Media Group Inc. released 2002

MR. JOSHUA *Lethal Weapon* soundtrack CD Bacchus Media Group Inc. released 2002

THEY GOT MY DAUGHTER *Lethal Weapon* soundtrack CD Bacchus Media Group Inc. released 2002

WE'RE GETTING TOO OLD FOR THIS *Lethal Weapon* soundtrack CD Bacchus Media Group Inc. released 2002

THE WEAPON *Lethal Weapon* soundtrack CD Bacchus Media Group Inc. released 2002

NIGHTCLUB *Lethal Weapon* soundtrack CD Bacchus Media Group Inc. released 2002

Eric Clapton: electric guitar
David Sanborn: saxophone
Dean Garcia: bass
Laurence Cottle: bass
Michael Kamen: Kurzwell, keyboards
Henry Spinetti: drums

Producer: Michael Kamen
Engineer: not known

ERIC CLAPTON GUEST SESSION

REVOLUTION STUDIOS
11 Church Road, Cheadle Hulme, Cheshire
Session for Jon Astley

DECEMBER 1986

JANE'S GETTING SERIOUS (Jon Astley) *Everyone Loves The Pilot (Except The Crew)* CD Atlantic 7 81740-2 released 1987

Jon Astley: vocals, Fairlight
Eric Clapton: guitar
Richie Close: keyboards

Producers: Phil Chapman / Andy MacPherson
Engineer: Andy MacPherson

5

1987

Eric started the year with a UK tour that included six shows at London's Royal Albert Hall. The 1986 band were augmented by Dire Straits' Mark Knopfler on guitar. Their styles worked well together and the highlight was the lengthy "Same Old Blues" allowing all the band members to solo. Phil Collins was the special guest drummer at the last two London shows. Three of the Albert Hall shows were recorded for a potential live album, as were several U.S. shows, but nothing was released.

JANUARY 1987

AUGUST UK TOUR 1987

BAND LINEUP:
Eric Clapton: guitar, vocals
Mark Knopfler: guitar, vocals on "Money For Nothing"
Greg Phillinganes: keyboards
Nathan East: bass
Steve Ferrone: drums

3 January 1987, Apollo Theatre, Manchester (with the Big Town Playboys)

SETLIST: Crossroads / White Room / I Shot The Sheriff / Wanna Make Love To You / Take A Chance / Hung Up On Your Love / Miss You / Same Old Blues / Tearing Us Apart / Holy Mother / Badge / Let It Rain / Cocaine / Layla / Money For Nothing / Sunshine Of Your Love

4 January 1987, Apollo Theatre, Manchester (with the Big Town Playboys)

SETLIST: Crossroads / White Room / I Shot The Sheriff / Wanna Make Love To You / Hung Up On Your Love / Same Old Blues / Miss You / Tearing Us Apart / Holy Mother / Badge / Let It Rain / Cocaine / Layla / Money For Nothing / Sunshine Of Your Love

6 January 1987, Royal Albert Hall, London (with the Big Town Playboys)

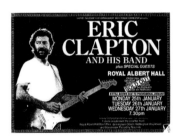

Advert for Eric Clapton's Royal Albert Hall shows in 1987.

SETLIST: Crossroads / White Room / I Shot The Sheriff / Wanna Make Love To You / Hung Up On Your Love / Wonderful Tonight / Miss You / Same Old Blues / Tearing Us Apart / Holy Mother / Badge / Let It Rain / Cocaine / Layla / Money For Nothing / Sunshine Of Your Love

7 January 1987, Royal Albert Hall, London (with the Big Town Playboys)

SETLIST: Crossroads / White Room / I Shot The Sheriff / Hung Up On Your Love / Wonderful Tonight / Miss You / Same Old Blues / Tearing Us Apart / Holy Mother / Badge / Let It Rain / Cocaine / Layla / Money For Nothing / Sunshine Of Your Love

Mark Knopfler and Eric Clapton during Eric's first season at the Royal Albert Hall, 7 January 1987.

8 January 1987, Royal Albert Hall, London (with the Big Town Playboys)

SETLIST: Crossroads / White Room / I Shot The Sheriff / Hung Up On Your Love / Wonderful Tonight / Miss You / Same Old Blues / Tearing Us Apart / Holy Mother / Badge / Let It Rain / Cocaine / Layla / Money For Nothing[1] / Sunshine Of Your Love[1]

[1]with Steve Winwood on keyboards and vocals and Sting on vocals

10 January 1987, Royal Albert Hall, London (with the Big Town Playboys)

Concert recorded by the Rolling Stones Mobile Studio. Unreleased.

SETLIST: Crossroads / White Room / I Shot The Sheriff / Hung Up On Your Love / Wonderful Tonight / Miss You / Same Old Blues / Tearing Us Apart / Holy Mother / Badge / Let It Rain / Cocaine / Layla / Money For Nothing / Sunshine Of Your Love

11 January 1987, Royal Albert Hall, London (with the Big Town Playboys)

Concert recorded by the Rolling Stones Mobile Studio. Unreleased.

SETLIST: Crossroads / White Room / I Shot The Sheriff / Hung Up On Your Love / Wonderful Tonight / Miss You / Same Old Blues / Tearing Us Apart / Holy Mother / Badge / Let It Rain / Cocaine / Layla / Money For Nothing / Sunshine Of Your Love

Concert recorded by the Rolling Stones Mobile Studio. Unreleased. Phil Collins is also on drums this evening.

12 January 1987, Royal Albert Hall, London (with the Big Town Playboys)

Concert recorded by the Rolling Stones Mobile Studio. Unreleased. Phil Collins is also on drums this evening.

SETLIST: Crossroads / White Room / I Shot The Sheriff / Hung Up On Your Love / Wonderful Tonight / Miss You / Same Old Blues / Tearing Us Apart / Holy Mother / Badge / Let It Rain / Cocaine / Layla / Money For Nothing / Sunshine Of Your Love

AUGUST EUROPEAN TOUR 1987

BAND LINEUP:
Eric Clapton: guitar, vocals
Mark Knopfler: guitar, vocals on "Money For Nothing"[1]
Greg Phillinganes: keyboards
Nathan East: bass
Steve Ferrone: drums
[1]appears only on 17 January and 18 January

16 January 1987, Ahoy Hall, Rotterdam, Netherlands (with the Big Town Playboys)

No Mark Knopfler this evening.

SETLIST: Crossroads / White Room / I Shot The Sheriff / Hung Up On Your Love / Wonderful Tonight / Miss You / Same Old Blues / Tearing Us Apart / Holy Mother / Badge / Let It Rain / Cocaine / Layla / Sunshine Of Your Love

17 January 1987, Forest National, Bruxelles, Belgium (with the Big Town Playboys)

SETLIST: Crossroads / White Room / I Shot The Sheriff / Hung Up On Your Love / Wonderful Tonight / Miss You / Same Old Blues / Tearing Us Apart / Holy Mother / Badge / Let It Rain / Cocaine / Layla / Money For Nothing / Sunshine Of Your Love

18 January 1987, Le Zenith, Paris, France (with the Big Town Playboys)

Last show with Mark Knopfler.

SETLIST: Crossroads / White Room / I Shot The Sheriff / Hung Up On Your Love / Wonderful Tonight / Miss You / Same Old Blues / Tearing Us Apart / Holy Mother / Badge / Let It Rain / Cocaine / Layla / Money For Nothing / Sunshine Of Your Love / Further On Up The Road

20 January 1987, Westfalenhalle, Dortmund, Germany (with the Big Town Playboys)

SETLIST: Crossroads / White Room / I Shot The Sheriff / Hung Up On Your Love / Wonderful Tonight / Miss You / Same Old Blues / Tearing Us Apart / Holy Mother / Badge / Let It Rain / Cocaine / Layla / Sunshine Of Your Love

21 January 1987, Sporthalle, Hamburg, Germany (with the Big Town Playboys)

SETLIST: Crossroads / White Room / I Shot The Sheriff / Hung Up On Your Love / Wonderful Tonight / Miss You / Same Old Blues / Tearing Us Apart / Holy Mother / Badge / Let It Rain / Cocaine/ Layla / Sunshine Of Your Love

22 January 1987, Festhalle, Frankfurt, Germany (with the Big Town Playboys)

SETLIST: Crossroads / White Room / I Shot The Sheriff / Hung Up On Your Love / Wonderful Tonight / Miss You / Same Old Blues / Tearing Us Apart / Holy Mother / Badge / Let It Rain / Cocaine / Layla / Sunshine Of Your Love

23 January 1987, Olympiahalle, Munich, Germany (with the Big Town Playboys)

SETLIST: Crossroads / White Room / I Shot The Sheriff / Hung Up On Your Love / Wonderful Tonight / Miss You / Same Old Blues / Tearing Us Apart / Holy Mother / Badge / Let It Rain / Cocaine / Layla / Sunshine Of Your Love

26 January 1987, Palatrussardi, Milan, Italy (with the Big Town Playboys)

SETLIST: Crossroads / White Room / I Shot The Sheriff / Hung Up On Your Love / Wonderful Tonight / Miss You / Same Old Blues / Tearing Us Apart / Holy Mother / Badge / Let It Rain / Cocaine / Layla / Behind The Mask / Sunshine Of Your Love

29 January 1987, Palaeur, Rome, Italy (with the Big Town Playboys)

SETLIST: Crossroads / White Room / I Shot The Sheriff / Hung Up On Your Love / Wonderful Tonight / Miss You / Same Old Blues / Tearing Us Apart / Holy Mother / Badge / Let It Rain / Cocaine / Layla / Behind The Mask / Sunshine Of Your Love

30 January 1987, Palasport, Florence, Italy (with the Big Town Playboys)

SETLIST: Crossroads / White Room / I Shot The Sheriff / Hung Up On Your Love / Wonderful Tonight / Miss You / Same Old Blues / Tearing Us Apart / Holy Mother / Badge / Let It Rain / Cocaine / Layla / Behind The Mask / Sunshine Of Your Love

MARCH 1987

27 March 1987, Cranleigh Golf and Country Club, Cranleigh, Surrey (local charity concert)

SETLIST: Tulsa Time / Behind The Mask / Walking The Dog / Route 66 / Crossroads / Lay Down Sally / Black Magic Woman / The Bear / Alberta / Tearing Us Apart / Knock On Wood / Ramblin' On My Mind / Hi Heel Sneakers / Boogie Woogie / Walking On Sunset / Sunshine Of Your Love / I Loved Another Woman / Cocaine / Further On Up The Road

AUGUST U.S. TOUR 1987

APRIL 1987

BAND LINEUP:
Eric Clapton: guitar, vocals
Greg Phillinganes: keyboards
Nathan East: bass
Phil Collins: drums

Support act Robert Cray would join Eric on "Further On Up The Road" on most nights.

8 April 1987–9 April 1987, rehearsals at the Warfield Theatre, San Francisco

11 April 1987, Coliseum, Oakland, California (with Robert Cray)

SETLIST: Crossroads / White Room / I Shot The Sheriff / Hung Up On Your Love / Wonderful Tonight / Miss You / Same Old Blues / Tearing Us Apart / Holy Mother / Badge / Let It Rain / Cocaine / Layla / Behind The Mask / Sunshine Of Your Love

13 April 1987, Pacific Amphitheatre, Costa Mesa, California (with Robert Cray)

SETLIST: Crossroads / White Room / I Shot The Sheriff / Hung Up On Your Love / Wonderful Tonight / Miss You / Same Old Blues / Tearing Us Apart / Holy Mother / Badge / Let It Rain / Cocaine / Layla / Further On Up The Road / Sunshine of Your Love

14 April 1987, Forum, Los Angeles, California (with Robert Cray)

SETLIST: Crossroads / White Room / I Shot The Sheriff / Hung Up On Your Love / Wonderful Tonight / Miss You / Same Old Blues / Tearing Us Apart / Holy Mother / Badge / Let It Rain / Cocaine / Layla / Further On Up The Road / Sunshine of Your Love

B.B. KING
TELEVISON SPECIAL 1987

15 April 1987, Ebony Showcase Theatre, Los Angeles, California (on his day off, Eric participates in the filming of a B.B. King television special. It was broadcast in the U.S. on 12 November 1987 on HBO/CINEMAX. Wonderful to see footage of Eric and Stevie Ray Vaughan playing together in the same band. Tragically, Paul Butterfield died three weeks after the filming and when the show was released it was dedicated to his memory)

SETLIST:

Why I Sing The Blues (B.B. King) *A Blues Session–B.B. King & Friends* VHS video released 1987

B.B. King: vocals, guitar
Albert King: vocals, guitar
Eric Clapton: guitar
Stevie Ray Vaughan: guitar
Phil Collins: drums
Paul Butterfield: harmonica
Dr. John: keyboards
Etta James: vocals
Gladys Knight: vocals
Chaka Khan: vocals
Billy Ocean: vocals
Not known: bass
Not known: drums
Not known: horns

The Thrill Is Gone (Roy Hawkins / Rick Darnell) *A Blues Session–B.B. King & Friends* VHS video released 1987

B.B. King: vocals, guitar
Eric Clapton: guitar
Phil Collins: drums
Paul Butterfield: harmonica
Not known: bass
Not known: drums
Not known: horns
Not known: horns

Let The Good Times Roll (B.B. King) *A Blues Session–B.B. King & Friends* VHS video released 1987

B.B. King: vocals, guitar
Albert King: vocals, guitar
Eric Clapton: guitar
Stevie Ray Vaughan: guitar
Phil Collins: drums
Paul Butterfild: hamonica
Dr. John: keyboards
Etta James: vocals
Gladys Knight: vocals
Chaka Khan: vocals
Billy Ocean: vocals
Not known: bass
Not known: drums
Not known: horns

Take My Hand Precious Lord (Thomas A. Dorsey / George Nelson Allen) *A Blues Session–B.B. King & Friends* VHS video released 1987

B.B. King: guitar
Albert King: guitar
Eric Clapton: guitar
Stevie Ray Vaughan: guitar
Phil Collins: drums
Paul Butterfield: harmonica
Dr. John: keyboards
Etta James: vocals
Gladys Knight: vocals
Chaka Khan: vocals

Billy Ocean: vocals
Not known: bass
Not known: drums
Not known: horns
Producer: Ken Ehrlich

16 April 1987, McNichols Arena, Denver, Colorado (with Robert Cray)

SETLIST: Crossroads / White Room / I Shot The Sheriff / Hung Up On Your Love / Wonderful Tonight / Miss You / Same Old Blues / Tearing Us Apart / Holy Mother / Badge / Let It Rain / Cocaine / Layla / Sunshine Of Your Love

18 April 1987, Civic Center, St. Paul, Minnesota (with Robert Cray)

SETLIST: Crossroads / White Room / I Shot The Sheriff / Hung Up On Your Love / Wonderful Tonight / Miss You / Same Old Blues / Tearing Us Apart / Holy Mother / Badge / Let It Rain / Cocaine / Layla / Sunshine Of Your Love

19 April 1987, Rosemont Horizon, Rosemont, Illinois (with Robert Cray)

SETLIST: Crossroads / White Room / I Shot The Sheriff / Hung Up On Your Love / Wonderful Tonight / Miss You / Same Old Blues / Tearing Us Apart / Holy Mother / Badge / Let It Rain / Cocaine / Layla / Further On Up The Road / Sunshine Of Your Love

BUDDY GUY JAM 1987

19 April 1987, Limelight Club, Chicago, Illinois

After Eric's set at the Rosemont Horizon, Eric along with Phil Collins, Robert Cray, and Richard Cousins head to the Limelight Club in Chicago where Buddy Guy is playing. Buddy had already played his first set and the stage hands prepared the stage for the special guests by bringing on extra amps, microphones, etc. After an hour, they join Sunnyland Slim, Sugar Blue, James Cotton, Konika Kress, Eddie Lusk, and Buddy Guy for a one-hour jam session.

SETLIST: Everyday I Have The Blues / My Time After Awhile / Blue Monday / Stone Crazy / Funky Jam / Goin' Down / Sunshine Of Your Love / Sweet Little Angel

Eric Clapton jams with Buddy Guy at the Limelight Club, Chicago, Illinois.

21 April 1987, Market Square Arena, Indianapolis, Indiana (with Robert Cray)

SETLIST: Crossroads / White Room / I Shot The Sheriff / Hung Up On Your Love / Wonderful Tonight / Miss You / Same Old Blues / Tearing Us Apart / Holy Mother / Badge / Let It Rain / Cocaine / Layla / Further On Up The Road

22 April 1987, Joe Louis Arena, Detroit, Michigan (with Robert Cray)

SETLIST: Crossroads / White Room / I Shot The Sheriff / Hung Up On Your Love / Wonderful Tonight / Miss You / Same Old Blues / Tearing Us Apart / Holy Mother / Badge / Let It Rain / Cocaine / Layla / Sunshine Of Your Love

23 April 1987, Richfield Coliseum, Cleveland, Ohio (with Robert Cray)

SETLIST: Crossroads / White Room / I Shot The Sheriff / Hung Up On Your Love / Wonderful Tonight / Miss You / Same Old Blues / Tearing Us Apart / Holy Mother / Badge / Let It Rain / Cocaine / Layla / Sunshine Of Your Love

25 April 1987, Capitol Centre, Largo, Maryland (with Robert Cray)

SETLIST: Crossroads / White Room / I Shot The Sheriff / Hung Up On Your Love / Wonderful Tonight / Miss You / Same Old Blues / Tearing Us Apart / Holy Mother / Badge / Let It Rain / Cocaine / Layla / Further On Up The Road / Sunshine Of Your Love

26 April 1987, Civic Center, Providence, Rhode Island (with Robert Cray)

SETLIST: Crossroads / White Room / I Shot The Sheriff / Hung Up On Your Love / Wonderful Tonight / Miss You / Same Old Blues / Tearing Us Apart / Holy Mother / Badge / Let It Rain / Cocaine / Layla / Further On Up The Road / Sunshine Of Your Love

Concert is recorded officially but remains unreleased.

27 April 1987, Madison Square Garden, New York City (with Robert Cray)

SETLIST: Crossroads / White Room / I Shot The Sheriff / Hung Up On Your Love / Wonderful Tonight / Miss You / Same Old Blues / Tearing Us Apart / Holy Mother / Badge / Let It Rain / Cocaine / Layla / Further On Up The Road / Sunshine Of Your Love

Concert recorded officially but remains unreleased.

MAY 1987

LIONEL RICHIE JAM 1987

6 May 1987, Wembley Arena, Wembley, London (guest appearance with Lionel Richie on "Tonight Will Be Alright" and "Brickhouse." Steve Gadd was the drummer for the tour and Eric asked his manager if they could get Gadd to join his band for the next tour. Roger Forrester drily replied that he could not afford him!)

Eric Clapton joins friend Lionel Richie on stage at Wembley Arena on 6 May 1987.

IAN BOTHAM PUB GIG 1987

30 May 1987, Crown at Martley (Eric plays Ian Bothams's local pub after losing a bet with Ian. Eric joins Stan Webb for the evening session)

JUNE 1987

PRINCE'S TRUST CONCERTS 1987

5 June 1987, Wembley Arena, Wembley, London

While My Guitar Gently Weeps unreleased

Eric Clapton: guitar
George Harrison: guitar, vocals
Jeff Lynne: guitar
Ringo Starr: drums
Phil Collins: drums
Elton John: piano
Jools Holland: keyboards
Mark King: bass
Ray Cooper: percussion
John Thirkell: horns
Gary Barnacle: horns
Peter Throne: horns
Mel Collins: horns
George Chandler: backing vocals
Jimmy Helms: backing vocals
Jimmy Chambers: backing vocals

Wonderful Tonight unreleased

Eric Clapton: guitar, vocals
Phil Collins: drums
Ray Cooper: tambourine
Jools Holland: keyboards
Mark Lindup: keyboards
Mark King: bass
Midge Ure: guitar
George Chandler: backing vocals
Jimmy Helms: backing vocals

Jimmy Chambers: backing vocals
Jimmy Chambers: backing vocals

Behind The Mask unreleased

Eric Clapton: guitar, vocals
Phil Collins: drums
Jools Holland: keyboards
Mark Lindup: keyboards
Mark King: bass
Midge Ure: guitar
John Thirkell: horns
Gary Barnacle: horns
Peter Throne: horns
Mel Collins: horns
George Chandler: backing vocals
Jimmy Helms: backing vocals
Jimmy Chambers: backing vocals

With A Little Help From My Friends unreleased

Eric Clapton: guitar
George Harrison: guitar, vocals
Jeff Lynne: guitar, vocals
Ringo Starr: vocals, tambourine
Phil Collins: drums
Elton John: vocals
Jools Holland: keyboards
Mark King: bass
Ray Cooper: percussion
John Thirkell: horns
Gary Barnacle: horns
Peter Throne: horns
Mel Collins: horns
George Chandler: backing vocals
Jimmy Helms: backing vocals
Jimmy Chambers: backing vocals
Dave Edmonds: guitar
Bryan Adams: vocals
Labi Siffre: vocals
Paul Young: vocals
Midge Ure: vocals, guitar

6 June 1987, Wembley Arena, Wembley, London

While My Guitar Gently Weeps *The Prince's Trust Concert 1987* CD A&M 396 931-2 released November 1987 / VHS video

Eric Clapton: guitar
George Harrison: guitar, vocals
Jeff Lynne: guitar
Ringo Starr: drums
Phil Collins: drums
Elton John: piano
Jools Holland: keyboards
Mark King: bass
Ray Cooper: percussion

John Thirkell: horns
Gary Barnacle: horns
Peter Throne: horns
Mel Collins: horns
George Chandler: backing vocals
Jimmy Helms: backing vocals
Jimmy Chambers: backing vocals

Wonderful Tonight *The Prince's Trust Concert 1987* CD A&M 396 931-2 released November 1987 / VHS video

Eric Clapton: guitar, vocals
Phil Collins: drums
Ray Cooper: tambourine
Jools Holland: keyboards
Mark Lindup: keyboards
Mark King: bass
Midge Ure: guitar
George Chandler: backing vocals
Jimmy Helms: backing vocals
Jimmy Chambers: backing vocals

Behind The Mask *The Prince's Trust Concert 1987* CD A&M 396 931-2 released November 1987 / VHS video

Eric Clapton: guitar, vocals
Phil Collins: drums
Jools Holland: keyboards
Mark Lindup: keyboards
Mark King: bass
Midge Ure: guitar
John Thirkell: horns
Gary Barnacle: horns
Peter Throne: horns
Mel Collins: horns
George Chandler: backing vocals
Jimmy Helms: backing vocals
Jimmy Chambers: backing vocals

With A Little Help From My Friends *The Prince's Trust Concert 1987* CD A&M 396 931-2 released November 1987 / VHS video

Eric Clapton: guitar
George Harrison: guitar, vocals
Jeff Lynne: guitar, vocals
Ringo Starr: vocals, tambourine
Phil Collins: drums
Elton John: vocals
Jools Holland: keyboards
Mark King: bass
Ray Cooper: percussion
John Thirkell: horns
Gary Barnacle: horns
Peter Throne: horns
Mel Collins: horns
George Chandler: backing vocals
Jimmy Helms: backing vocals
Jimmy Chambers: backing vocals

Dave Edmonds: guitar
Bryan Adams: vocals
Labi Siffre: vocals
Paul Young: vocals
Midge Ure: vocals, guitar

Producer: Midge Ure
Engineer: Doug Hopkins
Recorded by: RAK Mobile

TINA TURNER WITH ERIC CLAPTON 1987

18 June 1987, Wembley Arena, Wembley, London (guest appearance with Tina Turner)

Eric Clapton joins Tina Turner on stage at Wembley Arena on 18 June 1987.

BAND LINEUP:

Tina Turner: vocals
Eric Clapton: guitar, vocals
Jamie Ralston: guitar, vocals
Laurie Wisefield: guitar
Bob Feit: bass guitar, vocals
Jack Bruno: drums
Stevie Scales: percussion
John Miles: guitar, vocals
Ollie Marland: keyboards, vocals
Deric Dyer: saxophone, keyboards

Tearing Us Apart (Eric Clapton / Greg Phillinganes) *Live In Europe* 2CD Capitol CDP 7 90126 2 released 1988

Producer: John Hudson
Engineer: Mike Ging
Recorded by: The Manor Mobile

JULY 1987

ISLAND RECORDS 25th BIRTHDAY PARTY 1987

4 July 1987, Pinewood Studios, Iver, Buckinghamshire (Island Records 25th birthday party)

Eric joined the Island Allstars for a version of Bob Marley's "I Shot The Sheriff." Later on Eric participated in a jam session with Ringo Starr, Andy Summers, Buckwheat Zydeco, John Martyn, and others. "I Shot The Sheriff" was released on the VHS video called *Alright Now* in 1987.

Eric Clapton and John Martyn jamming at Pinewood Studios, Iver, Buckinghamshire, for Island Records' 25th Birthday Party.

JAM WITH BUCKWHEAT ZYDECO 1987

20 July 1987, S.O.B.'s, 204 Varick Street, New York City (Eric attends the release party for Buckwheat Zydeco's *On A Night Like This* album and jams with him and his band on a set of blues)

AUGUST 1987

14 August 1987, Finchley Cricket Club, East End Road, London (Eric jams with Chicken Shack at a charity cricket show)

SETLIST: Everyday I Have The Blues / The Thrill Is Gone / Rich Man's Blues / Cocaine / Sweet Sixteen / I'd Rather Go Blind / Going Up, Going Down / Long Distance Call / Further On Up The Road / I'm Tore Down

Jack Bruce and Eric Clapton jamming on the terrace at Hurtwood Edge in Surrey some time in August. Part of this sequence was used for a South Bank Show *television special on Eric in 1987.*

SEPTEMBER 1987

ROOMFUL OF BLUES JAM 1987

4 September 1987, Lone Star Cafe, New York City (guest appearance with Ronnie Earl's Roomful of Blues)

OCTOBER 1987

SOUTH BANK SHOW FILMING 1987

6 October 1987, Ronnie Scott's Club, Soho, London

Eric joins Buddy Guy at Ronnie Scott's before a specially invited audience for an afternoon filming session for a *South Bank Show* television program dedicated to Eric. The filming took up most of the afternoon and in between camera film changes, the band played just for the crowd in attendance.

BAND LINEUP:
Buddy Guy: guitar, vocals
Mark Knopfler: guitar, vocals on "Money For Nothing"
Eric Clapton: guitar, vocals
Chris Stainton: piano
Greg Rzab: bass
Gerry Porter: drums

Buddy Guy and Eric Clapton jam at Ronnie Scott's Club in London's Soho for a special television show to be broadcast later in 1987.

SETLIST: Sweet Home Chicago (without Eric) (Take 1) / Sweet Home Chicago (without Eric) (Take 2) / Down In The Bottom / Play The Blues / Key To The Highway / Walking The Dog / Stormy Monday (Take 1) / Real Mother For Ya / Stormy Monday (Take 2) / Chicken Heads / Jam / Worried Life Blues (Take 1) / Worried Life Blues (breaks down) / Worried Life Blues (Take 2) / Worry Worry / Chicken Heads / I Just Wanna Make Love To You / Jam

Above is the complete setlist for the afternoon, including songs played during down time in filming.

BROADCAST SETLIST: Key To The Highway / Stormy Monday / Worried Life Blues / Sweet Home Chicago (without Eric) / Chicken Heads / Jam

These were the only numbers filmed. Unfortunately due to a technical problem, Buddy's guitar was largely missing from the mix in the broadcast. So you can see Buddy wailing away on the guitar, but with hardly any sound due to a mixing error in editing the footage for television. Eric was very disappointed when he saw the broadcast. A true stereo mix tape was located during research for the proposed Eric Clapton anthology project in 2005 and was sourced direct from the mixing desk. Hopefully one day a new edition of the broadcast will be made available with the correct soundtrack restored.

> **"**They showed some of it on TV, late hours. I watched some of that and was very disappointed with the sound mix because you can hardly hear Buddy. And I thought that was sad.**"**
>
> **—ERIC CLAPTON**

ERIC CLAPTON BUDDY GUY JAM 1987

9 October 1987, Dingwalls Club, Camden, London (Eric makes a guest appearance with Buddy Guy)

BAND LINEUP:
Buddy Guy: guitar, vocals
Eric Clapton: guitar, vocals
John Porter: guitar
Greg Rzab: bass
Gerry Porter: drums

SETLIST: Stormy Monday / The Things That I Used To Do / Rock Me Baby / It's Still Called The Blues / Sweet Home Chicago / Chicken Heads / Jam / I Just Wanna Make Love To You / Long Distance Call / My Time After A While / Knock On Wood / Sweet Sixteen / Why Worry / Strange Brew / Going Down

Eric Clapton at Dingwalls in Camden on 9 October 1987.

AUGUST AUSTRALIA / JAPAN TOUR 1987

BAND LINEUP:
Eric Clapton: guitar, vocals
Alan Clark: keyboards
Nathan East: bass
Steve Ferrone: drums

23 October 1987, Entertainment Center, Sydney, Australia

SETLIST: Crossroads / White Room / I Shot The Sheriff / Run / Wonderful Tonight / Same Old Blues / Miss You / It's In The Way That You Use It / Tearing Us Apart / Holy Mother / Badge / Let It Rain / Cocaine / Layla / Sunshine Of Your Love / Further On Up The Road

24 October 1987, Entertainment Center, Brisbane, Australia

SETLIST: Crossroads / White Room / I Shot The Sheriff / Run / Wonderful Tonight / Same Old Blues / Miss You / It's In The Way That You Use It / Tearing Us Apart / Holy Mother / Badge / Let It Rain / Cocaine / Layla / Sunshine Of Your Love / Further On Up The Road

27 October 1987, Sports and Entertainment Center, Melbourne, Australia

SETLIST: Crossroads / White Room / I Shot The Sheriff / Run / Wonderful Tonight / Same Old Blues / Miss You / It's In The Way That You Use It / Tearing Us Apart / Holy Mother / Badge / Let It Rain / Cocaine / Layla / Sunshine Of Your Love / Further On Up The Road

28 October 1987, Sports and Entertainment Center, Melbourne, Australia

SETLIST: Crossroads / White Room / I Shot The Sheriff / Wonderful Tonight / Run / Same Old Blues / Tearing Us Apart / Holy Mother / Badge / Let It Rain / Cocaine / Layla / Behind The Mask / Sunshine Of Your Love / Further On Up The Road

NOVEMBER 1987

2 November 1987, Budokan, Tokyo, Japan

SETLIST: Crossroads / White Room / I Shot The Sheriff / Wonderful Tonight / Run / Same Old Blues / Tearing Us Apart / Holy Mother / Badge / Let It Rain / Cocaine / Layla / Behind The Mask / Sunshine Of Your Love / Further On Up The Road

4 November 1987, Budokan, Tokyo, Japan

SETLIST: Crossroads / White Room / I Shot The Sheriff / Wonderful Tonight / Run / Same Old Blues / Tearing Us Apart / Holy Mother / Badge / Let It Rain / Cocaine / Layla / Behind The Mask / Sunshine Of Your Love / Further On Up The Road

5 November 1987, Budokan, Tokyo, Japan

SETLIST: Crossroads / White Room / I Shot The Sheriff / Wonderful Tonight / Run / Same Old Blues / Tearing Us Apart / Holy Mother / Badge / Let It Rain / Cocaine / Layla / Behind The Mask / Sunshine Of Your Love / Further On Up The Road

7 November 1987, Nagoya Gym, Nagoya, Japan

SETLIST: Crossroads / White Room / I Shot The Sheriff / Wonderful Tonight / Run / Same Old Blues / Tearing Us Apart / Holy Mother / Badge / Let It Rain / Cocaine / Layla / Behind The Mask / Sunshine Of Your Love / Further On Up The Road

9 November 1987, Osaka Jo Hall, Osaka, Japan

SETLIST: Crossroads / White Room / I Shot The Sheriff / Wonderful Tonight / Run / Same Old Blues / Tearing Us Apart / Holy Mother / Badge / Let It Rain / Cocaine / Layla / Behind The Mask / Sunshine Of Your Love / Further On Up The Road

DECEMBER 1987

19 December 1987, Village Hall, Dunsfold, Surrey (charity show with Gary Brooker)

RECORDING SESSIONS 1987
ERIC CLAPTON GUEST SESSION
STUDIO ZERKALL
Germany
Session for Jack Bruce

WAITING ON A WORD (Jack Bruce / Pete Brown) *Somethin' Else* CD CMP CD1001 released 1993

Jack Bruce: vocals, bass, piano
Eric Clapton: guitar
Peter Weihe: rhythm guitar
Stuart Elliot: drums
Trilok Gurtu: percussion

WILLPOWER (Jack Bruce / Pete Brown) *Somethin' Else* CD CMP CD1001 released 1993

Jack Bruce: vocals, bass, keyboards
Eric Clapton: guitar
Clem Clempson: rhythm guitar
Stuart Elliot: drums
Bruce Fowler: trombone
Walt Fowler: trumpet
Gerd Dudek: tenor saxophone
Uli Lask: alto sxophone

SHIPS IN THE NIGHT (Jack Bruce / Pete Brown) *Somethin' Else* CD CMP CD1001 released 1993

Jack Bruce: vocals, bass, piano, keyboards, cello
Eric Clapton: guitar
Peter Weihe: acoustic guitar
Maggie Reilly: vocals
Stuart Elliot: drums

Producers: Jack Bruce / Walter Quintus
Engineer: Walter Quintus

ERIC CLAPTON GUEST SESSION

AIR STUDIOS
Waterworks Estate, Montserrat, West Indies
Session for Sting

MARCH 1987

THEY DANCE ALONE (Sting) *Nothing Like The Sun* CD A&M Records CD 6402, DX 2163 released October 1987

Sting: bass, vocals
Eric Clapton: guitar
Chet Atkins: acoustic guitar
Mark Knopfler: guitar
Fareed Haque: guitar
Manu Katche: drums
Kenny Kirkland: keyboards
Mino Cinelu: vocoder, percussion
Brandford Marsalis: saxophone
Ruben Blades: Spanish voice

WE'LL BE TOGETHER (Sting) (alternate version with Eric Clapton) *Fields Of Gold The Best Of Sting 1984-1985* CD A&M 540 307 2 released 1994

Sting: bass, vocals
Eric Clapton: electric guitar, solo
Andy Newmark: additional drums
Manu Katche: drums
Kenny Kirkland: keyboards
Mino Cinelu: vocoder, percussion
Brandford Marsalis: saxophone

Producers: Sting / Neil Dorfsman
Engineer: Neil Dorfsman

> **"**On 'They Dance Alone' I'm playing a Gibson Chet Atkins, which is a gut string solid guitar. But if you look at the credits on that track you will see there are other guitar players. The way it is mixed you can just hear me, very barely in some places. Because I know that I played, I can recognize it, otherwise you wouldn't know.
>
> I don't know why. I think perhaps he's a perfectionist. I played on about three or four other tracks on the album. That was in Montserrat. Sting wasn't there because his mother had just died. I then went to New York where I knew he'd be, just to see what his reaction was, and he wanted me to change a few things. So I played some of it again and he seemed pleased. But then when he mixed it down, he obviously decided there was too much going on, so he mixed it out.
>
> I think it is sad in a way that some of that stuff gets lost. However, it is not lost forever, because it has got to be there somewhere. He knows best. It's his music, isn't it?**"**
>
> **—ERIC CLAPTON**

ERIC CLAPTON GUEST SESSION

[FPSHOT] FRIAR PARK STUDIOS
Henley On Thames, Oxfordshire
Session for George Harrison

MARCH 1987

CLOUD NINE (George Harrison) *Cloud Nine* CD Dark Horse 925643 2 released November 1987

THAT'S WHAT IT TAKES (George Harrison / Jeff Lynne / Gary Wright) *Cloud Nine* CD Dark Horse 925643 2 released November 1987

DEVIL'S RADIO (George Harrison) *Cloud Nine* CD Dark Horse 925643 2 released November 1987

WRECK OF THE HESPERUS (George Harrison) *Cloud Nine* CD Dark Horse 925643 2 released November 1987

George Harrison: guitar, vocals
Eric Clapton: guitar
Jeff Lynne: bass, guitar
Elton John: keyboards
Gery Wright: keyboards
Jim Keltner: drums
Ringo Starr: drums
Ray Cooper: percussion
Jim Horn: saxophone

Producers: George Harrison / Jeff Lynne
Engineer: Richard Dodd

"Eric Clapton plays on four tracks; Eric has the end solo on 'That's What It Takes,' he plays on 'Devil's Radio,' 'Wreck Of The Hesperus,' and on the title track. And then Elton John plays electric piano on 'Cloud Nine'—and he plays piano on 'Devil's Radio' and, I believe, 'Wreck Of The Hesperus.' All the remaining stuff: bass is Jeff; keyboards, Oberheim is Jeff; and guitars are me and Jeff. All the little twiddly parts that just crop up, like autoharps, is just me and Jeff, and we also do all the backing voices."

—GEORGE HARRSION

POWER STATION STUDIOS
441 West 53rd Street,
New York City
Session for
Michelob advert

SEPTEMBER 1987

In 1987, Anheuser-Busch launched their "The Night Belongs to Michelob" campaign with a series of commercials involving popular rock and roll artists of the day such as Steve Winwood and Phil Collins. They also signed up Eric Clapton. The problem was that he was a practicing alchoholic at the time, so it seemed a somewhat controversial and perhaps ill-advised move to participate in such a campaign promoting the wonders of Michelob beer in America. Eric was seen in adverts on television and magazines. As soon as he admitted to his condition, the contract was terminated. It did at least provide us with a new and exciting version of JJ Cale's "After Midnight."

AFTER MIDNIGHT (JJ Cale) A-side CD single / *Crossroads* box set Polydor 835 261-2 released 1988

Eric Clapton: guitar, vocals
Alan Clark: keyboards
Nathan East: bass
Andy Newmark: drums

Producers: Peter McHugh / Jim Harris
Engineer: Justin Neibank

6

1988

Eric's 1988 UK concerts were instant sell-outs and the Royal Albert Hall shows were extended to nine nights to satisfy demand and could have been extended by even more. The year also marked Eric's twenty-fifth anniversary as a professional musician and the prospect of a set consisting of numbers drawn from various periods in his illustrious career were anticipated.

Mark Knopfler from Dire Straits was in the band again, as he had been in 1987. Alan Clark, another member of Dire Straits, was recruited to replace Greg Phillinganes, who had gone off to be musical director for Michael Jackson's huge *Bad* world tour. Two further new recruits to the band were the glamorous and talented backing vocalists Tessa Niles and Katie Kissoon, whose combined CVs read like a Who's Who of the music world. Also new, Ray Cooper, the zany and very talented percussionist from Elton John's band among others. His on stage antics are always a crowd pleaser and his years with Eric always brought a smile to the crowds lucky enough to see the shows. The remainder of the band were the same as in 1987.

Throughout the tour, a confident white-suited Eric Clapton strolled center stage to lead his band through a set that inexplicably differed little from 1987. Although his playing was faultless, his judgment and obvious disinterest in doing anything adventurous from his massive back catalog was a major dissapointment to many. Considering that a career-spanning 4CD box set called *Crossroads* was due for release to celebrate his twenty-five years in the business, it seemed strange not to delve deeper into his back catalog.

The expanded group presented Eric with the opportunity of giving his repertoire a larger canvas to play with and most numbers benefited from having a fuller sound. A handsome silver-covered anniversary program that traced Eric's career with some beautiful photos and memorabilia quickly sold out and became quite collectable over the years.

The remainder of 1988 was hectic for Eric. Charity concerts and soundtrack work kept him busy until the end of summer when he toured North America and Japan ending towards the middle of November. By this time the 1989 Royal Albert Hall concerts had already sold out!

JANUARY 1988

25th ANNIVERSARY UK TOUR 1988

BAND LINEUP:
Eric Clapton: guitar, vocals
Mark Knopfler: guitar, vocals
Nathan East: bass
Steve Ferrone: drums
Alan Clark: keyboards
Ray Cooper: percussion
Tessa Niles: backing vocals
Katie Kissoon: backing vocals

22 January 1988, National Exhibition Centre, Birmingham

SETLIST: Crossroads / White Room / I Shot The Sheriff / Wonderful Tonight / Run / Same Old Blues / Tearing Us Apart / Holy Mother / Badge / Let It Rain / Cocaine / A

Remark You Made / Layla / Behind The Mask / Sunshine Of Your Love / Money For Nothing / Further On Up The Road

23 January 1988, National Exhibition Centre, Birmingham

SETLIST: Crossroads / White Room / I Shot The Sheriff / Wonderful Tonight / Run / Same Old Blues / Tearing Us Apart / Holy Mother / Badge / Let It Rain / Cocaine / A Remark You Made / Layla / Behind The Mask / Sunshine Of Your Love / Money For Nothing / Further On Up The Road

25 January 1988, Royal Albert Hall, London

SETLIST: Crossroads / White Room / I Shot The Sheriff / Wonderful Tonight / Run / Same Old Blues / Tearing Us Apart / Holy Mother / Badge / Let It Rain / Cocaine / A Remark You Made / Layla / Behind The Mask / Sunshine Of Your Love / Money For Nothing / Further On Up The Road

26 January 1988, Royal Albert Hall, London

SETLIST: Crossroads / White Room / I Shot The Sheriff / Wonderful Tonight / Run / Same Old Blues / Tearing Us Apart / Holy Mother / Badge / Let It Rain / Cocaine / A Remark You Made / Layla / Behind The Mask / Sunshine Of Your Love / Money For Nothing / Further On Up The Road

27 January 1988, Royal Albert Hall, London

Mark Knopfler and Eric Clapton during Eric's residency at the Royal Albert Hall in London, January 1988.

SETLIST: Crossroads / White Room / I Shot The Sheriff / Wonderful Tonight / Run / Same Old Blues / Tearing Us Apart / Holy Mother / Badge / Let It Rain / Cocaine / A Remark You Made / Layla / Behind The Mask / Sunshine Of Your Love / Money For Nothing / Further On Up The Road

29 January 1988, Royal Albert Hall, London

SETLIST: Crossroads / White Room / I Shot The Sheriff / Wonderful Tonight / Run / Same Old Blues / Tearing Us Apart / Holy Mother / Badge / Let It Rain / Cocaine / A Remark You Made / Layla / Behind The Mask / Sunshine Of Your Love / Money For Nothing / Further On Up The Road

30 January 1988, Royal Albert Hall, London

SETLIST: Crossroads / White Room / I Shot The Sheriff / Wonderful Tonight / Run / Same Old Blues / Tearing Us Apart / Holy Mother / Badge / Let It Rain / Cocaine / A Remark You Made / Layla / Behind The Mask / Sunshine Of Your Love / Money For Nothing / Further On Up The Road

31 January 1988, Royal Albert Hall, London

SETLIST: Crossroads / White Room / I Shot The Sheriff / Wonderful Tonight / Run / Same Old Blues / Tearing Us Apart / Holy Mother / Badge / Let It Rain / Cocaine / A Remark You Made / Layla / Behind The Mask / Sunshine Of Your Love / Money For Nothing / Further On Up The Road

FEBRUARY 1988

2 February 1988, Royal Albert Hall, London

SETLIST: Crossroads / White Room / I Shot The Sheriff / Wonderful Tonight / Run / Same Old Blues / Tearing Us Apart / Holy Mother / Badge / Let It Rain / Cocaine / A Remark You Made / Layla / Behind The Mask / Sunshine Of Your Love / Money For Nothing / Further On Up The Road

3 February 1988, Royal Albert Hall, London

SETLIST: Crossroads / White Room / I Shot The Sheriff / Wonderful Tonight / Run / Same Old Blues / Tearing Us Apart / Holy Mother / Badge / Let It Rain / Cocaine / A Remark You Made / Layla / Behind The Mask / Sunshine Of Your Love / Money For Nothing / Further On Up The Road

4 February 1988, Royal Albert Hall, London

SETLIST: Crossroads / White Room / I Shot The Sheriff / Wonderful Tonight / Run / Same Old Blues / Tearing Us Apart / Holy Mother / Badge / Let It Rain / Cocaine / A Remark You Made / Layla / Behind The Mask / Sunshine Of Your Love / Money For Nothing / Further On Up The Road

7 February 1988, Civic Hall, Guildford, Surrey

Phil Collins plays drums alongside Steve Ferrone for the whole set.

Eric and Elton John at the Guildford Civic Hall, Surrey, on 7 February 1988.

SETLIST: Crossroads / White Room / I Shot The Sheriff / Wonderful Tonight / Run / Same Old Blues[1] / Tearing Us Apart[1] / Holy Mother[1] / Badge[1] / Let It Rain[1] / Cocaine[1]/ A Remark You Made[1] / Layla[1] / Behind The Mask[1] / Sunshine Of Your Love[1] / Money For Nothing[1] / Further On Up The Road[1]

[1]with Elton John

MAY 1988

30 May 1988–31 May 1988, Brixton Academy, Brixton, London (rehearsing with Dire Starits for upcoming Nelson Mandela concert)

JUNE 1988

1 June 1988–3 June 1988, Brixton Academy, Brixton, London (rehearsing with Dire Starits for upcoming Nelson Mandela concert)

PRINCE'S TRUST CONCERTS 1988

BAND LINEUP:
Eric Clapton: guitar, vocals
Mark Knopfler: guitar, vocals
Elton John: keyboards, vocals
Phil Collins: drums, vocals
Steve Ferrone: drums
Nathan East: bass
Katie Kissoon: vocals
Tessa Niles: vocals

4 June 1988, Brixton Academy, Brixton, London (Eric rehearses for the Prince's Trust concerts)

5 June 1988, Brixton Academy, Brixton, London (afternoon rehearsals with Dire Starits for upcoming Nelson Mandela concert)

5 June 1988, Royal Albert Hall, London (Prince's Trust Concert)

SETLIST: Behind The Mask / Cocaine / Money For Nothing / I Don't Wanna Go On With You Like That / Layla / With A Little Help From My Friends[1]

[1]This last song was sung by Joe Cocker with most of the other artists from the concert including Midge Ure, the Bee Gees, T 'Pau, and Wet Wet Wet

The entire show was broadcast on the *King Biscuit Flower Hour* in 1988, and highlights were released as a home video.

6 June 1988, Brixton Academy, Brixton, London (afternoon rehearsals with Dire Straits for upcoming Nelson Mandela concert)

6 June 1988, Royal Albert Hall, London (Prince's Trust Concert)

SETLIST: Behind The Mask / Cocaine / Money For Nothing / I Don't Wanna Go On With You Like That / Layla / With A Little Help From My Friends

7 June 1988, Brixton Academy, Brixton, London (rehearsals with Dire Straits for upcoming Nelson Mandela concert)

DIRE STRAITS-NELSON MANDELA WARM-UP SHOWS 1988

8 June 1988, Hammersmith Odeon, London

SETLIST: Walk Of Life / Sultans Of Swing / Romeo And Juliet / Money For Nothing / Brothers In Arms / Tunnel Of Love / Wonderful Tonight / Solid Rock / Going Home

9 June 1988, Hammersmith Odeon, London

SETLIST: Walk Of Life / Sultans O f Swing / Romeo And Juliet / Money For Nothing / Brothers In Arms / Tunnel Of Love / Wonderful Tonight / Solid Rock / Going Home

NELSON MANDELA 70th BIRTHDAY TRIBUTE CONCERT 1988

BAND LINEUP:
Eric Clapton: guitar, vocals
Mark Knopfler: guitar, vocals
Alan Clark: keyboards
Guy Fletcher: keyboards
John Illsley: bass
Terry Williams: drums
Chris White: saxophone

10 June 1988, Wembley Stadium, Wembley, London (Dire Straits and Eric do a soundcheck at Wembley in preparation for tomorrow's show)

11 June 1988, Wembley Stadium, Wembley, London

Many stars came out for this day-long concert to celebrate Nelson Mandela's 70th Birthday Tribute at London's Wembley Stadium. The eleven-hour concert was broadcast on both radio and television worldwide. The lineup was diverse mixing soul, pop, world, and a little comedy in almost equal measure. The order of appearance was as follows: Farafina Drummers, Sting, George Michael, the Eurythmics, the Arnhelmland Dancers, the Amabutho Male Chorus, Lenny Henry, Al Green, Joe Cocker, Jonathan Butler, Freddie Jackson, Ashford and Simpson, Natalie Cole, Fry & Laurie, Tracy Chapman (the first of two appearances), Wet Wet Wet, Tony Hadley, Joan Armatrading, Midge Ure and Phil Collins, Paul Carrack, Fish, Paul Young, Curt Smith, Bryan Adams, the Bee Gees, Jonas Gwangwa, Salif Keita, Youssou N'Dour, Jackson Browne and Youssou N'Dour, Sly and Robby with Aswad, Mahlathini and the Mahotella Wueens, UB40 and guest Chrissie Hynde, Whoopi Goldberg, Tracy Chapman (second appearance), Hugh Masakela and Miriam Makeba, Courtney Pine and I Dance Jazz Dancers, Simple Minds, Simple Minds with guests Peter Gabriel, Steven Van Zandt, David Sanborn, Jerry Dammers, Harry Enfield, Amampondo, Whitney Houston, Salt-N-Pepa, Derek B, Stevie Wonder, Fat Boys with Chubby Checker, Billy Connolly, Dire Straits with Eric Clapton, Jessye Norman.

SETLIST: Walk Of Life / Sultans Of Swing / Romeo And Juliet / Money For Nothing / Brothers In Arms / Wonderful Tonight / Solid Rock

30 June 1988, rehearsals for Wintershall charity show

JULY 1988

1 July 1988, rehearsals for Wintershall charity show

WINTERSHALL 1988

2 July 1988, Wintershall Estate, Bramley, Surrey

Charity show in aid of the King Edward VII Hospital with the Band Du Lac.

BAND DU LAC LINEUP:
Eric Clapton: guitar, vocals
Gary Brooker: keyboards, vocals
Phil Collins: drums, vocals
Andy Fairweather Low: guitar, vocals
Howard Jones: keyboards
Mike Rutherford: guitar
Henry Spinetti: drums
Jody Linscott: percussion

Rick Wills: bass
Frank Mead: saxophone
Mel Collins: saxophone
Vicky Brown: backing vocals
Sam Brown: backing vocals
Carol Kenyon: backing vocals

SETLIST: Celebration / Yes Indeed / Behind The Mask / Celebrate Our Love / I Missed Again / Stop / Conquistador / Throwing It All Away / Limelight / All I Need / Gin House / It's In The Way That You Use It / No One Is To Blame / Echoes In The Night / Wide-Eyed And Legless / You Can't Hurry Love / You Know I Love You / A Salty Dog / Inside Out / Hold On I'm Coming / Soothe Me / You Don't Know Like I Know / I Want To Know What Love Is / Whiter Shade Of Pale / The Night Time Is The Right Time / Cocaine / Medley: Turn It On Again / Everybody Needs Somebody To Love / Satisfaction / Midnight Hour / Turn It On Again / I Wish

Phil Collins, Mike Rutherford, and Eric in their best Blues Brothers disguise at Wintershall on 2 July 1988.

25th ANNIVERSAY U.S. / CANADIAN TOUR 1988

AUGUST 1988

21 August 1988–31 August 1988, rehearsals in Dallas for upcoming U.S. / Canada tour

SEPTEMBER 1988

BAND LINEUP:
Eric Clapton: guitar, vocals
Mark Knopfler: guitar, vocals
Alan Clark: keyboards
Nathan East: bass
Steve Ferrone: drums
Jody Linscott: percussion
Katie Kissoon: backing vocals
Tessa Niles: backing vocals

1 September 1988, Starplex Amphitheatre, Dallas, Texas (with Buckwheat Zydeco)

SETLIST: Crossroads / White Room / I Shot The Sheriff / Motherless Children / Lay Down Sally / Wonderful Tonight / After Midnight / Tearing Us Apart / Can't Find My Way Home / Same Old Blues / Behind The Mask / Sunshine Of Your Love / Ramblin' On My Mind / Cocaine / A Remark You Made / Layla / Money For Nothing / Further On Up The Road

2 September 1988, Lakefront Arena, New Orleans, Louisiana (with Buckwheat Zydeco)

SETLIST: Crossroads / White Room / I Shot The Sheriff / Lay Down Sally / Wonderful Tonight / Tearing Us Apart / After Midnight / Can't Find My Way Home / Motherless Children / Same Old Blues / Cocaine / A Remark You Made / Layla / Money For Nothing / Sunshine Of Your Love

4 September 1988, Civic Arena, Pittsburgh, Pennsylvania (with Buckwheat Zydeco)

SETLIST: Crossroads / White Room / I Shot The Sheriff / Motherless Children / Lay Down Sally / Wonderful Tonight / After Midnight / Tearing Us Apart / Can't Find My Way Home / Behind The Mask / Sunshine Of Your Love / Ramblin' On My Mind / Cocaine / A Remark You Made / Layla / Money For Nothing / Further On Up The Road

6 September 1988, Meadowlands Arena, East, Rutherford, New Jersey (with Buckwheat Zydeco)

SETLIST: Crossroads / White Room / I Shot The Sheriff / Lay Down Sally / Wonderful Tonight / Tearing Us Apart

/ After Midnight / Can't Find My Way Home / Behind The Mask / Sunshine Of Your Love / Same Old Blues / Cocaine / A Remark You Made / Layla / Money For Nothing / Further On Up The Road

7 September 1988, Spectrum, Philadelphia, Pennsylvania (with Buckwheat Zydeco)

SETLIST: Crossroads / White Room / I Shot The Sheriff / Lay Down Sally / Wonderful Tonight / Tearing Us Apart / After Midnight / Can't Find My Way Home / Motherless Children / Same Old Blues / Cocaine / A Remark You Made / Layla / Money For Nothing / Sunshine Of Your Love

8 September 1988, Capitol Centre, Largo, Maryland (with Buckwheat Zydeco)

SETLIST: Crossroads / White Room / I Shot The Sheriff / Lay Down Sally / Wonderful Tonight / Tearing Us Apart / Can't Find My Way Home / Badge / Same Old Blues / Cocaine / A Remark You Made / Layla / Money For Nothing / Sunshine Of Your Love

10 September 1988, Civic Center, Hartford, Connecticut (with Buckwheat Zydeco)

SETLIST: Crossroads / White Room / I Shot The Sheriff / Lay Down Sally / Wonderful Tonight / Tearing Us Apart / After Midnight / Can't Find My Way Home / Motherless Children / Same Old Blues / Cocaine / A Remark You Made / Layla / Money For Nothing / Sunshine Of Your Love

11 September 1988, Nassau Veterans Memorial Coliseum, Uniondale, New York (with Buckwheat Zydeco)

SETLIST: Crossroads / White Room / I Shot The Sheriff / Lay Down Sally / Wonderful Tonight / Tearing Us Apart / After Midnight / Can't Find My Way Home / Motherless Children / Same Old Blues / Cocaine / A Remark You Made / Layla / Money For Nothing / Sunshine Of Your Love

13 September 1988, Great Woods Center for the Performing Arts, Mansfield, Massachusetts (with Buckwheat Zydeco)

SETLIST: Crossroads / White Room / I Shot The Sheriff / Lay Down Sally / Wonderful Tonight / Tearing Us Apart / After Midnight / Can't Find My Way Home / Badge / Same Old Blues / Cocaine / A Remark You Made / Layla / Money For Nothing / Sunshine Of Your Love

14 September 1988, Great Woods Center for the Performing Arts, Mansfield, Massachusetts (with Buckwheat Zydeco)

SETLIST: Crossroads / White Room / I Shot The Sheriff / Lay Down Sally / Wonderful Tonight / Tearing Us Apart / After Midnight / Can't Find My Way Home / Badge / Same Old Blues / Cocaine / A Remark You Made / Layla / Money For Nothing / Sunshine Of Your Love

16 September 1988, Palace of Auburn Hills, Auburn Hills, Michigan (with Buckwheat Zydeco)

SETLIST: Crossroads / White Room / I Shot The Sheriff / Lay Down Sally / Wonderful Tonight / Tearing Us Apart / After Midnight / Can't Find My Way Home / Badge / Same Old Blues / Cocaine / A Remark You Made / Layla / Money For Nothing / Sunshine Of Your Love

17 September 1988, Alpine Valley, Milwaukee, Wisconsin (with Buckwheat Zydeco)

SETLIST: Crossroads / White Room / I Shot The Sheriff / Lay Down Sally / Wonderful Tonight / Tearing Us Apart / After Midnight / Same Old Blues / Badge / Let It Rain / Cocaine / A Remark You Made / Layla / Money For Nothing / Sunshine Of Your Love

19 September 1988, Fiddler's Green, Denver, Colorado (with Buckwheat Zydeco)

SETLIST: Crossroads / White Room / I Shot The Sheriff / Lay Down Sally / Wonderful Tonight / Tearing Us Apart / After Midnight / Can't Find My Way Home / Badge / Same Old Blues / Cocaine / A Remark You Made / Layla / Money For Nothing / Sunshine Of Your Love

21 September 1988, Shoreline Amphitheater, San Francisco, California (with Buckwheat Zydeco)

SETLIST: Crossroads / White Room / I Shot The Sheriff / Lay Down Sally / Wonderful Tonight / Tearing Us Apart / After Midnight / Can't Find My Way Home / Badge /

Same Old Blues / Cocaine / A Remark You Made / Layla / Money For Nothing / Sunshine Of Your Love

22 September 1988, Arco Arena, Sacramento, California (with Buckwheat Zydeco)

SETLIST: Crossroads / White Room / I Shot The Sheriff / Lay Down Sally / Wonderful Tonight / Tearing Us Apart / After Midnight / Can't Find My Way Home / Badge / Same Old Blues / Cocaine / A Remark You Made / Layla / Money For Nothing / Sunshine Of Your Love

23 September 1988, Irvine Meadows Amphitheatre, Lugana Hills, California (with Buckwheat Zydeco)

SETLIST: Crossroads / White Room / I Shot The Sheriff / Lay Down Sally / Wonderful Tonight / Tearing Us Apart / After Midnight / Can't Find My Way Home / Badge / Same Old Blues / Cocaine / A Remark You Made / Layla / Money For Nothing / Sunshine Of Your Love

LITTLE FEAT JAM 1988

24 September 1988, Pantages Theatre, Los Angeles, California

Eric joins Little Feat during their encore of "Apolitical Blues." Bonnie Raitt had joined the band for several numbers in their main set but did not return for the encores.

ELTON JOHN JAM 1988

25 September 1988, Hollywood Bowl, Los Angeles, California

Eric joins Elton John and his band for "Saturday Night's Alright For Fighting."

26 September 1988, Memorial Coliseum, Portland, Oregon (with Buckwheat Zydeco)

SETLIST: Crossroads / White Room / I Shot The Sheriff / Lay Down Sally / Wonderful Tonight / Tearing Us Apart / After Midnight / Can't Find My Way Home / Badge / Same Old Blues / Cocaine / A Remark You Made / Layla / Money For Nothing / Sunshine Of Your Love

27 September 1988, Tacoma Dome, Tacoma, Washington (with Buckwheat Zydeco)

SETLIST: Crossroads / White Room / I Shot The Sheriff / Lay Down Sally / Wonderful Tonight / Tearing Us Apart / After Midnight / Can't Find My Way Home / Badge / Same Old Blues / Cocaine / A Remark You Made / Layla / Money For Nothing / Sunshine Of Your Love

28 September 1988, PNE Coliseum, Vancouver, British Columbia, Canada (with Buckwheat Zydeco)

SETLIST: Crossroads / White Room / I Shot The Sheriff / Lay Down Sally / Wonderful Tonight / Tearing Us Apart / After Midnight / Can't Find My Way Home / Badge / Same Old Blues / Cocaine / A Remark You Made / Layla / Money For Nothing / Sunshine Of Your Love

30 September 1988, Canadian Airlines Saddledome, Calgary, Alberta, Canada (with Buckwheat Zydeco)

SETLIST: Crossroads / White Room / I Shot The Sheriff / Lay Down Sally / Wonderful Tonight / Tearing Us Apart / After Midnight / Can't Find My Way Home / Badge / Same Old Blues / Cocaine / A Remark You Made / Layla / Money For Nothing / Sunshine Of Your Love

OCTOBER 1988

1 October 1988, Saskatchewan Place, Saskatoon, Saskatchewan, Canada (with Buckwheat Zydeco)

SETLIST: Crossroads / White Room / I Shot The Sheriff / Lay Down Sally / Wonderful Tonight / Tearing Us Apart / After Midnight / Can't Find My Way Home / Badge / Same Old Blues / Cocaine / A Remark You Made / Layla / Money For Nothing / Sunshine Of Your Love

3 October 1988, Winnipeg Arena, Winnipeg, Manitoba, Canada (with Buckwheat Zydeco)

SETLIST: Crossroads / White Room / I Shot The Sheriff / Lay Down Sally / Wonderful Tonight / Tearing Us Apart / After Midnight / Can't Find My Way Home / Badge / Same Old Blues / Cocaine / A Remark You Made / Layla / Money For Nothing / Sunshine Of Your Love

4 October 1988, MET Sports Center, Minneapolis, Minnesota (with Buckwheat Zydeco)

SETLIST: Crossroads / White Room / I Shot The Sheriff / Lay Down Sally / Wonderful Tonight / Tearing Us Apart / After Midnight / Can't Find My Way Home / Badge / Same Old Blues / Cocaine / A Remark You Made / Layla / Money For Nothing / Sunshine Of Your Love

6 October 1988, Forum, Montreal, Quebec, Canada (with Buckwheat Zydeco)

SETLIST: Crossroads / White Room / I Shot The Sheriff / Lay Down Sally / Wonderful Tonight / Tearing Us Apart / After Midnight / Can't Find My Way Home / Badge / Same Old Blues / Cocaine / A Remark You Made / Layla / Money For Nothing / Sunshine Of Your Love

7 October 1988, Maple Leaf Gardens, Toronto, Ontario, Canada (with Buckwheat Zydeco)

SETLIST: Crossroads / White Room / I Shot The Sheriff / Lay Down Sally / After Midnight / Wonderful Tonight / Tearing Us Apart / Can't Find My Way Home / Badge / Same Old Blues / Cocaine / A Remark You Made / Layla / Money For Nothing / Sunshine Of Your Love

8 October 1988, Copps Coliseum, Hamilton, Ontario, Canada (with Buckwheat Zydeco)

SETLIST: Why Does Love Got To Be So Sad

Eric joins opening act Buckwheat Zydeco for the Derek and the Dominos classic.

SETLIST: Crossroads / White Room / I Shot The Sheriff / Lay Down Sally / Wonderful Tonight / Tearing Us Apart / After Midnight / Can't Find My Way Home / Badge / Same Old Blues / Cocaine / A Remark You Made / Layla / Money For Nothing / Sunshine Of Your Love

JACK BRUCE JAM 1988

11 October 1988, Bottom Line, New York City (Eric joins Jack Bruce and his band for a jam)

BAND LINEUP:
Jack Bruce: bass, vocals
Anton Fier: drums
Pat Thrall: guitar

David Bravo: keyboards
Eric Clapton: guitar

SETLIST: Spoonful / Sunshine Of Your Love

25th ANNIVERSARY JAPAN TOUR 1988

BAND LINEUP:
Eric Clapton: guitar, vocals
Mark Knopfler: guitar, vocals
Elton John: piano, keyboards[1]
Alan Clark: keyboards
Nathan East: bass
Steve Ferrone: drums
Ray Cooper: percussion
Katie Kissoon: backing vocals
Tessa Niles: backing vocals

26 October 1988–29 October 1988, rehearsals at Ramza's Gym, Tokyo

31 October 1988, Rainbow Hall, Nagoya, Japan

SETLIST: Crossroads / White Room / I Shot The Sheriff / Lay Down Sally / Wonderful Tonight / Tearing Us Apart / Can't Find My Way Home / After Midnight / Money For Nothing / Candle In the Wind[1] / I Guess That's Why They Call It The Blues[1] / I Don't Wanna Go On With You Like That[1] / I'm Still Standing[1] / Daniel[1] / Cocaine[1] / Layla[1] / Solid Rock[1] / Saturday Night's Alright For Fighting[1] / Sunshine Of Your Love[1]

NOVEMBER 1988

2 November 1988, Tokyo Dome, Tokyo, Japan

SETLIST: Crossroads / White Room / I Shot The Sheriff / Lay Down Sally / Wonderful Tonight / Tearing Us Apart / Can't Find My Way Home / After Midnight / Money For Nothing / Candle In the Wind / I Guess That's Why They Call It The Blues / I Don't Wanna Go On With You Like That / I'm Still Standing / Daniel / Cocaine / Layla / Solid Rock / Saturday Night's Alright For Fighting / Sunshine Of Your Love

Edited highlights from this show were later broadcast on Japanese televison and radio.

4 November 1988, Budokan, Tokyo, Japan

SETLIST: Crossroads / White Room / I Shot The Sheriff / Lay Down Sally / Wonderful Tonight / Tearing Us Apart / Can't Find My Way Home / After Midnight / Money For Nothing[1,2] / Candle In the Wind / I Guess That's Why They Call It The Blues / I Don't Wanna Go On With You Like That / I'm Still Standing / Daniel / Cocaine / Layla / Solid Rock / Saturday Night's Alright For Fighting / Sunshine Of Your Love

[2]with Sting on vocals

5 November 1988, Osaka Stadium, Osaka, Japan

SETLIST: Crossroads / White Room / I Shot The Sheriff / Lay Down Sally / Wonderful Tonight / Tearing Us Apart / Can't Find My Way Home / After Midnight / Money For Nothing / Candle In the Wind[1] / I Guess That's Why They Call It The Blues[1] / I Don't Wanna Go On With You Like That[1] / I'm Still Standing[1] / Daniel[1] / Cocaine[1] / Layla[1] / Solid Rock[1] / Saturday Night's Alright For Fighting[1] / Sunshine Of Your Love[1]

CELIA HAMMOND TRUST CONCERT WITH JEFF BECK 1988

28 November 1988, Hard Rock Cafe, 150 Old Park Lane, London

Event for Celia Hammond's animal charities at London's Hard Rock Café on 28 November 1988. L to R: Jeff Beck, Mitch Mitchell, Eric Clapton, Noel Redding.

Event for Celia Hammond's animal charities at London's Hard Rock Café on 28 November 1988. Jeff Beck and Eric Clapton are in the crowd.

Eric and Jeff Beck along with Mitch Mitchell on drums and Noel Redding on bass play a charity gig for the Celia Hammond Trust. Celia was Jeff's girlfriend and Jeff was, and is, very much into supporting animal rescue charities.

DECEMBER 1988

23 December 1988, Village Hall, Dunsfold, Surrey (Eric joins Gary Brooker and No Stiletto Shoes for a local charity concert)

RECORDING SESSIONS 1988

ERIC CLAPTON GUEST SESSION

TOWN HOUSE STUDIOS 150 Goldhawk Road, London Guitar overdub for Buckwheat Zydeco

MARCH 1988

Eric overdubs a guitar solo on a version of Derek and the Dominos' "Why Does Love Got To Be So Sad."

WHY DOES LOVE GOT TO BE SO SAD (Eric Clapton/ Bobby Whitlock)
Taking It Home CD Island 842603 released 1988

Buckwheat Zydeco: vocals, accordion, keyboards
Eric Clapton: lead guitar

Lee Allen Zeno : bass
Melvin Veazie: guitar
Robert James Ahearn: guitar
Herman "Rat" Brown: drums
Patrick Landry: trumpet
Anthony Butler: alto saxophone
Lisa Mednick: backing vocals
Allison Young: backing vocals

Producer: Rob Fraboni
Engineer: Rob Fraboni

"He wasn't there when I did it. This session came about through a mutual friend, Rob Fraboni, who produced 'No Reason To Cry.' He is just a dear old friend of mine and when I was in New York late 1987 he introduced me, and in fact I went to see Buckwheat play. I got up and jammed with him and one thing led to another. Buckwheat was offered some material. He chose 'Why Does Love Got To Be So Sad,' the Dominos' song. When Rob came to England earlier this year, he brought over the tape with him. I played on the thing, two takes. And I played it just like I did on the Dominos' album."

—ERIC CLAPTON

"We had originally met Eric Clapton outside of London at Island Records' 25th anniversary party at Pinewood Studios. Buck sat in on the Hammond B3 during an all-star jam featuring Clapton, Ringo Starr, Andy Summers of the Police, and others. Buck arrived via the rear of the stage, after the jam had already begun, without Clapton noticing him. As soon as Eric peeled off one of his gorgeous blues–rock solos, Buck matched it on the organ and bumped it a notch. Eric responded and upped the ante. Buck topped him. Clapton then came back even stronger. A furious 'cutting contest' ensued and the crowd of about 6,000 hipsters went wild as this ordinary all-star jam took off. Then, in the middle of a solo, Eric quit and turned around to see who had been so deftly challenging him; he stuck out his hand and with a broad smile said, 'I'm Eric Clapton, who are you?' Eric became a Buckwheat Zydeco fan. That summer he came to New York especially for our record release party for *On A Night Like This,* at S.O.B's, and played a fabulous blues set with the band. Hoping to capture the excitement of Buck and Clapton's interplay, I suggested that we do the plaintive, wailing, Derek and the Dominos' tune 'Why Does Love Got To Be So Sad?' We cut our tracks at Southlake Studio, leaving room for Eric to overdub his guitar. Clapton's

friend and sometime collaborator, Rob Fraboni, took the master tape to England where Eric added his guitar work. Apparently Clapton was as pleased with the result as we were because he offered us the opening slot on his summer and fall 1988 North American tour, and then, the following January, twelve nights with him at the Royal Albert Hall in London."

—TED FOX
(Buckwheat Zydeco's manager)

TOWN HOUSE STUDIOS
150 Goldhawk Road, London
Sessions for *Buster* soundtrack

25 MARCH 1988

THE ROBBERY (Anne Dudley) *Buster* soundtrack CD US Atlantic 81905-2 / UK Virgin CDV2544 released September 1988

Anne Dudley: synthesizers
Eric Clapton: guitar

Producer: Anne Dudley

"I just played guitar. It was part of the score. The robbery scene, which is quite early on in the film, was where Anne Dudley, who was the lady who wrote the music, wanted some guitar playing. I was just playing a part that she had already written down for a guitar. It is not very long but it is quite effective."

—ERIC CLAPTON

TOWN HOUSE STUDIOS
150 Goldhawk Road, London
and
OLYMPIC STUDIOS
117 Church Road, London
Sessions for
Homeboy soundtrack

23 APRIL 1988–29 APRIL 1988

TRAVELLING EAST *Homeboy* soundtrack CD UK Virgin CDV 2574 / US 7 91241-2 released 1989

JOHNNY *Homeboy* soundtrack CD UK Virgin CDV 2574 / US 7 91241-2 released 1989

BRIDGE *Homeboy* soundtrack CD UK Virgin CDV 2574 / US 7 91241-2 released 1989

DIXIE *Homeboy* soundtrack CD UK Virgin CDV 2574 / US 7 91241-2 released 1989

RUBY'S LOFT *Homeboy* soundtrack CD UK Virgin CDV 2574 / US 7 91241-2 released 1989

COUNTRY BIKIN' *Homeboy* soundtrack CD UK Virgin CDV 2574 / US 7 91241-2 released 1989

RUBY *Homeboy* soundtrack CD UK Virgin CDV 2574 / US 7 91241-2 released 1989

PARTY *Homeboy* soundtrack CD UK Virgin CDV 2574 / US 7 91241-2 released 1989

TRAINING *Homeboy* soundtrack CD UK Virgin CDV 2574 / US 7 91241-2 released 1989

FINAL FIGHT *Homeboy* soundtrack CD UK Virgin CDV 2574 / US 7 91241-2 released 1989

CHASE *Homeboy* soundtrack CD UK Virgin CDV 2574 / US 7 91241-2 released 1989

DIXIE 2 *Homeboy* soundtrack CD UK Virgin CDV 2574 / US 7 91241-2 released 1989

HOMEBOY *Homeboy* soundtrack CD UK Virgin CDV 2574 / US 7 91241-2 released 1989

Eric Clapton: guitar, Dobro
Michael Kamen: keyboards
Steve Ferrone: drums
Nathan East: bass

Producer: Frazer Kennedy

> **"**I worked in collaboration with Michael Kamen initially, but then Michael had to move on to another project and I took over on my own. I played Dobro on one track—I don't play it very often. It's funny, because I'd forgotten how unique that sound is. And when you play it for other people they go crazy. You really have to work at it for three to four weeks without touching anything else to get back to your good state of playing.**"**
>
> **—ERIC CLAPTON**

OLYMPIC STUDIOS
117 Church Road, London
Sessions for *Peace In Our Time* soundtrack

7 MAY–8 MAY 1988, 14 MAY 1988–15 MAY 1988, 21 MAY 1988

Various instrumental numbers.

> **"**I just did some film music for a TV documentary about the beginning of the Second World War, because it's the fiftieth year of the Munich Agreement with Hitler and Chamberlain, and a Czechoslavakian company asked me to do the music and I was a bit lost when I first thought about it. . . . And when I saw the footage, which is archive black and white material, I just wrote a very simple kind of blues progression and got some string players in and set it to a kind of philharmonic setting and it still works, which is an example of the fact that I always think from a blues point of view and try to frame it in different ways to make it palatable.**"**
>
> **—ERIC CLAPTON**

ERIC CLAPTON GUEST SESSION
SPACEWARD STUDIOS
Old School, Stretham, Cambridge
Guitar overdub for Jonathan (Yoni) Nameri

MAY 1988

Another one of Eric's more obscure sessions that has generated a lot of misinformation all over the Internet. After having spoken to both Dave Stewarts, I can confirm that the one from the Eurythmics had nothing to do with this recording. It is the other Dave Stewart (as in Dave Stewart and Barbara Gaskin) who contributed keyboards. The other players were Nico Ramsden on guitar, Nigel Olsson on drums, Deon Estus on bass. The session was booked under the name of Jonathan Nameri. All lyrics were sung in Hebrew and were recorded both in England and Israel. I spoke with Jonathan who lives in Israel and he confirmed the session details to me.

The album was only released in Israel by NMC records in 1989.

THE WAY OF THE EAGLE (Yoni Nameri) *Silence From Another World* album NMC CBS463260-1 released 1989
Yoni Nameri: vocals
Eric Clapton: guitar solo

Dave Stewart: keyboards
Deon Estus: bass
Nigel Olsson: drums
Nico Ramsden: guitar

Producer: Nick Bradford
Engineer: Nick Bradford

> **"**It happened by coincidence really. It was done in the studio I was recording at for the album. Eric only played the solo, that's all. It was as a favor for me. Nigel Olsson, Elton John's drummer, is on it as well as Nico Ramsden and Dave Stewart.**"**
>
> —**JONATHAN (YONI) NAMERI**

ERIC CLAPTON GUEST SESSION

TOWN HOUSE STUDIOS 150 Goldhawk Road, London Session for Davina McCall demos

15 JUNE 1988—25 JUNE 1988

At the risk of sounding harsh, Davina was a far better presenter than singer. Not surprisingly, these tracks were never released.

THE VERY LAST TIME unreleased

I'M TOO GOOD FOR YOU unreleased

STICKY SITUATION unreleased

Davina McCall: vocals
Eric Clapton: guitar
Not known: bass
Not known: drums
Not known: keyboards

Producers: Eric Clapton / Rob Fraboni

ERIC CLAPTON GUEST SESSION

TONE DEAF STUDIO Nettlebed, Oxfordshire Session for Jim Capaldi

JULY 1988

YOU ARE THE ONE (Jim Capaldi / C. Parren) *Some Come Running* CD Island Records 259 439 released 1988

Jim Capaldi: vocals, drums
Eric Clapton: guitar
Peter Vale: bass
Mike Waters: guitar

OH LORD WHY LORD (P. Trim / M. Bouchety) *Some Come Running* CD Island Records 259 439 released 1988

Jim Capaldi: vocals, drums
Eric Clapton: guitar
George Harrison: guitar
Rosko Gee: bass
Chris Parren: keyboards

Producer: Jim Capaldi
Engineer: Andy MacPherson

> **"**I played on two tracks. In fact I played on more, but I think two tracks are going to be released. I drove over to a studio he was using in Marlow and I just overdubbed it in no time at all. It's a very good sounding record.**"**
>
> —**ERIC CLAPTON**

> **"**Tone Deaf was a whacky place where sheep occasionally wandered into the control room. Alan Rogan and Lee Dixon were both there too.
>
> I think he may be mistaken about further tracks but of course he may not be. I have learned not to trust exclusively to my own recollection of events. There was certainly nothing further which was released but we may have tried something out on the day in the time we had left. I recall they arrived after lunch and had to move on promptly by late afternoon.**"**
>
> —**JOHN TAYLOR**
> (Jim Cipaldi's manager)

ERIC CLAPTON GUEST SESSION

THE SMOKEHOUSE STUDIOS 120 Pennington Street, London Session for Gail Ann Dorsey

JULY 1988

WASTED COUNTRY (Gail Ann Dorsey) *The Corporate World* CD WEA Records 244046-2 released 1988 / *Wasted Country (Wasted Mix)* 12" single in picture sleeve WEA Records YZ194T released 1988 / *Wasted Country (Wasted Mix)* 3" CD single WEA Records 2477032 released 1988

Gail Ann Dorsey: bass, guitar, backing vocals
Eric Clapton: guitar, guitar solo
Bub Roberts: guitar
Steve Ferrone: Akai Linn drums
Ted Hayton: MPC-60 drum program
Marcel East: keyboards
Nathan East: keyboards, backing vocals
Jerry Hey: horn arrangement, trumpet
Garry Grant: trumpet
Bill Reichenbach: trombone
Kim Hutchcroft: baritone and tenor saxophones

Producer: Nathan East
Engineer: Ted Hayton

"It was a great track and Eric's solo is instantly recognizable as him just by the first couple of notes. I played the riffing guitar throughout and was pleased that on the instrumental ending and fade Eric and I had some good interplay happening (more evident on the 12-inch mix).

Gail had the same amp Eric used (new Fender blah blah) and I caught her writing down his amp settings!!! Needless to say it didn't sound the same.

Doing that session was a great buzz for me because it was Eric's early records with Cream that really inspired me to play the guitar. I never thought that many years later we would play on the same record."

—BUB ROBERTS
(guitarist)

ERIC CLAPTON GUEST SESSION
SKYLINE STUDIOS
36 West 37th Sreet,
New York City
Session for Carole King

DECEMBER 1988

CITY STREETS CD Capitol CDP 7-90885 released 1989
Carole King: vocals, synthesizers

Eric Clapton: guitar
Rudy Guess: guitar
Wayne Pedzwater: bass
Steve Ferrone: drums
Jimmy Bralower: tambourine
Michael Brecker: tenor saxophone

AIN'T THAT THE WAY CITY STREETS CD Capitol CDP 7-90885 released 1989

Carole King: vocals, piano, organ
Eric Clapton: guitar
Wayne Pedzwater: bass
Steve Ferrone: drums
Sammy Figueroa: percussion

Producers: Carole King / Rudy Guess
Engineer: James Farber

7

1989

Most of November and December 1988 and January 1989 were spent preparing material for a new album that would be recorded in New York during March and April 1989. In January Eric went to see Womack and Womack play at Dingwalls in Camden. He was invited up for a jam which he enjoyed. Womack and Womack presented him with a song for his next album, "Lead Me On." But first, he had to play his now regular run of shows at the Royal Albert Hall. These shows were now starting to attract fans from all over the world who wanted to make a pilgrimage to one of Eric's legendary residencies at this historic venue. A further three nights had been added this year making a total of twelve nights. They could have doubled the dates and they still would not have met the high demand for tickets.

This year the Albert Hall shows were split into two groups. The first six shows were comprised of a four-piece lineup with Eric on guitar and vocals, Nathan East on bass and backing vocals, Greg Phillinganes on keyboards and backing vocals, and Phil Collins on drums and vocals. The setlist had at last changed, if only slightly, which was a welcome surprise to the Albert Hall veterans. Included were a rousing version of the Philip Bailey hit "Easy Lover," and even better, the emotive Derek and the Dominos classic "Bell Bottom Blues."

For the following six shows Eric augmented the band once again with Mark Knopfler on guitar, Alan Clark on keyboards, Ray Cooper on percussion, Tessa Niles and Katie Kissoon on backing vocals, and Steve Ferrone on drums replacing Phil Collins. The set changed again very slightly with the inclusion of "Lay Down Sally" and the *August* outtake "Wanna Make Love To You." Mark Knopfler was now practically a permanent fixture, but was quickly wearing out his welcome in the eyes of certain fans. Shame, as the two of them worked well together and their guitar styles complemented each other well.

As soon as the Albert Hall run ended, Eric and Michael Kamen entered the studio to record the theme tune for the next Bond movie, *License To Kill*. They spent the whole of 7 February working on the song before settling on a master they were happy with. The original James Bond theme guitar player, Vic Flick, was invited to the session as he would be helping provide guitar work for the orchestrations in the film soundtrack. The track is quite spectacular with a killer solo by Eric and Vic providing Bondish licks in the background. There was talk of getting songwriter B. A. Robertson to write a set of lyrics, but ultimately it was felt that Kamen had not enough experience to write a Bond theme song which was a great dissapointment to him. He did do a grand job on the film's orchestrations though. Furthermore, disputes over money and Eric having to appear in a promo video shoot were said to be other factors in the number not being used.

Eric happily walked away and went off to New York to record what would be a hugely successful album for him, *Journeyman*.

JANUARY 1989

10 January 1989, Dingwalls Club, Camden, London (Eric joins Womack And Womack for a few numbers)

UK TOUR 1989

FOUR-PIECE BAND LINEUP:
Eric Clapton: guitar, vocals
Nathan East: bass, vocals
Greg Phillinganes: keyboards, vocals
Phil Collins: drums, vocals

16 January 1989, City Hall, Sheffield (with Buckwheat Zydeco)

SETLIST: Crossroads / White Room / I Shot The Sheriff / After Midnight / Wonderful Tonight / Wanna Make Love To You / Bell Bottom Blues / Can't Find My Way Home / Forever Man / Same Old Blues / Knockin' On Heaven's Door / Tearing Us Apart / Cocaine / Layla / Easy Lover / Behind The Mask / Sunshine Of Your Love

17 January 1989, City Hall, Newcastle upon Tyne (with Buckwheat Zydeco)

SETLIST: Crossroads / White Room / I Shot The Sheriff / Bell Bottom Blues / Wanna Make Love To You / Wonderful Tonight / After Midnight / Can't Find My Way Home / Forever Man / Knockin' On Heaven's Door / Same Old Blues / Tearing Us Apart / Cocaine / Layla / Easy Lover / Behind The Mask / Sunshine Of Your Love

18 January 1989, Playhouse, Edinburgh, Scotland (with Buckwheat Zydeco)

SETLIST: Crossroads / White Room / I Shot The Sheriff / Bell Bottom Blues / Wonderful Tonight / After Midnight / Can't Find My Way Home / Forever Man / Same Old Blues / Knockin' On Heaven's Door / Easy Lover / Tearing Us Apart / Cocaine / Layla / Behind The Mask / Sunshine Of Your Love

20 January 1989, Royal Albert Hall, London (with Buckwheat Zydeco)

SETLIST: Crossroads / White Room / I Shot The Sheriff / Bell Bottom Blues / After Midnight / Wonderful Tonight / Can't Find My Way Home / Forever Man / Same Old Blues / Knockin' On Heaven's Door / Easy Lover / Tearing Us Apart / Cocaine / A Remark You Made / Layla / Behind The Mask / Sunshine Of Your Love

21 January 1989, Royal Albert Hall, London (with Buckwheat Zydeco)

SETLIST: Crossroads / White Room / I Shot The Sheriff / Bell Bottom Blues / After Midnight / Wonderful Tonight / Can't Find My Way Home / Forever Man / Same Old Blues / Knockin' On Heaven's Door / Easy Lover / Tearing Us Apart / Cocaine / A Remark You Made / Layla / Behind The Mask / Sunshine Of Your Love

22 January 1989, Royal Albert Hall, London (with Buckwheat Zydeco)

Eric Clapton at the Royal Albert Hall, January 1989.

SETLIST: Crossroads / White Room / I Shot The Sheriff / Bell Bottom Blues / After Midnight / Wonderful Tonight / Can't Find My Way Home / Forever Man / Same Old Blues / Knockin' On Heaven's Door / Easy Lover / Tearing Us Apart / Cocaine / A Remark You Made / Layla / Behind The Mask / Sunshine Of Your Love

24 January 1989, Royal Albert Hall, London (with Buckwheat Zydeco)

SETLIST: Crossroads / White Room / I Shot The Sheriff / Bell Bottom Blues / After Midnight / Wonderful Tonight

/ Can't Find My Way Home / Forever Man / Same Old Blues / Knockin' On Heaven's Door / Easy Lover / Tearing Us Apart / Cocaine / A Remark You Made / Layla / Behind The Mask / Sunshine Of Your Love

25 January 1989, Royal Albert Hall, London (with Buckwheat Zydeco)

SETLIST: Crossroads / White Room / I Shot The Sheriff / Bell Bottom Blues / After Midnight / Wonderful Tonight / Can't Find My Way Home / Forever Man / Same Old Blues / Knockin' On Heaven's Door / Easy Lover / Tearing Us Apart / Cocaine / A Remark You Made / Layla / Behind The Mask / Sunshine Of Your Love

26 January 1989, Royal Albert Hall, London (with Buckwheat Zydeco)

SETLIST: Crossroads / White Room / I Shot The Sheriff / Bell Bottom Blues / After Midnight / Wonderful Tonight / Can't Find My Way Home / Forever Man / Same Old Blues / Knockin' On Heaven's Door / Easy Lover / Tearing Us Apart / Cocaine / A Remark You Made / Layla / Behind The Mask / Sunshine Of Your Love

NINE-PIECE BAND LINEUP:
Eric Clapton: guitar, vocals
Mark Knopfler: guitar, vocals
Nathan East: bass
Steve Ferrone: drums
Alan Clark: keyboards
Greg Phillinganes: keyboards
Ray Cooper: percussion
Tessa Niles: backing vocals
Katie Kissoon: backing vocals

28 January 1989, Royal Albert Hall, London (with Buckwheat Zydeco)

SETLIST: Crossroads / White Room / I Shot The Sheriff / Bell Bottom Blues / Lay Down Sally / Wonderful Tonight / Wanna Make Love To You / After Midnight[1] / Can't Find My Way Home[1] / Forever Man / Same Old Blues / Tearing Us Apart / Cocaine / A Remark You Made / Layla / Behind The Mask / Sunshine Of Your Love

[1] with Carole King vocals

Mark Knopfler at the Royal Albert Hall, January 1989.

29 January 1989, Royal Albert Hall, London (with Buckwheat Zydeco)

SETLIST: Crossroads / White Room / I Shot The Sheriff / Bell Bottom Blues / Lay Down Sally / Wonderful Tonight / Wanna Make Love To You / After Midnight / Can't Find My Way Home / Forever Man / Same Old Blues / Tearing Us Apart / Cocaine / A Remark You Made / Layla / Behind The Mask / Sunshine Of Your Love

30 January 1989, Royal Albert Hall, London (with Buckwheat Zydeco)

SETLIST: Crossroads / White Room / I Shot The Sheriff / Bell Bottom Blues / Lay Down Sally / Wonderful Tonight / Wanna Make Love To You / After Midnight / Can't Find My Way Home / Forever Man / Same Old Blues / Tearing Us Apart / Cocaine / A Remark You Made / Layla / Behind The Mask / Sunshine Of Your Love

FEBRUARY 1989

1 February 1989, Royal Albert Hall, London (with Buckwheat Zydeco)

SETLIST: Crossroads / White Room / I Shot The Sheriff / Bell Bottom Blues / Lay Down Sally / Wonderful Tonight

/ Wanna Make Love To You / After Midnight / Can't Find My Way Home / Forever Man / Same Old Blues / Tearing Us Apart / Cocaine / A Remark You Made / Layla / Solid Rock / Behind The Mask / Sunshine Of Your Love

2 February 1989, Royal Albert Hall, London (with Buckwheat Zydeco)

SETLIST: Crossroads / White Room / I Shot The Sheriff / Bell Bottom Blues / Lay Down Sally / Wonderful Tonight / Wanna Make Love To You / After Midnight / Can't Find My Way Home / Forever Man / Same Old Blues / Tearing Us Apart / Cocaine / A Remark You Made / Layla / Solid Rock / Behind The Mask / Sunshine Of Your Love

3 February 1989, Royal Albert Hall, London (with Buckwheat Zydeco)

SETLIST: Crossroads / White Room / I Shot The Sheriff / Bell Bottom Blues / Lay Down Sally / Wonderful Tonight / Wanna Make Love To You / After Midnight / Can't Find My Way Home / Forever Man / Same Old Blues / Tearing Us Apart / Cocaine / A Remark You Made / Layla / Solid Rock / Behind The Mask / Sunshine Of Your Love

MAY 1989

JAM WITH CARL PERKINS 1989

9 May 1989, Bottom Line, New York City (Eric jams with Carl Perkins)

SETLIST: Mean Woman Blues / Matchbox / Rock 'N' Roll Medley / Going Down The Road Feelin' Bad

FIRST INTERNATIONAL ROCK AWARDS CEREMONY 1989

31 May 1989, 69th Regiment Armory, New York City

Hollywood has the Oscars, Broadway has its Tony, so why shouldn't rock and roll have its very own statuette? The International Rock Awards changed all that in 1989 by holding an extravaganza at Manhattan's 69th Regiment Armory, where musicians could own their own throphy, a twelve-inch bronze miniature of Elvis. Hence the name, Elvis Awards.

The event was televised live. The stage set was a bizarre collection of styrofoam columns, and the following guests all turned up: Robert Palmer, Lou Reed, David Bowie with Tin Machine, Eric Clapton, Alice Cooper, and Keith Richards. Quite a few people did not show up in person for their awards, such as Bono, Sting, Phil Collins, and Madonna.

Keith Richards presented the Best Guitarist Award to Eric, and Keith was presented the Living Legend Award. The evening of course had to finish with the obligatory jam. Tonight it was "I Hear You Knocking."

BAND LINEUP:
Eric Clapton: guitar, vocals
Keith Richards: guitar, vocals
Dave Edmunds: guitar, vocals
Jeff Healey: guitar
Vernon Reid: guitar
Waddy Wachtel: guitar
Bobby Keys: saxophone
Clarence Clemons: saxophone
Ivan Neville: keyboards
Charley Drayton: bass
Steve Jordan: drums
Sarah Dash: vocals
Tina Turner: vocals

I HEAR YOU KNOCKING (Smiley Lewis) broadcast on television

JULY 1989

WINTERSHALL 1989

1 July 1989, Wintershall Estate, Bramley, Surrey, (charity show in aid of the King Edward VII Hospital)

BAND LINEUP:
Gary Brooker: vocals, keyboards
Eric Clapton: guitar, vocals
Andy Fairweather Low: guitar, vocals
Mike Rutherford: guitar

Dave Bronze: bass
Steve Winwood: keyboards, vocals
Mel Collins: saxophone
Frank Mead: saxophone
Phil Collins: drums, vocals
Gary Hammond: percussion
Henry Spinetti: drums
Vicki Brown: backing vocals
Sam Brown: backing vocals
Margo Buchanan: backing vocals
Carol Kenyon: backing vocals

Eric Clapton as part of Band Du Lac at Wintershall on 1 July 1989.

SETLIST: Pick Up The Pieces / Ain't That Peculiar / Can I Get A Witness / Freedom Overspill / Lead Me To The Water / All I Need Is A Miracle / Old Love / Stop In The Name Of Love / You Don't Know Like I Know / Respect / Throwing It All Away / A Bridge Across The Water / Lay Down Sally / Souvenir Of London / Roll With It / Stop / I Am A Pilgrim / Loco In Acapulco / Gin House / The Living Years / Cocaine / A Whiter Shade Of Pale / Twisting The Night Away / You Can't Hurry Love / Night Time Is The Right Time / Gimme Some Lovin'

EUROPEAN / MIDDLE EASTERN / AFRICAN TOUR 1989

BAND LINEUP:
Eric Clapton: guitar, vocals
Phil Palmer: guitar
Nathan East: bass
Steve Ferrone: drums
Alan Clark: keyboards
Ray Cooper: percussion
Katie Kissoon: backing vocals
Tessa Niles: backing vocals

6 July 1989, Statenhal, Den Haag, Netherlands

7 July 1989, Statenhal, Den Haag, Netherlands

SETLIST: Crossroads / White Room / I Shot The Sheriff / Bell Bottom Blues / Lay Down Sally / Wonderful Tonight / Wanna Make Love To You / After Midnight / Can't Find My Way Home / Forever Man / Same Old Blues / Tearing Us Apart / Cocaine / Layla / Badge / Sunshine Of Your Love

9 July 1989, Hallenstadion, Zürich, Switzerland
10 July 1989, Hallenstadion, Zürich, Switzerland
13 July 1989, Sultan's Pool, Jerusalem, Israel

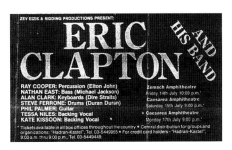

Advert for Israeli shows in July 1989.

SETLIST: Crossroads / White Room / I Shot The Sheriff / Bell Bottom Blues / Lay Down Sally / Wonderful Tonight / Wanna Make Love To You / After Midnight / Can't Find My Way Home / Forever Man / Same Old Blues / Tearing Us Apart / Cocaine / Layla / Badge / Sunshine Of Your Love

14 July 1989, Zemach Amphitheatre, Zemach, Israel

15 July 1989, Caesarea Amphitheatre, Qesari, Israel

17 July 1989, Caesarea Amphitheatre, Qesari, Israel

22 July 1989, Somhlolo National Stadium, Mbabane, Swaziland

25 July 1989, Conference Center, Harare, Zimbabwe

26 July 1989, Conference Center, Harare, Zimbabwe

28 July 1989, Boipuso Hall, Gaborone, Botswana

30 July 1989, Machava National Stadium, Maputo, Mozambique

SEPTEMBER 1989

JAM WITH ZUCCHERO FORNACIARI 1989

28 September 1989, Da Campo Boario, Rome, Italy (guest appearance with Zucchero Fornaciari on "Wonderful World," a song the two had recorded in New York back in March)

OCTOBER 1989

JAM WITH ELTON JOHN 1989

7 October 1989, Madison Square Garden, New York City (Eric joins Elton John for "Rocket Man")

JAM WITH THE ROLLING STONES 1989

10 October 1989, Shea Stadium, New York City (Eric joins the Rolling Stones for "Little Red Rooster." The show is recorded)

JAM WITH THE ROLLING STONES 1989

19 October 1989, Coliseum, Los Angeles, California (Eric joins the Rolling Stones for "Little Red Rooster." The show is recorded)

NIGHT MUSIC WITH DAVID SANBORN 1989

25 October 1989, *Night Music with David Sanborn,* NBC Television Studios, Rockefeller Center, New York City

SETLIST:

Hard Times (Ray Charles)
Eric Clapton: guitar, vocals
Hiram Bullock: guitar
Omar Hajim: drums
Tom Barney: bass
David Sanborn: saxophone
Greg Phillinganes: piano
Phillipe Saisse: keyboards

Don Alias: percussion
Not known: horn section

Old Love (Eric Clapton / Robert Cray)
Eric Clapton: guitar, vocals
Robert Cray: guitar
Hiram Bullock: guitar
Omar Hakim: drums
Tom Barney: bass
Greg Phillinganes: piano
Phillipe Saisse: keyboards
Don Alias: percussion

Before You Accuse Me (Ellas McDaniel)
Eric Clapton: guitar, vocals
Robert Cray: guitar
Hiram Bullock: guitar
Omar Hakim: drums
Tom Barney: bass
David Sanborn: saxophone
Greg Phillinganes: piano
Phillipe Saisse: keyboards
Don Alias: percussion
Not known: horn section

SUE LAWLEY'S *SATURDAY MATTERS* 1989

28 October 1989, *Satuday Matters,* BBC Studios, Shepherds Bush, London (Eric appears on Sue Lawley's television chat show alongside Pete Townshend. As well as being interviewed, Eric and Pete play an acoustic version of "Standing Around Crying")

NOVEMBER 1989

PARENTS FOR SAFE FOOD CONCERT 1989

18 November 1989, Royal Albert Hall, London (the Parents For Safe Food charity show is recorded and filmed but has never been released)

SETLIST:

Edge Of Darkness (Eric Clapton / Michael Kamen)
unreleased

Eric Clapton: guitar
Andy Newmark: drums
Ray Cooper: percussion
Organic Symphony Orchestra
Conductor: Carl Davis

TINA TURNER PARTY AT THE REFORM CLUB 1989

26 November 1989, Reform Club, St. James, London

Eric Joins Tina Turner on stage.

DECEMBER 1989

JAM WITH THE ROLLING STONES 1989

19 December 1989, Convention Center, Atlantic City, New Jersey.

Eric joins the Rolling Stones. The show is recorded and televised as well as being broadcast thoughout the U.S. on radio.

SETLIST:

Little Red Rooster (Willie Dixon) *Flashpoint* CD Rolling Stones Records US CK 47456 / UK 468135 2 released 1991

Mick Jagger: vocals
Keith Richards: guitar
Bill Wyman: bass
Charlie Watts: drums
Ron Wood: guitar
Chuck Leavell: keyboards
Matt Clifford: keyboards
Eric Clapton: guitar

Boogie Chillin (John Lee Hooker) radio and television broadcast only

John Lee Hooker: guitar, vocals
Mick Jagger: vocals
Keith Richards: guitar
Bill Wyman: bass
Charlie Watts: drums
Ron Wood: guitar
Chuck Leavell: keyboards
Matt Clifford; keyboards
Eric Clapton: guitar

Producers: Chris Kimsey / Mick Jagger / Keith Richards
Engineers: Richard Sullivan / Spencer May

GARY BROOKER'S CHRISTMAS SHOW 1989

23 December 1989, Chiddingfold Club, Woodside Road, Chiddingfold, Surrey

BAND LINEUP:
Eric Clapton: guitar
Gary Brooker: vocals, piano
Henry Spinetti: drums
Andy Fairweather Low: guitar, vocals
Dave Bronze: bass
Frank Mead: saxophone

SETLIST: Lucille / In The Midnight Hour / Let The Good Times Roll / La Booga Rooga / Big Black Cadillac / Mary Anne / Too Much Monkey Business / Bright Lights Big City / Hit The Road Jack / Shotgun / Wide Eyed And Legless / Never Make Your Move Too Soon / Ubangi Stomp / Jesus Is On The Mainline / Lead Me To The Water / Let It Rock / That's All Right Mama / Rhythm Bound / Let It Rock / Gin House / Little Queenie

RECORDING SESSIONS 1989
TOWN HOUSE STUDIOS
150 Goldhawk Road, London
Session for *Licence To Kill* soundtrack

7 FEBRUARY 1989

LICENCE TO KILL THEME (Michael Kamen / Eric Clapton) unreleased

Eric Clapton: guitar
Vic Flick: guitar
Ray Cooper: percussion
Steve Ferrone: drums
Michael Kamen: keyboards

Producer: Michael Kamen
Engineer: Stephen McLaughlin

> "Clapton and Kamen had come up with a theme and in the process of recording it they asked me to put in some low guitar 'Bondish' riffs, which I did. The only other name I can remember who played at the session is Ray Cooper, the guy that plays percussion with Elton John. I brought along the original guitar I used on the James Bond theme in the sixties. We worked on it all day and by the end it sounded really good."
>
> —VIC FLICK

ERIC CLAPTON GUEST SESSION

POWER STATION STUDIOS
441 West 53rd Street,
New York City
Session for Zucchero Fornaciari

3 MARCH 1989

WONDERFUL WORLD (Frank Musker / Zucchero Fornaciari) *Oro Incenso & Birra'* CD Polydor 839539 released June 1989 / *Zucchero* CD London Records 511 962-2 released November 1990 / maxi-CD London records LONCD 300 with radio and full-length version released November 1990 / Another version using Eric's original solo was released on *Zu & Co.* Polydor 981 095-2 released May 2004 with a vocal duet between Zucchero and Eric. The percussionist from the original recording, Rosario Jermano, is replaced by Luciano Luisi on programming and keyboards. Worth noting a video clip of the original recording session in 1989 of "Wonderful World" at the Power Station can be found on the extras section on the *Zucchero: Zu & Co. Live at the Royal Albert Hall London* DVD released May 2004.

Zucchero Fornaciari: vocals
Eric Clapton: guitar
Corrado Rustici: guitar, keyboards
Polo Jones: bass
Giorgio Francis: drums
David Sancious: keyboards
Rosario Jermano: percussion

Producer: Corrado Rustici

ERIC CLAPTON GUEST SESSION

THE HIT FACTORY
421 West 54th Street,
New York City
Session for Cyndi Lauper

APRIL 1989

INSECURIOUS (Desmond Child / Cyndi Lauper / Diane Warren) *A Night To Remember* CD Epic 7599-26280-1 released May 1989

Cyndi Lauper: vocals
Eric Clapton: guitar
Steve Ferrone: drums
Jeff Bova: keyboards
Daryl Jones: bass
Carole Steele: percussion

Producers: Cyndi Lauper / Lennie Petzie
Engineer: E. T. Thorngren

> "Cyndi Lauper asked me to play my part exactly like I did on 'White Room.' That angered me. What about the music I'm making now? How did I play that then? I didn't remember how I played on 'White Room' because that was so long ago! And I didn't want to have to listen to the original recordings just to find out how to play that session! But such an experience is good for my ego, because it knocks me right down and I have to be a working musician just to get the job done."
>
> —ERIC CLAPTON

POWER STATION STUDIOS
441 West 53rd Street,
New York City
Session for Elton John / Bernie Taupin tribute

APRIL 1989

THE BORDER SONG (Elton John / Bernie Taupin) *Two Rooms: Celebrating The Songs Of Elton John and Bernie Taupin* CD Mercury 845 750-2 released October 1991

Eric Clapton: guitar, vocals
Greg Phillinganes: keyboards
Jeff Bova: synth horns
Alan Clark: synthesizer
Robby Knodor: synthesizer
Daryl Jones: bass
Steve Ferrone: drums
Carol Steele: tambourine
Michael Brecker: tenor saxophone
George Young: tenor saxophone
Ronnie Cuber: baritone saxophone
Alan Rubin: trumpet
Dave Bargeron: trombone
Reverend Timothy Wright Washington Temple Concert Choir

Producers: Eric Clapton / Truman Stiles

Engineer: Dave O'Donnell

POWER STATION STUDIOS
441 West 53rd Street,
New York City
Session for *Journeyman*

MARCH 1989—APRIL 1989

PRETENDING (Jerry Lynn Williams) *Journeyman* CD Duck 9 26074-2 released November 1989

Eric Clapton: guitar, vocals
Chaka Khan: backing vocals
Nathan East: bass, backing vocals
Carol Steele: congas
Jimmy Bralower: drum programming
Jerry Williams: guitar, harmony vocals, backing vocals
Alan Clark: Hammond B3 organ, synthesizer horns
Greg Phillinganes: piano
Jeff Bova: synthesizer horns, synthesizer organ

NO ALIBIS (Jerry Lynn Williams) *Journeyman* CD Duck 9 26074-2 released November 1989

Eric Clapton: guitar, vocals
Chaka Khan: backing vocals
Lani Groves: backing vocals
Nathan East: bass, backing vocals
Jimmy Bralower: drum programming
Daryl Hall: harmony vocals
Greg Phillinganes: keyboards, backing vocals
Carol Steele: percussion
Richard Tee: piano
Robby Kondor: synthesizer programming

OLD LOVE (Eric Clapton / Robert Cray) *Journeyman* CD Duck 9 26074-2 released November 1989

Eric Clapton: guitar, vocals
Nathan East: bass
Jim Keltner: drums, tambourine
Robert Cray: guitar
Richard Tee: piano
Robby Kondor: synth piano
Alan Clark: synth strings
Gary Burton: vibes

HARD TIMES (Ray Charles) *Journeyman* CD Duck 9 26074-2 released November 1989

Eric Clapton: guitar, vocals
Hank Crawford: alto saxophone
David "Fathead" Newman: tenor saxophone
Jon Faddis: trumpet
Lou Solof: trumpet
Ronnie Cuber: baritone saxophone
Nathan East: bass
Steve Ferrone: drums
Greg Phillinganes: piano
John Tropea: rhythm guitar

HOUND DOG (Jerry Leiber / Mike Stoller) *Journeyman* CD Duck 9 26074-2 released November 1989

Eric Clapton: guitar, vocals
Nathan East: bass
Jim Keltner: drums, percussion
Robert Cray: guitar
Richard Tee: piano

Robby Kondor: synthesizer
Roger Forrester and Friends: barking!

BEFORE YOU ACCUSE ME (Elias MCDaniel) *Journeyman* CD Duck 9 26074-2 released November 1989

Eric Clapton: guitar, vocals
Nathan East: bass
Jim Keltner: drums
Robert Cray: guitar
Richard Tee: piano
Robby Kondor: synthesizer

BREAKING POINT (Marty Grebb / Jerry Lynn Willaims) *Journeyman* CD Duck 9 26074-2 released November 1989

Eric Clapton: guitar, vocals
David Sanborn: alto saxophone
Tawatha Agee: backing vocals
Vaneese Thomas: backing vocals
Nathan East: bass
Jim Keltner: drums, drum programming
Steve Ferrone: hi-hat
Greg Phillinganes: keyboards
Carol Steele: percussion
Jeff Bova: synthesizer and drum programming, sequenced bass and organ

ANYTHING FOR YOUR LOVE (Jerry Lynn Williams) *Journeyman* CD Duck 9 26074-2 released November 1989

Eric Clapton: guitar, vocals
Nathan East: bass
Jim Keltner: drums
Robert Cray: guitar
Greg Phillinganes: keyboards
Robby Kondor: keyboards, bass harmonica, vocoder, drum programming
Richard Tee: piano
Jeff Bova: additional synthesizer programming

RUN SO FAR (George Harrison) *Journeyman* CD Duck 9 26074-2 released November 1989

Eric Clapton: guitar, vocals
George Harrison: guitar, harmony vocals
Darryl Jones: bass
Jimmy Bralower: drum programming
Jim Keltner: drums and drum programming
Carol Steele: percussion
Robby Kondor: synthesizer programming
Greg Phillinganes: synthesizer
Rob Mounsey: synthesizer
Alan Clark: synthesizer

LEAD ME ON (Cecil Womack / Linda Womack) *Journeyman* CD Duck 9 26074-2 released November 1989

Eric Clapton: guitar, vocals
Cecil Womack: acoustic guitar, vocals
Nathan East: bass
Steve Ferrone: drums
Richard Tee: electric piano
Carol Steele: percussion
Robby Kilgore: synthesizer
Linda Womack: vocals
Arif Mardin: string arrangement

THAT KIND OF WOMAN (George Harrison) *Nobody's Child* CD Warner Bros. 7599-26280-1 released 1990

Eric Clapton: guitar, vocals
George Harrison: guitar, harmony vocals
Nathan East: bass
Jim Keltner: drums and drum programming

Robby Kondor: synthesizer programming
Rob Mounsey: synthesizer

RUNNING ON FAITH (Jerry Lynn Williams) (electric version) *Journeyman*
CD Duck 9 26074-2 released November 1989

Eric Clapton: guitar, vocals
Lani Groves: backing vocals
Nathan East: bass, backing vocals
Steve Ferrone: drums
Alan Clark: Hammond B3 organ
Greg Phillinganes: piano, backing vocals
Carol Steele: tambourine
Reverend Timothy Wright Washington Temple Concert Choir

RUNNING ON FAITH (Jerry Lynn Williams) (Dobro version) unreleased

Eric Clapton: Dobro, guitar, vocals
Lani Groves: backing vocals
Nathan East: bass, backing vocals
Steve Ferrone: drums
Alan Clark: Hammond B3 organ
Greg Phillinganes: piano, backing vocals
Carol Steele: tambourine
Reverend Timothy Wright Washington Temple Concert Choir

SOMETHING ABOUT YOU unreleased

FOREVER unreleased

DON'T TURN YOUR BACK unreleased

MURDOCH'S MEN unreleased

HIGHER POWER unreleased

Producer: Russ Titelman
Engineers: Dave O'Donnell / Dave Wittman / Jack Joseph Puig / Steve "Barney" Chase

> **❝**I had a subconscious feeling that we didn't want this album to be filled with too many similar tracks. We could have made a pure R&B album, or a pure blues album, or just a straight rock album because we had enough material to make it that way. I'm like that—I will deliberately choose a lot of opposites, if I'm given complete control, which my producer Russ Titelman gave to me.**❞**
>
> **—ERIC CLAPTON**

> **❝**I can't remember the other George songs but in retrospect both songs ['That Kind Of Woman,' 'Run So Far'] could have gone on *Journeyman* had we dropped 'Breaking Point.' They didn't record any of the other songs George presented.**❞**
>
> **—RUSS TITELMAN**

POWER STATION STUDIOS 441 West 53rd Street, New York City Session for *Lethal Weapon 2* soundtrack

APRIL 1989

KNOCKIN' ON HEAVEN'S DOOR (Bob Dylan) *Lethal Weapon 2* soundtrack CD Warner Bros. 9 25985-2 released 1989

RIGGS (Eric Clapton / Michael Kamen) *Lethal Weapon 2* soundtrack CD Warner Bros. 9 25985-2 released 1989

THE EMBASSY (Eric Clapton / Michael Kamen) *Lethal Weapon 2* soundtrack CD Warner Bros. 9 25985-2 released 1989

RIGGS AND ROGER (Eric Clapton / Michael Kamen) *Lethal Weapon 2* soundtrack CD Warner Bros. 9 25985-2 released 1989

LEO (Eric Clapton / Michael Kamen) *Lethal Weapon 2* soundtrack CD Warner Bros. 9 25985-2 released 1989

GOODNIGHT RIKA (Eric Clapton / Michael Kamen) *Lethal Weapon 2* soundtrack CD Warner Bros. 9 25985-2 released 1989

THE STILT HOUSE (Eric Clapton / Michael Kamen) *Lethal Weapon 2* soundtrack CD Warner Bros. 9 25985-2 released 1989

THE SHIPYARD (David Sanborn) *Lethal Weapon 2* soundtrack CD Warner Bros. 9 25985-2 released 1989

Eric Clapton: guitar
David Sanborn: alto saxophone
Michael Kamen: Kurzweil
Greg Phillinganes: keyboards
Tom Barney: bass
Sonny Emory: drums
Lew Soloff: trumpet on "Leo"
Randy Crawford: vocals on "Knockin' On Heaven's Door"

Producer: Michael Kamen
Engineer: Stephen McLaughlin

TOWN HOUSE STUDIOS 150 Goldhawk Road, London Session for *Journeyman*

JUNE 1989

BAD LOVE (Eric Clapton / Mick Jones) *Journeyman* CD Duck 9 26074-2 released November 1989

Eric Clapton: guitar, vocals
Pino Palladino: bass
Phil Collins: drums, harmony vocals, backing vocals
Phil Palmer: guitar
Alan Clark: keyboards
Katie Kasoon: backing vocals
Tessa Niles: backing vocals

Producer: Russ Titelman

"Warner Bros. wanted another 'Layla.' I thought, well if you sit down and write a song in a formulated way, it's not so hard. You think, 'What was "Layla" comprised of? A fiery intro modulated into the first verse, and a chorus with a riff around it.' I had this stuff in my head, so I just juggled it around, and Mick Jones came in to help tidy up. He was the one who said, 'You should put a "Badge" middle in there.' So we did that. Although it sounds like a cold way of doing it, it actually took on its own life."

—ERIC CLAPTON

ERIC CLAPTON GUEST SESSION

TOWN HOUSE STUDIOS
150 Goldhawk Road, London
Session for Phil Collins

JUNE 1989

I WISH IT WOULD RAIN (Phil Collins) *But Seriously* CD Virgin CDV 2620 released November 1989

Phil Collins: drums, keyboards, tambourine
Eric Clapton: guitar
Pino Palladino: bass

Producers: Phil Collins / Hugh Padgham
Engineer: Hugh Padgham

ERIC CLAPTON GUEST SESSION

MATRIX STUDIOS
35 Little Russell Street, London
Session for Brendan Croker

AUGUST 1989

THIS KIND OF LIFE (Brendan Croker) *Brendan Croker And The Five O'Clock Shadows* CD UK Silvertone ORE CD 505 / US Silvertone ZD 74218 released September 1989

Brendan Croker: vocals, acoustic guitar
Eric Clapton: vocals
Marcus Cliffe: bass
Steve Goulding: drums
Preston Heyman: percussion

Producer: John Porter
Engineer: Kenney Jones

Eric injured his hand at a charity cricket match a few days before the session and was unable to play the guitar. On this occasion he lent his vocal talents instead.

TOWN HOUSE STUDIOS
150 Goldhawk Road, London
Session for
Communion soundtrack

DECEMBER 1989

COMMUNION TITLE MUSIC (Eric Clapton) unreleased
INCIDENTAL MUSIC (Eric Clapton) unreleased
Eric Clapton: guitar
Alan Clark: keyboards, synthesizers

Producer: not known
Engineer: not known

1990

Hot on the heels of a hit single ("Bad Love") and album (*Journeyman*), Eric hit the road. The world tour started in the UK with some dates in Birmingham before arriving at his favorite venue, the Royal Albert Hall in London. The adverts proudly advertised a record-breaking eighteen nights which would be split into different lineups over the period. The first six shows would be a stripped-down, four-piece band, the second set of six shows would be a thirteen-piece band which also included a horn section, and the last six shows would be split into three nights of blues and three nights backed by the National Philharmonic Orchestra.

These shows really set a new benchmark for Eric and it was wisely decided to record them and even celebrate the event with a couple of special BBC exclusive broadcasts. America would not be left out as the last night of the four-piece band show on 24 February was recorded and given to America's Westwood One, who broadcast it as part of their hugely popular *Superstar Concert Series* in a slightly edited form.

JOURNEYMAN UK TOUR 1990

FOUR-PIECE BAND LINEUP:

Eric Clapton: guitar, vocals
Nathan East: bass
Steve Ferrone: drums
Greg Phillinganes: keyboards

JANUARY 1990

14 January 1990, National Exhibition Centre, Birmingham, Midlands (with Zucchero Fornaciari)

SETLIST: Pretending / White Room / I Shot The Sheriff / Running On Faith / Breaking Point / Can't Find My Way Home / Bad Love / Lay Down Sally / Hard Times / Before You Accuse Me / No Alibis / Old Love / Tearing Us Apart / Wonderful Tonight / Cocaine / A Remark You Made / Layla / Crossroads

15 January 1990, National Exhibition Centre, Birmingham, Midlands (with Zucchero Fornaciari)

SETLIST: Pretending / White Room / I Shot The Sheriff / Running On Faith / Breaking Point / Can't Find My Way Home / Bad Love / Lay Down Sally / Hard Times / Before You Accuse Me / No Alibis / Old Love / Tearing Us Apart / Wonderful Tonight / Cocaine / A Remark You Made / Layla / Crossroads

16 January 1990, National Exhibition Centre, Birmingham, Midlands (with Zucchero Fornaciari)

SETLIST: Pretending / White Room / I Shot The Sheriff / Running On Faith / Breaking Point / Can't Find My Way Home / Bad Love / Lay Down Sally / Hard Times / Before You Accuse Me / No Alibis / Old Love / Tearing Us Apart / Wonderful Tonight / Cocaine / A Remark You Made / Layla / Crossroads

18 January 1990, Royal Albert Hall, London (with Zucchero Fornaciari)

SETLIST: Pretending / Running On Faith / Breaking Point / I Shot The Sheriff / White Room / Can't Find My Way Home / Bad Love / Lay Down Sally / Before You Accuse Me / No Alibis / Old Love / Tearing Us Apart / Wonderful Tonight / Cocaine / A Remark You Made / Layla / Crossroads / Sunshine Of Your Love

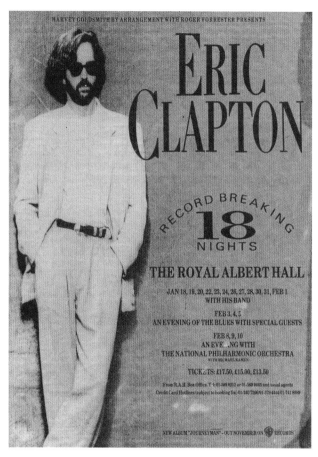

Press advert for a record-breaking eighteen nights at the Royal Albert Hall in 1990.

19 January 1990, Royal Albert Hall, London (with Zucchero Fornaciari)

SETLIST: Pretending / Before You Accuse Me / Breaking Point / I Shot The Sheriff / White Room / Can't Find My Way Home / Bad Love / Lay Down Sally / Running On Faith / No Alibis / Old Love / Tearing Us Apart / Wonderful Tonight / Cocaine / A Remark You Made / Layla / Crossroads

20 January 1990, Royal Albert Hall, London (with Zucchero Fornaciari)

SETLIST: Pretending / Running On Faith / Breaking Point / I Shot The Sheriff / White Room / Can't Find My Way Home / Bad Love / Lay Down Sally / Before You Accuse Me / No Alibis / Old Love / Tearing Us Apart / Wonderful Tonight / Cocaine / A Remark You Made / Layla / Crossroads / Sunshine Of Your Love

22 January 1990, Royal Albert Hall, London (with Zucchero Fornaciari)

SETLIST: Pretending / Running On Faith / Breaking Point / I Shot The Sheriff / White Room / Can't Find My Way Home / Bad Love / Lay Down Sally / Before You Accuse Me / Same Old Blues / Tearing Us Apart / Wonderful Tonight / Cocaine / A Remark You Made / Layla / Crossroads / Sunshine Of Your Love

23 January 1990, Royal Albert Hall, London (with Zucchero Fornaciari)

SETLIST: Pretending / Running On Faith / Breaking Point / I Shot The Sheriff / White Room / Can't Find My Way Home / Bad Love / Lay Down Sally / Before You Accuse Me / Same Old Blues / Tearing Us Apart / Wonderful Tonight / Cocaine / A Remark You Made / Layla / Crossroads / Sunshine Of Your Love

24 January 1990, Royal Albert Hall, London (with Zucchero Fornaciari)

"Running On Faith," "White Room," and "Sunshine Of Your Love" from this show can be found on *24 Nights* 2CD set Duck Records released October 1991. Most of the show was also broadcast at a later date in America on Westwood One's *Superstars in Concert* series. This show is also filmed.

SETLIST: Pretending / Running On Faith / Breaking Point / I Shot The Sheriff / White Room / Can't Find My Way Home / Bad Love / Lay Down Sally / Before You Accuse Me / Old Love / No Alibis / Tearing Us Apart / Wonderful Tonight / Cocaine / A Remark You Made / Layla / Knocking On Heaven's Door[1] / Crossroads[1] / Sunshine Of Your Love[1]

[1] with Phil Collins on tambourine and vocals

BIG BAND LINEUP:

Eric Clapton: guitar, vocals
Nathan East: bass
Steve Ferrone: drums
Greg Phillinganes: keyboards
Phil Palmer: guitar
Alan Clark: keyboards
Ray Cooper: percussion
Tessa Niles: backing vocals
Katie Kissoon: backing vocals
Ronnie Cuber: saxophone
Randy Brecker: trumpet
Louis Marini: saxophone
Alan Rubin: trumpet

26 January 1990, Royal Albert Hall, London (with Zucchero Fornaciari)

SETLIST: Pretending / Running On Faith / Breaking Point / I Shot The Sheriff / White Room / Can't Find My Way Home / Bad Love / Lay Down Sally / Before You Accuse Me / Old Love / No Alibis / Tearing Us Apart / Wonderful Tonight / Cocaine / A Remark You Made / Layla / Crossroads / Sunshine Of Your Love

27 January 1990, Royal Albert Hall, London (with Zucchero Fornaciari)

SETLIST: Pretending / Running On Faith / Breaking Point / I Shot The Sheriff / White Room / Can't Find My Way Home / Bad Love / Lay Down Sally / Before You Accuse Me / Old Love / No Alibis / Tearing Us Apart / Wonderful Tonight / Cocaine / A Remark You Made / Layla / Crossroads / Sunshine Of Your Love

28 January 1990, Royal Albert Hall, London (with Zucchero Fornaciari)

SETLIST: Pretending / Running On Faith / Breaking Point / I Shot The Sheriff / White Room / Can't Find My Way Home / Bad Love / Before You Accuse Me / Old Love / No Alibis / Tearing Us Apart / Wonderful Tonight / Cocaine / A Remark You Made / Layla / Crossroads / Sunshine Of Your Love

30 January 1990, Royal Albert Hall, London (with Zucchero Fornaciari)

SETLIST: Pretending / Running On Faith / Breaking Point / I Shot The Sheriff / White Room / Can't Find My Way Home / Bad Love / Before You Accuse Me / Old Love / No Alibis / Tearing Us Apart / Wonderful Tonight / Cocaine / A Remark You Made / Layla / Crossroads / Sunshine Of Your Love

31 January 1990, Royal Albert Hall, London (with Zucchero Fornaciari)

SETLIST: Pretending / Running On Faith / Breaking Point / I Shot The Sheriff / White Room / Can't Find My Way Home / Bad Love / Before You Accuse Me / Old Love / No Alibis / Tearing Us Apart / Wonderful Tonight / Cocaine / A Remark You Made / Layla / Crossroads / Sunshine Of Your Love

FEBRUARY 1990

1 February 1990, Royal Albert Hall, London (with Zucchero Fornaciari)

The show is filmed.

SETLIST: Pretending / Running On Faith / Breaking Point / I Shot The Sheriff / White Room / Can't Find My Way Home / Bad Love / Before You Accuse Me / Old Love / No Alibis[1] / Tearing Us Apart / Wonderful Tonight / Cocaine / A Remark You Made / Layla / Crossroads / Sunshine Of Your Love

[1] with Jerry Lynn Williams on vocals

BLUES NIGHTS 1990

3 February 1990, Royal Albert Hall, London (with Zucchero Fornaciari)

Complete show broadcast live on BBC Radio 1.

SETLIST: Key To The Highway / Worried Life Blues / All Your Love / Have You Ever Loved A Woman / Standing Around Crying / Long Distance Call / Johnnie's Boogie / Going Down Slow / You Belong To Me / Cry For Me / Howling For My Baby / Same Thing / Money / Five Long Years / Everything Gonna Be Alright / Something On Your

Mind / My Time After A While / Sweet Home Chicago / Hoochie Coochie Man / Wee Wee Baby

4 February 1990, Royal Albert Hall, London (with Zucchero Fornaciari)

SETLIST: Key To The Highway / Worried Life Blues / Better Watch Yourself / Have You Ever Loved A Woman / Johnnie's Boogie / Standing Around Crying / Long Distance Call / Going Down Slow / You Belong To Me / Cry For Me / Howling For My Baby / Same Thing / Money / Five Long Years / Something On Your Mind / Everything Gonna Be Alright / Sweet Home Chicago / My Time After A While

5 February 1990, Royal Albert Hall, London (with Zucchero Fornaciari)

"Worried Life Blues," "Watch Yourself," and "Have You Ever Loved A Woman" from this show can be found on *24 Nights* 2CD set Duck Records released October 1991. The show is also filmed.

SETLIST: Key To The Highway / Worried Life Blues / Watch Yourself / Have You Ever Loved A Woman / Johnnie's Boogie / Standing Around Crying / Long Distance Call / Going Down Slow / You Belong To Me / Cry For Me / Howling For My Baby / Same Thing / Money / Five Long Years / Something On Your Mind / Everything Gonna Be Alright / Sweet Home Chicago / My Time After A While / Wee Wee Baby

ORCHESTRA NIGHTS 1990

8 February 1990, Royal Albert Hall, London

SETLIST: Layla Introduction / Crossroads / Bell Bottom Blues / Lay Down Sally / Holy Mother / I Shot The Sheriff / Hard Times / Can't Find My Way Home / Edge of Darkness / Old Love / Wonderful Tonight / White Room / Concerto for Electric Guitar And Orchestra: First Movement / Concerto For Electric Guitar And Orchestra: Second Movement / Layla / Sunshine Of Your Love

9 February 1990, Royal Albert Hall, London

"Bell Bottom Blues" and "Hard Times" from this show

can be found on *24 Nights* 2CD set Duck Records released October 1991. The show is filmed.

SETLIST: Layla Introduction / Crossroads / Bell Bottom Blues / Lay Down Sally / Holy Mother / I Shot The Sheriff / Hard Times / Can't Find My Way Home / Edge Of Darkness / Old Love / Wonderful Tonight / White Room / Concerto For Electric Guitar And Orchestra: First Movement / Concerto For Electric Guitar And Orchestra: Second Movement / Layla / Sunshine Of Your Love

10 February 1990, Royal Albert Hall, London

Complete show broadcast live on BBC Radio 1.

SETLIST: Layla Introduction / Crossroads / Bell Bottom Blues / Lay Down Sally / Holy Mother / I Shot The Sheriff / Hard Times / Can't Find My Way Home / Edge Of Darkness / Old Love / Wonderful Tonight / White Room / Concerto For Electric Guitar And Orchestra: First Movement / Concerto For Electric Guitar And Orchestra: Second Movement / Layla / Sunshine Of Your Love

JOURNEYMAN SCANDINAVIAN/EUROPEAN TOUR 1990

14 February 1990, Icehall, Helsinki, Finland (with Zucchero Fornaciari)

SETLIST: Pretending / Running On Faith / Breaking Point / I Shot The Sheriff / White Room / Can't Find My Way Home / Bad Love / Before You Accuse Me / Old Love / No Alibis / Tearing Us Apart / Wonderful Tonight / Cocaine / A Remark You Made / Layla / Crossroads / Sunshine Of Your Love

16 February 1990, Globen, Stockholm, Sweden (with Zucchero Fornaciari)

SETLIST: Pretending / Running On Faith / Breaking Point / I Shot The Sheriff / White Room / Can't Find My Way Home / Bad Love / Before You Accuse Me / Old Love / No Alibis / Tearing Us Apart / Wonderful Tonight / Cocaine / A Remark You Made / Layla / Crossroads / Sunshine Of Your Love

17 February 1990, Skedsmohallen, Oslo, Norway (with Zucchero Fornaciari)

SETLIST: Pretending / Running On Faith / Breaking Point / I Shot The Sheriff / White Room / Can't Find My Way Home / Bad Love / Before You Accuse Me / Old Love / No Alibis / Tearing Us Apart / Wonderful Tonight / Cocaine / A Remark You Made / Layla / Crossroads / Sunshine Of Your Love

19 February 1990, KB-Hallen, Copenhagen, Denmark (with Zucchero Fornaciari)

SETLIST: Pretending / Running On Faith / Breaking Point / I Shot The Sheriff / White Room / Can't Find My Way Home / Bad Love / Before You Accuse Me / Old Love / No Alibis / Tearing Us Apart / Wonderful Tonight / Cocaine / A Remark You Made / Layla / Crossroads / Sunshine Of Your Love

20 February 1990, Sporthalle, Hamburg, Germany (with Zucchero Fornaciari)

SETLIST: Pretending / Running On Faith / Breaking Point / I Shot The Sheriff / White Room / Can't Find My Way Home / Bad Love / Before You Accuse Me / Old Love / No Alibis / Tearing Us Apart / Wonderful Tonight / Cocaine / A Remark You Made / Layla / Crossroads / Sunshine Of Your Love

22 February 1990, Forest National, Bruxelles, Belgium (with Zucchero Fornaciari)

SETLIST: Pretending / Running On Faith / Breaking Point / I Shot The Sheriff / White Room / Can't Find My Way Home / Bad Love / Before You Accuse Me / Old Love / Tearing Us Apart / Wonderful Tonight / Cocaine / A Remark You Made / Layla / Sunshine Of Your Love

23 February 1990, Grugahalle, Essen, Germany (with Zucchero Fornaciari)

SETLIST: not known

24 February 1990, Statenhal, Den Haag, Netherlands (with Zucchero Fornaciari)

SETLIST: Pretending / No Alibis / Running On Faith / I Shot The Sheriff / White Room / Can't Find My Way Home / Bad Love / Hard Times[1] / Before You Accuse Me[1] / Old Love / Tearing Us Apart / Wonderful Tonight / Cocaine / A Remark You Made / Layla / Tulips From Amsterdam / Sunshine Of Your Love

[1] with Billy Preston on organ and vocals

26 February 1990, Palatrussardi, Milano, Italy (with Zucchero Fornaciari)

SETLIST: Pretending / No Alibis / Running On Faith / I Shot The Sheriff / White Room / Can't Find My Way Home / Bad Love / Before You Accuse Me / Old Love / Tearing Us Apart / Wonderful Tonight / Cocaine / A Remark You Made / Layla / Crossroads / Sunshine Of Your Love

27 February 1990, Palatrussardi, Milano, Italy (with Zucchero Fornaciari)

SETLIST: Pretending / No Alibis / Running On Faith / I Shot The Sheriff / White Room / Can't Find My Way Home / Bad Love / Before You Accuse Me / Old Love / Tearing Us Apart / Wonderful Tonight / Cocaine / A Remark You Made / Layla / Crossroads / Volare / Sunshine Of Your Love

MARCH 1990

1 March 1990, Olympiahalle, München, Germany (with Zucchero Fornaciari)

SETLIST: Pretending / No Alibis / Running On Faith / I Shot The Sheriff / White Room / Can't Find My Way Home / Bad Love / Before You Accuse Me / Old Love / Tearing Us Apart / Wonderful Tonight / Cocaine / A Remark You Made / Layla / Crossroads / Sunshine Of Your Love

3 March 1990, Le Zenith, Paris, France (with Zucchero Fornaciari)

SETLIST: Pretending / No Alibis / Running On Faith / I Shot The Sheriff / White Room / Can't Find My Way Home / Bad Love / Before You Accuse Me / Old Love

/ Tearing Us Apart / Wonderful Tonight / Cocaine / A Remark You Made / Layla / Crossroads / Sunshine Of Your Love

4 March 1990, Le Zenith, Paris, France (with Zucchero Fornaciari)

SETLIST: Pretending / No Alibis / Running On Faith / I Shot The Sheriff / White Room / Can't Find My Way Home / Bad Love / Before You Accuse Me / Old Love / Tearing Us Apart / Wonderful Tonight / Cocaine / A Remark You Made / Layla / Crossroads / Sunshine Of Your Love

5 March 1990, Festhalle, Frankfurt, Germany (with Zucchero Fornaciari)

SETLIST: Pretending / No Alibis / Running On Faith / I Shot The Sheriff / White Room / Can't Find My Way Home / Bad Love / Before You Accuse Me / Old Love / Tearing Us Apart / Wonderful Tonight / Cocaine / A Remark You Made / Layla / Crossroads / Sunshine Of Your Love

SATURDAY NIGHT LIVE 1990

24 March 1990, *Saturday Night Live* television show, NBC Studios, Rockefeller Center, New York City

ERIC AND HIS BAND SETLIST: No Alibis / Pretending / Wonderful Tonight

ERIC WITH *SATURDAY NIGHT LIVE* HOUSE BAND SETLIST: Born Under A Bad Sign / Hideaway (shown as credits rolled and continued in the studio after the broadcast ended)

JOURNEYMAN U.S. TOUR 1990

28 March 1990, Omni, Atlanta, Georgia

SETLIST: Pretending / No Alibis / Running On Faith / I Shot The Sheriff / White Room / Can't Find My Way

Home / Bad Love / Before You Accuse Me / Old Love / Tearing Us Apart / Wonderful Tonight / Cocaine / A Remark You Made / Layla / Crossroads / Sunshine Of Your Love

30 March 1990, Charlotte Coliseum, Charlotte, North Carolina

SETLIST: Pretending / No Alibis / Running On Faith / I Shot The Sheriff / White Room / Can't Find My Way Home / Bad Love / Before You Accuse Me / Old Love / Tearing Us Apart / Wonderful Tonight / Cocaine / A Remark You Made / Layla / Crossroads / Sunshine Of Your Love

31 March 1990, Dean E. Smith Center, Chapel Hill, North Carolina

APRIL 1990

2 April 1990, Madison Square Garden, New York City

SETLIST: Pretending / Before You Accuse Me / Running On Faith / I Shot The Sheriff / White Room / Can't Find My Way Home / Bad Love / No Alibis[1] / Old Love / Tearing Us Apart / Wonderful Tonight / Cocaine / A Remark You Made / Layla / Crossroads / Sunshine Of Your Love

[1]with Daryl Hall on vocals

3 April 1990, Meadowlands Arena, East Rutherford, New Jersey

SETLIST: Pretending / Before You Accuse Me / Running On Faith / I Shot The Sheriff / White Room / Can't Find My Way Home / Bad Love / Lay Down Sally / No Alibis / Old Love / Tearing Us Apart / Wonderful Tonight / Cocaine / A Remark You Made / Layla / Crossroads / Sunshine Of Your Love

4 April 1990, Spectrum, Philadelphia, Pennsylvania

SETLIST: Pretending / Before You Accuse Me / Running On Faith / I Shot The Sheriff / White Room / Can't Find My Way Home / Bad Love / Lay Down Sally / No Alibis / Old Love / Tearing Us Apart / Wonderful Tonight /

Cocaine / A Remark You Made / Layla / Crossroads / Sunshine Of Your Love

6 April 1990, Nassau Coliseum, Uniondale, New York

SETLIST: Pretending / No Alibis / Running On Faith / I Shot The Sheriff / White Room / Can't Find My Way Home / Bad Love / Before You Accuse Me / After Midnight / Old Love / Tearing Us Apart / Wonderful Tonight / Cocaine / A Remark You Made / Layla / Crossroads / Sunshine Of Your Love

7 April 1990, Carrier Dome, Syracuse, New York

SETLIST: Pretending / No Alibis / Running On Faith / I Shot The Sheriff / White Room / Can't Find My Way Home / Bad Love / Before You Accuse Me / After Midnight / Old Love / Tearing Us Apart / Wonderful Tonight / Cocaine / A Remark You Made / Layla / Crossroads / Sunshine Of Your Love

9 April 1990, Centrum, Worcester, Massachusetts

SETLIST: Pretending / No Alibis / Running On Faith / I Shot The Sheriff / White Room / Can't Find My Way Home / Bad Love / Before You Accuse Me / Old Love / Tearing Us Apart / Wonderful Tonight / Cocaine / A Remark You Made / Layla / Crossroads / Sunshine Of Your Love

10 April 1990, Centrum, Worcester, Massachusetts

SETLIST: Pretending / No Alibis / Running On Faith / I Shot The Sheriff / White Room / Can't Find My Way Home / Bad Love / Before You Accuse Me / Old Love / Tearing Us Apart / Wonderful Tonight / Cocaine / A Remark You Made / Layla / Crossroads / Sunshine Of Your Love

12 April 1990, Civic Center, Hartford, Connecticut

SETLIST: Pretending / No Alibis / Running On Faith / I Shot The Sheriff / White Room / Can't Find My Way Home / Bad Love / Before You Accuse Me / After Midnight / Old Love / Tearing Us Apart / Wonderful Tonight / Cocaine / A Remark You Made / Layla / Crossroads / Sunshine Of Your Love

13 April 1990, Civic Center, Hartford, Connecticut

SETLIST: Pretending / No Alibis / Running On Faith / I Shot The Sheriff / White Room / Can't Find My Way Home / Bad Love / Before You Accuse Me / After Midnight / Old Love / Tearing Us Apart / Wonderful Tonight / Cocaine / A Remark You Made / Layla / Crossroads / Sunshine Of Your Love

15 April 1990, Palace of Auburn Hills, Auburn Hills, Michigan

SETLIST: Pretending / No Alibis / Running On Faith / I Shot The Sheriff / White Room / Can't Find My Way Home / Bad Love / Before You Accuse Me[1] / After Midnight[1] / Old Love / Tearing Us Apart / Wonderful Tonight / Cocaine / A Remark You Made / Layla / Crossroads / Sunshine Of Your Love

[1] with Stevie Ray Vaughan on guitar

16 April 1990, Riverfront Coliseum, Cincinnati, Ohio

SETLIST: Pretending / No Alibis / Running On Faith / I Shot The Sheriff / White Room / Can't Find My Way Home / Bad Love / Before You Accuse Me / After Midnight / Old Love / Tearing Us Apart / Wonderful Tonight / Cocaine / A Remark You Made / Layla / Crossroads / Sunshine Of Your Love

17 April 1990, Richfield Coliseum, Cleveland, Ohio

SETLIST: Pretending / No Alibis / Running On Faith / I Shot The Sheriff / White Room / Can't Find My Way Home / Bad Love / Before You Accuse Me / After Midnight / Old Love / Tearing Us Apart / Wonderful Tonight / Cocaine / A Remark You Made / Layla / Crossroads / Sunshine Of Your Love

19 April 1990, Market Square Arena, Indianapolis, Indiana

SETLIST: Pretending / No Alibis / Running On Faith / I Shot The Sheriff / White Room / Can't Find My Way Home / Bad Love / Before You Accuse Me / After Midnight / Old Love / Tearing Us Apart / Wonderful Tonight / Cocaine / A Remark You Made / Layla / Crossroads / Sunshine Of Your Love

20 April 1990, Hilton Coliseum, Ames, Iowa

SETLIST: Pretending / No Alibis / Running On Faith / I Shot The Sheriff / White Room / Can't Find My Way Home / Bad Love / Before You Accuse Me / Old Love / Tearing Us Apart / Wonderful Tonight / Cocaine / A Remark You Made / Layla / Crossroads / Sunshine Of Your Love

21 April 1990, Arena, St. Louis, Missouri

SETLIST: Pretending / No Alibis / Running On Faith / I Shot The Sheriff / White Room / Can't Find My Way Home / Bad Love / Before You Accuse Me / Old Love / Tearing Us Apart / Wonderful Tonight / Cocaine / A Remark You Made / Layla / Crossroads / Sunshine Of Your Love

23 April 1990, Lakefront Arena, New Orleans, Louisiana

SETLIST: Pretending / No Alibis / Running On Faith / I Shot The Sheriff / White Room / Can't Find My Way Home / Bad Love / Before You Accuse Me / Old Love / Tearing Us Apart / Wonderful Tonight / Cocaine / A Remark You Made / Layla / Crossroads / Sunshine Of Your Love

24 April 1990, Summit, Houston, Texas

SETLIST: Pretending / No Alibis / Running On Faith / I Shot The Sheriff / White Room / Can't Find My Way Home / Bad Love / Before You Accuse Me / Old Love / Tearing Us Apart / Wonderful Tonight / Cocaine / A Remark You Made / Layla / Crossroads / Sunshine Of Your Love

25 April 1990, Reunion Arena, Dallas, Texas

SETLIST: Pretending / No Alibis / Running On Faith / I Shot The Sheriff / White Room / Can't Find My Way Home / Bad Love / Before You Accuse Me / Old Love / Tearing Us Apart / Wonderful Tonight / Cocaine / A Remark You Made / Layla / Crossroads[1] / Sunshine Of Your Love[1]

[1]with Jamie Oldaker sitting in on drums

The band sing "Happy Birthday" to Steve Ferrone just before "A Remark You Made."

27 April 1990, McNichols Arena, Denver, Colorado

SETLIST: Pretending / No Alibis / Running On Faith / I Shot The Sheriff / White Room / Can't Find My Way Home / Bad Love / Before You Accuse Me / Old Love / Tearing Us Apart / Wonderful Tonight / Cocaine / A Remark You Made / Layla / Crossroads / Sunshine Of Your Love

29 April 1990, Tingley Coliseum, Albuquerque, New Mexico

SETLIST: Pretending / No Alibis / Running On Faith / I Shot The Sheriff / White Room / Can't Find My Way Home / Bad Love / Before You Accuse Me / Old Love / Tearing Us Apart / Wonderful Tonight / Cocaine / A Remark You Made / Layla / Crossroads / Sunshine Of Your Love

30 April 1990, ASU Activity Center, Phoenix, Arizona

SETLIST: Pretending / No Alibis / Running On Faith / I Shot The Sheriff / White Room / Can't Find My Way Home / Bad Love / Before You Accuse Me / Old Love / Tearing Us Apart / Wonderful Tonight / Cocaine / A Remark You Made / Layla / Crossroads / Sunshine Of Your Love

MAY 1990

1 May 1990, Forum, Los Angeles, California

Poster for Eric Clapton concert at the Forum in Los Angeles, California, on 1 May 1990.

SETLIST: Pretending / No Alibis / Running On Faith / I Shot The Sheriff / White Room / Can't Find My Way Home / Bad Love / Before You Accuse Me / Old Love / Tearing Us Apart / Wonderful Tonight / Cocaine / A Remark You Made / Layla / Instrumental Jam[1] / Crossroads[1] / Sunshine Of Your Love

[1]with George Harrison on guitar

3 May 1990, Sports Arena, San Diego, California

SETLIST: Pretending / No Alibis / Running On Faith / I Shot The Sheriff / White Room / Can't Find My Way Home / Bad Love / Before You Accuse Me / Old Love / Tearing Us Apart / Wonderful Tonight / Cocaine / A Remark You Made / Layla / Crossroads / Sunshine Of Your Love

4 May 1990, Pacific Amphitheatre, Costa Mesa, California

SETLIST: Pretending / No Alibis / Running On Faith / I Shot The Sheriff / White Room / Can't Find My Way Home / Bad Love / Before You Accuse Me / Old Love / Tearing Us Apart / Wonderful Tonight / Cocaine / A Remark You Made / Layla / Crossroads / Sunshine Of Your Love

5 May 1990, Shoreline Amphitheater, San Francisco, California

SETLIST: Pretending / No Alibis / Running On Faith / I Shot The Sheriff / White Room / Can't Find My Way Home / Bad Love / Before You Accuse Me / Old Love / Tearing Us Apart / Wonderful Tonight / Cocaine / A Remark You Made / Layla / Crossroads / Sunshine Of Your Love

JUNE 1990

INTERNATIONAL ROCK AWARDS REHEARSAL 1990

5 June 1990, 69th Regiment Armory, New York City

Eric and his band do a soundcheck for tomorrow's show.

BAND LINEUP:
Eric Clapton: guitar, vocals
Phil Palmer: guitar
Greg Phillinganes: keyboards
Alan Clark: keyboards
Nathan East: bass, voals
Steve Ferrone: drums
Ray Cooper: percussion
Katie Kissoon: backing vocals
Tessa Niles: backing vocals

SETLIST: Born Under A Bad Sign / Bad Boy / I Was Made To Love Her / Signed, Sealed, Delivered / Before You Accuse Me (Verion 1) / Before You Accuse Me (Version 2) / Who Do You Love / I Want Candy (jam) / Sweet Home Chicago / Who Do You Love / I Want Candy (jam)

INTERNATIONAL ROCK AWARDS 1990

6 June 1990, International Rock Awards, 69th Regiment Armory, New York City (Eric received a Lifetime Achievement Award at this ABC Television/Tall Pony production)

SETLIST:

Before You Accuse Me (Ellas McDaniel) broadcast
Eric Clapton: guitar, vocals
Phil Palmer: guitar
Greg Phillinganes: keyboards
Alan Clark: keyboards
Nathan East: bass, vocals
Steve Ferrone: drums
Ray Cooper: percussion
Katie Kissoon: backing vocals
Tessa Niles: backing vocals

Sweet Home Chicago (Robert Johnson) broadcast
Eric Clapton: guitar, vocals
Phil Palmer: guitar
Greg Phillinganes: keyboards
Alan Clark: keyboards
Nathan East: bass, vocals
Steve Ferrone: drums
Ray Cooper: percussion
Katie Kissoon: backing vocals
Tessa Niles: backing vocals
Buddy Guy: guitar, vocals
Joe Perry: guitar

Steven Tyler: vocals, harmonica
Billy Joel: keyboards
Richie Sambora: guitar
Bo Diddley: guitar
Sam Kinison: guitar
Gary Busey: guitar
Lou Reed: guitar
Dave Stewart: guitar
Neil Schon: guitar

Producer: Anthony Eaton
Recorded by: Record Plant Mobile

NORDOFF-ROBBINS KNEBWORTH CONCERT 1990

30 June 1990, Knebworth Park, Knebworth, Hertfordshire (concert in aid of the Nordoff–Robbins Music Therapy Centre and the BRIT School for Performing Arts. Some 120,000 fans gathered for this historic event featuring a legendary combination of top British rock artists: Phil Collins with Genesis, Paul McCartney, Pink Floyd, Robert Plant with Jimmy Page, Cliff Richard and the Shadows, Status Quo, Tears For Fears, Dire Straits, Elton John, and Eric Clapton)

Elton John, Eric Clapton, and Phil Palmer on stage at the Nordoff-Robbins Music Therapy Concert at Knebworth, 30 June 1990.

BAND LINEUP:
Eric Clapton: guitar, vocals
Phil Palmer: guitar
Greg Phillinganes: keyboards
Alan Clark: keyboards
Nathan East: bass, vocals
Steve Ferrone: drums
Ray Cooper: percussion
Katie Kissoon: backing vocals

Tessa Niles: backing vocals

SPECIAL GUESTS WHERE INDICATED:
Mark Knopfler: guitar, vocals
Guy Fletcher: keyboards
John Illsley: bass
Elton John: keyboards, vocals

SETLIST:

Pretending (Jerry Lynn Williams) broadcast live on BBC Radio 1

Before You Accuse Me (Ellas McDaniel) broadcast live on BBC Radio 1 / *Live At Knebworth* DVD Eagle Vision EREDV273 released October 2002

Old Love (Eric Clapton / Robert Cray) broadcast live on BBC Radio 1

Tearing Us Apart (Eric Clapton / Greg Phillinganes) broadcast live on BBC Radio 1 / *Live At Knebworth* DVD Eagle Vision EREDV273 released October 2002

Solid Rock (Mark Knopfler) [1, 2, 3] broadcast live on BBC Radio 1 / *Live At Knebworth* DVD Eagle Vision EREDV273 released October 2002

I Think I Love You Too Much (Mark Knopfler) [1, 2, 3] broadcast live on BBC Radio 1 / *Live At Knebworth* 2CD Eagle EDGCD410 released March 2010 / *Live At Knebworth* DVD Eagle Vision EREDV273 released October 2002

Money For Nothing (Mark Knopfler / Sting) [1,2,3] broadcast live on BBC Radio 1 / *Live At Knebworth* 2CD Eagle EDGCD410 released March 2010 / *Live At Knebworth* DVD Eagle Vision EREDV273 released October 2002

Sacrifice (Elton John / Bernie Taupin) [1, 4] broadcast live on BBC Radio 1 / *Live At Knebworth* DVD Eagle Vision EREDV273 released October 2002

Sad Songs (Elton John / Bernie Taupin) [1, 4] broadcast live on BBC Radio 1 / *Live At Knebworth* 2CD Eagle EDGCD410 released March 2010 / *Live At Knebworth* DVD Eagle Vision EREDV273 released October 2002

Saturday Night's Alright For Fighting (Elton John / Bernie Taupin) [1, 4] 1broadcast live on BBC Radio 1 / *Live At Knebworth* 2CD Eagle EDGCD410 released March 2010

Sunshine Of Your Love (Jack Bruce / Pete Brown / Eric Clapton) [1, 4] broadcast live on BBC Radio 1 / Live At Knebworth 2CD Eagle EDGCD410 released March 2010

/ Live At Knebworth DVD Eagle Vision EREDV273 released October 2002

[1]with Mark Knopfler on guitar and vocals
[2]with Guy Fletcher on keyboards
[3]with John Illsley on bass
[4]with Elton John on keyboards and vocals

Producers: Chris Kimsey / Steve Smith
Recorded by: Fleetwood Mobile (video) / Advision Mobile (audio)

JULY 1990

JOURNEYMAN U.S. TOUR 1990

BAND LINEUP:
Eric Clapton: guitar, vocals
Phil Palmer: guitar
Greg Phillinganes: keyboards
Alan Clark: keyboards
Nathan East: bass, vocals
Steve Ferrone: drums
Ray Cooper: percussion
Katie Kissoon: backing vocals
Tessa Niles: backing vocals

21-22 July 1990, rehearsals at Miami Arena, Miami, Florida

23 July 1990, Miami Arena, Miami, Florida

SETLIST: Pretending / No Alibis / Running On Faith / I Shot The Sheriff / White Room / Can't Find My Way Home / Bad Love / Before You Accuse Me / Old Love / Tearing Us Apart / Wonderful Tonight / Cocaine / Layla / Crossroads / Sunshine Of Your Love

25 July 1990, Orlando Arena, Orlando, Florida

SETLIST: Pretending / No Alibis / Running On Faith / I Shot The Sheriff / White Room / Can't Find My Way Home / Bad Love / Before You Accuse Me / Old Love / Badge / Wonderful Tonight / Cocaine / A Remark You Made / Layla / Crossroads / Sunshine Of Your Love

27 July 1990, Suncoast Dome, St. Petersburg, Florida

SETLIST: Pretending / No Alibis / Running On Faith / I Shot The Sheriff / White Room / Can't Find My Way Home / Bad Love / Before You Accuse Me / Old Love / Badge / Wonderful Tonight / Cocaine / A Remark You Made / Layla / Crossroads / Sunshine Of Your Love

28 July 1990, Lakewood Amphitheatre, Atlanta, Georgia

SETLIST: Pretending / No Alibis / Running On Faith / I Shot The Sheriff / White Room / Can't Find My Way Home / Bad Love / Before You Accuse Me / Old Love / Badge / Wonderful Tonight / Cocaine / A Remark You Made / Layla / Crossroads / Sunshine Of Your Love

30 July 1990, Starwood Amphitheatre, Nashville, Tennessee

SETLIST: Pretending / No Alibis / Running On Faith / I Shot The Sheriff / White Room / Can't Find My Way Home / Bad Love / Before You Accuse Me / Old Love / Badge / Wonderful Tonight / Cocaine / A Remark You Made / Layla / Crossroads / Sunshine Of Your Love

31 July 1990, Mid-South Coliseum, Memphis, Tennessee

SETLIST: Pretending / No Alibis / Running On Faith / I Shot The Sheriff / White Room / Can't Find My Way Home / Bad Love / Before You Accuse Me / Old Love / Badge / Wonderful Tonight / Cocaine / A Remark You Made / Layla / Crossroads / Sunshine Of Your Love

AUGUST 1990

2 August 1990, Coliseum, Greensboro, North Carolina

SETLIST: Pretending / No Alibis / Running On Faith / I Shot The Sheriff / White Room / Can't Find My Way Home / Bad Love / Before You Accuse Me / Old Love / Badge / Wonderful Tonight / Cocaine / A Remark You Made / Layla / Crossroads / Sunshine Of Your Love

3 August 1990, Capitol Centre, Washington, D.C.

SETLIST: Pretending / No Alibis / Running On Faith / I Shot The Sheriff / White Room / Can't Find My Way Home / Bad Love / Before You Accuse Me / Old Love

/ Badge / Wonderful Tonight / Cocaine / A Remark You Made / Layla / Crossroads / Sunshine Of Your Love

4 August 1990, Capitol Centre, Washington, D.C.

SETLIST: Pretending / No Alibis / Running On Faith / I Shot The Sheriff / White Room / Can't Find My Way Home / Bad Love / Before You Accuse Me / Old Love / Badge / Wonderful Tonight / Cocaine / A Remark You Made / Layla / Crossroads / Sunshine Of Your Love

6 August 1990, Meadowlands Arena, East Rutherford, New Jersey

SETLIST: Pretending / No Alibis / Running On Faith / I Shot The Sheriff / White Room / Can't Find My Way Home / Bad Love / Before You Accuse Me / Old Love / Badge / Wonderful Tonight / Cocaine / A Remark You Made / Layla / Crossroads / Sunshine Of Your Love

7 August 1990, Meadowlands Arena, East Rutherford, New Jersey

SETLIST: Pretending / No Alibis / Running On Faith / I Shot The Sheriff / White Room / Can't Find My Way Home / Bad Love / Before You Accuse Me / Old Love / Badge / Wonderful Tonight / Cocaine / A Remark You Made / Layla / Crossroads / Sunshine Of Your Love

9 August 1990, Great Woods, Boston, Massachusetts

SETLIST: Pretending / No Alibis / Running On Faith / I Shot The Sheriff / White Room / Can't Find My Way Home / Bad Love / Before You Accuse Me / Old Love / Badge / Wonderful Tonight / Cocaine / A Remark You Made / Layla / Crossroads / Sunshine Of Your Love

10 August 1990, Great Woods, Boston, Massachusetts

SETLIST: Pretending / No Alibis / Running On Faith / I Shot The Sheriff / White Room / Can't Find My Way Home / Bad Love / Before You Accuse Me / Old Love / Badge / Wonderful Tonight / Cocaine / A Remark You Made / Layla / Crossroads / Sunshine Of Your Love

11 August 1990, Great Woods, Boston, Massachusetts

SETLIST: Pretending / No Alibis / Running On Faith / I Shot The Sheriff / White Room / Can't Find My Way Home / Bad Love / Before You Accuse Me / Old Love / Badge / Wonderful Tonight / Cocaine / A Remark You Made / Layla / Crossroads / Sunshine Of Your Love

13 August 1990, Performing Arts Center, Saratoga Springs, New York

SETLIST: Pretending / No Alibis / Running On Faith / I Shot The Sheriff / White Room / Can't Find My Way Home / Bad Love / Before You Accuse Me / Old Love / Badge / Wonderful Tonight / Cocaine / A Remark You Made / Layla / Crossroads / Sunshine Of Your Love

14 August 1990, Spectrum, Philadelphia, Pennsylvania

SETLIST: Pretending / No Alibis / Running On Faith / I Shot The Sheriff / White Room / Can't Find My Way Home / Bad Love / Before You Accuse Me / Old Love / Badge / Wonderful Tonight / Cocaine / A Remark You Made / Layla / Crossroads / Sunshine Of Your Love

15 August 1990, Spectrum, Philadelphia, Pennsylvania

SETLIST: Pretending / No Alibis / Running On Faith / I Shot The Sheriff / White Room / Can't Find My Way Home / Bad Love / Before You Accuse Me / Old Love / Badge / Wonderful Tonight / Cocaine / A Remark You Made / Layla / Crossroads / Sunshine Of Your Love

17 August 1990, Nassau Veterans Memorial Coliseum, Uniondale, New York

SETLIST: Pretending / No Alibis / Running On Faith / I Shot The Sheriff / White Room / Can't Find My Way Home / Bad Love / Before You Accuse Me / Old Love / Badge / Wonderful Tonight / Cocaine / A Remark You Made / Layla / Crossroads / Sunshine Of Your Love

18 August 1990, Nassau Veterans Memorial Coliseum, Uniondale, New York

SETLIST: Pretending / No Alibis / Running On Faith / I Shot The Sheriff / White Room / Can't Find My Way Home / Bad Love / Before You Accuse Me / Old Love / Badge / Wonderful Tonight / Cocaine / A Remark You Made / Layla / Crossroads / Sunshine Of Your Love

21 August 1990, Blossom Music Center, Cleveland, Ohio

SETLIST: Pretending / No Alibis / Running On Faith / I Shot The Sheriff / White Room / Can't Find My Way Home / Bad Love / Before You Accuse Me / Old Love / Badge / Wonderful Tonight / Cocaine / A Remark You Made / Layla / Crossroads / Sunshine Of Your Love

22 August 1990, Pine Knob Pavilion, Detroit, Michigan

SETLIST: Pretending / No Alibis / Running On Faith / I Shot The Sheriff / White Room / Can't Find My Way Home / Bad Love / Before You Accuse Me / Old Love / Badge / Wonderful Tonight / Cocaine / A Remark You Made / Layla / Crossroads / Sunshine Of Your Love

23 August 1990, Riverbend Music Theatre, Cincinnati, Ohio

SETLIST: Pretending / No Alibis / Running On Faith / I Shot The Sheriff / White Room / Can't Find My Way Home / Bad Love / Before You Accuse Me / Old Love / Badge / Wonderful Tonight / Cocaine / A Remark You Made / Layla / Crossroads / Sunshine Of Your Love

25 August 1990, Alpine Valley, East Troy, Wisconsin

SETLIST: Pretending / No Alibis / Running On Faith / I Shot The Sheriff / White Room / Can't Find My Way Home / Bad Love / Before You Accuse Me / Old Love / Badge / Wonderful Tonight / Cocaine / A Remark You Made / Layla / Crossroads[1] / Sunshine Of Your Love[1]

[1] with Jeff Healey on guitar

26 August 1990, Alpine Valley, East Troy, Wisconsin

SETLIST: Pretending / No Alibis / Running On Faith / I Shot The Sheriff / White Room / Can't Find My Way Home / Bad Love / Before You Accuse Me / Old Love / Badge / Wonderful Tonight / Cocaine / A Remark You Made / Layla / Sunshine Of Your Love / Sweet Home Chicago[1]

[1] with Stevie Ray Vaughan, Jimmie Vaughan, Robert Cray, and Buddy Guy on guitars

After the concert, one of the helicopters carrying Stevie Ray Vaughan and several members of Eric's crew crashed, killing all on board. It was very foggy and pilot error was listed as the cause of the accident. After much reflecting and debate it was decided to carry on the tour as a tribute to Stevie, but it was one of the hardest decisions Eric and the band ever made.

28 August 1990, Sandstone Amphitheatre, Kansas City, Kansas

SETLIST: Pretending / No Alibis / Running On Faith / I Shot The Sheriff / White Room / Can't Find My Way Home / Bad Love / Before You Accuse Me / Old Love / Badge / Wonderful Tonight / Cocaine / A Remark You Made / Layla / Crossroads / Sunshine Of Your Love

29 August 1990, Arena, St. Louis, Missouri

SETLIST: Pretending / No Alibis / Running On Faith / I Shot The Sheriff / White Room / Can't Find My Way Home / Bad Love / Before You Accuse Me / Old Love / Badge / Wonderful Tonight / Cocaine / A Remark You Made / Layla / Crossroads / Sunshine Of Your Love

31 August 1990, Thompson-Boling Arena, Knoxville, Tennessee

SETLIST: Pretending / No Alibis / Running On Faith / I Shot The Sheriff / White Room / Can't Find My Way Home / Bad Love / Before You Accuse Me / Old Love / Badge / Wonderful Tonight / Cocaine / A Remark You Made / Layla / Crossroads / Sunshine Of Your Love

SEPTEMBER 1990

1 September 1990, Oak Mountain Amphitheatre, Birmingham, Alabama

SETLIST: Pretending / No Alibis / Running On Faith / I Shot The Sheriff / White Room / Can't Find My Way Home / Bad Love / Before You Accuse Me / Old Love / Badge / Wonderful Tonight / Cocaine / A Remark You Made / Layla / Crossroads / Sunshine Of Your Love

2 September 1990, Coast Coliseum, Biloxi, Mississippi

SETLIST: Pretending / No Alibis / Running On Faith / I Shot The Sheriff / White Room / Can't Find My Way Home / Bad Love / Before You Accuse Me / Old Love

/ Badge / Wonderful Tonight / Cocaine / A Remark You Made / Layla / Crossroads / Sunshine Of Your Love

JOURNEYMAN SOUTH AMERICAN TOUR 1990

BAND LINEUP:
Eric Clapton: guitar, vocals
Phil Palmer: guitar
Greg Phillinganes: keyboards
Nathan East: bass, vocals
Steve Ferrone: drums
Ray Cooper: percussion
Katie Kissoon: backing vocals
Tessa Niles: backing vocals

29 September 1990, Estadio Nacional, Santiago, Chile

SETLIST: Pretending / No Alibis / Running On Faith / I Shot The Sheriff / White Room / Can't Find My Way Home / Bad Love / Before You Accuse Me / Old Love / Badge / Wonderful Tonight / Cocaine / A Remark You Made / Layla / Crossroads / Sunshine Of Your Love

OCTOBER 1990

3 October 1990, Estadio Centemario, Montevideo, Uruguay

SETLIST: Pretending / No Alibis / Running On Faith / I Shot The Sheriff / White Room / Can't Find My Way Home / Bad Love / Before You Accuse Me / Old Love / Badge / Wonderful Tonight / Cocaine / A Remark You Made / Layla / Crossroads / Sunshine Of Your Love

5 October 1990, Estadio River Plate, Buenos Aires, Argentina

SETLIST: Pretending / No Alibis / Running On Faith / I Shot The Sheriff / White Room / Can't Find My Way Home / Bad Love / Before You Accuse Me / Old Love / Badge / Wonderful Tonight / Cocaine / A Remark You Made / Layla / Crossroads / Sunshine Of Your Love

7 October 1990, Praca da Apoteose, Rio de Janeiro, Brazil

SETLIST: Pretending / No Alibis / Running On Faith / I Shot The Sheriff / White Room / Can't Find My Way Home / Bad Love / Before You Accuse Me / Old Love / Badge / Wonderful Tonight / Cocaine / A Remark You Made / Layla / Crossroads / Sunshine Of Your Love

9 October 1990, Ginasio Nilson Nelson, Brasilia, Brazil

SETLIST: Pretending / No Alibis / Running On Faith / I Shot The Sheriff / White Room / Can't Find My Way Home / Bad Love / Before You Accuse Me / Old Love / Badge / Wonderful Tonight / Cocaine / A Remark You Made / Layla / Crossroads / Sunshine Of Your Love

11 October 1990, Ginasio Mineirinho, Belo Horizonte, Brazil

SETLIST: Pretending / No Alibis / Running On Faith / I Shot The Sheriff / White Room / Can't Find My Way Home / Bad Love / Before You Accuse Me / Old Love / Badge / Wonderful Tonight / Cocaine / A Remark You Made / Layla / Crossroads / Sunshine Of Your Love

13 October 1990, Orlando Scarpelli Stadium, Florianopolis, Brazil

SETLIST: Pretending / No Alibis / Running On Faith / I Shot The Sheriff / White Room / Can't Find My Way Home / Bad Love / Before You Accuse Me / Old Love / Badge / Wonderful Tonight / Cocaine / A Remark You Made / Layla / Crossroads / Sunshine Of Your Love

16 October 1990, Ginasio Gigantinho, Porto Alegre, Brazil

SETLIST: Pretending / No Alibis / Running On Faith / I Shot The Sheriff / White Room / Can't Find My Way Home / Bad Love / Before You Accuse Me / Old Love / Badge / Wonderful Tonight / Cocaine / A Remark You Made / Layla / Crossroads / Sunshine Of Your Love

19 October 1990, Olympia, São Paulo, Brazil

SETLIST: Pretending / No Alibis / Running On Faith / I Shot The Sheriff / White Room / Can't Find My Way

Home / Bad Love / Before You Accuse Me / Old Love / Badge / Wonderful Tonight / Cocaine / A Remark You Made / Layla / Crossroads / Sunshine Of Your Love

20 October 1990, Olympia, São Paulo, Brazil

SETLIST: Pretending / No Alibis / Running On Faith / I Shot The Sheriff / White Room / Can't Find My Way Home / Bad Love / Before You Accuse Me / Old Love / Badge / Wonderful Tonight / Cocaine / A Remark You Made / Layla / Crossroads / Sunshine Of Your Love

21 October 1990, Olympia, São Paulo, Brazil

SETLIST: Pretending / No Alibis / Running On Faith / I Shot The Sheriff / White Room / Can't Find My Way Home / Bad Love / Before You Accuse Me / Old Love / Badge / Wonderful Tonight / Cocaine / A Remark You Made / Layla / Crossroads / Sunshine Of Your Love

JOURNEYMAN AUSTRALIA TOUR 1990

BAND LINEUP:
Eric Clapton: guitar, vocals
Phil Palmer: guitar
Greg Phillinganes: keyboards
Nathan East: bass, vocals
Steve Ferrone: drums
Ray Cooper: percussion
Katie Kissoon: backing vocals
Tessa Niles: backing vocals

NOVEMBER 1990

4 November 1990, depart for Auckland, New Zealand
6 November 1990, arrive in Auckland, New Zealand
7 November 1990, Supertop, Auckland, New Zealand

SETLIST: Pretending / No Alibis / Running On Faith / I Shot The Sheriff / White Room / Can't Find My Way Home / Bad Love / Before You Accuse Me / Old Love / Badge / Wonderful Tonight / Cocaine / A Remark You Made / Layla / Crossroads / Sunshine Of Your Love

8 November 1990, Supertop, Auckland, New Zealand

SETLIST: Pretending / No Alibis / Running On Faith / I Shot The Sheriff / White Room / Can't Find My Way Home / Bad Love / Before You Accuse Me / Old Love / Badge / Wonderful Tonight / Cocaine / A Remark You Made / Layla / Crossroads / Sunshine Of Your Love

9 November 1990, fly to Canberra, Australia
10 November 1990, Royal Theatre Canberra, Australia

SETLIST: Pretending / No Alibis / Running On Faith / I Shot The Sheriff / White Room / Can't Find My Way Home / Bad Love / Before You Accuse Me / Old Love / Badge / Wonderful Tonight / Cocaine / A Remark You Made / Layla / Crossroads / Sunshine Of Your Love

11 November 1990, day off
12 November 1990, Festival Theatre, Adelaide, Australia

SETLIST: Pretending / No Alibis / Running On Faith / I Shot The Sheriff / White Room / Can't Find My Way Home / Bad Love / Before You Accuse Me / Old Love / Badge / Wonderful Tonight / Cocaine / A Remark You Made / Layla / Crossroads / Sunshine Of Your Love

13 November 1990, Festival Theatre, Adelaide, Australia

SETLIST: Pretending / No Alibis / Running On Faith / I Shot The Sheriff / White Room / Can't Find My Way Home / Bad Love / Before You Accuse Me / Old Love / Badge / Wonderful Tonight / Cocaine / A Remark You Made / Layla / Crossroads / Sunshine Of Your Love

14 November 1990, day off
15 November 1990, National Tennis Center, Melbourne, Australia

SETLIST: Pretending / No Alibis / Running On Faith / I Shot The Sheriff / White Room / Can't Find My Way Home / Bad Love / Before You Accuse Me / Old Love / Badge / Wonderful Tonight / Cocaine / A Remark You Made / Layla / Crossroads / Sunshine Of Your Love

16 November 1990, Entertainment Center, Sydney, Australia

SETLIST: Pretending / No Alibis / Running On Faith / I Shot The Sheriff / White Room / Can't Find My Way Home / Bad Love / Before You Accuse Me / Old Love

/ Badge / Wonderful Tonight / Cocaine / A Remark You Made / Layla / Crossroads / Sunshine Of Your Love

17 November 1990, Entertainment Center, Sydney, Australia

SETLIST: Pretending / No Alibis / Running On Faith / I Shot The Sheriff / White Room / Can't Find My Way Home / Bad Love / Before You Accuse Me / Old Love / Badge / Wonderful Tonight / Cocaine / A Remark You Made / Layla / Crossroads / Sunshine Of Your Love

18 November 1990, day off

19 November 1990, Entertainment Center, Brisbane, Australia

SETLIST: Pretending / No Alibis / Running On Faith / I Shot The Sheriff / White Room / Can't Find My Way Home / Bad Love / Before You Accuse Me / Old Love / Badge / Wonderful Tonight / Cocaine / A Remark You Made / Layla / Crossroads / Sunshine Of Your Love

20 November 1990, fly to Singapore

JOURNEYMAN FAR EAST TOUR 1990

BAND LINEUP:
Eric Clapton: guitar, vocals
Phil Palmer: guitar
Greg Phillinganes: keyboards
Nathan East: bass, vocals
Steve Ferrone: drums
Ray Cooper: percussion
Katie Kissoon: backing vocals
Tessa Niles: backing vocals

24 November 1990, Singapore Indoor Stadium, Singapore, Singapore

SETLIST: Pretending / No Alibis / Running On Faith / I Shot The Sheriff / White Room / Can't Find My Way Home / Bad Love / Before You Accuse Me / Old Love / Badge / Wonderful Tonight / A Remark You Made / Layla / Crossroads / Sunshine Of Your Love

26 November 1990, Negara Stadium, Kuala Lumpur, Malaysia

SETLIST: Pretending / No Alibis / Running On Faith / I Shot The Sheriff / White Room / Can't Find My Way Home / Bad Love / Before You Accuse Me / Old Love / Badge / Wonderful Tonight / A Remark You Made / Layla / Crossroads / Sunshine Of Your Love

29 November 1990, Coliseum, Hong Kong

SETLIST: Pretending / No Alibis / Running On Faith / I Shot The Sheriff / White Room / Can't Find My Way Home / Bad Love / Before You Accuse Me / Old Love / Badge / Wonderful Tonight / Cocaine / A Remark You Made / Layla / Crossroads / Sunshine Of Your Love

DECEMBER 1990

4 December 1990, Budokan, Tokyo, Japan

SETLIST: Pretending / No Alibis / Running On Faith / I Shot The Sheriff / White Room / Can't Find My Way Home / Bad Love / Before You Accuse Me / Old Love / Badge / Wonderful Tonight / Cocaine / A Remark You Made / Layla / Crossroads / Sunshine Of Your Love

5 December 1990, Budokan, Tokyo, Japan

SETLIST: Pretending / No Alibis / Running On Faith / I Shot The Sheriff / White Room / Can't Find My Way Home / Bad Love / Before You Accuse Me / Old Love / Badge / Wonderful Tonight / Cocaine / A Remark You Made / Layla / Crossroads / Sunshine Of Your Love

6 December 1990, Budokan, Tokyo, Japan

SETLIST: Pretending / No Alibis / Running On Faith / I Shot The Sheriff / White Room / Can't Find My Way Home / Bad Love / Before You Accuse Me / Old Love / Badge / Wonderful Tonight / Cocaine / A Remark You Made / Layla / Crossroads / Sunshine Of Your Love

9 December 1990, Yoyogi Olympic Pool, Tokyo

SETLIST: Pretending / No Alibis / Running On Faith / I Shot The Sheriff / White Room / Can't Find My Way Home / Bad Love / Before You Accuse Me / Old Love / Badge / Wonderful Tonight / Cocaine / A Remark You Made / Layla / Crossroads / Sunshine Of Your Love

10 December 1990, Rainbow Hall, Nagoya, Japan

SETLIST: Pretending / No Alibis / Running On Faith / I Shot The Sheriff / White Room / Can't Find My Way Home / Bad Love / Before You Accuse Me / Old Love / Badge / Wonderful Tonight / Cocaine / A Remark You Made / Layla / Crossroads / Sunshine Of Your Love

11 December 1990, Castle Hall, Osaka, Japan

SETLIST: Pretending / No Alibis / Running On Faith / I Shot The Sheriff / White Room / Can't Find My Way Home / Bad Love / Before You Accuse Me / Old Love / Badge / Wonderful Tonight / Cocaine / A Remark You Made / Layla / Crossroads / Sunshine Of Your Love

13 December 1990, Yokohama Arena, Yokohama, Japan

SETLIST: Pretending / No Alibis / Running On Faith / I Shot The Sheriff / White Room / Can't Find My Way Home / Bad Love / Before You Accuse Me / Old Love / Badge / Wonderful Tonight / Cocaine / Auld Lang Syne / A Remark You Made / Layla / Crossroads / Sunshine Of Your Love

RECORDING SESSIONS 1990
ERIC CLAPTON GUEST SESSION
SARM WEST STUDIOS
8-10 Basing Street, London
Session for Michael Kamen

MARCH 1990

SANDRA (Michael Kamen) *Concerto For Saxophone And Orchestra* CD Warner Bros. 7599-26157-2 released November 1990

Michael Kamen: oboe, keyboards
Eric Clapton: guitar
David Sanborn: saxophone
Elliott Randall: guitar
Terry Reed: acoustic guitar
Pino Palladino: bass

Ray Cooper: percussion
Gary Wallace: drums
Producers: Michael Kamen / Stephen McLaughlin
Engineer: John McLure

ERIC CLAPTON GUEST SESSION
RED BIRD STUDIO
Leonard, Oklahoma

JUNE 1990

Initial demo sessions made at Jerry Wiliams's home studio. Eric overdubbed his guitar at the Power Station.

POWER STATION
441 West 53rd Street, New York City
Guitar overdub for Jerry Lynn Williams

SEPTEMBER 1990

SENDING ME ANGELS (Jerry Lynn Williams / Frankie Miller) *The Peacemaker* CD Viceroy Music 37 237-422 released 1996

Jerry Lynn Williams: vocals, synth bass, strings, piano
Eric Clapton: guitar
Marty Grebb: Hammond B3 organ
Tom "T-Bone" Wolk: accordion
Mickey Curry: drums

WHAT'S THIS WORLD COMING TO (Jerry Lynn Williams) *The Peacemaker* CD Viceroy Music 37 237-422 released 1996

Jerry Lynn Williams: vocals, piano, synth strings
Eric Clapton: guitar
John Oates: synth strings, bass
Nicky Hopkins: synth, keyboards
Jimmy Bralower: drum programming

YOU BETTER ROCK ME BABY (Jerry Lynn Williams) *The Peacemaker* CD Viceroy Music 37 237-422 released 1996

Jerry Lynn Williams: vocals, rhythm guitar, synth bass
Eric Clapton: guitar
John Oates: synth strings, bass
Nicky Hopkins: piano
Chris Green: drum programming

Producer: Jerry Lynn Williams
Engineer: Peter Moshay

> "We recorded *The Peacemaker* at both Red Bird Studio (the studio I built for Jerry at his house in Leonard, Oklahoma) and also at A-Pawling Studio, New York City. The album and many songs were produced by John Oates, who also co-wrote some songs with Jerry. Eric overdubbed his solos in New York."
>
> **—PETER MOSHAY**
> (engineer)

ELECTRIC LADY STUDIOS
52 West 8th Street,
New York City
Overdub session for
Honda Cars advert in
Japan

SEPTEMBER 1990

BAD LOVE (Eric Clapton / Mick Jones) unreleased

Eric overdubs some new guitar lines and licks over the original backing track which was used in an advert for Honda cars on Japanese television.

ERIC CLAPTON GUEST SESSION

THE HIT FACTORY
421 West 54th Street,
New York City
Session for Lamont Dozier

SEPTEMBER 1990

THAT AIN'T ME (Lamont Dozier) *Inside Seduction* CD Atlantic released 1991

HOLD ON TIGHT (Lamont Dozier) unreleased

Lamont Dozier: vocals
Eric Clapton: guitar
Phil Collins: drums
Ryo Okumoto: keyboards, programming
David Boroff: saxophone

Producers: Lamont Dozier / Phil Collins
Engineer: Reginald Dozier

> "I don't think people realize how good a singer he is. It's very easy to work with Lamont because he writes such straightforward material."
>
> **—ERIC CLAPTON**

9

1991

The year began very much in the same way 1990 had with a spectacular run of shows at the Royal Albert Hall. Only this time, it turned out to be over a record-breaking twenty-four nights. Once again, Eric tasked himself with offering the public a choice of music. You could choose a stripped-down four-piece lineup, an augmented nine-piece lineup, a to-die-for blues lineup, and for those with a more cultural taste, the orchestra nights. Something for everyone really.

Rehearsals for the four-piece and nine-piece bands started at the Point in Dublin where Eric played two warmup shows. After that an amazingly well structured rehearsal plan at the Albert Hall was put together. As the first six shows were underway in the evening, Eric rehearsed the next segment during the day. So when the four-piece band performed, they'd rehearse with the nine-piece band during the day. Then, when the nine-piece band took over at night, they'd rehearse with the blues band during the day. Two further days of rehearsals with the blues guests took place at Bray Studios in Windsor.

Rehearsals for the fourth and final segment with the National Philharmonic Orchestra took place at the Royal College of Music, conveniently located behind the Royal Albert Hall. Michael Kamen was the conductor. The orchestra shows were not without problems as Eric's amp had to be completely isolated to protect the very delicate ears of some of the orchestra members in the near vicinity. Eric had to make do with a monitor wedge that played his guitar back at very low volumes.

Every single night at the Royal Albert Hall was recorded with a portable recording unit based under the stage. Russ Titelman was taking care of the recording process. One night of each format was also filmed and segments of audio and film were used in Eric's *24 Nights* live double album and video/DVD.

These shows were a huge success, but had been a lot of hard work and pressure for Eric. Within a few short weeks of the shows ending, Eric was on a well-earned break in New York with his son, Conor. The unimaginable happened on 20 March when Conor accidently fell to his death from a highrise apartment window. It was heartbreaking, horrific, and an absolute tragedy.

Understandably, Eric walked away from any work he had planned and went to Antigua. There, he found some comfort in writing highly personnal songs that were first and foremost for himself. Eventually, as part of his grieving process he felt able to share some of them with the world. There had been huge compassion for Eric and Lori Del Santo, Conor's mother, and sharing these intimate lyrics was a brave thing to do.

Russ Titelman was left in charge of choosing tracks for the double live album.

JOURNEYMAN UK / IRELAND TOUR 1991

JANUARY 1991

21 January 1991–25 January 1991, four-piece rehearsals at the Point, Dublin, Ireland

26 January 1991–29 January 1991, nine-piece rehearsals at the Point, Dublin, Ireland

30 January 1991, day off

FOUR-PIECE BAND LINEUP:
Eric Clapton: guitar, vocals
Nathan East: bass, vocals
Greg Phillinganes: keyboards
Phil Collins: drums

31 January 1991, The Point, Dublin, Ireland

SETLIST: Pretending / No Alibis / Running On Faith / I Shot The Sheriff / White Room / Can't Find My Way Home / Bad Love / Knockin' On Heaven's Door / Before You Accuse Me / Old Love / Wonderful Tonight / Cocaine / Layla / Crossroads / Sunshine of Your Love

FEBRUARY 1991

1 February 1991, day off

2 February 1991, the Point, Dublin, Ireland

SETLIST: Pretending / No Alibis / Running On Faith / I Shot The Sheriff / White Room / Can't Find My Way Home / Bad Love / Knockin' On Heaven's Door / Before You Accuse Me / Old Love / Badge / Wonderful Tonight / Cocaine / Layla / Crossroads / Sunshine of Your Love

The program on the right with the Peter Blake artwork was withdrawn within a few days of release and replaced with the cover on the left. The Peter Blake cover is now rare and collectable.

3 February 1991, day off

4 February 1991, day off

5 February 1991, Royal Albert Hall, London, England

SETLIST: Pretending / No Alibis / Running On Faith / I Shot The Sheriff / White Room / Bad Love / Knocking

On Heaven's Door / Before You Accuse Me / Old Love / Badge / Wonderful Tonight / Cocaine / Layla / Crossroads / Sunshine Of Your Love

6 February 1991, Royal Albert Hall, London

SETLIST: Pretending / No Alibis / Running On Faith / I Shot The Sheriff / White Room / Can't Find My Way Home / Bad Love / Knockin' On Heaven's Door / Before You Accuse Me / Old Love / Badge / Wonderful Tonight / Cocaine / Layla / Crossroads / Sunshine of Your Love

7 February 1991, Royal Albert Hall, London

SETLIST: Pretending / No Alibis / Running On Faith / I Shot The Sheriff / White Room / Can't Find My Way Home / Bad Love / Knocking On Heaven's Door / Before You Accuse Me / Old Love / Badge / Wonderful Tonight / Cocaine / A Remark You Made / Layla / Crossroads / Sunshine Of Your Love

8 February 1991, day off

FOUR-PIECE BAND LINEUP:
Eric Clapton: guitar, vocals
Nathan East: bass
Greg Phillinganes: keyboards
Steve Ferrone: drums

9 February 1991, Royal Albert Hall, London

SETLIST: Pretending / No Alibis / Running On Faith / I Shot The Sheriff / White Room / Can't Find My Way Home / Bad Love / Before You Accuse Me / Old Love / Badge / Wonderful Tonight / Cocaine / A Remark You Made / Layla / Crossroads / Sunshine Of Your Love

10 February 1991, Royal Albert Hall, London

"Badge" from this show can be found on *24 Nights* 2CD set Duck Records released October 1991.

SETLIST: Pretending / No Alibis / Running On Faith / I Shot The Sheriff / White Room / Can't Find My Way Home / Bad Love / Before You Accuse Me / Old Love / Badge / Wonderful Tonight / Cocaine / A Remark You Made / Layla / Crossroads / Sunshine Of Your Love

11 February 1991, Royal Albert Hall, London

SETLIST: Pretending / No Alibis / Running On Faith / I Shot The Sheriff / White Room / Can't Find My Way Home / Bad Love / Before You Accuse Me / Old Love / Badge / Wonderful Tonight / Cocaine / A Remark You Made / Layla / Crossroads / Sunshine Of Your Love

12 February 1991, day off

NINE-PIECE BAND LINEUP:
Eric Clapton: guitar, vocals
Phil Palmer: guitar
Greg Phillinganes: keyboards
Chuck Leavell: keyboards
Nathan East: bass, vocals
Steve Ferrone: drums
Ray Cooper: percussion
Katie Kissoon: backing vocals
Tessa Niles: backing vocals

13 February 1991, Royal Albert Hall, London

SETLIST: Pretending / No Alibis / Running On Faith / I Shot The Sheriff / White Room / Can't Find My Way Home / Bad Love / Before You Accuse Me / Old Love / Badge / Wonderful Tonight / Thank You (Falettinme Be Mice Elf Agin) / Cocaine / A Remark You Made / Layla / Crossroads / Sunshine of Your Love

14 February 1991, Royal Albert Hall, London

SETLIST: Pretending / No Alibis / Running On Faith / I Shot The Sheriff / White Room / Can't Find My Way Home / Bad Love / Before You Accuse Me / Old Love / Badge / Wonderful Tonight / Thank You (Falettinme Be Mice Elf Agin) / Cocaine / A Remark You Made / Layla / Sunshine of Your Love

15 February 1991, Royal Albert Hall, London

SETLIST: Pretending / Running On Faith / I Shot The Sheriff / White Room / Can't Find My Way Home / Bad Love / Before You Accuse Me / Old Love / Badge / Wonderful Tonight / Thank You (Falettinme Be Mice Elf Agin) / Cocaine / A Remark You Made / Layla / Crossroads / Sunshine of Your Love

16 February 1991, day off
17 February 1991, Royal Albert Hall, London

Complete show broadcast live on BBC Radio 1.

SETLIST: Pretending / No Alibis / Running On Faith / I Shot The Sheriff / White Room / Can't Find My Way Home / Bad Love / Before You Accuse Me / Old Love / Badge / Wonderful Tonight / Thank You (Falettinme Be Mice Elf Agin) / Cocaine / A Remark You Made / Layla / Crossroads / Sunshine of Your Love

18 February 1991, Royal Albert Hall, London

"Pretending," "Bad Love," "Old Love," and "Wonderful Tonight" from this show can be found on *24 Nights* 2CD set Duck Records released October 1991. "No Alibis," "I Shot The Sheriff," and "Cocaine" were released on various CD singles of "Wonderful Tonight."

SETLIST: Pretending / No Alibis / Running On Faith / I Shot The Sheriff / White Room / Can't Find My Way Home / Bad Love / Before You Accuse Me / Old Love / Badge / Wonderful Tonight / Thank You (Falettinme Be Mice Elf Agin) / Cocaine / A Remark You Made / Layla / Crossroads / Sunshine of Your Love

19 February 1991, Royal Albert Hall, London

SETLIST: Pretending / No Alibis / Running On Faith / I Shot The Sheriff / White Room / Can't Find My Way Home / Bad Love / Before You Accuse Me / Old Love / Badge / Wonderful Tonight / Thank You (Falettinme Be Mice Elf Agin) / Cocaine / A Remark You Made / Layla / Crossroads / Sunshine of Your Love

20 February 1991–21 February 1991, blues rehearsals, Bray Studios, Windsor, Berkshire
22 February 1991, day off

BLUES NIGHTS 1991

BAND LINEUP:
Eric Clapton: guitar, vocals
Jimmie Vaughan: guitar, vocals
Chuck Leavell: keyboards

Jerry Portnoy: harmonica
Joey Spampinato: bass
Jamie Oldaker: drums
Johnnie Johnson: piano, vocals[1]
Albert Collins: guitar, vocals[2]
Robert Cray: guitar, vocals[3]
Buddy Guy: guitar, vocals[4]

23 February 1991, Royal Albert Hall, London

SETLIST: Watch Yourself / Hoodoo Man / Hideaway / Standing Around Crying / All Your Love / Have You Ever Loved A Woman / That's All Right / Key To The Highway / Wee Wee Baby / Johnnie's Boogie[1] / Tanqueray[1] / Travelin' South[2] / Lights Are On But Nobody's Home[2] / Black Cat Bone[2] / I've Been Abused[2, 3] / Reconsider Baby[2, 3] / Stranger Blues[2, 3] / Hoochie Coochie Man[2, 3, 4] / Little By Little[2, 3, 4] / My Time After A While[2, 3, 4] / Sweet Home Chicago[2, 3, 4]

24 February 1991, Royal Albert Hall, London

SETLIST: Watch Yourself / Hoodoo Man / Hideaway / Standing Around Crying / All Your Love / Have You Ever Loved A Woman / That's All Right / Key To The Highway / Wee Wee Baby / Johnnie's Boogie[1] / Tanqueray[1] / Travelin' South[2] / Lights Are On But Nobody's Home[2] / Black Cat Bone[2] / I've Been Abused[2, 3] / Reconsider Baby[2, 3] / Stranger Blues[2, 3] / Hoochie Coochie Man[2, 3, 4] / Little By Little[2, 3, 4] / My Time After A While[2, 3, 4] / Sweet Home Chicago[2, 3, 4] Stranger Blues[1, 2] / Hoochie Coochie Man[1, 2, 3] / Little By Little[1, 2, 3] / My Time After A While[1, 2, 3] / Sweet Home Chicago[1, 2, 3]

25 February 1991, Royal Albert Hall, London

Complete show broadcast on BBC Radio 1.

SETLIST: Watch Yourself / Hoodoo Man / Hideaway / Standing Around Crying / All Your Love / Have You Ever Loved A Woman / That's All Right / Key To The Highway / Wee Wee Baby / Johnnie's Boogie[1] / Tanqueray[1] / Travelin' South[2] / Lights Are On But Nobody's Home[2] / Black Cat Bone[2] / I've Been Abused[2, 3] / Reconsider Baby[2, 3] / Stranger Blues[2, 3] / Hoochie Coochie Man[2, 3, 4] / Little By Little[2, 3, 4] / My Time After A While[2, 3, 4] / Sweet Home Chicago[2, 3, 4]

26 February 1991, day off

27 February 1991, Royal Albert Hall, London

SETLIST: Watch Yourself / Hoodoo Man / Hideaway / Standing Around Crying / All Your Love / Have You Ever Loved A Woman / That's All Right / Key To The Highway / Wee Wee Baby / Johnnie's Boogie[1] / Tanqueray[1] / Travelin' South[2] / Lights Are On But Nobody's Home[2] / Black Cat Bone[2] / I've Been Abused[2, 3] / Reconsider Baby[2, 3] / Stranger Blues[2, 3] / Hoochie Coochie Man[2, 3, 4] / Little By Little[2, 3, 4] / My Time After A While[2, 3, 4] / Sweet Home Chicago[2, 3, 4]

28 February 1991, Royal Albert Hall, London

"Hoodoo Man" from this show can be found on *24 Nights* 2CD set Duck Records released October 1991.

SETLIST: Watch Yourself / Hoodoo Man / Hideaway / Standing Around Crying / All Your Love / Have You Ever Loved A Woman / That's All Right / Key To The Highway / Wee Wee Baby / Johnnie's Boogie[1] / Tanqueray[1] / Travelin' South[2] / Lights Are On But Nobody's Home[2] / Black Cat Bone[2] / I've Been Abused[2, 3] / Reconsider Baby[2, 3] / Stranger Blues[2, 3] / Hoochie Coochie Man[2, 3, 4] / Little By Little[2, 3, 4] / My Time After A While[2, 3, 4] / Sweet Home Chicago[2, 3, 4]

MARCH 1991

1 March 1991, Royal Albert Hall, London

SETLIST: Watch Yourself / Hoodoo Man / Hideaway / Standing Around Crying / All Your Love / Have You Ever Loved A Woman / That's All Right / Key To The Highway / Wee Wee Baby / Johnnie's Boogie[1] / Tanqueray[1] / Travelin' South[2] / Lights Are On But Nobody's Home[2] / Black Cat Bone[2] / I've Been Abused[2, 3] / Reconsider Baby[2, 3] / Stranger Blues[2, 3] / Hoochie Coochie Man[2, 3, 4] / Little By Little[2, 3, 4] / My Time After A While[2, 3, 4] / Sweet Home Chicago[2, 3, 4]

2 March 1991, day off

ORCHESTRA NIGHTS 1991

BAND LINEUP:
Eric Clapton: guitar, vocals
Steve Ferrone: drums
Nathan East: bass
Phil Palmer: guitar

Chuck Leavell: keyboards
Greg Phillinganes: keyboards
Ray Cooper: percussion
Tessa Niles: backing vocals
Katie Kissoon: backing vocals
National Philharmonic Orchestra
Michael Kamen: conductor

3 March 1991, Royal Albert Hall, London

SETLIST: Crossroads / Bell Bottom Blues / Holy Mother / I Shot The Sheriff / Hard Times / Can't Find My Way Home / Edge Of Darkness / Old Love / Wonderful Tonight / White Room / Concerto For Electric Guitar / Layla / Sunshine Of Your Love

4 March 1991, Royal Albert Hall, London

Eric Clapton during the Orchestra Nights, March 1991.

SETLIST: Crossroads / Bell Bottom Blues / Holy Mother / I Shot The Sheriff / Hard Times / Can't Find My Way Home / Edge Of Darkness / Old Love / Wonderful Tonight / White Room / Concerto For Electric Guitar / Layla / Sunshine Of Your Love

5 March 1991, Royal Albert Hall, London

SETLIST: Crossroads / Bell Bottom Blues / Holy Mother / I Shot The Sheriff / Hard Times / Can't Find My Way Home / Edge Of Darkness / Old Love / Wonderful Tonight / White Room / Concerto For Electric Guitar / Layla / Sunshine Of Your Love

6 March 1991, day off

7 March 1991, Royal Albert Hall, London

SETLIST: Crossroads / Bell Bottom Blues / Holy Mother / I Shot The Sheriff / Hard Times / Can't Find My Way Home / Edge Of Darkness / Old Love / Wonderful

Tonight / White Room / Concerto For Electric Guitar / Layla / Sunshine Of Your Love

8 March 1991, Royal Albert Hall, London

"Edge of Darkness" from this show can be found on *24 Nights* 2CD set Duck Records released October 1991.

SETLIST: Crossroads / Bell Bottom Blues / Holy Mother / I Shot The Sheriff / Hard Times / Can't Find My Way Home / Edge Of Darkness / Old Love / Wonderful Tonight / White Room / Concerto For Electric Guitar / Layla / Sunshine Of Your Love

9 March 1991, Royal Albert Hall, London

SETLIST: Crossroads / Bell Bottom Blues / Holy Mother / I Shot The Sheriff / Hard Times / Can't Find My Way Home / Edge Of Darkness / Old Love / Wonderful Tonight / White Room / Concerto For Electric Guitar / Layla / Sunshine Of Your Love

> **"**All twenty-four nights were recorded but memory fails on which takes were used from which nights. We brought in a facility from New York in cases and set up in the basement under the stage. John Harris was the engineer. The album was mixed in New York City at the Power Station by Alex Haas.**"**
>
> **—RUSS TITELMAN**

SEPTEMBER 1991

4 September 1991, Roxy Los Angeles, California (Eric joins Buddy Guy for a jam)

SUNDAY COMICS 1991

26 September 1991, *Sunday Comics,* Palace, Hollywood, Los Angeles, California (Eric joins the house band from this popular comedy variety show. The musical director of the house band is Nathan East, Eric's bass player. The show is broadcast 29 September 1991. They play "Further On Up The Road")

HOUSE BAND LINEUP:
Nathan East: bass
Michael Thompson: guitar

Randy Waldman: keyboards
Mike Baird: drums
Danny Pelfry: saxophone

DECEMBER 1991

ROCK LEGENDS TOUR WITH GEORGE HARRISON 1991

George was not fond of touring, especially since he had lost his voice on his 1974 U.S. tour. Other than the occasional guest appearance, he had not toured since then. Eric helped persuade him to try again and suggested Japan as a good place to tour with respectful and appreciative audiences. He also offered to back George with his band. George agreed and a tour was announced to huge worldwide acclaim. Sadly, other than a one-off show at the Royal Albert Hall, George did not tour again. Luckily, we have a well-recorded double live album as a permanent souvenir from the tour. Although not included on the album, Eric played a mini set of hits in the middle of each show.

EQUIPMENT USED ON THE TOUR

GEORGE HARRISON

GUITARS:
Roy Buchanan / Bluesmaster electric guitar No. 6 by Fliz Bros.

Fender unknown 12-string electric guitar (gold)

Fender / Stratocaster Eric Clapton Model (red)

Gibson / Les Paul Standard '60

Gibson / J-2000 custom acoustic guitar

AMPLIFIER:
Fender / Bassman (re-issue model)

EFFECTS:
James Demeter / Tube Direct

MXR / Dynacomp

Boss / CE3 Chorus

Ibanez / Tube Screamer

Ibanez / Digital Delay

ERIC CLAPTON

GUITARS:
Fender / Stratocaster Eric Clapton Model (black)

Gibson / J-185 acoustic

AMPLIFIER:
Soldano / Amplifier (Marshall cabinets with electro-voice speakers)

EFFECTS:
Tri Stereo Chorus Model 618

TC Electronics / 2290

Pete Conish Rack

PA SYSTEM:
Showco / Prism System 5-way speaker

Macro-Teck / 2400 power amp

Showco / Custom 5-way Original Crossover Network

Showco / DG-4023 equalizer

Aphex noise gate limiter

BSS / DPR402 and dbx / 903 compresser and limiter

Showco / Original 32ch + 20ch mixer

BAND LINEUP:
George Harrison: guitar, vocals
Eric Clapton: guitar, vocals
Nathan East: bass, vocals
Steve Ferrone: drums
Chuck Leavell: keyboards
Greg Phillinganes: keyboards
Ray Cooper: percussion
Andy Fairweather Low: guitar
Katie Kissoon: backing vocals
Tessa Niles: backing vocals

1 December 1991, Yokohama Arena, Yokohama, Japan

SETLIST: I Want To Tell You / Old Brown Shoe / Taxman / Give Me Love (Give Me Peace On Earth) / If I Needed Someone / Something / Fish On The Sand / Love Comes To Everyone / What Is Life / Dark Horse / Piggies / Pretending / Old Love / Badge / Wonderful Tonight / Got My Mind Set On You / Cloud Nine / Here Comes The Sun

/ My Sweet Lord / All Those Years Ago / Cheer Down / Devil's Radio / Isn't It A Pity / While My Guitar Gently Weeps / Roll Over Beethoven

2 December 1991, Castle Hall, Osaka, Japan

SETLIST: I Want To Tell You / Old Brown Shoe / Taxman / Give Me Love (Give Me Peace On Earth) / If I Needed Someone / Something / Fish On The Sand / What Is Life / Dark Horse / Piggies / Pretending / Old Love / Badge / Wonderful Tonight / Got My Mind Set On You / Cloud Nine / Here Comes The Sun / My Sweet Lord / All Those Years Ago / Cheer Down / Devil's Radio / Isn't It A Pity / While My Guitar Gently Weeps / Roll Over Beethoven

3 December 1991, Castle Hall, Osaka, Japan

SETLIST: I Want To Tell You / Old Brown Shoe / Taxman / Give Me Love (Give Me Peace On Earth) / If I Needed Someone / Something / What Is Life / Dark Horse / Piggies / Pretending / Old Love / Badge / Wonderful Tonight / Got My Mind Set On You / Cloud Nine / Here Comes The Sun / My Sweet Lord / All Those Years Ago / Cheer Down / Devil's Radio / Isn't It A Pity / While My Guitar Gently Weeps / Roll Over Beethoven

5 December 1991, Nagoya International Showcase Hall, Nagoya, Japan

SETLIST: I Want To Tell You / Old Brown Shoe / Taxman / Give Me Love (Give Me Peace On Earth) / If I Needed Someone / Something / What Is Life / Dark Horse / Piggies / Pretending / Old Love / Badge / Wonderful Tonight / Got My Mind Set On You / Cloud Nine / Here Comes The Sun / My Sweet Lord / All Those Years Ago / Cheer Down / Devil's Radio / Isn't It A Pity / While My Guitar Gently Weeps / Roll Over Beethoven

6 December 1991, Hiroshima Sun Plaza, Hiroshima, Japan

SETLIST: I Want To Tell You / Old Brown Shoe / Taxman / Give Me Love (Give Me Peace On Earth) / If I Needed Someone / Something / What Is Life / Dark Horse / Piggies / Pretending / Old Love / Badge / Wonderful Tonight / Got My Mind Set On You / Cloud Nine / Here Comes The Sun / My Sweet Lord / All Those Years Ago / Cheer Down / Devil's Radio / Isn't It A Pity / While My Guitar Gently Weeps / Roll Over Beethoven

9 December 1991, Fukuoka International Center Hall, Fukuoka, Japan

SETLIST: I Want To Tell You / Old Brown Shoe / Taxman / Give Me Love (Give Me Peace On Earth) / If I Needed Someone / Something / What Is Life / Dark Horse / Piggies / Pretending / Old Love / Badge / Wonderful Tonight / Got My Mind Set On You / Cloud Nine / Here Comes The Sun / My Sweet Lord / All Those Years Ago / Cheer Down / Devil's Radio / Isn't It A Pity / While My Guitar Gently Weeps / Roll Over Beethoven

10 December 1991, Castle Hall, Osaka, Japan

SETLIST: I Want To Tell You / Old Brown Shoe / Taxman / Give Me Love (Give Me Peace On Earth) / If I Needed Someone / Something / What Is Life / Dark Horse / Piggies / Pretending / Old Love / Badge / Wonderful Tonight / Got My Mind Set On You / Cloud Nine / Here Comes The Sun / My Sweet Lord / All Those Years Ago / Cheer Down / Devil's Radio / Isn't It A Pity / While My Guitar Gently Weeps / Roll Over Beethoven

11 December 1991, Castle Hall, Osaka, Japan

SETLIST:

I Want To Tell You (George Harrison) unreleased

Old Brown Shoe (George Harrison) unreleased

Taxman (George Harrison) unreleased

Give Me Love (Give Me Peace On Earth) (George Harrison) unreleased

If I Needed Someone (George Harrsion) *George Harrison Live In Japan* 2CD Dark Horse 94665 released July 1992

Something (George Harrison) unreleased

What Is Life (George Harrison) unreleased

Dark Horse (George Harrison) *George Harrison Live In Japan* 2CD Dark Horse 94665 released July 1992

Piggies (George Harrison) unreleased

Pretending (Jerry Williams) unreleased

Old Love (Eric Clapton, Robert Cray) unreleased

Badge (Eric Clapton, George Harrison) unreleased

Wonderful Tonight (Eric Clapton) unreleased

Got My Mind Set On You (Rudy Clark) unreleased

Cloud Nine (George Harrison) unreleased

Here Comes The Sun (George Harrison) unreleased

My Sweet Lord (George Harrison) unreleased

All Those Years Ago (George Harrison) unreleased

Cheer Down (George Harrison, Tom Petty) unreleased

Devil's Radio (George Harrison) unreleased

Isn't It A Pity (George Harrison) unreleased

While My Guitar Gently Weeps (George Harrison) unreleased

Roll Over Beethoven (Chuck Berry) unreleased

12 December 1991, Castle Hall, Osaka, Japan

SETLIST:

I Want To Tell You (George Harrison) unreleased

Old Brown Shoe (George Harrison) unreleased

Taxman (George Harrison) unreleased

Give Me Love (Give Me Peace On Earth) (George Harrison) unreleased

If I Needed Someone (George Harrsion) unreleased

Something (George Harrison) *George Harrison Live In Japan* 2CD Dark Horse 94665 released July 1992

What Is Life (George Harrison) unreleased

Dark Horse (George Harrison) unreleased

Piggies (George Harrison) unreleased

Pretending (Jerry Williams)

Old Love (Eric Clapton / Robert Cray) unreleased

Badge (Eric Clapton / George Harrison) unreleased

Wonderful Tonight (Eric Clapton) unreleased

Got My Mind Set On You (Rudy Clark) unreleased

Cloud Nine (George Harrison) unreleased

Here Comes The Sun (George Harrison) *George Harrison Live In Japan* 2CD Dark Horse 94665 released July 1992

My Sweet Lord (George Harrison) unreleased

All Those Years Ago (George Harrison) unreleased

Cheer Down (George Harrison, Tom Petty) unreleased

Devil's Radio (George Harrison) unreleased

Isn't It A Pity (George Harrison) unreleased

While My Guitar Gently Weeps (George Harrison) unreleased

Roll Over Beethoven (Chuck Berry) unreleased

14 December 1991, Tokyo Dome, Tokyo, Japan

SETLIST:

I Want To Tell You (George Harrison) unreleased

Old Brown Shoe (George Harrison) unreleased

Taxman (George Harrison) unreleased

Give Me Love (Give Me Peace On Earth) (George Harrison) unreleased

If I Needed Someone (George Harrison) unreleased

Something (George Harrison) unreleased

What Is Life (George Harrison) unreleased

Dark Horse (George Harrison) unreleased

Piggies (George Harrison) unreleased

Pretending (Jerry Williams) unreleased

Old Love (Eric Clapton, Robert Cray) unreleased

Badge (Eric Clapton, George Harrison) unreleased

Wonderful Tonight (Eric Clapton) unreleased

Got My Mind Set On You (Rudy Clark) unreleased

Cloud Nine (George Harrison) unreleased

Here Comes The Sun (George Harrison) unreleased

My Sweet Lord (George Harrison) unreleased

All Those Years Ago (George Harrison) unreleased

Cheer Down (George Harrison, Tom Petty) unreleased

Devil's Radio (George Harrison) unreleased

Isn't It A Pity (George Harrison) unreleased

While My Guitar Gently Weeps (George Harrison) (composite of this night and 17 December 1991 on *George Harrison Live In Japan* 2CD Dark Horse 94665 released July 1992

Roll Over Beethoven (Chuck Berry) unreleased

15 December 1991, Tokyo Dome, Tokyo, Japan

SETLIST:

I Want To Tell You (George Harrison) *George Harrison Live In Japan* 2CD Dark Horse 94665 released July 1992

Old Brown Shoe (George Harrison) unreleased

Taxman (George Harrison) *George Harrison Live In Japan* 2CD Dark Horse 94665 released July 1992

Give Me Love (Give Me Peace On Earth) (George Harrison) *George Harrison Live In Japan* 2CD Dark Horse 94665 released July 1992

If I Needed Someone (George Harrison) unreleased

Something (George Harrison) unreleased

What Is Life (George Harrison) unreleased

Dark Horse (George Harrison) unreleased

Piggies (George Harrison) *George Harrison Live In Japan* 2CD Dark Horse 94665 released July 1992

Pretending (Jerry Williams) unreleased

Old Love (Eric Clapton / Robert Cray) unreleased

Badge (Eric Clapton / George Harrison) unreleased

Wonderful Tonight (Eric Clapton) unreleased

Got My Mind Set On You (Rudy Clark) *George Harrison Live In Japan* 2CD Dark Horse 94665 released July 1992

Cloud Nine (George Harrison) *George Harrison Live In Japan* 2CD Dark Horse 94665 released July 1992

Here Comes The Sun (George Harrison) unreleased

My Sweet Lord (George Harrison) *George Harrison Live In Japan* 2CD Dark Horse 94665 released July 1992

All Those Years Ago (George Harrison) *George Harrison Live In Japan* 2CD Dark Horse 94665 released July 1992

Cheer Down (George Harrison / Tom Petty) *George Harrison Live In Japan* 2CD Dark Horse 94665 released July 1992

Devil's Radio (George Harrison) *George Harrison Live In Japan* 2CD Dark Horse 94665 released July 1992

Isn't It A Pity (George Harrison) *George Harrison Live In Japan* 2CD Dark Horse 94665 released July 1992

While My Guitar Gently Weeps (George Harrison)

Roll Over Beethoven (Chuck Berry) *George Harrison Live In Japan* 2CD Dark Horse 94665 released July 1992

17 December 1991, Tokyo Dome, Tokyo, Japan

SETLIST:

I Want To Tell You (George Harrison) unreleased

Old Brown Shoe (George Harrison) *George Harrison Live In Japan* 2CD Dark Horse 94665 released July 1992

Taxman (George Harrison) unreleased

Give Me Love (Give Me Peace On Earth) (George Harrison) unreleased

If I Needed Someone (George Harrison) unreleased

Something (George Harrison) unreleased

What Is Life (George Harrison) *George Harrison Live In Japan* 2CD Dark Horse 94665 released July 1992

Dark Horse (George Harrison) unreleased

Piggies (George Harrison) unreleased

Pretending (Jerry Williams) unreleased

Old Love (Eric Clapton, Robert Cray) unreleased

Badge (Eric Clapton, George Harrison) unreleased

Wonderful Tonight (Eric Clapton) unreleased

Got My Mind Set On You (Rudy Clark) unreleased

Cloud Nine (George Harrison) unreleased

Here Comes The Sun (George Harrison) unreleased

My Sweet Lord (George Harrison) unreleased

All Those Years Ago (George Harrison) unreleased

Cheer Down (George Harrison, Tom Petty) unreleased

Devil's Radio (George Harrison) unreleased

Isn't It A Pity (George Harrison) unreleased

While My Guitar Gently Weeps (George Harrison) composite of this night and 14 December 1991 on *George Harrison Live In Japan* 2CD Dark Horse 94665 released July 1992

Roll Over Beethoven (Chuck Berry) unreleased

RECORDING SESSIONS 1991
ABBEY ROAD STUDIOS
3 Abbey Road, London
Session for "Concerto for Electric Guitar"

MARCH 1991

Several attempts were made to record a studio version of the "Concerto For Electric Guitar," but for Eric at least, the moment had passed and the project was abandoned and never revisited.

CONCERTO FOR ELECTRIC GUITAR unreleased

Producer: Michael Kamen

ERIC CLAPTON GUEST SESSION

BATTERY STUDIOS
1 Maybury Gardens, London
Session for Buddy Guy

MARCH 1991

This was one of the first albums John Porter produced after moving to America in 1990, even though the album ended up being recorded in London, and it secured him his first Grammy Award. Hard to believe now, but Buddy's career was in the doldrums at this point and he needed a great album to bring him back to the attention of the critics and record-buying public. John felt the album should have some high-profile guests to help raise awareness of the release. Eric was an obvious choice as he was a friend of Buddy's and had played with him on several occasions in London as well as in Chicago and was on board straight away.

Buddy was in town as he was appearing with Eric at the Royal Albert Hall during the blues nights. It made sense to record the album at that point. Jeff Beck and Mark Knopfler also lent their talents to the album which went on to sell over a million copies and revitalized Buddy's career. He continues to amaze and thrill crowds wherever he plays.

EARLY IN THE MORNING (Leo Hickman / Louis Jordan / Dallas Bartley) *Damn Right I've Got The Blues* CD Silvertone ORE 516 released 1991

Buddy Guy: vocals, guitar
Eric Clapton: guitar
Jeff Beck: guitar
Neil Hubbard: guitar
Pete Wingfield: piano
Mick Weaver: organ
Greg Rzab: bass
Richie Hayward: drums
Andre Love: trumpet
Wayne Jackson: saxophone

Producer: John Porter
Engineer: Tony Platt

ERIC CLAPTON GUEST SESSION

NOMIS STUDIOS
45-53 Sinclair Road, Barons Court, London
Session for Johnnie Johnson

MARCH 1991

Eric overdubs his guitar on two tracks for Johnnie Johnson's album.

CREEK MUD (Johnnie Johnson / Tom Ardolino) *Johnnie B Bad* CD Nonesuch released 1992.

BLUES #572 (Johnnie Johnson) *Johnnie B Bad* Nonesuch CD released 1992

Johnnie Johnson: piano, vocals
Eric Clapton: guitar
Joey Spampinato: bass, background vocals
Bernie Worrell: keyboard
Steve Ferguson: guitar, vocals
Tom Ardolino: drums

Producer: Terry Adams
Engineer: Ted Mayton

ERIC CLAPTON GUEST SESSION

TOWN HOUSE STUDIOS
150 Goldhawk Road, London
Session for Richie Sambora

MARCH 1991

Eric overdubs a solo on "Mr. Bluesman" in London for Richie Sambora's solo album.

MR. BLUESMAN (Richie Sambora) *Stranger In This Town* CD Mercury 848 895-2 released 1991

Richie Sambora, lead guitarist with Bon Jovi, had met Eric Clapton at the International Rock Awards in June 1990. He mentioned to Eric how he had been a huge influence on him in his own musical upbringing. A few months later, when Sambora started working on his first solo album, *Stranger In This Town,* his partner encouraged him to contact Eric Clapton about guesting on a track he had written about a young boy wanting to be a guitar player. The number was called "Mr Bluesman" and was also about Richie wanting to be like Eric. He decided to send Eric a demo of the song along with a heartfelt letter which in part included the following compelling words: "I had to ask you to be on my first solo record because if you had the chance to ask Robert Johnson to be on your first record, I'm sure you would have."

> **❝**Richie came to London with the tape, and I showed up at the studio. He gave me a gift, which was a massive 12-string Taylor guitar with my name on it. It was magnificent. Then he put the tape on, and I realized instantly that I was completely out of my depth. The song wasn't what I expected it to be, and I had to sit down and go down to the bottom of my socks and pull up whatever I had to make it work. It took hours, and I sweated buckets. He was sitting there, watching me go through this. It was the kind of thing you would like to go off and do in private, because you're going to make all your worst mistakes right there in front of everybody. Reality comes in the door.**❞**
>
> **—ERIC CLAPTON**
> (*Rolling Stone,* 17 October 1991)

THE VILLAGE RECORDER 1616 Butler Avenue, Los Angeles, California Session for *Rush* soundtrack

AUGUST 1991

NEW RECRUIT *Rush* soundtrack CD Reprise 9 26794 released 1992

TRACKS AND LINES *Rush* soundtrack CD Reprise 9 26794 released 1992

REALIZATION *Rush* soundtrack CD Reprise 9 26794 released 1992

KRISTEN AND JIM *Rush* soundtrack CD Reprise 9 26794 released 1992

PRELUDE FUGUE *Rush* soundtrack CD Reprise 9 26794 released 1992

COLD TURKEY *Rush* soundtrack CD Reprise 9 26794 released 1992

WILL GAINES *Rush* soundtrack CD Reprise 9 26794 released 1992 (arranged by Eric Clapton, Randy Kerber, and Russ Titelman)

HELP ME UP (Eric Clapton / Will Jennings) *Rush* soundtrack CD Reprise 9 26794 released 1992

Eric Clapton: guitar, vocals
Randy Kerber: organ

Nathan East: bass
Steve Ferone: drums
Lenny Castro: percussion
Greg Phillinganes: piano
Bill Champlin: backing vocals
Jenni Muldaur: backing vocals
Lani Groves: backing vocals
Vaneese Thomas: backing vocals

DOUBLE TROUBLE (Otis Rush) unreleased

HOOCHIE COOCHIE MAN (Willie Dixon) unreleased

DON'T KNOW WHICH WAY TO GO (Al Perkins / Willie Dixon) *Rush* soundtrack CD Reprise 9 26794 released 1992

Eric Clapton: guitar
Buddy Guy: guitar, vocals
Greg Phillinganes: organ
Nathan East: bass
Steve Ferrone: drums
Chuck Leavell: piano

TEARS IN HEAVEN (Eric Clapton / Will Jennings) *Rush* soundtrack CD Reprise 9 26794 released 1992

Eric Clapton: guitar, Dobro, vocals
Jimmy Bralower: drum machine
Gayle Levant: Celtic harp
Jay Dee Maness: pedal steel guitar
Randy Kerber: synthesizer
Nathan East: bass
Lenny Castro: percussion

Producer: Russ Titelman
Engineers: Ed Cherney / Jeff DeMorris

> **❝**One of the assistants at Village had the machine in 'safe' when they were doing either 'Hoochie Coochie Man' or 'Double Trouble' (or both). The only sound that exists is on a video somewhere. Those performances were mighty.
>
> 'Tears In Heaven' was completed when we were recording the *Rush* soundtrack and used specifically for the movie. Eventually the unplugged version overshadowed the original recording which won the Grammy for Record of the Year off of the *Rush* soundtrack while the *Unplugged* album won for Album of the Year—so we actually won Grammys on two different albums from the same artist in the same year. I think that is unprecedented in Grammy history. The other songs were 'Circus Left Town' and 'My Father's Eyes,' but not recorded during that time.**❞**
>
> **—RUSS TITELMAN**

> **"**For *Rush* I've been playing very, very quietly, so if I hit a note and hold it with vibrato you can hear it just sizzling against the fret. But not very loud. You have to strain to hear it. And I love that. It's different from the big, big sound people are more used to. **"**
>
> —ERIC CLAPTON

> **"**There are already six songs which I've started recording in Los Angeles. The songs are about my son. I've three on tape and there are three more. And every day I start to work on other ones. It's happening all the time. I'm writing continually because I need to. This is the way I repair myself from the tragedy.**"**
>
> —ERIC CLAPTON

ERIC CLAPTON GUEST SESSION

ABBEY ROAD STUDIOS
3 Abbey Road, London
Session for Kate Bush

SEPTEMBER 1991

AND SO IS LOVE (Kate Bush) *The Red Shoes* CD EMI CDEMD 1047 released November 1993

Kate Bush: vocals, keyboard
Eric Clapton: guitar
Stuart Elliott: drums
Gary Brooker: Hammond B3 organ
John Giblin: bass

Producer: Kate Bush

VILLAGE RECORDER
1616 Butler Avenue,
Los Angeles, California
Session for new songs

OCTOBER 1991

CIRCUS LEFT TOWN unreleased

MY FATHER'S EYES unreleased

LONELY STRANGER unreleased

Producer: not known
Engineer: not known

ERIC CLAPTON GUEST SESSION

POWER STATION STUDIOS
441 West 53rd Street,
New York City
Session for David Sanborn

NOVEMBER 1991

FULL HOUSE (Marcus Miller / David Sanborn) *Upfront* CD Elektra 7559-61272-2 released 1992

David Sanborn: alto saxophone
Eric Clapton: guitar
Marcus Miller: bass clarinet, keyboards, bass
Steve Jordan: drums
Ricky Peterson: Hammond B3 organ
Chris Bruce: rhythm guitar
Don Alias: congas
John Purcell: tenor saxophone
Randy Brecker: trumpet
Dave Bargeron: trombone

Producer: Marcus Miller
Engineer: Joe Ferla

10

1992

1992

U2's The Edge presented the Yardbirds with their award at the 7th Annual Induction Ceremony for the Rock and Roll Hall of Fame on 15 January. Although he was nominated as a member of the Yardbirds, Eric did not participate at the ceremony as he was committed to record an *MTV Unplugged* show which took place the very next day in England.

The *Unplugged* all-acoustic show, which was filmed and recorded by MTV, took place on Soundstage 1 at Bray Studios in front of a very lucky 300 fans who had won tickets in a competition via BBC's Radio 1. The resultant album proved to be a huge success and helped put the *MTV Unplugged* format on the map.

A sold-out UK tour followed, culminating in Eric's sixth season of concerts at the Royal Albert Hall. Buoyed by the success of the unplugged format, this year Eric introduced a sit-down set of acoustic numbers which included the huge worldwide hit "Tears In Heaven." A long two-part U.S. tour followed, in the middle of which Eric did a stadium tour of the UK and Europe with Elton John on a double headliner basis. Eric was back in America in August with Elton John in tow for several shows as in Europe.

Eric was in Los Angeles on 9 September to receive an MTV Best Video Award for "Tears In Heaven." Eric, backed by his band, played the song live. Another big event was playing at Bob Dylan's 30th Anniversary Concert at New York's Madison Square Garden on 16 October. The concert also featured Neil Young, Roger McGuinn, George Harrison, Tracy Chapman, and The Band among many others.

JANUARY 1992

MTV UNPLUGGED 1992

16 January 1992, Soundstage 1, Bray Studios, Windsor, Berkshire

Eric plays an unplugged performance for MTV which would prove to be a spectacular success.

BAND LINEUP:
Eric Clapton: guitar, vocals
Andy Fairweather Low: guitar
Nathan East: bass
Steve Ferrone: drums
Chuck Leavell: keyboards
Ray Cooper: percussion
Tessa Niles: backing vocals
Katie Kissoon: backing vocals

SETLIST:

Signe (Eric Clapton) unreleased

Before You Accuse Me (Ellas MCDaniel) *Unplugged* CD Reprise US 9 45024-2 / UK 9362-45024-2 released August 1992

Hey Hey (Big Bill Broonzy) *Unplugged* CD Reprise US 9 45024-2 / UK 9362-45024-2 released August 1992

Tears In Heaven (Eric Clapton / Will Jennings) unreleased

Circus Has Left Town (Eric Clapton) unplugged television broadcast only

Lonely Stranger (Eric Clapton) *Unplugged* CD Reprise US 9 45024-2 / UK 9362-45024-2 released August 1992

Nobody Knows You When You're Down And Out (Jimmy Cox) *Unplugged* CD Reprise US 9 45024-2 / UK 9362-45024-2 released August 1992

Layla (Eric Clapton / Jim Gordon) *Unplugged* CD Reprise US 9 45024-2 / UK 9362-45024-2 released August 1992

Signe (Take 2) (Eric Clapton) unreleased

My Father's Eyes (Eric Clapton) unreleased

Running On Faith (Jerry Lynn Williams)

Walkin' Blues (Robert Johnson)

Alberta (traditional) *Unplugged* CD Reprise US 9 45024-2 / UK 9362-45024-2 released August 1992

San Francisco Bay Blues (Jesse Fuller) unreleased

Malted Milk (Robert Johnson) unreleased

Signe (Take 3) (Eric Clapton) *Unplugged* CD Reprise US 9 45024-2 / UK 9362-45024-2 released August 1992

Tears In Heaven (Take 2) (Eric Clapton / Will Jennings) *Unplugged* CD Reprise US 9 45024-2 / UK 9362-45024-2 released August 1992

My Father's Eyes (Take 2) (Eric Clapton) *Unplugged* CD Reprise US 9 45024-2 / UK 9362-45024-2 released August 1992

Rollin' And Tumblin' (Muddy Waters) *Unplugged* CD Reprise US 9 45024-2 / UK 9362-45024-2 released August 1992

Running On Faith (Take 2) (Jerry Lynn Williams) *Unplugged* CD Reprise US 9 45024-2 / UK 9362-45024-2 released August 1992

Walkin' Blues (Take 2) (Robert Johnson) *Unplugged* CD Reprise US 9 45024-2 / UK 9362-45024-2 released August 1992

San Francisco Bay Blues (Take 2) (Jesse Fuller) *Unplugged* CD Reprise US 9 45024-2 / UK 9362-45024-2 released August 1992

Malted Milk (Take 2) (Robert Johnson) *Unplugged* CD Reprise US 9 45024-2 / UK 9362-45024-2 released August 1992

Worried Life Blues (Big Maceo Merriweather) unreleased

Old Love (Eric Clapton / Robert Cray) *Unplugged* CD Reprise US 9 45024-2 / UK 9362-45024-2 released August 1992

> "Eric didn't want it released because it wasn't intended for a CD release. I think he felt he might have done some things differently had he had that in mind. We know the result. We ran the show and then did the second half over. We used the first half of Take 1 and the second half from the redo. 'Rollin' and Tumblin'" was just a jam they played during the break between takes. Luckily we pushed 'record' on the tape machine.**"**
>
> **—RUSS TITELMAN**

U.K. TOUR 1992

BAND LINEUP:
Eric Clapton: guitar, vocals
Andy Fairweather Low: guitar
Nathan East: bass
Steve Ferrone: drums
Chuck Leavell: keyboards
Ray Cooper: percussion
Tessa Niles: backing vocals
Katie Kissoon: backing vocals

Eric Clapton at the Brighton Centre, Brighton, East Sussex, 1 February 1992.

FEBRUARY 1992

1 February 1992, Brighton Centre, Brighton, East Sussex

SETLIST: Anything For Your Love / Pretending / I Shot The Sheriff / Running On Faith / My Father's Eyes / She's Waiting / Circus Left Town / Tears In Heaven / Signe / Before You Accuse Me / Old Love / Badge / Wonderful Tonight / Tearing Us Apart / Layla / Crossroads / Sunshine Of Your Love

3 February 1992, National Indoor Arena, Birmingham

SETLIST: Anything For Your Love / Pretending / I Shot The Sheriff / Running On Faith / My Father's Eyes / She's

Waiting / Circus Left Town / Tears In Heaven / Signe / Before You Accuse Me / Old Love / Badge / Wonderful Tonight / Tearing Us Apart / Layla / Crossroads / Sunshine Of Your Love

4 February 1992, National Indoor Arena, Birmingham

SETLIST: She's Waiting / Anything For Your Love / I Shot The Sheriff / Running On Faith / My Father's Eyes / Tearing Us Apart / Circus Left Town / Tears In Heaven / Signe / Pretending / Before You Accuse Me / Old Love / Badge / Wonderful Tonight / White Room / Layla / Crossroads / Sunshine Of Your Love

5 February 1992, National Indoor Arena, Birmingham

SETLIST: She's Waiting / Anything For Your Love / I Shot The Sheriff / Running On Faith / My Father's Eyes / Tearing Us Apart / Circus Left Town / Tears In Heaven / Signe / Before You Accuse Me / Old Love / Badge / Wonderful Tonight / White Room / Layla / Crossroads / Sunshine Of Your Love

7 February 1992, Sheffield Arena, Sheffield, South Yorkshire

SETLIST: She's Waiting / Anything For Your Love / I Shot The Sheriff / Running On Faith / My Father's Eyes / Before You Accuse Me / Circus Left Town / Tears In Heaven / Signe / Tearing Us Apart / Old Love / Badge / Wonderful Tonight / White Room / Layla / Crossroads / Sunshine Of Your Love

8 February 1992, Sheffield Arena, Sheffield, South Yorkshire

SETLIST: White Room / Pretending / Anything For Your Love / I Shot The Sheriff / My Father's Eyes / Running On Faith / She's Waiting / Circus Left Town / Tears In Heaven / Signe / Before You Accuse Me / Tearing Us Apart / Old Love / Badge / Wonderful Tonight / Layla / Crossroads / Sunshine Of Your Love

12 February 1992, Royal Albert Hall, London

SETLIST: White Room / Pretending / Anything For Your Love / Running On Faith / My Father's Eyes / She's Waiting / Circus Left Town / Tears In Heaven / Signe /

Before You Accuse Me / Tearing Us Apart / Old Love / Badge / Wonderful Tonight / Layla / Crossroads / Sunshine Of Your Love

13 February 1992, Royal Albert Hall, London

SETLIST: White Room / Pretending / Anything For Your Love / I Shot The Sheriff / Running On Faith / My Father's Eyes / She's Waiting / Circus Has Left Town / Tears In Heaven / Signe / Malted Milk / Nobody Knows You When You're Down And Out / Tearing Us Apart / Before You Accuse Me / Old Love / Badge / Wonderful Tonight / Layla / Crossroads / Sunshine Of Your Love

14 February 1992, Royal Albert Hall, London

SETLIST: White Room / Pretending / Anything For Your Love / I Shot The Sheriff / Running On Faith / My Father's Eyes / She's Waiting / Circus Has Left Town / Tears In Heaven / Signe / Malted Milk / Nobody Knows You When You're Down And Out / Tearing Us Apart / Before You Accuse Me / Old Love / Badge / Wonderful Tonight / Layla / Crossroads / Sunshine Of Your Love

16 February 1992, Royal Albert Hall, London

SETLIST: White Room / Pretending / Anything For Your Love / I Shot The Sheriff / Running On Faith / My Father's Eyes / She's Waiting / Circus Has Left Town / Tears In Heaven / Signe / Malted Milk / Nobody Knows You When You're Down And Out / Tearing Us Apart / Before You Accuse Me / Old Love / Badge / Wonderful Tonight / Layla / Crossroads / Sunshine Of Your Love

17 February 1992, Royal Albert Hall, London

SETLIST: White Room / Pretending / Anything For Your Love / I Shot The Sheriff / Running On Faith / My Father's Eyes / She's Waiting / Circus Has Left Town / Tears In Heaven / Signe / Malted Milk / Nobody Knows You When You're Down And Out / Tearing Us Apart / Before You Accuse Me / Old Love / Badge / Wonderful Tonight / Layla / Crossroads / Sunshine Of Your Love

18 February 1992, Royal Albert Hall, London

SETLIST: White Room / Pretending / Anything For Your Love / I Shot The Sheriff / Running On Faith / My

Father's Eyes / She's Waiting / Circus Has Left Town / Tears In Heaven / Signe / Malted Milk / Nobody Knows You When You're Down And Out / Tearing Us Apart / Before You Accuse Me / Old Love / Badge / Wonderful Tonight / Layla / Crossroads / Sunshine Of Your Love

22 February 1992, Royal Albert Hall, London

SETLIST: White Room / Pretending / Anything For Your Love / I Shot The Sheriff / Running On Faith / My Father's Eyes / She's Waiting / Circus Has Left Town / Tears In Heaven / Signe / Malted Milk / Nobody Knows You When You're Down And Out / Tearing Us Apart / Before You Accuse Me / Old Love / Badge / Wonderful Tonight / Layla / Crossroads / Sunshine Of Your Love

23 February 1992, Royal Albert Hall, London

SETLIST: White Room / Pretending / Anything For Your Love / I Shot The Sheriff / Running On Faith / My Father's Eyes / She's Waiting / Circus Has Left Town / Tears In Heaven / Signe / Malted Milk / Nobody Knows You When You're Down And Out / Tearing Us Apart / Before You Accuse Me / Old Love / Badge / Wonderful Tonight / Layla / Crossroads / Sunshine Of Your Love

24 February 1992, Royal Albert Hall, London

SETLIST: White Room / Pretending / Anything For Your Love / I Shot The Sheriff / Running On Faith / My Father's Eyes / She's Waiting / Circus Has Left Town / Tears In Heaven / Signe / Malted Milk / Nobody Knows You When You're Down And Out / Tearing Us Apart / Before You Accuse Me / Old Love / Badge / Wonderful Tonight / Layla / Crossroads / Sunshine Of Your Love

SUE LAWLEY PROGRAM 1992

25 February 1992, *The Sue Lawley Program,* a Granada Television Production for ITV (Eric Clapton talks to Sue Lawley about his life in music, his battle with drink and drugs, and the death of his son, in whose memory he gives the first TV performance of the song "Tears In Heaven." The program had been filmed at Eric's home in January 1992)

26 February 1992, Royal Albert Hall, London

SETLIST: White Room / Pretending / Anything For Your Love / I Shot The Sheriff / Running On Faith / My Father's Eyes / She's Waiting / Circus Has Left Town / Tears In Heaven / Signe / Malted Milk / Nobody Knows You When You're Down And Out / Tearing Us Apart / Before You Accuse Me / Old Love / Badge / Wonderful Tonight / Layla / Crossroads / Sunshine Of Your Love

27 February 1992, Royal Albert Hall, London

SETLIST: White Room / Pretending / Anything For Your Love / I Shot The Sheriff / Running On Faith / My Father's Eyes / She's Waiting / Circus Has Left Town / Tears In Heaven / Signe / Malted Milk / Nobody Knows You When You're Down And Out / Tearing Us Apart / Before You Accuse Me / Old Love / Badge / Wonderful Tonight / Layla / Crossroads / Sunshine Of Your Love

28 February 1992, Royal Albert Hall, London

SETLIST: White Room / Pretending / Anything For Your Love / I Shot The Sheriff / Running On Faith / My Father's Eyes / She's Waiting / Circus Has Left Town / Tears In Heaven / Signe / Malted Milk / Nobody Knows You When You're Down And Out / Tearing Us Apart / Before You Accuse Me / Old Love / Badge / Wonderful Tonight / Layla / Crossroads / Sunshine Of Your Love

MARCH 1992

2 March 1992, Scottish Exhibition and Conference Centre, Glasgow, Scotland

SETLIST: White Room / Pretending / Anything For Your Love / I Shot The Sheriff / Running On Faith / My Father's Eyes / She's Waiting / Circus Has Left Town / Tears In Heaven / Signe / Malted Milk / Nobody Knows You When You're Down And Out / Tearing Us Apart / Before You Accuse Me / Old Love / Badge / Wonderful Tonight / Layla / Crossroads / Sunshine Of Your Love

3 March 1992, Scottish Exhibition and Conference Centre, Glasgow, Scotland

SETLIST: White Room / Pretending / Anything For Your Love / I Shot The Sheriff / Running On Faith / My Father's Eyes / She's Waiting / Circus Has Left Town /

Tears In Heaven / Signe / Malted Milk / Nobody Knows You When You're Down And Out / Tearing Us Apart / Before You Accuse Me / Old Love / Badge / Wonderful Tonight / Layla / Crossroads / Sunshine Of Your Love

APRIL 1992

U.S. TOUR 1992 (First leg)

BAND LINEUP:
Eric Clapton: guitar, vocals
Andy Fairweather Low: guitar
Nathan East: bass
Steve Ferrone: drums
Chuck Leavell: keyboards
Ray Cooper: percussion
Gina Foster: backing vocals
Katie Kissoon: backing vocals

16 April 1992, depart for Dallas

17 April 1992–23 April 1992, rehearsals in Las Colinas, Dallas, Texas

24 April 1992, day off

25 April 1992, Reunion Arena, Dallas, Texas

SETLIST: White Room / Pretending / Anything For Your Love / I Shot The Sheriff / Running On Faith / She's Waiting / Circus Has Left Town / Tears In Heaven / Before You Accuse Me / Tearing Us Apart / Old Love / Badge / Wonderful Tonight / Layla / Crossroads / Sunshine Of Your Love

26 April 1992, day off

27 April 1992, Lakefront Arena, New Orleans, Louisiana

SETLIST: White Room / Pretending / Anything For Your Love / I Shot The Sheriff / Running On Faith / She's Waiting / Circus Has Left Town / Tears In Heaven / Before You Accuse Me / Tearing Us Apart / Old Love / Badge / Wonderful Tonight / Layla / Crossroads / Sunshine Of Your Love

28 April 1992, Civic Centre, Birmingham, Alabama

SETLIST: White Room / Pretending / Anything For Your Love / I Shot The Sheriff / Running On Faith / She's Waiting / Circus Has Left Town / Tears In Heaven / Before You Accuse Me / Tearing Us Apart / Old Love / Badge / Wonderful Tonight / Layla / Crossroads / Sunshine Of Your Love

29 April 1992, Pyramid, Memphis, Tennessee

SETLIST: White Room / Pretending / Anything For Your Love / I Shot The Sheriff / Running On Faith / She's Waiting / Circus Has Left Town / Tears In Heaven / Before You Accuse Me / Tearing Us Apart / Old Love / Badge / Wonderful Tonight / Layla / Crossroads / Sunshine Of Your Love

30 April 1992, day off

MAY 1992

1 May 1992, Thompson-Boling Arena, Knoxville, Tennessee

SETLIST: White Room / Pretending / Anything For Your Love / I Shot The Sheriff / Running On Faith / She's Waiting / Circus Has Left Town / Tears In Heaven / Before You Accuse Me / Tearing Us Apart / Old Love / Badge / Wonderful Tonight / Layla / Crossroads / Sunshine Of Your Love

2 May 1992, Charlotte Coliseum, Charlotte, North Carolina

SETLIST: White Room / Pretending / Anything For Your Love / I Shot The Sheriff / Running On Faith / She's Waiting / Circus Has Left Town / Tears In Heaven / Before You Accuse Me / Tearing Us Apart / Old Love / Badge / Wonderful Tonight / Layla / Crossroads / Sunshine Of Your Love

3 May 1992, day off

4 May 1992, Spectrum, Philadelphia, Pennsylvania

SETLIST: White Room / Pretending / Anything For Your Love / I Shot The Sheriff / Running On Faith / She's Waiting / Circus Has Left Town / Tears In Heaven / Before You Accuse Me / Tearing Us Apart / Old Love / Badge

/ Wonderful Tonight / Layla / Crossroads / Sunshine Of Your Love

5 May 1992, Spectrum, Philadelphia, Pennsylvania

SETLIST: White Room / Pretending / Anything For Your Love / I Shot The Sheriff / Running On Faith / She's Waiting / Circus Has Left Town / Tears In Heaven / Before You Accuse Me / Tearing Us Apart / Old Love / Badge / Wonderful Tonight / Layla / Crossroads / Sunshine Of Your Love

6 May 1992, Civic Centre, Hartford, Connecticut

SETLIST: White Room / Pretending / Anything For Your Love / I Shot The Sheriff / Running On Faith / She's Waiting / Circus Has Left Town / Tears In Heaven / Before You Accuse Me / Tearing Us Apart / Old Love / Badge / Wonderful Tonight / Layla / Crossroads / Sunshine Of Your Love

7 May 1992, day off
8 May 1992, Meadowlands Arena, East Rutherford, New Jersey

SETLIST: White Room / Pretending / Anything For Your Love / I Shot The Sheriff / Running On Faith / She's Waiting / Circus Has Left Town / Tears In Heaven / Before You Accuse Me / Tearing Us Apart / Old Love / Badge / Wonderful Tonight / Layla / Crossroads / Sunshine Of Your Love

9 May 1992, day off
10 May 1992, Capitol Centre, Washington, D.C.

SETLIST: White Room / Pretending / Anything For Your Love / I Shot The Sheriff / Running On Faith / She's Waiting / Circus Has Left Town / Tears In Heaven / Before You Accuse Me / Tearing Us Apart / Old Love / Badge / Wonderful Tonight / Layla / Crossroads / Sunshine Of Your Love

11 May 1992, Dean E. Smith Center, Chapel Hill, North Carolina

SETLIST: White Room / Pretending / Anything For Your Love / I Shot The Sheriff / Running On Faith / She's Waiting / Circus Has Left Town / Tears In Heaven / Before

You Accuse Me / Tearing Us Apart / Old Love / Badge / Wonderful Tonight / Layla / Crossroads / Sunshine Of Your Love

12 May 1992, day off
13 May 1992, Rosemont Horizon, Rosemont, Illinois

SETLIST: White Room / Pretending / Anything For Your Love / I Shot The Sheriff / Running On Faith / She's Waiting / Circus Has Left Town / Tears In Heaven / Before You Accuse Me / Tearing Us Apart / Old Love / Badge / Wonderful Tonight / Layla / Crossroads / Sunshine Of Your Love

14 May 1992, Rosemont Horizon, Rosemont, Illinois

SETLIST: White Room / Pretending / Anything For Your Love / I Shot The Sheriff / Running On Faith / She's Waiting / Circus Has Left Town / Tears In Heaven / Before You Accuse Me / Tearing Us Apart / Old Love / Badge / Wonderful Tonight / Layla / Crossroads / Sunshine Of Your Love

16 May 1992, Bradley Center, Milwaukee, Wisconsin

SETLIST: White Room / Pretending / Anything For Your Love / I Shot The Sheriff / Running On Faith / She's Waiting / Circus Has Left Town / Tears In Heaven / Before You Accuse Me / Tearing Us Apart / Old Love / Badge / Wonderful Tonight / Layla / Crossroads / Sunshine Of Your Love

17 May 1992, Target Center, Minneapolis, Minnesota

SETLIST: White Room / Pretending / Anything For Your Love / I Shot The Sheriff / Running On Faith / She's Waiting / Circus Has Left Town / Tears In Heaven / Before You Accuse Me / Tearing Us Apart / Old Love / Badge / Wonderful Tonight / Layla / Crossroads / Sunshine Of Your Love

18 May 1992, day off
19 May 1992, Market Square Arena, Indianapolis, Indiana

SETLIST: White Room / Pretending / Anything For Your Love / I Shot The Sheriff / Running On Faith / She's Waiting / Circus Has Left Town / Tears In Heaven / Before You Accuse Me / Tearing Us Apart / Old Love / Badge

/ Wonderful Tonight / Layla / Crossroads / Sunshine Of Your Love

20 May 1992, Richfield Coliseum, Cleveland, Ohio

SETLIST: White Room / Pretending / Anything For Your Love / I Shot The Sheriff / Running On Faith / She's Waiting / Circus Has Left Town / Tears In Heaven / Before You Accuse Me / Tearing Us Apart / Old Love / Badge / Wonderful Tonight / Layla / Crossroads / Sunshine Of Your Love

21 May 1992, Riverfront Coliseum, Cincinnati, Ohio

SETLIST: White Room / Pretending / Anything For Your Love / I Shot The Sheriff / Running On Faith / She's Waiting / Circus Has Left Town / Tears In Heaven / Before You Accuse Me / Tearing Us Apart / Old Love / Badge / Wonderful Tonight / Layla / Crossroads / Sunshine Of Your Love

22 May 1992, day off
23 May 1992, Omni Theatre, Atlanta, Georgia

SETLIST: White Room / Pretending / Anything For Your Love / I Shot The Sheriff / Running On Faith / She's Waiting / Circus Has Left Town / Tears In Heaven / Before You Accuse Me / Tearing Us Apart / Old Love / Badge / Wonderful Tonight / Layla / Crossroads / Sunshine Of Your Love

24 May 1992, Suncoast Dome, St. Petersburg, Florida

SETLIST: White Room / Pretending / Anything For Your Love / I Shot The Sheriff / Running On Faith / She's Waiting / Circus Has Left Town / Tears In Heaven / Before You Accuse Me / Tearing Us Apart / Old Love / Badge / Wonderful Tonight / Layla / Crossroads / Sunshine Of Your Love

25 May 1992, Miami Arena, Miami, Florida

SETLIST: White Room / Pretending / Anything For Your Love / I Shot The Sheriff / Running On Faith / She's Waiting / Circus Has Left Town / Tears In Heaven / Before You Accuse Me / Tearing Us Apart / Old Love / Badge / Wonderful Tonight / Layla / Crossroads / Sunshine Of Your Love

29 May 1992, Grosvenor House Hotel, London (Eric attends the Rhythm of Fashion Show)

EUROPEAN TOUR 1992

JUNE 1992

14 June 1992–15 June 1992, rehearsals in Gent, Belgium
16 June 1992, Flanders Expo, Gent, Belgium

SETLIST: White Room / Pretending / Anything For Your Love / I Shot The Sheriff / Running On Faith / She's Waiting / Tears In Heaven / Before You Accuse Me / Tearing Us Apart / Old Love / Badge / Wonderful Tonight / Layla / Crossroads / Sunshine Of Your Love

17 June 1992, day off
18 June 1992, Hippodrome de Vincennes, Paris, France (with Elton John and Bonnie Raitt)

SETLIST: White Room / Pretending / I Shot The Sheriff / Running On Faith / She's Waiting / Tears In Heaven / Before You Accuse Me / Old Love / Badge / Wonderful Tonight / Layla / Crossroads

19 June 1992, Stadion Feyenoord, Rotterdam, Netherlands (with Elton John and Bonnie Raitt)

SETLIST: White Room / Pretending / Anything For Your Love / I Shot The Sheriff / Running On Faith / She's Waiting / Circus Has Left Town / Tears In Heaven / Before You Accuse Me / Tearing Us Apart / Old Love / Badge / Wonderful Tonight / Layla / Crossroads / Sunshine Of Your Love

20 June 1992, day off
21 June 1992, Olympiahalle, München, Germany (with Joe Cocker)

SETLIST: not known

22 June 1992, Waldbühne, Berlin, Germany (with Joe Cocker)

SETLIST: White Room / Pretending / I Shot The Sheriff / Running On Faith / She's Waiting / Tears In Heaven /

Before You Accuse Me / Old Love / Badge / Wonderful Tonight / Layla / Crossroads

23 June 1992, Westfalenhalle, Dortmund, Germany (with Tony Joe White)

SETLIST: White Room / Pretending / Anything For Your Love / I Shot The Sheriff / Running On Faith / She's Waiting / Circus Has Left Town / Tears In Heaven / Before You Accuse Me / Tearing Us Apart / Old Love / Badge / Wonderful Tonight / Layla / Crossroads / Sunshine Of Your Love

24 June 1992–25 June 1992, days off

26 June 1992, Wembley Stadium, Wembley, London (with Elton John, Curtis Stigers, and Bonnie Raitt)

SETLIST: White Room / Pretending / I Shot The Sheriff / Running On Faith / She's Waiting / Tears In Heaven / Before You Accuse Me / Old Love / Badge / Wonderful Tonight / Layla / Crossroads / Sunshine Of Your Love

ELTON JOHN SETLIST: Runaway Train[1]

[1]Eric joins Elton John during his set

27 June 1992, Wembley Stadium, Wembley, London (with Elton John, Curtis Stigers, and Bonnie Raitt)

SETLIST: White Room / Pretending / I Shot The Sheriff / Running On Faith / She's Waiting / Tears In Heaven / Blues All Day Long[1] / Before You Accuse Me / Old Love / Badge / Wonderful Tonight / Layla / Crossroads / Sunshine Of Your Love

[1]with Jimmy Rogers

28 June 1992, Wembley Stadium, London (with Elton John, Curtis Stigers, and Bonnie Raitt)

SETLIST: White Room / Pretending / I Shot The Sheriff / Running On Faith / She's Waiting / Tears In Heaven / Before You Accuse Me[1] / Old Love / Badge / Wonderful Tonight / Layla / Crossroads / Sunshine Of Your Love

[1]with Bonnie Raitt

Elton John headlines the double bill today and for the finale encore of "The Bitch Is Back" he is joined by Eric, Bonnie Raitt, Curtis Stigers, and Brian May.

29 June 1992–30 June 1992, days off

JULY 1992

1 July 1992–2 July 1992, days off

3 July 1992, Stade de la Pontaise, Lausanne, Switzerland (with Elton John, Curtis Stigers, and Bonnie Raitt)

SETLIST: not known

4 July 1992, St. Jakobshalle, Basel, Switzerland (with Elton John, Curtis Stigers, and Bonnie Raitt)

SETLIST: not known

5 July 1992, day off

6 July 1992, Stadio Communale, Bologna, Italy (with Elton John, Curtis Stigers, and Bonnie Raitt)

SETLIST: White Room / Pretending / Anything For Your Love / I Shot The Sheriff / Running On Faith / She's Waiting / Circus Has Left Town / Tears In Heaven / Before You Accuse Me / Tearing Us Apart[1] / Old Love / Badge / Wonderful Tonight / Layla / Crossroads / Sunshine Of Your Love

[1]with Zucchero Fornaciari

7 July 1992–9 July 1992, days off

10 July 1992, Stadio Brianteo, Monza, Italy (w   ith Elton John, Curtis Stigers, and Bonnie Raitt)

SETLIST: White Room / Pretending / I Shot The Sheriff / Running On Faith / She's Waiting / Tears In Heaven / Before You Accuse Me / Old Love / Badge / Wonderful Tonight / Layla / Crossroads / Sunshine Of Your Love

11 July 1992, day off

12 July 1992, Le Casino, Montreux, Switzerland

SETLIST: White Room / Pretending / Anything For Your Love / I Shot The Sheriff / Running On Faith / She's Waiting / Tears In Heaven / Before You Accuse Me / Old Love / Badge / Wonderful Tonight / Layla / Crossroads / Sunshine Of Your Love

AUGUST 1992

U.S. TOUR 1992 (Second leg)

8 August 1992, depart for Pittsburgh, Pennsylvania

9 August 1992–10 August 1992, rehearsals at Civic Arena, Pittsburgh, Pennsylvania

11 August 1992, Civic Arena, Pittsburgh, Pennsylvania (with Curtis Stigers)

SETLIST: White Room / Pretending / Anything For Your Love / I Shot The Sheriff / Running On Faith / She's Waiting / Tears In Heaven / Before You Accuse Me / Tearing Us Apart / Old Love / Badge / Wonderful Tonight / Layla / Crossroads / Sunshine Of Your Love

12 August 1992, day off

13 August 1992, Meadowbrook Amphitheater, Rochester Hills, Michigan   (jam with Little Feat)

SETLIST: Mellow Down Easy / Say Man / Apolitical Blues

14 August 1992, Palace of Auburn Hills, Auburn Hills, Michigan (with Curtis Stigers)

SETLIST: White Room / Pretending / Anything For Your Love / I Shot The Sheriff / Running On Faith / She's Waiting / Tears In Heaven / Before You Accuse Me / Tearing Us Apart / Old Love / Badge / Wonderful Tonight / Layla / Crossroads / Sunshine Of Your Love

15 August 1992–16 August 1992, days off

17 August 1992, Great Woods Center for the Performing Arts, Mansfield, Massachusetts (with Curtis Stigers)

SETLIST: White Room / Pretending / Anything For Your Love / I Shot The Sheriff / Running On Faith / She's Waiting / Tears In Heaven / Before You Accuse Me / Old Love / Badge / Wonderful Tonight / Layla / Crossroads / Sunshine Of Your Love

18 August 1992, Great Woods Center for the Performing Arts, Mansfield, Massachusetts (with Curtis Stigers)

SETLIST: White Room / Pretending / Anything For Your Love / I Shot The Sheriff / Running On Faith / She's Waiting / Tears In Heaven / Before You Accuse Me / Old Love / Badge / Wonderful Tonight / Layla / Crossroads / Sunshine Of Your Love

19 August 1992, Performing Arts Center, Saratoga Springs, New York (with Curtis Stigers)

SETLIST: White Room / Pretending / Anything For Your Love / I Shot The Sheriff / Running On Faith / She's Waiting / Tears In Heaven / Before You Accuse Me / Old Love / Badge / Wonderful Tonight / Layla / Crossroads / Sunshine Of Your Love

20 August 1992, day off

21 August 1992, Shea Stadium, Flushing, New York (with Elton John)

SETLIST: White Room / Pretending / Anything For Your Love / I Shot The Sheriff / Running On Faith / She's Waiting / Tears In Heaven / Before You Accuse Me / Tearing Us Apart / Old Love / Badge / Wonderful Tonight / Layla / Crossroads / Sunshine Of Your Love

Eric came out for a duet on "Runaway Train" during Elton John's set.

22 August 1992, Shea Stadium, Flushing, New York (with Elton John)

SETLIST: White Room / Pretending / Anything For Your Love / I Shot The Sheriff / Running On Faith / She's Waiting / Tears In Heaven / Before You Accuse Me / Tearing Us Apart / Old Love / Badge / Wonderful Tonight / Layla / Crossroads / Sunshine Of Your Love

Eric came out for a duet on "Runaway Train" during Elton John's set.

23 August 1992, day off

24 August 1992, Poplar Creek Music Theater, Hoffman Estates, Illinois (with Curtis Stigers)

SETLIST: White Room / Pretending / Anything For Your Love / I Shot The Sheriff / Running On Faith / She's Waiting / Tears In Heaven / Before You Accuse Me /

Tearing Us Apart / Old Love / Badge / Wonderful Tonight / Layla / Crossroads / Sunshine Of Your Love

25 August 1992, Riverport Amphitheater, St. Louis, Missouri (with Curtis Stigers)

SETLIST: White Room / Pretending / Anything For Your Love / I Shot The Sheriff / Running On Faith / She's Waiting / Tears In Heaven / Before You Accuse Me / Tearing Us Apart / Old Love / Badge / Wonderful Tonight / Layla / Crossroads / Sunshine Of Your Love

26 August 1992–28 August 1992, days off

29 August 1992, Dodger Stadium, Los Angeles, California (with Elton John)

Eric came out for a duet on "Runaway Train" during Elton John's set.

SETLIST: White Room / Pretending / Anything For Your Love / I Shot The Sheriff / Running On Faith / She's Waiting / Tears In Heaven / Before You Accuse Me / Tearing Us Apart / Old Love / Badge / Wonderful Tonight / Layla / Crossroads / Sunshine Of Your Love

30 August 1992, Dodger Stadium, Los Angeles, California (with Elton John)

Eric came out for a duet on "Runaway Train" during Elton John's set.

SETLIST: White Room / Pretending / Anything For Your Love / I Shot The Sheriff / Running On Faith / She's Waiting / Tears In Heaven / Before You Accuse Me / Tearing Us Apart / Old Love / Badge / Wonderful Tonight / Layla / Crossroads / Sunshine Of Your Love

31 August 1992, day off

SEPTEMBER 1992

1 September 1992–2 September 1992, days off

3 September 1992, Shoreline Amphitheatre, San Francisco, California (with Curtis Stigers)

SETLIST: White Room / Pretending / Anything For Your Love / I Shot The Sheriff / Running On Faith / She's Waiting / Tears In Heaven / Before You Accuse Me / Old

Love / Badge / Wonderful Tonight / Layla / Crossroads / Sunshine Of Your Love

4 September 1992, Shoreline Amphitheatre, San Francisco, California (with Curtis Stigers)

SETLIST: White Room / Pretending / Anything For Your Love / I Shot The Sheriff / Running On Faith / She's Waiting / Tears In Heaven / Before You Accuse Me / Old Love / Badge / Wonderful Tonight / Layla / Crossroads / Sunshine Of Your Love

5 September 1992, day off

6 September 1992, Tacoma Dome, Tacoma, Washington (with Curtis Stigers)

SETLIST: White Room / Pretending / Anything For Your Love / I Shot The Sheriff / Running On Faith / She's Waiting / Tears In Heaven / Before You Accuse Me / Old Love / Badge / Wonderful Tonight / Layla / Crossroads / Sunshine Of Your Love

MTV AWARDS

9 September 1992, UCLA Pauley Pavilion, Los Angeles, California MTV Awards (Eric wins award for Best Male Video for "Tears In Heaven" and plays a version of the song with his band. The whole event is broadcast on television)

OCTOBER 1992

BOB DYLAN'S 30th ANNIVERSARY CONCERT 1992

16 October 1992, Madison Square Garden, New York City

Eric is one of the many guests performing tonight to celebrate Bob Dylan's 30th anniversary as a recording artist. The event is filmed and recorded.

Love Minus Zero–No Limit (Bob Dylan) *Bob Dylan The 30th Anniversary Concert Celebration* VHS video CMV 49165 2 released August 1993

Eric Clapton: guitar, vocals
G. E. Smith: guitar
Steve Cropper: guitar
Booker T. Jones: keyboards
Donald "Duck" Dunn: bass
Anton Fig: drums

Don't Think Twice, It's All Right (Bob Dylan) *Bob Dylan The 30th Anniversary Concert Celebration* CD Columbia 474000 2 / *Bob Dylan The 30th Anniversary Concert Celebration* VHS video CMV 49165 2 released August 1993

Eric Clapton: guitar, vocals
G. E. Smith: guitar
Steve Cropper: guitar
Booker T. Jones: keyboards
Donald "Duck" Dunn: bass
Anton Fig: drums
Jim Keltner: drums

My Back Pages (Bob Dylan) *Bob Dylan The 30th Anniversary Concert Celebration* CD Columbia 474000 2 / *Bob Dylan The 30th Anniversary Concert Celebration* VHS video CMV 49165 2 released August 1993

Bob Dylan: acoustic guitar, vocals
Roger McGuinn: guitar, vocals
Tom Petty: guitar
Neil Young: guitar
George Harrsion: guitar
Eric Clapton: guitar, vocals
G. E. Smith: guitar
Steve Cropper: guitar
Booker T. Jones: keyboards
Donald "Duck" Dunn: bass
Anton Fig: drums
Al Kooper: organ
Stan Lynch: percussion

Knockin' On Heaven's Door (Bob Dylan) *Bob Dylan The 30th Anniversary Concert Celebration* CD Columbia 474000 2 / *Bob Dylan The 30th Anniversary Concert Celebration* VHS video CMV 49165 2 released August 1993

Bob Dylan: acoustic guitar, vocals
Roger McGuinn: guitar, vocals
Tom Petty: guitar
Neil Young: guitar
George Harrsion: guitar
Eric Clapton: guitar, vocals
G. E. Smith: guitar
Steve Cropper: guitar
Booker T. Jones: keyboards
Donald "Duck" Dunn: bass
Anton Fig: drums
Al Kooper: organ
Stan Lynch: percussion

Ron Wood: guitar
June Carter Cash: backing vocals
Mary Chapin Carpenter: backing vocals
Sinead O'Connor: backing vocals
Rosanne Cash: backing vocals
Clancy Brothers: backing vocals
Richie Havens: backing vocals
John Mellencamp: backing vocals
Tracy Chapman: backing vocals
Kris Kristofferson: backing vocals
Producers: Jeff Rosen / Don DeVito
Engineers: Vic Anesini / Phil Gitomer / Peter Hefter / Sean McClintock

DECEMBER 1992

NEW YEAR'S EVE DANCE 1992

31 December 1992, Woking Leisure Centre, Woking, Surrey (the first of Eric's traditional New Year's Eve Dance shows at this venue)

Eric and his band are called the Character Defects.

BAND LINEUP:
Eric Clapton: guitar, vocals
Alan Darby: guitar
Chris Stainton: keyboards
Gary Brooker: keyboards, vocals
Dave Bronze: bass
Henry Spinetti: drums
Jackie: vocals
Maggie Ryder: vocals

SETLIST 1: I Feel So Good / Knock On Wood / Sweet Home Chicago / Five Long Years / I Heard It Through The Grapevine[1] / Little Queenie / Everyday I Have The Blues / I Drink The Wine[2] / Stormy Monday / Love Letter[3]

[1]with Jackie on lead vocals
[2]with Alan Darby on lead vocals
[3]with Maggie Ryder on lead vocals

SETLIST 2: Midnight Hour / Auld Lang Syne / Lay Down Sally / Wonderful Tonight / Cocaine / Layla / A Whiter Shade Of Pale / Everybody Needs Somebody To Love / Good Golly Miss Molly

RECORDING SESSIONS 1992

ERIC CLAPTON GUEST SESSION

TOWN HOUSE
150 Goldhawk Road, London
Session for Elton John

MARCH 1992

RUNAWAY TRAIN (Elton John / Bernie Taupin / Olle Romo) *Lethal Weapon 3* soundtrack CD Reprise 7599-26989-2 released June 1992 / *The One* CD Rocket Record Company 512 360-2 released June 1992

Although the song will appear on Elton's *The One* album, the track is also used on the soundtrack of *Lethal Weapon 3*.

Elton John: keyboards, vocals
Eric Clapton: guitar, vocals
Pino Paladino: bass
Ollie Romo: drums
Davey Johnstone: guitar
Guy Babylon: keyboards
Joniece Jamison: backing vocals
Carole Fredericks: backing vocals
Beckie Bell: backing vocals

Producer: Chris Thomas
Engineer: Andy Bradfield

SARM WEST STUDIOS
8-10 Basing Street, London
Session for *Lethal Weapon 3*

26 MARCH 1992–6 APRIL 1992

GRAB THE CAT *Lethal Weapon 3* soundtrack CD Reprise 7599-26989-2 released June 1992

LEO GETZ GOES TO THE HOCKEY GAME *Lethal Weapon 3* soundtrack CD Reprise 7599-26989-2 released June 1992

DARRYL DIES *Lethal Weapon 3* soundtrack CD Reprise 7599-26989-2 released June 1992

RIGGS AND ROG *Lethal Weapon 3* soundtrack CD Reprise 7599-26989-2 released June 1992

ROGER'S BOAT *Lethal Weapon 3* soundtrack CD Reprise 7599-26989-2 released June 1992

ARMOUR PIERCING BULLETS *Lethal Weapon 3* soundtrack CD Reprise 7599-26989-2 released June 1992

GOD JUDGES US BY OUR SCARS *Lethal Weapon 3* soundtrack CD Reprise 7599-26989-2 released June 1992

LORNA - A QUIET EVENING BY THE FIRE *Lethal Weapon 3* soundtrack CD Reprise 7599-26989-2 released June 1992

Eric Clapton: guitar
Michael Kamen: keyboards
David Sanborn: saxophone

Producers: Michael Kamen / Stephen McLaughlin

Once again, Eric and Michael Kamen were called upon to provide the soundtrack to the latest in the popular series of *Lethal Weapon* films, as they had for the first two films. The pressure was on as the film was due to launch in a couple of months and Eric only had a week or so to get it done due to his own work schedule. As well as the basic score, it was decided to record a "buddy" duet as the films basically featured a buddy team of Mel Gibson and Danny Glover, and this song would provide a unifying theme. The buddy in this case turned out to be Sting. Eric sent him a cassette with some ideas for the basis of the song. Sting spent a few days adding a melody and bridge. As Eric was preparing for a large U.S. tour, operations moved over to New York in April for the recording of Eric and Sting's new song which had its tempo set by a Zippo lighter. Sting's lyrics were tailored to suit Eric, but in the end Eric asked Sting to sing the song.

BMG STUDIOS
1540 Broadway
New York City
Session for *Lethal Weapon 3*

11 APRIL 1992–13 APRIL 1992

IT'S PROBABLY ME (Sting / Michael Kamen / Eric Clapton) *Lethal Weapon 3* soundtrack CD Reprise 7599-26989-2 released June 1992 / CD single A&M 390 883-2 released June 1992 / *Ten Summoner's Tales* A&M 31454 0070 2 released March 1993

Eric Clapton: electric and acoustic guitars
Sting: vocals, bass
Michael Kamen: keyboards
David Sanborn: saxophone
Steve Gadd: drums
Don Alias: percussion

Greater New York Alumni Orchestra: strings
Producers: Michael Kamen / Stephen McLaughlin

> "Eric kept picking out these bluesy chords of the basic *Lethal Weapon* theme, re-examining the melody line and in this quick, continuous clicking motion, he'd simultaneously light one cigarette after another with his Zippo. Click! Fump! Click! It was a three-part ritual: the metal lighter case popping open, the flick of ignition, and the shutting of the case. Stephen McLaughlin, who was co-producing the sessions, decided to sample the Zippo and reshuffle its sequence."
>
> **—MICHAEL KAMEN**
> (*Billboard*, 20 June 1992)

> "There's a maturity in Eric's work that we need and there's an integrity there that gets better and better. I've always thought he was one of the greatest 'feel' players ever. I walked around the property listening to the cassette of rough ideas and I especially liked the percussive motif of the lighter sounds and the way the guitar chords moved. So I worked out a melody that would go over the theme's changes, and my pop training told me it also needed an old-fashioned bridge."
>
> **—STING**
> (*Billboard*, 20 June 1992)

ERIC CLAPTON GUEST SESSION

RECORD PLANT
1032 North Sycamore Avenue, Los Angeles, California
Session for Ray Charles

SEPTEMBER 1992

NONE OF US ARE FREE (Brenda Russell / Barry Marr / Cynthia Weil) *My World* CD Warner Bros. 7599-26735-2 released March 1993

Ray Charles: vocals
Eric Clapton: guitar solo
Donny Nguyen: drum, percussion programming
Abe Laboriel: bass
Barry Mann: synthesizer
Guy Moon: synthesizer
Steve Lindley: Wurlitzer, synth horns
Enrico De Paoli: percussion
Lee Thornburg: horns
Doug Norwine: horns
Paulinho da Costa: percussion
Mavis Staples: backing vocals
Brenda Russell: backing vocals
Maxanne Lewis: backing vocals
Phil Perry: backing vocals

Producer: Richard Perry
Engineer: Mike Brooks

11

1993

The year started remarkably with a Cream reunion, albeit for only three numbers. They were being inducted into the Rock and Roll Hall of Fame along with other bands such as the Doors, with a huge event at the Century Plaza Hotel in Los Angeles. This was the news that so many people had waited years for but never thought possible. Clearly the magic was still there and it was certainly an emotional night for all three of them—Jack Bruce, Ginger Baker, and Eric— but Eric was not ready for a proper reunion and went back to his solo career with the now traditional Royal Albert Hall residency.

JANUARY 1993

11 January 1993, Power Plant, North Hollywood, California

Eric Clapton, Jack Bruce, and Ginger Baker rehearse for tomorrow's Rock and Roll Hall of Fame induction. As well as multiple takes of the three numbers they would be performing at the show, they also jam as a way of getting warmed up. Many say that the rehearsals were far better than the actual show.

ROCK AND ROLL HALL OF FAME CONCERT 1993

12 January 1993, Century Plaza Hotel, Los Angeles, California (Cream are inducted into the Hall Of Fame)

BAND LINEUP:
Eric Clapton: guitar, vocals
Jack Bruce: vocals, bass
Ginger Baker: drums

SETLIST: Sunshine Of Your Love / Born Under A Bad Sign / Crossroads

All three tracks are available on Time Life's *Rock And Roll Hall Of Fame Museum Live* box set of DVDs and the audio can be purchased from ITunes.

> **"**Doing that Hall of Fame gig made me realize that people love it still. We are seriously looking at doing reunion dates, probably sooner rather than later. I know Eric's keen— maybe I've got to instigate it myself to make it happen.**"**
> **—JACK BRUCE**

The world would have to wait until 2005 for the reunion to take place. In the meantime, Jack and Ginger went off with Gary Moore as B.B.M. (Bruce Baker Moore) with varying degrees of success and controversy. They managed a tour and an album, but Ginger and Gary did not get on particularly well and the band were doomed before a second album could be attempted.

FEBRUARY 1993

ROYAL ALBERT HALL RESIDENCY 1993

In many ways, these were very important shows. It was the start of Eric taking control of his own destiny which would eventually lead to a split with his manager in 1998. Eric's musical identity is steeped in blues tradition, yet he had never played an all-blues show since leaving John Mayall back in 1966. This year we got that in spades. It was Eric's blues history lesson for those who cared to listen. Luckily most of the audience did. The odd one or two walked out because they wanted to hear the hits. It was their loss.

The shows were measured in their presentation starting with acoustic and moving to electric guitar with a stellar band providing the perfect backdrop for the sound he wanted to achieve. These were realistic interpretations of classic songs from people who had inspired him since childhood. He treated them with due respect. The only odd one out was a new song by Eric called "Hear Me Calling" which he had written the previous year. It was a modern blues song that fit well in the repertoire.

Eric would develop his blues shows for the next few years into something really special. Included among all was the recording of an all-blues album.

BAND LINEUP:
Eric Clapton: guitar, vocals
Andy Fairweather Low: guitar
Chris Stainton: keyboards
Jerry Portnoy: harmonica
Donald "Duck" Dunn: bass
Richie Hayward: drums

20 February 1993, Royal Albert Hall, London (with Jimmie Vaughan)

SETLIST: How Long Blues / Alabama Women / Terraplane Blues / From Four Until Late / Kid Man Blues / County Jail / 32-20 / Chicago Breakdown / Hey Hey / Walkin' Blues / Long Distance Call / Blow Wind Blow / Blues With A Feeling / Tell Me Mama / Key To The Highway / Juke / Going Away / Blues Leave Me Alone / Coming Home / Meet Me At The Bottom / Forty Four Blues / It's My Life / Love Her With A Feeling / Tore Down / Born Under

A Bad Sign / Let Me Love You Baby / All Your Love / Groaning The Blues / Hear Me Calling / Ain't Nobody's Business / Further On Up The Road

21 February 1993, Royal Albert Hall, London (with Jimmie Vaughan)

SETLIST: Hey Hey / Walkin' Blues / Long Distance Call / Blow Wind Blow / Key To The Highway / Tell Me Mama / Juke / How Long Blues / Alabama Women / Terraplane Blues / From Four Until Late / Kid Man Blues / County Jail / 32-20 / Chicago Breakdown / Blues Leave Me Alone / Going Away / Coming Home / Meet Me At The Bottom / Forty Four Blues / It's My Life / Love Her With A Feeling / Tore Down / Born Under A Bad Sign / Let Me Love You Baby / All Your Love / Groaning The Blues / Hear Me Calling / Ain't Nobody's Business / Sweet Home Chicago[1]

[1] with Jimmie Vaughan

Eric Clapton gives a blues history lesson at the Royal Albert Hall in London in February 1993.

22 February 1993, Royal Albert Hall, London (with Jimmie Vaughan)

SETLIST: How Long Blues / Alabama Women / Terraplane Blues / From Four Until Late / Kid Man Blues / County Jail / 32-20 / Chicago Breakdown / Hey Hey / Walkin' Blues / Long Distance Call / Blow Wind Blow / Key To The Highway / Tell Me Mama / Juke / Blues Leave Me Alone / Going Away / Coming Home / Meet Me At The Bottom / Forty Four Blues / It's My Life / Love Her With A Feeling / Tore Down / Born Under A Bad Sign / Let Me Love You Baby / All Your Love / Groaning The Blues / Hear Me Calling / Ain't Nobody's Business / Sweet Home Chicago

23 February 1993, Royal Albert Hall, London (with Jimmie Vaughan)

SETLIST: How Long Blues / Alabama Women / Terraplane Blues / From Four Until Late / Kid Man Blues / County Jail / 32-20 / Chicago Breakdown / Hey Hey / Walkin' Blues / Long Distance Call / Blow Wind Blow / Key To The Highway / Tell Me Mama / Juke / Blues Leave Me Alone / Going Away / Coming Home / Meet Me At The Bottom / Forty Four Blues / It's My Life / Love Her With A Feeling / Tore Down / Born Under A Bad Sign / Let Me Love You Baby / All Your Love / Groaning The Blues / Hear Me Calling / Ain't Nobody's Business / Sweet Home Chicago

Eric Clapton at the Royal Albert Hall in London in 1993.

GRAMMY AWARDS 1993

24 February 1993, Shrine Auditorium, Los Angeles, California (Eric flies to Los Angeles to attend and perform at the Grammy Awards)

SETLIST: Tears In Heaven

Eric takes home a staggering six Grammy Awards:

Record Of The Year for "Tears In Heaven" awarded to Eric Clapton and Russ Titelman, producer

Album Of The Year for *Unplugged* awarded to Eric Clapton and Russ Titelman, producer

Song Of The Year for "Tears In Heaven" awarded to Eric Clapton and Will Jennings, composers.

Best Male Rock Vocal Performance for *Unplugged* awarded to Eric Clapton

Best Male Pop Vocal Performance for "Tears In Heaven" awarded to Eric Clapton

Best Rock Song for "Layla" awarded to Eric Clapton and Jim Gordon, composers

26 February 1993, Royal Albert Hall, London (with Jimmie Vaughan)

SETLIST: How Long Blues / Alabama Women / Terraplane Blues / From Four Until Late / Kid Man Blues / County Jail / 32-20 / Chicago Breakdown / Hey Hey / Walkin' Blues / Long Distance Call / Blow Wind Blow / Key To The Highway / Tell Me Mama / Juke / Blues Leave Me Alone / Going Away / Coming Home / Meet Me At The Bottom / Forty Four Blues / It's My Life / Love Her With A Feeling / Tore Down / Born Under A Bad Sign / Let Me Love You Baby / All Your Love / Groaning The Blues / Hear Me Calling / Ain't Nobody's Business / Sweet Home Chicago[1]

[1]with Buddy Guy and Jimmie Vaughan on guitars and vocals

27 February 1993, Royal Albert Hall, London (with Jimmie Vaughan)

SETLIST: How Long Blues / Alabama Women / Terraplane Blues / From Four Until Late / Kid Man Blues / County Jail / 32-20 / Chicago Breakdown / Hey Hey / Walkin' Blues / Long Distance Call / Blow Wind Blow / Key To The Highway / Tell Me Mama / Juke / Blues Leave Me Alone / Going Away / Coming Home / Meet Me At The Bottom / Forty Four Blues / It's My Life / Love Her With A Feeling / Tore Down / Born Under A Bad Sign / Let Me Love You Baby / All Your Love / Groaning The Blues / Hear Me Calling / Ain't Nobody's Business / Sweet Home Chicago

MARCH 1993

1 March 1993, Royal Albert Hall, London (with Jimmie Vaughan)

SETLIST: How Long Blues / Alabama Women / Terraplane Blues / From Four Until Late / Kidman Blues / County Jail / 32-20 / Chicago Breakdown / Hey Hey / Walkin' Blues / Long Distance Call / Blow Wind Blow / Key To The

Highway / Tell Me Mama / Duke / Blues Leave Me Alone / Goin' Away Baby / Coming Home / Meet Me In The Bottom / Forty Four Blues / It's My Life / Love Her With A Feeling / Tore Down / Born Under A Bad Sign / Let Me Love You Baby / All My Love / Groaning The Blues / Hear Me Calling / Ain't Nobody's Business / Sweet Home Chicago

2 March 1993, Royal Albert Hall, London (with Jimmie Vaughan)

SETLIST: How Long Blues / Alabama Women / Terraplane Blues / From Four Until Late / Kidman Blues / County Jail / 32-20 / Chicago Breakdown / Hey Hey / Walking Blues / Long Distance Call / Blow Wind Blow / Key To The Highway / Tell Me Mama / Duke / Blues Leave Me Alone / Goin' Away Baby / Coming Home / Meet Me In The Bottom / Forty Four Blues / It's My Life / Love Her With A Feeling / Tore Down / Born Under A Bad Sign / Let Me Love You Baby / All My Love / Groaning The Blues / Hear Me Calling / Ain't Nobody's Business / Sweet Home Chicago

3 March 1993, Royal Albert Hall, London (with Jimmie Vaughan)

SETLIST: How Long Blues / Alabama Women / Terraplane Blues / From Four Until Late / Kidman Blues / County Jail / 32-20 / Chicago Breakdown / Hey Hey / Walking Blues / Long Distance Call / Blow Wind Blow / Key To The Highway / Tell Me Mama / Duke / Blues Leave Me Alone / Goin' Away Baby / Coming Home / Meet Me In The Bottom / Forty Four Blues / It's My Life / Love Her With A Feeling / Tore Down / Born Under A Bad Sign / Let Me Love You Baby / Groaning The Blues / Hear Me Calling / Ain't Nobody's Business / Sweet Home Chicago[1]

[1]with Jimmie Vaughan

5 March 1993, Royal Albert Hall, London (with Jimmie Vaughan)

SETLIST: How Long Blues / Alabama Women / Terraplane Blues / From Four Until Late / Kidman Blues / County Jail Blues / 32-20 / Chicago Breakdown / Hey Hey / Walkin' Blues / Long Distance Call / Blues Before Sunrise / Key To The Highway / Tell Me Mama / Juke / Blues Leave Me Alone / Goin' Away Baby / Coming Home / Meet Me In

The Bottom / Forty Four Blues / It's My Life / Love Her With A Feeling / Tore Down / Born Under A Bad Sign / Let Me Love You Baby / Groaning The Blues / Hear Me Calling / Ain't Nobody's Business / Sweet Home Chicago

6 March 1993, Royal Albert Hall, London (with Jimmie Vaughan)

SETLIST: How Long Blues / Alabama Women / Terraplane Blues / From Four Until Late / Kidman Blues / County Jail Blues / 32-20 / Chicago Breakdown / Hey Hey / Walkin' Blues / Long Distance Call / Blues Before Sunrise / Key To The Highway / Tell Me Mama / Juke / Blues Leave Me Alone / Goin' Away Baby / Coming Home / Meet Me In The Bottom / Forty Four Blues / It's My Life / Love Her With A Feeling / Tore Down / Born Under A Bad Sign / Let Me Love You Baby / Groaning The Blues / Hear Me Calling / Ain't Nobody's Business / Sweet Home Chicago

7 March 1993, Royal Albert Hall, London (with Jimmie Vaughan)

SETLIST: How Long Blues / Alabama Women / Terraplane Blues / From Four Until Late / Kidman Blues / County Jail Blues / 32-20 / Chicago Breakdown / Hey Hey / Walkin' Blues / Long Distance Call / Blow Wind Blow / Key To The Highway / Tell Me Mama / Juke / Blues Leave Me Alone / Goin' Away Baby / Coming Home / Meet Me In the Bottom / Forty Four Blues / It's My Life / Love Her With A Feeling / Tore Down / Born Under A Bad Sign / Let Me Love You Baby / Groaning The Blues / Hear Me Calling / Ain't Nobody's Business / Sweet Home Chicago

The last six shows were recorded during this run, but only two tracks from an unknown night were released in September 1994. The two numbers in question were: "County Jail Blues" (Alfred Fields) and "32-20" (Big Maceo Merriweather).

JUNE 1993

APOLLO THEATER HALL OF FAME CONCERT 1993

15 June 1993, Apollo Theater, New York City (special gala evening and concert for the first Annual Apollo

Theater Hall of Fame with Bryan Adams, Jeff Beck, Regina Belle, Thelma Carpenter, Eric Clapton, Albert Collins, Robert De Niro, Danny Glover, Al Green, Buddy Guy, Chuck Jackson, B.B. King, Ben E. King, Bobby McKnight, Teddy Pendergrass, Smokey Robinson, Diana Ross, Robin Williams, Orchestra: Frank Owens, Brian Brake, Tom Barney, Ray Chew, Steve Bargonetti, Warren Smith, Kamau Adilitu, John Longo, Steve Furtado, Dennis Wilson, Benny Powell, Jerome Richardson, Frank Wess, Charles Davis)

SETLIST:

Rock Me Baby broadcast on television

B.B. King: guitar, vocals
Eric Clapton: guitar
Ray Chew: keyboards
Steve Bargonetti: guitar
Brian Brake: drums
Tom Barney: bass

Sweet Little Angel broadcast on television

B.B. King: guitar, vocals
Eric Clapton: guitar
Jeff Beck: guitar
Albert Collins: guitar
Ray Chew: keyboards
Steve Bargonetti: guitar
Brian Brake: drums
Tom Barney: bass

Let The Good Times Roll broadcast on television

B.B. King: guitar, vocals
Eric Clapton: guitar, vocals
Jeff Beck: guitar
Albert Collins: guitar
Buddy Guy: guitar
Ray Chew: keyboards
Steve Bargonetti: guitar
Brian Brake: drums
Tom Barney: bass
Al Green: vocals
Diana Ross: vocals
Ben E. King: vocals
Bryan Adams: vocals

SEPTEMBER 1993

RUINS CONCERT 1993

18 September 1993, Cowdray Park, Midhurst, West Sussex (charity concert with the Ruins featuring Eric Clapton, David Gilmour, Phil Collins, Mike Rutherford, and others)

SETLIST: Stone Free / Old Love / Gimmie Some Lovin' / Can I Get A Witness

OCTOBER 1993

CHEMICAL DEPENDENCY CENTRE PROJECT CHARITY CONCERTS 1993

BAND LINEUP:
Eric Clapton: guitar, vocals
Joe Cocker: vocals
Chris Stainton: keyboards
Andy Fairweather Low: guitar
Donald "Duck" Dunn: bass
Richie Hayward: drums
Jerry Portnoy: harmonica
Katie Kissoon: vocals
Maggie Ryder: vocal
Roddy Lorimer: trumpet
Tim Sanders: tenor saxophone
Simon Clarke: baritone saxophone

1 October 1993, National Indoor Arena, Birmingham (with Nine Below Zero, ZZ Top)

SETLIST: White Room / Badge / Wonderful Tonight / Stone Free / Burning Of The Midnight Lamp / Circus Left Town / Tears In Heaven / Feelin' Alright[1] / Lonely Avenue[1] / Leave Your Hat On[1] / Hard Times[1] / Unchain My Heart[1] / Cocaine / Groaning The Blues / Crossroads / Ain't Nobody's Business / Layla

[1]with Joe Cocker on vocals

Joe Cocker and Eric Clapton at the Chemical Dependency Centre Project Charity concerts at the National Exhibition Centre, Birmingham, October 1993.

2 October 1993, National Exhibition Centre, Birmingham (with Nine Below Zero, ZZ Top)

Eric Clapton in Birmingham in October 1993.

SETLIST: White Room / Badge / Wonderful Tonight / Stone Free / Burning Of The Midnight Lamp / Circus Left Town / Tears In Heaven / Feelin' Alright[1] / Lonely Avenue[1] / You Can Leave Your Hat On[1] / Hard Times[1] / Unchain My Heart[1] / Groaning The Blues / Crossroads / Ain't Nobody's Business / Layla / Sweet Home Chicago[2]

[1]with Joe Cocker on vocals

[2]with Billy Gibbons on guitar, Dusty Hill on bass, both from ZZ Top

3 October 1993, Sheffield Arena, Sheffield, South Yorkshire (with Nine Below Zero, ZZ Top)

SETLIST: White Room / Badge / Wonderful Tonight / Stone Free / Burning Of The Midnight Lamp / Circus Left Town / Tears In Heaven / Feelin' Alright[1] / Lonely Avenue[1] / You Can Leave Your Hat On[1] / Hard Times[1] / Unchain My Heart[1] / Groaning The Blues / Crossroads / Ain't Nobody's Business / Sweet Home Chicago[2]

[1]with Joe Cocker on vocals
[2]with Billy Gibbons on guitar, Dusty Hill on bass (both from ZZ Top), Dennis Greaves on guitar, Gerry McAvoy on tambourine, Brendan O'Neill on congas, and Alan Glen on harmonica (all members of Nine Below Zero), and Joe Cocker on vocals

JAPAN TOUR 1993

BAND LINEUP:
Eric Clapton: guitar, vocals
Andy Fairweather Low: guitar
Nathan East: bass, vocals
Chris Stainton: keyboards
Richie Hayward: drums
Jerry Portnoy: harmonica
Roddy Lorimer: trumpet
Tim Sanders: tenor saxophone
Simon Clarke: baritone saxophone
Katie Kissoon: backing vocals
Maggie Ryder: backing vocals

6 October 1993, depart for Japan

7 October 1993, arrive in Japan

8 October 1993–10 October 1993, rehearsals in Tokyo

12 October 1993, Budokan, Tokyo, Japan

SETLIST: Malted Milk / Terraplane Blues / How Long Blues / 32-20 / Kidman Blues / County Jail Blues / Forty Four Blues / Blues Leave Me Alone / Tell Me Mama / White Room / Badge / Wonderful Tonight / Stone Free / Circus Left Town / Tears In Heaven / Crossroads / Tearing Us Apart / Groaning The Blues / Cocaine / Ain't Nobody's Business / Layla

13 October 1993, Budokan, Tokyo, Japan

SETLIST: Malted Milk / Terraplane Blues / How Long Blues / 32-20 / Kidman Blues / County Jail Blues / Forty Four Blues / Blues Leave Me Alone / Tell Me Mama / White Room / Badge / Wonderful Tonight / Stone Free / Circus Left Town / Tears In Heaven / Crossroads / Tearing Us Apart / Groaning The Blues / Cocaine / Ain't Nobody's Business / Layla

14 October 1993, Rainbow Hall, Nagoya, Japan

SETLIST: Malted Milk / Terraplane Blues / How Long Blues / 32-20 / Kidman Blues / County Jail Blues / Forty Four Blues / Blues Leave Me Alone / Tell Me Mama / White Room / Badge / Wonderful Tonight / Stone Free / Circus Left Town / Tears In Heaven / Crossroads / Tearing Us Apart / Groaning The Blues / Cocaine / Ain't Nobody's Business / Layla

15 October 1993, day off
16 October 1993, day off
17 October 1993, Kokusai Centre, Fukuoka, Japan

SETLIST: Malted Milk / Terraplane Blues / How Long Blues / 32-20 / Kidman Blues / County Jail Blues / Forty Four Blues / Blues Leave Me Alone / Tell Me Mama / White Room / Badge / Wonderful Tonight / Stone Free / Circus Left Town / Tears In Heaven / Crossroads / Tearing Us Apart / Groaning The Blues / Cocaine / Ain't Nobody's Business / Layla

18 October 1993, Castle Hall, Osaka, Japan

SETLIST: Malted Milk / Terraplane Blues / How Long Blues / 32-20 / Kidman Blues / County Jail Blues / Forty Four Blues / Blues Leave Me Alone / Tell Me Mama / White Room / Badge / Wonderful Tonight / Stone Free / Circus Left Town / Tears In Heaven / Crossroads / Tearing Us Apart / Groaning The Blues / Cocaine / Ain't Nobody's Business / Layla

19 October 1993, Castle Hall, Osaka, Japan

SETLIST: Malted Milk / Terraplane Blues / How Long Blues / 32-20 / Kidman Blues / County Jail Blues / Forty Four Blues / Blues Leave Me Alone / Tell Me Mama / White Room / Badge / Wonderful Tonight / Stone Free / Circus Left Town / Tears In Heaven / Crossroads / Tearing

Us Apart / Groaning The Blues / Cocaine / Ain't Nobody's Business / Layla

20 October 1993, day off
21 October 1993, Budokan, Tokyo, Japan

SETLIST: Malted Milk / Terraplane Blues / How Long Blues / 32-20 / Kidman Blues / County Jail Blues / Forty Four Blues / Blues Leave Me Alone / Tell Me Mama / White Room / Badge / Wonderful Tonight / Stone Free / Circus Left Town / Tears In Heaven / Crossroads / Tearing Us Apart / Groaning The Blues / Cocaine / Ain't Nobody's Business / Layla

22 October 1993, Budokan, Tokyo, Japan

SETLIST: Malted Milk / Terraplane Blues / How Long Blues / 32-20 / Kidman Blues / County Jail Blues / Forty Four Blues / Blues Leave Me Alone / Tell Me Mama / White Room / Badge / Wonderful Tonight / Stone Free / Circus Left Town / Tears In Heaven / Crossroads / Tearing Us Apart / Groaning The Blues / Cocaine / Ain't Nobody's Business / Layla

23 October 1993, Yokohama Arena, Yokohama, Japan

SETLIST: Malted Milk / Terraplane Blues / How Long Blues / 32-20 / Kidman Blues / County Jail Blues / Forty Four Blues / Blues Leave Me Alone / Tell Me Mama / White Room / Badge / Wonderful Tonight / Stone Free / Circus Left Town / Tears In Heaven / Crossroads / Tearing Us Apart / Groaning The Blues / Cocaine / Ain't Nobody's Business / Layla

24 October 1993, day off
25 October 1993, Budokan, Tokyo, Japan

SETLIST: Malted Milk / Terraplane Blues / How Long Blues / 32-20 / Kidman Blues / County Jail Blues / Forty Four Blues / Blues Leave Me Alone / Tell Me Mama / White Room / Badge / Wonderful Tonight / Stone Free / Circus Left Town / Tears In Heaven / Crossroads / Tearing Us Apart / Groaning The Blues / Cocaine / Ain't Nobody's Business / Layla

26 October 1993, Budokan, Tokyo, Japan

SETLIST: Malted Milk / Terraplane Blues / How Long Blues / 32-20 / Kidman Blues / County Jail Blues / Forty Four Blues / Blues Leave Me Alone / Tell Me Mama / White Room / Badge / Wonderful Tonight / Stone Free / Circus Left Town / Tears In Heaven / Crossroads / Tearing Us Apart / Groaning The Blues / Cocaine / Ain't Nobody's Business / Layla

27 October 1993, Budokan, Tokyo, Japan

SETLIST: Malted Milk / Terraplane Blues / How Long Blues / 32-20 / Kidman Blues / County Jail Blues / Forty Four Blues / Blues Leave Me Alone / Tell Me Mama / White Room / Badge / Wonderful Tonight / Stone Free / Circus Left Town / Tears In Heaven / Crossroads / Tearing Us Apart / Groaning The Blues / Cocaine / Ain't Nobody's Business / Layla

28 October 1993, day off

29 October 1993, day off

30 October 1993, Yokohama Arena, Yokohama, Japan

SETLIST: Malted Milk / Terraplane Blues / How Long Blues / 32-20 / Kidman Blues / County Jail Blues / Forty Four Blues / Blues Leave Me Alone / Tell Me Mama / White Room / Badge / Wonderful Tonight / Stone Free / Circus Left Town / Tears In Heaven / Crossroads / Tearing Us Apart / Groaning The Blues / Cocaine / Ain't Nobody's Business / Layla

31 October 1993, Budokan, Tokyo, Japan

SETLIST: Malted Milk / Terraplane Blues / How Long Blues / 32-20 / Kidman Blues / County Jail Blues / Forty Four Blues / Blues Leave Me Alone / Tell Me Mama / White Room / Badge / Wonderful Tonight / Stone Free / Circus Left Town / Tears In Heaven / Crossroads / Tearing Us Apart / Groaning The Blues / Cocaine / Ain't Nobody's Business / Layla

1 November 1993, return home

DECEMBER 1993

NEW YEAR'S EVE DANCE 1993

31 December 1993, Woking Leisure Centre, Woking, Surrey

Eric and his band are called the Resentments.

BAND LINEUP:
Eric Clapton: guitar, vocals
Alan Darby: guitar
Chris Stainton: keyboards
Dave Bronze: bass
Richie Hayward: drums
Maggie Ryder: vocals
Helen Jennor: vocals
Zara: vocals

SETLIST 1: Everyday I Have The Blues / Knock On Wood / Sweet Home Chicago / Someday After A While / After Midnight / Love Letters / Rollin' Man[1] / Because The Night[3] / Knockin' On Heaven's Door / I Feel So Good

[1]with Alan Darby on lead vocals

SETLIST 2: Midnight Hour / I Drink The Wine[1] / Five Long Years / Crazy Love[2] / Lay Down Sally / Wonderful Tonight / Cocaine / Stone Free / Layla / Crossroads

[1]with Alan Darby on lead vocals
[2]with Helen Jennor on lead vocals
[3]with Zara on lead vocals

RECORDING SESSIONS 1993

ROBBIE ROBERTSON HOME STUDIO

JANUARY 1993

Eric and Robbie record some demos and throw some ideas around. They will eventually record together in 2008, using these demos as the basis of an album along with new material.

THE RIGHT MISTAKE (Robbie Robertson) (demo) *How To Become Clairvoyant* deluxe 2CD 429 Records FTN17822 released April 2011

HE DON'T LIVE HERE NO MORE (Robbie Robertson) (demo) *How To Become Clairvoyant* deluxe 2CD 429 Records FTN17822 released April 2011

FEAR OF FALLING (Eric Clapton / Robbie Robertson) (demo) *How To Become Clairvoyant* deluxe 2CD 429 Records FTN17822 released April 2011

THIS IS WHERE I GET OFF (Robbie Robertson) (demo) *How To Become Clairvoyant* deluxe 2CD 429 Records FTN17822 released April 2011

MADAME X (demo) (Eric Clapton) *How To Become Clairvoyant* deluxe 2CD 429 Records FTN17822 released April 2011

WON'T BE BACK (Eric Clapton / Robbie Robertson) (demo) available only on Japanese edition of *How To Become Clairvoyant* CD

HIT FACTORY
421 West 54th Street, New York City
Session for Curtis Mayfield Tribute

AUGUST 1993

YOU MUST BELIEVE ME (Curtis Mayfield) *A Tribute To Curtis Mayfield* CD Warner Bros. 9362-45500-2 released February 1994

Eric Clapton: guitar, lead vocals
Nile Rodgers: guitar
Sterling Campbell: drums
Barry Campbell: bass guitar
Richard Hilton: keyboards
John Powe: backing vocals
Shawn Powe: backing vocals
Demetrius Peete: backing vocals
John Clay: backing vocals

Producer: Nile Rogers
Engineer: Gary Tole

HIT FACTORY
421 West 54th Street, New York City

AUGUST 1993

STONE FREE (Jimi Hendrix) *Stone Free: A Tribute To Jimi Hendrix* CD Reprise Records released November 1993

Eric Clapton: guitar, vocals
Bernard Edwards: bass
Tony Thompson: drums
Nile Rodgers: guitar
Richard Hilton: keyboards
John Clay: backing vocals
John Powe: backing vocals
Demetrius Peete: backing vocals
Shawn Powe: backing vocals

BURNING OF THE MIDNIGHT LAMP (Jimi Hendrix) *Power of Soul: A Tribute to Jimi Hendrix* CD Experience Hendrix EXP2281 released May 2004

Eric Clapton: guitar, vocals
Bernard Edwards: bass
Tony Thompson: drums
Nile Rodgers: guitar
Richard Hilton: keyboards
John Clay: backing vocals
John Powe: backing vocals
Demetrius Peete: backing vocals
Shawn Powe: backing vocals

Producer: Nile Rogers
Engineer: Gary Tole

OLYMPIC RECORDING STUDIOS
117-123 Church Road, Barnes, London
Sessions for *From The Cradle*

NOVEMBER 1993, DECEMBER 1993, MARCH 1994

BLUES BEFORE SUNRISE (Leroy Carr) *From The Cradle* CD Reprise 9362-45735-2 released September 1994

THIRD DEGREE (Eddie Boyd, Willie Dixon) *From The Cradle* CD Reprise 9362-45735-2 released September 1994

RECONSIDER BABY (Lowell Fulson) *From The Cradle* CD Reprise 9362-45735-2 released September 1994

HOOCHIE COOCHIE MAN (Willie Dixon) *From The Cradle* CD Reprise 9362-45735-2 released September 1994

FIVE LONG YEARS (Eddie Boyd) *From The Cradle* CD Reprise 9362-45735-2 released September 1994

I'M TORE DOWN (Sonny Thompson) *From The Cradle* CD Reprise 9362-45735-2 released September 1994

HOW LONG BLUES (Leroy Carr) *From The Cradle* CD Reprise 9362-45735-2 released September 1994

GOIN' AWAY BABY (James Lane) *From The Cradle* CD Reprise 9362-45735-2 released September 1994

BLUES LEAVE ME ALONE (James Lane) *From The Cradle* CD Reprise 9362-45735-2 released September 1994

SINNER'S PRAYER (Lowell Glenn, Lowell Fulson) *From The Cradle* CD Reprise 9362-45735-2 released September 1994

MOTHERLESS CHILD (Barbeque Bob) *From The Cradle* CD Reprise 9362-45735-2 released September 1994

IT HURTS ME TOO (Elmore James) *From The Cradle* CD Reprise 9362-45735-2 released September 1994

SOMEDAY AFTER A WHILE (Freddy King / Sonny Thomson) *From The Cradle* CD Reprise 9362-45735-2 released September 1994

STANDING ROUND CRYING (McKinley Morganfield) *From The Cradle* CD Reprise 9362-45735-2 released September 1994

DRIFTING BLUES (Charles Brown / Johnny Moore / Eddie Williams) *From The Cradle* CD Reprise 9362-45735-2 released September 1994

GROANING THE BLUES (Willie Dixon) *From The Cradle* CD Reprise 9362-45735-2 released September 1994

Eric Clapton: guitar, vocals

Dave Bronze: bass
Jim Keltner: drums
Andy Fairweather Low: guitar
Jerry Portnoy: harmonica
Chris Stainton: keyboards
Roddy Lorimer: trumpet
Simon Clarke: baritone saxophone
Tim Sanders: tenor saxophone
Richie Hayward: percussion on "How Long Blues"

Producers: Eric Clapton / Russ Titelman
Engineers: Alan Douglas / Alan Haas ("How Long Blues")

> **"**All of *From the Cradle* was live. They played songs over and over until we got the right take, leaving a song if it wasn't happening and going back to it. Many spectacular solos are in the can but the best playing and singing from our various takes is on that album. Eric chose the songs. Ideas were being thrown around the studio and a couple may have been used from those suggestions.**"**
>
> **—RUSS TITELMAN**

Recorded live in the studio with no overdubs or edits except for Dobro oververdub on "How Long Blues" and drum overdub on "Motherless Child." Horns arranged and played by the Kick Horns.

Eric used approximately fifty guitars during the *Cradle* sessions from his personal collection, including a dot-neck Gibson ES-335 (a tobacco sunburst model from the early 60s), and his famous cherry red ES-335. He also used an Olympic white Eric Clapton Model Strat from the Fender Custom Shop, several different Gibson L-5s, Byrdlands, and some Super 400s. He played straight through a Soldano SLO-100. The acoustic guitars used on the album included several Martin acoustics, his Tony Zemaitis 12-string (known as "Ivan the Terrible" with a heart-shaped motif), and several resonator guitars (Dobros) in different tunings. Clapton used an old Fender Twin amp with no effects and occasionally an old Fender Champ, plus a Silverface Fender Deluxe and a Blonde Showman head.

When Eric went out on the road to promote the album in 1994 and 1995, many of these made the trip with him. A good number of these guitars were later sold by Eric at auctions held in 1999 and 2004 to help raise funds for Crossroads Centre in Antigua.

12

1994

1994

Clearly, the blues were becoming more and more of a feature in Eric's concerts, much to the delight of fans. This was a bold move on his behalf and his manager was not as keen on this direction as Eric was. In December 1993 he had entered Olympic Studios in Barnes to start sessions for an all-blues album that would feature songs that had had some meaning to him in his life. Although there were several numbers that could have been recorded, he was very selective about what would be used. The resulting tours during 1994 and 1995 showed Eric at his best. Highlights were the U.S. club shows as well as the Japanese tour in 1995 where Eric had never played better. I have no idea where he was channeling his playing from, but it was simply breathtaking. It made his playing on the Bluesbreakers album seem amateurish. Yes, that's how good he was.

JANUARY 1994

19 January 1994, Waldorf Astoria Hotel, Grand Ballroom, New York (9th Annual Induction Ceremony for the Rock and Roll Hall of Fame. Eric inducted The Band and joined them for a performance of "The Weight")

BAND LINEUP:
Eric Clapton: guitar, vocals
Robbie Robertson: guitar
Anton Fig: drums
Levon Helm: drums
Paul Schaffer: keyboards
Rick Danko: bass
Garth Hudson: accordion

SETLIST:

The Weight (Robbie Robertson) available on Time Life's *Rock And Roll Hall Of Fame Museum Live* box set of DVDs and the audio can be purchased from iTunes.

U.K. TOUR 1994

FEBRUARY 1994

Eric's equipment for this tour consisted of a 12-string acoustic guitar, a Martin 6-string acoustic guitar, Dobro, blonde Gibson Byrdland, brown sunburst Gibson ES-175, white Fender Stratocaster, black Fender Stratocaster for slide work, brown sunburst Gibson ES-335, cherry red Gibson ES-335.

BAND LINEUP:
Eric Clapton: guitar, vocals
Andy Fairweather Low: guitar
Jerry Portnoy: harmonica
Chris Stainton: keyboards
Dave Bronze: bass
Steve Gadd: drums
Roddy Lorimer: trumpet
Tim Sanders: tenor saxophone
Simon Clarke: baritone saxophone

16 February 1994, Apollo Theatre, Manchester (with Nine Below Zero)

SETLIST: not known

Eric Clapton with Dobro at the Royal Albert Hall in London, February 1994.

20 February 1994, Royal Albert Hall, London (with Nine Below Zero)

SETLIST: Terraplane Blues / Come On In My Kitchen / Malted Milk / How Long Blues / Kidman Blues / County Jail / Forty Four Blues / Standing Around Crying / Goin' Away Baby / Blues All Day Long / Hoochie Coochie Man / It Hurts Me Too / Blues Before Sunrise / Someday After A While / Tore Down / White Room / Badge / Wonderful Tonight / Stone Free / Circus / Tears In Heaven / Five Long Years / Tearing Us Apart / Crossroads / Groaning The Blues / Layla / Ain't Nobody's Business

21 February 1994, Royal Albert Hall, London (with Nine Below Zero)

SETLIST: Terraplane Blues / Come On In My Kitchen / Malted Milk / How Long Blues / Kidman Blues / County Jail Blues / Forty Four Blues / Standing Around Crying / Going Away / Blues All Day Long / Hoochie Coochie Man / Hurts Me Too / Blues Before Sunrise / Someday After A While / Tore Down / White Room / Badge / Wonderful Tonight / Stone Free / Circus Left Town / Tears In Heaven / Five Long Years / Tearing Us Apart / Crossroads / Groaning The Blues / Layla / Ain't Nobody's Business

22 February 1994, Royal Albert Hall, London (with Nine Below Zero)

SETLIST: Terraplane Blues / Come On In My Kitchen / Malted Milk / How Long Blues / Kidman Blues / County Jail / Forty Four Blues / Standing Around Crying / Goin' Away Baby / Blues All Day Long / Hoochie Coochie Man / It Hurts Me Too / Blues Before Sunrise / Someday After A While / Tore Down / White Room / Badge / Wonderful Tonight / Stone Free / Circus / Tears In Heaven / Five

Long Years / Tearing Us Apart / Crossroads / Groaning The Blues / Layla / Ain't Nobody's Business

24 February 1994, Royal Albert Hall, London (with Nine Below Zero)

SETLIST: Terraplane Blues / Come On In My Kitchen / Malted Milk / How Long Blues / Kidman Blues / County Jail / Forty Four Blues / Standing Around Crying / Goin' Away Baby / Blues All Day Long / Hoochie Coochie Man / It Hurts Me Too / Blues Before Sunrise / Someday After A While / Tore Down / White Room / Badge / Wonderful Tonight / Stone Free / Circus / Tears In Heaven / Five Long Years / Tearing Us Apart / Crossroads / Groaning The Blues / Layla / Ain't Nobody's Business

25 February 1994, Royal Albert Hall, London (with Nine Below Zero)

SETLIST: Terraplane Blues / Come On In My Kitchen / Malted Milk / How Long Blues / Kidman Blues / County Jail / Forty Four Blues / Standing Around Crying / Goin' Away Baby / Blues All Day Long / Hoochie Coochie Man / It Hurts Me Too / Blues Before Sunrise / Someday After A While / Tore Down / White Room / Badge / Wonderful Tonight / Stone Free / Circus / Tears In Heaven / Five Long Years / Tearing Us Apart / Crossroads / Groaning The Blues / Layla / Ain't Nobody's Business

26 February 1994, Royal Albert Hall, London (with Nine Below Zero)

SETLIST: Terraplane Blues / Come On In My Kitchen / Malted Milk / How Long Blues / Kidman Blues / County Jail / Forty Four Blues / Standing Around Crying / Goin' Away Baby / Blues All Day Long / Hoochie Coochie Man / It Hurts Me Too / Blues Before Sunrise / Someday After A While / Tore Down / White Room / Badge / Wonderful Tonight / Stone Free / Circus / Tears In Heaven / Five Long Years / Tearing Us Apart / Crossroads / Groaning The Blues / Layla / Ain't Nobody's Business

28 February 1994, Royal Albert Hall, London (with Nine Below Zero) (100th Eric Clapton show at the Royal Albert Hall)

SETLIST: Terraplane Blues / Come On In My Kitchen / Malted Milk / How Long Blues / Kidman Blues / County Jail Blues / Forty Four Blues / Standin' Around Cryin' /

Going Away / Blues All Day Long / Hoochie Coochie Man / Hurts Me Too / Blues Before Sunrise / Someday After A While / Tore Down / White Room / /Badge / Wonderful Tonight / Stone Free / Circus Left Town / Tears In Heaven / Five Long Years / Tearing Us Apart / Crossroads / Groaning The Blues / Layla / Ain't Nobody's Business

MARCH 1994

1 March 1994, Royal Albert Hall, London (with Nine Below Zero)

SETLIST: Terraplane Blues / Come On In My Kitchen / Malted Milk / How Long Blues / Kidman Blues / County Jail / Forty Four Blues / Standing Around Crying / Goin' Away Baby / Blues All Day Long / Hoochie Coochie Man / It Hurts Me Too / Blues Before Sunrise / Someday After A While / Tore Down / White Room / Badge / Wonderful Tonight / Stone Free / Circus / Tears In Heaven / Five Long Years / Tearing Us Apart / Crossroads / Groaning The Blues / Layla / Ain't Nobody's Business

2 March 1994, Royal Albert Hall, London (with Nine Below Zero)

SETLIST: Terraplane Blues / Come On In My Kitchen / Malted Milk / How Long Blues / Kidman Blues / County Jail / Forty Four Blues / Standing Around Crying / Goin' Away Baby / Blues All Day Long / Hoochie Coochie Man / It Hurts Me Too / Blues Before Sunrise / Someday After A While / Tore Down / White Room / Badge / Wonderful Tonight / Stone Free / Circus / Tears In Heaven / Five Long Years / Tearing Us Apart / Crossroads / Groaning The Blues / Layla / Ain't Nobody's Business

4 March 1994, Royal Albert Hall, London (with Nine Below Zero)

SETLIST: Terraplane Blues / Come On In My Kitchen / Malted Milk / How Long Blues / Kidman Blues / County Jail / Forty Four Blues / Standing Around Crying / Goin' Away Baby / Blues All Day Long / Hoochie Coochie Man / It Hurts Me Too / Blues Before Sunrise / Someday After A While / Tore Down / White Room / Badge / Wonderful Tonight / Stone Free / Circus / Tears In Heaven / Five Long Years / Tearing Us Apart / Crossroads / Groaning The Blues / Layla / Ain't Nobody's Business

5 March 1994, Royal Albert Hall, London (with Nine Below Zero)

SETLIST: Terraplane Blues / Kind Hearted Woman / Malted Milk / How Long Blues / Kidman Blues / County Jail / Forty Four Blues / Standing Around Crying / Goin' Away Baby / Blues All Day Long / Hoochie Coochie Man / It Hurts Me Too / Blues Before Sunrise / Someday After A While / Tore Down / White Room / Badge / Wonderful Tonight / Stone Free / Circus / Tears In Heaven / Five Long Years / Tearing Us Apart / Crossroads / Groaning The Blues / Layla / Ain't Nobody's Business

6 March 1994, Royal Albert Hall, London (with Nine Below Zero)

SETLIST: Terraplane Blues / Kind Hearted Woman / Malted Milk / How Long Blues / Kidman Blues / County Jail / Forty Four Blues / Standing Around Crying / Goin' Away Baby / Blues All Day Long / Hoochie Coochie Man / It Hurts Me Too / Blues Before Sunrise / Someday After A While / Tore Down / White Room / Badge / Wonderful Tonight / Stone Free / Circus / Tears In Heaven / Five Long Years / Tearing Us Apart / Crossroads / Groaning The Blues / Layla / Ain't Nobody's Business

MAY 1994

T.J. MARTELL FOUNDATION BENEFIT 1994

2 May 1994, Avery Fisher Hall, New York City (benefit for the T.J. Martell Foundation)

SETLIST: Terraplane Blues / Malted Milk / How Long Blues / Kidman Blues / County Jail Blues / Forty Four Blues / Blues All Day Long / Going Away / Standing Around Crying / Hoochie Coochie Man / It Hurts Me Too / Blues Before Sunrise / Third Degree / Reconsider Baby / Someday After A While / I'm Tore Down / Five Long Years / Born Under A Bad Sign / Groaning The Blues / Crossroads / Ain't Nobody's Business

JUNE 1994

RONNIE WOOD BIRTHDAY BASH 1994

5 June 1994, 606 Club, Chelsea (Eric jams with Ronnie Wood who was celebrating his 47th birthday four days late. Others present included Mick Jagger, Bill Wyman, and Slash)

SEPTEMBER 1994

SATURDAY NIGHT LIVE 1994

24 September 1994, *Saturday Night Live* TV Show, NBC Studios, Rockefeller Center, New York City (Eric was the musical guest for the first episode of *Saturday Night Live's* twentieth season)

BAND LINEUP:
Eric Clapton: guitar, vocals
Andy Fairweather Low: guitar
Chris Stainton: keyboards
Dave Bronze: bass
Andy Newmark: drums
Jerry Portnoy: harmonica
Simon Clarke: baritone saxophone
Roddy Lorimer: trumpet
Tim Sanders: tenor saxophone

SETLIST: I'm Tore Down / Five Long Years

28 September 1994, Manhattan Center Studios, New York City

Rehearsals for the forthcoming U.S. tour. Parts of the last rehearsal before the start of the *Nothing But The Blues* Tour on this date are televised in different countries as a promotion for the *From The Cradle* album.

SETLIST: Hoochie Coochie Man / I'm Tore Down / Sinner's Prayer / Motherless Child / Malted Milk / Born Under A Bad Sign / Someday After A While / It

Hurts Me Too / Forty Four Blues / Five Long Years / Crossroads / Ain't Nobody's Business / Drifting Blues[1]

[1] only shown on one edition of the broadcast

OCTOBER 1994

NOTHING BUT THE BLUES U.S. TOUR 1994

BAND LINEUP:
Eric Clapton: guitar, vocals
Andy Fairweather Low: guitar
Jerry Portnoy: harmonica
Chris Stainton: keyboards
Dave Bronze: bass
Andy Newmark: drums
Roddy Lorimer: trumpet
Tim Sanders: tenor saxophone
Simon Clarke: baritone saxophone

3 October 1994, Forum, Montreal, Quebec, Canada (with Jimmie Vaughan and the Tilt-A-Whirl Band)

SETLIST: not known

5 October 1994, Maple Leaf Gardens, Toronto, Ontario, Canada (with Jimmie Vaughan and the Tilt-A-Whirl Band)

SETLIST: Kidman Blues / County Jail / Gonna Cut Your Head / Blues All Day Long / Standing Around Crying / Hoochie Coochie Man / It Hurts Me Too / Blues Before Sunrise / Third Degree / Reconsider Baby / Sinner's Prayer / Can't Judge Nobody / Someday After A While / Tore Down / Have You Ever Loved A Woman / Crosscut Saw / Five Long Years / Born Under A Bad Sign / Groaning The Blues / Crossroads / Ain't Nobody's Business / Sweet Home Chicago[1]

[1] with Jimmie Vaughan on guitar and vocals

6 October 1994, Maple Leaf Gardens, Toronto, Ontario, Canada (with Jimmie Vaughan and the Tilt-A-Whirl Band)

SETLIST: Motherless Child / Malted Milk / How Long Blues / Kidman Blues / County Jail / Forty Four

Blues / Blues All Day Long / Going Away / Standing Around Crying / Hoochie Coochie Man / It Hurts Me Too / Blues Before Sunrise / Third Degree / Reconsider Baby / Sinner's Prayer / Can't Judge Nobody / Someday After A While / Tore Down / Have You Ever Loved A Woman / Crosscut Saw / Five Long Years / Born Under A Bad Sign / Groaning The Blues / Crossroads / Ain't Nobody's Business / Sweet Home Chicago[1]

[1]with Jimmie Vaughan on guitar and vocals

8 October 1994, Madison Square Garden, New York City (with Jimmie Vaughan and the Tilt-A-Whirl Band)

SETLIST: Motherless Child / Malted Milk / How Long Blues / Kidman Blues / County Jail / Forty Four Blues / Blues All Day Long / Going Away / Standing Around Crying / Hoochie Coochie Man / It Hurts Me Too / Blues Before Sunrise / Third Degree / Reconsider Baby / Sinner's Prayer / I Can't Judge Nobody / Someday After A While / Tore Down / Have You Ever Loved A Woman / Crosscut Saw / Five Long Years / Born Under A Bad Sign / Groaning the Blues / Crossroads / Ain't Nobody's Business If I Do / Sweet Home Chicago[1]

[1]with Jimmie Vaughan on guitar and vocals

9 October 1994, Madison Square Garden, New York City (with Jimmie Vaughan and the Tilt-A-Whirl Band)

SETLIST: Motherless Child / Malted Milk / How Long Blues / Kidman Blues / County Jail / Forty Four Blues / Blues Leave Me Alone / Going Away Baby / Standing Around Crying / Hoochie Coochie Man / It Hurts Me Too / Blues Before Sunrise / Third Degree / Reconsider Baby / Sinners Prayer / I Can't Judge Nobody / Someday After A While / Tore Down / Have You Ever Loved A Woman / Crosscut Saw / Five Long Years / Born Under A Bad Sign / Groaning The Blues / Crossroads / Ain't Nobody's Business / Sweet Home Chicago[1]

[1]with Jimmie Vaughan on guitar and vocals

10 October 1994, Madison Square Garden, New York City (with Jimmie Vaughan and the Tilt-A-Whirl Band)

SETLIST: Motherless Child / Malted Milk / How Long Blues / Kidman Blues / County Jail / Forty Four Blues / Blues All Day Long / Goin' Away Baby / Standing Around Crying / Hoochie Coochie Man / It Hurts Me

Too / Blues Before Sunrise / Third Degree / Reconsider Baby / Sinner's Prayer / Can't Judge Nobody / Someday After A While / Tore Down / Have You Ever Loved A Woman / Crosscut Saw / Five Long Years / Born Under A Bad Sign / Groaning The Blues / Crossroads / Ain't Nobody's Business / Sweet Home Chicago[1]

[1]with Jimmie Vaughan on guitar and vocals

12 October 1994, Capitol Centre, Washington, D.C. (with Jimmie Vaughan and the Tilt-A-Whirl Band)

SETLIST: Motherless Child / Malted Milk / How Long Blues / Kidman Blues / County Jail / Forty Four Blues / Blues All Day Long / Goin' Away Baby / Standing Around Crying / Hoochie Coochie Man / It Hurts Me Too / Blues Before Sunrise / Third Degree / Reconsider Baby / Sinner's Prayer / Can't Judge Nobody / Someday After A While / Tore Down / Have You Ever Loved A Woman / Crosscut Saw / Five Long Years / Born Under A Bad Sign / Groaning The Blues / Crossroads / Ain't Nobody's Business / Sweet Home Chicago[1]

[1]with Jimmie Vaughan on guitar and vocals

13 October 1994, Civic Center, Hartford, Connecticut (with Jimmie Vaughan and the Tilt-A-Whirl Band)

SETLIST: Motherless Child / Malted Milk / How Long Blues / Kidman Blues / County Jail / Forty Four Blues / Blues Leave Me Alone / Going Away / Standing Around Crying / Hoochie Coochie Man / It Hurts Me Too / Blues Before Sunrise / Third Degree / Reconsider Baby / Sinner's Prayer / Can't Judge Nobody / Someday After A While / Tore Down / Have You Ever Loved A Woman / Crosscut Saw / Five Long Years / Born Under A Bad Sign / Groaning The Blues / Crossroads / Ain't Nobody's Business / Sweet Home Chicago[1]

[1]with Jimmie Vaughan on guitar and vocals

14 October 1994, Centrum, Worcester, Massachusetts (with Jimmie Vaughan and the Tilt-A-Whirl Band)

SETLIST: Motherless Child / Malted Milk / How Long Blues / Kidman Blues / County Jail / Forty Four Blues / Blues All Day Long / Going Away Baby / Standing Around Crying / Hoochie Coochie Man / It Hurts Me Too / Blues Before Sunrise / Third Degree / Reconsider Baby / Sinner's Prayer / Can't Judge Nobody / Someday

After A While / Tore Down / Have You Ever Loved A Woman / Crosscut Saw / Five Long Years / Born Under A Bad Sign / Groaning The Blues / Crossroads / Ain't Nobody's Business / Sweet Home Chicago[1]

[1]with Jimmie Vaughan on guitar and vocals

16 October 1994, Civic Arena, Pittsburgh, Pennsylvania (with Jimmie Vaughan and the Tilt-A-Whirl Band)

SETLIST: Motherless Child / Malted Milk / How Long Blues / Kidman Blues / County Jail / Forty Four Blues / Blues All Day Long / Going Away Baby / Standing Around Crying / Hoochie Coochie Man / It Hurts Me Too / Blues Before Sunrise / Third Degree / Reconsider Baby / Sinner's Prayer / Can't Judge Nobody / Someday After A While / Tore Down / Have You Ever Loved A Woman / Crosscut Saw / Five Long Years / Born Under A Bad Sign / Groaning The Blues / Crossroads / Ain't Nobody's Business / Sweet Home Chicago[1]

[1]with Jimmie Vaughan on guitar and vocals

17 October 1994, Riverfront Coliseum, Cincinnati, Ohio (with Jimmie Vaughan and the Tilt-A-Whirl Band)

SETLIST: not known

18 October 1994, Gateway Arena, Cleveland, Ohio (with Jimmie Vaughan and the Tilt-A-Whirl Band)

SETLIST: Motherless Child / Malted Milk / How Long Blues / Kidman Blues / County Jail / Forty Four Blues / Blues All Day Long / Going Away / Standing Around Crying / Hoochie Coochie Man / Hurts Me Too / Blues Before Sunrise / Third Degree / Reconsider Baby / Sinner's Prayer / Someday After A While / Tore Down / Have You Ever Loved A Woman / Crosscut Saw / Five Long Years / Born Under A Bad Sign / Groaning The Blues / Crossroads / Ain't Nobody's Business / Sweet Home Chicago[1]

[1]with Jimmie Vaughan on guitar and vocals

20 October 1994, Palace of Auburn Hills, Auburn Hills, Michigan (with Jimmie Vaughan and the Tilt-A-Whirl Band)

SETLIST: not known

21 October 1994, United Center, Chicago, Illinois (with Jimmie Vaughan and the Tilt-A-Whirl Band)

SETLIST: Motherless Child / Malted Milk / How Long Blues / Kidman Blues / County Jail / Forty Four Blues / Blues All Day Long / Standing Around Crying / Hoochie Coochie Man / It Hurts Me Too / Blues Before Sunrise / Third Degree / Reconsider Baby / Sinner's Prayer / Can't Judge Nobody / Someday After A While / Tore Down / Have You Ever Loved A Woman / Crosscut Saw / Five Long Years / Born Under A Bad Sign / Groaning The Blues / Crossroads / Ain't Nobody's Business / Sweet Home Chicago[1]

[1]with Jimmie Vaughan on guitar and vocals

23 October 1994, Market Square Arena, Indianapolis, Indiana (with Jimmie Vaughan and the Tilt-A-Whirl Band)

SETLIST: Motherless Child / Malted Milk / How Long Blues / Kidman Blues / County Jail / Forty Four Blues / Blues Leave Me Alone / Standing Around Crying / Hoochie Coochie Man / It Hurts Me Too / Blues Before Sunrise / Third Degree / Reconsider Baby / Sinner's Prayer / Can't Judge Nobody / Someday After A While / Tore Down / Have You Ever Loved A Woman / Crosscut Saw / Five Long Years / Born Under A Bad Sign / Groaning The Blues / Ain't Nobody's Business / Sweet Home Chicago[1]

[1]with Jimmie Vaughan on guitar and vocals

24 October 1994, Bradley Center, Milwaukee, Wisconsin (with Jimmie Vaughan and the Tilt-A-Whirl Band)

SETLIST: Motherless Child / Malted Milk / How Long Blues / Kidman Blues / County Jail / Forty Four Blues / Blues Leave Me Alone / Standing Around Crying / Hoochie Coochie Man / It Hurts Me Too / Blues Before Sunrise / Third Degree / Reconsider Baby / Sinner's Prayer / Can't Judge Nobody / Someday After A While / Tore Down / Have You Ever Loved A Woman / Crosscut Saw / Five Long Years / Born Under A Bad Sign / Groaning The Blues / Ain't Nobody's Business / Sweet Home Chicago[1]

[1]with Jimmie Vaughan on guitar and vocals

26 October 1994, Pyramid, Memphis, Tennessee (with Jimmie Vaughan and the Tilt-A-Whirl Band)

SETLIST: Motherless Child / Malted Milk / Blues / Kidman Blues / County Jail / Forty Four Blues / Blues All Day Long / Standing Around Crying / Hoochie Coochie Man / It Hurts Me Too / Blues Before Sunrise / Third Degree / Reconsider Baby / Sinner's Prayer / Can't Judge Nobody / Someday After A While / Tore Down / Have You Ever Loved A Woman / Crosscut Saw / Five Long Years / Born Under A Bad Sign / Groaning The Blues / Crossroads / Ain't Nobody's Business / Sweet Home Chicago[1]

[1]with Jimmie Vaughan on guitar and vocals

27 October 1994, Kiel Auditorium, St. Louis, Missouri
(with Jimmie Vaughan and the Tilt-A-Whirl Band)

SETLIST: Motherless Child / Malted Milk / How Long Blues / Kidman Blues / County Jail / Forty Four Blues / Blues Leave Me Alone / Standing Around Crying / Hoochie Coochie Man / It Hurts Me Too / Blues Before Sunrise / Third Degree / Reconsider Baby / Sinner's Prayer / Can't Judge Nobody / Someday After A While / Tore Down / Have You Ever Loved A Woman / Crosscut Saw / Five Long Years / Born Under A Bad Sign / Groaning The Blues / Crossroads / Ain't Nobody's Business / Sweet Home Chicago[1]

[1]with Jimmie Vaughan on guitar and vocals

28 October 1994 Kemper Arena, Kansas City, Kansas
(with Jimmie Vaughan and the Tilt-A-Whirl Band)

SETLIST: Motherless Child / Malted Milk / How Long Blues / Kidman Blues / County Jail / Forty Four Blues / Blues All Day Long / Standing Around Crying / Hoochie Coochie Man / It Hurts Me Too / Blues Before Sunrise / Third Degree / Reconsider Baby / Sinner's Prayer / Can't Judge Nobody / Someday After A While / Tore Down / Have You Ever Loved A Woman / Crosscut Saw / Five Long Years / Born Under A Bad Sign / Groaning The Blues / Crossroads / Ain't Nobody's Business / Kansas City[1]

[1]with Jimmie Vaughan on guitar and vocals

30 October 1994, McNichols Arena, Denver, Colorado
(with Jimmie Vaughan and the Tilt-A-Whirl Band)

SETLIST: Motherless Child / Malted Milk / How Long Blues / Kidman Blues / County Jail Blues / Forty Four Blues / Blues All Day Long / Standing Around Crying / Hoochie Coochie Man / It Hurts Me Too / Blues Before Sunrise / Third Degree / Reconsider Baby / Sinner's Prayer

/ Can't Judge Nobody / Someday After A While / I'm Tore Down / Have You Ever Loved A Woman / Crosscut Saw / Five Long Years / Crossroads / Groaning The Blues / Ain't Nobody's Business / Sweet Home Chicago[1]

[1]with Jimmie Vaughan on guitar and vocals

31 October 1994, McNichols Arena, Denver, Colorado
(with Jimmie Vaughan and the Tilt-A-Whirl Band)

SETLIST: not known

NOVEMBER 1994

2 November 1994, America West Arena, Phoenix, Arizona
(with Jimmie Vaughan and the Tilt-A-Whirl Band)

SETLIST: Motherless Child / Malted Milk / How Long Blues / Kidman Blues / County Jail / Forty Four Blues / Blues Leave Me Alone / Standing Around Crying / Hoochie Coochie Man / It Hurts Me Too / Blues Before Sunrise / Third Degree / Reconsider Baby / Sinner's Prayer / Can't Judge Nobody / Someday After A While / I'm Tore Down / Have You Ever Loved A Woman / Crosscut Saw / Five Long Years / Crossroads / Groaning The Blues / Ain't Nobody's Business / Sweet Home Chicago[1]

[1]with Jimmie Vaughan on guitar and vocals

3 November 1994, Forum, Los Angeles, California

SETLIST: Motherless Child / Malted Milk / How Long Blues / Kidman Blues / County Jail / Forty Four Blues / Blues Leave Me Alone / Standing Around Crying / Hoochie Coochie Man / It Hurts Me Too / Blues Before Sunrise / Third Degree / Reconsider Baby / Sinner's Prayer / I Can't Judge Nobody / Someday After A While / I'm Tore Down / Have You Ever Loved A Woman / Crosscut Saw / Five Long Years / Crossroads / Groaning The Blues / Ain't Nobody's Business / Sweet Home Chicago[1]

[1]with Jimmie Vaughan on guitar and vocals

4 November 1994, San Jose Arena, San Jose, Californiia

SETLIST: Motherless Child / Malted Milk / How Long Blues / Kidman Blues / County Jail / Forty Four Blues / Blues Leave Me Alone / Standing Around Crying /

Hoochie Coochie Man / It Hurts Me Too / Blues Before Sunrise / Third Degree / Reconsider Baby / Sinner's Prayer / I Can't Judge Nobody / Someday After A While / I'm Tore Down / Have You Ever Loved A Woman / Crosscut Saw / Five Long Years / Crossroads / Groaning The Blues / Ain't Nobody's Business / Sweet Home Chicago[1]

[1]with Jimmie Vaughan on guitar and vocals

FROM THE CRADLE CLUB DATES 1994

7 November 1994, Fillmore West, San Francisco, California

SETLIST: Motherless Child / Malted Milk / How Long Blues / Kidman Blues / County Jail / Forty Four Blues / Blues All Day Long / Standing Around Crying / Hoochie Coochie Man / It Hurts Me Too / Blues Before Sunrise / Third Degree / Reconsider Baby / Sinner's Prayer / I Can't Judge Nobody / Someday After A While / Tore Down / Have You Ever Loved A Woman / Crosscut Saw / Five Long Years / Crossroads / Groaning The Blues /Ain't Nobody's Business

Martin Scorsese filmed tonight's show on a single camera as a test run in preparation for the filming of the following two nights at the Fillmore. They were used for a documentary called *Nothing But The Blues*. The film traced the history of the blues with Eric Clapton discussing who had influenced him throughout his career, with video clips of performances by Howlin' Wolf, Buddy Guy, Muddy Waters, B.B. King, among others, and interspersed with footage of Eric from the Fillmore shows. The film was shown once on PBS Television but sadly never received an official home-video release. In early summer 1995, Warner/Reprise produced a limited number of copies to be used for promotion. These also feature a unique stunning electric performance of "Drifting Blues" not shown on the PBS release.

8 November 1994, Fillmore West, San Francisco, California

SETLIST: Motherless Child / Malted Milk / How Long Blues / Kidman Blues / County Jail / Forty Four Blues / Blues All Day Long / Standing Around Crying / Hoochie Coochie Man / It Hurts Me Too / Blues Before Sunrise / Third Degree / Reconsider Baby / Sinner's Prayer / Can't Judge Nobody / Early In The Morning / Everyday I Have The Blues / Someday After A While / Tore Down / Have You Ever Loved A Woman / Crossroads / Groaning The Blues / Five Long Years / Ain't Nobody's Business

"Motherless Child," "Malted Milk," "How Long Blues," "Forty Four Blues," "Blues All Day Long," "Standing Around Crying," "It Hurts Me Too," "Reconsider Baby," "Sinner's Prayer," "Everyday I Have The Blues," "Tore Down," "Five Long Years," "Groaning The Blues" and "Ain't Nobody's Business" are used from this show by Martin Scorsese for his unreleased *Nothing But The Blues* documentary.

9 November 1994, Fillmore West, San Francisco, California

SETLIST: Motherless Child / Malted Milk / How Long Blues / Kidman Blues / County Jail / Forty Four Blues / Blues All Day Long / Standing Around Crying / Hoochie Coochie Man / It Hurts Me Too / Blues Before Sunrise / Third Degree / Reconsider Baby / Sinner's Prayer / Can't Judge Nobody / Early In The Morning / Too Bad / Someday After A While / Tore Down / Have You Ever Loved A Woman / Crosscut Saw / Drifting Blues / Crossroads / Groaning The Blues / Five Long Years / Ain't Nobody's Business

"Early In The Morning," "Someday After A While," "Have You Ever Loved A Woman," "Drifting Blues," and "Crossroads" are used from this show by Martin Scorsese for his unreleased *Nothing But The Blues* documentary.

11 November 1994, House Of Blues, Los Angeles, California

SETLIST: Motherless Child / Malted Milk / How Long Blues / Kidman Blues / County Jail / Forty Four Blues / Blues All Day Long / Standing Around Crying / Hoochie Coochie Man / It Hurts Me Too / Blues Before Sunrise / Third Degree / Reconsider Baby / Sinner's Prayer / Can't Judge Nobody / Early In The Morning / Let Me Love You Baby / Someday After A While / Tore Down / Have You Ever Loved A Woman / Crosscut Saw / Five Long Years / Crossroads / Groaning The Blues / Ain't Nobody's Business

12 November 1994, House of Blues, Los Angeles, California

SETLIST: Motherless Child / Malted Milk / How Long Blues / Kidman Blues / County Jail / Forty Four Blues / Blues All Day Long / Going Away / Standing Around Crying / Hoochie Coochie Man / It Hurts Me Too / Blues Before Sunrise / Third Degree / Reconsider Baby / Sinner's Prayer / Can't Judge Nobody / Early In The Morning / Everyday I Have The Blues / Someday After A While / Tore Down / Have You Ever Loved A Woman / Crosscut Saw / Five Long Years / Crossroads / Groaning The Blues / Ain't Nobody's Business

13 November 1994, House of Blues, Los Angeles, California

SETLIST: Motherless Child / Malted Milk / How Long Blues / Kidman Blues / County Jail / Forty Four Blues / Blues All Day Long / Standing Around Crying / Hoochie Coochie Man / It Hurts Me Too / Blues Before Sunrise / Third Degree / Reconsider Baby / Sinner's Prayer / Can't Judge Nobody / Early In The Morning / Everyday I Have The Blues / Someday After A While / Tore Down / Have You Ever Loved A Woman / Crosscut Saw / Five Long Years / Crossroads / Groaning The Blues / Let Me Love You Baby / Ain't Nobody's Business

16 November 1994, Legends, Chicago, Illinois

SETLIST: Motherless Child / Malted Milk / How Long Blues / Kidman Blues / County Jail / Forty Four Blues / Blues All Day Long / Going Away / Standing Around Crying / Hoochie Coochie Man / It Hurts Me Too / Blues Before Sunrise / Third Degree / Reconsider Baby / Sinner's Prayer / You Can't Judge Nobody / Early In The Morning / Everyday I Have The Blues / Someday After A While / Tore Down / Have You Ever Loved A Woman / Crosscut Saw / Five Long Years / Crossroads / Groaning The Blues / Ain't Nobody's Business

17 November 1994, Legends, Chicago, Illinois

SETLIST: Motherless Child / Malted Milk / How Long Blues / Kidman Blues / County Jail / Forty Four Blues / Blues All Day Long / Standing Around Crying / Hoochie Coochie Man / It Hurts Me Too / Blues Before Sunrise / Third Degree / Reconsider Baby / Sinner's Prayer / Can't Judge Nobody / Early In The Morning / Everyday I Have The Blues / Someday After A While / Tore Down / Have You Ever Loved A Woman / Crosscut Saw / Five Long Years / Crossroads / Groaning The Blues / Ain't Nobody's Business

18 November 1994, Legends, Chicago, Illinois

SETLIST: not known

21 November 1994, House of Blues, New Orleans, Louisiana

SETLIST: not known

22 November 1994, House of Blues, New Orleans, Louisiana

SETLIST: Motherless Child / Malted Milk / How Long Blues / Kidman Blues / County Jail / Forty Four Blues / Blues All Day Long / Going Away / Standing Around Crying / Hoochie Coochie Man / It Hurts Me Too / Blues Before Sunrise / Third Degree / Reconsider Baby / Sinner's Prayer / Can't Judge Nobody / Early In The Morning / Everyday I Have The Blues / Someday After A While / Tore Down / Have You Ever Loved A Woman / Crosscut Saw / Groaning The Blues / Crossroads / Five Long Years / Blues Jam[1] / What A Shame[1]

[1]with Clarence Gatemouth Brown on guitar and vocals

23 November 1994, House of Blues, New Orleans, Louisiana

SETLIST: Motherless Child / Malted Milk / How Long Blues / Kidman Blues / County Jail / Forty Four Blues / Blues All Day Long / Going Away / Standing Around Crying / Hoochie Coochie Man / It Hurts Me Too / Blues Before Sunrise / Third Degree / Reconsider Baby / Sinner's Prayer / Can't Judge Nobody / Early In The Morning / Let Me Love You Baby / Someday After A While / Tore Down / Have You Ever Loved A Woman / Crosscut Saw / Five Long Years / Crossroads / Groaning The Blues / Everyday I Have The Blues / Ain't Nobody's Business

26 November 1994, Irving Plaza, New York City

SETLIST: Motherless Child / Malted Milk / How Long Blues / Kidman Blues / County Jail / Forty Four Blues / Blues All Day Long / Going Away / Standing Around Crying / Hoochie Coochie Man / It Hurts Me Too / Blues Before Sunrise / Third Degree / Reconsider Baby / Sinner's Prayer / Can't Judge Nobody / Early In The Morning / Everyday I Have The Blues / Someday After A While / Tore Down / Have You Ever Loved A Woman / Crosscut Saw / Five Long Years / Crossroads / Groaning The Blues / Sweet Home Chicago / Ain't Nobody's Business

27 November 1994, Irving Plaza, New York City

SETLIST: Motherless Child / Malted Milk / How Long Blues / Kidman Blues / County Jail / Forty Four Blues / Blues All Day Long / Going Away / Standing Around Crying / Hoochie Coochie Man / It Hurts Me Too / Blues Before Sunrise / Third Degree / Reconsider Baby / Sinner's Prayer / Can't Judge Nobody / Early In The Morning / Everyday I Have The Blues / Someday After A While / Tore Down / Have You Ever Loved A Woman / Crosscut Saw / Drifting Blues / Crossroads / Groaning The Blues / Ain't Nobody's Business

28 November 1994, Irving Plaza, New York City

SETLIST: Motherless Child / Malted Milk / How Long Blues / Kidman Blues / County Jail / Forty Four Blues / Blues Leave Me Alone / Standing Around Crying / Going Away / Hoochie Coochie Man / It Hurts Me Too / Blues Before Sunrise / Third Degree / Reconsider Baby / Sinner's Prayer / Before You Accuse Me / Early In The Morning / Everyday I Have The Blues / Someday After A While / Tore Down / Have You Ever Loved A Woman / Crosscut Saw / Black Cat Bone / Five Long Years / Crossroads / Groaning The Blues / Ain't Nobody's Business

The final performance of the U.S. 1994 blues tour. A stunning performance. "Black Cat Bone" was only performed at this show.

DECEMBER 1994

NEW YEAR'S EVE DANCE 1994

31 December 1994, Woking Leisure Centre, Woking, Surrey

Eric and his band are called the Promises.

BAND LINEUP:
Eric Clapton: guitar, vocals
Alan Darby: guitar, vocals
Chris Stainton: keyboards
Dave Bronze: bass
Andy Newmark: drums
Roddy Lorimer: trumpet
Tim Sanders: tenor saxophone
Simon Clarke: baritone saxophone
Maggie Ryder: vocals
Helen Jennor: vocals

SETLIST 1: In The Midnight Hour / Blues Leave Me Alone / Lay Down Sally / Wonderful Tonight / Five Long Years / I Can't Make You Love Me[1] / It Hurts Me Too / Blues Before Sunrise / Rollin' Man[2]

SETLIST 2: Knock On Wood / Knockin' On Heaven's Door / Tore Down / Have You Ever Loved A Woman / Reconsider Baby / Drift Away[3] / Everyday I Have The Blues / I Hardly Ever Do[2] / Cocaine / Someday After A While / Let Me Love You Baby

[1] with Maggie Ryder on lead vocals
[2] with Alan Darby on lead vocals
[3] with Helen Jennor on lead vocals

RECORDING SESSIONS 1994

ERIC CLAPTON GUEST SESSION

SNAKE RANCH STUDIOS 90 Lots Road, Chelsea, London Session for Bill Wyman

APRIL 1994

MELODY (Mick Jagger / Keith Richards) *Struttin' Our Stuff* CD UK BMG 74321 51441 2 released September 1997 / US VEL-79708-2 released February 1998

Bill Wyman: bass
Terry Taylor: guitar
Graham Broad: drums
Beverly Skeete: vocals
Georgie Fame: vocals, Hammond B3 organ
Eric Clapton: guitar
Frank Mead: saxophone
Nick Payn: saxophone
Martin Drover: trumpet
Dave Hartley: piano

GEE BABY AIN'T I GOOD TO YOU (Don Redman / Andy Razaf) *Anyway The Wind Blows* CD BMG 74321 59523 2 released February 1999

Bill Wyman: bass
Terry Taylor: guitar
Graham Broad: drums
Georgie Fame: vocals, Hammond B3 organ
Eric Clapton: guitar
Dave Hartley: piano
Frank Mead: saxophone
Nick Payn: saxophone
Melanie Redmond: backing vocals
Debi Doss: backing vocals
Keeley Smith: backing vocals

Producer: Bill Wyman
Engineer: Stuart Epps

ERIC CLAPTON GUEST SESSION

METROPOLIS STUDIOS
Power House, 70 Chiswick High Road, London
Session for Comic Relief single

JUNE 1994

LOVE CAN BUILD A BRIDGE (Naomi Judd / Paul Overstreet / John Barlow Jarvis) CD single London Records 850 069-2 released March 1995

Cher: vocals
Chrissie Hynde: vocals
Neneh Cherry: vocals
Eric Clapton: guitar overdub

Producer: Peter Asher
Engineer: Frank Wolf

ERIC CLAPTON GUEST SESSION

OCEAN WAY RECORDING
6050 Sunset Boulevard, Hollywood, California
Session for Jimmy Rogers

NOVEMBER 1994

BLUES ALL DAY LONG (Jimmy Rogers) *Blues Blues Blues* CD Atlantic
Jimmy Rogers: guitar, vocals (verses 1, 3, 5)

Eric Clapton: guitar, vocals (verses 2, 4, and some choruses)
Carey Bell: harmonica
Johnnie Johnson: piano
Jimmy D. Lane: guitar
Freddie Crawford: bass
Ted Harvey: drums

THAT'S ALL RIGHT (Jimmy Rogers)

Jimmy Rogers: guitar, vocals (verses 1, 3, 5)
Eric Clapton: guitar, vocals (verses 2, 4, and choruses)
Carey Bell: harmonica
Johnnie Johnson: piano
Jimmy D. Lane: guitar
Freddie Crawford: bass
Ted Harvey: drums

GONNA SHOOT YOU RIGHT DOWN (BOOM BOOM) (John Lee Hooker / John Koenig / Jimmy Rogers)

Jimmy Rogers: guitar, vocals (verses 2, 4, 5, 7)
Eric Clapton: guitar
Jimmy Page: guitar
Robert Plant: vocals (verses 1, 3, 6, 7)
Carey Bell: harmonica
Johnnie Johnson: piano
Jimmy D. Lane: guitar
Freddie Crawford: bass
Ted Harvey: drums

Producer: John Koenig
Engineer: Michael C .Ross

Jimmy Page and Robert Plant's contributions were recorded at Pearl Sound, Detroit, Michigan, when they were touring the U.S. as Page & Plant in April 1995.

13

1995

FEBRUARY 1995

FROM THE CRADLE UK TOUR 1995

BAND LINEUP:
Eric Clapton: guitar, vocals
Andy Fairweather Low: guitar
Jerry Portnoy: harmonica
Chris Stainton: keyboards
Dave Bronze: bass
Steve Gadd: drums
Roddy Lorimer: trumpet
Tim Sanders: tenor saxophone
Simon Clarke: baritone saxophone

15 February 1995, Scottish Exhibition and Conference Centre, Glasgow, Scotland (with Clarence Gatemouth Brown)

SETLIST: Motherless Child / Malted Milk / Four Until Late / How Long Blues / Kidman Blues / County Jail / I'm Gonna Cut Your Head / Forty Four Blues / Blues All Day Long / Standing Around Crying / Hoochie Coochie Man / It Hurts Me Too / Blues Before Sunrise / Third Degree / Reconsider Baby / Sinner's Prayer / Bad Boy / Everyday I Have The Blues / Double Trouble / Someday After A While / Tore Down / Have You Ever Loved A Woman / Crosscut Saw / Five Long Years / Crossroads / Groaning The Blues / Got My Mojo Working / Ain't Nobody's Business

16 February 1995, Sheffield Arena, Sheffield, South Yorkshire (with Clarence Gatemouth Brown)

SETLIST: Motherless Child / Malted Milk / Four Until Late / How Long Blues / Kidman Blues / County Jail / I'm Gonna Cut Your Head / Forty Four Blues / Blues All Day Long / Standing Around Crying / Hoochie Coochie Man / It Hurts Me Too / Blues Before Sunrise / Third Degree / Reconsider Baby / Sinner's Prayer / Everyday I Have The Blues / Early In The Morning / Someday After A While / Tore Down / Have You Ever Loved A Woman / Crosscut Saw / Five Long Years / Crossroads / Got My Mojo Working / Ain't Nobody's Business

19 February 1995, Royal Albert Hall, London (with Clarence Gatemouth Brown)

SETLIST: Motherless Child / Malted Milk / From Four Until Late / How Long Blues / Kidman Blues / County Jail / I'm Gonna Cut Your Head / Forty Four Blues / Blues All Day Long / Standing Around Crying / Hoochie Coochie Man / It Hurts Me Too / Blues Before Sunrise / Third Degree / Reconsider Baby / Sinner's Prayer / Everyday I Have The Blues / Early In The Morning / Someday After A While / Tore Down / Have You Ever Loved A Woman / Crosscut Saw / Five Long Years / Got My Mojo Working / Ain't Nobody's Business

20 February 1995, Royal Albert Hall, London (with Clarence Gatemouth Brown)

SETLIST: Motherless Child / Malted Milk / From Four Until Late / How Long Blues / Kidman Blues / I'm Gonna Cut Your Head / Forty Four Blues / Blues All Day Long /

Standing Around Crying / Hoochie Coochie Man / It Hurts Me Too / Blues Before Sunrise / Third Degree / Reconsider Baby / Sinner's Prayer / Everyday I Have The Blues / Early In The Morning / Can't Judge Nobody / Someday After A While / Tore Down / Have You Ever Loved A Woman / Crosscut Saw / Five Long Years / Crossroads / Got My Mojo Working / Ain't Nobody's Business

Eric plays a Gibson L5 at the Royal Albert Hall in February 1995. To his left is Nathan East on bass.

21 February 1995, Royal Albert Hall, London (with Clarence Gatemouth Brown) (benefit for the Chemical Dependency Centre)

SETLIST: Motherless Child / Malted Milk / Four Until Late / How Long Blues / Kidman Blues / I'm Gonna Cut Your Head / Forty Four Blues / Blues All Day Long / Hoochie Coochie Man / Got My Mojo Working / It Hurts Me Too / Blues Before Sunrise / Third Degree / Reconsider Baby / Sinner's Prayer / Bad Boy / Everyday I Have The Blues / Double Trouble / Someday After A While / Tore Down / Have You Ever Loved A Woman / Crosscut Saw / Five Long Years / Crossroads / Ain't Nobody's Business

23 February 1995, Royal Albert Hall, London (with Clarence Gatemouth Brown)

SETLIST: Motherless Child / Malted Milk / Four Until Late / How Long Blues / Kidman Blues / I'm Gonna Cut Your Head / Forty Four Blues / Blues All Day Long / Standing Around Crying / Hoochie Coochie Man / It Hurts Me Too / Blues Before Sunrise / Third Degree / Reconsider Baby / Sinner's Prayer / Everyday I Have The Blues / Double Trouble / Bad Boy / Got My Mojo Working / Someday After A While / Tore Down / Have

You Ever Loved A Woman / Crosscut Saw / Five Long Years / Crossroads / Ain't Nobody's Business

24 February 1995, Royal Albert Hall, London (with Clarence Gatemouth Brown)

SETLIST: Motherless Child / Malted Milk / Four Until Late / How Long Blues / Kidman Blues / I'm Gonna Cut Your Head / Forty Four Blues / Blues All Day Long / Standing Around Crying / Hoochie Coochie Man / It Hurts Me / Blues Before Sunrise / Third Degree / Reconsider Baby / Sinner's Prayer / Everyday I Have The Blues / Early In The Morning / Can't Judge Nobody / Someday After A While / Tore Down / Have You Ever Loved A Woman / Crosscut Saw / Five Long Years / Crossroads / Got My Mojo Working / Ain't Nobody's Business

25 February 1995, Royal Albert Hall, London (with Clarence Gatemouth Brown)

SETLIST: Motherless Child / Malted Milk / Four Until Late / How Long Blues / Kidman Blues / I'm Gonna Cut Your Head / Forty Four Blues / Blues All Day Long / Standing Around Crying / Hoochie Coochie Man / It Hurts Me Too / Blues Before Sunrise / Third Degree / Reconsider Baby / Sinner's Prayer / Everyday I Have The Blues / Early In The Morning / Before You Accuse Me / Someday After A While / Tore Down / Have You Ever Loved A Woman / Crosscut Saw / Five Long Years / Crossroads / Got My Mojo Working / Ain't Nobody's Business

27 February 1995, Royal Albert Hall, London (with Clarence Gatemouth Brown)

SETLIST: Motherless Child / Malted Milk / Four Until Late / How Long Blues / Kidman Blues / I'm Gonna Cut Your Head / Forty Four Blues / Blues All Day Long / Standing Around Crying / Hoochie Coochie Man / It Hurts Me Too / Blues Before Sunrise / Third Degree / Reconsider Baby / Sinner's Prayer / Everyday I Have The Blues / Early In The Morning / Before You Accuse Me / Someday After A While / Tore Down / Have You Ever Loved A Woman / Crosscut Saw / Five Long Years / Crossroads / Ain't Nobody's Business

28 February 1995, Royal Albert Hall, London (with Clarence Gatemouth Brown)

SETLIST: Motherless Child / Malted Milk / Four Until Late / How Long Blues / Kidman Blues / I'm Gonna Cut Your Head / Forty Four Blues / Blues All Day Long / Standing Around Crying / Hoochie Coochie Man / It Hurts Me Too / Blues Before Sunrise / Third Degree / Reconsider Baby / Sinner's Prayer / Everyday I Have The Blues / Early In The Morning / Before You Accuse Me / Someday After A While / Tore Down / Have You Ever Loved A Woman / Crosscut Saw / Five Long Years / Crossroads / Ain't Nobody's Business

MARCH 1995

1 March 1995, Royal Albert Hall, London (with Clarence Gatemouth Brown)

SETLIST: Motherless Child / Malted Milk / Four Until Late / How Long Blues / Kidman Blues / I'm Gonna Cut Your Head / Forty Four Blues / Blues All Day Long / Standing Around Crying / Hoochie Coochie Man / It Hurts Me Too / Blues Before Sunrise / Third Degree / Reconsider Baby / Sinner's Prayer / Everyday I Have The Blues / Early In The Morning / Before You Accuse Me / Someday After A While / Tore Down / Have You Ever Loved A Woman / Crosscut Saw / Five Long Years / Crossroads / Got My Mojo Working

3 March 1995, Royal Albert Hall, London (with Clarence Gatemouth Brown)

SETLIST: Motherless Child / Malted Milk / Four Until Late / How Long Blues / Kidman Blues / I'm Gonna Cut Your Head / Forty Four Blues / Blues All Day Long / Standing Around Crying / Hoochie Coochie Man / It Hurts Me Too / Blues Before Sunrise / Third Degree / Reconsider Baby / Sinner's Prayer / Everyday I Have The Blues / Double Trouble / Before You Accuse Me / Someday After A While / Tore Down / Have You Ever Loved A Woman / Crosscut Saw / Five Long Years / Crossroads / Got My Mojo Working / Ain't Nobody's Business

4 March 1995, Royal Albert Hall, London (with Clarence Gatemouth Brown)

SETLIST: Motherless Child / Malted Milk / Four Until Late / How Long Blues / Kidman Blues / I'm Gonna Cut Your Head / Forty Four Blues / Blues All Day Long / Standing Around Crying / Hoochie Coochie Man / It Hurts Me Too / Blues Before Sunrise / Third Degree / Reconsider Baby / Sinner's Prayer / Everyday I Have The Blues / Double Trouble / Before You Accuse Me / Someday After A While / Tore Down / Have You Ever Loved A Woman / Crosscut Saw / Five Long Years / Crossroads / Ain't Nobody's Business

5 March 1995, Royal Albert Hall, London (with Clarence Gatemouth Brown)

SETLIST: Motherless Child / Malted Milk / Four Until Late / How Long Blues / Kidman Blues / I'm Gonna Cut Your Head / Forty Four Blues / Blues All Day Long / Standing Around Crying / Hoochie Coochie Man / It Hurts Me Too / Blues Before Sunrise / Third Degree / Reconsider Baby / Sinner's Prayer / Everyday I Have The Blues / Double Trouble / Before You Accuse Me / Someday After A While / Tore Down / Have You Ever Loved A Woman / Crosscut Saw / Five Long Years / Crossroads / Got My Mojo Working / Ain't Nobody's Business

7 March 1995, National Indoor Arena, Birmingham (with Clarence Gatemouth Brown)

SETLIST: Motherless Child / Malted Milk / Four Until Late / How Long Blues / Kidman Blues / I'm Gonna Cut Your Head / Forty Four Blues / Blues All Day Long / Standing Around Crying / Hoochie Coochie Man / It Hurts Me Too / Blues Before Sunrise / Third Degree / Reconsider Baby / Sinner's Prayer / Everyday I Have The Blues / Double Trouble / Before You Accuse Me / Someday After A While / Tore Down / Have You Ever Loved A Woman / Crosscut Saw / Five Long Years / Crossroads / Got My Mojo Working

APRIL 1995

FROM THE CRADLE SCANDINAVIAN / EUROPEAN TOUR 1995

5 April 1995, Spektrum, Oslo, Norway (with Clarence Gatemouth Brown)

SETLIST: Motherless Child / Malted Milk / Four Until Late / How Long Blues / Kidman Blues / I'm Gonna Cut Your Head / Forty Four Blues / Blues All Day Long / Standing Around Crying / Hoochie Coochie Man / It Hurts Me Too / Blues Before Sunrise / Third Degree / Reconsider Baby / Sinner's Prayer / Everyday I Have The Blues / Early In The Morning / Before You Accuse Me / Someday After A While / Tore Down / Have You Ever Loved A Woman / Crosscut Saw / Five Long Years / Crossroads / Got My Mojo Working / Ain't Nobody's Business

7 April 1995, Spektrum, Oslo, Norway (with Clarence Gatemouth Brown)

SETLIST: not known

8 April 1995, Globen, Stockholm, Sweden (with Clarence Gatemouth Brown)

SETLIST: not known

10 April 1995, Forum, Copenhagen, Denmark (with Clarence Gatemouth Brown)

SETLIST: Motherless Child / Malted Milk / Four Until Late / How Long Blues / Kidman Blues / I 'm I'm Gonna Cut Your Head / Forty Four Blues / Blues All Day Long / Standing Around Crying / Hoochie Coochie Man / It Hurts Me Too / Blues Before Sunrise / Third Degree / Reconsider Baby / Sinner's Prayer / Everyday I Have The Blues / Double Trouble / Before You Accuse Me / Someday After A While / Tore Down / Have You Ever Loved A Woman / Crosscut Saw / Five Long Years / Crossroads / Got My Mojo Working / Ain't Nobody's Business

11 April 1995, Forum, Copenhagen, Denmark (with Clarence Gatemouth Brown)

SETLIST: Motherless Child / Malted Milk / Four Until Late / How Long Blues / Kidman Blues / I 'm I'm Gonna Cut Your Head / Forty Four Blues / Blues All Day Long / Standing Around Crying / Hoochie Coochie Man / It Hurts Me Too / Blues Before Sunrise / Third Degree / Reconsider Baby / Sinner's Prayer / Everyday I Have The Blues / Early In The Morning / Before You Accuse Me / Someday After A While / Tore Down / Have You Ever Loved A Woman / Crosscut Saw / Five Long Years / Crossroads / Ain't Nobody's Business

13 April 1995, Deutschlandhalle, Berlin, Germany (with Clarence Gatemouth Brown)

SETLIST: Motherless Child / Malted Milk / From Four Until Late / How Long Blues / Kidman Blues / I'm Gonna Cut Your Head / Forty Four Blues / Blues All Day Long / Standing Around Crying / Hoochie Coochie Man / It Hurts Me Too / Blues Before Sunrise / Third Degree / Reconsider Baby / Sinner's Prayer / Everyday I Have The Blues / Groaning The Blues / Before You Accuse Me / Someday After A While / Tore Down / Have You Ever Loved A Woman / Crosscut Saw / Five Long Years / Crossroads / Ain't Nobody's Business

14 April 1995, Stadthalle, Bremen, Germany (with Clarence Gatemouth Brown)

SETLIST: Motherless Child / Malted Milk / From Four Until Late / How Long Blues / Kidman Blues / I'm Gonna Cut Your Head / Forty Four Blues / Blues All Day Long / Standing Around Crying / Hoochie Coochie Man / It Hurts Me Too / Blues Before Sunrise / Third Degree / Reconsider Baby / Sinner's Prayer / Everyday I Have The Blues / Double Trouble / Before You Accuse Me / Someday After A While / Tore Down / Have You Ever Loved A Woman / Crosscut Saw / Five Long Years / Crossroads / Ain't Nobody's Business

15 April 1995, Flanders Expo, Gent, Belgium (with Clarence Gatemouth Brown)

SETLIST: Motherless Child / Malted Milk / Four Until Late / How Long Blues / Kidman Blues / I'm Gonna Cut Your Head / Forty Four Blues / Blues All Day Long / Standing Around Crying / Hoochie Coochie Man / Got My Mojo Working / It Hurts Me Too / Third Degree / Reconsider Baby / Sinner's Prayer / Everyday I Have The Blues / Early In The Morning / Before You Accuse Me / Someday After A While / I'm Tore Down / Have You Ever Loved A Woman / Crosscut Saw / Five Long Years / Crossroads / Ain't Nobody's Business

17 April 1995, Ahoy Hall, Rotterdam, Netherlands (with Clarence Gatemouth Brown)

SETLIST: Motherless Child / Malted Milk / Four Until Late / How Long Blues / Kidman Blues / I'm Gonna Cut Your Head / Forty Four Blues / Blues All Day Long / Standing Around Crying / Hoochie Coochie Man / Got

My Mojo Working / It Hurts Me Too / Third Degree / Reconsider Baby / Sinner's Prayer / Everyday I Have The Blues / Early In The Morning / Before You Accuse Me / Someday After A While / Tore Down / Have You Ever Loved A Woman / Crosscut Saw / Five Long Years / Crossroads / Sweet Home Chicago / Ain't Nobody's Business

18 April 1995, Ahoy Hall, Rotterdam, Netherlands (with Clarence Gatemouth Brown)

SETLIST: Motherless Child / Malted Milk / Four Until Late / How Long Blues / Kidman Blues / County Jail Blues / Forty Four Blues / Blues All Day Long / Standing Around Crying / Hoochie Coochie Man / It Hurts Me Too / Blues Before Sunrise / Third Degree / Reconsider Baby / Sinner's Prayer / Groaning The Blues / Before You Accuse Me / Someday After A While / Tore Down / Have You Ever Loved A Woman / Crosscut Saw / Five Long Years / Crossroads / Sweet Home Chicago[1]

[1] with Clarence Gatemouth Brown on guitar

19 April 1995, MECC, Maastricht, Netherlands (with Clarence Gatemouth Brown)

SETLIST: Motherless Child / Malted Milk / Four Until Late / How Long Blues / Kidman Blues / I'm Gonna Cut Your Head / Forty Four Blues / Blues All Day Long / Standing Around Crying / Hoochie Coochie Man / It Hurts Me Too / Blues Before Sunrise / Third Degree / Reconsider Baby / Sinner's Prayer / Everyday I Have The Blues / Double Trouble / Before You Accuse Me / Someday After A While / Tore Down / Have You Ever Loved A Woman / Crosscut Saw / Five Long Years / Crossroads / Sweet Home Chicago / Ain't Nobody's Business

21 April 1995, Bercy, Paris, France (with Clarence Gatemouth Brown)

SETLIST: Motherless Child / Malted Milk / From Four Until Late / How Long Blues / Kidman Blues / I'm Gonna Cut Your Head / Forty Four Blues / Blues Leave Me Alone / Standing Around Crying / Hoochie Coochie Man / It Hurts Me Too / Blues Before Sunrise / Third Degree / Reconsider Baby / Sinner's Prayer / Everyday I Have The Blues / Early In The Morning / Before You Accuse Me / Someday After A While / Tore Down / Crossroads

/ Five Long Years / Sweet Home Chicago / Ain't Nobody's Business

22 April 1995, Bercy, Paris, France (with Clarence Gatemouth Brown)

SETLIST: Motherless Child / Malted Milk / From Four Until Late / How Long Blues / Kidman Blues / I'm Gonna Cut Your Head / Forty Four Blues / Blues Leave Me Alone / Standing Around Crying / Hoochie Coochie Man / It Hurts Me Too / Blues Before Sunrise / Third Degree / Reconsider Baby / Sinner's Prayer / Everyday I Have The Blues / Early In The Morning / Before You Accuse Me / Someday After A While / Tore Down / Crossroads / Five Long Years / Sweet Home Chicago / Ain't Nobody's Business

24 April 1995, Festhalle, Frankfurt, Germany (with Clarence Gatemouth Brown)

SETLIST: Motherless Child / Malted Milk / From Four Until Late / How Long Blues / Kidman Blues / I'm Gonna Cut Your Head / Forty Four Blues / Blues Leave Me Alone / Standing Around Crying / Hoochie Coochie Man / It Hurts Me Too / Blues Before Sunrise / Third Degree / Reconsider Baby / Sinner's Prayer / Everyday I Have The Blues / Double Trouble / Before You Accuse Me / Someday After A While / I'm Tore Down / Have You Ever Loved A Woman / Crossroads / Five Long Years / Ain't Nobody's Business

25 April 1995, Westfalenhalle, Dortmund, Germany (with Clarence Gatemouth Brown)

SETLIST: Motherless Child / Malted Milk / From Four Until Late / How Long Blues / Kidman Blues / I'm Gonna Cut Your Head / Forty Four Blues / Blues Blues Blues / Standing Around Crying / Hoochie Coochie Man / It Hurts Me Too / Blues Before Sunrise / Third Degree / Reconsider Baby / Sinner's Prayer / Everyday I Have The Blues / Early In The Morning / Before You Accuse Me / Someday After A While / Tore Down / Crosscut Saw / Crossroads / Five Long Years / Ain't Nobody's Business

27 April 1995, Olympiahalle, Munich, Germany (with Clarence Gatemouth Brown)

SETLIST: Motherless Child / Malted Milk / Four Until Late / How Long Blues / Kidman Blues / I'm Gonna

Cut Your Head / Forty Four Blues / Blues All Day Long / Standing Around Crying / Hoochie Coochie Man / It Hurts Me Too / Blues Before Sunrise / Third Degree / Reconsider Baby / Sinner's Prayer / Everyday I Have The Blues / Early In The Morning / Before You Accuse Me / Someday After A While / Tore Down / Have You Ever Loved A Woman / Crossroads / Five Long Years / Ain't Nobody's Business

28 April 1995, Hallenstadion, Zurich, Switzerland (with Clarence Gatemouth Brown)

SETLIST: Motherless Child / Malted Milk / From Four Until Late / How Long Blues / Kidman Blues / I'm Gonna Cut Your Head / Forty Four Blues / Blues Leave Me Alone / Standing Around Crying / Hoochie Coochie Man / It Hurts Me Too / Blues Before Sunrise / Third Degree / Reconsider Baby / Sinner's Prayer / Everyday I Have The Blues / Early In The Morning / Before You Accuse Me / Someday After A While / I'm Tore Down / Have You Ever Loved A Woman / Got My Mojo Working / Five Long Years / Crossroads / Ain't Nobody's Business

30 April 1995, Palaeur, Rome, Italy (with Clarence Gatemouth Brown)

SETLIST: Motherless Child / Malted Milk / From Four Until Late / How Long Blues / Kidman Blues / I'm Gonna Cut Your Head / Forty Four Blues / Blues All Day Long / Standing Around Crying / Hoochie Coochie Man / It Hurts Me Too / Reconsider Baby / Sinner's Prayer / Everyday I Have The Blues / Double Trouble / Before You Accuse Me / Someday After A While / Tore Down / Have You Ever Loved A Woman / Five Long Years / Crossroads / Ain't Nobody's Business

MAY 1995

1 May 1995, Filaforum, Milan, Italy (with Clarence Gatemouth Brown)

SETLIST: Motherless Child / Malted Milk / Four Until Late / How Long Blues / Kidman Blues / I'm Gonna Cut Your Head / Forty Four Blues / Blues All Day Long / Standing Around Crying / Hoochie Coochie Man / It Hurts Me Too / Blues Before Sunrise / Third Degree / Reconsider Baby / Sinner's Prayer / Everyday I Have The

Blues / Groaning The Blues / Before You Accuse Me / Someday After A While / Got My Mojo Workin' / Five Long Years / Crossroads / Ain't Nobody's Business

2 May 1995, Filaforum, Milan, Italy (with Clarence Gatemouth Brown)

SETLIST: not known

4 May 1995, Palau San Jordi, Barcelona, Spain (with Clarence Gatemouth Brown)

SETLIST: Motherless Child / Malted Milk / Four Until Late / How Long Blues / Kidman Blues / I'm Gonna Cut Your Head / Forty Four Blues / Blues All Day Long / Standing Around Crying / Hoochie Coochie Man / It Hurts Me Too / Blues Before Sunrise / Third Degree / Reconsider Baby / Sinner's Prayer / Everyday I Have The Blues / Double Trouble / Before You Accuse Me / Someday After A While / Tore Down / Have You Ever Loved A Woman / Crossroads / Five Long Years / Sweet Home Chicago / Ain't Nobody's Business

5 May 1995, Palau San Jordi, Barcelona, Spain (with Clarence Gatemouth Brown)

SETLIST: Motherless Child / Malted Milk / Four Until Late / How Long Blues / Kidman Blues / I'm Gonna Cut Your Head / Forty Four Blues / Blues Leave Me Alone / Standing Around Crying / Hoochie Coochie Man / It Hurts Me Too / Blues Before Sunrise / Third Degree / Reconsider Baby / Sinner's Prayer / Everyday I Have The Blues / Groaning The Blues / Before You Accuse Me / Someday After A While / Got My Mojo Working / Five Long Years / Crossroads / Ain't Nobody's Business

STEVIE RAY VAUGHAN TRIBUTE SHOWS 1995

11 May 1995, *Austin City Limits* TV show, University of Texas Campus, Austin, Texas

Ain't Gone 'N' Give Up On Love (Stevie Ray Vaughan) *A Tribute To Stevie Ray Vaughan* CD Epic 485067 2 released August 1996 / also on DVD

Eric Clapton: guitar, vocals
Bill Willis: Hammond B3
Denny Freeman: piano

George Rains: drums
Tommy Shannon: bass

Six Strings Down (Art Neville / C. Neville / E. Kolb / K. Smith / Jimmie Vaughan) *A Tribute To Stevie Ray Vaughan* CD Epic 485067 2 released August 1996 / also on DVD

Jimmie Vaughan: guitar, vocals
Eric Clapton: guitar, vocals
Buddy Guy: guitar
Robert Cray: guitar, vocals
B.B. King: guitar, vocals
Bonnie Raitt: slide guitar, vocals
Dr. John: percussion, vocals
Art Neville: keyboards
Bill Willis: Hammond B3 organ
Denny Freeman: piano
George Rains: drums
Tommy Shannon: bass

Tick Tock (Jimmie Vaughan / Nile Rogers / Jerry Lynne Williams) *A Tribute To Stevie Ray Vaughan* CD Epic 485067 2 released August 1996 / also on DVD

Jimmie Vaughan: guitar
Eric Clapton: guitar
Buddy Guy: guitar
Robert Cray: guitar
B.B. King: guitar, vocals
Bonnie Raitt: slide guitar
Dr. John: percussion
Art Neville: tambourine
Bill Willis: Hammond B3 organ
Denny Freeman: piano
George Rains: drums
Tommy Shannon: bass
Leroy Burns: vocals
Dennis King: vocals
Reginald "Briz" Brisbon: vocals

SRV Shuffle (Jimmie Vaughan) *A Tribute To Stevie Ray Vaughan* CD Epic 485067 2 released August 1996 / also on DVD

Jimmie Vaughan: guitar
Eric Clapton: guitar
Buddy Guy: guitar
Robert Cray: guitar
B.B. King: guitar, vocals
Bonnie Raitt: slide guitar
Dr. John: piano
Art Neville: tambourine
Bill Willis: Hammond B3 organ
George Rains: drums
Tommy Shannon: bass

Producer: Jimmie Vaughan
Engineer: David Hough

12 May 1995, Music Hall, Austin, Texas

Great jam session at the Music Hall in Austin with Eric, Jimmie Vaughan and the Tilt-A-Whirl Band, Robert Cray, and Buddy Guy.

TILT-A-WHIRL BAND LINEUP:
Bill Willis: Hammond B3 organ
Denny Freeman: piano, guitar
George Rains: drums

JIMMIE VAUGHAN, ROBERT CRAY, ERIC CLAPTON SETLIST: Reconsider Baby / Third Degree

JIMMIE VAUGHAN, ROBERT CRAY, ERIC CLAPTON, BUDDY GUY SETLIST: Sweet Home Chicago / I Can't Quit You Baby / Same Thing / Further On Up The Road / Let Me Love You Baby / Wee Wee Baby / Early In The Morning / Can't Judge Nobody / Love Struck Baby / Six Strings Down

AUGUST 1995

FROM THE CRADLE U.S. TOUR 1995

BAND LINEUP:
Eric Clapton: guitar, vocals
Andy Fairweather Low: guitar, vocals
Jerry Portnoy: harmonica
Chris Stainton: keyboards
Dave Bronze: bass
Steve Gadd: drums
Roddy Lorimer: trumpet
Tim Sanders: tenor saxophone
Simon Clarke: baritone saxophone

28 August 1995, Reunion Arena, Dallas, Texas (with Clarence Gatemouth Brown)

SETLIST: Motherless Child / Malted Milk / Four Until Late / How Long Blues / Kidman Blues / I'm Gonna Cut Your Head / Forty Four Blues / Blues All Day Long / Standing Around Crying / Hoochie Coochie Man / It Hurts Me Too / Blues Before Sunrise / Third Degree /

Reconsider Baby / Sinner's Prayer / Everyday I Have The Blues / Early In The Morning / Before You Accuse Me / Someday After A While / Tore Down / Have You Ever Loved A Woman / Crossroads / Five Long Years / Ain't Nobody's Business

30 August 1995, Frank Erwin Centre, Austin, Texas (with Clarence Gatemouth Brown)

SETLIST: not known

31 August 1995, Summit, Houston, Texas (with Clarence Gatemouth Brown)

SETLIST: Motherless Child / Malted Milk / Born Too Late / How Long Blues / Kidman Blues / I'm Gonna Cut Your Head / Forty Four Blues / Blues All Day Long / Standing Around Crying / Hoochie Coochie Man / It Hurts Me Too / Blues Before Sunrise / Third Degree / Reconsider Baby / Sinner's Prayer / Groaning The Blues / Before You Accuse Me / Someday After A While / I'm Tore Down / Have You Ever Loved A Woman / Crossroads / Five Long Years / Ain't Nobody's Business

SEPTEMBER 1995

2 September 1995, Omni Theatre, Atlanta, Georgia (with Clarence Gatemouth Brown)

SETLIST: Motherless Child / Malted Milk / Born Too Late / How Long Blues / Kidman Blues / I'm Gonna Cut Your Head / Forty Four Blues / Blues All Day Long / Standing Around Crying / Hoochie Coochie Man / It Hurts Me Too / Blues Before Sunrise / Third Degree / Reconsider Baby / Sinner's Prayer / Groaning The Blues / Before You Accuse Me / Someday After A While / I'm Tore Down / Have You Ever Loved A Woman / Crossroads / Five Long Years / Ain't Nobody's Business

3 September 1995, Thompson-Boling Arena, Knoxville, Tennessee (with Clarence Gatemouth Brown)

SETLIST: Motherless Child / Malted Milk / Four Until Late / How Long Blues / Kidman Blues / I'm Gonna Cut Your Head / Forty Four Blues / Blues All Day Long / Standing Around Crying / Hoochie Coochie Man / It Hurts Me Too / Blues Before Sunrise / Third Degree /

Reconsider Baby / Sinner's Prayer / Everyday I Have The Blues / Double Trouble / Before You Accuse Me / Someday After A While / Tore Down / Have You Ever Loved A Woman / Crossroads / Five Long Years / Ain't Nobody's Business

5 September 1995, Miami Arena, Miami, Florida (with Clarence Gatemouth Brown)

SETLIST: Motherless Child / Malted Milk / Four Until Late / How Long Blues / Kidman Blues / I'm Gonna Cut Your Head / Forty Four Blues / Blues All Day Long / Standing Around Crying / Hoochie Coochie Man / It Hurts Me Too / Blues Before Sunrise / Third Degree / Reconsider Baby / Sinner's Prayer / Everyday I Have The Blues / Groaning The Blues / Before You Accuse Me / Someday After A While / Tore Down / Have You Ever Loved A Woman / Crossroads / Five Long Years / Ain't Nobody's Business

6 September 1995, Miami Arena, Miami, Florida (with Clarence Gatemouth Brown)

SETLIST: Motherless Child / Malted Milk / Four Until Late / How Long Blues / Kidman Blues / I'm Gonna Cut Your Head / Forty Four Blues / Blues All Day Long / Standing Around Crying / Hoochie Coochie Man / It Hurts Me Too / Blues Before Sunrise / Third Degree / Reconsider Baby / Sinner's Prayer / Everyday I Have The Blues / Double Trouble / Before You Accuse Me / Someday After A While / Tore Down / Have You Ever Loved A Woman / Crossroads / Five Long Years / Ain't Nobody's Business

7 September 1995, Thunderdome, St. Petersburg, Florida (with Clarence Gatemouth Brown)

SETLIST: Motherless Child / Malted Milk / Four Until Late / How Long Blues / Kidman Blues / I'm Gonna Cut Your Head / Forty Four Blues / Blues All Day Long / Standing Around Crying / Hoochie Coochie Man / It Hurts Me Too / Blues Before Sunrise / Third Degree / Reconsider Baby / Sinner's Prayer / Everyday I Have The Blues / Early In The Morning / Before You Accuse Me / Someday After A While / Tore Down / Have You Ever Loved A Woman / Crossroads / Five Long Years / Ain't Nobody's Business

9 September 1995, Dean E. Smith Center, Chapel Hill, North Carolina (with Clarence Gatemouth Brown)

SETLIST: Motherless Child / Malted Milk / Four Until Late / How Long Blues / Kidman Blues / I'm Gonna Cut Your Head / Forty Four Blues / Blues All Day Long / Standing Around Crying / Hoochie Coochie Man / It Hurts Me Too / Blues Before Sunrise / Third Degree / Reconsider Baby / Sinner's Prayer / Everyday I Have The Blues / Early In The Morning / Before You Accuse Me / Someday After A While / Tore Down / Have You Ever Loved A Woman / Crossroads / Five Long Years / Ain't Nobody's Business

10 September 1995, Charlotte Coliseum, Charlotte, North Carolina (with Clarence Gatemouth Brown)

SETLIST: not known

11 September 1995, U.S. Air Arena, Landover, Maryland (with Clarence Gatemouth Brown)

SETLIST: not known

13 September 1995, Spectrum, Philadelphia, Pennsylvania (with Clarence Gatemouth Brown)

SETLIST: Motherless Child / Malted Milk / Four Until Late / How Long Blues / Kidman Blues / I'm Gonna Cut Your Head / Forty Four Blues / Blues All Day Long / Standing Around Crying / Hoochie Coochie Man / It Hurts Me Too / Blues Before Sunrise / Third Degree / Reconsider Baby / Sinner's Prayer / Everyday I Have The Blues / Groaning The Blues / Before You Accuse Me / Someday After A While / Tore Down / Have You Ever Loved A Woman / Crossroads / Five Long Years / Ain't Nobody's Business

14 September 1995, Spectrum, Philadelphia, Pennsylvania (with Clarence Gatemouth Brown)

SETLIST: not known

15 September 1995, Centrum, Worcester, Massachusetts (with Clarence Gatemouth Brown)

SETLIST: Motherless Child / Malted Milk / Four Until Late / How Long Blues / Kidman Blues / I'm Gonna

Cut Your Head / Forty Four Blues / Blues All Day Long / Standing Around Crying / Hoochie Coochie Man / It Hurts Me Too / Blues Before Sunrise / Third Degree / Reconsider Baby / Sinner's Prayer / Everyday I Have The Blues / Early In The Morning / Before You Accuse Me / Someday After A While / Tore Down / Crossroads / Five Long Years / Ain't Nobody's Business

17 September 1995, Madison Square Garden, New York City (with Clarence Gatemouth Brown)

SETLIST: Motherless Child / Malted Milk / Four Until Late / How Long Blues / Kidman Blues / I'm Gonna Cut Your Head / Forty Four Blues / Blues All Day Long / Standing Around Crying / Hoochie Coochie Man / It Hurts Me Too / Blues Before Sunrise / Third Degree / Reconsider Baby / Sinner's Prayer / Everyday I Have The Blues / Groaning The Blues / Before You Accuse Me / Someday After A While / Tore Down / Have You Ever Loved A Woman / Crossroads / Five Long Years / Ain't Nobody's Business

18 September 1995, Madison Square Garden, New York City (with Clarence Gatemouth Brown)

SETLIST: Motherless Child / Malted Milk / Four Until Late / How Long Blues / Kidman Blues / I'm Gonna Cut Your Head / Forty Four Blues / Blues All Day Long / Standing Around Crying / Hoochie Coochie Man / It Hurts Me Too / Blues Before Sunrise / Third Degree / Reconsider Baby / Sinner's Prayer / Everyday I Have The Blues / Early In The Morning / Before You Accuse Me / Someday After A While / Tore Down / Have You Ever Loved A Woman / Crossroads / Five Long Years / Ain't Nobody's Business

19 September 1995, Nassau Veterans Memorial Coliseum, Uniondale, New York (with Clarence Gatemouth Brown)

SETLIST: Motherless Child / Malted Milk / Four Until Late / How Long Blues / Kidman Blues / I'm Gonna Cut Your Head / Forty Four Blues / Blues All Day Long / Standing Around Crying / Hoochie Coochie Man / It Hurts Me Too / Blues Before Sunrise / Third Degree / Reconsider Baby / Sinner's Prayer / Everyday I Have The Blues / Early In The Morning / Before You Accuse Me / Someday After A While / Tore Down / Have You Ever

Loved A Woman / Crossroads / Five Long Years / Ain't Nobody's Business

21 September 1995, Memorial Auditorium, Buffalo, New York (with Clarence Gatemouth Brown)

SETLIST: Motherless Child / Malted Milk / Four Until Late / How Long Blues / Kidman Blues / I'm Gonna Cut Your Head / Forty Four Blues / Blues All Day Long / Standing Around Crying / Hoochie Coochie Man / It Hurts Me Too / Blues Before Sunrise / Third Degree / Reconsider Baby / Sinner's Prayer / Everyday I Have The Blues / Groaning The Blues / Before You Accuse Me / Someday After A While / Tore Down / Have You Ever Loved A Woman / Crossroads / Five Long Years / Ain't Nobody's Business

23 September 1995, Palace of Auburn Hills, Auburn Hills, Michigan (with Clarence Gatemouth Brown)

SETLIST: Motherless Child / Malted Milk / Four Until Late / How Long Blues / Kidman Blues / I'm Gonna Cut Your Head / Forty Four Blues / Blues All Day Long / Standing Around Crying / Hoochie Coochie Man / It Hurts Me Too / Blues Before Sunrise / Third Degree / Reconsider Baby / Early In The Morning / Everyday I Have The Blues / Double Trouble / Before You Accuse Me / Someday After A While / Tore Down / Have You Ever Loved A Woman / Crossroads / Five Long Years / Ain't Nobody's Business

24 September 1995, United Center, Chicago, Illinois (with Clarence Gatemouth Brown)

SETLIST: Motherless Child / Malted Milk / Four Until Late / How Long Blues / Kidman Blues / I'm Gonna Cut Your Head / Forty Four Blues / Blues All Day Long / Standing Around Crying / Hoochie Coochie Man / It Hurts Me Too / Blues Before Sunrise / Third Degree / Reconsider Baby / Sinner's Prayer / Everyday I Have The Blues / Early In The Morning / Before You Accuse Me / Someday After A While / Tore Down / Have You Ever Loved A Woman / Crossroads / Five Long Years / Sweet Home Chicago[1]

[1] with Buddy Guy on guitar

OCTOBER 1995

FROM THE CRADLE JAPAN TOUR 1995

BAND LINEUP:
Eric Clapton: guitar, vocals
Steve Gadd: drums
Chris Stainton: keyboards
Dave Bronze: bass
Andy Fairweather Low: guitar
Jerry Portnoy: harmonica
Roddy Lorimer: trumpet
Tim Saunders: saxophone
Simon Clarke: saxophone

1 October 1995, Yoyogi Olympic Pool, Tokyo, Japan

SETLIST: Motherless Child / Malted Milk / Four Until Late / How Long Blues / Kidman Blues / I'm Gonna Cut Your Head / Forty Four Blues / Blues All Day Long / Standing Around Crying / Hoochie Coochie Man / It Hurts Me Too / Blues Before Sunrise / Third Degree / Reconsider Baby / Sinner's Prayer / Everyday I Have The Blues / Groaning The Blues / Before You Accuse Me / Someday After A While / Tore Down / Have You Ever Loved A Woman / Crossroads / Five Long Years / Ain't Nobody's Business

2 October 1995, Yoyogi Olympic Pool, Tokyo, Japan

SETLIST: Motherless Child / Malted Milk / Four Until Late / How Long Blues / Kidman Blues / I'm Gonna Cut Your Head / Forty Four Blues / Blues All Day Long / Standing Around Crying / Hoochie Coochie Man / It Hurts Me Too / Third Degree / Reconsider Baby / Sinner's Prayer / Everyday I Have The Blues / Early In The Morning / Before You Accuse Me / Someday After A While / Tore Down / Have You Ever Loved A Woman / Crossroads / Five Long Years / Ain't Nobody's Business

3 October 1995, Yoyogi Olympic Pool, Tokyo, Japan

SETLIST: Motherless Child / Malted Milk / Four Until Late / How Long Blues / Kidman Blues / I'm Gonna

Cut Your Head / Forty Four Blues / Blues All Day Long / Standing Around Crying / Hoochie Coochie Man / It Hurts Me Too / Third Degree / Reconsider Baby / Sinner's Prayer / Everyday I Have The Blues / Double Trouble / Before You Accuse Me / Someday After A While / Tore Down / Have You Ever Loved A Woman / Crossroads / Five Long Years / Ain't Nobody's Business

5 October 1995, Yoyogi Olympic Pool, Tokyo, Japan

SETLIST: Motherless Child / Malted Milk / Four Until Late / How Long Blues / Kidman Blues / I'm Gonna Cut Your Head / Forty Four Blues / Blues All Day Long / Standing Around Crying / Hoochie Coochie Man / It Hurts Me Too / Third Degree / Reconsider Baby / Sinner's Prayer / Everyday I Have The Blues / Groaning The Blues / Before You Accuse Me / Someday After A While / Tore Down / Have You Ever Loved A Woman / Crossroads / Five Long Years / Ain't Nobody's Business

6 October 1995, Yoyogi Olympic Pool, Tokyo, Japan

SETLIST: Motherless Child / Malted Milk / Four Until Late / How Long Blues / Kidman Blues / I'm Gonna Cut Your Head / Forty Four Blues / Blues All Day Long / Standing Around Crying / Hoochie Coochie Man / It Hurts Me Too / Third Degree / Reconsider Baby / Sinner's Prayer / Everyday I Have The Blues / Early In The Morning / Before You Accuse Me / Someday After A While / Tore Down / Have You Ever Loved A Woman / Crossroads / Five Long Years / Ain't Nobody's Business

8 October 1995, Castle Hall, Osaka, Japan

SETLIST: Motherless Child / Malted Milk / Four Until Late / How Long Blues / Kidman Blues / I'm Gonna Cut Your Head / Forty Four Blues / Blues All Day Long / Standing Around Crying / Hoochie Coochie Man / It Hurts Me Too / Blues Before Sunrise / Third Degree / Reconsider Baby / Sinner's Prayer / Everyday I Have The Blues / Double Trouble / Before You Accuse Me / Someday After A While / Tore Down / Have You Ever Loved A Woman / Crossroads / Five Long Years / Ain't Nobody's Business

9 October 1995, Castle Hall, Osaka, Japan

SETLIST: Motherless Child / Malted Milk / Four Until Late / How Long Blues / Kidman Blues / I'm Gonna Cut Your Head / Forty Four Blues / Blues All Day Long / Standing Around Crying / Hoochie Coochie Man / It Hurts Me Too / Third Degree / Reconsider Baby / Sinner's Prayer / Everyday I Have The Blues / Groaning The Blues / Before You Accuse Me / Someday After A While / Tore Down / Have You Ever Loved A Woman / Crossroads / Five Long Years / Ain't Nobody's Business

11 October 1995, Budokan, Tokyo, Japan

SETLIST: Motherless Child / Malted Milk / Four Until Late / How Long Blues / Kidman Blues / I'm Gonna Cut Your Head / Forty Four Blues / Blues Leave Me Alone / Standing Around Crying / Hoochie Coochie Man / It Hurts Me Too / Third Degree / Reconsider Baby / Sinner's Prayer / Everyday I Have The Blues / Early In The Morning / Before You Accuse Me / Someday After A While / I'm Tore Down / Have You Ever Loved A Woman / Crossroads / Five Long Years / Ain't Nobody's Business

12 October 1995, Budokan, Tokyo, Japan

SETLIST: Motherless Child / Malted Milk / Four Until Late / How Long Blues / Kidman Blues / I'm Gonna Cut Your Head / Forty Four Blues / Blues All Day Long / Standing Around Crying / Hoochie Coochie Man / It Hurts Me Too / Blues Before Sunrise / Third Degree / Reconsider Baby / Sinner's Prayer / Everyday I Have The Blues / Groaning The Blues / Before You Accuse Me / Someday After A While / Tore Down / Have You Ever Loved A Woman / Crossroads / Five Long Years / Ain't Nobody's Business

13 October 1995, Budokan, Tokyo, Japan

SETLIST: Motherless Child / Malted Milk / From Four Until Late / How Long Blues / Kidman Blues / I'm Gonna Cut Your Head / Forty Four Blues / Blues Leave Me Alone / Standing Around Crying / Hoochie Coochie Man / It Hurts Me Too / Third Degree / Reconsider Baby / Sinner's Prayer / Everyday I Have The Blues / Double Trouble / Before You Accuse Me / Someday After A While / I'm Tore Down / Have You Ever Loved A Woman / Crossroads / Five Long Years / Ain't Nobody's Business

DECEMBER 1995

JOOLS HOLLAND HOOTENANNY 1995

13 December 1995, BBC Television Centre Studios, Wood
Lane, London (filming for *Jools Holland Hootenanny*
show broadcast on 31 December 1995)

SETLIST:

Such A Night (with Dr. John and the Jools Holland
Rhythm & Blues Orchestra) broadcast

Eric Clapton: guitar, vocals
Dr. John: piano, vocals
Andy Fairweather Low: guitar
Mark Flanagan: guitar
Jools Holland: electric piano
Christopher Holland: organ
Dave Swift: bass
Gilson Lavis: drums
Phil Veacock: saxophone
Lisa Grahame: saxophone
Michael Rose: saxophone
Derek Nash: saxophone
Nick Lunt: baritone saxophone
Rico Rodriguez: trombone
Roger Goslyn: trombone
Fayyaz Virji: trombone
Winston Rollins: trombone
Jason McDermid: trumpet
Jon Scott: trumpet
Chris Storr: trumpet
Not known: percussion

Reconsider Baby broadcast

Eric Clapton: guitar, vocals
Andy Fairweather Low: guitar
Mark Flanagan: guitar
Jools Holland: electric piano
Christopher Holland: organ
Dave Swift: bass
Gilson Lavis: drums
Phil Veacock: saxophone
Lisa Grahame: saxophone
Michael Rose: saxophone
Derek Nash: saxophone
Nick Lunt: baritone saxophone
Rico Rodriguez: trombone
Roger Goslyn: trombone
Fayyaz Virji: trombone
Winston Rollins: trombone

Jason McDermid: trumpet
Jon Scott: trumpet
Chris Storr: trumpet
Not known: percussion

There Must Be A Better World Somewhere (with Dr.
John and the Jools Holland Rhythm & Blues Orchestra)
broadcast

Eric Clapton: guitar, vocals
Dr. John: piano, vocals
Andy Fairweather Low: guitar
Mark Flanagan: guitar
Jools Holland: electric piano
Christopher Holland: organ
Dave Swift: bass
Gilson Lavis: drums
Phil Veacock: saxophone
Lisa Grahame: saxophone
Michael Rose: saxophone
Derek Nash: saxophone
Nick Lunt: baritone saxophone
Rico Rodriguez: trombone
Roger Goslyn: trombone
Fayyaz Virji: trombone
Winston Rollins: trombone
Jason McDermid: trumpet
Jon Scott: trumpet
Chris Storr: trumpet
Not known: percussion

Third Degree broadcast

Eric Clapton: guitar, vocals
Andy Fairweather Low: guitar
Mark Flanagan: guitar
Jools Holland: electric piano
Christopher Holland: organ
Dave Swift: bass
Gilson Lavis: drums
Phil Veacock: saxophone
Lisa Grahame: saxophone
Michael Rose: saxophone
Derek Nash: saxophone
Nick Lunt: baritone saxophone
Rico Rodriguez: trombone
Roger Goslyn: trombone
Fayyaz Virji: trombone
Winston Rollins: trombone
Jason McDermid: trumpet
Jon Scott: trumpet
Chris Storr: trumpet
Not known: percussion

Jump For Joy (with the Jools Holland Rhythm & Blues
Orchestra) broadcast

Eric Clapton: guitar, vocals
Dick Dale: guitar

David McAlmont: vocals
Andy Fairweather Low: guitar
Dr. John: piano
Mark Flanagan: guitar
Jools Holland: electric piano
Christopher Holland: organ
Dave Swift: bass
Gilson Lavis: drums
Phil Veacock: saxophone
Lisa Grahame: saxophone
Michael Rose: saxophone
Derek Nash: saxophone
Nick Lunt: baritone saxophone
Rico Rodriguez: trombone
Roger Goslyn: trombone
Fayyaz Virji: trombone
Winston Rollins: trombone
Jason McDermid: trumpet
Jon Scott: trumpet
Chris Storr: trumpet
Not known: percussion
Director: Janet Fraser-Crook
Producer: Mark Cooper

15 and 16 December 1995, Chiddingfold Club, Surrey (Eric plays with Gary Brooker and friends for a couple of charity concerts)

NEW YEAR'S EVE DANCE 1995

31 December 1995, Woking Leisure Centre, Surrey

Eric and his band are called the Traditions.

BAND LINEUP:
Eric Clapton: guitar, vocals
Alan Darby: guitar
Paul Wassif: guitar
Chris Stainton: keyboards
Dave Bronze: bass
Steve Gadd: drums
Helen Jennor: vocals

SETLIST 1: Layla / Blues Leave Me Alone / Have You Ever Loved A Woman / Wonderful Tonight / Rollin' Man[1] / Crazy Love[2] / He Ain't Heavy, He's My Brother / Lay Down Sally / I'm Tore Down

[1]with Alan Darby on lead vocals
[2]with Helen Jennor on lead vocals

SETLIST 2: Midnight Hour / Knockin' On Heaven's Door / Cocaine / Everyday I Have The Blues / Five Long Years

RECORDING SESSIONS 1995
OLYMPIC STUDIOS
117 Church Road, London

MARCH 1995

Granada Televison commissioned a documentary about the history of the song "Danny Boy" and how it has transcended national and musical barriers, including comments from various people on the song, musical interpretations, and archival footage. Various musicians contributed to the filming such as Van Morrison, Marianne Faithfull, and Eric Clapton among others. Eric was filmed at Olympic Studios performing an instrumental version on acoustic guitar.

DANNY BOY (traditional) *Change The World* CD single Reprise 9362-43727-2 released 1996
Eric Clapton: acoustic guitar
Producer: not known
Engineer: not known

ERIC CLAPTON GUEST SESSION
SOUND CITY STUDIOS
15456 Cabrito Road, Van Nuys, California
Session for Taj Mahal *Phantom Blues*

MAY 1995

HERE IN THE DARK (Bernard Anders) *Phantom Blues* CD Private Music 0100582139-2 released 1996
Taj Mahal: vocals
Eric Clapton: lead guitar
Tony Braunagel: drums
Jon Cleary: piano
Larry Fulcher: bass
Johnny Lee Schell: guitar
Joe Sublett: tenor saxophone
Darrell Leonard: trumpet

LOVE HER WITH A FEELING (Sonny Thompson / Freddie King) *Phantom Blues* CD Private Music 0100582139-2 released 1996

Taj Mahal: vocals
Eric Clapton: lead guitar
Tony Braunagel: drums
Mick Weaver: organ
Jon Cleary: piano
Larry Fulcher: bass
Johnny Lee Schell: tenor saxophone
Darrell Leonard: trumpet

Producer: John Porter
Engineer: Joe McGrath

> "The stark, gritty blues feel of these songs is really due to Eric Clapton's guitar. John Porter, who produced my current two albums, and who helped me put an outstanding band together, is a good friend of Eric's and used to play guitar in his band. We've been talking about working with Eric for awhile now, and the schedules finally jived. I think Eric's work is so good, these songs could stand as instrumentals. He really put everything into it, from start to finish."
>
> —TAJ MAHAL
> (from the liner notes)

ERIC CLAPTON GUEST SESSION
SIGMA STUDIOS
212 North 12th Street, Philadelphia, Pennsylvania
Session for Clarence Gatemouth Brown

14 SEPTEMBER 1995

BLUES POWER (Eric Clapton / Leon Russell) *Long Way Home* CD Verve

Clarence Gatemouth Brown: vocals, guitar
Eric Clapton: guitar
Jim Keltner: drums
Willie Weeks: bass
George Bitzer: Hammond B3 organ, piano

Producer: Jim Bateman
Engineer: Jay Newland

1996

1996

JANUARY 1996

11 January 1996, Ronnie Scott's Club, Soho, London (Eric jams with Dr. John and his band for a proposed live album. Although a live album from the dates at Ronnie Scott's is released in 1997 as *Trippin' Live,* none of the tracks with Eric are released)

13 January 1966, Ronnie Scott's Club, Soho, London (Eric jams again with Dr. John and his band for the proposed live album. None of the material with Eric was used on the released CD)

BAND LINEUP:
Dr. John: piano, vocals
Alvin Tyler: tenor saxophone
Charlie Miller: trumpet, fluglehorn
Ronnie Cuber: baritone saxophone
David Barard: bass, vocals
Herman V. Ernest III: drums, vocals
Bobby Broom: guitar, vocals

Producer: Dr. John
Co-producer: Chuck Vincent
Engineers: Chris Lewis / Chris Turgenson

U.K. TOUR 1996

BAND LINEUP:
Eric Clapton: guitar, vocals
Andy Fairweather Low: rhythm guitar
Jerry Portnoy: harmonica
Chris Stainton: keyboards

Dave Bronze: bass
Steve Gadd: drums
Tessa Niles: backing vocals
Katie Kissoon: backing vocals
Roddy Lorimer: trumpet
Tim Sanders: tenor saxophone
Simon Clarke: baritone saxophone

FEBRUARY 1996

16 February 1996, Nynex Centre, Manchester (with the Big Town Playboys)

Eric and his band at Nynex Centre, Manchester. L to R: Chris Stainton, Steve Gadd, Andy Fairweather Low, Dave Bronze, Eric Clapton, Katie Kissoon, Tessa Niles.

SETLIST: Badge / Bell Bottom Blues / Knockin' On Heaven's Door / Lay Down Sally / Wonderful Tonight / I Shot The Sheriff / Old Love / Behind The Mask / White Room / Sunshine Of Your Love / Circus Left Town / Tears In Heaven / My Father's Eyes / Alberta / Layla /

Reconsider Baby / Third Degree / Tearing Us Apart / Hoochie Coochie Man / I'm Tore Down / Have You Ever Loved A Woman / It Hurts Me Too / Five Long Years / Everyday I Have The Blues / Before You Accuse Me

18 February 1996, Royal Albert Hall, London

SETLIST: Badge / Bell Bottom Blues / Knockin' On Heaven's Door / Lay Down Sally / Wonderful Tonight / I Shot The Sheriff / Old Love / Behind The Mask / White Room / Sunshine Of Your Love / Circus Left Town / Tears In Heaven / My Father's Eyes / Alberta / Layla / Reconsider Baby / Third Degree / Tearing Us Apart / Hoochie Coochie Man / I'm Tore Down / Have You Ever Loved A Woman / It Hurts Me Too / Five Long Years / Everyday I Have The Blues / Before You Accuse Me

19 February 1996, Royal Albert Hall, London

SETLIST: Badge / Bell Bottom Blues / Knockin' On Heaven's Door / Lay Down Sally / Wonderful Tonight / I Shot The Sheriff / Old Love / White Room / Sunshine Of Your Love / Circus Left Town / Tears In Heaven / My Father's Eyes / Alberta / Layla / Tearing Us Apart / Third Degree / Hoochie Coochie Man / I'm Tore Down / Have You Ever Loved A Woman / It Hurts Me Too / Five Long Years / Everyday I Have The Blues / Before You Accuse Me

20 February 1996, Royal Albert Hall, London

SETLIST: Badge / Bell Bottom Blues / Knockin' On Heaven's Door / Lay Down Sally / Wonderful Tonight / I Shot The Sheriff / Old Love / White Room / Sunshine Of Your Love / Circus Left Town / Tears In Heaven / My Father's Eyes / San Francisco Bay Blues / Layla / Hoochie Coochie Man / Tearing Us Apart / Groaning The Blues / I'm Tore Down / Have You Ever Loved A Woman / Crossroads / Five Long Years / Everyday I Have The Blues / Before You Accuse Me

22 February 1996, Royal Albert Hall, London

SETLIST: Ain't Nobody's Business / Hoochie Coochie Man / Tearing Us Apart / It Hurts Me Too / I'm Tore Down / Have You Ever Loved A Woman / Five Long Years / Circus Left Town / Tears In Heaven / My Father's Eyes / Alberta / Layla / Badge / Bell Bottom Blues / Lay Down

Sally / Wonderful Tonight / I Shot The Sheriff / Old Love / White Room / Sunshine Of Your Love / Everyday I Have The Blues / Before You Accuse Me

23 February 1996, Royal Albert Hall, London

SETLIST: Hoochie Coochie Man / It Hurts Me Too / I'm Tore Down / Have You Ever Loved A Woman / Tearing Us Apart / Five Long Years / Ain't Nobody's Business / Circus Left Town / Tears In Heaven / My Father's Eyes / Alberta / Layla / Badge / Bell Bottom Blues / Lay Down Sally / Wonderful Tonight / I Shot The Sheriff / Old Love / White Room / Sunshine Of Your Love / Everyday I Have The Blues / Before You Accuse Me

Jerry Portnoy and Eric Clapton at the Royal Albert Hall, 23 February 1996.

24 February 1996, Royal Albert Hall, London

SETLIST: Hoochie Coochie Man / Blues Leave Me Alone / I'm Tore Down / Have You Ever Loved A Woman / Tearing Us Apart / Five Long Years / Bell Bottom Blues / Circus Left Town / Tears In Heaven / My Father's Eyes / Alberta / Layla / Badge / Bell Bottom Blues / Lay Down Sally / Wonderful Tonight / I Shot The Sheriff / Old Love / White Room / Sunshine Of Your Love / Everyday I Have The Blues / Ain't Nobody's Business / Before You Accuse Me

26 February 1996, Royal Albert Hall, London

SETLIST: Badge / Hoochie Coochie Man / Bell Bottom Blues / I Shot The Sheriff / Wonderful Tonight / Lay Down Sally / Five Long Years / Circus Left Town / Tears In Heaven / My Father's Eyes / Alberta / Layla / Tearing

Us Apart / Old Love / I'm Tore Down / Have You Ever Loved A Woman / White Room / Sunshine Of Your Love / Everyday I Have The Blues / Before You Accuse Me

27 February 1996, Royal Albert Hall, London

SETLIST: Badge / Hoochie Coochie Man / Bell Bottom Blues / I Shot The Sheriff / It Hurts Me Too / Wonderful Tonight / Five Long Years / Circus Left Town / Tears In Heaven / My Father's Eyes / Alberta / Layla / Tearing Us Apart / Old Love / I'm Tore Down / Have You Ever Loved A Woman / White Room / Sunshine Of Your Love / Everyday I Have The Blues / Before You Accuse Me[1]

[1]with Zucchero Fornaciari on vocals

28 February 1996 Royal Albert Hall, London

SETLIST: Badge / Hoochie Coochie Man / Bell Bottom Blues / I Shot The Sheriff / It Hurts Me Too / Wonderful Tonight / Five Long Years / Circus Left Town / Tears In Heaven / My Father's Eyes / Alberta / Layla / Tearing Us Apart / Old Love / I'm Tore Down / Have You Ever Loved A Woman / White Room / Sunshine Of Your Love / Everyday I Have The Blues / Ain't Nobody's Business / Before You Accuse Me

MARCH 1996

1 March 1996, Royal Albert Hall, London

SETLIST: Badge / Hoochie Coochie Man / Bell Bottom Blues / I Shot The Sheriff / It Hurts Me Too / Wonderful Tonight / Five Long Years / Circus Left Town / Tears In Heaven / My Father's Eyes / Alberta / Layla / Tearing Us Apart / Old Love / I'm Tore Down / Have You Ever Loved A Woman / White Room / Sunshine Of Your Love / Everyday I Have The Blues / Before You Accuse Me

2 March 1996, Royal Albert Hall, London

SETLIST: Badge / Hoochie Coochie Man / Bell Bottom Blues / I Shot The Sheriff / It Hurts Me Too / Wonderful Tonight / Five Long Years / Circus Left Town / Tears In Heaven / My Father's Eyes / Alberta / Layla / Tearing Us Apart / Old Love / I'm Tore Down / Have You Ever

Loved A Woman / White Room / Sunshine Of Your Love / Everyday I have The Blues / Before You Accuse Me

3 March 1996, Royal Albert Hall, London

SETLIST: Badge / Hoochie Coochie Man / Bell Bottom Blues / I Shot The Sheriff / It Hurts Me Too / Wonderful Tonight / Five Long Years / Circus Left Town / Tears In Heaven / My Father's Eyes / Alberta / Layla / Tearing Us Apart / Old Love / Tore Down / Have You Ever Loved A Woman / White Room / Sunshine Of Your Love / Everyday I Have The Blues / Ain't Nobody's Business / Before You Accuse Me

PRINCE'S TRUST CONCERT 1996

19 March 1996, Royal Albert Hall, London (special gala evening in aid of the Prince's Trust. Among the artists appearing are Eric, Shirley Bassey, Barry Manilow, David Frost, Cannon & Ball. Eric only plays one number)

BAND LINEUP:
Eric Clapton: guitar
Jerry Portnoy: harmonica
Steve Gadd: washboard

SETLIST: Alberta (traditional) broadcast on Carlton television

MAY 1996

VH1 *DUETS* 1996

9 May 1996, Roseland Ballroom, New York City

Filming of the popular VH1 *Duets* program. Tonight's show was with Eric Clapton and Dr. John. Eric and the good doctor are in top form.

BAND LINEUP:
Eric Clapton: guitar, vocals
Dr. John: keyboards, guitar, vocals

Bobby Broom: guitar
David Barard: bass
Herman Ernest: drums
Bashiri Johnson: percussion
Ronnie Cuber: baritone saxophone
Andy Snitzer: tenor saxophone
Randy Brecker: trumpet

SETLIST:

Right Place, Wrong Time broadcast

St. James Infirmary broadcast

Third Degree not broadcast

How Long Blues broadcast

Roberta broadcast

Walk On Gilded Splinters not broadcast

Wang-Dang-Doodle not broadcast

Reconsider Baby not broadcast

Be Positive not broadcast

Tipitina not broadcast

Layla broadcast

Director: Michael Simon guitar, vocals
Producer: Joel Stillerman

BUDDY GUY JAM 1996

28 May 1996, Shepherds Bush Empire, Shepherds Bush, London.

Eric joins Buddy Guy and his band for a couple of numbers, none of which are recorded.

BAND LINEUP:
Buddy Guy: guitar, vocals
Eric Clapton: guitar
Scott Holt: guitar
Tony Z: keyboards
Greg Rzab: bass
Ray Allison: drums

SETLIST: Red House / Strange Brew

JUNE 1996

WAR CHILD BENEFIT CONCERT 1996

20 June 1996, Parco Novi Sad, Modena, Italy

SETLIST:

Holy Mother (Eric Clapton / Stephen Bishop) *Pavarotti & Friends for War Child* Decca 452 900-2 released December 1996

Luciano Pavarotti: vocals
Eric Clapton: guitar, vocals
Greg Phillinganes: keyboards
Pino Palladino: bass
Steve Gadd: drums
East London Gospel Choir
Torino Philharmonic Orchestra

Third Degree (Eddie Boyd / Willie Dixon) *Pavarotti & Friends for War Child* Decca 452 900-2 released December 1996

Eric Clapton: guitar, vocals
Greg Phillinganes: keyboards
Pino Palladino: bass
Steve Gadd: drums

Run, Baby, Run (Sheryl Crow / Bill Bottrell / David Baerwald) *Pavarotti & Friends for War Child* Decca 452 900-2 released December 1996

Sheryl Crow: vocals, guitar
Eric Clapton: guitar, vocals
Rob Mathis: guitar
Greg Phillinganes: keyboards
Pino Palladino: bass
Steve Gadd: drums
Torino Philharmonic Orchestra

Un Piccolo Aiuto (Zucchero Fornaciari) *Pavarotti & Friends for War Child* VHS video Decca 074102-3 released December 1996

Zucchero Fornaciari: vocals
Eric Clapton: lead acoustic guitar and solo
Polo Jones: bass
Mario Schilirò: acoustic guitar
Luciano Luisi: keyboards
Torino Philharmonic Orchestra

Live Like Horses (Elton John / Bernie Taupin) *Pavarotti & Friends for War Child* Decca 452 900-2 released December 1996

Elton John: piano, vocals
Luciano Pavarotti: vocals
Eric Clapton: guitar
Rob Mathis: guitar
Greg Phillinganes: keyboards
Pino Palladino: bass
Steve Gadd: drums
Torino Philharmonic Orchestra
East London Gospel Choir
Sheryl Crow: backing vocals
Liza Minnelli: backing vocals
Joan Osborne: backing vocals
Zucchero Fornaciari: backing vocals
Ligabue: backing vocals
Litfiba: backing vocals
The Kelly Family: backing vocals
Jon Secada: backing vocals

Producer: Phil Ramone
Engineers: Pete Lewis / Philip Siney
Recorded by: RAI mobile

MASTERCARD MASTERS OF MUSIC FOR THE PRINCE'S TRUST CONCERT 1996

29 June 1996, Hyde Park, London

BAND LINEUP:
Eric Clapton: guitars, vocals
Dave Bronze: bass
Steve Gadd: drums
Andy Fairweather Low: guitar, vocals
Jerry Portnoy: harmonica
Chris Stainton: keyboards
Roddy Lorimer: horns
Simon Clarke: horns
Tim Sanders: horns
Katie Kissoon: backing vocals
Tessa Niles: backing vocals
East London Gospel Choir[1]

SETLIST:

Layla (Eric Clapton / Jim Gordon) *Live In Hyde Park* DVD Warner Bros. released November 2001

Badge (Eric Clapton / George Harrison) *Live In Hyde Park* DVD Warner Bros. released November 2001

Hoochie Coochie Man (Willie Dixon) *Live In Hyde Park* DVD Warner Bros. released November 2001

I Shot The Sheriff (Bob Marley) *Live In Hyde Park* DVD Warner Bros. released November 2001

It Hurts Me Too (Elmore James) *Live In Hyde Park* DVD Warner Bros. released November 2001

Wonderful Tonight (Eric Clapton) *Live In Hyde Park* DVD Warner Bros. released November 2001

Five Long Years (Eddie Boyd) *Live In Hyde Park* DVD Warner Bros. released November 2001

Tearing Us Apart (Eric Clapton / Greg Phillinganes) *Live In Hyde Park* DVD Warner Bros. released November 2001

Old Love (Eric Clapton / Robert Cray) *Live In Hyde Park* DVD Warner Bros. released November 2001

I'm Tore Down (Freddie King) *Live In Hyde Park* DVD Warner Bros. released November 2001

Have You Ever Loved A Woman (Billy Myles) *Live In Hyde Park* DVD Warner Bros. released November 2001

Eric in Modena, Italy, 20 June 1996.

Eric Clapton and Luciano Pavarotti in concert, Modena, Italy, 20 June 1996.

White Room (Jack Bruce / Pete Brown) *Live In Hyde Park* DVD Warner Bros. released November 2001

Everyday I Have The Blues (T-Bone Walker) *Live In Hyde Park* DVD Warner Bros. released November 2001

Holy Mother[1] (Eric Clapton / Stephen Bishop) *Live In Hyde Park* DVD Warner Bros. released November 2001

[1]with the East London Gospel Choir
Film director: Julia Knowles
Sound produced by: Simon Climie

SEPTEMBER 1996

GIORGIO ARMANI SHOW 1996

12 September 1996, 69th Regiment Armory, New York City (Giorgio Armani Gala)

Eric Clapton was invited to play at the 69th Regiment Armory on Lexington Avenue by fashion designer Giorgio Armani who was celebrating the opening of his two stores on Madison Avenue. Other guests included Mariah Carey, Winona Ryder, the Duchess of York, and Mike Tyson who were also treated to a preview of Armani's spring 1997 collection by fifty models.

BAND LINEUP:
Eric Clapton: guitar, vocals
Greg Phillinganes: keyboards
Nathan East: bass
Steve Gadd: drums

SETLIST: Crossroads / Pretending / Going Down Slow / Tearing Us Apart[1]

[1]Sheryl Crow vocals

OCTOBER 1996

SHERYL CROW JAM 1996

11 October 1996, Viper Room, Sunset Boulevard, West Hollywood, California (Eric Clapton and Greg Phillinganes both join Sheryl Crow and her band for a couple of numbers. Eric and guitarist Todd Wolf tear it up on a spectacular version of Willie Dixon's "I Can't Quit You Baby")

SETLIST: I Can't Quit You Baby / The Na-Na Song

SHERYL CROW JAM 1996

31 October 1996, Elysee Montmartre, Paris (Eric joins Sheryl Crow for the last four numbers in her set)

SETLIST: Home / Ordinary Morning / Sway / Superstar

NOVEMBER 1996

SHERYL CROW JAM 1996

18 November 1996, Shepherds Bush Empire, Shepherds Bush, London (Eric joins Sheryl Crow for four numbers)

SETLIST: Home / The Na-Na Song / Superstar / Ordinary Morning

SHERYL CROW JAM 1996

19 November 1996, Shepherds Bush Empire, Shepherds Bush, London (Eric joins Sheryl Crow for three numbers)

SETLIST: Home / The Na-Na Song / Ordinary Morning

SHERYL CROW JAM 1996

26 November 1996, Shepherds Bush Empire, Shepherds Bush, London (Eric joins Sheryl Crow for two numbers. The majority of the concert is released first on VHS video and later on DVD)

SETLIST:

Home (Sheryl Crow) unreleased

Ordinary Morning (Sheryl Crow) *Live From London* VHS video VVL 054 0883 released 1997 / *Live From London* DVD edition released by Universal June 2005

Sheryl Crow: vocals, keyboards
Eric Clapton: guitar solo
Todd Wolfe: guitar
Jeff Trott: guitar
Tim Smith: bass
Jim Bogios: drums
R. S. Bryan: guitar

Show is filmed and recorded.

DECEMBER 1996

NEW YEAR'S EVE DANCE 1996

31 December 1996, Woking Leisure Centre, Woking, Surrey

Eric and his band are called Men Without Legs.

BAND LINEUP:
Eric Clapton: guitar, vocals
Alan Darby: guitar
Paul Wassif: guitar
Chris Stainton: keyboards
Simon Climie: keyboards
Dave Bronze: bass
Steve Gadd: drums

FIRST SET: Before You Accuse Me / Layla / I'm Tore Down / Have You Ever Loved A Woman / Lay Down Sally / Wonderful Tonight / I Hardly Ever Do[1] / Knock On Wood / It Hurts Me Too / Everyday I Have The Blues

[1]with Alan Darby on lead vocals

SECOND SET: Midnight Hour / Reconsider Baby / Hoochie Coochie Man / Knockin' On Heaven's Door / Blues Before Sunrise / Rollin' Man[1] / Someday After A While / Cocaine / Five Long Years / Sunshine Of Your Love

[1]with Alan Darby on lead vocals

RECORDING SESSIONS 1996

OLYMPIC STUDIOS
117 Church Road, London
Session for *The Van* soundtrack

JANUARY 1996

Eric records several pieces of incidental music for the soundtrack of Roddy Doyle's *The Van* film. Some of it is just Eric on acoustic accompanied by Jerry Portnoy on harmonica and some is with his band. Eric is a natural at film soundtracks and captures the moment perfectly. Unfortunately, no soundtrack was released. The only way to hear the music is to buy the DVD of the film.

Eric Clapton: acoustic guitar, electric guitar
Andy Fairweather Low: guitars
Chris Stainton: keyboards
Jerry Portnoy: harmonica
Steve Gadd: drums

Music recorded by: Alan Douglas

VILLAGE RECORDERS
1616 Butler Avenue, Los Angeles, California
Session for *Phenomenon* soundtrack

MARCH 1996

CHANGE THE WORLD (Tommy Sims / Gordon Kennedy / Wayne Kirkpatrick) CD single Reprise 9362-43727-2 released 1996

Eric Clapton: acoustic guitar, vocals
Kenny "Babyface" Edmonds: acoustic guitar, keyboards, drum programming

Producer: Kenneth "Babyface" Edmonds
Engineer: Brad Gilderman

ERIC CLAPTON GUEST SESSION

THE RECORD PLANT
1032 North Sycamore Avenue, Los Angeles, California

Session for Babyface

MAY 1996

TALK TO ME (Kenneth Edmonds) *The Day* CD EPIC EK 67293 released October 1996

Kenneth "Babyface" Edmonds: vocals, acoustic guitar, keyboards
Eric Clapton: guitar
Michael Thompson: guitar
Nathan East: bass
John Robinson: drums
De De O'Neal: backing vocals
Marc Nelson: backing vocals
Shanice: backing vocals
Sheila E: percussion

Producer: Babyface
Engineer: Brad Gilderman, Thom Russo

OCEAN WAY RECORDING 6050 Sunset Boulevard, Hollywood, California Session for Giorgio Armani Fashion Show / TDF

AUGUST 1996

Eric asked for Simon Climie's help in putting togther some music for an upcoming Giorgio Armani fashion show. The two of them started in Climie's small Pro Tools–equipped facility in the UK before moving operations to L.A. where they continued their collaboration in conjunction with Alan Douglas at Ocean Way Recording. Some of the music later made it onto a low-key release by TDF (Totally Dysfunctional Family) with Eric under the guise of X-Sample. In fact Eric dedicated a fair bit of time to the TDF project later in England after the sessions for *Pilgrim* had finished.

PARCHMENT

HEAD ABOVE WATER

TWICE SHY

UNDERWEAR

BACK TO YOU

ANGELICA

SIENNA

DONNA

ANGELICA (ACOUSTIC)

RIPSTOP

GIRL ON BEACH

Producers: Simon Climie / Eric Clapton
Engineer: Alan Douglas

OCEAN WAY RECORDING 6050 Sunset Boulevard, Hollywood, California Sessions for *Pilgrim*

SEPTEMBER 1996

and

OLYMPIC STUDIOS 117 Church Road, London Sessions for *Pilgrim*

NOVEMBER 1996

The initial sessions for the album that would become *Pilgrim* took place at Ocean Way Recording in Los Angeles. Starting on 2 September 1996, Eric had a tight four-piece band with him in the studio and produced some memorable songs with a good groove and funky edge. The band was Steve Gadd, Nathan East, and Greg Phillinganes. Things boded well for a great sounding record. Eric, however, had other ideas. He changed his mind often during these initial sessions putting on new guitar parts and solos resulting in completely different sounding numbers. This proved quite frustrating.

Sessions moved from Los Angeles to Olympic Studios in Barnes, London, in November 1996 where Eric started to take a more assertive role in the direction the album should move in. Ninety-five percent of the material recorded in L.A. was basically scrapped, even though there was more than enough to make a great album. But Eric didn't feel it was current enough. Ultimately this would prove to be a creative faux pas. He liked American R&B and hip hop grooves and wanted to head in that direction. Basically, Eric wanted

Pilgrim to have a heavily sequenced, contemporary sound; just like the records he was listening to at the time. The danger is that songs can sound dated very quickly due to a particular production style.

Around twenty numbers had been worked on over time as the project progressed in different locations. Eventually, fourteen made it onto the finished album, most of which were written by Eric himself. There were a couple co-written with Simon Climie, and then there was Bob Dylan's "Born In Time." Bob had originally offered this outtake from the *No Mercy* album sessions to Eric in 1989. Eric loved it and was going to record it at the time only to find that Dylan had re-recorded a new version on his 1990 *Under The Red Sky* album. When Eric found out it was being released, he decided not to record it. Bob persevered though, as he sent Eric another demo of the song in 1996 and clearly felt that Eric should record a version of it.

Eric came back to Olympic in early January 1997 to record music for the soundtrack of the *Nil By Mouth* film. Work on *Pilgrim* started again in mid-January with subsequent re-recordings, and re-re-recordings that dragged on until November 1997.

"Broken Hearted" is the only one of the live band tracks from the original sessions to have actually made it onto the finished album. Even then programmed drums had been added.

ERIC CLAPTON GUEST SESSION
OLYMPIC SOUND STUDIOS
117 Church Road, Barnes, London
Session for *Eternal*

DECEMBER 1996

SOMEDAY (Alan Menken / Stephen Schwartz) CD single EMI 724388317320 / *Before The Rain* CD EMI EMD 1103 released March 1997

Easther Bennett: vocals
Vernie Bennett: vocals
Kelle Bryan: vocals
Louise Nurding: vocals
Eric Clapton: acoustic guitar
Nick Ingham: string arrangement

Producer: Simon Climie

ERIC CLAPTON GUEST SESSION
OLYMPIC SOUND STUDIOS
117 Church Road, Barnes, London
Guitar overdub for Albert King

WHEN YOU WALK OUT THAT DOOR (Ike Darby) unreleased

In 1996 Eric also added an overdub to an Albert King number, "When You Walk Out That Door," which was due to form part of a two-volume set of the materiel Albert was working on before he passed away. It remains unreleased.

15

1997

FEBRUARY 1997

GRAMMY AWARDS 1997

26 February 1997, Madison Square Garden, New York City

The National Academy of Recording Arts & Sciences (NARAS) presented the 39th Annual Grammy Awards at New York's Madison Square Garden. Eric took trophies home for Record of the Year and Male Pop Vocal for the song "Change the World" from the *Phenomenon* soundtrack. The song's writers, Gordon Kennedy, Wayne Kirkpatrick, and Tommy Sims, also won a Grammy for Song of the Year. Eric also shared a win with Jimmie Vaughan, Bonnie Raitt, Robert Cray, B.B. King, Buddy Guy, Dr. John, and Art Neville for Best Rock Instrumental Performance for "SRV Shuffle," from the *A Tribute To Stevie Ray Vaughan* album.

Eric and Kenneth "Babyface" Edmonds performed the hit single "Change The World" live. The show was broadcast live on radio and TV. The television show was watched by about 1.5 billion people in 170 countries.

BAND LINEUP:
Eric Clapton: guitar, vocals
Kenneth "Babyface" Edmonds: guitar, vocals

SETLIST: Change The World (broadcast on television)

JULY 1997

LEGENDS EUROPEAN JAZZ FESTIVAL TOUR 1997

BAND LINEUP:
Eric Clapton: guitar, vocals
Marcus Miller: bass
David Sanborn: saxophone
Joe Sample: keyboards
Steve Gadd: drums

3 July 1997, Auditorium Stravinsky, Montreux, Switzerland

SETLIST: Full House / Snakes / Ruthie / Marcus #1 / Going Down Slow / Peeper / Suggestion / Third Degree / First Song–Tango Blues / Put It Where You Want It / Jelly Roll / In A Sentimental Mood / Layla / Everyday I Have The Blues

4 July 1997, Jazz Festival, Auditorium Stravinsky, Montreux, Switzerland

Whole show released on DVD/Blu-ray Eagle Vision in September 2005.

SETLIST: Full House / Marcus #1 / Ruthie / Snakes / Going Down Slow / Peeper / Suggestions / Third Degree / First Song–Tango Blues / Put It Where You Want It / Jelly Roll / In A Sentimental Mood / Layla / Everyday I Have The Blues

5 July 1997, Jazz A Vienne, Théâtre Romain, Vienne, France

SETLIST: Full House / Marcus #1 / Ruthie / Snakes / Going Down Slow / Peeper / Suggestions / Third Degree / First Song–Tango Blues / Put It Where You Want It / Jelly Roll / Sentimental / Layla / Everyday I Have The Blues

7 July 1997, Istanbul Jazz Festival, Cemil Topuzlu Amphitheatre, Istanbul, Turkey

SETLIST: Full House / Marcus #1 / Ruthie / Snakes / Going Down Slow / Peeper / Suggestions / Third Degree / First Song–Tango Blues / Put It Where You Want It / Jelly Roll / Sentimental / Layla / Everyday I Have The Blues

8 July 1997, Vienna Jazz Festival, Stadthalle, Vienna, Austria

SETLIST: Full House / Marcus #1 / Ruthie / Snakes / Going Down Slow / Peeper / Suggestions / Third Degree / First Song–Tango Blues / Put It Where You Want It / Jelly Roll / Sentimental / Layla / Everyday I Have The Blues / So Far Away

9 July 1997, Tivoli Garden, Copenhagen, Denmark

SETLIST: Full House / Marcus #1 / Ruthie / Snakes / Going Down Slow / Peeper / Suggestions / Third Degree / First Song–Tango Blues / Put It Where You Want It / Jelly Roll / Sentimental / Layla / Everyday I Have The Blues

11 July 1997, North Sea Jazz Festival, Statenhal, Den Haag, Netherlands

The show is filmed and recorded.

SETLIST: Full House / Marcus #1 / Ruthie / Snakes / Going Down Slow / Peeper / Suggestions / Third Degree / First Song–Tango Blues / Put It Where You Want It / Jelly Roll / Sentimental / Layla

11 July 1997, North Sea Jazz Festival, Statenhal, Den Haag, Netherlands (guest appearance with Robert Cray. After the *Legends* concert, Robert Cray performs in the same hall and is joined by Eric Clapton for "Right Next Door")

12 July 1997, Molde International Jazz Festival, Romsdalsmuseet, Molde, Norway

SETLIST: Full House / Marcus #1 / Ruthie / Snakes / Going Down Slow / Peeper / Suggestions / Third Degree / First Song–Tango Blues / Put It Where You Want It / Jelly Roll / Sentimental / Layla / Everyday I Have The Blues

13 July 1997, Umbria Jazz Festival, Villa Fidelia, Spello, Umbria, Italy

SETLIST: Full House / Marcus #1 / Ruthie / Snakes / Going Down Slow / Peeper / Suggestions / Third Degree / First Song–Tango Blues / Put It Where You Want It / Jelly Roll / Sentimental / Layla / Everyday I Have The Blues

15 July 1997, Rocce Rosse & Blues Festival, Red Cliffs of Arbatax, Sardinia, Italy

SETLIST: Full House / Marcus #1 / Ruthie / Snakes / Going Down Slow / Peeper / Suggestions / Third Degree / First Song–Tango Blues/ Put It Where You Want It / Jelly Roll / Sentimental / Layla / Everyday I Have The Blues

17 July 1997, Vitoria-Gasteiz Jazz Festival, Polideportivo Mendizorroza, Vitoria, Spain

The show is filmed and recorded.

SETLIST: Full House / Snakes / Ruthie / Marcus #1 / Going Down Slow / Peeper / Suggestions / Third Degree / First Song–Tango Blues/ Put It Where You Want It / Jelly Roll / Sentimental / Layla / Everyday I Have The Blues

SEPTEMBER 1997

MUSIC FOR MONTSERRAT 1997

15 September 1997, Royal Albert Hall, London

A one-off supergroup came together at the request of George Martin with the aim of raising funds for the volcano-ravaged island of Montserrat. The event was billed as the biggest charity concert of the decade with all the participants playing for free. As well as being televised in forty countries, the concert was also filmed for video release. Eric can be seen using his gold Fender Stratocaster.

Paul McCartney, Sting, Mark Knopfler, and Eric Clapton at the Royal Albert Hall for the Concert for Montserrat, 15 September 1997.

Money For Nothing

Mark Knopfler: vocals, guitar
Eric Clapton: guitar
Phil Palmer: guitar
Phil Collins: drums
Ian Thomas: drums
Guy Fletcher: keyboards
Ray Cooper: percussion
John Gidling: bass
Sting: vocals

Broken Hearted

Eric Clapton: acoustic guitar, vocals

Layla

Eric Clapton: acoustic guitar, vocals
Mark Knopfler: electric guitar

Same Old Blues

Eric Clapton: guitar, vocals
Mark Knopfler: guitar
Phil Collins: drums
Pino Paladino: bass
Ray Cooper: percussion
Jools Holland: piano
Chris Stainton: keyboards

Golden Slumbers / Carry That Weight / The End

Paul McCartney: piano, guitar, vocals
Eric Clapton: guitar
Mark Knopfler: guitar
Phil Palmer: guitar
Robby McIntosh: guitar
Phil Collins: drums
Ian Thomas: drums

Ray Cooper: percussion
Paul "Wix" Wickens: keyboards
John Gidling: bass
Guy Fletcher: keyboards
Foundation Philharmonic Orchestra
London Community Gospel Choir

Hey Jude

Paul McCartney: piano, vocals
Eric Clapton: guitar
Mark Knopfler: guitar
Phil Palmer: acoustic guitar
Robby McIntosh: guitar
Paul "Wix" Wickens: keyboards
Midge Ure: acoustic guitar
Phil Collins: drums
Ian Thomas: drums
John Gidling: bass
Elton John: keyboards, vocals
Carl Perkins: vocals
Sting: vocals
Ray Cooper: percussion
Robert Greenidge: steel drums
Jools Holland: piano
Elton John: piano
Alphonsus "Arrow" Cassel: vocals
Jimmy Buffett: vocals
Foundation Philharmonic Orchestra
London Community Gospel Choir

Kansas City

Paul McCartney: vocals
Eric Clapton: guitar
Mark Knopfler: guitar
Phil Palmer: guitar
Robby McIntosh: guitar
Paul "Wix" Wickens: keyboards
Midge Ure: acoustic guitar
Phil Collins: drums
Ian Thomas: drums
Carl Perkins: guitar, vocals
Sting: bass
Ray Cooper: percussion
Robert Greenidge: percussion
Jools Holland: piano
Elton John: piano
Alphonsus "Arrow" Cassel: vocals
Jimmy Buffett: vocals

Producer: George Martin

All the above songs can be found on the *Music For Montserrat* DVD via Eagle Vision which was released in 2003.

UNPLUGGED WITH BABYFACE 1997

25 September 1997, Hammerstein Ballroom, New York City (*MTV Unplugged* session with Babyface)

SETLIST:

Change The World *Babyface MTV Unplugged NYC 1997* CD Epic EK 68779 released November 1997 / *Babyface MTV Unplugged NYC 1997* DVD Sony Music released August 2001

Talk To Me *Babyface MTV Unplugged NYC 1997* CD Epic EK 68779 released November 1997 / *Babyface MTV Unplugged NYC 1997* DVD Sony Music released August 2001

Eric Clapton: guitar, vocals
Michael Thompson: guitar
Wayne Linsey: keyboards
Tim Carmon: keyboards
Bo Watson: keyboards
Reggie Griffin: guitar, keyboards, saxophone
Nathan East: bass
Ricky Lawson: drums
Sheila E.: percussion
Kevon Edmonds: vocals
Melvin Edmonds: vocals
Mark Nelson: vocals
Shanice Wilson: vocals
Beverly Crowder: vocals
Lynne Linsey: vocals

Producer: Alex Coletti

FAR EAST / JAPAN TOUR 1997

BAND LINEUP:
Eric Clapton: guitar, vocals
Andy Fairweather Low: rhythm guitar
Joe Sample: piano
Chris Stainton: keyboards
Dave Bronze: bass
Steve Gadd: drums
Katie Kissoon: backing vocals
Tessa Niles: backing vocals

OCTOBER 1997

9 October 1997, Olympic Gymnasium, Seoul, South Korea

SETLIST: Layla / Change The World / Nobody Knows You When You're Down And Out / Tears In Heaven / Going Down Slow / Broken Hearted / Pilgrim / Sick And Tired / I Shot The Sheriff / Wonderful Tonight / I'm Tore Down / Have You Ever Loved A Woman / Tearing Us Apart / Cocaine / Old Love / Everyday I Have The Blues / Before You Accuse Me

10 October 1997, Olympic Gymnasium, Seoul, South Korea

SETLIST: Layla / Change The World / Nobody Knows You When You're Down And Out / Tears In Heaven / Going Down Slow / Broken Hearted / Pilgrim / Sick And Tired / I Shot The Sheriff / Wonderful Tonight / Tore Down / Have You Ever Loved A Woman / Tearing Us Apart / Cocaine / Old Love / Sunshine Of Your Love / Everyday I Have The Blues / Before You Accuse Me

13 October 1997, Budokan, Tokyo, Japan

SETLIST: Layla / Change The World / Nobody Knows You When You're Down And Out / Tears In Heaven / Going Down Slow / Broken Hearted / Pilgrim / Sick And Tired / I Shot The Sheriff / Wonderful Tonight / Tore Down / Have You Ever Loved A Woman / Cocaine / Tearing Us Apart / Old Love / Sunshine Of Your Love / Everyday I Have The Blues / Before You Accuse Me

14 October 1997, Budokan, Tokyo, Japan

SETLIST: Layla / Change The World / Nobody Knows You When You're Down And Out / Tears In Heaven / Going Down Slow / Broken Hearted / Pilgrim / Sick And Tired / I Shot The Sheriff / Wonderful Tonight / Tore Down / Have You Ever Loved A Woman / Cocaine / Tearing Us Apart / Old Love / Sunshine Of Your Love / Everyday I Have The Blues / Before You Accuse Me

16 October 1997, Budokan, Tokyo, Japan

SETLIST: Layla / Change The World / Nobody Knows You When You're Down And Out / Tears In Heaven / Going

Down Slow / Broken Hearted / Pilgrim / Sick And Tired / I Shot The Sheriff / Wonderful Tonight / Tore Down / Have You Ever Loved A Woman / Cocaine / Tearing Us Apart / Old Love / Sunshine Of Your Love / Everyday I Have The Blues / Before You Accuse Me

17 October 1997, Budokan, Tokyo, Japan

SETLIST: Layla / Change The World / Nobody Knows You When You're Down And Out / Tears In Heaven / Going Down Slow / Broken Hearted / Pilgrim / Before You Accuse Me / I Shot The Sheriff / Wonderful Tonight / Tore Down / Have You Ever Loved A Woman / Cocaine / Tearing Us Apart / Old Love / Sunshine Of Your Love / Everyday I Have The Blues

20 October 1997, Marine Messe, Fukuoka, Japan

SETLIST: Layla / Change The World / Nobody Knows You When You're Down And Out / Tears In Heaven / Going Down Slow / Broken Hearted / Pilgrim / Before You Accuse Me / I Shot The Sheriff / Wonderful Tonight / Tore Down / Have You Ever Loved A Woman / Cocaine / Tearing Us Apart / Old Love / Sunshine Of Your Love / Everyday I Have The Blues

21 October 1997, Osaka Castle Hall, Osaka, Japan

SETLIST: Layla / Change The World / Nobody Knows You When You're Down And Out / Tears In Heaven / Going Down Slow / Broken Hearted / Pilgrim / Before You Accuse Me / I Shot The Sheriff / Wonderful Tonight / Tore Down / Have You Ever Loved A Woman / Cocaine / Tearing Us Apart / Old Love / Sunshine Of Your Love / Everyday I Have The Blues

22 October 1997, Osaka Castle Hall, Osaka, Japan

SETLIST: Layla / Change The World / Nobody Knows You When You're Down And Out / Tears In Heaven / Going Down Slow / Broken Hearted / Pilgrim / Before You Accuse Me / I Shot The Sheriff / Wonderful Tonight / Tore Down / Have You Ever Loved A Woman / Cocaine / Tearing Us Apart / Old Love / Sunshine Of Your Love / Everyday I Have The Blues

24 October 1997, Green Arena, Hiroshima, Japan

SETLIST: Layla / Change The World / Nobody Knows You When You're Down And Out / Tears In Heaven / Going Down Slow / Broken Hearted / Pilgrim / Before You Accuse Me / I Shot The Sheriff / Wonderful Tonight / Tore Down / Have You Ever Loved A Woman / Cocaine / Tearing Us Apart / Old Love / Sunshine Of Your Love / Everyday I Have The Blues

25 October 1997, Rainbow Hall, Nagoya, Japan

SETLIST: Layla / Change The World / Nobody Knows You When You're Down And Out / Tears In Heaven / Going Down Slow / Broken Hearted / Pilgrim / Before You Accuse Me / I Shot The Sheriff / Wonderful Tonight / Tore Down / Have You Ever Loved A Woman / Cocaine / Tearing Us Apart / Old Love / Sunshine Of Your Love / Everyday I Have The Blues

27 October 1997, Budokan, Tokyo, Japan

SETLIST: Layla / Change The World / Nobody Knows You When You're Down And Out / Tears In Heaven / Going Down Slow / Broken Hearted / Pilgrim / Before You Accuse Me / I Shot The Sheriff / White Room / Wonderful Tonight / Tore Down / Have You Ever Loved A Woman / Cocaine / Tearing Us Apart / Old Love / Sunshine Of Your Love / Everyday I Have The Blues

This show is filmed for the launch of Direct TV in Japan and was broadcast in November 1997. Cream's "White Room" makes its only appearance in the setlist during this tour. The new numbers were not allowed to be broadcast for fear that they would be bootlegged before an official release.

28 October 1997, Budokan, Tokyo, Japan

SETLIST: Layla / Change The World / Nobody Knows You When You're Down And Out / Tears In Heaven / Going Down Slow / Broken Hearted / Pilgrim / Before You Accuse Me / I Shot The Sheriff / Wonderful Tonight / Tore Down / Have You Ever Loved A Woman / Cocaine / Tearing Us Apart / Old Love / Sunshine Of Your Love / Everyday I Have The Blues

30 October 1997, Budokan, Tokyo, Japan

SETLIST: Layla / Change The World / Nobody Knows You When You're Down And Out / Tears In Heaven / Going Down Slow / Broken Hearted / Pilgrim / Before You Accuse Me / I Shot The Sheriff / Wonderful Tonight / Tore Down / Have You Ever Loved A Woman / Cocaine / Tearing Us Apart / Old Love / Sunshine Of Your Love / Everyday I Have The Blues

31 October 1997, Budokan, Tokyo, Japan

SETLIST: Layla / Change The World / Nobody Knows You When You're Down And Out / Tears In Heaven / Going Down Slow / Broken Hearted / Pilgrim / Before You Accuse Me / I Shot The Sheriff / Wonderful Tonight / Tore Down / Have You Ever Loved A Woman / Cocaine / Tearing Us Apart / Old Love / Sunshine Of Your Love / Everyday I Have The Blues

DECEMBER 1997

NEW YEAR'S EVE DANCE 1997

31 December 1997, Woking Leisure Centre, Woking, Surrey

Eric and his band are called the Spiritual Tools.

BAND LINEUP:
Eric Clapton: guitar, vocals
Paul Wassif: guitar
Alan Darby: guitar, vocals
Andy Fairweather Low: guitar, vocals
Chris Stainton: keyboards
Dave Bronze: bass
Henry Spinetti: drums
Kevin Rowland: vocals

SETLIST 1: Reconsider Baby / Hoochie Coochie Man / Knockin' On Heaven's Door / Rollin' Man[1] / Someday After A While / Cocaine / Five Long Years / You'll Never Walk Alone / Sunshine Of Your Love / Everyday I Have The Blues

[1] with Alan Darby on lead vocals

SETLIST 2: Midnight Hour / I'm Tore Down / Have You Ever Loved A Woman / Lay Down Sally / Wonderful Tonight / I Hardly Ever Do[1] / Knock On Wood / Gin House / Layla

[1] with Alan Darby on lead vocals

RECORDING SESSIONS 1997
OLYMPIC STUDIOS
117 Church Road,
Session for *Nil By Mouth* soundtrack

JANUARY 1997

Eric records the soundtrack to *Nil By Mouth*. It was Gary Oldman's debut as a writer and director. A soundtrack was never released. The film depicts the harsh realities of growing up on a council estate and is quite harrowing to watch. The music is recorded by Alan Douglas.

ERIC CLAPTON GUEST SESSION
OLYMPIC STUDIOS
117 Church Road, Barnes, London
Sessions for Tony Rich Project

FEBRUARY 1997

Eric was really into Tony Rich's music and after seeing him in concert in London in 1996, he asked him if he could come and lend his vocal talents to the album he was in the process of recording (*Pilgrim*). Tony agreed and the two of them headed off to Olympic Studios after the gig. It ended up as a quid pro quo setup with Eric agreeing to add some guitar parts to Tony's *Birdseye* album. Rich flew over to England in February 1997 with tapes for his new album and Eric added his guitar work on several tracks. It ended up a deliberately low-key affair with no real mention of Eric's participation other than a capital *E* next to "guitar" in the credits for his appearance on the various tracks. The smooth R&B grooves would be an influence on how *Pilgrim* would sound.

NO TIME SOON (Tony Rich) *Birdseye* CD LaFace 73008 26042 2 released August 1998

Tony Rich: drums, keyboards, vocals
Jose Jeffries: keyboards, bass, shaker
Peter Moore: classical acoustic guitar
LaMarquis Jefferson: bass
Eric Clapton: electric guitar, slide guitar

THOUGHTS OF LEAVIN' (Joe Rich / Don Dubose) *Birdseye* CD LaFace 73008 26042 2 released August 1998

Tony Rich: drums, keyboards, vocals
Cedric Anderson: percussion
Peter Moore: acoustic guitar
LaMarquis Jefferson: bass
Eric Clapton: electric guitar

MY STOMACH HURTS (Tony Rich) *Birdseye* CD LaFace 73008 26042 2 released August 1998

Tony Rich: drums, keyboards, vocals
Cedric Anderson: percussion
Peter Moore: acoustic guitar
LaMarquis Jefferson: bass
Eric Clapton: electric guitar
Meko: female background vocals

Producer: Tony Rich
Engineer: Girdy Garnvarn

> **"**We were touring in the UK, and had a gig in London. At soundcheck, Steve Powell [road manager] told us that Tony had been invited to sing on one of Eric's projects, and the session would happen that night. The band was pretty excited about the prospect of meeting a living legend, but Steve told us that only Tony could go. Of course no one could sleep until Tony returned with the play-by-play. He told us that Eric was very gracious, and they had a great time. At the end of the session, Eric thanked Tony and asked him if he could do anything for him in return. Tony asked Eric to return the favor by playing on *Birdseye*. Eric agreed. For me, trading licks with Slow Hand was a dream come true, but, unfortunately, most of the public could only speculate that Eric Clapton actually played on *Birdseye* because allegedly, one of the record company executives at Eric's label accused Tony of using Eric's name to promote his own album by including it in the liner notes. To avoid problems, Tony used the initial *E*.**"**
>
> **—PETER MOORE**
> (guitarist on *Birdseye*)

> **"**There were some allegations that I had him on the album as some type of promotional stunt, but I don't have to have anyone on my album to promote my album. Me and Eric are friends and I wanted him to play guitar, he wanted to sing backup, and we just exchanged favors. There wasn't any money involved. I didn't pay him, he didn't pay me, it was just like that. It was real cool though. Eric really wanted to be a part of playing some guitar parts, but he didn't really want to play it up. He just wanted to be one of the musicians like all the other guys that I use. So we're happy that we did exchange our talents with each other.**"**
>
> **—TONY RICH**
> (*MTV News*)

ERIC CLAPTON GUEST SESSION

MARCUS RECORDING STUDIOS
17-21 Wyfold Road, Fulham, London
Session for BeBe Winans

FEBRUARY 1997

THIS SONG (BeBe Winans / Marc Harris) *BeBe Winans* CD Atlantic 8304-2 released October 1997

BeBe Winans: vocals
Eric Clapton: guitar
Luke Smith: piano
Steve Williams: percussion
Nigel Lowis: keyboards
London Session Orchestra: strings
Lawrence Johnson: backing vocals
Priscilla May Jones: backing vocals
Lain Gray: backing vocals
Fay Simpson: backing vocals

Producer: BeBe Winans / Nigel Lowis
Engineer: Gareth Lacking

SILLY MAN (Tony Rich) *Birdseye* CD LaFace 73008 26042 2 released August 1998
Tony Rich: keyboards, acoustic guitar, drums, vocals
Peter Moore: acoustic guitar
LaMarquis Jefferson: bass
Cedric Anderson: additional drums, percussion
Eric Clapton: electric guitar, slide guitar

ERIC CLAPTON GUEST SESSION

SHOWLINE STUDIOS 915 Lakeshore Boulevard East, Toronto, Ontario

Session for *Blues Brothers 2000* film and soundtrack

26 AUGUST 1997

HOW BLUE CAN YOU GET (Jane Feather) (Take 3) *Blues Brothers 2000* CD Universal UD53116 released February 1998

Eric Clapton: guitar, vocals
B.B. King: guitar, vocals
Bo Diddley: guitar, vocals
Jimmy Vaughan: guitar, vocals
Jeff "Skunk" Baxter: guitar
Travis Tritt: guitar, vocals
Steve Winwood: organ, vocals
Dr. John: vocals, piano
Charlie Musselwhite: vocals, harmonica
Billy Preston: synthesizer, vocals
Jack DeJonette: drums
Jon Faddis: trumpet
Joshua Redman: tenor saxophone
Grover Washington, Jr.,: baritone saxophone
Clarence Clemons: tenor saxophone, vocals, tambourine
Isaac Hayes: vocals
Koko Taylor: vocals
Lou Rawls: vocals
Gary U.S. Bonds: vocals
Tommy McDonnell: vocals
Willie Weeks: bass

NEW ORLEANS (Joseph Royster / Frank Guida) (Take 3) *Blues Brothers 2000* CD Universal UD53116 released February 1998

Eric Clapton: guitar, vocals
B.B. King: guitar, vocals
Bo Diddley: guitar, vocals
Jimmy Vaughan: guitar, vocals
Jeff "Skunk" Baxter: guitar
Travis Tritt: guitar, vocals
Steve Winwood: organ, vocals
Dr. John: vocals, piano
Charlie Musselwhite: vocals, harmonica
Billy Preston: synthesizer, vocals
Jack DeJonette: drums
Jon Faddis: trumpet
Joshua Redman: tenor saxophone
Grover Washington, Jr.: baritone saxophone
Clarence Clemons: tenor saxophone, vocals, tambourine
Isaac Hayes: vocals
Koko Taylor: vocals
Lou Rawls: vocals
Gary U.S. Bonds: vocals
Tommy McDonnell: vocals
Willie Weeks: bass
Steve Cropper: guitar
Matt Murphy: guitar
Donald "Duck" Dunn: bass
Anton Fig: drums
Paul Shaffer: piano, organ
Leon Pendarvis: piano, organ
Lou Marini: saxophone
Alan Rubin: trumpet
Birch Johnson: trombone

JAM unreleased

Eric Clapton: guitar
B.B. King: guitar
Bo Diddley: guitar

"That remote was done at Showline Studios [a big film soundstage] on Lakeshore Bouelvard in Toronto on 26 August 1997. My company did all the multitrack audio recording for songs in the movie that were recorded live, including a James Brown song that was included after the credit roll. It was done on 48-eight track analog (we had two 24-track Ampex MM1200 recorders and a 50-input Neotek Elite console).

They had built a set inside the soundstage to resemble the House of Blues in New Orleans. We couldn't start setting the stage till after midnight as they were shooting dialog scenes there all day. We set up till 5:00 a.m., went home for two hours of sleep, then came back at 8:00 a.m. for the big finale concert shoot. They only had all the musicians in town for the one day, so we did three takes of each song.

Steve Cropper was in the mobile with me producing. (I got to hear things like 'Doug would you like to hear Stevie Winwood play organ now,' 'OK.' Steve thought that Jimmy Vaughan's guitar tone was a bit bassy and asked me to ask him to change it. I told him that I thought it would mean more if Steve Cropper told him to change it.

I didn't actually speak to Clapton, but he was smiling all day long, surrounded by his heroes. The guitar section was Clapton, B.B. King, Bo Diddley, Jimmy Vaughan, Travis Tritt, and Jeff "Skunk" Baxter. Keyboard section: Stevie Winwood, Billy Preston, Dr. John. Horn section: Grover Washington, Jr., Joshua Redmond, Clarence Clemons, Charlie Musselwhite was on harmonica. Background vocals included Isaac Hayes, Gary U.S. Bonds, Koko Taylor, and others. Musical director: Paul Shaffer.

They used the last take of each song: one Gator Boys ('How Blue Can You Get'), one Blues Brothers ('Lovelight'), and one with both bands combined ('New Orleans'). There was an instrumental jam afterwards that was recorded but not used. I think we were finished shooting by about 5:00 p.m. There were no overdubs, it was all totally live off the floor."

—DOUG MCCLEMENT

(engineer)

Jimmy Vaughan: guitar
Jeff "Skunk" Baxter: guitar
Travis Tritt: guitar
Steve Winwood: organ
Dr. John: vocals, piano
Charlie Musselwhite: harmonica
Billy Preston: synthesizer
Jack DeJonette: drums
Jon Faddis: trumpet
Joshua Redman: tenor saxophone
Grover Washington, Jr.: baritone saxophone
Clarence Clemons: tenor saxophone, vocals, tambourine
Willie Weeks: bass
Steve Cropper: guitar
Matt Murphy: guitar
Donald "Duck" Dunn: bass
Anton Fig: drums
Paul Shaffer: piano, organ
Leon Pendarvis: piano, organ
Lou Marini: saxophone
Alan Rubin: trumpet
Birch Johnson: trombone

Producer: Paul Shaffer
Engineer: Doug McClement
Recorded by: LiveWire Remote Recorders

ERIC CLAPTON GUEST SESSION

TOWN HOUSE STUDIOS 150 Goldhawk Road, London Session For B.B. King

AUGUST 1997

ROCK ME BABY (Joe Josea / B.B. King) *Deuces Wild* CD MCA MCD11722 released November 1997

B.B. King: guitar, vocals
Eric Clapton: guitar
Paul Carrack: Hammond B3 organ
Pino Paladino: bass
Paulinho Da Costa: percussion
Simon Climie: programming
Paul Waller: programming

Producer: John Porter

OCEAN WAY RECORDING 6050 Sunset Boulevard, Los Angeles, California

and

OLYMPIC STUDIOS 117 Church Road, London Sessions for *Pilgrim*

SEPTEMBER 1996– DECEMBER 1997

Eric admitted ahead of his Japanese tour in October 1997, "I've been in the studio for almost a year trying to make a good record. I've never worked this hard in making a studio album before. I don't know why it suddenly became so important but I really want to make a good one, so I'm taking my time. We are going over to Japan just to try out a few of these new songs."

MY FATHER'S EYES (Eric Clapton) *Pilgrim* CD Reprise 46577 released March 1998

Eric Clapton: guitar, vocals
Nathan East: bass
Paul Waller: drum programming
Steve Gadd: drums
Andy Fairweather Low: guitar
Simon Climie: keyboards
Chris Stainton: Hammond B3 organ
Joe Sample: piano
Chyna: backing vocals

RIVER OF TEARS (Eric Clapton / Simon Climie) *Pilgrim* CD Reprise 46577 released March 1998

Eric Clapton: guitar, vocals
Luis Jardim: bass, percussion
Paul Waller: drum programming
Simon Climie: keyboards, bass synthesizer, backing vocals
Chyna: backing vocals
Nick Ingman: string arrangement
London Session Orchestra: strings

PILGRIM (Eric Clapton / Simon Climie) *Pilgrim* CD Reprise 46577 released March 1998

Eric Clapton: guitar, vocals
Simon Climie: drum programming, keyboards, backing vocals
Paul Carrack: Hammond B3 organ
Chyna: backing vocals
Nick Ingman: string arrangement
London Session Orchestra: strings

BROKEN HEARTED (Eric Clapton / Greg Phillinganes) *Pilgrim* CD Reprise 46577 released March 1998
Eric Clapton: guitar, vocals
Nathan East: bass
Paul Waller: drum programming
Steve Gadd: drums
Greg Phillinganes: keyboards
Simon Climie: keyboard programming
Paul Brady: backing vocals, tin whistle
Chyna: backing vocals

ONE CHANCE (Eric Clapton / Simon Climie) *Pilgrim* CD Reprise 46577 released March 1998
Eric Clapton: guitar, vocals
Pino Paladino: bass
Paul Waller: drum programming

Simon Climie: keyboards
Paul Carrack: Hammond B3 organ
Chyna: backing vocals
Nick Ingman: string arrangement
London Session Orchestra: strings

CIRCUS (Eric Clapton) *Pilgrim* CD Reprise 46577 released March 1998

Eric Clapton: guitar, vocals
Nathan East: bass
Paul Waller: drum programming
Simon Climie: keyboards
Chyna: backing vocals

GOING DOWN SLOW (St. Louis Jimmy) *Pilgrim* CD Reprise 46577 released March 1998

Eric Clapton: guitar, vocals
Pino Paladino: bass
Paul Waller: drum programming
Simon Climie: keyboards
Paul Carrack: Hammond B3 organ, Wurlitzer
Nick Ingman: string arrangement
London Session Orchestra: strings

FALL LIKE RAIN (Eric Clapton)

Eric Clapton: guitar, vocals, backing vocals
Nathan East: bass
Paul Waller: drum programming
Simon Climie: keyboards

BORN IN TIME (Bob Dylan) *Pilgrim* CD Reprise 46577 released March 1998

Eric Clapton: guitar
Pino Paladino: bass
Paul Waller: drum programming
Simon Climie: keyboards
Kenny Edmonds: backing vocals
Luis Jardim: percussion
Nick Ingman: string arrangement
London Session Orchestra: strings

SICK AND TIRED (Eric Clapton / Simon Climie) *Pilgrim* CD Reprise 46577 released March 1998

Eric Clapton: guitar, vocals
Simon Climie: drum programming, keyboards
Paul Carrack: Hammond B3 organ
Nick Ingman: string arrangement
London Session Orchestra: strings

NEEDS HIS WOMAN (Eric Clapton) *Pilgrim* CD Reprise 46577 released March 1998

Eric Clapton: guitar, vocals

Tony Rich: backing vocals
Nathan East: bass
Paul Waller: drum programming
Greg Phillinganes: keyboards

SHE'S GONE (Eric Clapton / Simon Climie) *Pilgrim* CD Reprise 46577 released March 1998

Eric Clapton: guitar, vocals
Pino Paladino: bass
Paul Waller: drum programming
Steve Gadd: drums
Simon Climie: keyboards
Chyna: backing vocals
Paul Carrack: Hammond B3 organ

YOU WERE THERE (Eric Clapton) *Pilgrim* CD Reprise 46577 released March 1998

Eric Clapton: guitar, vocals
Dave Bronze: bass
Simon Climie: drum programming, keyboard programming, backing vocals
Steve Gadd: drums
Chris Stainton: Hammond B3 organ
Joe Sample: piano
Chyna: backing vocals
Nick Ingman: string arrangement
London Session Orchestra: strings

INSIDE OF ME (Eric Clapton / Simon Climie) *Pilgrim* CD Reprise 46577 released March 1998

Eric Clapton: guitar, vocals
Paul Waller: drum programming
Simon Climie: keyboards
Chyna: backing vocals
Nick Ingman: string arrangement
London Session Orchestra: strings
Ruth Kelly-Clapton: spoken verse

THEME FROM A MOVIE THAT NEVER HAPPENED (Eric Clapton) orchestral bonus track on Japanese edition of *Pilgrim* CD Reprise WPCR-1400 released March 1998 / *My Father's Eyes* 4-track CD single UK WEA / Reprise/Duck Records W0443CD released March 1998

Eric Clapton: guitar
Nick Ingman: string arrangement
London Session Orchestra: strings

MODERN GIRL (Eric Clapton) unreleased (re-recorded for the *Reptile* sessions)

Producers: Eric Clapton / Simon Climie
Engineer: Alan Douglas

OLYMPIC STUDIOS
117 Church Road, London
Sessions for T.D.F.

NOVEMBER 1997

BLUE ROCK (Simon Climie / X-Sample) *T.D.F. Retail Therapy* CD Reprise 9362-46489-2 released October 1999

ANGELICA (Simon Climie / X-Sample) *T.D.F. Retail Therapy* CD Reprise 9362-46489-2 released October 1999

PNOM-SEN (Simon Climie / X-Sample) *T.D.F. Retail Therapy* CD Reprise 9362-46489-2 released October 1999

SNO-GOD (Simon Climie / X-Sample) *T.D.F. Retail Therapy* CD Reprise 9362-46489-2 released October 1999

SIENNA (Simon Climie / X-Sample) T.D.F. *Retail Therapy* CD Reprise 9362-46489-2 released October 1999

SEVEN (Simon Climie / X-Sample) *T.D.F. Retail Therapy* CD Reprise 9362-46489-2 released October 1999

ANGELICA'S DREAM (Simon Climie / X-Sample) *T.D.F. Retail Therapy* CD Reprise 9362-46489-2 released October 1999

WHAT SHE WANTS (Simon Climie / X-Sample) *T.D.F. Retail Therapy* CD Reprise 9362-46489-2 released October 1999

DONNA (Simon Climie / X-Sample) *T.D.F. Retail Therapy* CD Reprise 9362-46489-2 released October 1999

RIP STOP (Simon Climie / X-Sample) *T.D.F. Retail Therapy* CD Reprise 9362-46489-2 released October 1999

WHAT ELSE (Simon Climie / X-Sample) *T.D.F. Retail Therapy* CD Reprise 9362-46489-2 released October 1999

X Sample: guitar
Paul Waller: drum programming
Tony Rich: vocals on "What She Wants"
Sheryl Crow: vocals on "What She Wants"
B.B. King: featured sample in "Seven"
Nick Ingman: string arrangement on "What Else"

Producers: X Sample / Simon Climie
Engineer: Alan Douglas

16

1998

The year 1998 was all about *Pilgrim* and the promoting of that album. Eric toured for most of the year.

MARCH 1998

PILGRIM U.S. TOUR 1998

BAND LINEUP:
Eric Clapton: guitar, vocals
Andy Fairweather Low: guitar, vocals
Nathan East: bass, vocals
Alan Darby: guitar, vocals
Tim Carmon: keyboards, vocals
Kenneth Crouch: keyboards
Ricky Lawson: drums
Katie Kissoon: backing vocals
Chyna: backing vocals
Charlean Hines: backing vocals
Nick Ingman: conductor of 20-piece orchestra

30 March 1998, Civic Center, St. Paul, Minnesota (with Distant Cousins)

SETLIST: My Father's Eyes / Pilgrim / One Chance / River Of Tears / Going Down Slow / Born In Time / She's Gone / Tears In Heaven / Circus / Layla / Needs His Woman / Change The World / Old Love / Sick And Tired / Have You Ever Loved A Woman / I Shot The Sheriff /

Wonderful Tonight / Tearing Us Apart / Sunshine Of Your Love / Crossroads

APRIL 1998

2 April 1998, Kemper Arena, Kansas City, Kansas (with Distant Cousins)

SETLIST: My Father's Eyes / One Chance / Pilgrim / River Of Tears / Going Down Slow / Born In Time / She's Gone / Tears In Heaven / Circus / Layla / Change The World / Old Love / Sick And Tired / Have You Ever Loved A Woman / I Shot The Sheriff / Wonderful Tonight / Tearing Us Apart / Sunshine Of Your Love / Crossroads

3 April 1998, Kiel Center, St. Louis, Missouri (with Distant Cousins)

SETLIST: My Father's Eyes / Pilgrim / One Chance / River of Tears / Going Down Slow / Born In Time / She's Gone / Tears In Heaven / Layla / Change The World / Old Love / Sick And Tired / Have You Ever Loved A Woman / I Shot The Sheriff / Wonderful Tonight / Tearing Us Apart / Sunshine Of Your Love / Crossroads

5 April 1998, Mark of the Quad Cities, Moline, Illinois (with Distant Cousins)

SETLIST: My Father's Eyes / Pilgrim / One Chance / River Of Tears / Going Down Slow / She's Gone / Tears In Heaven / Layla / Change The World / Old Love / Sick And Tired / Have You Ever Loved A Woman / I Shot The

Sheriff / Wonderful Tonight / Tearing Us Apart / Sunshine Of Your Love

6 April 1998, Bradley Center, Milwaukee, Wisconsin (with Distant Cousins)

SETLIST: My Father's Eyes / Pilgrim / One Chance / River Of Tears / Going Down Slow / She's Gone / Tears In Heaven / Layla / Change The World / Old Love / Sick And Tired / Have You Ever Loved A Woman / I Shot The Sheriff / Wonderful Tonight / Tearing Us Apart / Sunshine of Your Love

8 April 1998, Palace of Auburn Hills, Auburn Hills, Michigan (with Distant Cousins)

SETLIST: My Father's Eyes / Pilgrim / One Chance / River Of Tears / Going Down Slow / She's Gone / Tears In Heaven / Layla / Change The World / Old Love / Sick And Tired / Have You Ever Loved A Woman / I Shot The Sheriff / Wonderful Tonight / Tearing Us Apart / Sunshine of Your Love

9 April 1998, United Center, Chicago, Illinois (with Distant Cousins)

SETLIST: My Father's Eyes / Pilgrim / One Chance / River Of Tears / Going Down Slow / She's Gone / Tears In Heaven / Layla / Change The World / Old Love / Sick And Tired / Have You Ever Loved A Woman / I Shot The Sheriff / Wonderful Tonight / Tearing Us Apart / Cocaine / Sunshine Of Your Love

10 April 1998, United Center, Chicago, Illinois (with Distant Cousins)

SETLIST: My Father's Eyes / Pilgrim / One Chance / River Of Tears / Going Down Slow / She's Gone / Tears In Heaven / Layla / Change The World / Old Love / Crossroads / Have You Ever Loved A Woman / I Shot The Sheriff / Wonderful Tonight / Tearing Us Apart / Cocaine / Sunshine Of Your Love / Sweet Home Chicago[1]

[1] with Buddy Guy on guitar and vocals

12 April 1998, Gund Arena, Cleveland, Ohio (with Distant Cousins)

SETLIST: My Father's Eyes / Pilgrim / One Chance / River Of Tears / Going Down Slow / She's Gone / Tears In Heaven / Layla / Change The World / Old Love / Crossroads / Have You Ever Loved A Woman / I Shot The Sheriff / Wonderful Tonight / Tearing Us Apart / Cocaine / Sunshine Of Your Love

14 April 1998, Fleet Center, Boston, Massachusetts (with Distant Cousins)

SETLIST: My Father's Eyes / Pilgrim / One Chance / River Of Tears / Going Down Slow / She's Gone / Tears In Heaven / Layla / Change The World / Old Love / Crossroads / Have You Ever Loved A Woman / I Shot The Sheriff / Wonderful Tonight / Tearing Us Apart / Cocaine / Sunshine Of Your Love

15 April 1998, First Union Center, Philadelphia, Pennsylvania (with Distant Cousins)

SETLIST: My Father's Eyes / Pilgrim / One Chance / River Of Tears / Going Down Slow / She's Gone / Tears In Heaven / Layla / Change The World / Old Love / Crossroads / Have You Ever Loved A Woman / I Shot The Sheriff / Wonderful Tonight / Tearing Us Apart / Cocaine / Sunshine Of Your Love

16 April 1998, MCI Center, Washington, D.C. (with Distant Cousins)

SETLIST: My Father's Eyes / Pilgrim / One Chance / River Of Tears / Going Down Slow / She's Gone / Tears In Heaven / Layla / Change The World / Old Love / Crossroads / Have You Ever Loved A Woman / I Shot The Sheriff / Wonderful Tonight / Tearing Us Apart / Cocaine / Sunshine Of Your Love

18 April 1998, Madison Square Garden, New York City (with Distant Cousins)

SETLIST: My Father's Eyes / Pilgrim / One Chance / River Of Tears / Going Down Slow / She's Gone / Tears In Heaven / Layla / Change The World / Old Love / Crossroads / Have You Ever Loved A Woman / I Shot The Sheriff / Wonderful Tonight / Tearing Us Apart / Cocaine / Sunshine Of Your Love

19 April 1998, Madison Square Garden, New York City (with Distant Cousins)

SETLIST: My Father's Eyes / Pilgrim / One Chance / River Of Tears / Going Down Slow / She's Gone / Tears In Heaven / Layla / Change The World / Old Love / Crossroads / Have You Ever Loved A Woman / I Shot The Sheriff / Wonderful Tonight / Tearing Us Apart / Cocaine / Sunshine Of Your Love

20 April 1998, Madison Square Garden, New York City (with Distant Cousins)

SETLIST: My Father's Eyes / Pilgrim / One Chance / River Of Tears / Going Down Slow / She's Gone / Tears In Heaven / Layla / Change The World / Old Love / Crossroads / Have You Ever Loved A Woman / I Shot The Sheriff / Wonderful Tonight / Tearing Us Apart / Cocaine / Sunshine Of Your Love

22 April 1998, Charlotte Coliseum, Charlotte, North Carolina (with Distant Cousins)

SETLIST: My Father's Eyes / Pilgrim / One Chance / River Of Tears / Going Down Slow / She's Gone / Tears In Heaven / Layla / Change The World / Old Love / Crossroads / Have You Ever Loved A Woman / I Shot The Sheriff / Wonderful Tonight / Tearing Us Apart / Cocaine / Sunshine Of Your Love

23 April 1998, Thompson-Boling Arena, Knoxville, Tennessee (with Distant Cousins)

SETLIST: My Father's Eyes / Pilgrim / One Chance / River Of Tears / Going Down Slow / She's Gone / Tears In Heaven / Layla / Change The World / Old Love / Crossroads / Have You Ever Loved A Woman / I Shot The Sheriff / Wonderful Tonight / Tearing Us Apart / Cocaine / Sunshine Of Your Love

25 April 1998, Miami Arena, Miami, Florida (with Distant Cousins)

SETLIST: My Father's Eyes / Pilgrim / One Chance / River Of Tears / Going Down Slow / She's Gone / Tears In Heaven / Layla / Change The World / Old Love / Crossroads / Have You Ever Loved A Woman / I Shot The Sheriff / Wonderful Tonight / Tearing Us Apart / Cocaine / Sunshine Of Your Love

26 April 1998, Ice Palace Arena, Tampa, Florida (with Distant Cousins)

SETLIST: My Father's Eyes / Pilgrim / One Chance / River Of Tears / Going Down Slow / She's Gone / Tears In Heaven / Layla / Change The World / Old Love / Crossroads / Have You Ever Loved A Woman / I Shot The Sheriff / Wonderful Tonight / Tearing Us Apart / Cocaine / Sunshine Of Your Love

MAY 1998

PILGRIM U.S. TOUR 1998 (Second leg)

BAND LINEUP:
Eric Clapton: guitar, vocals
Andy Fairweather Low: guitar, vocals
Nathan East: bass, vocals
Alan Darby: guitar, vocals
Tim Carmon: keyboards, vocals
Kenneth Crouch: keyboards
Ricky Lawson: drums
Katie Kissoon: backing vocals
Chyna: backing vocals
Charlean Hines: backing vocals
Nick Ingman: conductor of 20-piece orchestra

11 May 1998, Civic Arena, Pittsburgh, Pennsylvania (with Distant Cousins)

SETLIST: My Father's Eyes / Pilgrim / One Chance / River Of Tears / Going Down Slow / She's Gone / Drifting Blues / Tears In Heaven / Layla / Change The World / Old Love / Crossroads / Have You Ever Loved A Woman / I Shot The Sheriff / Wonderful Tonight / Tearing Us Apart / Cocaine / Sunshine Of Your Love

12 May 1998, Crown, Cincinnati, Ohio (with Distant Cousins)

SETLIST: My Father's Eyes / Pilgrim / One Chance / River Of Tears / Going Down Slow / She's Gone / Drifting Blues / Tears In Heaven / Layla / Change The World / Old Love / Crossroads / Have You Ever Loved A Woman / I Shot The Sheriff / Wonderful Tonight / Tearing Us Apart / Cocaine / Sunshine Of Your Love

14 May 1998, Dean E. Smith Center, Chapel Hill, North Carolina (with Distant Cousins)

SETLIST: My Father's Eyes / Pilgrim / One Chance / River Of Tears / Going Down Slow / She's Gone / Drifting Blues / Tears In Heaven / Layla / Change The World / Old Love / Crossroads / Have You Ever Loved A Woman / I Shot The Sheriff / Wonderful Tonight / Tearing Us Apart / Cocaine / Sunshine Of Your Love

16 May 1998, Nashville Arena, Nashville, Tennessee (with Distant Cousins)

SETLIST: My Father's Eyes / Pilgrim / One Chance / River Of Tears / Going Down Slow / She's Gone / Drifting Blues / Tears In Heaven / Layla / Change The World / Old Love / Crossroads / Have You Ever Loved A Woman / I Shot The Sheriff / Wonderful Tonight / Tearing Us Apart / Cocaine / Sunshine Of Your Love

17 May 1998, Pyramid, Memphis, Tennessee (with Distant Cousins)

SETLIST: My Father's Eyes / Pilgrim / One Chance / River Of Tears / Going Down Slow / She's Gone / Drifting Blues / Tears In Heaven / Layla / Change The World / Old Love / Crossroads / Have You Ever Loved A Woman / I Shot The Sheriff / Wonderful Tonight / Tearing Us Apart / Cocaine / Sunshine Of Your Love

19 May 1998, Compaq Center, Houston, Texas (with Distant Cousins)

SETLIST: My Father's Eyes / Pilgrim / One Chance / River Of Tears / Going Down Slow / She's Gone / Drifting Blues / Tears In Heaven / Layla / Change The World / Old Love / Crossroads / Have You Ever Loved A Woman / I Shot The Sheriff / Wonderful Tonight / Tearing Us Apart / Cocaine / Sunshine Of Your Love

20 May 1998, Super Dome, New Orleans, Louisiana (with Distant Cousins)

SETLIST: My Father's Eyes / Pilgrim / One Chance / River Of Tears / Going Down Slow / She's Gone / Drifting Blues / Tears In Heaven / Layla / Change The World / Old Love / Crossroads / Have You Ever Loved A Woman / I Shot The Sheriff / Wonderful Tonight / Tearing Us Apart / Cocaine / Sunshine Of Your Love

22 May 1998, Reunion Arena, Dallas, Texas (with Distant Cousins)

SETLIST: My Father's Eyes / Pilgrim / One Chance / River Of Tears / Going Down Slow / She's Gone / Drifting Blues / Tears In Heaven / Layla / Change The World / Old Love / Crossroads / Have You Ever Loved A Woman / I Shot The Sheriff / Wonderful Tonight / Cocaine / Sunshine Of Your Love

23 May 1998, Alamo Dome, San Antonio, Texas (with Distant Cousins)

SETLIST: My Father's Eyes / Pilgrim / One Chance / River Of Tears / Going Down Slow / She's Gone / Drifting Blues / Tears In Heaven / Layla / Change The World / Old Love / Crossroads / Have You Ever Loved A Woman / I Shot The Sheriff / Wonderful Tonight / Cocaine / Sunshine Of Your Love

25 May 1998, America West Arena, Phoenix, Arizona (with Distant Cousins)

SETLIST: My Father's Eyes / Pilgrim / One Chance / River Of Tears / Going Down Slow / She's Gone / Drifting Blues / Tears In Heaven / Layla / Change The World / Old Love / Crossroads / Have You Ever Loved A Woman / I Shot The Sheriff / Wonderful Tonight / Cocaine / Sunshine Of Your Love

26 May 1998, Cox Arena, San Diego, California (with Distant Cousins)

SETLIST: My Father's Eyes / Pilgrim / One Chance / River Of Tears / Going Down Slow / She's Gone / Drifting Blues / Tears In Heaven / Layla / Change The World / Old Love / Crossroads / Have You Ever Loved A Woman / I Shot The Sheriff / Wonderful Tonight / Cocaine / Sunshine Of Your Love

27 May 1998, Forum, Los Angeles, California (with Distant Cousins)

SETLIST: My Father's Eyes / Pilgrim / One Chance / River Of Tears / Going Down Slow / She's Gone / Drifting Blues / Tears In Heaven / Layla / Change The World / Old Love / Crossroads / Have You Ever Loved A Woman / I Shot The Sheriff / Wonderful Tonight / Cocaine / Sunshine Of Your Love

29 May 1998, The Pond, Anaheim, California (with Distant Cousins)

SETLIST: My Father's Eyes / Pilgrim / One Chance / River Of Tears / Going Down Slow / She's Gone / Drifting Blues / Tears In Heaven / Layla / Change The World / Old Love / Crossroads / Have You Ever Loved A Woman / I Shot The Sheriff / Wonderful Tonight / Cocaine / Sunshine Of Your Love

30 May 1998, MGM Grand, Las Vegas, Nevada (with Distant Cousins)

SETLIST: My Father's Eyes / Pilgrim / One Chance / River Of Tears / Going Down Slow / She's Gone / Drifting Blues / Tears In Heaven / Layla / Change The World / Old Love / Crossroads / Have You Ever Loved A Woman / I Shot The Sheriff / Wonderful Tonight / Cocaine / Sunshine Of Your Love

JUNE 1998

1 June 1998, San Jose Arena, San Jose, California (with Distant Cousins)

SETLIST: My Father's Eyes / Pilgrim / One Chance / River Of Tears / Going Down Slow / She's Gone / Drifting Blues / Tears In Heaven / Layla / Change The World / Old Love / Crossroads / Have You Ever Loved A Woman / I Shot The Sheriff / Wonderful Tonight / Cocaine / Sunshine Of Your Love

2 June 1998, Arco Arena, Sacramento, California (with Distant Cousins)

SETLIST: My Father's Eyes / Pilgrim / One Chance / River Of Tears / Going Down Slow / She's Gone / Drifting Blues / Tears In Heaven / Layla / Change The World / Old Love / Crossroads / Have You Ever Loved A Woman / I Shot The Sheriff / Wonderful Tonight / Cocaine / Sunshine Of Your Love

4 June 1998, Idaho Center, Boise, Idaho (with Distant Cousins)

SETLIST: My Father's Eyes / Pilgrim / One Chance / River Of Tears / Going Down Slow / She's Gone / Drifting

Blues / Tears In Heaven / Layla / Change The World / Old Love / Crossroads / Have You Ever Loved A Woman / I Shot The Sheriff / Wonderful Tonight / Cocaine / Sunshine Of Your Love

5 June 1998, Rose Gardens, Portland, Oregon (with Distant Cousins)

SETLIST: My Father's Eyes / Pilgrim / One Chance / River Of Tears / Going Down Slow / She's Gone / Drifting Blues / Tears In Heaven / Layla / Change The World / Old Love / Crossroads / Have You Ever Loved A Woman / I Shot The Sheriff / Wonderful Tonight / Cocaine / Sunshine Of Your Love

6 June 1998, Key Arena, Seattle, Washington (with Distant Cousins)

SETLIST: My Father's Eyes / Pilgrim / One Chance / River Of Tears / Going Down Slow / She's Gone / Drifting Blues / Tears In Heaven / Layla / Change The World / Old Love / Crossroads / Have You Ever Loved A Woman / I Shot The Sheriff / Wonderful Tonight / Cocaine / Sunshine Of Your Love

SEPTEMBER 1998

PILGRIM U.S. / CANADIAN TOUR 1998

5 September 1998, San Jose University, Event Center, San Jose, California (World Convention of Narcotics Anonymous) (with Jeffrey Gaines)

SETLIST: My Father's Eyes / Pilgrim / One Chance / River Of Tears / Going Down Slow / She's Gone / Circus / Tears In Heaven / Layla / Change The World / Old Love / Crossroads / Have You Ever Loved A Woman / I Shot The Sheriff / Wonderful Tonight / Cocaine / Before You Accuse Me[1] / Sunshine Of Your Love

[1] with Jimmy Vaughan

6 September 1998, New Arena, Oakland, California

SETLIST: My Father's Eyes / Pilgrim / One Chance / River Of Tears / Going Down Slow / She's Gone / Drifting Blues / Tears In Heaven / Layla / Change The World / Old Love / Crossroads / Have You Ever Loved A Woman / I Shot The Sheriff / Wonderful Tonight / Cocaine / Sunshine Of Your Love

8 September 1998, General Motors Place, Vancouver, British Columbia, Canada

SETLIST: My Father's Eyes / Pilgrim / One Chance / River Of Tears / Going Down Slow / She's Gone / Drifting Blues / Tears In Heaven / Layla / Change The World / Old Love / Crossroads / Have You Ever Loved A Woman / Tearing Us Apart / Wonderful Tonight / Cocaine / Sunshine Of Your Love

10 September 1998, Canadian Airlines Saddledome, Calgary, Alberta, Canada

SETLIST: My Father's Eyes / Pilgrim / One Chance / River Of Tears / Going Down Slow / She's Gone / Drifting Blues / Alberta / Tears In Heaven / Layla / Change The World / Old Love / Crossroads / Have You Ever Loved A Woman / Tearing Us Apart / Wonderful Tonight / Cocaine / Sunshine Of Your Love

11 September 1998, Edmonton Coliseum, Edmonton, Alberta, Canada

SETLIST: My Father's Eyes / Pilgrim / One Chance / River Of Tears / Going Down Slow / She's Gone / Drifting Blues / Alberta / Tears In Heaven / Layla / Change The World / Old Love / Crossroads / Have You Ever Loved A Woman / Tearing Us Apart / Wonderful Tonight / Cocaine / Sunshine Of Your Love

15 September 1998, Corel Centre, Ottawa, Ontario, Canada (with Bonnie Raitt)

SETLIST: My Father's Eyes / Pilgrim / One Chance / River Of Tears / Going Down Slow / She's Gone / Drifting Blues / Tears In Heaven / Layla / Change The World / Old Love / Crossroads / Have You Ever Loved A Woman / I Shot The Sheriff / Wonderful Tonight / Cocaine / Before You Accuse Me[1]

[1]with Bonnie Raitt

17 September 1998, Sky Dome, Toronto, Ontario, Canada (with Bonnie Raitt)

SETLIST: My Father's Eyes / Pilgrim / One Chance / River Of Tears / Going Down Slow / She's Gone / Drifting Blues / Tears In Heaven / Layla / Change The World / Old Love / Crossroads / Have You Ever Loved A Woman / I Shot The Sheriff / Wonderful Tonight / Cocaine / Before You Accuse Me[1]

[1]with Bonnie Raitt

18 September 1998, Molson Centre, Montreal, Quebec, Canada (with Bonnie Raitt)

SETLIST: My Father's Eyes / Pilgrim / One Chance / River Of Tears / Going Down Slow / She's Gone / Drifting Blues / Tears In Heaven / Layla / Change The World / Old Love / Crossroads / Have You Ever Loved A Woman / I Shot The Sheriff / Wonderful Tonight / Cocaine / Before You Accuse Me[1]

[1]with Bonnie Raitt

CITY OF HOPE 1998

24 September 1998, Paramount Studios, Los Angeles, California (Eric and his band play a benefit concert for Hollywood's City of Hope National Medical Center. Other acts included Steven Seagal and his band, G. Sheppard, Misti Pierson. The event was hosted by Colleen Camp Goldwyn, wife of Paramount Studios President John Goldwyn)

OCTOBER 1998

PILGRIM UK / EUROPEAN TOUR 1998

BAND LINEUP:
Eric Clapton: guitar, vocals
Andy Fairweather Low: guitar, vocals
Nathan East: bass, vocals
Alan Darby: guitar, vocals
Tim Carmon: keyboards, vocals
Kenneth Crouch: keyboards
Steve Gadd: drums

Katie Kissoon: backing vocals
Chyna: backing vocals
Charlean Hines: backing vocals
Nick Ingman: conductor of 20-piece orchestra

13 October 1998, National Exhibition Centre, Birmingham
(with Bonnie Raitt)

Eric Clapton on the UK Pilgrim *Tour, October 1998.*

SETLIST: My Father's Eyes / Pilgrim / One Chance / River Of Tears / Going Down Slow / She's Gone / Drifting Blues / Tears In Heaven / Layla / Change The World / Old Love / Crossroads / Have You Ever Loved A Woman / Wonderful Tonight / I Shot The Sheriff / Cocaine / Before You Accuse Me[1]

[1]with Bonnie Raitt

15 October 1998, Earls Court Arena, London

SETLIST: My Father's Eyes / Pilgrim / One Chance / River Of Tears / Going Down Slow / She's Gone / Drifting Blues / Tears In Heaven / Layla / Change The World / Old Love / Crossroads / Have You Ever Loved A Woman / I Shot The Sheriff / Wonderful Tonight / Cocaine / Before You Accuse Me[1] / You Were There

[1]with Bonnie Raitt

16 October 1998, Earls Court Arena, London

SETLIST: My Father's Eyes / Pilgrim / One Chance / River Of Tears / Going Down Slow / She's Gone / Drifting Blues / Tears In Heaven / Layla / Change The World / Old Love / Crossroads / Have You Ever Loved

A Woman / I Shot The Sheriff / Wonderful Tonight / Cocaine / Everyday I Have The Blues[1] / Blues Jam[1]

[1]with Bonnie Raitt and B.B. King

17 October 1998, Earls Court Arena, London

SETLIST: My Father's Eyes / Pilgrim / One Chance / River Of Tears / Going Down Slow / She's Gone / Drifting Blues / Tears In Heaven / Layla / Change The World / Old Love / Crossroads / Have You Ever Loved A Woman / I Shot The Sheriff / Wonderful Tonight / Cocaine / Before You Accuse Me[1]

[1]with Bonnie Raitt

19 October 1998, Olympiahalle, Munich, Germany

SETLIST: My Father's Eyes / Pilgrim / One Chance / River Of Tears / Going Down Slow / She's Gone / Drifting Blues / Tears In Heaven / Layla / Change The World / Old Love / Crossroads / Have You Ever Loved A Woman / I Shot The Sheriff / Wonderful Tonight / Cocaine / Sunshine Of Your Love

20 October 1998, Festhalle, Frankfurt, Germany

SETLIST: My Father's Eyes / Pilgrim / One Chance / River Of Tears / Going Down Slow / She's Gone / Drifting Blues / Tears In Heaven / Layla / Change The World / Old Love / Crossroads / Have You Ever Loved A Woman / I Shot The Sheriff / Wonderful Tonight / Cocaine / So Many Roads[1]

[1]with Bonnie Raitt

23 October 1998, Palasport Casalecchio, Bologna, Italy

SETLIST: My Father's Eyes / Pilgrim / One Chance / River Of Tears / Going Down Slow / She's Gone / Drifting Blues / Tears In Heaven / Layla / Change The World / Old Love / Crossroads / Have You Ever Loved A Woman / I Shot The Sheriff / Wonderful Tonight / Cocaine / Killing Floor[1]

[1]with Bonnie Raitt

24 October 1998, Filaforum, Milan, Italy

SETLIST: My Father's Eyes / Pilgrim / One Chance / River Of Tears / Going Down Slow / She's Gone / Drifting Blues / Tears In Heaven / Layla / Change The World / Old Love / Crossroads / Have You Ever Loved A Woman / I Shot The Sheriff / Wonderful Tonight / Cocaine / Dust My Broom[1]

[1]with Bonnie Raitt

26 October 1998, Palau San Jordi, Barcelona, Spain

SETLIST: My Father's Eyes / Pilgrim / One Chance / River Of Tears / Going Down Slow / She's Gone / Drifting Blues / Tears In Heaven / Layla / Change The World / Old Love / Crossroads / Have You Ever Loved A Woman / I Shot The Sheriff / Wonderful Tonight / Cocaine / Rollin' And Tumblin'[1]

[1]with Bonnie Raitt

27 October 1998, Le Dôme, Marseille, France

SETLIST: My Father's Eyes / Pilgrim / One Chance / River Of Tears / Going Down Slow / She's Gone / Drifting Blues / Tears In Heaven / Layla / Change The World / Old Love / Crossroads / Have You Ever Loved A Woman / I Shot The Sheriff / Wonderful Tonight / Cocaine / Rock Me Baby[1]

[1]with Bonnie Raitt

29 October 1998, Le Zenith, Paris, France

SETLIST: My Father's Eyes / Pilgrim / One Chance / River Of Tears / Going Down Slow / She's Gone / Drifting Blues / Tears In Heaven / Layla / Change The World / Old Love / Crossroads / Have You Ever Loved A Woman / I Shot The Sheriff / Wonderful Tonight / Cocaine / Rock Me Baby[1]

[1]with Bonnie Raitt

30 October 1998, Le Zenith, Paris, France

SETLIST: My Father's Eyes / Pilgrim / One Chance / River Of Tears / Going Down Slow / She's Gone / Drifting Blues / Tears In Heaven / Layla / Change The World / Old Love / Crossroads / Have You Ever Loved A Woman / I Shot The Sheriff / Wonderful Tonight / Cocaine / Everyday I Have The Blues[1]

[1]with Bonnie Raitt and Michel Petrucian

31 October 1998, Hallenstadion, Zürich, Switzerland

SETLIST: My Father's Eyes / Pilgrim / One Chance / River Of Tears / Going Down Slow / She's Gone / Drifting Blues / Tears In Heaven / Layla / Change The World / Old Love / Crossroads / Have You Ever Loved A Woman / I Shot The Sheriff / Wonderful Tonight / Cocaine / Sunshine Of Your Love[1]

[1]with Bonnie Raitt

NOVEMBER 1998

2 November 1998, Flanders Expo, Gent, Belgium

SETLIST: My Father's Eyes / Pilgrim / One Chance / River Of Tears / Going Down Slow / She's Gone / Drifting Blues / Tears In Heaven / Layla / Change The World / Old Love / Crossroads / Have You Ever Loved A Woman / I Shot The Sheriff / Wonderful Tonight / Cocaine / Sunshine Of Your Love[1]

[1]with Bonnie Raitt

3 November 1998, Ahoy Hall, Rotterdam, Netherlands

SETLIST: My Father's Eyes / Pilgrim / One Chance / River Of Tears / Going Down Slow / She's Gone / Drifting Blues / Tears In Heaven / Layla / Change The World / Old Love / Crossroads / Have You Ever Loved A Woman / Tearing Us Apart / Wonderful Tonight / Cocaine / Rock Me Baby[1]

[1]with Bonnie Raitt

4 November 1998, Ahoy Hall, Rotterdam, Netherlands

SETLIST: My Father's Eyes / Pilgrim / One Chance / River Of Tears / Going Down Slow / She's Gone / Drifting Blues / Tears In Heaven / Layla / Change The World / Old Love / Crossroads / Have You Ever Loved A Woman / Tearing Us Apart / Wonderful Tonight / Cocaine / Before You Accuse Me[1]

[1]with Bonnie Raitt

PILGRIM EUROPEAN TOUR 1998 (Second leg)

20 November 1998, Max Schmeling Halle, Berlin, Germany (with Jimmie Vaughan and the Tilt-A-Whirl Band)

SETLIST: My Father's Eyes / Pilgrim / One Chance / River Of Tears / Going Down Slow / She's Gone / Blues Leave Me Alone / Tears In Heaven / Layla / Change The World / Old Love / Crossroads / Have You Ever Loved A Woman / Tearing Us Apart / Wonderful Tonight / Cocaine / Sunshine Of Your Love

21 November 1998, Max Schmeling Halle, Berlin, Germany (with Jimmie Vaughan and the Tilt-A-Whirl Band)

SETLIST: My Father's Eyes / Pilgrim / One Chance / River Of Tears / Going Down Slow / She's Gone / Blues Leave Me Alone / Tears In Heaven / Layla / Change The World / Old Love / Crossroads / Have You Ever Loved A Woman / I Shot The Sheriff / Wonderful Tonight / Cocaine / Before You Accuse Me[1]

[1]with Jimmie Vaughan

23 November 1998, Thialf Stadium, Heerenveen, Netherlands (with Jimmie Vaughan and the Tilt-A-Whirl Band)

SETLIST: My Father's Eyes / Pilgrim / One Chance / River Of Tears / Going Down Slow / She's Gone / Drifting Blues / Tears In Heaven / Layla / Change The World / Old Love / Crossroads / Have You Ever Loved A Woman / Tearing Us Apart / Wonderful Tonight / Cocaine / Before You Accuse Me[1]

[1]with Jimmie Vaughan

25 November 1998, Spektrum, Oslo, Norway (with Jimmie Vaughan and the Tilt-A-Whirl Band)

SETLIST: My Father's Eyes / Pilgrim / One Chance / River Of Tears / Going Down Slow / She's Gone / Drifting Blues / Tears In Heaven / Layla / Change The World / Old Love / Crossroads / Have You Ever Loved A Woman / Tearing Us Apart / Wonderful Tonight / Cocaine / Sunshine Of Your Love

27 November 1998, Hartwall Arena, Helsinki, Finland (with Jimmie Vaughan and the Tilt-A-Whirl Band)

SETLIST: My Father's Eyes / Pilgrim / One Chance / River Of Tears / Going Down Slow / She's Gone / Drifting Blues / Tears In Heaven / Layla / Change The World / Old Love / Crossroads / Have You Ever Loved A Woman / Tearing Us Apart / Wonderful Tonight / Cocaine / Before You Accuse Me[1]

[1]with Jimmie Vaughan

28 November 1998, Hartwall Arena, Helsinki, Finland (with Jimmie Vaughan and the Tilt-A-Whirl Band)

SETLIST: My Father's Eyes / Pilgrim / One Chance / River Of Tears / Going Down Slow / She's Gone / Drifting Blues / Tears In Heaven / Layla / Change The World / Old Love / Crossroads / Have You Ever Loved A Woman / Tearing Us Apart / Wonderful Tonight / Cocaine / Before You Accuse Me[1]

[1]with Jimmie Vaughan

30 November 1998, Scandinavium, Gothenberg, Sweden (with Jimmie Vaughan and the Tilt-A-Whirl Band)

SETLIST: My Father's Eyes / Pilgrim / One Chance / River Of Tears / Going Down Slow / She's Gone / Drifting Blues / Tears In Heaven / Layla / Change The World / Wonderful Tonight / Crossroads / Have You Ever Loved A Woman / Cocaine / Before You Accuse Me[1]

[1]with Jimmie Vaughan

DECEMBER 1998

2 December 1998, Globen, Stockholm, Sweden (with Jimmie Vaughan and the Tilt-A-Whirl Band)

SETLIST: My Father's Eyes / Pilgrim / One Chance / River Of Tears / Going Down Slow / She's Gone / Blues Leave Me Alone / Tears In Heaven / Layla / Change The World / Old Love / Crossroads / Have You Ever Loved A Woman / Cocaine / Wonderful Tonight / Sunshine Of Your Love / Before You Accuse Me[1]

[1]with Jimmie Vaughan

3 December 1998, Forum, Copenhagen, Denmark (with Jimmie Vaughan and the Tilt-A-Whirl Band)

SETLIST: My Father's Eyes / Pilgrim / One Chance / River Of Tears / Going Down Slow / She's Gone / Drifting Blues / Tears In Heaven / Layla / Change The World / Old Love / Crossroads / Have You Ever Loved A Woman / Wonderful Tonight / Cocaine / Before You Accuse Me[1]

[1]with Jimmie Vaughan

4 December 1998, Forum, Copenhagen, Denmark (with Jimmie Vaughan and the Tilt-A-Whirl Band)

SETLIST: My Father's Eyes / Pilgrim / One Chance / River Of Tears / Going Down Slow / She's Gone / Blues Leave Me Alone / Tears In Heaven / Layla / Change The World / Old Love / Crossroads / Have You Ever Loved A Woman / Wonderful Tonight / Cocaine / Before You Accuse Me[1]

[1]with Jimmie Vaughan

6 December 1998, Ostseehalle, Kiel, Germany (with Jimmie Vaughan and the Tilt-A-Whirl Band)

SETLIST: My Father's Eyes / Pilgrim / One Chance / River Of Tears / Going Down Slow / She's Gone / Drifting Blues / Tears In Heaven / Layla / Change The World / Old Love / Crossroads / Have You Ever Loved A Woman / Wonderful Tonight / Sunshine Of Your Love / Before You Accuse Me[1]

[1]with Jimmie Vaughan

7 December 1998, Cologne Arena, Cologne, Germany (with Jimmie Vaughan and the Tilt-A-Whirl Band)

SETLIST: My Father's Eyes / Pilgrim / One Chance / River Of Tears / Going Down Slow / She's Gone / Drifting Blues / Tears In Heaven / Layla / Change The World / Old Love / Crossroads / Have You Ever Loved A Woman / Wonderful Tonight / Cocaine / Before You Accuse Me[1]

[1]with Jimmie Vaughan

9 December 1998, Westfalenhalle, Dortmund, Germany (with Jimmie Vaughan and the Tilt-A-Whirl Band)

SETLIST: My Father's Eyes / Pilgrim / One Chance / River Of Tears / Going Down Slow / She's Gone / Drifting Blues / Tears In Heaven / Layla / Change The World / Old Love / Crossroads / Have You Ever Loved A Woman / Wonderful Tonight / Cocaine / Before You Accuse Me[1]

[1]with Jimmie Vaughan

10 December 1998, Messehalle, Hannover, Germany (with Jimmie Vaughan and the Tilt-A-Whirl Band)

SETLIST: My Father's Eyes / Pilgrim / One Chance / River Of Tears / Going Down Slow / She's Gone / Early In The Morning / Tears In Heaven / Layla / Change The World / Old Love / Crossroads / Have You Ever Loved A Woman / Wonderful Tonight / Sunshine Of Your Love / Before You Accuse Me[1]

[1]with Jimmie Vaughan

11 December 1998, Messehalle, Hannover, Germany (with Jimmie Vaughan and the Tilt-A-Whirl Band)

SETLIST: My Father's Eyes / Pilgrim / One Chance / River Of Tears / Going Down Slow / She's Gone / Early In The Morning / Tears In Heaven / Layla / Change The World / Old Love / Crossroads / Have You Ever Loved A Woman / Wonderful Tonight / Cocaine / Before You Accuse Me[1]

[1]with Jimmie Vaughan

AFTER NEW YEAR'S EVE SHOW WITH DAVID SANBORN 1998

14 December 1998, *After New Year's Eve Show With David Sanborn,* Unitel Television Studio 55, New York City

Hosted by David Sanborn, the *After New Year's Eve Show* recording took place on 14 December 1998 and was broadcast by ABC at 1:00 a.m. on 1 January 1999. The guests were Eric Clapton, Cassandra Wilson, and D'Angelo and Gang Starr, with Marcus Miller as musical director. The whole show was released on DVD in Japan.

BAND LINEUP:

David Sanborn: saxophone
Marcus Miller: bass
Dean Brown: guitar
Ricky Peterson: keyboards
Don Alias: percussion
Gene Lake: drums
Steve Gadd: drums

SETLIST:

Crossroads Eric Clapton, vocals

Going Down Slow Eric Clapton, vocals

Sunshine Of Your Love Eric Clapton, D'Angelo vocals

Use Me D'Angelo vocals, Eric on guitar

I'll Take You There the whole band with all guests and Eric on guitar

SPECIAL OLYMPICS CONCERT 1998

17 December 1998, White House, Washington, D.C. (gala for the 30th anniversary of the Special Olympics. The event was billed as "A Very Special Christmas From Washington, D.C." Artists including Eric Clapton, Jon Bon Jovi, Sheryl Crow, Mary J. Blige, Vanessa Williams, Run-D.M.C., and Tracy Chapman performed favorite Christmas classics at a generally invitation-only concert hosted by Whoopi Goldberg for about 200 people including President and Mrs. Clinton)

BAND LINEUP:

Leon Pendarvis: keyboards
Richie Rosenberg: trombone
Shawn Pelton: drums, percussion
Bobby Bandiera: guitar
Ed Manion: saxophone
Timmy Cappello: saxophone
Michael Mancini: keyboards
Sue Williams: bass
Mike Spengler: trumpet

SETLIST:

Merry Christmas Baby (Johnny Dudley Moore / Lou Baxter) Sheryl Crow, Eric Clapton

Christmas Tears (Sonny Thompson / Robert Charles Wilson) Eric Clapton

Gimme One Reason (Tracy Chapman) Tracy Chapman, Eric Clapton

Christmas Blues (Henry Vestine / Adolfo De La Parra / Alan Wilson / Larry Taylor / Robert Hite) John Popper, Eric Clapton

Santa Claus Is Coming To Town (J. Fred Coots / Haven Gillespie) everyone

The event was taped and premiered on TNT on Sunday, 20 December 1998.

RECORDING SESSIONS 1998
UNKNOWN STUDIO (Probably Olympic in Barnes)

MARCH 1998

Eric recorded some incidental music for the *Lethal Weapon 4* film which was released in July 1998. No soundtrack was released.

ERIC CLAPTON GUEST SESSION
OLYMPIC STUDIOS
117 Church Road, London
Guitar overdub for The Band

MARCH 1998

LAST TRAIN TO MEMPHIS (Levon Helm / Bobby Charles) *Jubilation* CD River North Records 51416 1420 2 released September 1998

Levon Helm: lead vocal, triangle, acoustic guitar, harmonica, mandolin, drums
Randy Ciarlante: drums, percussion, backing vocals
Rick Danko: string bass, background vocals
Marie Spinosa: percussion, background vocals
Jim Weider: guitar
Garth Hudson: accordion, piano, tenor saxophone
Aaron Hurwitz: backing vocals

Eric Clapton: lead guitar, rhythm guitar
Producers: Aaron Hurwitz / The Band

> "Levon was very excited about this CD and wrote a letter to Eric about recording on the Levon and Bobby Charles tune 'Last Train To Memphis.' I know we were under pressure from the label to finish so I sent Eric the tracks and he recorded his parts. I am not sure where. He sent them back to my studio where we were mixing and put the song together. It must have been in the spring of '98."
>
> **—AARON HURWITZ**

ERIC CLAPTON GUEST SESSION

OCEAN WAY RECORDING 6050 West Sunset Boulevard, Los Angeles, California

Session for John Lee Hooker

MAY 1998

Although *The Best Of Friends* is essentially a best-of compilation, this CD does contain a few new recordings, one of which is this killer rendition of "Boogie Chillin" with Eric on lead guitar.

BOOGIE CHILLIN (John Lee Hooker / Bernard Besman) *The Best Of Friends* CD US Virgin 8 46424 2 / UK Pointblank VPBCD 49 released October 1998

John Lee Hooker: vocals, guitar
Eric Clapton: guitar
Reggie McBride: bass
Jim Keltner: drums
Johnny Lee Schell: guitar
Rich Kirch: guitar
Bill Payne: keyboards

Producers: John Porter / Mike Kappus

17

1999

FEBRUARY 1999

30th ANNUAL NAACP IMAGE AWARDS 1999

14 February 1999, Civic Auditorium, Pasadena, California (30th Annual NAACP Image Awards ceremony)

Some of the most famous African-Americans in the entertainment industry were present at this star-studded gala hosted by the nation's oldest and largest civil rights organization, which celebrated its 90th birthday in 1999.

At the awards ceremony, actor Will Smith was named Entertainer of the Year and former Chicago Bulls star Michael Jordan was honored with the Jackie Robinson Sports Award. Other honorees included entertainer Harry Belafonte, who received the Chairman's Award recognizing special achievement; opera singer Kathleen Battle and blues legend B.B. King, both of whom received the Hall of Fame Award; and Grammy-nominated singer Lauryn Hill, who was given the Presidential Award.

The musical highlight of the evening was a tribute to B.B. King by guitarists Eric Clapton and George Benson. B.B. King received a standing ovation when he came on stage and picked up his guitar to join in on a performance of "Rock Me Baby."

BAND LINEUP:
Eric Clapton: guitar
George Benson: guitar
B.B. King: guitar

SETLIST: Rock Me Baby

The show was broadcast on 4 March 1999 on the FX Network.

41st ANNUAL GRAMMY AWARDS 1999

24 February, 1999 Shrine Auditorium, Los Angeles, California.

Eric Clapton attends the 41st Annual Grammy Awards where he receives two nominations in the category of Male Pop Vocal Performance for "My Father's Eyes" and in the Best Pop Album category for *Pilgrim*. He picked up his thirteenth career Grammy when "My Father's Eyes" won in the category of Best Male Pop Vocal Performance.

Ten days after last playing with B.B. King, Eric again plays another version of "Rock Me Baby" with him at tonight's ceremony which is broadcast live on CBS.

BAND LINEUP:
Eric Clapton: guitar
B.B. King: guitar

SETLIST: Rock Me Baby

THE RHYTHM & BLUES FOUNDATION 10th ANNUAL PIONEER AWARDS 1999

25 February 1999, Sony Studios Lot, Culver City, California.

The 10th Rhythm & Blues Foundation's annual Pioneer Awards take place tonight at Sony Studios in Culver City. The ceremony was honoring John Lee Hooker with the Lifetime Achievement Award. Patti LaBelle and the Bluebelles, Isaac Hayes, Barbara Lewis, Ashford and Simpson, and Dionne Warwick all also received Pioneer Awards.

Eric Clapton and Bonnie Raitt presented the 1999 R&B Lifetime Achievement Award to John Lee Hooker. Afterwards, Bonnie Raitt and John Lee Hooker played their Grammy-winning performance of Hooker's "I'm In The Mood" with Eric Clapton. Later on, a special tribute to John Lee Hooker took place in the form of a guitar jam, when Raitt and Hooker were joined by Eric, Maceo Parker, Keb Mo, Robert Lockwood, Jr., Larry Graham, Hubert Sumlin, Kevin Eubanks, Wyclef Jean, and others for an all-star finale on Hooker's "Boogie Chillin." In addition to his role as honorary chairman, Ronald O. Perelman, a drummer, participated in the guitar jam.

I'm In The Mood unreleased

John Lee Hooker: vocals
Eric Clapton: guitar
Bonnie Raitt: slide guitar, vocals

Boogie Chillin unreleased

John Lee Hooker: guitar, vocals
Bonnie Raitt: slide guitar
Eric Clapton: guitar
Maceo Parker: saxophone
Keb Mo: guitar
Robert Lockwood, Jr.: guitar
Larry Graham: bass
Hubert Sumlin: guitar
Kevin Eubanks: guitar
Wyclef Jean: vocals
Ronald O. Perelman: drums

MARCH 1999

ROCK AND ROLL HALL OF FAME CONCERT 1999

15 March 1999, Waldorf Astoria Hotel, Grand Ballroom, New York City (14th Annual Induction Ceremony for the Rock and Roll Hall of Fame)

There was a lot of sadness hanging over the event this year as Dusty Springfield had died a couple of weeks before the induction ceremony. Lauryn Hill, Puff Daddy, and D'Angelo were the young artists on hand this year to salute the 1999 inductees which included Curtis Mayfield, Del Shannon, Bruce Springsteen, and Paul McCartney among others. After an evening of inductions, the musicians and various friends hit the stage for the hugely popular all-star jam that the induction ceremonies have become known for. The jam started on a high note with Bruce Springsteen and the E Street Band performing three of their classic numbers, "Promised Land," "Backstreets," and "Tenth Avenue Freeze-Out" before Bruce called soul legend Wilson Pickett to the stage to sing "Midnight Hour." Billy Joel, another inductee, jumped in on keyboards.

Eric Clapton and D'Angelo came on next and played a beautiful version of Curtis Mayfield's "I've Been Trying." Billy Joel followed with a rendition of Del Shannon's "Runaway." Next up were Eric Clapton along with Bonnie Raitt and Paul McCartney playing Carl Perkins's "Blue Suede Shoes" backed by Paul Shaffer's band.

Billy Joel came back on stage singing lead vocals on "What'd I Say" along with Dion, Bonnie Raitt, and Chris Isaak, with Eric on guitar. Paul Shaffer was jumping around the stage and sharing a mic with Dion.

Next up were Bruce Springsteen, Nils Lofgren, and Bono who took lead vocals on Curtis Mayfield's "People Get Ready." Lauryn Hill provided backing vocals. At the song's close, Billy Joel played the opening chords to the Beatles classic "Let It Be." Billy took the first verse with Paul McCartney jumping in on the chorus. Paul then took over lead vocals and was backed by Lauryn Hill, Eric Clapton, Bonnie Raitt, Melissa Etheridge, the Staple Singers, and Wilson Pickett. The evening could not have ended on a better note.

An edited version of the evening aired exclusively on

VH1 on 17 March 1999.

HOUSE BAND:
Paul Shaffer: musical director, keyboards, vocals
Anton Fig: drums
Felicia Collins: guitar, vocals
Sid McGinnis: guitar
Will Lee: bass
Tom Malone: horns
Bruce Kapler: horns
Al Chez: horns

INDIVIDUAL ARTISTS:
Eric Clapton: guitar vocals
D'Angelo: keyboards, vocals
Paul McCartney: vocals
Billy Joel: keyboards, vocals

SETLIST:

I've Been Trying Eric with D'Angelo; available on Time Life's *Rock And Roll Hall Of Fame Museum Live* box set of DVDs and the audio can be purchased from iTunes

Blue Suede Shoes with Paul McCartney and Billy Joel; available on Time Life's *Rock And Roll Hall Of Fame Museum Live* box set of DVDs and the audio can be purchased from iTunes

What'd I Say with Paul McCartney and Billy Joel; available on Time Life's *Rock And Roll Hall Of Fame Museum Live* box set of DVDs and the audio can be purchased from iTunes

People Get Ready (with all stars) unreleased

Let It Be (with all stars) available on Time Life's *Rock And Roll Hall Of Fame Museum Live* box set of DVDs and the audio can be purchased from iTunes

MAY 1999

FRANK SKINNER SHOW 1999

20 May 1999, London Studios, Upper Ground, London (*Frank Skinner Show*, Season 3, Episode 6. Eric Clapton on string bass and vocals, Frank Skinner on guitar and vocals, and Zoe Ball on washboard

attempt to play an impromtu version of "Rock Island Line")

JUNE 1999

GIORGIO ARMANI GALA EVENING FOR CHRISTIE'S CLAPTON GUITAR AUCTION 1999

12 June 1999, Quixote Studios, West Hollywood, California

Italian fashion designer Giorgio Armani held an evening event for his friend Eric Clapton at Quixote Studios in West Hollywood. The invitation-only event previewed forty of the one hundred Clapton guitars which went up for auction at Christie's New York on 24 June 1999 in a benefit for Crossroads Centre at Antigua.

The 500 guests were treated to a two-hour concert with Jimmy Vaughan and the Tilt-A-Whirl Band. Eric joined the band for around thirty minutes.

George Harrison and Eric Clapton attend a party for a special preview of Eric's guitar auction at Christie's in London on 3 June 1999.

BAND LINEUP:
Eric Clapton: guitar, vocals
Jimmie Vaughan: guitar
George Rains: drums
Bill Willis: Hammond B3 organ
Billy Pitman: guitar

SETLIST: Reconsider Baby / Drifting Blues / Everyday I Have The Blues / Boom Bapa Boom / Wee Wee Baby / Instrumental Jam

ERIC CLAPTON AND FRIENDS CROSSROADS CONCERT 1999

30 June 1999, Madison Square Garden, New York City

BAND LINEUP:
Eric Clapton: guitar, vocals
Andy Fairweather Low: guitar
Nathan East: bass
Steve Gadd: drums
Tim Carmon: keyboards
David Delhomme: keyboards
Katie Kissoon: backing vocals
Tessa Niles: backing vocals

SPECIAL GUESTS:
David Sanborn
Sheryl Crow
Mary J Blige
Bob Dylan

ERIC CLAPTON AND HIS BAND SET

My Father's Eyes unreleased

Hoochie Coochie Man *Eric Clapton & Friends in Concert: A Benefit for the Crossroads Centre at Antigua* DVD Warner Bros. released October 1999

Reconsider Baby unreleased

Pilgrim unreleased

River Of Tears *Eric Clapton & Friends in Concert: A Benefit for the Crossroads Centre at Antigua* DVD Warner Bros. released October 1999

ERIC CLAPTON AND HIS BAND WITH DAVID SANBORN SET

Going Down Slow *Eric Clapton & Friends in Concert: A Benefit for the Crossroads Centre at Antigua* DVD Warner Bros. released October 1999

ERIC CLAPTON AND HIS BAND WITH SHERYL CROW SET

My Favorite Mistake *Eric Clapton & Friends in Concert: A Benefit for the Crossroads Centre at Antigua* DVD Warner Bros. released October 1999

Makes You Happy unreleased

Run Baby Run unreleased

Leaving Las Vegas unreleased

Difficult Kind *Eric Clapton & Friends in Concert: A Benefit for the Crossroads Centre at Antigua* DVD Warner Bros. released October 1999

ERIC CLAPTON AND HIS BAND WITH SHERYL CROW AND DAVID SANBORN SET

Little Wing *Eric Clapton & Friends in Concert: A Benefit for the Crossroads Centre at Antigua* DVD Warner Bros. released October 1999

ERIC CLAPTON AND HIS BAND WITH MARY J. BLIGE SET

Do Right Woman unreleased

Be Happy *Eric Clapton & Friends in Concert: A Benefit for the Crossroads Centre at Antigua* DVD Warner Bros. released October 1999

Joy *Eric Clapton & Friends in Concert: A Benefit for the Crossroads Centre at Antigua* DVD Warner Bros. released October 1999

Love No Limit unreleased

My Life unreleased

Everything unreleased

Not Gonna Cry *Eric Clapton & Friends in Concert: A Benefit for the Crossroads Centre at Antigua* DVD Warner Bros. released October 1999

ERIC CLAPTON AND HIS BAND SET

Tears In Heaven *Eric Clapton & Friends in Concert: A Benefit for the Crossroads Centre at Antigua* DVD Warner Bros. released October 1999

ERIC CLAPTON AND HIS BAND WITH DAVID SANBORN SET

Change The World *Eric Clapton & Friends in Concert: A Benefit for the Crossroads Centre at Antigua* DVD Warner Bros. released October 1999

ERIC CLAPTON AND HIS BAND SET

Old Love *Eric Clapton & Friends in Concert: A Benefit for the Crossroads Centre at Antigua* DVD Warner Bros. released October 1999

Badge unreleased

Wonderful Tonight *Eric Clapton & Friends in Concert: A Benefit for the Crossroads Centre at Antigua* DVD Warner Bros. released October 1999

ERIC CLAPTON AND HIS BAND WITH DAVID SANBORN SET

Layla *Eric Clapton & Friends in Concert: A Benefit for the Crossroads Centre at Antigua* DVD Warner Bros. released October 1999

ERIC CLAPTON AND HIS BAND WITH BOB DYLAN SET

Don't Think Twice *Eric Clapton & Friends in Concert: A Benefit for the Crossroads Centre at Antigua* DVD Warner Bros. released October 1999

It Takes A Lot To Laugh, It Takes A Train To Cry unreleased

Born In Time (dueting with Eric) unreleased

Leopard-Skin Pillbox Hat unreleased

It's Not Dark Yet unreleased

Crossroads (dueting with Eric) *Eric Clapton & Friends in Concert: A Benefit for the Crossroads Centre at Antigua* DVD Warner Bros. released October 1999

ENCORES

Sunshine Of Your Love (all artists on stage) *Eric Clapton & Friends in Concert: A Benefit for the Crossroads Centre at Antigua* DVD Warner Bros. released October 1999

Bright Lights, Big City (all artists on stage) unreleased

SEPTEMBER 1999

SHERYL CROW AND FRIENDS IN CENTRAL PARK 1999

14 September 1999, Central Park, East Meadow, New York City

Eric performed only two songs and joined in the encore. The whole show was broadcast on television and a CD of edited highlights was released in December 1999.

Eric Clapton and Sheryl Crow, Central Park, East Meadow, New York, 14 September 1999.

SETLIST:

White Room (Jack Bruce / Pete Brown) *Sheryl Crow And Friends: Live From Central Park* CD A&M Records 069490574-2 released December 1999

Little Wing (Jimi Hendrix) unreleased

Sheryl Crow: guitar, vocals
Eric Clapton: guitar, vocals
Jim Bogios: drums
Peter Stroud: guitar
Mike Rowe: keyboards
Tim Smith: guitar
Mattew Brubeck: bass

Tombstone Blues (Bob Dylan) *Sheryl Crow And Friends: Live From Central Park* CD A&M Records 069490574-2 released December 1999

Sheryl Crow: guitar, vocals
Jim Bogios: drums
Peter Stroud: guitar
Mike Rowe: keyboards
Tim Smith: guitar
Matthew Brubeck: bass
Keith Richards: guitar
Eric Clapton: guitar
Emily Robison: slide guitar
Martie Seidel: fiddle
Ash Sood: tambourine
Stevie Nicks: tambourine
Chrissie Hynde: vocals
Natalie Maines: vocals
Sarah McLachlan: vocals
Producer: Sheryl Crow

OCTOBER 1999

CONCERT OF THE CENTURY 1999

23 October 1999, Concert of the Century for VH1, Save the Music, White House, South Lawn, Washington, D.C.

SETLIST:

Ramblin' On My Mind (Robert Johnson) broadcast on VH1

Eric Clapton: Dobro, vocals

All Along The Watchtower (Bob Dylan) broadcast on VH1

Lenny Kravitz: acoustic guitar, vocals
Eric Clapton: guitar
Craig Ross: acoustic guitar
Cindy Blackman: drums
Jack Daley: bass
George Laks: keyboards
Sunovia Piere: tamborine
Nehemiah Heild: tambourine

The Thrill Is Gone (Roy Hawkins / Rick Darnell) broadcast on VH1

B.B. King: guitar, vocals
Eric Clapton: guitar, vocals
Paul Shaffer: keyboards
Anton Fig: drums
Will Lee: bass
Sid McGinnis: guitar
Felicia Collins: guitar
Tom Malone: saxophone
Bruce Kapler: saxophone
Al Chez: trumpet

Eric joined a varied group of celebrities and musicians performing at the White House for VH1's Concert of the Century on 23 October 1999. The event was hosted by President Clinton and First Lady Hillary Clinton. The 800 invitation-only concertgoers sat in a large pavillion on the White House's South Lawn. The concert was aired live on VH1 nationally in the U.S. and featured artists such as Garth Brooks, Sheryl Crow, Gloria Estefan with 'N Sync, Al Green, B.B. King, John Fogerty, Lenny Kravitz, John Mellencamp, Melissa Ethridge, and Eric of course. There were also several celebrities introducing the musicians, including

Angela Bassett, Robert DeNiro, Calista Flockhart, Gwyneth Paltrow, Sarah Jessica Parker, Keri Russell, Meryl Streep, Muhammed Ali, and Kevin Spacey. All of the performers were backed by musical director Paul Shaffer and his band.

Eric opened this special two-hour concert with "Ramblin' On My Mind." The show was highlighted by three powerful duets: Lenny Kravitz and Eric Clapton performing a rousing "All Along The Watchtower"; Clapton teaming up with B.B. King on "The Thrill Is Gone," a song the two guitar legends seemed destined to perform together.

NOVEMBER 1999

ALLEGRO AWARDS 1999

2 November 1999, Phoenix House and Musicians' Assistance Program's Allegro Awards Gala, Universal City, California.

Eric Clapton was honored with the Stevie Ray Vaughan Award as part of the Phoenix House and Musicians' Assistance Program's First Annual Allegro Awards. The award was presented to Eric by Bonnie Raitt and was created to honor the memory of Vaughan and to recognize outstanding musicians who give something back to the community. In Eric's case, it was for establishing the Crossroads Centre in Antigua. After the presentation, Eric joined in with Bonnie Raitt, Jimmie Vaughan, and Dr. John for a couple of blues jams. He played his white Fender Stratocaster and the set was filmed for archival purposes only.

BAND LINEUP:
Eric Clapton: guitar
Bonnie Raitt: slide guitar
Jimmie Vaughan: guitar
Dr. John: keyboards
George Rains: drums
Billy Pitman: rhythm guitar
Bill Willis: keyboards

SETLIST: Blues Jam 1 / Blues Jam 2

4 November 1999, The Complex, Los Angeles, California (Japan Tour rehearsals are recorded for later radio broacast in various countries)

JAPAN TOUR 1999

BAND LINEUP:
Eric Clapton: guitar, vocals
Nathan East: bass
Steve Gadd: drums
Andy Fairweather Low: guitar, vocals
Dave Delhomme: keyboards
Katie Kissoon: backing vocals
Tessa Niles: backing vocals

9 November 1999, Budokan, Tokyo, Japan

SETLIST: My Father's Eyes / Hoochie Coochie Man / Reconsider Baby / Going Down Slow / River of Tears / Pilgrim / She's Gone / Ramblin' On My Mind / Bell Bottom Blues / Tears In Heaven / Change The World / Gin House / Cocaine / Old Love / Badge / Wonderful Tonight / Layla / Sunshine Of Your Love / Before You Accuse Me

11 November 1999, Gymnasium, Nagoya, Japan

SETLIST: My Father's Eyes / Pilgrim / River of Tears / Going Down Slow / Hoochie Coochie Man / Reconsider Baby / She's Gone / Ramblin' On My Mind / Tears In Heaven / Bell Bottom Blues / Change The World / Gin House / Cocaine / Have You Ever Loved A Woman / Badge / Wonderful Tonight / Layla / Sunshine Of Your Love

13 November 1999, Marine Messe, Fukuoka, Japan

SETLIST: My Father's Eyes / Pilgrim / River Of Tears / Going Down Slow / Hoochie Coochie Man / Have You Ever Loved A Woman / She's Gone / Ramblin' On My Mind / Tears In Heaven / Bell Bottom Blues / Change The World / Gin House / Cocaine / Old Love / Badge / Wonderful Tonight / Layla / Sunshine Of Your Love

15 November 1999, Castle Hall, Osaka, Japan

SETLIST: My Father's Eyes / Pilgrim / River Of Tears / Going Down Slow / Hoochie Coochie Man / Have You Ever Loved A Woman / She's Gone / Ramblin' On My Mind / Tears In Heaven / Bell Bottom Blues / Change The World / Gin House / Cocaine / Old Love / Badge / Wonderful Tonight / Layla / Before You Accuse Me

16 November 1999, Castle Hall, Osaka, Japan

SETLIST: My Father's Eyes / Pilgrim / River Of Tears / Hoochie Coochie Man / Going Down Slow / She's Gone / Ramblin' On My Mind / Tears In Heaven / Bell Bottom Blues / Change The World / Gin House / Cocaine / Old Love / Badge / Wonderful Tonight / Layla / Sunshine Of Your Love

17 November 1999, Castle Hall, Osaka, Japan

SETLIST: My Father's Eyes / Pilgrim / River Of Tears / Going Down Slow / Hoochie Coochie Man / She's Gone / Ramblin' On My Mind / Tears In Heaven / Bell Bottom Blues / Change The World / Gin House / Cocaine / Old Love / Badge / Wonderful Tonight / Layla / Sunshine Of Your Love

19 November 1999, Budokan, Tokyo, Japan

SETLIST: My Father's Eyes / Pilgrim / River Of Tears / Going Down Slow / Hoochie Coochie Man / She's Gone / Ramblin' On My Mind / Tears In Heaven / Bell Bottom Blues / Change The World / Gin House / Cocaine / Have You Ever Loved A Woman / Badge / Wonderful Tonight / Layla / Before You Accuse Me

20 November 1999, Budokan, Tokyo, Japan

SETLIST: My Father's Eyes / Pilgrim / River Of Tears / Hoochie Coochie Man / Going Down Slow / She's Gone / Ramblin' On My Mind / Tears In Heaven / Bell Bottom Blues / Change The World / Gin House / Cocaine / Wonderful Tonight / Badge / Have You Ever Loved A Woman / Layla / Before You Accuse Me

22 November 1999, Budokan, Tokyo, Japan

SETLIST: My Father's Eyes / Pilgrim / River Of Tears / Going Down Slow / Hoochie Coochie Man / She's Gone / Ramblin' On My Mind / Tears In Heaven / Bell Bottom Blues / Change The World / Gin House / Cocaine / Wonderful Tonight / Badge / Have You Ever Loved A Woman / Layla / Sunshine Of Your Love

24 November 1999, Yokohama Arena, Yokohama, Japan (this show was aired on television via NHK satellite broadcasting in Japan)

SETLIST: My Father's Eyes / Pilgrim / River Of Tears / Going Down Slow / Hoochie Coochie Man / She's Gone / Ramblin' On My Mind / Tears In Heaven / Bell Bottom Blues / Change The World / Gin House / Cocaine / Wonderful Tonight / Badge / Have You Ever Loved A Woman / Layla / Sunshine Of Your Love

26 November 1999, Budokan, Tokyo, Japan

SETLIST: My Father's Eyes / Pilgrim / River Of Tears / Going Down Slow / Hoochie Coochie Man / She's Gone / Ramblin' On My Mind / Tears In Heaven / Bell Bottom Blues / Change The World / Gin House / Cocaine / Wonderful Tonight / Badge / Have You Ever Loved A Woman / Layla / Sunshine Of Your Love

27 November 1999, Budokan, Tokyo, Japan

SETLIST: My Father's Eyes / Pilgrim / River Of Tears / Going Down Slow / She's Gone / Ramblin' On My Mind / Tears In Heaven / Before You Accuse Me / Bell Bottom Blues / Change The World / Gin House / Cocaine / Wonderful Tonight / Badge / Have You Ever Loved A Woman / Layla / Sunshine Of Your Love

29 November 1999, Budokan, Tokyo, Japan

SETLIST: My Father's Eyes / Pilgrim / River Of Tears / Going Down Slow / She's Gone / Ramblin' On My Mind / Tears In Heaven / Before You Accuse Me / Bell Bottom Blues / Change The World / Gin House / Cocaine / Wonderful Tonight / Badge / Stormy Monday / Layla / Sunshine Of Your Love

30 November 1999, Budokan, Tokyo, Japan

SETLIST: My Father's Eyes / Pilgrim / River Of Tears / Going Down Slow / She's Gone / Ramblin' On My Mind / Tears In Heaven / Before You Accuse Me / Bell Bottom Blues / Change The World / Gin House / Cocaine / Wonderful Tonight / Badge / Stormy Monday / Layla / Sunshine Of Your Love

DECEMBER 1999

NEW YEAR'S EVE DANCE 1999

31 December 1999, Woking Leisure Centre, Woking, Surrey

Eric and his band are called the Grave Emotional And Mental Disorders.

BAND LINEUP:
Eric Clapton: guitar, vocals
Andy Fairweather Low: guitar, vocals
Dave Bronze: bass
Steve Gadd: drums
Simon Climie: piano

SETLIST 1: Knock On Wood / Reconsider Baby / Tore Down / Have You Ever Loved A Woman / If Paradise Was Half As Nice / Lay Down Sally / Wonderful Tonight / Sunshine Of Your Love

SETLIST 2: Midnight Hour / Hoochie Coochie Man / Knockin' On Heaven's Door / Stormy Monday / Cocaine / Gin House / Five Long Years / Layla / Everyday I Have The Blues

RECORDING SESSIONS 1999

UNKNOWN STUDIO
Session for *Runaway Bride* soundtrack
FEBRUARY 1999

BLUE EYES BLUE (Dinae Warren) *Runaway Bride* CD Columbia 494873 2 released July 1999

Eric Clapton: guitar, vocals
Nathan East: bass
Steve Ferrone: drums
Darryl Crooks: guitar
Tim Pierce: guitar
Jamie Muhoberac: keyboards
Greg Curtis: keyboards, backing vocals, programming
Luis Conte: percussion
Mike Fasano: percussion

Producer: Rob Cavallo
Engineer: Allen Sides

PARAMOUNT SCORING
Stage M, Paramount Pictures Studios, Hollywood, California
Session for *The Story Of Us* soundtrack

FEBRUARY 1999

Rob Reiner got in touch with Eric about doing the soundtrack for his film. He had sent Eric a preview copy of the film and after watching it Eric did some demos which he sent back to Rob, who was thrilled to hear what Eric had done. Eric came over to Los Angeles and spent a day in the studio to record his parts.

GET LOST (Eric Clapton) *The Story Of Us* soundtrack CD Reprise 9 47608-2 released November 1999

Eric Clapton: guitar, vocals
Nathan East: bass
JR Robinson: drummer
Lenny Castro: percussion
Randy Kerber: keyboards

A SPOON IS JUST A SPOON (Eric Clapton / Marc Shaiman) *The Story Of Us* soundtrack CD Reprise 9 47608-2 released November 1999

THE GIRL IN THE PIT HELMET (Eric Clapton / Marc Shaiman) *The Story Of Us* soundtrack CD Reprise 9 47608-2 released November 1999

FIGHTING (Eric Clapton / Marc Shaiman) *The Story Of Us* soundtrack CD Reprise 9 47608-2 released November 1999

EMPTY NEST (Eric Clapton / Marc Shaiman) *The Story Of Us* soundtrack CD Reprise 9 47608-2 released November 1999

TOUCHING FEET UNDER THE COVERS (Eric Clapton / Marc Shaiman) *The Story Of Us* soundtrack CD Reprise 9 47608-2 released November 1999

EVERYTHING I LOVE IS IN THIS BED (Eric Clapton / Marc Shaiman) *The Story Of Us* soundtrack CD Reprise 9 47608-2 released November 1999

DRY CLEANING / GET LOST (Eric Clapton) *The Story Of Us* soundtrack CD Reprise 9 47608-2 released November 1999

FAMILY BED (Eric Clapton / Marc Shaiman) *The Story Of Us* soundtrack CD Reprise 9 47608-2 released November 1999

BUSY BABY MONTAGE (Eric Clapton / Marc Shaiman) *The Story Of Us* soundtrack CD Reprise 9 47608-2 released November 1999

SILENT DRIVE TO CAMP (Eric Clapton / Marc Shaiman) *The Story Of Us* soundtrack CD Reprise 9 47608-2 released November 1999

CAMP MONTAGE (Eric Clapton / Marc Shaiman) *The Story Of Us* soundtrack CD Reprise 9 47608-2 released November 1999

EPIPHANY AT THE BISTRO (Eric Clapton / Marc Shaiman) *The Story Of Us* soundtrack CD Reprise 9 47608-2 released November 1999

BEN TAKES THE APARTMENT (Eric Clapton / Marc Shaiman) *The Story Of Us* soundtrack CD Reprise 9 47608-2 released November 1999

WRITING MONTAGE (Eric Clapton / Marc Shaiman) *The Story Of Us* soundtrack CD Reprise 9 47608-2 released November 1999

PICTURES ON A WALL (Eric Clapton / Marc Shaiman) *The Story Of Us* soundtrack CD Reprise 9 47608-2 released November 1999

LET'S GO TO CHOW FUN (Eric Clapton / Marc Shaiman) *The Story Of Us* soundtrack CD Reprise 9 47608-2 released November 1999

Eric Clapton: acoustic guitar
Producers: Eric Clapton / Marc Shaiman

ERIC CLAPTON GUEST SESSION

RECORD PLANT
1032 North
Sycamore Avenue,
Los Angeles, California
Session for Santana

1 MARCH 1999

THE CALLING (Carlos Santana / Chester Thompson / Freddie Stone / Linda Graham) *Supernatural* CD Arista 88697 48080 2 released June 1999

Carlos Santana: guitar, percussion
Eric Clapton: guitar
Chester Thompson: keyboards
Mike Mani: programming
Tony Lindsay: vocals
Jeanie Tracy: vocals

Producers: Carlos Santana / Clive Davis
Engineer: Steve Fontano

ERIC CLAPTON GUEST SESSION

SONY MUSIC STUDIOS
460 West 54th Street,
New York City
Session for Mary J. Blige

JUNE 1999

GIVE ME YOU (Diane Warren) *Mary* CD MCA Records US MCAD-11929 / UK 111 976-2 released August 1999

Mary J. Blige: vocals, backing vocals
Eric Clapton: guitar
Paulette McWilliams: backing vocals
Nate-Love Clemons: bass synthesizer
Michael "Big Mike" Clemons: drums
Paul Pesco: guitar
Manuel Seal: acoustic piano, electric piano
Paul Riser: strings

Producer: Manuel Seal
Recorded by: Steve Eigner

ERIC CLAPTON GUEST SESSION

OLYMPIC STUDIOS
117 Church Road, London,
Session for Jack Bruce

DECEMBER 1999

SUNSHINE OF YOUR LOVE (Jack Bruce / Pete Brown / Eric Clapton) *Shadows In The Air* CD Sanctuary SANCD84 released 2001

Jack Bruce: bass, vocals
Eric Clapton: guitar, vocals
Milton Cardona: congas
Richie Flores: congas
Robby Ameen: drums
El Negro Horecio Herendez: drums
Andy Gonzalez: bass
Changuito Luis Quintas: congas, Quinto, timbales

WHITE ROOM (Jack Bruce / Pete Brown) *Shadows In The Air* CD Sanctuary SANCD84 released 2001

Jack Bruce: bass, vocals
Eric Clapton: guitar, vocals
Milton Cardona: congas
Richie Flores: congas
Robby Ameen: drums
El Negro Horecio Herendez: drums
Andy Gonzalez: bass
Changuito Luis Quintas: congas, quinto, timbales
Malcolm Bruce: guitar, synthesizer

Producers: Kip Hanrahan / Jack Bruce
Engineer: John Fausty

> "When I heard the way the tracks came out, I thought it would be so great to have Eric, especially, singing because that's a double lead vocal—to see the difference in the voices after all these years. I didn't imagine he would play with the fire he did. He really played quite amazingly. We had a lovely time doing it—quite moving in fact."
>
> —JACK BRUCE
> (*Billboard*, 21 July 2001)

18

2000

FEBRUARY 2000

CURTIS MAYFIELD MEMORIAL CONCERT 2000

22 February 2000, First African Methodist Episcopal Church, Los Angeles, California

Over 300 musicians and parishioners gathered on Tuesday, 22 February, at the First AME Church in South Los Angeles, the oldest black congregation in the city of Los Angeles. They were there to pay tribute to soul legend Curtis Mayfield, who died in December 1999. Stevie Wonder sang "Gypsy Woman," an early hit by the Impressions from the sixties. Eric Clapton sang "I've Been Trying," along with the surviving Impressions. Lauryn Hill sang a solo version of "The Makings Of You."

The enthusiastic crowd clapped and swayed along to Curtis Mayfield's music, played against the backdrop of a beautiful church mural depicting the cultural pride, slave history, and social triumphs of African-Americans. The finale was the highlight with "It's All Right" which was followed by a rousing fifteen-minute version of "Amen," with Eric on guitar, Stevie Wonder on keyboards, and Lauryn Hill singing with the Impressions and the First AME Freedom Choir.

Eric and the Impressions rehearse the day before in a studio.

BAND LINEUP:
Eric Clapton: guitar, vocals
Nathan East: bass
Greg Phillinganes: keyboards
Larry Williams: saxophone
Jerry Hey: trumpet
Jeff Baxter: guitar
Narada Michael Walden: drums
Myung Jackson: percussion
Penny Ford: backing vocal
Kipper Jones: backing vocals
Fred White: backing vocals
Richard Brian: backing vocals
Stevie Wonder: keyboards on "Amen"
Lauryn Hill: vocals on "Amen"
First AME Freedom Choir

THE IMPRESSIONS:
Sam Gooden: vocals
Fred Cash: vocals
Ralph Johnson: vocals
Vandy Hampton: vocals
Gary Underwood: vocals

SETLIST: I've Been Trying / It's All Right / Amen

MARCH 2000

ROCK AND ROLL HALL OF FAME 2000

6 March 2000, Waldorf Astoria Hotel, New York City, (15th Annual Induction Ceremony for the Rock and Roll Hall Of Fame)

Ahmet Ertegun, the Chairman of the Rock and Roll Hall of Fame Foundation, opened the evening with a speech. This was followed by a night of inductions. At around midnight, Eric Clapton was presented with his award by Robbie Robertson, The Band's former guitarist and songwriter. Eric was already a member of the Rock And Roll Hall Of Fame, having been inducted in 1992 as a member of the Yardbirds and again in 1993 as a member of Cream. After a quick two-minute acceptance speech, Eric played "Tears In Heaven" and "Further On Up The Road." As always, the evening concluded with an all-star jam, which included the inductees and the presenters. Natalie Cole started the jam with Bobby Troup's "Route 66." After about two minutes, the band went into a vamp and took off with guitar solos from Bonnie Raitt on slide, followed by Robbie Robertson and then Eric Clapton, who just tore it up.

SETLIST:

Tears In Heaven available on Time Life's *Rock And Roll Hall Of Fame Museum Live* box set of DVDs and the audio can be purchased from iTunes

Further On Up The Road available on Time Life's *Rock And Roll Hall Of Fame Museum Live* box set of DVDs and the audio can be purchased from iTunes

Route 66 (all-star jam) available on Time Life's *Rock And Roll Hall Of Fame Museum Live* box set of DVDs and the audio can be purchased from iTunes

An edited version of the event was broadcast on VH1 on 8 March 2000 at 9:00 p.m.

B.B. KING JAM

19 March 2000, B.B. King's Blues Club, 1000 Universal Center Drive, Universal City, California (Eric joins B.B. King for his set)

BERNIE ECCLESTONE CHARITY GALA 2000

19 April 2000, Dorchester Hotel, Park Lane, London (Formula One boss Bernie Ecclestone holds a charity gala to mark the Formula One World Championship's 50th anniversary. The evening raised nearly $3 million for the National Society for the Prevention of Cruelty to Children. Musical entertainment was in the form of former World Champion Damon Hill on guitar, Jools Holland on piano, Eddie Jordan on drums, Eric Clapton on guitar, and Jamiroquai's vocalist Jason Kay)

BOBBY WHITLOCK AND ERIC CLAPTON ON *LATER WITH JOOLS HOLLAND* 2000

25 April 2000, BBC Television Centre, Wood Lane, London (Eric plays three numbers with ex-Dominos member Bobby Whitlock for the *Later With Jools Holland* television show which is broadcast on the 29 April)

SETLIST:

Wing And A Prayer
Bobby Whitlock: vocals, piano
Eric Clapton: guitar
Mark Flanagan: guitar
Jools Holland: organ
Dave Swift: bass
Gilson Lavis: drums
Phil Veacock: saxophone
Joy Rose: backing vocals
Lorraine McIntosh: backing vocals

Bell Bottom Blues
Bobby Whitlock: vocals, piano
Eric Clapton: guitar, vocals
Mark Flanagan: guitar
Jools Holland: organ
Dave Swift: bass

"One day the phone rang and it was a voice that I vaguely remembered but knew in a funny sort of way. It was Mark Cooper asking how I was doing and if I would be interested in coming over to London and doing a guest spot on the *Jools Holland Show*. I told him that I would love to, but it was just a matter of when it was to happen. He told me that it was within a few months. That shook me because I didn't want to be seen in the shape that I was in. I knew how bad off I was because of the drugs and alcohol. I told him thank you and hung up the phone, just shaking my head and wondering how in the world am I going to be up to this.

Several days passed and Mark phoned again. This time he asked what I thought about having Eric Clapton on my show. He said that they had asked Eric and he said that he would love to be on my segment. He said that Eric had changed his schedule around just for this as he was on his way to Tokyo to be with Carlos Santana then he was to come back and he was doing what was to be *Riding With The King* with B.B. King. I told him to give me a few days. The real problem was that I was completely strung out on pills and alcohol and was embarrassed to be in Eric's company in the shape that I was in physically and psychologically.

Mark rang a few days later and I told him that I would be very happy to have Eric on my show and was really looking forward to it. I had to really start trying to get myself together then. At least I had a reason and a purpose to finally deal with myself. I just wished every time that I took a pill or had a drink that it was the last one and that it all had never started in the first place. But it had. Now my day of reckoning was nigh upon me.

The day came that I was to leave for the airport to go do the show. I was pretty steady and was feeling quite confident about it all. About three hours out of Heathrow Airport I started losing control of myself. The wine and the meds were running my mouth again for me. I became beligerant and was almost escorted off of the plane and into the arms of the police at the airport but somehow managed to convince them that I was sincerely sorry for my actions. And I was, I hated being that way.

I was staying at the Inn on the Park in London. The first thing in the morning after my arrival was rehearsal for the show at the BBC soundstage. I was on time but running behind in my head. I was pretty much in a state of confusion as I didn't have anybody looking after me, like a road manager. I arrived at the studio and walked through the outside door directly into the soundstage. The band and everyone were already there and had been running through things and waiting for me. My piano was straight across the room from where I had entered so I walked directly to it, not looking at the band and who was in it. I couldn't see very well until my eyes adjusted to the inside lights. The record executive walked up to me as I sat down at the piano and said that I had walked straight past Eric Clapton and didn't say a word to him. I didn't see him! I walked over to Eric and apologized. He understood everything and knew me very well. Unfortunately, not much had changed except my age. We ran through a few numbers that Jools had selected for me to do off of my current CD, *It's About Time,* 'A Wing And A Prayer' and 'Bell Bottom Blues,' then Jools asked if we could do something to what I had been warming up with. Turns out it was a song that I had written years ago titled 'Southern Gentleman.' It's a groovy song to play on piano. We all went through everything and the band was absolutley great! It consisted of Jools's band the Engine Room, plus Eric and two background singers.

All in all, it was a pretty damn good band. I distinctly remember Eric sitting on his amp directly across from me with his legs crossed and his guitar in his lap with his arms folded gently across the top of it. He was so peaceful and serene and had an aura about him that completely captivated me. My focus at that moment was directly on him and it was as if I had tunnel vision and could see no one else except for Eric at the end of it. We looked at each other like that before many times when we were playing. Totally in the moment, only this moment the entire planet would be watching and I was about to come unglued in front of it. Or so it seemed to me. I knew then what I had to do when I got back home. I had to take care of business now and worry about me later after I got back to the States.

I saw Eric a few years ago and we were talking about this very same show. He said that he thought that I was just nervous. I told him that I was very nearly about to come unglued in front of the planet and knew it too as it was all going down. Time and again I get the proof in my own life that God does exist. Because there would be no other way for all of this to transpire and have such an outcome were it not divinely inspired and orchestrated. Six months later I had an awakening and have been alcohol- and drug-free ever since. That was October 13, 2000."

—BOBBY WHITLOCK

Gilson Lavis: drums
Joy Rose: backing vocals
Lorraine McIntosh: backing vocals

Southern Gentleman

Bobby Whitlock: vocals, piano
Eric Clapton: guitar
Mark Flanagan: guitar
Jools Holland: organ
Dave Swift: bass
Gilson Lavis: drums
Phil Veacock: saxophone

> ❝I did indeed play with Eric and Bobby Whitlock on the recordings in 2000. It was a long time ago now but I think the songs we performed were 'Southern Gentleman,' 'Bell Bottom Blues,' and 'On A Wing And A Prayer.' I have to say, this was highly unusual for us to play three songs with a guest on *Later,* it's usually two at the most. We did a rehearsal with both Bobby and Eric. The personnel was myself on bass guitar, Gilson [Lavis] on drums, and of course Eric, but this time Jools played organ, and we were joined by our regular guitarist Mark and one of our saxophone players, Phil Veacock. Great recordings and such an enjoyable experience!
>
> It's funny, I've just gone back to watch these clips as I've not seen them for many years, and on all of these performances I'm using a Fender Jazz bass, which is very unusual for me as my main and favorite instrument is a Fender Precision.❞
>
> —DAVE SWIFT
> (bassist with Jools Holland)

SANTANA JAM 2000

28 April 2000, Budokan, Tokyo, Japan (Eric jams with Santana)

BAND LINEUP:

Carlos Santana: guitar
Eric Clapton: guitar
Andy Vargas: vocals
Tony Lindsay: vocals
Chester Thompson: keyboards
Benny Rietveld: bass
Rodney Holmes: drums
Raul Rekow: congas
Karl Perazzo: timbales

SETLIST: Batuka / No One To Depend On / Taboo / The Calling / Apache / Smooth / Soul Sacrifice / Jingo

Just before playing "Batuka" Carlos Santana walked up to the mic and introduced Eric Clapton who walked on from the right side of the backstage area. He was holding a Fender SRV (Stevie Ray Vaughan) Signature Stratocaster model which he plugged into a Fender twin amp. It was not his usual Tweed amp, but one borrowed from the Santana band for the evening. Together they played "Batuka" which led into "No One To Depend On" followed by "Taboo" / "The Calling." The jam lasted for around twenty minutes and Eric was firing off some great solos and clearly having a ball with a beaming smile on his face. Eric went off for a break while Santana ended their main set with "Black Magic Woman" and "Oye Como Va." Santana came back on for a fifty-minute encore accompanied by Eric playing "Apache," "Smooth," "Soul Sacrifice," and "Jingo." They sounded remarkably tight considering they had only rehearsed once immediately before the show in Budokan.

MAY 2000

DR. JOHN JAM 2000

23 May 2000, Blue Note Club, Tokyo (Eric joined Dr. John for one number tonight. Eric was a regular visitor at the club when touring Japan over the years, but had never played here. He had gone there to see Marcus Miller, Jim Hall, and Nile Rogers among others)

Dr. John was playing a residency at the club from Monday 22 May to Friday 27 May and was familiar with the club, having played there several times before. Eric dropped by on the evening of 23 May at around quarter past nine for the second show of the evening. He sat in the audience and enjoyed Dr. John's performance. Then, after "Right Place, Wrong Time" he walked up onto the stage to the surprise and delight of the small crowd. He borrowed a yellow-colored Fender Stratocaster from Dr. John's guitarist, Renard Poche, and the band started a C major double shuffle called "Bad Rock Blues." After the number was finished, Eric returned to his seat and watched the remainder of the show.

BAND LINEUP:

Dr. John: piano, vocals
Eric Clapton: guitar
Renard Poche: guitar
David Barard: bass
Herman Ernest: drums

SETLIST: Bad Rock Blues

DECEMBER 2000

NEW YEAR'S EVE DANCE 2000

31 December 2000, Woking Leisure Centre, Woking, Surrey

Eric and his band are called Concious Contact.

BAND LINEUP:

Eric Clapton: guitar, vocals
Andy Fairweather Low: guitar, vocals
Dave Bronze: bass
Henry Spinetti: drums
Gary Brooker: keyboards, vocals

SETLIST 1: Reconsider Baby / Rock And Roll Music / Mary Anne / Stagger Lee / Hoochie Coochie Man / Lay Down Sally / St. James Infirmary / Peter Gunn / If Paradise Was Half As Nice / Hold On / Wonderful Tonight / Shake, Rattle And Roll

SETLIST 2: In The Midnight Hour / Stormy Monday / Poison Ivy / Too Much Monkey Business / Blueberry Hill / Tore Down / Knockin' On Heaven's Door / Let's Work Together / I Shall Not Be Moved / Can't Judge A Book / Five Long Years / Cocaine / A Whiter Shade Of Pale / Little Queenie

RECORDING SESSIONS 2000

OCEAN WAY RECORDING 6050 Sunset Boulevard, Hollywood, California Sessions with B.B. King for *Riding With The King*

JANUARY 2000—FEBRUARY 2000

Ever since the two guitarists had jammed together back at the Café Au Go Go in New York in 1967, they had wanted to collaborate on a project. Time just went by and the two only ever managed the odd jam or one-off session. It would not be until 2000 that they finally made their true collaboration happen.

Eric flew to L.A. in early January to start laying down tracks for his joint project with B.B. King. The recording would take up to the begining of April, including mixing and mastering. In preperation Eric had made a selection of potential tracks for the two of them to record. This included five B.B. King numbers which surprised B.B. because he hadn't played these since the fifties and had forgotten how to play them in the right way. In fact he admitted that Eric knew them better than he did. The only track that caused some concern was Johnny Mercer's and Harold Arlen's "Come Rain Or Come Shine" because B.B. felt that the number just would not suit his style. Eric asked him to at least give it a try because he felt it would work well. Sure enough, after one take, B.B. knew that Eric had been correct.

The album went double-platinum (two million in certified sales) and won the Grammy for Best Traditional Blues Album.

RIDING WITH THE KING (John Hiatt) *Riding With The King* CD Reprise 9362-47612-2 released June 2000

Eric Clapton: guitar, vocals
B.B. King: guitar, vocals
Andy Fairweather Low: guitar
Doyle Bramhall II: guitar
Steve Gadd: drums
Nathan East: bass
Tim Carmon: Hammond B3 organ
Joe Sample: piano, Wurlitzer
Susannah Melvoin: backing vocals
Wendy Melvoin: backing vocals
Paul Waller: drum programming

TEN LONG YEARS (Jules Taub, B.B. King) *Riding With The King* CD Reprise 9362-47612-2 released June 2000

Eric Clapton: guitar
B.B. King: guitar, vocals

Andy Fairweather Low: guitar
Doyle Bramhall II: guitar
Steve Gadd: drums
Nathan East: bass
Tim Carmon: Hammond B3 organ
Joe Sample: Wurlitzer
Paul Waller: drum programming

KEY TO THE HIGHWAY (Big Bill Broonzy, Charlie Segar) *Riding With The King* CD Reprise 9362-47612-2 released June 2000

Eric Clapton: guitar, vocals
B.B. King: guitar, vocals
Steve Gadd: drums
Nathan East: bass
Tim Carmon: Hammond B3 organ
Paul Waller: drum programming

MARRY YOU (Doyle Bramhall II, Susannah Melvoin, Craig Ross, Charlie Segar) *Riding With The King* CD Reprise 9362-47612-2 released June 2000

Eric Clapton: guitar, vocals
B.B. King: guitar, vocals
Andy Fairweather Low: guitar
Doyle Bramhall II: guitar, backing vocals
Steve Gadd: drums
Nathan East: bass
Tim Carmon: Hammond B3 organ
Susannah Melvoin: backing vocals
Wendy Melvoin: backing vocals
Paul Waller: drum programming

THREE O'CLOCK BLUES (Lowell Fulson, B.B. King, Jules Taub) *Riding With The King* CD Reprise 9362-47612-2 released June 2000

Eric Clapton: guitar, vocals
B.B. King: guitar, vocals
Steve Gadd: drums
Nathan East: bass
Tim Carmon: Hammond B3 organ
Joe Sample: piano

HELP THE POOR (Charles Singleton) *Riding With The King* CD Reprise 9362-47612-2 released June 2000

Eric Clapton: guitar, vocals
B.B. King: guitar, vocals
Andy Fairweather Low: guitar
Doyle Bramhall II: guitar
Jimmie Vaughan: guitar
Steve Gadd: drums
Nathan East: bass
Tim Carmon: Hammond B3 organ
Joe Sample: Rhodes

I WANNA BE (Doyle Bramhall II, Charlie Sexton) *Riding With The King* CD Reprise 9362-47612-2 released June 2000

Eric Clapton: guitar, vocals
B.B. King: guitar, vocals
Andy Fairweather Low: guitar
Doyle Bramhall II: guitar, backing vocals
Steve Gadd: drums
Nathan East: bass
Tim Carmon: Hammond B3 organ
Joe Sample: Wurlitzer
Susannah Melvoin: backing vocals
Wendy Melvoin: backing vocals
Paul Waller: drum programming

WORRIED LIFE BLUES (Sam Hopkins, Big Maceo Merriweather) *Riding With The King* CD Reprise 9362-47612-2 released June 2000

Eric Clapton: guitar, vocals
B.B. King: guitar, vocals
Steve Gadd: drums
Nathan East: bass
Paul Waller: drum programming

DAYS OF OLD (Jules Taub, B.B. King) *Riding With The King* CD Reprise 9362-47612-2 released June 2000

Eric Clapton: guitar, vocals
B.B. King: guitar, vocals
Andy Fairweather Low: guitar
Doyle Bramhall II: guitar
Steve Gadd: drums
Nathan East: bass
Tim Carmon: Hammond B3 organ
Joe Sample: piano
Susannah Melvoin: backing vocals
Wendy Melvoin: backing vocals
Paul Waller: drum programming

WHEN MY HEART BEATS LIKE A HAMMER (B.B. King, Jules Taub) *Riding With The King* CD Reprise 9362-47612-2 released June 2000

Eric Clapton: guitar
B.B. King: guitar, vocals
Andy Fairweather Low: guitar
Doyle Bramhall II: guitar
Steve Gadd: drums
Nathan East: bass
Tim Carmon: Hammond B3 organ
Joe Sample: piano
Paul Waller: drum programming

HOLD ON, I'M COMIN' (Isaac Hayes, David Porter) *Riding With The King* CD Reprise 9362-47612-2 released June 2000

Eric Clapton: guitar, vocals
B.B. King: guitar, vocals
Andy Fairweather Low: guitar
Doyle Bramhall II: guitar
Steve Gadd: drums
Nathan East: bass
Tim Carmon: Hammond B3 organ
Joe Sample: Wurlitzer
Susannah Melvoin: backing vocals
Wendy Melvoin: backing vocals
Paul Waller: drum programming

COME RAIN OR COME SHINE (Harold Arlen, Johnny Mercer) *Riding With The King* CD Reprise 9362-47612-2 released June 2000

Eric Clapton: guitar, vocals
B.B. King: guitar, vocals
Andy Fairweather Low: guitar
Doyle Bramhall II: guitar
Steve Gadd: drums
Nathan East: bass
Tim Carmon: Hammond B3 organ
Joe Sample: piano
Susannah Melvoin: backing vocals
Wendy Melvoin: backing vocals
Paul Waller: drum programming
Arif Mardin: string arrangement and orchestration

LET ME LOVE YOU (B.B. King / Jules Taub) *Riding With The King* Japanese CD single only Warner WPCR10801 released June 2000

Eric Clapton: guitar
B.B. King: guitar, vocals
Andy Fairweather Low: guitar
Doyle Bramhall II: guitar

Steve Gadd: drums
Nathan East: bass
Tim Carmon: Hammond B3 organ
Joe Sample: piano
Arif Mardin: string arrangement and orchestration

Producers: Eric Clapton / Simon Climie
Engineer: Alan Douglas

RECORD ONE STUDIOS
13849 Ventura Boulevard, Sherman Oaks, California
Sessions for *Reptile*

SEPTEMBER 2000

Eric had been so thrilled with the way the session with B.B. King had gone that he recalled the same team that he used on *Riding With The King*—but without B.B. of course.

After a couple of weeks Eric knew that it just wasn't happening. He quickly realized that B.B.'s presence had been such a vital component in the success of their session together and that without him, some other influence would need to come into play for his solo album to be a success.

Eric had a break in the sessions when he went on a fishing trip in Vancouver, Canada. He also met up with family members and they got talking about his uncle Adrian, who had passed away earlier in the year. Because of Eric's early dysfunctional childhood, he had believed his uncle was his brother. He had been a big influence in Eric's life and he now became the catalyst for Eric's newfound motivation for heading back to the recording studios to continue sessions for the album that would be called *Reptile*. The title was also related to his uncle as it was used as a term of endearment among people living in Ripley, a little village in Surrey where Eric was born. He also looked back to the *Layla* and *461 Ocean Boulevard* albums where there would be a healthy mix of covers and originals. He followed the same pattern during these sessions with cover songs by Stevie Wonder, JJ Cale, and James Taylor. Eric ended up producing a fine album that still sounds great today.

OLYMPIC STUDIOS
117 Churck Road, London
Final sessions for *Reptile*

OCTOBER 2000

Eric books the Olympic Studios in Barnes to add some new vocals and strings to the new album started in Los Angeles in September.

REPTILE (Eric Clapton) *Reptile* CD Reprise / Duck 9362-47966-2 released March 2001

Eric Clapton: guitar
Pino Paladino: bass
Steve Gadd: drums
Paul Carrack: keyboards
Paulinho Da Costa: percussion
Paul Waller: drum programming

GOT YOU ON MY MIND (Joe Thomas / Howard Briggs) *Reptile* CD Reprise / Duck 9362-47966-2 released March 2001

Eric Clapton: guitar, vocals
Nathan East: bass
Steve Gadd: drums
Andy Fairweather Low: guitar
Doyle Bramhall II: guitar
Billy Preston: Hammond B3 organ
The Impressions: backing vocals

TRAVELIN' LIGHT (JJ Cale) *Reptile* CD Reprise / Duck 9362-47966-2 released March 2001

Eric Clapton: guitar, vocals
Nathan East: bass
Steve Gadd: drums
Andy Fairweather Low: guitar
Doyle Bramhall II: guitar
Joe Sample: electric piano
Tim Carmon: Hammond B3 organ
Paulinho Da Costa: percussion
Paul Waller: drum programming
The Impressions: backing vocals

BELIEVE IN LIFE (Eric Clapton) *Reptile* CD Reprise / Duck 9362-47966-2 released March 2001

Eric Clapton: guitar, vocals
Nathan East: bass
Steve Gadd: drums
Andy Fairweather Low: guitar
Doyle Bramhall II: guitar
Joe Sample: electric piano
Tim Carmon: Hammond B3 organ
Paulinho Da Costa: percussion
Paul Waller: drum programming
The Impressions: backing vocals

COME BACK BABY (Ray Charles) *Reptile* CD Reprise / Duck 9362-47966-2 released March 2001

Eric Clapton: guitar, vocals
Nathan East: bass
Steve Gadd: drums
Andy Fairweather Low: guitar
Doyle Bramhall II: guitar
Billy Preston: Hammond B3 organ
Tim Carmon: piano
Paulinho Da Costa: percussion
Paul Waller: drum programming
The Impressions: backing vocals

BROKEN DOWN (Simon Climie / Dennis Morgan) *Reptile* CD Reprise / Duck 9362-47966-2 released March 2001

Eric Clapton: guitar, vocals
Nathan East: bass
Steve Gadd: drums
Andy Fairweather Low: guitar
Doyle Bramhall II: guitar
Joe Sample: electric piano
Billy Preston: piano
Paulinho Da Costa: percussion
Paul Waller: drum programming
Nick Ingman: string arrangement

FIND MYSELF (Eric Clapton) *Reptile* CD Reprise / Duck 9362-47966-2 released March 2001

Eric Clapton: guitar, vocals
Nathan East: bass
Steve Gadd: drums
Andy Fairweather Low: guitar
Doyle Bramhall II: guitar
Tim Carmon: Hammond B3 organ
Paulinho Da Costa: percussion
The Impressions: backing vocals

I AIN'T GONNA STAND FOR IT (Stevie Wonder) *Reptile* CD Reprise / Duck 9362-47966-2 released March 2001

Eric Clapton: guitar, vocals
Nathan East: bass
Steve Gadd: drums
Andy Fairweather Low: guitar
Doyle Bramhall II: guitar
Billy Preston: piano
Joe Sample: electric piano
Tim Carmon: Hammond B3 organ
Paulinho Da Costa: percussion
Paul Waller: drum programming
The Impressions: backing vocals

I WANT A LITTLE GIRL (Murray Mencher / Billy Moll) *Reptile* CD Reprise / Duck 9362-47966-2 released March 2001

Eric Clapton: guitar, vocals
Nathan East: bass
Steve Gadd: drums
Andy Fairweather Low: guitar
Doyle Bramhall II: guitar
Billy Preston: piano
Tim Carmon: Hammond B3 organ
Paulinho Da Costa: percussion
The Impressions: backing vocals

SECOND NATURE (Eric Clapton / Simon Climmie / Dennis Morgan) *Reptile* CD Reprise / Duck 9362-47966-2 released March 2001

Eric Clapton: guitar, vocals
Pino Paladino: bass
Steve Gadd: drums
Paul Carrack: electric piano, Hammond B3 organ
Paul Waller: drum programming
The Impressions: backing vocals

DON'T LET ME BE LONELY TONIGHT (James Taylor) *Reptile* CD Reprise / Duck 9362-47966-2 released March 2001

Eric Clapton: guitar, vocals
Nathan East: bass
Steve Gadd: drums
Andy Fairweather Low: guitar
Doyle Bramhall II: guitar
Joe Sample: electric piano
Tim Carmon: Hammond B3 organ

Paulinho Da Costa: percussion
Paul Waller: drum programming
The Impressions: backing vocals
Nick Ingman: string arrangement

MODERN GIRL (Eric Clapton) *Reptile* CD Reprise / Duck 9362-47966-2 released March 2001

Eric Clapton: guitar, vocals
Nathan East: bass
Steve Gadd: drums
Andy Fairweather Low: guitar
Doyle Bramhall II: guitar
Tim Carmon: synthesizer
The Impressions: backing vocals
Nick Ingman: string arrangement

SUPERMAN INSIDE (Eric Clapton / Doyle Bramhall II / Susannah Melvoin) *Reptile* CD Reprise / Duck 9362-47966-2 released March 2001

Eric Clapton: guitar, vocals
Nathan East: bass
Steve Gadd: drums
Andy Fairweather Low: guitar
Doyle Bramhall II: guitar
Billy Preston: Hammond B3 organ
Tim Carmon: piano
Paulinho Da Costa: percussion
Paul Waller: drum programming
The Impressions: backing vocals

SON & SYLVIA (Eric Clapton) *Reptile* CD Reprise / Duck 9362-47966-2 released March 2001

Eric Clapton: guitar
Nathan East: bass
Steve Gadd: drums
Andy Fairweather Low: guitar
Doyle Bramhall II: guitar
Billy Preston: harmonica
Joe Sample: piano, electric piano
Tim Carmon: synthesizer
Paulinho Da Costa: percussion
Nick Ingman: string arrangement

LOSING HAND (Charles Calhoun) *Reptile* CD Warner Music Japan WPCR-11100 / *Ain't Gonna Stand For It* CD single Reprise W555CD released May 2001

Eric Clapton: guitar, vocals
Nathan East: bass
Steve Gadd: drums
Andy Fairweather Low: guitar
Doyle Bramhall II: guitar
Tim Carmon: Hammond B3 organ
Joe Sample: piano, electric piano
Paulinho Da Costa: percussion

JOHNNY GUITAR (Peggy Lee / Victor Young) *I Ain't Gonna Stand For It* CD single Reprise W555CD released May 2001

Eric Clapton: guitar
Nathan East: bass
Steve Gadd: drums
Andy Fairweather Low: guitar
Doyle Bramhall II: guitar
Tim Carmon: Hammond B3 organ
Joe Sample: piano
Paulinho Da Costa: percussion

Producers: Eric Clapton / Simon Climie
Engineer: Alan Douglas

ERIC CLAPTON GUEST SESSION

O'HENRY STUDIOS
200 Magnolia Boulevard, Burbank, California
Session for the Crickets and Their Buddies

28 MARCH 2000

SOMEONE SOMEONE (Edwin Greines Cohen / Norman Petty) *The Crickets And Their Buddies* CD Sovereign Artists 1952 released 2004

PEGGY SUE (Buddy Holly) unreleased

MAYBE BABY (Buddy Holly / Norman Petty) unreleased

Joe B. Mauldin bass
Jerry Allison: drums
Eric Clapton: guitar, vocals
JJ Cale: acoustic guitar, backing vocals
Jeffrey "CJ" Vanston: piano, Hammond B3 organ
Johnny Rivers: backing vocals

Producer: Greg Ladanyi

> "It was one of those days that make all the hard work worth it. CJ played piano and B3 on six songs on a tribute to Buddy Holly and the Crickets with the original Crickets and guest star Eric Clapton. JJ Cale and Johnny Rivers showed up and grabbed a mic to make it a very special day indeed."
> —GREG LADANY
> (producer)

ERIC CLAPTON GUEST SESSION

SHOWPLACE RECORDING STUDIOS

347 South Salem Street, Dover, New Jersey
Session for Hubert Sumlin

MARCH 2000

Eric records two tracks with Hubert Sumlin in New Jersey for Hubert's *Plays Muddy* album. As the title suggests, it was to be a tribute to Muddy Waters. Tracks recorded are "I'm Ready" and "Long Distance Call." They feature Levon Helm on drums, David Maxwell on piano, Paul Oscher on harp, Mudcat Ward on bass, and Bob Margolin on guitar. Keith Richards also participated in the sessions on "Two Trains Runnin'" with just him and Hubert. The album was delayed for several years and when it eventually came out in January 2005 it was retitled *About Them Shoes*. It was nominated for the 2006 Grammy for Best Traditional Blues Album.

I'M READY (Willie Dixon) *About Them Shows* CD Tone-Cool Records TCL-CD-51609 released January 2005

Hubert Sumlin: guitar
Eric Clapton: guitar, vocals
Bob Margolin: guitar
Levon Helm: drums
Paul Oscher: harmonica
Mudcat Ward: bass
Dave Maxwell: keyboards
George Receli: percussion

LOND DISTANCE CALL (McKinley Morganfield) *About Them Shows* CD Tone-Cool Records TCL-CD-51609 released January 2005

Hubert Sumlin: guitar
Eric Clapton: guitar, vocals
Bob Margolin: guitar
Levon Helm: drums
Paul Oscher: harmonica
Mudcat Ward: bass
Dave Maxwell: keyboards
Blondie Chaplin: percussion

Producer: Rob Fraboni
Engineer: Ben Elliott

2001

During the 2001 *Reptile* Tour, several changes were made in Eric Clapton's stage setup. He initially started out using copies of his old Fender Tweed Twins, built by Fender under the supervision of John Suhr. Partway through the tour, Eric went off of them and started using 3x10 Fender Vibro Kings with 2x12 extension cabinets built by the Fender Custom Shop. He also continued to use a Leslie speaker driven by a Marshall JCM800 Lead Series 1959 head. Due to its proximity on stage to drummer Steve Gadd, the box was also soundproofed.

JANUARY 2001

Rehearsals for the *Reptile* Tour take place at Bray Studios. Part of the rehearsals are filmed for adocumentary simply called *Eric Clapton And Friends*. Sadly, the documentary was never given a general release.

OFFICIAL TOUR PRESS RELEASE:
A veteran chronicler of Latin American music, Jana Bokova enlisted cinematographer Javier Aguirresarobe (*The Others*) to document three days of rehearsals leading up to Clapton's 2001 world tour. What they capture is loose and improvisational—a glimpse behind the scenes at how one of the best in the business gets ready for the spotlight. The reverence shown for the guitar god by his own band is undeniable in this love letter to a living rock and roll legend.

Jana Bokova had been approached by Clapton to make the video clip for his latest CD, Reptile. He had kept an eye on her career as documentary and feature director for many years, her career as documentary and feature director for many years, and wanted her particular visual style. She arrived to film at Bray Studios, where Eric and a group of the greatest names in rock and blues music were rehearsing for their forthcoming tour. She brought over from Spain the leading cameraman Javier Aguirresarobe, who had just shot to fame in Hollywood for his work on the Amenabar film *The Others,* starring Nicole Kidman. As shooting began, Clapton allowed Jana and her crew to film more and more of the songs in rehearsal. Jana picked up a DV camera herself, unable to resist filming the rehearsal process as it went along—those intimate moments when the Maestro and his friends worked tirelessly at creating new ideas and variations for their music. Eric Clapton is known as a perfectionist, and his hard-working band includes some of the other great survivors in rock and rhythm & blues including guitarist Andy Fairweather Low and Steve Gadd. Then the legendary four-man group the Impressions arrived to back Eric's vocals, injecting some of their celebrated gospel sounds into the lineup. Clapton had admired them since he had been a teenage fan himself. So Bokova's film crew became a part of the family for the three days, and this film is a distillation of the hard work and play of Clapton and friends at rehearsal before they set off for a grueling twelve months on tour.

> **"**I play for the band, we play for each other. With the audience, I don't try to read their minds. I think if we do it for one another to please ourselves, and we're happy, then that is contagious. Whereas if we try to patronize the audience that would be indulging and they would sense that. I think the only secret is to be in the moment, you know. Not to think ahead about what I'm going to do. . . . Bottom line, the secret is to listen to what everyone else is doing, and that will tell me what to do. Just generally to get out of my head, to turn off my brain, because if I try to calculate it, I'll get it wrong. Thinking it doesn't work with music . . . you just have to feel it, and listen.**"**
>
> **—ERIC CLAPTON**

WYCLEF JEAN FOUNDATION CONCERT 2001

19 January 2001, Carnegie Hall, New York City (benefit for the Wyclef Jean Foundation / Clef's Kids)

Wyclef Jean had the distinction of being the first hip hop artist to perform at the pretigious Carnegie Hall in New York. He played host and entertainer to an all-star benefit on behalf of his self-titled foundation. During the concert he demonstrated his versatility by mixing Bach with hip hop, jazz with rap, and by collaborating with such diverse artists as Whitney Houston, Eric Clapton, and Stevie Wonder.

Eric used the occasion to show off his new "Crashocaster" (aka Crash 1) guitar. It was its first public appearance as well as being the first in Eric's series of "Grafitti" Stratocasters that would be taken on the road for the huge worldwide *Reptile* Tour. The Carnegie audience went wild as soon as Eric played the first few notes of "Wonderful Tonight," which for tonight's show he performed with a light reggae tilt. He also played on a new Wyclef Jean composition titled "My Song" and appeared with most of the night's entertainers for the show closer, "Guantanamera." The concert was released on DVD/Blu-ray as *All Star Jam at Carnegie Hall* via Eagle Rock.

REPTILE UK TOUR 2001

With a new album comes a new world tour to promote it. Surprisingly, *Reptile* received mixed reviews from the press and fans alike. Despite that it remains one of the best albums he's released, with great production, stylish playing, and good songs. Reviews of the shows were also mixed. Long-term fans felt he was coasting, and regular sound problems marred many shows on the European leg of the tour. Behind the scenes, Eric told the sound guys in no uncertain terms to get their act together.

As the tour progressed, it felt at times that Eric really wasn't there, so it came as no surprise when he announced some sort of semi-retirement early on in the U.S. tour by saying he could no longer face doing these long gruelling tours.

Eric always seems to be in a bit of a no-win situation. Long-term fans want constant variety. On this particular tour, the fans wanted to hear "Tell The Truth," "Blues Power," "Got To Get Better In A Little While," and numerous other gems that had been neglected for far too long. Eric struggles before every tour to come up with a setlist that will hopefully please everyone. But one thing is certain, the big hits must be played for the casual concertgoer who would be very dissapointed not to hear "Wonderful Tonight," "Layla," and "Tears In Heaven." And I guess you have to respect that.

BAND LINEUP:
Eric Clapton: guitar, vocals
Nathan East: bass, vocals
Andy Fairweather Low: guitar, vocals
Steve Gadd: drums
Paulinho Da Costa: percussion
David Sancious: keyboards, vocals
The Impressions: backing vocals

FEBRUARY 2001

3 February 2001, Royal Albert Hall, London (with Doyle Bramhall II and Smokestack)

Eric Clapton at the Royal Albert Hall, 3 February 2001.

SETLIST: Key To The Highway / Reptile / Tears In Heaven / Bell Bottom Blues / Change The World / My Father's Eyes / River Of Tears / Going Down Slow / She's Gone / It's Alright[1] / Finally Got Myself Together[1] / Got You On My Mind[1] / I Ain't Gonna Stand For It[1] / Don't Let Me Be Lonely Tonight[1] / Travelin' Light[1] / Hoochie Coochie Man / Five Long Years / I Shot The Sheriff / Badge / Wonderful Tonight / Layla / Sunshine Of Your Love / Somewhere Over The Rainbow

[1]with the Impressions on vocals

4 February 2001, Royal Albert Hall, London (with Doyle Bramhall II and Smokestack)

SETLIST: Key To The Highway / Reptile / Tears In Heaven / Bell Bottom Blues / Change The World / My Father's Eyes / River Of Tears / Going Down Slow / She's Gone / It's Alright[1] / Finally Got Myself Together[1] / Got You On My Mind[1] / I Ain't Gonna Stand For It[1] / Don't Let Me Be Lonely Tonight[1] / Travelin' Light[1] / Hoochie Coochie Man / Five Long Years / I Shot The Sheriff / Badge / Wonderful Tonight / Layla / Sunshine Of Your Love / Somewhere Over The Rainbow

[1]with the Impressions on vocals

6 February 2001, Royal Albert Hall, London (with Doyle Bramhall II and Smokestack)

SETLIST: Key To The Highway / Reptile / Tears In Heaven / Bell Bottom Blues / Change The World / My

Father's Eyes / River Of Tears / Going Down Slow / She's Gone / It's Alright[1] / Finally Got Myself Together[1] / Got You On My Mind[1] / I Ain't Gonna Stand For It[1] / Travelin' Light[1] / Hoochie Coochie Man[1] / Have You Ever Loved A Woman / Badge / Wonderful Tonight / Layla / Sunshine Of Your Love / Somewhere Over The Rainbow

[1]with the Impressions on vocals

7 February 2001, Royal Albert Hall, London (under medical advice Eric was reluctantly forced to cancel this evening's concert due to a cold and sore throat. Had he not done that, there was a strong possiblilty that more shows would have been canceled)

9 February 2001, Royal Albert Hall, London (with Doyle Bramhall II and Smokestack)

SETLIST: Drifting Blues / Reptile / Tears In Heaven / Bell Bottom Blues / Change The World / My Father's Eyes / River Of Tears / Going Down Slow / She's Gone / It's Alright[1] / Finally Got Myself Together[1] / Got You On My Mind[1] / I Ain't Gonna Stand For It[1] / Don't Let Me Be Lonely Tonight[1] / Travelin' Light[1] / Hoochie Coochie Man / Cocaine / Badge / Wonderful Tonight / Layla / Sunshine Of Your Love / Somewhere Over The Rainbow

[1]with the Impressions on vocals

10 February 2001, Royal Albert Hall, London (with Doyle Bramhall II and Smokestack)

Eric Clapton at the Royal Albert Hall, 10 February 2001.

SETLIST: Key To The Highway / Reptile / Tears In Heaven / Bell Bottom Blues / Change The World / My Father's Eyes / River Of Tears / Going Down Slow / She's Gone / It's Alright[1] / Finally Got Myself Together[1] / Got You On My Mind[1] / I Ain't Gonna Stand For It[1] / Don't Let Me Be Lonely Tonight[1] / Travelin' Light[1] / Hoochie Coochie Man / Have You Ever Loved A Woman / Badge / Wonderful Tonight / Layla / Sunshine Of Your Love / Somewhere Over The Rainbow

[1]with the Impressions on vocals

12 February 2001, Sheffield Arena, Sheffield, South Yorkshire (with Doyle Bramhall II and Smokestack)

SETLIST: Key To The Highway / Reptile / Tears In Heaven / Bell Bottom Blues / Change The World / My Father's Eyes / River Of Tears / Going Down Slow / She's Gone / It's Alright[1] / Finally Got Myself Together[1] / Got You On My Mind[1] / I Ain't Gonna Stand For It[1] / Don't Let Me Be Lonely Tonight[1] / Travelin' Light[1] / Hoochie Coochie Man / Have You Ever Loved A Woman / Badge / Wonderful Tonight / Layla / Sunshine Of Your Love / Somewhere Over The Rainbow

[1]with the Impressions on vocals

14 February 2001, Manchester Evening News Arena, Manchester (with Doyle Bramhall II and Smokestack)

SETLIST: Key To The Highway / Reptile / Tears In Heaven / Bell Bottom Blues / Change The World / My Father's Eyes / River Of Tears / Going Down Slow / She's Gone / It's Alright[1] / Finally Got Myself Together[1] / Got You On My Mind[1] / I Ain't Gonna Stand For It[1] / Don't Let Me Be Lonely Tonight[1] / Travelin' Light[1] / Hoochie Coochie Man / Have You Ever Loved A Woman / Badge / Wonderful Tonight / Layla / Sunshine Of Your Love / Somewhere Over The Rainbow

[1]with the Impressions on vocals

16 February 2001, National Exhibition Centre, Birmingham (with Doyle Bramhall II and Smokestack)

SETLIST: Key To The Highway / Reptile / Tears In Heaven / Bell Bottom Blues / Change The World / My Father's Eyes / River Of Tears / Going Down Slow / She's Gone / It's Alright[1] / Finally Got Myself Together[1] / Got You On My Mind[1] / I Ain't Gonna Stand For It[1] / Don't Let Me Be

Lonely Tonight[1] / Travelin' Light[1] / Hoochie Coochie Man / Five Long Years / Badge / Wonderful Tonight / Layla / Sunshine Of Your Love / Somewhere Over The Rainbow

[1]with the Impressions on vocals

REPTILE EUROPEAN / SCANDINAVIAN / RUSSIAN TOUR 2001

BAND LINEUP:
Eric Clapton: guitar
Nathan East: bass, vocals
Andy Fairweather Low: guitar, vocals
Steve Gadd: drums
Paulinho Da Costa: percussion
David Sancious: keyboards, vocals

20 February 2001, Pavilhão Atlântico, Lisbon, Portugal (with Doyle Bramhall II and Smokestack)

SETLIST: Key To The Highway / Reptile / Tears In Heaven / Bell Bottom Blues / Change The World / My Father's Eyes / River Of Tears / Going Down Slow / She's Gone / Got You On My Mind / I Ain't Gonna Stand For It / Don't Let Me Be Lonely Tonight / Badge / Hoochie Coochie Man / Cocaine / Have You Ever Loved A Woman / Wonderful Tonight / Layla / Sunshine Of Your Love / Somewhere Over The Rainbow

22 February 2001, Palacio de los Deportes, Madrid, Spain (with Doyle Bramhall II and Smokestack)

SETLIST: Key To The Highway / Reptile / Tears In Heaven / Bell Bottom Blues / Change The World / My Father's Eyes / River Of Tears / Going Down Slow / She's Gone / Got You On My Mind / Travelin' Light / Don't Let Me Be Lonely Tonight / Badge / Hoochie Coochie Man / Five Long Years / Cocaine / Wonderful Tonight / Layla / Sunshine Of Your Love / Somewhere Over The Rainbow

23 February 2001, Palacio de los Deportes, Madrid, Spain (with Doyle Bramhall II and Smokestack)

SETLIST: Key To The Highway / Reptile / Tears In Heaven / Bell Bottom Blues / Change The World / My Father's Eyes / River Of Tears / Going Down Slow / She's Gone / Got You On My Mind / Travlin' Light / Don't Let Me Be

Lonely Tonight / White Room / Hoochie Coochie Man / Stormy Monday / Cocaine / Wonderful Tonight / Layla / Sunshine Of Your Love / Somewhere Over The Rainbow

25 February 2001, Palau Sant Jordi, Barcelona, Spain (with Doyle Bramhall II and Smokestack)

SETLIST: Key To The Highway / Reptile / Tears In Heaven / Bell Bottom Blues / Change The World / My Father's Eyes / River Of Tears / Going Down Slow / She's Gone / Got You On My Mind / Travelin' Light / Don't Let Me Be Lonely Tonight / Badge / Hoochie Coochie Man / Have You Ever Loved A Woman / Cocaine / Wonderful Tonight / Layla / Sunshine Of Your Love / Somewhere Over The Rainbow

26 February 2001, Le Zenith, Toulouse, France (with Doyle Bramhall II and Smokestack)

SETLIST: Key To The Highway / Reptile / Tears In Heaven / Bell Bottom Blues / Change The World / My Father's Eyes / River Of Tears / Going Down Slow / She's Gone / Got You On My Mind / Don't Let Me Be Lonely Tonight / Travelin' Light / White Room / Hoochie Coochie Man / Five Long Years / Cocaine / Wonderful Tonight / Layla / Sunshine Of Your Love / Somewhere Over The Rainbow

28 February 2001, Palasport, Florence, Italy (with Doyle Bramhall II and Smokestack)

SETLIST: Key To The Highway / Reptile / Tears In Heaven / Bell Bottom Blues / Change The World / My Father's Eyes / River Of Tears / Going Down Slow / She's Gone / Got You On My Mind / Travelin' Light / Don't Let Me Be Lonely Tonight / Badge / Hoochie Coochie Man / Stormy Monday / Cocaine / Wonderful Tonight / Layla / Sunshine Of Your Love / Somewhere Over The Rainbow

MARCH 2001

2 March 2001, Fila Forum, Milan, Italy (with Doyle Bramhall II and Smokestack)

SETLIST: Key To The Highway / Reptile / Tears In Heaven / Bell Bottom Blues / Change The World / My Father's Eyes / River Of Tears / Going Down Slow / She's Gone / Got You On My Mind / Travelin' Light / Don't Let Me Be

Lonely Tonight / White Room / Hoochie Coochie Man / Have You Ever Loved A Woman / Cocaine / Wonderful Tonight / Layla / Sunshine Of Your Love / Somewhere Over The Rainbow

3 March 2001, BPA Palas, Pesaro, Italy (with Doyle Bramhall II and Smokestack)

SETLIST: Key To The Highway / Reptile / Tears In Heaven / Bell Bottom Blues / Change The World / My Father's Eyes / River Of Tears / Going Down Slow / She's Gone / Got You On My Mind / Don't Let Me Be Lonely Tonight / Travelin' Light / Badge / Hoochie Coochie Man / Stormy Monday / Cocaine / Wonderful Tonight / Layla / Sunshine Of Your Love / Somewhere Over The Rainbow

5 March 2001, Hallenstadion, Zurich, Switzerland (with Doyle Bramhall II and Smokestack)

SETLIST: Key To The Highway / Reptile / Tears In Heaven / Bell Bottom Blues / Change The World / My Father's Eyes / River Of Tears / Going Down Slow / She's Gone / Got You On My Mind / Don't Let Me Be Lonely Tonight / Travelin' Light / Badge / Hoochie Coochie Man / Have You Ever Loved A Woman / Cocaine / Wonderful Tonight / Layla / Sunshine Of Your Love / Somewhere Over The Rainbow

6 March 2001, Schleyerhalle, Stuttgart, Germany (with Doyle Bramhall II and Smokestack)

SETLIST: Key To The Highway / Reptile / Tears In Heaven / Bell Bottom Blues / Change The World / My Father's Eyes / River Of Tears / Going Down Slow / She's Gone / Got You On My Mind / Don't Let Me Be Lonely Tonight / Travelin' Light / Badge / Hoochie Coochie Man / Stormy Monday / Cocaine / Wonderful Tonight / Layla / Sunshine Of Your Love / Somewhere Over The Rainbow

8 March 2001, Cologne Arena, Cologne, Germany (with Doyle Bramhall II and Smokestack)

SETLIST: Key To The Highway / Reptile / Tears In Heaven / Bell Bottom Blues / Change The World / My Father's Eyes / River Of Tears / Going Down Slow / She's Gone / Got You On My Mind / Don't Let Me Be Lonely Tonight / Travelin' Light / Badge / Hoochie Coochie Man / Stormy Monday / Cocaine / Wonderful Tonight / Layla / Sunshine Of Your Love / Somewhere Over The Rainbow

9 March 2001, Festhalle, Frankfurt, Germany (with Doyle Bramhall II and Smokestack)

SETLIST: Key To The Highway / Reptile / Tears In Heaven / Bell Bottom Blues / Change The World / My Father's Eyes / River Of Tears / Going Down Slow / She's Gone / Got You On My Mind / Don't Let Me Be Lonely Tonight / Travelin' Light / Badge / Hoochie Coochie Man / Five Long Years / Cocaine / Wonderful Tonight / Layla / Sunshine Of Your Love / Somewhere Over The Rainbow

20 March 2001, Palais Omnisports de Paris Bercy, Paris, France (with Doyle Bramhall II and Smokestack)

SETLIST: Key To The Highway / Reptile / Tears In Heaven / Bell Bottom Blues / Change The World / My Father's Eyes / River Of Tears / Going Down Slow / She's Gone / Got You On My Mind / Don't Let Me Be Lonely Tonight / Travelin' Light / Hoochie Coochie Man / Stormy Monday / Cocaine / Wonderful Tonight / Layla / Sunshine Of Your Love / Somewhere Over The Rainbow

21 March 2001, Palais Omnisports de Paris Bercy, Paris, France (with Doyle Bramhall II and Smokestack)

SETLIST: Key To The Highway / Reptile / Tears In Heaven / Bell Bottom Blues / Change The World / My Father's Eyes / River Of Tears / Going Down Slow / She's Gone / Got You On My Mind / Don't Let Me Be Lonely Tonight / Travelin' Light / Hoochie Coochie Man / Have You Ever Loved A Woman / Cocaine / Wonderful Tonight / Layla / Sunshine Of Your Love / Somewhere Over The Rainbow

23 March 2001, Flanders Expo, Ghent, Belgium (with Doyle Bramhall II and Smokestack)

SETLIST: Key To The Highway / Reptile / Tears In Heaven / Bell Bottom Blues / Change The World / My Father's Eyes / River Of Tears / Going Down Slow / She's Gone / Got You On My Mind / Don't Let Me Be Lonely Tonight / Travelin' Light / Hoochie Coochie Man / Five Long Years / Cocaine / Wonderful Tonight / Layla / Sunshine Of Your Love / Somewhere Over The Rainbow

25 March 2001, Ahoy Hall, Rotterdam, Netherlands (with Doyle Bramhall II and Smokestack)

SETLIST: Key To The Highway / Reptile / Tears In Heaven / Bell Bottom Blues / Change The World / My Father's Eyes / River Of Tears / Going Down Slow / She's Gone / Got You On My Mind / Don't Let Me Be Lonely Tonight / Travelin' Light / Hoochie Coochie Man / Five Long Years / Cocaine / Wonderful Tonight / Layla / Sunshine Of Your Love / Somewhere Over The Rainbow

26 March 2001, Ahoy Hall, Rotterdam, Netherlands (with Doyle Bramhall II and Smokestack)

SETLIST: Key To The Highway / Reptile / Tears In Heaven / Bell Bottom Blues / Change The World / My Father's Eyes / River Of Tears / Going Down Slow / She's Gone / Got You On My Mind / Don't Let Me Be Lonely Tonight / Travelin' Light / Hoochie Coochie Man / Stormy Monday / Cocaine / Wonderful Tonight / Layla / Sunshine Of Your Love / Somewhere Over The Rainbow

28 March 2001, Forum, Copenhagen, Denmark (with Doyle Bramhall II and Smokestack)

SETLIST: Key To The Highway / Reptile / Tears In Heaven / Bell Bottom Blues / Change The World / My Father's Eyes / River Of Tears / Going Down Slow / She's Gone / Got You On My Mind / Don't Let Me Be Lonely Tonight / Travelin' Light / Hoochie Coochie Man / Have You Ever Loved A Woman / Cocaine / Wonderful Tonight / Layla / Sunshine Of Your Love / Somewhere Over The Rainbow

29 March 2001, Forum, Copenhagen, Denmark (with Doyle Bramhall II and Smokestack)

SETLIST: Key To The Highway / Reptile / Tears In Heaven / Bell Bottom Blues / Change The World / My Father's Eyes / River Of Tears / Going Down Slow / She's Gone / Got You On My Mind / Don't Let Me Be Lonely Tonight / Superman Inside[1] / Hoochie Coochie Man[1] / Stormy Monday[1] / Cocaine / Wonderful Tonight / Layla / Sunshine Of Your Love / Somewhere Over The Rainbow

[1]with Doyle Bramhall II on guitar

31 March 2001, Scandinavium, Gothenburg, Sweden (with Doyle Bramhall II and Smokestack)

SETLIST: Key To The Highway / Reptile / Tears In Heaven / Bell Bottom Blues / Change The World / My Father's Eyes / River Of Tears / Going Down Slow / She's Gone / Got You On My Mind / Don't Let Me Be Lonely Tonight / Superman Inside[1] / Hoochie Coochie Man[1] / Five Long

Years[1] / Cocaine / Wonderful Tonight / Layla / Sunshine Of Your Love / Somewhere Over The Rainbow

[1]with Doyle Bramhall II on guitar

APRIL 2001

1 April 2001, Spektrum, Oslo, Norway (with Doyle Bramhall II and Smokestack)

SETLIST: Key To The Highway / Reptile / Tears In Heaven / Bell Bottom Blues / Change The World / My Father's Eyes / River Of Tears / Going Down Slow / She's Gone / Got You On My Mind / Don't Let Me Be Lonely Tonight / Travelin' Light / Superman Inside[1] / Hoochie Coochie Man[1] / Have You Ever Loved A Woman[1] / Cocaine / Wonderful Tonight / Layla / Sunshine Of Your Love / Somewhere Over The Rainbow

[1]with Doyle Bramhall II on guitar

3 April 2001, Globen, Stockholm, Sweden (with Doyle Bramhall II and Smokestack)

SETLIST: Key To The Highway / Reptile / Tears In Heaven / Bell Bottom Blues / Change The World / My Father's Eyes / River Of Tears / Going Down Slow / She's Gone / Got You On My Mind / Don't Let Me Be Lonely Tonight / Travelin' Light / Superman Inside[1] / Hoochie Coochie Man[1] / Five Long Years[1] / Cocaine / Wonderful Tonight / Layla / Sunshine Of Your Love / Somewhere Over The Rainbow

[1]with Doyle Bramhall II on guitar

5 April 2001, Hartwall Arena, Helsinki, Finland (with Doyle Bramhall II and Smokestack)

SETLIST: Key To The Highway / Reptile / Tears In Heaven / Bell Bottom Blues / Change The World / My Father's Eyes / River Of Tears / Going Down Slow / She's Gone / Got You On My Mind / Don't Let Me Be Lonely Tonight / Travelin' Light / Hoochie Coochie Man / Five Long Years / Cocaine / Wonderful Tonight / Layla / Sunshine Of Your Love / Somewhere Over The Rainbow

6 April 2001, Hartwall Arena, Helsinki, Finland (with Doyle Bramhall II and Smokestack)

SETLIST: Key To The Highway / Reptile / Tears In Heaven / Bell Bottom Blues / Change The World / My Father's Eyes / River Of Tears / Going Down Slow / She's Gone / Got You On My Mind / Don't Let Me Be Lonely Tonight / Travelin' Light / Hoochie Coochie Man / Have You Ever Loved A Woman / Cocaine / Wonderful Tonight / Layla / Sunshine Of Your Love / Somewhere Over The Rainbow

8 April 2001, Ice Palace, St Petersburg, Russia (with Doyle Bramhall II and Smokestack)

SETLIST: Key To The Highway / Reptile / Tears In Heaven / Bell Bottom Blues / Change The World / My Father's Eyes / River Of Tears / Going Down Slow / She's Gone / Got You On My Mind / Don't Let Me Be Lonely Tonight / Travelin' Light / Hoochie Coochie Man / Have You Ever Loved A Woman / White Room / Wonderful Tonight / Layla / Sunshine Of Your Love / Somewhere Over The Rainbow

10 April 2001, Kremlin Convention Centre, Moscow, Russia (with Doyle Bramhall II and Smokestack)

SETLIST: Key To The Highway / Reptile / Tears In Heaven / Bell Bottom Blues / Change The World / My Father's Eyes / River Of Tears / Going Down Slow / She's Gone / Got You On My Mind / Don't Let Me Be Lonely Tonight / Travelin' Light / Hoochie Coochie Man / Stormy Monday / Cocaine / Wonderful Tonight / Layla / Sunshine Of Your Love / Somewhere Over The Rainbow

11 April 2001, Kremlin Convention Centre, Moscow, Russia (with Doyle Bramhall II and Smokestack)

SETLIST: Key To The Highway / Reptile / Tears In Heaven / Bell Bottom Blues / Change The World / My Father's Eyes / River Of Tears / Going Down Slow / She's Gone / Got You On My Mind / Don't Let Me Be Lonely Tonight / Travelin' Light / Hoochie Coochie Man / Five Long Years / Cocaine / Wonderful Tonight / Layla / Sunshine Of Your Love / Somewhere Over The Rainbow

REPTILE U.S. TOUR 2001

BAND LINEUP:
Eric Clapton: guitar, vocals
Nathan East: bass, vocals

Andy Fairweather Low: guitar, vocals
Steve Gadd: drums
David Sancious: keyboards, guitar, vocals
Billy Preston: keyboards
The Impressions: vocals (between 21–25 May 2001)

MAY 2001

10 May 2001, Reunion Arena, Dallas, Texas (with Doyle Bramhall II and Smokestack)

SETLIST: Key To The Highway / Reptile / Tears In Heaven / Bell Bottom Blues / Change The World / My Father's Eyes / River Of Tears / Going Down Slow / She's Gone / I Want A Little Girl / Don't Let Me Be Lonely Tonight / Travelin' Light / Hoochie Coochie Man / Stormy Monday / Cocaine / Wonderful Tonight / Layla / Sunshine Of Your Love / Somewhere Over The Rainbow

12 May 2001, Alamo Dome, San Antonio, Texas (with Doyle Bramhall II and Smokestack)

SETLIST: Key To The Highway / Reptile / Got You On My Mind / Tears In Heaven / Bell Bottom Blues / Change The World / My Father's Eyes / River Of Tears / Going Down Slow / She's Gone / I Want A Little Girl / Don't Let Me Be Lonely Tonight / Travelin' Light / Hoochie Coochie Man / Have You Ever Loved A Woman / Badge / Wonderful Tonight / Layla / Sunshine Of Your Love / For All We Know

14 May 2001, Compaq Center, Houston, Texas (with Doyle Bramhall II and Smokestack)

SETLIST: Key To The Highway / Reptile / Got You On My Mind / Tears In Heaven / Bell Bottom Blues / Change The World / My Father's Eyes / River Of Tears / Going Down Slow / She's Gone / I Want A Little Girl / Don't Let Me Be Lonely Tonight / Travelin' Light / Hoochie Coochie Man[1] / Five Long Years[1] / Cocaine[1] / Wonderful Tonight[1] / Layla / Sunshine Of Your Love / Somewhere Over The Rainbow

[1]with Jimmie Vaughan on guitar

15 May 2001, New Orleans Arena, New Orleans, Louisiana (with Doyle Bramhall II and Smokestack)

SETLIST: Key To The Highway / Reptile / Got You On My Mind / Tears In Heaven / Bell Bottom Blues / Change The World / My Father's Eyes / River Of Tears / Going Down Slow / She's Gone / I Want A Little Girl / Don't Let Me Be Lonely Tonight / Travelin' Light / Hoochie Coochie Man / Stormy Monday / Cocaine / Wonderful Tonight / Layla / Sunshine Of Your Love / For All We Know

18 May 2001, National Car Rental Center, Sunrise, Florida (with Doyle Bramhall II and Smokestack)

SETLIST: Key To The Highway / Reptile / Got You On My Mind / Tears In Heaven / Bell Bottom Blues / Change The World / My Father's Eyes / River Of Tears / Going Down Slow / She's Gone / I Want A Little Girl / Don't Let Me Be Lonely Tonight / Travelin' Light / Hoochie Coochie Man / Have You Ever Loved A Woman / Cocaine / Wonderful Tonight / Layla / Sunshine Of Your Love / Somewhere Over The Rainbow

19 May 2001, Ice Palace Arena, Tampa, Florida (with Doyle Bramhall II and Smokestack)

SETLIST: Key To The Highway / Reptile / Got You On My Mind / Tears In Heaven / Bell Bottom Blues / Change The World / My Father's Eyes / River Of Tears / Going Down Slow / She's Gone / I Want A Little Girl / Don't Let Me Be Lonely Tonight / Travelin' Light / Hoochie Coochie Man / Stormy Monday / Cocaine / Wonderful Tonight / Layla / Sunshine Of Your Love / Somewhere Over The Rainbow

21 May 2001, Philips Arena, Atlanta, Georgia (with Doyle Bramhall II and Smokestack)

SETLIST: Key To The Highway / Reptile / Tears In Heaven / Bell Bottom Blues / Change The World / My Father's Eyes / River Of Tears / Going Down Slow / She's Gone / It's Alright[1] / Finally Got Myself Together[1] / Got You On My Mind[1] / Don't Let Me Be Lonely Tonight[1] / Travelin' Light[1] / Hoochie Coochie Man / Stormy Monday / Cocaine / Wonderful Tonight / Layla / Sunshine Of Your Love / Somewhere Over The Rainbow

[1]with the Impressions on vocals

22 May 2001, Pyramid, Memphis, Tennessee (with Doyle Bramhall II and Smokestack)

Billy Preston was unwell and missed this show. He would eventually rejoin the tour on 11 June in Boston.

SETLIST: Key To The Highway / Reptile / Tears In Heaven / Bell Bottom Blues / Change The World / My Father's Eyes / River Of Tears / Going Down Slow / She's Gone / It's Alright[1] / Finally Got Myself Together[1] / Got You On My Mind[1] / Don't Let Me Be Lonely Tonight[1] / Travelin' Light[1] / Hoochie Coochie Man / Have You Ever Loved A Woman / Cocaine / Wonderful Tonight / Layla / Sunshine Of Your Love / Somewhere Over The Rainbow[1]

[1]with the Impressions on vocals

24 May 2001, Gaylord Entertainment Center, Nashville, Tennessee (with Doyle Bramhall II and Smokestack)

SETLIST: Key To The Highway / Reptile / Tears In Heaven / Bell Bottom Blues / Change The World / My Father's Eyes / River Of Tears / Going Down Slow / She's Gone / It's Alright[1] / Finally Got Myself Together[1] / Got You On My Mind[1] / Don't Let Me Be Lonely Tonight[1] / Travelin' Light[1] / Hoochie Coochie Man / Stormy Monday / Cocaine / Wonderful Tonight / Layla / Sunshine Of Your Love / Somewhere Over The Rainbow[1]

[1]with the Impressions on vocals

25 May 2001, Charlotte Coliseum, Charlotte, North Carolina (with Doyle Bramhall II and Smokestack)

SETLIST: Key To The Highway / Reptile / Tears In Heaven / Bell Bottom Blues / Change The World / My Father's Eyes / River Of Tears / Going Down Slow / She's Gone / It's Alright[1] / Finally Got Myself Together[1] / Got You On My Mind[1] / Don't Let Me Be Lonely Tonight[1] / Travelin' Light[1] / Hoochie Coochie Man / Have You Ever Loved A Woman / Cocaine / Wonderful Tonight / Layla / Sunshine Of Your Love / Somewhere Over The Rainbow[1]

[1]with the Impressions on vocals

27 May 2001, MCI Center, Washington, D.C. (with Doyle Bramhall II and Smokestack)

SETLIST: Key To The Highway / Reptile / Got You On My Mind / Tears In Heaven / Bell Bottom Blues / Change The World / My Father's Eyes / River Of Tears / Going Down Slow / She's Gone / Don't Let Me Be Lonely Tonight / Travelin' Light / Hoochie Coochie Man / Five Long Years / Cocaine / Wonderful Tonight / Layla / Sunshine Of Your Love / Somewhere Over The Rainbow

30 May 2001, Bryce Jordan Center State College, University Park, Pennsylvania (with Doyle Bramhall II and Smokestack)

SETLIST: Key To The Highway / Reptile / Tears In Heaven / Bell Bottom Blues / Change The World / My Father's Eyes / River Of Tears / Going Down Slow / She's Gone / Don't Let Me Be Lonely Tonight / Travelin' Light / Hoochie Coochie Man / Have You Ever Loved A Woman / Cocaine / Wonderful Tonight / Layla / Sunshine Of Your Love / Somewhere Over The Rainbow

JUNE 2001

1 June 2001, Nationwide Arena, Columbus, Ohio (with Doyle Bramhall II and Smokestack)

SETLIST: Key To The Highway / Reptile / Got You On My Mind / Tears In Heaven / Bell Bottom Blues / Change The World / My Father's Eyes / River Of Tears / Going Down Slow / She's Gone / Don't Let Me Be Lonely Tonight / Travelin' Light / Hoochie Coochie Man / Stormy Monday / Cocaine / Wonderful Tonight / Layla / Sunshine Of Your Love / Somewhere Over The Rainbow

2 June 2001, Conseco Fieldhouse, Indianapolis, Indiana (with Doyle Bramhall II and Smokestack)

SETLIST: Key To The Highway / Reptile / Got You On My Mind / Tears In Heaven / Bell Bottom Blues / Change The World / My Father's Eyes / River Of Tears / Going Down Slow / She's Gone / Don't Let Me Be Lonely Tonight / Travelin' Light / Hoochie Coochie Man / Have You Ever Loved A Woman / Cocaine / Wonderful Tonight / Layla / Sunshine Of Your Love / Somewhere Over The Rainbow

4 June 2001, Gund Arena, Cleveland, Ohio (with Doyle Bramhall II and Smokestack)

SETLIST: Key To The Highway / Reptile / Got You On My Mind / Tears In Heaven / Bell Bottom Blues / Change The World / My Father's Eyes / River Of Tears / Going Down Slow / She's Gone / Don't Let Me Be Lonely Tonight / Travelin' Light / Hoochie Coochie Man /

Stormy Monday / Cocaine / Wonderful Tonight / Layla / Sunshine Of Your Love / Somewhere Over The Rainbow

6 June 2001, Palace of Auburn Hills, Auburn Hills, Michigan (with Doyle Bramhall II and Smokestack)

SETLIST: Key To The Highway / Reptile / Got You On My Mind / Tears In Heaven / Bell Bottom Blues / Change The World / My Father's Eyes / River Of Tears / Going Down Slow / She's Gone / Don't Let Me Be Lonely Tonight / Travelin' Light / Hoochie Coochie Man / Have You Ever Loved A Woman / Cocaine / Wonderful Tonight / Layla / Sunshine Of Your Love / Somewhere Over The Rainbow

9 June 2001, Air Canada Centre, Toronto, Ontario, Canada (with Doyle Bramhall II and Smokestack)

SETLIST: Key To The Highway / Reptile / Got You On My Mind / Tears In Heaven / Bell Bottom Blues / Change The World / My Father's Eyes / River Of Tears / Going Down Slow / She's Gone / Don't Let Me Be Lonely Tonight / Travelin' Light / Hoochie Coochie Man / Five Long Years / Cocaine / Wonderful Tonight / Layla / Sunshine Of Your Love / Somewhere Over The Rainbow

11 June 2001, Fleet Center, Boston, Massachusetts (with Doyle Bramhall II and Smokestack)

Billy Preston is back tonight after a break due to illness.

SETLIST: Key To The Highway / Reptile / Got You On My Mind / Tears In Heaven / Bell Bottom Blues / Change The World / My Father's Eyes / River Of Tears / Going Down Slow / She's Gone / I Want A Little Girl / Travelin' Light / Hoochie Coochie Man / Have You Ever Loved A Woman / Cocaine / Wonderful Tonight / Layla / Sunshine Of Your Love / Somewhere Over The Rainbow

12 June 2001, Fleet Center, Boston, Massachusetts (with Doyle Bramhall II and Smokestack)

SETLIST: Key To The Highway / Reptile / Got You On My Mind / Tears In Heaven / Bell Bottom Blues / Change The World / My Father's Eyes / River Of Tears / Going Down Slow / She's Gone / I Want A Little Girl / Travelin' Light / Hoochie Coochie Man / Five Long Years /

Cocaine / Wonderful Tonight / Layla / Sunshine Of Your Love / Somewhere Over The Rainbow

15 June 2001, HSBC Arena, Buffalo, New York (with Doyle Bramhall II and Smokestack)

SETLIST: Key To The Highway / Reptile / Got You On My Mind / Tears In Heaven / Bell Bottom Blues / Change The World / My Father's Eyes / River Of Tears / Going Down Slow / She's Gone / I Want A Little Girl / Travelin' Light / Hoochie Coochie Man / Stormy Monday / Cocaine / Wonderful Tonight / Layla / Sunshine Of Your Love / Somewhere Over The Rainbow

16 June 2001, Pepsi Arena, Albany, New York (with Doyle Bramhall II and Smokestack)

SETLIST: Key To The Highway / Reptile / Got You On My Mind / Tears In Heaven / Bell Bottom Blues / Change The World / My Father's Eyes / River Of Tears / Going Down Slow / She's Gone / I Want A Little Girl / Travelin' Light / Hoochie Coochie Man / Have You Ever Loved A Woman / Cocaine / Wonderful Tonight / Layla / Sunshine Of Your Love / Somewhere Over The Rainbow

17 June 2001, First Union Center, Philadelphia, Pennsylvania (with Doyle Bramhall II and Smokestack)

SETLIST: Key To The Highway / Reptile / Got You On My Mind / Tears In Heaven / Bell Bottom Blues / Change The World / My Father's Eyes / River Of Tears / Going Down Slow / She's Gone / I Want A Little Girl / Travelin' Light / Hoochie Coochie Man / Have You Ever Loved A Woman / Cocaine / Wonderful Tonight / Layla / Sunshine Of Your Love / For All We Know

21 June 2001, Madison Square Garden, New York City (with Doyle Bramhall II and Smokestack)

SETLIST: Key To The Highway / Reptile / Got You On My Mind / Tears In Heaven / Bell Bottom Blues / Change The World / My Father's Eyes / River Of Tears / Going Down Slow / She's Gone / I Want A Little Girl / Travelin' Light / Hoochie Coochie Man / Have You Ever Loved A Woman / Cocaine / Wonderful Tonight / Layla / Sunshine Of Your Love / Somewhere Over The Rainbow

22 June 2001, Madison Square Garden, New York City (with Doyle Bramhall II and Smokestack)

SETLIST: Drifting Blues / Reptile / Got You On My Mind / Tears In Heaven / Bell Bottom Blues / Change The World / My Father's Eyes / River Of Tears / Going Down Slow / She's Gone / I Want A Little Girl / Travelin' Light / Hoochie Coochie Man / Stormy Monday / Cocaine / Wonderful Tonight / Layla / Sunshine Of Your Love / Somewhere Over The Rainbow

23 June 2001, Madison Square Garden, New York City (with Doyle Bramhall II and Smokestack)

SETLIST: Drifting Blues / Reptile / Got You On My Mind / Tears In Heaven / Bell Bottom Blues / Change The World / My Father's Eyes / River Of Tears / Going Down Slow / She's Gone / I Want A Little Girl / Travelin' Light / Hoochie Coochie Man / Five Long Years / Cocaine / Wonderful Tonight / Layla / Sunshine Of Your Love / Somewhere Over The Rainbow

JULY 2001

PICNIC CONCERT BY THE CHAPEL ON THE LAKE 2001

7 July 2001, Wintershall Estate, Bramley, Surrey (Picnic Concert by the Chapel on the Lake charity show in aid of the Heart and Stroke Trust Endeavour [HASTE])

BAND DU LAC LINEUP:
Eric Clapton: guitar, vocals
Gary Brooker: keyboards, vocals
Andy Fairweather Low: guitar, vocals
Dave Bronze: bass
Henry Spinetti: drums
Mike Rutherford: guitar
Paul "Wix" Wickens: keyboards
Sam Brown: vocals
Margo Buchanon: vocals

SETLIST: Knock On Wood / Let's Work Together / Night And Day / All I Need Is A Miracle / We Shall Not Be Moved / Wonderful Tonight / Leave The Candle / Mojo Hannah / Before You Accuse Me / Stop / If Paradise Is Half As Nice / Poison Ivy / Stormy Monday / My Baby Just Cares For Me / The Weight / Good Golly Miss Molly / Gin House / Cocaine / A Whiter Shade Of Pale / Little Queenie

REPTILE U.S. TOUR 2001

By the second leg of the U.S. tour the band were really tight and were getting into a great groove most nights. Eric was clearly enjoying himself and Billy Preston even got to perform his classic "Will It Go Round In Circles" towards the end of the tour.

17 July 2001, Xcel Energy Center, St. Paul, Minnesota (with Doyle Bramhall II and Smokestack)

SETLIST: Key To The Highway / Reptile / Got You On My Mind / Tears In Heaven / Bell Bottom Blues / Change The World / My Father's Eyes / River Of Tears / Going Down Slow / She's Gone / I Want A Little Girl / Travelin' Light / Hoochie Coochie Man / Have You Ever Loved A Woman / Cocaine / Wonderful Tonight / Layla / Sunshine Of Your Love / Somewhere Over The Rainbow

19 July 2001, Fargo Dome, Fargo, North Dakota (with Doyle Bramhall II and Smokestack)

SETLIST: Key To The Highway / Reptile / Got You On My Mind / Tears In Heaven / Bell Bottom Blues / Change The World / My Father's Eyes / River Of Tears / Going Down Slow / She's Gone / I Want A Little Girl / Badge / Hoochie Coochie Man / Have You Ever Loved A Woman / Cocaine / Wonderful Tonight / Layla / Sunshine Of Your Love / Somewhere Over The Rainbow

21 July 2001, Bradley Center, Milwaukee, Wisconsin (with Doyle Bramhall II and Smokestack)

SETLIST: Key To The Highway / Reptile / Got You On My Mind / Tears In Heaven / Bell Bottom Blues / Change

The World / My Father's Eyes / River Of Tears / Going Down Slow / She's Gone / I Want A Little Girl / Badge / Hoochie Coochie Man / Stormy Monday / Cocaine / Wonderful Tonight / Layla / Sunshine Of Your Love / Somewhere Over The Rainbow

22 July 2001, Savvis Center, St. Louis, Missouri (with Doyle Bramhall II and Smokestack)

SETLIST: Key To The Highway / Reptile / Got You On My Mind / Tears In Heaven / Bell Bottom Blues / Change The World / My Father's Eyes / River Of Tears / Going Down Slow / She's Gone / Badge / Hoochie Coochie Man / Five Long Years / Cocaine / Wonderful Tonight / Layla / Sunshine Of Your Love / Somewhere Over The Rainbow

24 July 2001, United Center, Chicago, Illinois (with Doyle Bramhall II and Smokestack)

SETLIST: Key To The Highway / Reptile / Got You On My Mind / Tears In Heaven / Bell Bottom Blues / Change The World / My Father's Eyes / River Of Tears / Going Down Slow / She's Gone / I Want A Little Girl / Badge / Hoochie Coochie Man[1] / Stone Crazy / Blues Jam[1] / Cocaine / Wonderful Tonight / Layla / Sunshine Of Your Love / Somewhere Over The Rainbow

[1] with Buddy Guy on guitar and vocals

25 July 2001, United Center, Chicago, Illinois (with Doyle Bramhall II and Smokestack)

SETLIST: Key To The Highway / Reptile / Got You On My Mind / Tears In Heaven / Bell Bottom Blues / Change The World / My Father's Eyes / River Of Tears / Going Down Slow / She's Gone / I Want A Little Girl / Badge / Hoochie Coochie Man / Have You Ever Loved A Woman / Cocaine / Wonderful Tonight / Layla / Will It Go Round In Circles[1] / Somewhere Over The Rainbow

[1] with Billy Preston on lead vocals

27 July 2001, Mark of the Quad Cities, Moline, Illinois (with Doyle Bramhall II and Smokestack)

SETLIST: Key To The Highway / Reptile / Got You On My Mind / Tears In Heaven / Bell Bottom Blues / Change The World / My Father's Eyes / River Of Tears / Going Down Slow / She's Gone / I Want A Little Girl / Badge / Hoochie Coochie Man / Stormy Monday / Cocaine /

Wonderful Tonight / Layla / Will It Go Round In Circles[1] / Sunshine Of Your Love / Somewhere Over The Rainbow

[1] with Billy Preston on lead vocals

28 July 2001, Kemper Arena, Kansas City, Missouri (with Doyle Bramhall II and Smokestack)

SETLIST: Key To The Highway / Reptile / Got You On My Mind / Tears In Heaven / Bell Bottom Blues / Change The World / My Father's Eyes / River Of Tears / Going Down Slow / She's Gone / I Want A Little Girl / Badge / Hoochie Coochie Man / Five Long Years / Cocaine / Wonderful Tonight / Layla / Will It Go Round In Circles[1] / Sunshine Of Your Love / Somewhere Over The Rainbow

[1] with Billy Preston on lead vocals

30 July 2001, Pepsi Center Arena, Denver, Colorado (with Doyle Bramhall II and Smokestack)

SETLIST: Key To The Highway / Reptile / Got You On My Mind / Tears In Heaven / Bell Bottom Blues / Change The World / My Father's Eyes / River Of Tears / Going Down Slow / She's Gone / I Want A Little Girl / Badge / Hoochie Coochie Man / Stormy Monday / Cocaine / Wonderful Tonight / Blues Jam[1] / Layla / Will It Go Round In Circles[2] / Sunshine Of Your Love / Somewhere Over The Rainbow

[1] band plays while waiting for Eric's equipment to be repaired
[2] with Billy Preston on lead vocals

AUGUST 2001

1 August 2001, Delta Center, Salt Lake City, Utah (with Doyle Bramhall II and Smokestack)

SETLIST: Key To The Highway / Reptile / Got You On My Mind / Tears In Heaven / Bell Bottom Blues / Change The World / My Father's Eyes / River Of Tears / Going Down Slow / She's Gone / I Want A Little Girl / Badge / Hoochie Coochie Man / Five Long Years / Cocaine / Wonderful Tonight / Layla / Will It Go Round In Circles[1] / Sunshine Of Your Love / Somewhere Over The Rainbow

[1] with Billy Preston on lead vocals

2 August 2001, Idaho Center, Nampa, Idaho (with Doyle Bramhall II and Smokestack)

SETLIST: Key To The Highway / Reptile / Got You On My Mind / Tears In Heaven / Bell Bottom Blues / Change The World / My Father's Eyes / River Of Tears / Going Down Slow / She's Gone / I Want A Little Girl / Badge / Hoochie Coochie Man / Have You Ever Loved A Woman / Cocaine / Wonderful Tonight / Layla / Will It Go Round In Circles[1] / Sunshine Of Your Love / Somewhere Over The Rainbow

[1]with Billy Preston on lead vocals

4 August 2001, Key Arena, Seattle Center, Seattle, Washington (with Doyle Bramhall II and Smokestack)

SETLIST: Key To The Highway / Reptile / Got You On My Mind / Tears In Heaven / Bell Bottom Blues / Change The World / My Father's Eyes / River Of Tears / Going Down Slow / She's Gone / I Want A Little Girl / Badge / Hoochie Coochie Man / Stormy Monday / Cocaine / Wonderful Tonight / Layla / Will It Go Round In Circles[1] / Sunshine Of Your Love / Somewhere Over The Rainbow

[1]with Billy Preston on lead vocals

5 August 2001, General Motors Place, Vancouver, British Columbia, Canada (with Doyle Bramhall II and Smokestack)

SETLIST: Key To The Highway / Reptile / Got You On My Mind / Tears In Heaven / Bell Bottom Blues / Change The World / My Father's Eyes / River Of Tears / Going Down Slow / She's Gone / I Want A Little Girl / Badge / Hoochie Coochie Man / Have You Ever Loved A Woman / Cocaine / Wonderful Tonight / Layla / Sunshine Of Your Love / Somewhere Over The Rainbow

7 August 2001, Rose Garden Arena, Portland, Oregon (with Doyle Bramhall II and Smokestack)

SETLIST: Key To The Highway / Reptile / Got You On My Mind / Tears In Heaven / Bell Bottom Blues / Change The World / My Father's Eyes / River Of Tears / Going Down Slow / She's Gone / I Want A Little Girl / Badge / Hoochie Coochie Man / Have You Ever Loved A Woman / Cocaine / Wonderful Tonight / Layla / Will It Go Round In Circles[1] / Sunshine Of Your Love / Somewhere Over The Rainbow

[1]with Billy Preston on lead vocals

10 August 2001, ARCO Arena, Sacramento, California (with Doyle Bramhall II and Smokestack)

SETLIST: Key To The Highway / Reptile / Got You On My Mind / Tears In Heaven / Bell Bottom Blues / Change The World / My Father's Eyes / River Of Tears / Going Down Slow / She's Gone / I Want A Little Girl / Badge / Hoochie Coochie Man / Have You Ever Loved A Woman / Cocaine / Wonderful Tonight / Layla / Will It Go Round In Circles[1] / Sunshine Of Your Love / Somewhere Over The Rainbow

[1]with Billy Preston on lead vocals

11 August 2001, Oakland Arena, Oakland, California (with Doyle Bramhall II and Smokestack)

SETLIST: Key To The Highway / Reptile / Got You On My Mind / Tears In Heaven / Bell Bottom Blues / Change The World / My Father's Eyes / River Of Tears / Going Down Slow / She's Gone / I Want A Little Girl / Badge / Hoochie Coochie Man / Have You Ever Loved A Woman / Cocaine / Wonderful Tonight / Layla / Will It Go Round In Circles[1] / Sunshine Of Your Love / Somewhere Over The Rainbow

[1]with Billy Preston on lead vocals

13 August 2001, Thomas & Mack Center, Las Vegas, Nevada (with Doyle Bramhall II and Smokestack)

SETLIST: Key To The Highway / Reptile / Got You On My Mind / Tears In Heaven / Bell Bottom Blues / Change The World / My Father's Eyes / River Of Tears / Going Down Slow / She's Gone / I Want A Little Girl / Badge / Hoochie Coochie Man / Have You Ever Loved A Woman / Cocaine / Wonderful Tonight / Layla / Will It Go Round In Circles[1] / Sunshine Of Your Love / Somewhere Over The Rainbow

[1]with Billy Preston on lead vocals

15 August 2001, America West Arena, Phoenix, Arizona (with Doyle Bramhall II and Smokestack)

SETLIST: Key To The Highway / Reptile / Got You On My Mind / Tears In Heaven / Bell Bottom Blues / Change The World / My Father's Eyes / River Of Tears / Going Down Slow / She's Gone / I Want A Little Girl / Badge / Hoochie Coochie Man / Stormy Monday / Cocaine /

Wonderful Tonight / Layla / Will It Go Round In Circles[1] / Sunshine Of Your Love / Somewhere Over The Rainbow

[1] with Billy Preston on lead vocals

17 August 2001, Staples Center, Los Angeles, California (with Doyle Bramhall II and Smokestack)

Show recorded for *One More Car, One More Rider* double CD.

SETLIST: Key To The Highway / Reptile / Got You On My Mind / Tears In Heaven / Bell Bottom Blues / Change The World / My Father's Eyes / River Of Tears / Going Down Slow / She's Gone / I Want A Little Girl / Badge / Hoochie Coochie Man / Have You Ever Loved A Woman / Cocaine / Wonderful Tonight / Layla / Will It Go Round In Circles[1] / Sunshine Of Your Love / Somewhere Over The Rainbow

[1] with Billy Preston on lead vocals

18 August 2001, Staples Center, Los Angeles, California (with Doyle Bramhall II and Smokestack)

Show recorded for *One More Car, One More Rider* double CD. Complete show is filmed and released as *One More Rider, One More Car* DVD.

SETLIST: Key To The Highway / Reptile / Got You On My Mind / Tears In Heaven / Bell Bottom Blues / Change The World / My Father's Eyes / River Of Tears / Going Down Slow / She's Gone / I Want A Little Girl / Badge / Hoochie Coochie Man / Have You Ever Loved A Woman / Cocaine / Wonderful Tonight / Layla / Will It Go Round In Circles[1] / Sunshine Of Your Love / Somewhere Over The Rainbow

[1] with Billy Preston on lead vocals

REPTILE SOUTH AMERICA TOUR 2001

BAND LINEUP:
Eric Clapton: guitar, vocals
Nathan East: bass, vocals
Andy Fairweather Low: guitar, vocals
Steve Gadd: drums
David Sancious: keyboards, vocals, guitar
Greg Phillinganes: keyboards

OCTOBER 2001

4 October 2001, Estadio Nacional, Santiago, Chile (with Miguel "Botafogo" Vilanova)

SETLIST: Key To The Highway / Reptile / Got You On My Mind / Tears In Heaven / Bell Bottom Blues / Change The World / My Father's Eyes / River Of Tears / Going Down Slow / She's Gone / I Want A Little Girl / Badge / Hoochie Coochie Man / Have You Ever Loved A Woman / Cocaine / Wonderful Tonight / Layla / Sunshine Of Your Love / Somewhere Over The Rainbow

6 October 2001, Estadio River Plate, Buenos Aires, Argentina (with La Mississippi Blues Band and Memphis La Blusera)

SETLIST: Key To The Highway / Reptile / Got You On My Mind / Tears In Heaven / Bell Bottom Blues / Change The World / My Father's Eyes / River Of Tears / Going Down Slow / She's Gone / I Want A Little Girl / Badge / Hoochie Coochie Man / Stormy Monday / Cocaine / Wonderful Tonight / Layla / Sunshine Of Your Love / Somewhere Over The Rainbow

8 October 2001, Cilindro Municipal, Montevideo, Uruguay (support act not known)

SETLIST: Reptile / Got You On My Mind / Tears In Heaven / Bell Bottom Blues / Change The World / My Father's Eyes / River Of Tears / Going Down Slow / She's Gone / I Want A Little Girl / Badge / Hoochie Coochie Man / Have You Ever Loved A Woman / Cocaine / Wonderful Tonight / Layla / Sunshine Of Your Love / Somewhere Over The Rainbow

10 October 2001, Estádio Olímpico, Porto Alegre, Brazil (with Roberto Frejat)

SETLIST: Reptile / Got You On My Mind / Tears In Heaven / Bell Bottom Blues / Change The World / My Father's Eyes / River Of Tears / Going Down Slow / She's Gone / I Want A Little Girl / Badge / Hoochie Coochie Man / Have You Ever Loved A Woman / Cocaine / Wonderful Tonight / Layla / Sunshine Of Your Love / Somewhere Over The Rainbow

11 October 2001, Estádio do Pacaembu, São Paulo, Brazil (with Roberto Frejat)

SETLIST: Reptile / Got You On My Mind / Tears In Heaven / Bell Bottom Blues / Change The World / My Father's Eyes / River Of Tears / Going Down Slow / She's Gone / I Want A Little Girl / Badge / Hoochie Coochie Man / Stormy Monday / Cocaine / Wonderful Tonight / Layla / Sunshine Of Your Love / Somewhere Over The Rainbow

13 October 2001, Praça da Apoteose, Rio de Janeiro, Brazil (with Roberto Frejat)

SETLIST: Reptile / Got You On My Mind / Tears In Heaven / Bell Bottom Blues / Change The World / My Father's Eyes / River Of Tears / Going Down Slow / She's Gone / I Want A Little Girl / Badge / Hoochie Coochie Man / Have You Ever Loved A Woman / Cocaine / Wonderful Tonight / Layla / Sunshine Of Your Love / Somewhere Over The Rainbow

16 October 2001, Estacionamiento del Poliedro, Caracas, Venezuela (with Biella Da Costa)

SETLIST: Reptile / Got You On My Mind / Tears In Heaven / Bell Bottom Blues / Change The World / My Father's Eyes / River Of Tears / Going Down Slow / She's Gone / I Want A Little Girl / Badge / Hoochie Coochie Man / Five Long Years / Cocaine / Wonderful Tonight / Layla / Sunshine Of Your Love

19 October 2001, Foro Sol, Mexico City, Mexico (with Toto)

SETLIST: Reptile / Got You On My Mind / Tears In Heaven / Bell Bottom Blues / Change The World / My Father's Eyes / River Of Tears / Going Down Slow / She's Gone / I Want A Little Girl / Badge / Hoochie Coochie Man / Stormy Monday / Cocaine / Wonderful Tonight / Layla / Sunshine Of Your Love / Somewhere Over The Rainbow

THE CONCERT FOR NEW YORK CITY 2001

20 October 2001, Madison Square Garden, New York City (the benefit concert for the city of New York)

SETLIST:

Hoochie Coochie Man *The Concert For New York City* CD Columbia C2K 86270 released November 2001 / DVD SMV 54205 9 released 2002

Eric Clapton: guitar, vocals
Buddy Guy: guitar, vocals
Paul Shaffer: keyboards
Will Lee: bass
Anton Fig: drums

Everything's Gonna Be Alright *The Concert For New York City* CD Columbia C2K 86270 released November 2001 / DVD SMV 54205 9 released 2002

Eric Clapton: guitar, vocals
Buddy Guy: guitar, vocals
Paul Shaffer: keyboards
Will Lee: bass
Anton Fig:P drums

Let It Be (all-star finale) *The Concert For New York City* CD Columbia C2K 86270 released November 2001 / DVD SMV 54205 9 released 2002

Paul McCartney: vocals, guitar, piano
Rusty Anderson: guitar
Gabe Dixon: keyboards
Abe Laboriel, Jr.: drums
Billy Joel: keyboards
Eric Clapton: guitar
Sheryl Crow: vocals
Roger Daltrey: vocals
Pete Townshend: vocals
Jon Bon Jovi: vocals
Melissa Etheridge: vocals
Richie Sambora: vocals
James Taylor: vocals
Five For Fighting: vocals
Backstreet Boys: vocals
Jersey Levy: strings

Freedom (all-star finale) *The Concert For New York City* CD Columbia C2K 86270 released November 2001 / DVD SMV 54205 9 released 2002

Paul McCartney: vocals, guitar, piano
Rusty Anderson: guitar
Gabe Dixon: keyboards
Abe Laboriel, Jr.: drums
Billy Joel: keyboards
Eric Clapton: guitar
Sheryl Crow: vocals
Roger Daltrey: vocals
Pete Townshend: vocals
Jon Bon Jovi: vocals
Melissa Etheridge: vocals

Richie Sambora: vocals
James Taylor: vocals
Five For Fighting: vocals
Backstreet Boys: vocals
Jessey Levy: strings

Producers: Don DeVito / Bob Clearmountain /
Chuck Plotkin / Thom Cadley
Filmed by: MTV Remote Recording Services
Audio recorded by: Silver Studio Remote
Recording Services

REPTILE JAPAN TOUR 2001

BAND LINEUP:

Eric Clapton: guitar, vocals
Nathan East: bass, vocals
Andy Fairweather Low: guitar, vocals
Steve Gadd: drums
David Sancious: keyboards, vocals, guitar
Greg Phillinganes: keyboards, vocals

NOVEMBER 2001

19 November 2001, Castle Hall, Osaka, Japan

SETLIST: Key To The Highway / Reptile / Got You On My Mind / Tears In Heaven / Layla (acoustic) / Bell Bottom Blues / Change The World / My Father's Eyes / River Of Tears / Going Down Slow / She's Gone / I Want A Little Girl / Badge / Hoochie Coochie Man / Have You Ever Loved A Woman / Cocaine / Wonderful Tonight / Layla (electric) / Sunshine Of Your Love / Somewhere Over The Rainbow

21 November 2001, Castle Hall, Osaka, Japan

SETLIST: Key To The Highway / Reptile / Got You On My Mind / Tears In Heaven / Layla (acoustic) / Bell Bottom Blues / Change The World / My Father's Eyes / River Of Tears / Going Down Slow / She's Gone / I Want A Little Girl / Badge / Hoochie Coochie Man / Stormy Monday / Cocaine / Wonderful Tonight / Layla (electric) / Sunshine Of Your Love

22 November 2001, Castle Hall, Osaka, Japan

SETLIST: Key To The Highway / Reptile / Got You On My Mind / Tears In Heaven / Layla (acoustic) / Bell Bottom Blues / Change The World / River Of Tears / Going Down Slow / She's Gone / I Want A Little Girl / Badge / Hoochie Coochie Man / Five Long Years / Cocaine / Wonderful Tonight / Layla (electric) / Sunshine Of Your Love / Somewhere Over The Rainbow

Handbill for Eric's Japan tour in 2001.

SETLIST: Key To The Highway / Reptile / Got You On My Mind / Tears In Heaven / Layla (acoustic) / Bell Bottom Blues / Change The World / River Of Tears / Going Down Slow / She's Gone / I Want A Little Girl / Badge / Hoochie Coochie Man / Have You Ever Loved A Woman / Cocaine / Wonderful Tonight / Layla (electric) / Sunshine Of Your Love / Somewhere Over The Rainbow

26 November 2001, Marine Messe, Fukuoka, Japan

SETLIST: Key To The Highway / Reptile / Got You On My Mind / Tears In Heaven / Layla (acoustic) / Bell Bottom Blues / Change The World / River Of Tears / Going Down Slow / She's Gone / I Want A Little Girl / Badge

/ Hoochie Coochie Man / Stormy Monday / Cocaine / Wonderful Tonight / Layla (electric) / Sunshine Of Your Love / Somewhere Over The Rainbow

28 November 2001, Budokan, Tokyo, Japan

SETLIST: Key To The Highway / Reptile / Got You On My Mind / Tears In Heaven / Layla (acoustic) / Bell Bottom Blues / Change The World / River Of Tears / Going Down Slow / She's Gone / I Want A Little Girl / Badge / Hoochie Coochie Man / Have You Ever Loved A Woman / Cocaine / Wonderful Tonight / Layla (electric) / Sunshine Of Your Love / Somewhere Over The Rainbow

29 November 2001, Budokan, Tokyo, Japan

SETLIST: Key To The Highway / Reptile / Got You On My Mind / Tears In Heaven / Layla (acoustic) / Bell Bottom Blues / Change The World / River Of Tears / Going Down Slow / She's Gone / I Want A Little Girl / Badge / Hoochie Coochie Man / Stormy Monday / Cocaine / Wonderful Tonight / Layla (electric) / Sunshine Of Your Love / Somewhere Over The Rainbow

30 November 2001, Budokan, Tokyo, Japan

SETLIST: Key To The Highway / / Got You On My Mind / Tears In Heaven / Layla (acoustic) / Bell Bottom Blues / Change The World / River Of Tears / Going Down Slow / She's Gone / I Want A Little Girl / Badge / Hoochie Coochie Man / Have You Ever Loved A Woman / Cocaine / Wonderful Tonight / Layla (electric) / Sunshine Of Your Love / Somewhere Over The Rainbow

DECEMBER 2001

3 December 2001, Budokan, Tokyo, Japan

SETLIST: Key To The Highway / Reptile / Got You On My Mind / Tears In Heaven / Layla (acoustic) / Bell Bottom Blues / Change The World / River Of Tears / Going Down Slow / She's Gone / I Want A Little Girl / Badge / Hoochie Coochie Man / Have You Ever Loved A Woman / Cocaine / Wonderful Tonight / Layla (electric) / Sunshine Of Your Love / Somewhere Over The Rainbow

4 December 2001, Budokan, Tokyo, Japan (concert is broadcast on Japanese television)

The show is recorded as well as filmed and some tracks from this concert appear on the *One More Car, One More Rider* double CD.

SETLIST: Key To The Highway / Reptile / Got You On My Mind / Tears In Heaven / Layla (acoustic) / Bell Bottom Blues / Change The World / River Of Tears / Going Down Slow / She's Gone / I Want A Little Girl / Badge / Hoochie Coochie Man / Five Long Years / Cocaine / Wonderful Tonight / Layla (electric) / Sunshine Of Your Love / Somewhere Over The Rainbow

5 December 2001, Budokan, Tokyo, Japan

SETLIST: Key To The Highway / Reptile / Got You On My Mind / Tears In Heaven / Layla (acoustic) / Bell Bottom Blues / Change The World / River Of Tears / Going Down Slow / She's Gone / I Want A Little Girl / Badge / Hoochie Coochie Man / Stormy Monday / Cocaine / Wonderful Tonight / Layla (electric) / Sunshine Of Your Love / Somewhere Over The Rainbow

8 December 2001, Grandy 21, Sendai, Japan

SETLIST: Key To The Highway / Reptile / Got You On My Mind / Tears In Heaven / Layla (acoustic) / Bell Bottom Blues / Change The World / River Of Tears / Going Down Slow / She's Gone / I Want A Little Girl / Badge / Hoochie Coochie Man / Have You Ever Loved A Woman / Cocaine / Wonderful Tonight / Layla (electric) / Sunshine Of Your Love / Somewhere Over The Rainbow

10 December 2001, Budokan, Tokyo, Japan

SETLIST: Key To The Highway / Reptile / Got You On My Mind / Tears In Heaven / Layla (acoustic) / Bell Bottom Blues / Change The World / My Father's Eyes / River Of Tears / Going Down Slow / She's Gone / I Want A Little Girl / Badge / Hoochie Coochie Man / Have You Ever Loved A Woman / Cocaine / Wonderful Tonight / Layla (electric) / Sunshine Of Your Love / Somewhere Over The Rainbow

11 December 2001, Budokan, Tokyo, Japan

SETLIST: Key To The Highway / Reptile / Got You On My Mind / Tears In Heaven / Layla (acoustic) / Bell Bottom Blues / Change The World / My Father's Eyes / River Of Tears / Going Down Slow / She's Gone / I Want A Little Girl / Badge / Hoochie Coochie Man / Five Long Years / Cocaine / Wonderful Tonight / Layla (electric) / Sunshine Of Your Love / Somewhere Over The Rainbow

14 December 2001, Yokohama Arena, Yokohama, Japan

SETLIST: Key To The Highway / Reptile / Got You On My Mind / Tears In Heaven / Layla (acoustic) / Bell Bottom Blues / Change The World / River Of Tears / Going Down Slow / She's Gone / I Want A Little Girl / Badge / Hoochie Coochie Man / Stormy Monday / Cocaine / Wonderful Tonight / Layla (electric) / Sunshine Of Your Love / Somewhere Over The Rainbow

15 December 2001, Yokohama Arena, Yokohama, Japan

SETLIST: Key To The Highway / Reptile / Got You On My Mind / Tears In Heaven / Layla (acoustic) / Bell Bottom Blues / Change The World / My Father's Eyes / River Of Tears / Going Down Slow / She's Gone / I Want A Little Girl / Badge / Hoochie Coochie Man / Five Long Years / Cocaine / Wonderful Tonight / Layla (electric) / Sunshine Of Your Love / Somewhere Over The Rainbow

NEW YEAR'S EVE DANCE 2001

31 December 2001, Woking Leisure Centre, Woking, Surrey

Eric and his band are called the Usual Band.

BAND LINEUP:
Eric Clapton: guitar, vocals
Andy Fairweather Low: guitar, vocals
Gary Brooker: keyboards, vocals
Dave Bronze: bass, vocals
Henry Spinetti: drums
Paul Carrack: organ, vocals

SETLIST 1: Tempted / Before You Accuse Me / Good Golly Miss Molly / Wonderful Tonight / I Heard It Through The Grapevine / You Win Again / If Paradise Is Half As Nice / Knock On Wood / You Can't Judge A

Book / Hi-Heel Sneakers / Hoochie Coochie Man / Little Queenie

SETLIST 2: Midnight Hour / A Whiter Shade Of Pale / Reconsider Baby / How Sweet It Is / Stranger In My Home Town / Bring It On Home To Me / Lay Down Sally / Gin House / Five Long Years / Cocaine / Whole Lotta Shakin' / Shake, Rattle And Roll

RECORDING SESSIONS 2001

OLYMPIC STUDIOS
117 Church Road, London
Session for Sun Artists tribute

FEBRUARY 2001

JUST WALKIN' IN THE RAIN (Johnny Bragg / Buddy Killen / Robert Riley) *Good Rockin' Tonight* CD Sire 31165-2 released October 2001

Eric Clapton: guitar, vocals
The Impressions: vocals

Producers: Eric Clapton / Simon Climie / Ahmet Ertegun
Engineer: Simon Climmie

ERIC CLAPTON GUEST SESSION

MASTERLINK STUDIOS
114 17th Avenue South, Nashville, Tennessee
Session for Jamie Oldaker
Mad Dogs and Okies

23 MAY 2001

WAIT TILL DADDY GETS HOME (Vince Gill / Bob DiPiero) *Mad Dogs and Okies* CD Concord CCD-2267-2 released 2005

Vince Gill: vocals, electric guitar, acoustic guitar
Eric Clapton: electric guitar
Jamie Oldaker: drums
Walt Richmond: piano
Casey Van Beck: bass
Martin Crutchfield: guitar
Bekka Bramlett: backing vocals
Jenny Gill: backing vocals

POSITIVELY (Willis Alan Ramsey) *Mad Dogs and Okies* CD Concord CCD-2267-2 released 2005

Eric Clapton: acoustic guitar

Jamie Oldaker: drums
Walt Richmond: piano
Casey Van Beck: bass
Martin Crutchfield: guitar
Willis Alan Ramsey: acoustic slide
Fisk Jubilee Singers: background vocals

Producer: Jamie Oldaker
Engineer: Bobby Morse

ERIC CLAPTON GUEST SESSION

HELICON MOUNTAIN RECORDING STUDIOS
Pyramid Room, 2 Station Mews Terrace, London
Session for Jools Holland

4 SEPTEMBER 2001

WHAT WOULD I DO WITHOUT YOU (Ray Charles) *Small World Big Band*
CD Warner Bros. 0927 426562 released December 2001

Eric Clapton: guitar
Jools Holland: keyboards, vocals
Mark Flannagan: guitar
Gilson Lavis: drums
Dave Swift: bass
Chris Holland: organ
Jon Scott: trumpet
Jason McDermid: trumpet
Winston Rollins: trombone
Phil Veacock: saxophone
Michael Rose: saxophone
Lisa Grahame: saxophone
Pete Long: saxophone
Jackie Norrie: violin
Sally Herbert: violin
Anna Hemery: violin
Anne Stephenson: violin
Gina Ball: violin
Jayne Spencer: violin
Brian Wright: violin
Marina Solarek: violin
Dinah Beamish: cello
Nick Cooper: cello
Emily Burridge: cello
Alex Garnet: saxophone
Ray Gelato: saxophone
Abigail Trundle: cello
Jeff Moore: violin
Fenella Barton: violin
Anne Wood: violin
Julia Singleton: violin

Producer: Laurie Latham
Engineer: Laurie Latham

ERIC CLAPTON GUEST SESSION

QUAD STUDIOS
723 Seventh Avenue, New York City
Session for Paul McCartney

21 OCTOBER 2001

FREEDOM (Paul McCartney) CD single Parlaphone RS 6567 released November 2001 / hidden track on *Driving Rain* CD Parlaphone 535 5102 released November 2001

Paul McCartney: vocals, acoustic guitar, bass guitar
Rusty Anderson: rhythm guitar
Eric Clapton: lead guitar
Abe Laboriel, Jr.: drums

Producer: David Kahne

ERIC CLAPTON GUEST SESSION

HIROSHI FUJIWARA'S HOME STUDIO
Tokyo, Japan
Session for Hiroshi Fujiwara

DECEMBER 2001

MIME (Eric Clapton / Hiroshi Fujiwara) *Mellow Works Of Hiroshi Fujiwara* Victor VICL-61065 released March 2003

MIME (Alternate version) (Eric Clapton / Hiroshi Fujiwara) unreleased (only broadcst once on J-Wave on 20 March 2002 during an interview with Hiroshi Fujiwara)

MIME (K.U.D.O Remix) (Eric Clapton / Hiroshi Fujiwara) *Cappuccino* Victor VICL-61665 released January 2006

SKILL TACTICS (Eric Clapton / Hiroshi Fujiwara) unreleased

Hiroshi Fujiwara: guitar
Eric Clapton: guitar

Hiroshi Fujiwara is a very cool guy. In the eighties he was already an experienced DJ and had a good knowledge of hip hop. After visiting London he embraced the vibrancy of the punk scene, but was disappointed by the music he heard in clubs. He met Malcolm McLaren who advised him to visit New York where hip hop had a more healthy undergound scene than London. Once there he was influenced by the hip hop, skateboarding, and surfboard fashion culture, mainly Shawn Stussy. He brought back to Tokyo his melting pot of influences from his travels as a young man and became the leading light of the Harajuku fashion movement helping give exposure to brands and shops in the area. The importance of Harajuku was that it connected street culture to the fashion world. In 1996 he opened Ready Made, his first store in Harajuku. On top of his many other talents, he is also an accomplished guitarist.

Eric was a big fan of the famous Pride fights in Japan and had made numerous visits to Tokyo to see the events throughout 2000 and 2001. At the Tokyo Dome finals on 1 May 2000 Eric was on hand to deliver flowers to the fighters. When he was asked to write some music for a Pride event he was delighted to help. It was a collaboration with Hiroshi Fujiwara. "Skill Tactics" was the uptempo opening number which remains unreleased at the time of this writing. "Mime" was the mellow closing number and can be found on both *Mellow Works Of Hiroshi Fujiwara* and on the "Cappuccino" single.

20

2002
PARTY AT THE PALACE 2002

3 June 2002, Buckingham Palace, London

The year 2002 was the year of the Queen's Golden Jubilee and the whole of the UK was celebrating. To mark the occasion a huge concert was organized in the gardens at Buckingham Palace where Eric joined an all-star cast. Lucky ticket-holders had been allocated invitations by ballot to gain entry to the concert. It is believed that over a million people gathered outside the Palace to watch the concert on special cinema-style screens set up in all the nearby London parks and along the Mall.

Eric first came on stage during the early evening to join Brian Wilson midway through a medley of Beach Boys numbers. Eric plugged in and the two sang together on "The Warmth of the Sun."

Later in the evening, Eric delighted everyone by playing an electric version of "Layla."

The house band for the evening included Clapton regulars Phil Palmer on guitar, Pino Pallindino on bass, Ray Cooper on percussion, and Phil Collins on drums.

The evening culminated with Paul McCartney who sang a cheeky acoustic version of "Her Majesty" followed by "Blackbird." Beatles producer George Martin then gave a tribute to the late George Harrison and Eric came back on stage joining Paul McCartney for a haunting performance of "While My Guitar Gently Weeps." Eric returned at the end for an all-cast sing-along of "All You Need Is Love" and "Hey Jude."

The whole show was televised live and edited highlights were released on CD and DVD.

AUGUST 2002

FERRARI AND MASERATI CONCERT 2002

3 August 2002, Brands Hatch Racing Circuit, Fawkham, Longfield, Kent

Eric headlined a Ferrari and Maserati Festival concert at the Brands Hatch Racetrack. He was accompanied by Gary Brooker, Andy Fairweather Low, Henry Spinetti, and Dave Bronze for a storming show of old favorites as well as some well-chosen covers. Worth noting that Eric played his Gibson Byrdland for "Dust My Broom." Despite the torrential rain throughout most of the open-air show, Eric and the band put in a great set, highlighted by the appeareance of Albert Lee, his first live appearance with Eric in twenty years.

BAND LINEUP:
Eric Clapton: guitar, vocals
Gary Brooker: keyboards, vocals
Andy Fairweather Low: guitar, vocals
Albert Lee: guitar
Dave Bronze: bass
Henry Spinetti: drums

SETLIST: Knock On Wood / Reconsider Baby / Can't Judge A Book / Blue Monday / Sweet Little Rock 'N' Roller / Third Degree / If Paradise Is Half As Nice / Dust

My Broom / Knockin' On Heaven's Door / Good Golly Miss Molly / You Win Again / Got My Mojo Working / Hoochie Coochie Man / Mary Ann / Whole Lotta Shakin' / Gin House / Cocaine / Whiter Shade Of Pale / Five Long Years / Little Queenie / Shake, Rattle And Roll

OCTOBER 2002

CARL WILSON FOUNDATION CONCERT 2002

6 October 2002, UCLA Royce Hall, Los Angeles, California.

A benefit concert for the Carl Wilson Foundation, a multi-artist extravaganza, with different performers making several appearances throughout the evening. This year's concert was emceed by Van Dyke Parks.

BAND LINEUP:
Eric Clapton: guitar, vocals
Jeffrey Foskett: guitar
Bob Lizik: bass
Paul Mertens: saxophone
Darian Sahanaja: keyboards
Nik Wonder: guitar
Probyn Gregory: guitar,
Scott Bennett: keyboards
Jim Hines: drums
Mikey D'Amico: guitar

SETLIST: Stormy Monday / Layla

ALL-STAR BAND LINEUP:
Brian Wilson: vocals
Eric Clapton: guitar
Jeffrey Foskett: guitar, vocals, banjo, percussion
Bob Lizik: bass, vocals
Paul Mertens: woodwinds, harmonica, vocals, bass harmonica, bass flute, flute, piccolo, saxophone
Darian Sahanaja: keyboards, vibraphone, vocals
Nik Wonder: guitar, vocals
Probyn Gregory: guitar, French horn, trumpet, vocals, tannerin

Taylor Mills: vocals
Scott Bennett: vocals, keyboards, vibraphone, quinto, bicycle horn, tambourine
Jim Hines: drums
Mikey D'Amico: vocals, percussion, guitar
Matthew Sweet: backing vocals on encores "Surfin' U.S.A." and "Fun Fun Fun"
Carnie and Wendy Wilson: backing vocals on encores "Surfin' U.S.A." and "Fun Fun Fun"
Bill Medley: backing vocals on encores "Surfin' U.S.A." and "Fun Fun Fun"
Jackson Browne: backing vocals on encores "Surfin' U.S.A." and "Fun Fun Fun"
Dewey Bunnell: backing vocals on encores "Surfin' U.S.A." and "Fun Fun Fun"
Gerry Beckley backing vocals on encores "Surfin' U.S.A." and "Fun Fun Fun"

SETLIST: The Warmth Of The Sun / Good Vibrations / Barbara Ann / Surfin' U.S.A. / Fun Fun Fun

BET WALK OF FAME CONCERT 2002

19 October 2002, Black Entertainment Television's 8th Annual Walk Of Fame Gala, BET Studios 2, Washington, D.C.

This year's awardee was Stevie Wonder. His music touched the hearts of so many people spread over several generations and he was certainly deserving of all the accolades he'd already received. Eric was a big fan of Stevie's so he was thrilled to participate in the television tribute and actually got to play his favorite Stevie Wonder song in front of the man himself.

Eric played "Heaven Is 10 Zillion Light Years Away" followed by gospel stalwarts Kim Burrell and Fred Hammond singing "Heaven Help Us All" with Eric playing some cool guitar lines and solo.

The concert was broadcast on television on 29 October 2002.

SETLIST:

Heaven Is 10 Zillion Light Years Away (Stevie Wonder)
Eric Clapton: guitar, vocals
Reggie Young: guitar

Chris Vadala: saxophone
Dennis Wilson: trombone
Tommy Williams: trumpet
Chris Royal: trumpet
Greg Moore: keyboards
Charlie Young: bass
Fred Washington: bass
Leon Ndugu Chancler: drums
Munyungo Jackson: percussion
Patrick Gandy: piano
Kimberly Brewer: backing vocals
Keith John: backing vocals
Panzie Johnson: backing vocals
Lynne Linsey: backing vocals

Heaven Help Us All (Stevie Wonder)

Fred Hammond: vocals
Kim Burrell: vocals
Eric Clapton: guitar
Reggie Young: guitar
Chris Vadala: saxophone
Dennis Wilson: trombone
Tommy Williams: trumpet
Chris Royal: trumpet
Greg Moore: keyboards
Charlie Young: bass
Fred Washington: bass
Leon Ndugu Chancler: drums
Munyungo Jackson: percussion
Patrick Gandy: piano
Kimberly Brewer: backing vocals
Keith John: backing vocals
Panzie Johnson: backing vocals
Lynne Linsey: backing vocals
R.F.C. Choir

NOVEMBER 2002

CONCERT FOR GEORGE 2002

29 November, 2002, Royal Albert Hall, London

One of those "you should have been there" nights with Eric and an all-star band paying tribute to the late George Harrison at London's Royal Albert Hall. The music performed during the evening reflected George's musical tastes with Indian music, a little comedy from his Monty Python chums, and some of the world's finest rock musicians playing a stunning set comprised mainly of Harrison songs. The stage was bathed in flowers and the gentle relaxing scent of incense wafted through the hall. Eric came on stage and told the audience that the evening would be full of "beautiful music and warm feelings . . . a blessed occasion for me to share my love of George with you." Guests of honor were George's wife Olivia and their son, Dhani.

Eric was the musical director for the show and remained on stage for the majority of the concert, even joining the Ravi Shankar Orchestra in the first half of the concert playing some truly exceptional acoustic guitar soloing along with Ravi's forty-piece Indian orchestra. For the rock section of the evening, the house band consisted of Jeff Lynne, Andy Fairweather Low, Gary Brooker, Henry Spinetti, Albert Lee, Dhani Harrison, Chris Stainton, Jim Keltner, Ray Cooper, Jim Capaldi, and Dave Bronze. They were joined throughout the evening by Jools Holland, Sam Brown, Billy Preston, Paul McCartney, and Ringo Starr. Michael Kamen added orchestral arrangements to much of the set with a string orchestra. Among the many highlights for Eric Clapton fans was his beautifully melodic solo on "Isn't It A Pity." Another highlight was Paul McCartney and Eric on "Something" and "While My Guitar Gently Weeps." The concert finale consisted of Joe Brown playing an emotive version of "I'll See You In My Dreams" as red and yellow petals floated down from the ceiling. It was a fitting way to end a wonderful evening remembering George.

BAND LINEUP:
Eric Clapton: musical director, guitar, vocals
Dave Bronze: bass
Gary Brooker: keyboards
Jim Capaldi: drums
Ray Cooper: percussion
Andy Fairweather Low: guitar
Dhani Harrison: guitar
Jim Horn: tenor saxophone
Jim Keltner: drums
Marc Mann: guitar
Albert Lee: guitar
Katie Kissoon: backing vocals
Tessa Niles: backing vocals

SETLIST:

Sarve Shaam (traditional prayer, including a dedication by Ravi Shankar) *Concert For George* CD/DVD Warner Bros. released November 2003

Your Eyes (Ravi Shankar) *Concert For George* CD/DVD Warner Bros. released November 2003

```
Anoushka Shankar: sitar
Tanmoy Bose: tabla
```

The Inner Light (George Harrison) *Concert For George* CD/DVD Warner Bros. released November 2003

```
Anoushka Shankar: sitar
Jeff Lynne: lead vocals, acoustic guitar
Rajendara Prasanna: shahnai
Tanmoy Bose: tabla
Dhani Harrison: baking vocals, piano
```

Arpan (Ravi Shankar) *Concert For George* CD/DVD Warner Bros. released November 2003

```
Anoushka Shankar: sitar, conductor
Sukanya Shankar: vocal shloka
M. Balanchandar: mridangam
Rajendara Prasanna: shehnai
Vishwa Mohan Bhatt: mohan veena
Tanmoy Bose: tabla, dholak
Chandrasekhar, Balu Raghuraman: violins
Eric Clapton: acoustic guitar
Pedro Eustache: wind instruments
Sunil Gupta: flute
Anuradha Krishamurthi, O.S. Arun: lead vocals
Jane Lister: harp
Gaurav Mazumdar: sitar
Snehashish Mzumdar: mandolin
Ramesh Mishra: sarangi
Pirashanna Thevarajah: percussion
Kenji Ota: tanpura
Barry Phillips: cello
Emil Richards: marimba
Partho Sarathy: sarod
Hari Sivanesan, Sivaskti Sivanesan: veena
Boys and Girls Choir courtesy of Bharatiya
Vidya Bhavan
English Chamber Choir
London Metropolitan Orchestra (Andrew Brown,
Roger Chase, Chris Fish, Helen Hathorn, Lynda
Houghton, Ian Humphries, Zoe Martlew, Stella
Page, Debbie Widdup
Michael Kamen: string conductor, string
arrangements
```

Sit On My Face *Concert For George* DVD Warner Bros. released November 2003

The Lumberjack Song *Concert For George* DVD Warner Bros. released November 2003 (comic interlude with members of Monty Python: Michael Palin, Terry Jones, Eric Idle, and Terry Gilliam. Also performing are Neil Innes, Carol Cleveland, and Tom Hanks)

I Want to Tell You (Harrison) *Concert For George* CD/DVD Warner Bros. released November 2003

```
Jeff Lynne: lead vocals, rhythm guitar
```

If I Needed Someone (Harrison) *Concert For George* CD/DVD Warner Bros. released November 2003

```
Eric Clapton: lead vocals, rhythm guitar
```

Old Brown Shoe (George Harrison) *Concert For George* CD/DVD Warner Bros. released November 2003

```
Gary Brooker: lead vocals, electric piano
```

Give Me Love (Give Me Peace on Earth) (George Harrison) *Concert For George* CD/DVD Warner Bros. released November 2003

```
Jeff Lynne: lead vocals, acoustic guitar
```

Beware Of Darkness (George Harrison) *Concert For George* CD/DVD Warner Bros. released November 2003
```
Eric Clapton: lead vocals, rhythm guitar
```

Here Comes The Sun (George Harrison) *Concert For George* CD/DVD Warner Bros. released November 2003

```
Joe Brown: lead vocals, acoustic guitar
Neil Gauntlett: acoustic guitar
Dave "Rico" Nilo: bass
Phil Capaldi: drums
Andy Fairweather Low: electric guitar
```

That's The Way It Goes (George Harrison) *Concert For George* CD/DVD Warner Bros. released November 2003

```
Joe Brown: lead vocals, mandolin
Neil Gauntlett: slide guitar
Dave "Rico" Nilo: bass
Phil Capaldi: drums
```

Horse To The Water (George Harrison / Dhani Harrison) *Concert For George* DVD Warner Bros. released November 2003
```
Sam Brown: lead vocals
Jools Holland: piano
Jim Cipaldi: drums
```

Taxman (George Harrison) *Concert For George* CD/DVD Warner Bros. released November 2003

```
Tom Petty: lead vocals, rhythm guitar
Mike Campbell: lead guitar
Benmont Tench: electric piano
```

Ron Blair: bass
Steve Ferrone: drums
Scott Thurston: backing vocals, rythm guitar

I Need You (George Harrison) *Concert For George* CD/DVD Warner Bros. released November 2003

Tom Petty: lead vocals, 12-string acoustic rhythm guitar
Mike Campbell: lead guitar
Benmont Tench: electric piano
Ron Blair: bass
Steve Ferrone: drums
Scott Thurston: backing vocals, rhythm guitar

Handle With Care (George Harrison / Jeff Lynne / Roy Orbison / Tom Petty / Bob Dylan) *Concert For George* CD/DVD Warner Bros. released November 2003

Tom Petty: lead vocals, 12-string acoustic rhythm guitar
Jeff Lynne: lead vocals, rhythm guitar
Dhani Harrison: acoustic rhythm guitar
Scott Thurston: backing vocals, rhythm guitar, harmonica
Mike Campbell: lead guitar
Benmont Tench: electric piano
Ron Blair: bass
Steve Ferrone: drums
Jim Keltner: drums

Isn't It A Pity (George Harrison) *Concert For George* CD/DVD Warner Bros. released November 2003

Billy Preston: lead vocals, Hammond B3 organ
Eric Clapton: lead vocals, lead guitar

Photograph (Richard Starkey/George Harrison) *Concert For George* CD/DVD Warner Bros. released November 2003

Ringo Starr: lead vocals
Jim Horn: saxophone solo

Honey Don't (Carl Perkins) *Concert For George* CD/DVD Warner Bros. released November 2003

Ringo Starr: lead vocals
Albert Lee: lead guitar solo
Gary Brooker: piano solo
Billy Preston: Hammond B3 organ

For You Blue (George Harrison) *Concert For George* CD/DVD Warner Bros. released November 2003

Paul McCartney: lead vocals, acoustic guitar
Ringo Starr: drums
Marc Mann: slide guitar

Something (George Harrison) *Concert For George* CD/DVD Warner Bros. released November 2003

Paul McCartney: lead vocals, ukulele, acoustic rhythm guitar
Ringo Starr: drums
Eric Clapton: lead vocals, rhythm guitar
Marc Mann: lead guitar

All Things Must Pass (George Harrison) *Concert For George* CD/DVD Warner Bros. released November 2003

Paul McCartney: lead vocals, acoustic guitar
Ringo Starr: drums
Eric Clapton: acoustic guitar
Dhani Harrison: electric guitar

While My Guitar Gently Weeps (George Harrison) *Concert For George* CD/DVD Warner Bros. released November 2003

Eric Clapton: lead vocals, lead guitar
Paul McCartney: backing vocals, piano
Ringo Starr: drums
Dhani Harrison: acoustic guitar

My Sweet Lord (George Harrison) *Concert For George* CD/DVD Warner Bros. released November 2003

Billy Preston: lead vocals, Hammond B3 organ
Paul McCartney: piano
Eric Clapton: 12-string acoustic guitar
Dhani Harrison: backing vocals, acoustic guitar

Wah-Wah (George Harrison) *Concert For George* CD/DVD Warner Bros. released November 2003

Eric Clapton: rhythm guitar
Jeff Lynne: acoustic rhythm guitar
Billy Preston: lead vocals, Hammond B3 organ

I'll See You in My Dreams (Isham Jones / Gus Kahn) *Concert For George* CD/DVD Warner Bros. released November 2003

Joe Brown: lead vocals, ukulele
Neil Gauntlett: acoustic guitar
Dave "Rico" Nilo: bass
Jim Capaldi: drums

Producer: Jeff Lynne
Engineer: Ryan Ulyate

DECEMBER 2002

FERRARI CHRISTMAS PARTY 2002

14 December 2002, Palamalaguti di Bologna, Italy (Ferrari President Luca di Montezemolo and around 900 Ferrari staff, including team boss Jean Todt, race-pilots Michael Schumacher and Rubens Barrichello, and test drivers Luca Badoer and Luciano Burti, celebrated another successful year's work at the traditional Christmas party on the weekend of 13 December 2002 where special guests like Eric Clapton played)

BAND LINEUP:
Eric Clapton: guitar, vocals
Andy Fairweather Low: guitar, vocals
Dhani Harrison: guitar, vocals
Dave Bronze: bass
Gary Brooker: keyboards, vocals
Henry Spinetti: drums

SETLIST[1]**:** Knock On Wood / Reconsider Baby / Good Golly Miss Molly / You Win Again / Five Long Years / Wonderful Tonight / If I Needed Someone / Gin House / Whole Lotta Shakin' Goin' On / While My Guitar Gently Weeps / Stormy Monday / Cocaine / Whiter Shade of Pale / Layla / Little Queenie

[1]Courtesy of *Where's Eric* fan club magazine

DUNSFOLD CHARITY CONCERT 2002

20 December 2002, Dunsfold Village Hall, Dunsfold, Surrey (Eric turned up unannounced to play with his old friends No Stiletto Shoes. Although he remained seated throughout much of the set, Eric contributed some lovely guitar work, most notably on "Five Long Years" and "Gin House")

BAND LINEUP:
Eric Clapton: guitar, vocals
Gary Brooker: keyboards, vocals
Andy Fairweather Low: guitar, vocals

Nick Pentelow: saxophone
Dave Bronze: bass
Henry Spinetti: drums

SETLIST: Blueberry Hill / Gin House / Five Long Years / Can't Judge A Book / Good Golly Miss Molly / Whiter Shade Of Pale / Little Queenie / Shake, Rattle And Roll

NEW YEAR'S EVE DANCE 2002

31 December 2002, Woking Leisure Centre, Woking, Surrey

Eric and his band are called the Usual Band, as they had been in 2001.

BAND LINEUP:
Eric Clapton: guitar, vocals
Gary Brooker: piano, vocals
Andy Fairweather Low: guitar, vocals
Henry Spinetti: drums
Dave Bronze: bass, vocals

SETLIST 1: Knock On Wood / Reconsider Baby / Good Golly Miss Molly / Blueberry Hill / Five Long Years / Wonderful Tonight / Shake, Rattle And Roll / If Paradise Is Half As Nice / Cocaine

SETLIST 2: In The Midnight Hour / Can't Judge A Book / Gin House / While My Guitar Gently Weeps / Lay Down Sally / It's Only Make Believe / Whole Lotta Shakin' / Stormy Monday / Sweet Little Rock And Roller / Whiter Shade Of Pale / Layla / Little Queenie

RECORDING SESSIONS 2002
ERIC CLAPTON GUEST SESSION

ROCCABELLA STUDIOS
Cranleigh, Surrey
Session for Ringo Starr

JUNE 2002

NEVER WITHOUT YOU (Richard Starkey / Mark Hudson / Gary Nicholson) *Ringo Rama* CD KCH KOC-CD-8429 released March 2003 (the song is about George Harrison)

> "Eric's on two tracks on the album, but I really wanted him on this song because George loved Eric and Eric loved George. I wanted Eric to come and play that solo because I only wanted people on the track who George knew and loved."
>
> —RINGO STARR

IMAGINE ME THERE (Richard Starkey / Mark Hudson / Gary Burr) *Ringo Rama* CD KCH KOC-CD-8429 released March 2003

On the deluxe edition of *Ringo Rama*, you get a DVD with footage of Eric at the session as well as the guests.

Ringo Starr: drums, vocals
Eric Clapton: guitar
Mark Hudson: electric guitar, Wurlitzer organ, mellotron, keyboards, bass, background vocals
Charlie Hadon: upright bass on "Imagine Me There"
Gary Burr: acoustic guitar, bass, background vocals
Steve Dudas: guitar
Dean Grakal: 12-string acoustic guitar
Jim Cox: keyboards
Gary Nicholson: guitar

Producer: Mark Hudson

ERIC CLAPTON GUEST SESSION

SWEET TEA STUDIOS
700 Jackson Avenue East,
Oxford, Mississippi
Session for Buddy Guy

JULY 2002

CRAWLIN' KINGSNAKE (John Lee Hooker / Bernard Besman) *Blues Singer* CD Silvertone 01241-41843-2 released June 2003

Buddy Guy: guitar, vocals
Eric Clapton: acoustic lead guitar

B.B. King: acoustic lead guitar
Jim Keltner: drums
Jimbo Mathus: acoustic guitar
Tony Garnier: upright bass
The Perrys: handclaps

LUCY MAE (Frankie Lee Sims) *Blues Singer* CD Silvertone 01241-41843-2 released June 2003

Buddy Guy: guitar, vocals
Eric Clapton: acoustic lead guitar
Jim Keltner: drums
Jimbo Mathus: acoustic guitar
Tony Garnier: upright bass

Producer: Dennis Herring
Engineer: Jacquire King

ERIC CLAPTON GUEST SESSION

OCEAN WAY RECORDING
6050 Sunset Boulevard,
Los Angeles, California
Session for the
Crusaders

OCTOBER 2002

RURAL RENEWAL (Joe Sample) *Rural Renewal* CD US Verve 440 060 077-2 / UK 060 077-2 released March 2003

CREEPIN' (Joe Sample) *Rural Renewal* CD US Verve 440 060 077-2 / UK 060 077-2 released March 2003

Eric Clapton: electric guitar on "Creepin'," acoustic guitar on "Rural Renewal"
Freddie Washington: bass
"Stix" Hooper: drums
Dean Parks: guitar
Ray Parker, Jr.: guitar
Joe Sample: keyboards
Wilton Felder: tenor saxophone
Steve Baxter: trombone
Lenny Castro: percussion

Producer: Stewart Levine
Engineer: Rik Pekkonen

ERIC CLAPTON GUEST SESSION

OLYMPIC STUDIOS
117 Church Road,London

Guitar overdub for Kelly Price

DECEMBER 2002

AGAIN (Kelly Price) *Priceless* CD Def Soul 586 777-2 released April 2003

Kelly Price: vocals
Eric Clapton: guitar
Nunzio Signore: guitar
Bryon Sowell: keyboards
Jason Gaines: programming

Producer: Kelly Price
Eric's solo recorded by: Simon Climie

OLYMPIC STUDIOS 117 Church Road, London Session for *Conception: An Interpretation of Stevie Wonder's Songs*

DECEMBER 2002

HIGHER GROUND (Stevie Wonder) *Conception: An Interpretation of Stevie Wonder's Songs* CD Motown released March 2003

Eric Clapton: guitar, vocals
Billy Preston: clavinet, Hammond B3 organ
Nathan East: bass
Abe Laboriel, Jr.: drums
Jim Keltner: percussion

Producers: Eric Clapton / Simon Climie
Engineer: Alan Douglas

21

2003

The year started pretty quietly with a few charity shows, including an "unplugged" appearance at Eric's daughter's school in Sheffield. That was followed with a headlining concert at the Royal Albert Hall for Teenage Cancer Trust.

Eric accepted an invitation by Willie Nelson to play with him at the Beacon Theater in New York in April at a special concert celebrating Nelson's 70th birthday. The event was recorded and filmed.

Eric continued pretty much in the same way the year started by appearing at various charity concerts. Perhaps the most significant, not to mention anticipated, was a live reunion with his old boss, John Mayall, for UNICEF. This happened in Liverpool on 18 July and fans traveled from all over the globe to attend this special one-off show. Fans unable to attend the show were able to listen and watch it later as it was recorded and filmed. Mick Taylor and Chris Barber also played.

Eric was aware that at some point this year he would need to record a new album. He made plans to spend some of the summer alone at his house just outside Cannes in the South of France to write some new songs. Hoping to come away with at least six songs, he found the whole process difficult and eventually came away with only one song, "Run Home To Me." When Eric and his band entered the studio, the new album was temporarily put on hold in favor of recording a tribute album to Robert Johnson. It happened in an organic fashion and was certainly one of the best moves Eric made giving him a genuine passion that would be reflected on his hugely successful tour in 2004.

MARCH 2003

BIRKDALE SCHOOL 2003

18 March 2003, Birkdale School, Sheffield, South Yorkshire (Eric delighted pupils and parents at Sheffield's Birkdale School by hosting an evening of chat and music to raise money for the school and the Crossroads Centre in Antigua. His daughter, Ruth, was a pupil at the school. The show took place in the school hall where 790 lucky people witnessed a very special evening. Eric talked extensively about his life, music, and career, and his talk was interspersed with songs played on an acoustic guitar. At the end of the evening the audience was invited to ask questions which Eric was happy to answer. When finished he recieved a standing ovation for his talk and performance.

SETLIST: Nobody Knows You When You're Down And Out / Ramblin' On My Mind / Crossroads / Layla / Wonderful Tonight / Signe (partial) / Tears In Heaven

TEENAGE CANCER TRUST CONCERT 2003

25 March 2003, Royal Albert Hall, London (Teenage Cancer Trust Benefit Concert)

BAND LINEUP:
Eric Clapton: guitar, vocals
Andy Fairweather Low: guitar, vocals
Gary Brooker: keyboards, vocals

Henry Spinetti: drums
Dave Bronze: bass

Eric and his friends (No Stiletto Shoes) played to a packed Albert Hall as part of a special week of charity concerts which raised money for the Teenage Cancer Trust. A support set by Nigel Kennedy which overran by at least thirty minutes caused much annoyance in the crowd, not to mention backstage where Eric's crew were waiting to set up. But the little punk violinist simply kept ignoring signs from side stage to terminate his set. The end result was a shorter show by Eric, who played a mixture of hits, covers, and classics, to the delight of the crowd.

Eric Clapton, Royal Albert Hall, 25 March 2003.

SETLIST: Knock on Wood / Reconsider Baby / Can't Judge A Book / Blueberry Hill / Sweet Little Rock And Roller / Stormy Monday / If Paradise Is Half As Nice / Good Golly Miss Molly / You Win Again / Got My Mojo Workin' / Hoochie Coochie Man / Whole Lotta Shakin' / Gin House / Five Long Years / Cocaine / Whiter Shade of Pale / Layla / Little Queenie

APRIL 2003

WILLIE NELSON'S 70th BIRTHDAY CONCERT 2003

9 April 2003, Beacon Theater, New York City

Special concert celebrating Willie Nelson's 70th birthday. The nearly five-hour event was highlighted by Shania Twain and Toby Keith wheeling a guitar-shaped cake on stage to lead a rousing rendition of "Happy Birthday" for Willie Nelson. Also on stage were Lyle Lovett, Sheryl Crow, John Mellencamp, Kris Kristofferson, Kenny Chesney, Elvis Costello, Diana Krall, Leon Russell, Norah Jones, Steven Tyler, and Paul Shaffer.

The concert was filmed and recorded by USA Network which aired an edited version of the show as *Willie Nelson & Friends* on 26 May 2003.

Among the musical highlights was a duet between Willie Nelson and Eric Clapton on the song "Night Life" featuring some trademark blues guitar from Eric. The duet was by far the crowd's favorite of the night.

SETLIST:

NIGHT LIFE (Walt Breeland / Paul Buskirk / Willie Nelson) Willie Nelson & Friends Live & Kickin' CD Lost Highway B0000453-02IN04 2003 / *Willie Nelson & Friends Live & Kickin'* DVD Lost Highway released June 2003

MAY 2003

PAVAROTTI AND FRIENDS 2003

27 May 2003, Parco Novi Sad, Modena, Italy

Annual *Pavarotti and Friends* concert. This year the concert raised funds for the United Nations work on behalf of uprooted Iraqis under the banner "SOS Iraq." Although the show is filmed and recorded, the songs with Eric have not been released. Other artists who performed at the concert included Bono, Lionel Richie, Ricky Martin, Queen, Zucchero Fornaciari and Laura Pausini. The whole show was broadcast live on Italian television.

SETLIST: Stormy Monday / Holy Mother

JUNE 2003

BLOWIN' THE BLUES AWAY CONCERT 2003

2 June 2003, Apollo Theater, New York City

BAND LINEUP:

Wynton Marsalis: trumpet

Richard Johnson: piano

Reginald Veal: bass

Herlin Riley: drums

Victor Goines: tenor saxophone, clarinet

Wessell "Warm Daddy" Anderson: alto saxophone

Ronald Westray: trombone

SETLIST: I'm Not Rough[1] / Nobody Knows You When You're Down And Out[1] / Everyday I Have The Blues[2]

[1]with Eric Clapton
[2]with B.B. King and Eric Clapton
Recorded by: Remote Recording
Engineer: David Hewitt

B.B. King and Eric "Blowin' The Blues Away" at the Apollo Theater in New York on 2 June 2003.

> **"**One of the missions of Jazz at Lincoln Center is to document their events. Trying to capture the energy of an event featuring artists of this magnitude is hard under any circumstances. Remote Recording helped to create a great sounding recording, clearly showing the roots of jazz in the blues, and the wide influence of the blues. I'm so glad I chose David Hewitt and Remote Recording, they made a great-sounding live two-track recording, as well as a full multi-track backup easy, and fun! Which, when you consider the music being played, seems dead on target.**"**
>
> —SAM BERKOW
> (of SIA Acoustics)

> **"**The wonderful thing about this show was that all these great musicians were there to support a musical genre that they love, with no thought of monetary reward. Where else are you going to hear Willie Nelson play 'Milk Cow Blues' with the Wynton Marsalis Septet? It was a GALA in capital letters. Most fun I've had mixing a live-to-tape show in years!**"**
>
> —DAVID HEWITT

JULY 2003

LIVERPOOL POPS 2003

19 July 2003, Liverpool Pops, Liverpool King's Dock Arena, Liverpool

John Mayall and Friends including Eric Clapton played an exclusive concert for UNICEF at this year's Liverpool Summer Pops. It was the first show of *UNITE for UNICEF,* a concert series which aimed to raise awareness and generate funds for UNICEF UK's "End Child Exploitation Campaign."

BAND LINEUP:

John Mayall: vocals, organ, electric piano, harmonica

Eric Clapton: guitar, vocals on "Hoochie Coochie Man" and "Tore Down"

Joe Yuele: drums

Hank Van Sickle: bass

Tom Canning: keyboards

Buddy Whittington: guitar, vocals

Chris Barber: trombone[1]

Mick Taylor: guitar[2]

Eric Clapton reunites with John Mayall in Liverpool, 19 July 2003.

SETLIST:

No Big Hurry (John Mayall) *John Mayall 70th Birthday Concert* 2CD Eagle Records EDGCD246 / *John Mayall 70th Birthday Concert* DVD Eagle Rock released November 2003

Please Mr. Lofton[1] (John Mayall) *John Mayall 70th Birthday Concert* 2CD Eagle Records EDGCD246 / *John Mayall 70th Birthday Concert* DVD Eagle Rock released November 2003

Hideaway[1] (Freddie King, Sonny Thompson) *John Mayall 70th Birthday Concert* 2CD Eagle Records EDGCD246 / *John Mayall 70th Birthday Concert* DVD Eagle Rock released November 2003

All Your Love (Otis Rush) *John Mayall 70th Birthday Concert* 2CD Eagle Records EDGCD246 / *John Mayall 70th Birthday Concert* DVD Eagle Rock released November 2003

Have You Heard[1] (Lew Douglas, Charlie LaVere, Roy Rodde) *John Mayall 70th Birthday Concert* 2CD Eagle Records EDGCD246 / *John Mayall 70th Birthday Concert* DVD Eagle Rock released November 2003

Hoochie Coochie Man[1] (Willie Dixon) *John Mayall 70th Birthday Concert* 2CD Eagle Records EDGCD246 / *John Mayall 70th Birthday Concert* DVD Eagle Rock released November 2003

I'm Tore Down[1] (Thompson) *John Mayall 70th Birthday Concert* 2CD Eagle Records EDGCD246 / *John Mayall 70th Birthday Concert* DVD Eagle Rock released November 2003

Talk To Your Daughter[1] (A. Atkins / J.B. Lenoir) *John Mayall 70th Birthday Concert* 2CD Eagle Records EDGCD246 / *John Mayall 70th Birthday Concert* DVD Eagle Rock released November 2003

Producer: David Z / John Mayall

JUST FOR YOU JAPAN TOUR 2003

NOVEMBER 2003

BAND LINEUP:
Eric Clapton: guitar, vocals
Andy Fairweather Low: guitar, vocals
Nathan East: bass, vocals

Steve Gadd: drums
Chris Stainton: keyboards

15 November 2003, Green Arena, Hiroshima, Japan

SETLIST: Nobody Knows You When You're Down And Out / When You Got A Good Friend / Crossroads / I Shot The Sheriff / Bell Bottom Blues / Reconsider Baby / Can't Find My Way Home / White Room / I Want A Little Girl / Got My Mojo Working / Hoochie Coochie Man / Change The World / Before You Accuse Me / Kind Hearted Woman / Badge / Holy Mother / My Father's Eyes / River Of Tears / Lay Down Sally / Wonderful Tonight / Cocaine / Five Long Years / Knockin' On Heaven's Door / Layla / Sunshine Of Your Love / Somewhere Over The Rainbow

17 November 2003, Castle Hall, Osaka, Japan

SETLIST: When You Got A Good Friend / Crossroads / I Shot The Sheriff / Bell Bottom Blues / Reconsider Baby / Can't Find My Way Home / White Room / I Want A Little Girl / Got My Mojo Working / Hoochie Coochie Man / Change The World / Five Long Years / Kind Hearted Woman / Badge / Holy Mother / Lay Down Sally / Wonderful Tonight / Cocaine / Knockin' On Heaven's Door / Layla / Sunshine Of Your Love / Somewhere Over The Rainbow

19 November 2003, Castle Hall, Osaka, Japan

Handbill for Eric Clapton's tour of Japan in 2003.

SETLIST: When You Got A Good Friend / Crossroads / I Shot The Sheriff / Bell Bottom Blues / Reconsider Baby / Can't Find My Way Home / White Room / I Want A Little Girl / Got My Mojo Working / Hoochie Coochie

Man / Change The World / Five Long Years / Kind Hearted Woman / Badge / Holy Mother / Lay Down Sally / Wonderful Tonight / Coca ine / Knockin' On Heaven's Door / Layla / Sunshine Of Your Love / Somewhere Over The Rainbow

20 November 2003, Castle Hall, Osaka, Japan

SETLIST: When You Got A Good Friend / Crossroads / I Shot The Sheriff / Bell Bottom Blues / Reconsider Baby / Can't Find My Way Home / White Room / I Want A Little Girl / Got My Mojo Working / Hoochie Coochie Man / Change The World / Five Long Years / Kind Hearted Woman / Badge / River Of Tears / Lay Down Sally / Wonderful Tonight / Cocaine / Knockin' On Heaven's Door / Layla / Sunshine Of Your Love / Somewhere Over The Rainbow

22 November 2003, Rainbow Hall, Nagoya, Japan

SETLIST: When You Got A Good Friend / Crossroads / I Shot The Sheriff / Bell Bottom Blues / Reconsider Baby / Can't Find My Way Home / White Room / I Want A Little Girl / Got My Mojo Working / Hoochie Coochie Man / Change The World / Five Long Years / Badge / River Of Tears / Lay Down Sally / Wonderful Tonight / Cocaine / Knockin' On Heaven's Door / Layla / Sunshine Of Your Love / Somewhere Over The Rainbow

24 November 2003, Saitama Super Arena, Saitama, Japan

SETLIST: When You Got A Good Friend / Crossroads / I Shot The Sheriff / Bell Bottom Blues / Reconsider Baby / Can't Find My Way Home / White Room / I Want A Little Girl / Got My Mojo Working / Hoochie Coochie Man / Change The World / Kind Hearted Woman / Badge / Holy Mother / Lay Down Sally / Wonderful Tonight / Cocaine / Knockin' On Heaven's Door / Layla / Sunshine Of Your Love / Somewhere Over The Rainbow

26 November 2003, Yokohama Arena, Yokohama, Japan

SETLIST: When You Got A Good Friend / Crossroads / I Shot The Sheriff / Bell Bottom Blues / Reconsider Baby / Can't Find My Way Home / White Room / I Want A Little Girl / Got My Mojo Working / Hoochie Coochie Man / Change The World / Before You Accuse Me / Badge / River Of Tears / Lay Down Sally / Wonderful Tonight /

Cocaine / Knockin' On Heaven's Door / Layla / Sunshine Of Your Love / Somewhere Over The Rainbow

27 November 2003, Yokohama Arena, Yokohama, Japan

SETLIST: When You Got A Good Friend / Crossroads / I Shot The Sheriff / Bell Bottom Blues / Reconsider Baby / Can't Find My Way Home / White Room / I Want A Little Girl / Got My Mojo Working / Hoochie Coochie Man / Change The World / Before You Accuse Me / Kind Hearted Woman / Badge / Holy Mother / Lay Down Sally / Wonderful Tonight / Cocaine / Layla / Sunshine Of Your Love / Somewhere Over The Rainbow

29 November 2003, Budokan, Tokyo, Japan

SETLIST: When You Got A Good Friend / Crossroads / I Shot The Sheriff / Bell Bottom Blues / Reconsider Baby / Can't Find My Way Home / White Room / I Want A Little Girl / Got My Mojo Working / Hoochie Coochie Man / Change The World / Before You Accuse Me / Kind Hearted Woman / Badge / Holy Mother / Lay Down Sally / Wonderful Tonight / Cocaine / Layla / Sunshine Of Your Love / Somewhere Over The Rainbow

30 November 2003, Budokan, Tokyo, Japan

SETLIST: When You Got A Good Friend / Crossroads / I Shot The Sheriff / Bell Bottom Blues / Reconsider Baby / Can't Find My Way Home / White Room / I Want A Little Girl / Got My Mojo Working / Hoochie Coochie Man / Change The World / Before You Accuse Me / Kind Hearted Woman / Badge / River Of Tears / Lay Down Sally / Wonderful Tonight / Cocaine / Layla / Sunshine Of Your Love / Somewhere Over The Rainbow

DECEMBER 2003

2 December 2003, Budokan, Tokyo, Japan

SETLIST: When You Got A Good Friend / Crossroads / I Shot The Sheriff / Bell Bottom Blues / Reconsider Baby / Can't Find My Way Home / White Room / I Want A Little Girl / Got My Mojo Working / Hoochie Coochie Man / Change The World / Bright Lights, Big City / Kind Hearted Woman / Badge / Holy Mother / Lay Down Sally

/ Wonderful Tonight / Cocaine / Layla / Sunshine Of Your Love / Somewhere Over The Rainbow

3 December 2003, Budokan, Tokyo, Japan

SETLIST: When You Got A Good Friend / Crossroads / I Shot The Sheriff / Bell Bottom Blues / Reconsider Baby / Can't Find My Way Home / White Room / I Want A Little Girl / Got My Mojo Working / Hoochie Coochie Man / Change The World / Bright Lights, Big City / Kind Hearted Woman / Badge / Holy Mother / Lay Down Sally / Wonderful Tonight / Cocaine / Layla / Sunshine Of Your Love / Somewhere Over The Rainbow

5 December 2003, Grande 21, Sendai, Japan

SETLIST: When You Got A Good Friend / Crossroads / I Shot The Sheriff / Bell Bottom Blues / Reconsider Baby / Can't Find My Way Home / White Room / I Want A Little Girl / Got My Mojo Working / Hoochie Coochie Man / Change The World / Bright Lights, Big City / Kind Hearted Woman / Badge / Holy Mother / Lay Down Sally / Wonderful Tonight / Cocaine / Layla / Sunshine Of Your Love / Somewhere Over The Rainbow

7 December 2003, Sapporo Dome, Sapporo, Japan

SETLIST: When You Got A Good Friend / Crossroads / I Shot The Sheriff / Bell Bottom Blues / Reconsider Baby / Can't Find My Way Home / White Room / I Want A Little Girl / Got My Mojo Working / Hoochie Coochie Man / Change The World / Bright Lights, Big City / Kind Hearted Woman / Badge / Holy Mother / Lay Down Sally / Wonderful Tonight / Cocaine / Layla / Sunshine Of Your Love / Somewhere Over The Rainbow

9 December 2003, Budokan, Tokyo, Japan

SETLIST: When You Got A Good Friend / Crossroads / I Shot The Sheriff / Bell Bottom Blues / Reconsider Baby / Can't Find My Way Home / White Room / I Want A Little Girl / Got My Mojo Working / Hoochie Coochie Man / Change The World / Bright Lights, Big City / Kind Hearted Woman / Badge / Holy Mother / Lay Down Sally / Wonderful Tonight / Cocaine / Layla / Sunshine Of Your Love / Somewhere Over The Rainbow

10 December 2003, Budokan, Tokyo, Japan

SETLIST: When You Got A Good Friend / Crossroads / I Shot The Sheriff / Bell Bottom Blues / Reconsider Baby / Can't Find My Way Home / White Room / I Want A Little Girl / Got My Mojo Working / Hoochie Coochie Man / Change The World / Bright Lights, Big City / Kind Hearted Woman / Badge / Holy Mother / Lay Down Sally / Wonderful Tonight / Cocaine / Layla / Sunshine Of Your Love / Somewhere Over The Rainbow

12 December 2003, Budokan, Tokyo, Japan

SETLIST: When You Got A Good Friend / Crossroads / I Shot The Sheriff / Bell Bottom Blues / Reconsider Baby / Can't Find My Way Home / White Room / I Want A Little Girl / Got My Mojo Working / Hoochie Coochie Man / Change The World / Bright Lights, Big City / Kind Hearted Woman / Badge / Holy Mother / Lay Down Sally / Wonderful Tonight / Cocaine / Layla / Sunshine Of Your Love / Somewhere Over The Rainbow

13 December 2003, Budokan, Tokyo, Japan

SETLIST: Nobody Knows You When You're Down And Out / When You Got A Good Friend / Crossroads / I Shot The Sheriff / Bell Bottom Blues / Reconsider Baby / Can't Find My Way Home / White Room / I Want A Little Girl / Got My Mojo Working / Hoochie Coochie Man / Change The World / Bright Lights, Big City / Kind Hearted Woman / Badge / Holy Mother / Lay Down Sally / Wonderful Tonight / Cocaine / Layla / Sunshine Of Your Love / Somewhere Over The Rainbow

GARY BROOKER CHRISTMAS SHOW 2003

20 December 2003, Chinddingfold Club, Woodside Road, Chiddingfold, Surrey

Eric joins No Stiletto Shoes for Gary Brooker's traditional Christmas gig.

BAND LINEUP:
Gary Brooker: keyboards, vocals
Eric Clapton: guitar, vocals
Andy Fairweather Low: guitar, vocals
Dave Bronze: bass

Graham Broad: drums
Frank Mead: saxophone

No intermission this year and Eric played on the following numbers. Great show!

SETLIST: Nadine / A Mess Of Blues / If Paradise Is Half As Nice / Reconsider Baby / Hey Bo Diddley / Bright Lights, Big City / My Girl / Money (That's What I Want) / Gin House / O Come All Ye Faithful / Too Much Monkey Business / Poison Ivy / We Shall Not Be Moved / Little Liza Jane / Good Golly Miss Molly

NEW YEAR'S EVE DANCE 2003

31 December 2003, Woking Leisure Centre, Woking, Surrey (Eric had to cancel his appearance at the usual New Year's Eve dance)

RECORDING SESSIONS 2003

ERIC CLAPTON GUEST SESSION

HELICON MOUNTAIN RECORDING STUDIOS
Pyramid Room, 2 Station Mews Terrace, London
Session for Jools Holland

13 FEBRUARY 2003

MESSAGE TO MY SON (Holland / Burke / Clapton) *Jack O The Green Small World Big Band Friends* 3CD Radar 001CD released 2003

Eric Clapton: guitar
Solomon Burke: vocals
Jools Holland: keyboards, vocals
Dave Swift: bass
Gilson Lavis: drums, percussion
Chris Holland: organ
Phil Veacock: saxophone
Rob Wollard: cello
Frank Schaefer: cello

Abigail Trundle: cello
Dina Beamish: cello
Jayne Spencer: violin
Anne Stephenson: violin
Brian Wright: violin
Marina Solarek: violin
Peter Hanson: violin
Gini Ball: violin
Dermot Crehan: violin
Ian Mcleod: violin
Jocelyn Pook: viola
Ellen Blair: viola
Claire Orsler: viola
Lucy Morgan: viola
Mary Scully: double bass
Paddy Lannigan: double bass
Lynette Eaton: double bass
Jeremy Gordon: double bass

MABEL (Holland / Brown / Clapton) *Jack O The Green Small World Big Band Friends* 3CD Radar 001CD released 2003

Eric Clapton: guitar
Solomon Burke: vocals
Jools Holland: keyboards, vocals
Dave Swift: bass
Gilson Lavis: drums, percussion
Chris Holland: organ
Jon Scott: trumpet
Jason McDermid: trumpet
Winston Rollins: trombone
Phil Veacock: saxophone
Michael Rose: saxophone
Lisa Grahame: saxophone
Pete Long: saxophone
Nick Lunt: baritone saxophone
Fayaz Virgi: trombone
Claudia Fontaine: backing vocals
Louise Marshall: backing vocals
Helem McRobby: backing vocals

Producer: Laurie Latham
Engineer: Laurie Latham

ERIC CLAPTON GUEST SESSION

OLYMPIC STUDIOS
117 Church Road, Barnes, London
Guitar overdub for Brian Wilson

23 MAY 2003

CITY BLUES (Brian Wilson, Scott Bennett) *Gettin' In Over My Head* CD Rhino 8122-7647-2 released June 2004

Eric's solo is recorded by Alan Douglas.

> **"**The second duet recorded for the album was finished in London in May 2003. Brian was there to accept the prestigious Ivor Novello Award for Lifetime Achievement, and I was fortunate enough to accompany him both to the ceremony and to the studio the next day.
>
> We were staying in a posh hotel in London, and that morning, riding down the elevator, I asked what sort of sound he was looking for from Eric for 'City Blues.' Brian said, 'happy bluesy.' We arrived at Olympic Studios and were greeted by Mr. Clapton himself.
>
> Repairing to the booth (where Eric plugged directly into the board), Brian directed him through a half-dozen or more takes, alternately encouraging and inspiring the legendary guitarist, who offered up what may be the best lead guitar solo ever to grace a Brian Wilson production—instantly recognizable and instantly memorable.**"**
>
> **—DAVID LEAF**
> (from *Gettin' In Over My Head* liner notes)

OLYMPIC STUDIOS
117 Church Road,
Barnes, London
Sessions for *Me And Mr. Johnson* and *Back Home*

OCTOBER 2003

Eric and his band booked Olympic Studios to start sessions for what would eventually become *Back Home*. However, in between rehearsing new songs Eric and band would go off into Robert Johnson jams for fun and as a way to relax, and it quickly became apparent that this was more enjoyable. Suddenly the focus changed from recording a new album of original material into recording a dedicated Robert Johnson tribute. Eric had always had a passion for Johnson's music and the vulnerability expressed in his lyrics, and he now felt that he had matured enough to be able to do justice to the songs with his own life experience as a backdrop. Make no mistake, this is not an album of Eric attempting to replicate Johnson's songs, but rather Eric's interpretation of them, and it works beautifully. This was Eric's second dedicated blues album, the first being *From The Cradle*, and as always, you can hear how comfortable he is playing straight blues. *Me And Mr. Johnson* is a very different album from *From The Cradle*, not least because he plays the whole of this album with his fingers instead of a plectrum. So you do not get the natural attack he achieved on that album. Everything was done in one or two takes and the raw energy comes ripping out of the speakers with ferocious intensity. Eric recalled that the only two tracks that needed some extra work were "Last Fair Deal Gone Down" and "Stop Breaking Down," both of which needed new vocals by him; the rest was all done live. They were using the big room at Olympic and as everything was being recorded live; including vocals. Some of the instruments had to have baffle screens placed next to the amps to avoid too much leaking.

During sessions for this album, the electric guitars Eric used were a fifties Gibson Byrdland and Gibson L5, both with Alnico pickups, and an Eric Clapton Signature Fender Stratocaster (painted by graffiti artist Crash). These were largely played through an old Fender twin reverb amp. For acoustics, he played a vintage Martin OM-45 as well as a couple of his own Martin signature rosewood models. For the Dobro parts, he used an early seventies Dobro, reminiscent of the model Duane Allman used on the *Layla* sessions.

WHEN YOU GOT A GOOD FRIEND (Robert Johnson) *Me And Mr. Johnson* CD Reprise US 9362-48423-2 / UK 9362-48730-2 released March 2004

Eric Clapton: guitar, vocals
Nathan East: bass
Steve Gadd: drums
Andy Fairweather Low: guitar
Doyle Bramhall II: guitar
Jerry Portnoy: harmonica
Billy Preston: piano

LITTLE QUEEN OF SPADES (Robert Johnson) *Me And Mr. Johnson* CD Reprise US 9362-48423-2 / UK 9362-48730-2 released March 2004

Eric Clapton: guitar, vocals
Nathan East: bass
Steve Gadd: drums
Andy Fairweather Low: guitar
Doyle Bramhall II: slide guitar
Jerry Portnoy: harmonica
Billy Preston: Hammond B3 organ

THEY'RE RED HOT (Robert Johnson) *Me And Mr. Johnson* CD Reprise US 9362-48423-2 / UK 9362-48730-2 released March 2004

Eric Clapton: guitar, vocals
Nathan East: bass
Steve Gadd: drums
Andy Fairweather Low: acoustic guitar
Doyle Bramhall II: slide acoustic guitar
Jerry Portnoy: harmonica
Billy Preston: piano

ME AND THE DEVIL BLUES (Robert Johnson) *Me And Mr. Johnson* CD Reprise US 9362-48423-2 / UK 9362-48730-2 released March 2004

Eric Clapton: guitar, vocals

Nathan East: bass
Steve Gadd: drums
Andy Fairweather Low: guitar
Doyle Bramhall II: guitar
Jerry Portnoy: harmonica

TRAVELLING RIVERSIDE BLUES (Robert Johnson) *Me And Mr. Johnson*
CD Reprise US 9362-48423-2 / UK 9362-48730-2 released March 2004

Eric Clapton: guitar, vocals
Pino Palladino: bass
Jim Keltner: drums
Steve Gadd: drums
Andy Fairweather Low: guitar
Doyle Bramhall II: guitar
Jerry Portnoy: harmonica
Billy Preston: piano

LAST FAIR DEAL GONE DOWN (Robert Johnson) *Me And Mr. Johnson*
CD Reprise US 9362-48423-2 / UK 9362-48730-2 released March 2004

Eric Clapton: guitar, vocals
Nathan East: bass
Steve Gadd: drums
Andy Fairweather Low: guitar
Doyle Bramhall II: guitar
Billy Preston: piano

STOP BREAKIN' DOWN BLUES (Robert Johnson) *Me And Mr. Johnson*
CD Reprise US 9362-48423-2 / UK 9362-48730-2 released March 2004

Eric Clapton: guitar, vocals
Nathan East: bass
Steve Gadd: drums
Andy Fairweather Low: guitar
Doyle Bramhall II: guitar
Billy Preston: piano

MILKCOW'S CALF BLUES (Robert Johnson) *Me And Mr. Johnson* CD
Reprise US 9362-48423-2 / UK 9362-48730-2 released March 2004

Eric Clapton: guitar, vocals
Nathan East: bass
Steve Gadd: drums
Andy Fairweather Low: guitar
Doyle Bramhall II: guitar
Billy Preston: piano

MILKCOW'S CALF BLUES (Robert Johnson) (alternate version)
unreleased

KIND HEARTED WOMAN BLUES (Robert Johnson) *Me And Mr. Johnson*
CD Reprise US 9362-48423-2 / UK 9362-48730-2 released March 2004

Eric Clapton: guitar, vocals
Nathan East: bass
Steve Gadd: drums
Andy Fairweather Low: guitar
Doyle Bramhall II: guitar
Jerry Portnoy: harmonica
Billy Preston: piano

COME ON IN MY KITCHEN (Robert Johnson) *Me And Mr. Johnson* CD
Reprise US 9362-48423-2 / UK 9362-48730-2 released March 2004

Eric Clapton: Dobro, vocals
Nathan East: bass
Steve Gadd: drums
Andy Fairweather Low: guitar
Doyle Bramhall II: guitar
Jerry Portnoy: harmonica
Billy Preston: piano

COME ON IN MY KITCHEN (Robert Johnson) (alternate version)
unreleased

IF I HAD POSSESSION OVER JUDGMENT DAY (Robert Johnson) *Me And Mr. Johnson* CD Reprise US 9362-48423-2 / UK 9362-48730-2 released March 2004

Eric Clapton: guitar, vocals
Nathan East: bass
Steve Gadd: drums
Andy Fairweather Low: guitar
Doyle Bramhall II: guitar
Jerry Portnoy: harmonica
Billy Preston: piano

LOVE IN VAIN (Robert Johnson) *Me And Mr. Johnson* CD Reprise US 9362-48423-2 / UK 9362-48730-2 released March 2004

Eric Clapton: guitar, vocals
Nathan East: bass
Steve Gadd: drums
Andy Fairweather Low: guitar
Doyle Bramhall II: guitar
Jerry Portnoy: harmonica
Billy Preston: piano

32-20 BLUES (Robert Johnson) *Me And Mr. Johnson* CD Reprise US 9362-48423-2 / UK 9362-48730-2 released March 2004

Eric Clapton: guitar, vocals
Nathan East: bass
Steve Gadd: drums
Andy Fairweather Low: guitar
Doyle Bramhall II: guitar
Jerry Portnoy: harmonica
Billy Preston: piano

HELL HOUND ON MY TRAIL (Robert Johnson) *Me And Mr. Johnson* CD Reprise US 9362-48423-2 / UK 9362-48730-2 released March 2004

Eric Clapton: guitar, vocals
Nathan East: bass
Steve Gadd: drums
Andy Fairweather Low: guitar
Doyle Bramhall II: guitar
Jerry Portnoy: harmonica
Billy Preston: piano

Producers: Eric Clapton / Simon Climie
Engineer: Alan Douglas

ERIC CLAPTON GUEST SESSION

OLYMPIC STUDIOS
117 Church Road, Barnes, London
Guitar overdub for Jerry Lee Lewis

OCTOBER 2003

TROUBLE IN MIND (Richard M. Jones) *Last Man Standing* CD Artists First AFT-20001-2 released September 2006

Jerry Lee Lewis: piano, vocals
Eric Clapton: lead guitar
Jimmy Rip: guitar
Ken Lovelace: guitar
Jim Keltner: drums
Hutch Hutchinson: bass

Producers: Jimmy Rip / Steve Bing
Engineer: Steve Gamberonni

> **"**Eric was one of the first in on the *Last Man Standing* record, but he and Jerry did not record together. I sent the tracks to Simon Climie late in 2003, if my memory serves me. They may have been in the studio doing the *Me and Mr. Johnson* record. Simon sent back three or four beautiful E.C. blues tracks and I combined them into what's on the record.**"**
>
> **—JIMMY RIP**
> (producer)

ERIC CLAPTON GUEST SESSION

STUDIO D
Tokyo, Japan
Session for Hiroshi Fujiwara

NOVEMBER 2003

AIR ON A G STRING (Johann Sebastian Bach) *Classic Dub Classics* Crue-L Records KYTHMAK095DA released March 2005

CAPPUCCINO (Eric Clapton / Hiroshi Fujiwara) CD single Victor VICL-61665 released January 2006

Hiroshi Fujiwara: guitar
Yumi Matsutoya: vocals
Eric Clapton: acoustic guitar
Nathan East: bass

Producers: Hiroshi Fujiwara / Kohta Takahashi
Engineer: Kohta Takahashi

Eric not only collaborates musically with Hiroshi Fujiwara, but the two have also worked on two special Martin guitars. The first was the Bellezza Nera, which was released in the summer of 2004. It was very successful with a total of 476 guitars produced and is among the most popular limited editions in Martin history. Building on that success, the two later collaborated on the Martin Bellezza Bianca with a white finish, maple body, spruce top, mahogany neck, bound twenty-fret ebony fingerboard with mother-of-pearl snowflake inlays and mother-of-pearl "Bellezza Bianca" inlay, ebony headstock facing with mother-of-pearl flower alternative torch motif inlay, custom design rosette, herringbone top trim, ebony pin bridge, mother-of-pearl inlaid black endpins, silver-plated tuners and black pickguard, and a black hardshell contour case with bottle-green plush lining.

2004

Another year of extensive touring for Eric. This time he delighted fans by bringing out gems like "Walk Out In The Rain" as well as several numbers from the *Me And Mr. Johnson* album.

For his 2004 world tour, Eric Clapton used Cornell amplifiers with Tone Tubby speakers with hemp cones inside the cabinets for his electric guitars. Built by Dennis Cornell, the Eric Clapton Custom 80 (single channel) looks very much like a Fender Twin but sounds bluer with a lot more middle. Designed to his exact specifications, the Custom 80 is made from birch ply and covered in "Fender Tweed" that is treated to look old. He first used the Cornell / Eric Clapton Custom 80 at the Party At The Palace concert in June 2002. The manufacturer sold these amps in both single-channel and twin-channel models. In addition to this amp, Eric Clapton used a Fender Woody for the Robert Johnson set in the middle of each concert during the 2004 tour.

Clapton's effects pedals for the 2004 tour were limited to a tri-stereo chorus (Boss Chorus CE-3), a Leslie pedal, a Jim Dunlop 535 Crybaby wah-wah pedal (6-way selectable), and a box to switch from the amp to the Leslie or to select both. Eric did and does not use an overdrive pedal. He gets all of the overdrive from the 25dB boost in his guitar, a Fender Eric Clapton Signature Stratocaster. Eric used a Samson Synthetics wireless system on stage. His Martin 000-28EC goes through an Avalon DI box.

Since 2004, Eric Clapton has been using a Carlos Juan CP-1 Pickup in the Bellezza Nera model Martin guitar. These pickups are handbuilt in Germany by Carlos at his American Guitar Center. The Eric Clapton Signature Stratocasters are equipped with Fender Vintage Noiseless pickups.

Eric Clapton, Civic Hall, Guildford, 4 January 2004.

JANUARY 2004

THE LAST FLING 2004

4 January 2004, Civic Hall, Guildford, Surrey

Billed as The Last Fling, this was the final concert to take place at old Guildford Civic Hall, which was soon to be knocked down to make way for a state-of-the-art new entertainment venue. The concert billed as "Gary Brooker and Friends" was opened with a half-hour set by Judie Tzuke who was followed by the Jones Gang, featuring Kenny Jones, for an hour of rock classics by the Who, the Faces, Rod Stewart, Bad Company, and more.

The headliners, Gary Brooker and Friends, came on at 10:00 p.m. This was basically the usual lineup of No Stiletto Shoes. After a few numbers the first guests turned up on stage. Beverly Skeete and Colin Blunstone joined in on a few numbers. They were followed by ex-Manfred Mann singer Paul Jones for a couple of songs. After "Two Fools In Love," sung by Beverly Skeete, Gary Brooker announced Eric Clapton to the delight of the crowd. He remained on stage for the rest of the show. Other guests included Alvin Stardust, Leo Sayer, and Pete Solley who at the time were locals to Guildford and wanted to say a fond farewell to the Civic Hall.

The show was neither televised or recorded.

BAND LINEUP:
Gary Brooker: keyboards, vocals
Andy Fairweather Low: guitar, vocals
Henry Spinetti: drums
Dave Bronze: bass, vocals
Frank Mead: saxophone, percussion

GUESTS LINEUP:
Eric Clapton: guitar, vocals
Beverly Skeete: vocals
Colin Blunstone: vocals
Paul Jones: harmonica, vocals
Alvin Stardust: vocals
Leo Sayer: vocals
Pete Solley: organ

SETLIST:

Tequila

Let's Work Together

Lead Me To The Water (Beverly Skeete vocals)

Say You Don't Mind (Colin Blunstone vocals)

Time Of The Season (Beverly Skeete vocals; Colin Blunstone vocals)

She's Not There (Colin Blunstone vocals)

If Paradise Is Half As Nice (Andy Fairweather Low vocals)

Pretty Flamingo (Paul Jones vocals)

Work Song (Paul Jones vocals)

Help Me (Paul Jones vocals)

Two Fools In Love (Beverly Skeete vocals)

When You Got A Good Friend (Eric Clapton guitar, vocals; Beverly Skeete vocals)

Never Loved A Man (Eric Clapton guitar; Beverly Skeete vocals; Paul Jones harmonica)

Mustang Sally (Eric Clapton guitar; Beverly Skeete vocals)

I Put A Spell On You (Eric Clapton guitar; Beverly Skeete vocals)

Wonderful Tonight (Eric Clapton guitar, vocals) unreleased

Stagger Lee (Eric Clapton guitar; Alvin Stardust vocals)

Johnny B. Goode (Eric Clapton guitar; Alvin Stardust vocals)

My Girl (Eric Clapton guitar; Beverly Skeete vocals; Paul Jones vocals)

When I Need You (Eric Clapton guitar; Leo Sayer vocals, Beverly Skeete vocals)

Long Tall Glasses (Eric Clapton guitar; Leo Sayer vocals)

Gin House (Eric Clapton guitar; Andy Fairweather Low guitar, vocals)

Doo Wah Diddy (Eric Clapton guitar; Paul Jones vocals; Beverly Skeete vocals; Leo Sayer vocals)

A Whiter Shade Of Pale (Eric Clapton guitar; Pete Solley keyboards)

Cocaine (Eric Clapton guitar, vocals; Pete Solley keyboards)

We'll Meet Again (everyone)

MARCH 2004

FILM SESSION FOR *SESSIONS FOR ROBERT J* 2004

14 March 2004, Hookend Manor, Checkendon, Reading, Berkshire

This first session was recorded during rehearsals for the 2004 tour at Hookend Manor in Checkendon, Berkshire. On the DVD you see Eric getting out of his silver Porsche 911 and saying "good morning" to everyone before moving into the studio where the band are clearly having fun playing the blues. In between songs Eric is interviewed about Robert Johnson.

SESSION I (for *Sessions For Robert J.* CD/DVD, a companion project to *Me And Mr. Johnson*)

SETLIST: Let Kind Hearted Woman / They're Red Hot / Hellhound On My Trail / Sweet Home Chicago / When You've Got A Good Friend

ONE GENERATION 4 ANOTHER CONCERT 2004

15 March 2004, Royal Albert Hall, London (One Generation 4 Another fundraiser concert for the Lord Taverners charity, the official national charity for recreational cricket)

The concert raised more than £150,000 for the charity, which was established in 1950 to give children with special needs "a sporting chance." It supplies wheelchairs, minibuses, ponies, and swimming equipment to schools and colleges. Bill Wyman's Rhythm Kings played a short set to start the evening and remained on stage for the evening backing a variety of guest artists including the welcome return of Peter Green, Bob Geldof, Jools Holland, Gary Brooker, Paul Carrack, the Zombies, Geno Washington, and Roger Chapman. Eric Clapton agreed to play three songs and he did not dissapoint with some cutting guitar work earning a standing ovation from the crowd.

Eric played his custom Crash 3 Fender Stratocaster this evening. The guitar was sold for $321,100 during the second auction for the Crossroads Centre.

BAND LINEUP:
Eric Clapton: guitar, vocals
Bill Wyman: bass
Georgie Fame: organ
Mike Sanchez: piano
Terry Taylor: guitar
Graham Broad: drums
Frank Mead: saxophone
Nick Payn: saxophone, harmonica

SETLIST: When You Got A Good Friend / Little Queen Of Spades / Reconsider Baby

"After my fifteen years with the Big Town Playboys, within a year I was asked by Bill Wyman to join his Rhythm Kings who I then toured with for four years. The last time I met Eric was when we performed together at Royal Albert Hall on one of those Lord Taverners events where Bill Wyman's Rhythm Kings were the house band. We performed 'Reconsider Baby' and a couple of other classic blues tunes. That evening we also had Peter Green as a guest. That was one of the most frightening times of my life when at the last minute I was asked to sing 'Black Magic Woman' because 'Greeny' didn't want to sing it."
—MIKE SANCHEZ

ME AND MR. JOHNSON EUROPEAN TOUR 2004

BAND LINEUP:
Eric Clapton: guitar, vocals
Nathan East: bass, vocals
Chris Stainton: keyboards
Steve Gadd: drums
Doyle Bramhall II: guitar, vocals
Billy Preston: keyboards, vocals
Sharon White: backing vocals
Michelle John: backing vocals

24 March 2004, Palau Sant Jordi, Barcelona, Spain (with Robert Randolph and the Family Band)

SETLIST: Let It Rain / Hoochie Coochie Man / Bell Bottom Blues / Walk Out In The Rain / I Shot The Sheriff / When You Got A Good Friend / Milkcow's Calf Blues / Kind Hearted Woman / They're Red Hot / Hellhound On My Trail / Change The World / Got To Get Better In A Little While / I Want A Little Girl / Badge / Wonderful Tonight / Cocaine / Layla / Sunshine Of Your Love

26 March 2004, Zénith d'Auvergne, Cournon d'Auvergne, France (with Robert Randolph and the Family Band)

SETLIST: Let It Rain / Hoochie Coochie Man / Walk Out In The Rain / Bell Bottom Blues / Change The World / When You Got A Good Friend / Milkcow's Calf Blues / Kind Hearted Woman / They're Red Hot / Hellhound On My Trail / I Shot The Sheriff / Have You Ever Loved A Woman / Got To Get Better In A Little While / I Want A Little Girl / Badge / Wonderful Tonight / Cocaine / Layla / Sunshine Of Your Love[1] / Got My Mojo Working[1]

[1] with Robert Randolph on pedal steel guitar

28 March 2004, Hallenstadion, Zürich, Switzerland (with Robert Randolph and the Family Band)

SETLIST: Let It Rain / Hoochie Coochie Man / Walk Out In The Rain / Bell Bottom Blues / Change The World / When You Got A Good Friend / Milkcow's Calf Blues / Kind Hearted Woman / They're Red Hot / I Shot The Sheriff / Third Degree / Got To Get Better In A Little While / I Want A Little Girl / Badge / Wonderful Tonight / Cocaine / Layla / Sunshine Of Your Love[1] / Got My Mojo Working[1]

30 March 2004, Schleyerhalle, Stuttgart, Germany (with Robert Randolph and the Family Band)

SETLIST: Let It Rain / Hoochie Coochie Man / Walk Out In The Rain / Bell Bottom Blues / Change The World / When You Got A Good Friend / Milkcow's Calf Blues / Kind Hearted Woman / They're Red Hot / I Shot The Sheriff / Have You Ever Loved A Woman / Got To Get Better In A Little While / I Want A Little Girl / Badge / Wonderful Tonight / Cocaine / Layla / Sunshine Of Your Love¹ / Got My Mojo Working¹

¹with Robert Randolph on pedal steel guitar

31 March 2004, Olympiahalle, Munich, Germany (with Robert Randolph and the Family Band)

SETLIST: Let It Rain / Hoochie Coochie Man / Walk Out In The Rain / Bell Bottom Blues / Change The World / When You Got A Good Friend / Milkcow's Calf Blues / Kind Hearted Woman / They're Red Hot / I Shot The Sheriff / Have You Ever Loved A Woman / Got To Get Better In A Little While / I Want A Little Girl / Badge / Wonderful Tonight / Cocaine / Layla / Sunshine Of Your Love¹ / Got My Mojo Working¹

¹with Robert Randolph on pedal steel guitar

APRIL 2004

2 April 2004, Preussag Arena, Hannover, Germany (with Robert Randolph and the Family Band)

SETLIST: Let It Rain / Hoochie Coochie Man / Bell Bottom Blues / Got To Get Better In A Little While / Milkcow's Calf Blues / When You Got A Good Friend / They're Red Hot / Kind Hearted Woman / I Shot The Sheriff / I Want A Little Girl / Change The World / Have You Ever Loved A Woman / Badge / Wonderful Tonight / Cocaine / Layla / Sunshine Of Your Love¹ / Got My Mojo Working¹

¹with Robert Randolph on pedal steel guitar

3 April 2004, Color Line Arena, Hamburg, Germany (with Robert Randolph and the Family Band)

SETLIST: Let It Rain / Hoochie Coochie Man / Bell Bottom Blues / I Shot The Sheriff / Milkcow's Calf Blues / When You Got A Good Friend / They're Red Hot / Kind Hearted Woman / Change The World / I Want A Little Girl / Got To Get Better In A Little While / Have You Ever Loved A Woman / Badge / Wonderful Tonight / Cocaine / Layla / Sunshine Of Your Love¹ / Got My Mojo Working¹

¹with Robert Randolph on pedal steel guitar

6 April 2004, Palais Omnisports De Paris Bercy, Paris, France (with Robert Randolph and the Family Band)

SETLIST: Let It Rain / Hoochie Coochie Man / Bell Bottom Blues / I Shot The Sheriff / Milkcow's Calf Blues / When You Got A Good Friend / They're Red Hot / Kind Hearted Woman / Got To Get Better In A Little While / I Want A Little Girl / Change The World / Have You Ever Loved A Woman / Badge / Wonderful Tonight / Cocaine / Layla / Sunshine Of Your Love¹ / Got My Mojo Working¹

¹with Robert Randolph on pedal steel guitar

8 April 2004, Festhalle, Frankfurt, Germany (with Robert Randolph and the Family Band)

SETLIST: Let It Rain / Hoochie Coochie Man / Bell Bottom Blues / I Shot The Sheriff / Milkcow's Calf Blues / When You Got A Good Friend / They're Red Hot / Kind Hearted Woman / Got To Get Better In A Little While / I Want A Little Girl / Change The World / Have You Ever Loved A Woman / Badge / Wonderful Tonight / Layla / Cocaine / Sunshine Of Your Love¹ / Got My Mojo Working¹

¹with Robert Randolph on pedal steel guitar

9 April 2004, Sportpaleis, Antwerpen, Belgium (with Robert Randolph and the Family Band)

SETLIST: Let It Rain / Hoochie Coochie Man / Bell Bottom Blues / I Shot The Sheriff / Milkcow's Calf Blues / When You Got A Good Friend / They're Red Hot / Kind Hearted Woman / Got To Get Better In A Little While / I Want A Little Girl / Change The World / Have You Ever Loved A Woman / Badge / Wonderful Tonight / Layla / Cocaine / Sunshine Of Your Love¹ / Got My Mojo Working¹

¹with Robert Randolph on pedal steel guitar

11 April 2004, Ahoy Hall, Rotterdam, Netherlands (with Robert Randolph and the Family Band)

SETLIST: Let It Rain / Hoochie Coochie Man / Bell Bottom Blues / I Shot The Sheriff / Milkcow's Calf Blues / When You Got A Good Friend / They're Red Hot / Kind Hearted Woman / Got To Get Better In A Little While / I Want A Little Girl / Change The World / Have You Ever Loved A Woman / Badge / Wonderful Tonight / Layla / Cocaine / Sunshine Of Your Love[1] / Got My Mojo Working[1]

[1]with Robert Randolph on pedal steel guitar

12 April 2004, Ahoy Hall, Rotterdam, Netherlands (with Robert Randolph and the Family Band)

SETLIST: Let It Rain / Hoochie Coochie Man / Bell Bottom Blues / I Shot The Sheriff / Milkcow's Calf Blues / When You Got A Good Friend / They're Red Hot / Kind Hearted Woman / Got To Get Better In A Little While / I Want A Little Girl / Change The World / Have You Ever Loved A Woman / Badge / Wonderful Tonight / Layla / Cocaine / Sunshine Of Your Love[1] / Got My Mojo Working[1]

[1]with Robert Randolph on pedal steel guitar

14 April 2004, Westfalenhalle, Dortmund, Germany (with Robert Randolph and the Family Band)

SETLIST: Let It Rain / Hoochie Coochie Man / Walk Out In The Rain / Bell Bottom Blues / I Shot The Sheriff / Milkcow's Calf Blues / When You Got A Good Friend / They're Red Hot / Kind Hearted Woman / Got To Get Better In A Little While / Have You Ever Loved A Woman / Badge / Wonderful Tonight / Layla / Cocaine / Sunshine Of Your Love[1] / Got My Mojo Working[1]

[1]with Robert Randolph on pedal steel guitar

15 April 2004, Köln Arena, Köln, Germany (with Robert Randolph and the Family Band)

SETLIST: Let It Rain / Hoochie Coochie Man / Walk Out In The Rain / Bell Bottom Blues / I Shot The Sheriff / Milkcow's Calf Blues / When You Got A Good Friend / They're Red Hot / Kind Hearted Woman / Got To Get Better In A Little While / Have You Ever Loved A Woman / Badge / Wonderful Tonight / Layla / Cocaine / Sunshine Of Your Love[1] / Got My Mojo Working[1]

[1]with Robert Randolph on pedal steel guitar

17 April 2004, Parken, Copenhagen, Denmark (with Robert Randolph and the Family Band)

SETLIST: Let It Rain / Hoochie Coochie Man / Walk Out In The Rain / Bell Bottom Blues / I Shot The Sheriff / Milkcow's Calf Blues / When You Got A Good Friend / They're Red Hot / Kind Hearted Woman / Got To Get Better In A Little While / Have You Ever Loved A Woman / Badge / Wonderful Tonight / Layla / Cocaine / Sunshine Of Your Love[1] / Got My Mojo Working[1]

[1]with Robert Randolph on pedal steel guitar

23 April 2004, The Point, Dublin, Ireland (with Robert Randolph and the Family Band)

SETLIST: Let It Rain / Hoochie Coochie Man / Walk Out In The Rain / Bell Bottom Blues / I Shot The Sheriff / Milkcow's Calf Blues / When You Got A Good Friend / They're Red Hot / Kind Hearted Woman / Got To Get Better In A Little While / Have You Ever Loved A Woman / Badge / Wonderful Tonight / Layla / Cocaine / Sunshine Of Your Love[1] / Got My Mojo Working[1]

[1]with Robert Randolph on pedal steel guitar

24 April 2004, Odyssey Arena, Belfast, Northern Ireland (with Robert Randolph and the Family Band)

SETLIST: Let It Rain / Hoochie Coochie Man / Walk Out In The Rain / Bell Bottom Blues / I Shot The Sheriff / Milkcow's Calf Blues / When You Got A Good Friend / They're Red Hot / Kind Hearted Woman / Got To Get Better In A Little While / Have You Ever Loved A Woman / Badge / Wonderful Tonight / Layla / Cocaine / Sunshine Of Your Love[1] / Got My Mojo Working[1]

[1]with Robert Randolph on pedal steel guitar

This show was broadcast live by BBC Radio 2 as part of the BBC's *Music Live Festival In Ireland.* The broadcast cut into "Let It Rain" and missed the encores entirely.

26 April 2004, Scottish Exhibition and Conference Centre, Glasgow, Scotland (with Robert Randolph and the Family Band)

SETLIST: Let It Rain / Hoochie Coochie Man / Walk Out In The Rain / Bell Bottom Blues / I Shot The Sheriff

/ Milkcow's Calf Blues / When You Got A Good Friend / They're Red Hot / Kind Hearted Woman / Got To Get Better In A Little While / Have You Ever Loved A Woman / Badge / Wonderful Tonight / Layla / Cocaine / Sunshine Of Your Love[1] / Got My Mojo Working[1]

[1]with Robert Randolph on pedal steel guitar

27 April 2004, Telewest Arena, Newcastle (with Robert Randolph and the Family Band)

SETLIST: Let It Rain / Hoochie Coochie Man / Walk Out In The Rain / Bell Bottom Blues / I Shot The Sheriff / Milkcow's Calf Blues / When You Got A Good Friend / They're Red Hot / Kind Hearted Woman / Got To Get Better In A Little While / Have You Ever Loved A Woman / Badge / Wonderful Tonight / Layla / Cocaine / Sunshine Of Your Love[1] / Got My Mojo Working[1]

[1]with Robert Randolph on pedal steel guitar

29 April 2004, Manchester Evening News Arena, Manchester (with Robert Randolph and the Family Band)

SETLIST: Let It Rain / Hoochie Coochie Man / Walk Out In The Rain / Bell Bottom Blues / I Shot The Sheriff / Milkcow's Calf Blues / When You Got A Good Friend / They're Red Hot / Kind Hearted Woman / Got To Get Better In A Little While / Have You Ever Loved A Woman / Badge / Wonderful Tonight / Layla / Cocaine / Sunshine Of Your Love[1] / Got My Mojo Working[1]

[1]with Robert Randolph on pedal steel guitar

30 April 2004, National Exhibition Centre, Birmingham (with Robert Randolph and the Family Band)

SETLIST: Let It Rain / Hoochie Coochie Man / Walk Out In The Rain / Bell Bottom Blues / I Shot The Sheriff / Milkcow's Calf Blues / When You Got A Good Friend / They're Red Hot / Kind Hearted Woman / Got To Get Better In A Little While / Have You Ever Loved A Woman / Badge / Wonderful Tonight / Layla / Cocaine / Sunshine Of Your Love[1] / Got My Mojo Working[1]

[1]with Robert Randolph on pedal steel guitar

MAY 2004

2 May 2004, Hallam FM Arena, Sheffield, South Yorkshire (with Robert Randolph and the Family Band)

SETLIST: Let It Rain / Hoochie Coochie Man / Walk Out In The Rain / Bell Bottom Blues / I Shot The Sheriff / Milkcow's Calf Blues / When You Got A Good Friend / They're Red Hot / Kind Hearted Woman / Got To Get Better In A Little While / Have You Ever Loved A Woman / Badge / Wonderful Tonight / Layla / Cocaine / Sunshine Of Your Love[1] / Got My Mojo Working[1]

[1]with Robert Randolph on pedal steel guitar

Eric Clapton on wah wah at the Royal Albert Hall in London, 11 May 2004.

4 May 2004, Royal Albert Hall, London (with Robert Randolph and the Family Band)

SETLIST: Let It Rain / Hoochie Coochie Man / Walk Out In The Rain / I Want A Little Girl / I Shot The Sheriff / Me And The Devil Blues / They're Red Hot / Milkcow's Calf Blues / If I Had Possession Over Judgment Day / Kind Hearted Woman / Got To Get Better In A Little While / Have You Ever Loved A Woman / Badge / Wonderful Tonight / Layla / Cocaine / Sunshine Of Your Love[1] / Got My Mojo Working[1]

[1]with Robert Randolph on pedal steel guitar

Judgment Day / Kind Hearted Woman / Got To Get Better In A Little While / Have You Ever Loved A Woman / Badge / Wonderful Tonight / Layla / Cocaine / Sunshine Of Your Love[1] / Got My Mojo Working[1]

[1]with Robert Randolph on pedal steel guitar

The amazing Doyle Bramhall II, a perfect partner to Eric during the 2004 tour and beyond.

Eric Clapton and his custom painted Fender Strat at the Royal Albert Hall in London, 4 May 2004.

GUEST APPEARANCE WITH ZUCCHERO FORNACIARI 2004

6 May 2004, Royal Albert Hall, London (guest appearance with Zucchero Fornaciari)

Eric Clapton and Zucchero at the Royal Albert Hall in London, 6 May 2004.

Eric prepares for the final bow at the Royal Albert Hall on 4 May 2004.

5 May 2004, Royal Albert Hall, London (with Robert Randolph and the Family Band)

SETLIST: Let It Rain / Hoochie Coochie Man / Walk Out In The Rain / I Want A Little Girl / I Shot The Sheriff / Me And The Devil Blues / They're Red Hot / Milkcow's Calf Blues / If I Had Possession Over

BAND LINEUP:
Zucchero Fornaciari: vocals, guitar, piano
Eric Clapton: guitar
Polo Jones: bass
David Sancious: keyboards
Matteo Saggese: keyboards
Mario Schiliro: guitar
Adriano Molanari: drums
Lisa Hunt: backing vocals
Mino Vergnaghi: backing vocals
Elaine Jackson: backing vocals

SETLIST:

Hey Man (Zucchero Fornaciari / Eric Clapton) *Zu & Co. Live At The Royal Albert Hall* CD Universal released September 2005

Wonderful World (Zucchero Fornaciari / Eric Clapton) *Zu & Co. Live At The Royal Albert Hall* CD Universal released September 2005

7 May 2004, Royal Albert Hall, London (with Robert Randolph and the Family Band)

SETLIST: Let It Rain / Hoochie Coochie Man / Walk Out In The Rain / I Want A Little Girl / I Shot The Sheriff / Me And The Devil Blues / They're Red Hot / Milkcow's Calf Blues / If I Had Possession Over Judgment Day / Kind Hearted Woman / Got To Get Better In A Little While / Have You Ever Loved A Woman / Badge / Wonderful Tonight / Layla / Cocaine / Sunshine Of Your Love[1] / Got My Mojo Working[1]

[1]with Robert Randolph on pedal steel guitar

8 May 2004, Royal Albert Hall, London (with Robert Randolph and the Family Band)

Eric Clapton playing acoustic guitar at the Royal Albert Hall in London, May 2004.

SETLIST: Let It Rain / Hoochie Coochie Man / Walk Out In The Rain / I Want A Little Girl / I Shot The Sheriff / Me And The Devil Blues / They're Red Hot / Milkcow's Calf Blues / If I Had Possession Over Judgment Day / Kind Hearted Woman / Got To Get Better In A Little While / Have You Ever Loved A Woman / Badge / Wonderful Tonight / Layla / Cocaine / Sunshine Of Your Love

Robert Randolph does not jam with Eric tonight as his band are playing a club show in London.

10 May 2004, Royal Albert Hall, London (with Robert Randolph and the Family Band)

SETLIST: Let It Rain / Hoochie Coochie Man / Walk Out In The Rain / I Want A Little Girl / I Shot The Sheriff / Me And The Devil Blues / They're Red Hot / Milkcow's Calf Blues / If I Had Possession Over Judgment Day /

Kind Hearted Woman / Got To Get Better In A Little While / Five Long Years / Badge / Wonderful Tonight / Layla / Cocaine / Sunshine Of Your Love[1] / Got My Mojo Working[1]

[1]with Robert Randolph on pedal steel guitar

11 May 2004, Royal Albert Hall, London (with Robert Randolph and the Family Band)

Eric Clapton and Doyle Bramhall II at the Royal Albert Hall in London, 11 May 2004.

SETLIST: Let It Rain / Hoochie Coochie Man / Walk Out In The Rain / I Want A Little Girl / I Shot The Sheriff / Me And The Devil Blues / They're Red Hot / Milkcow's Calf Blues / If I Had Possession Over Judgment Day / Kind Hearted Woman / Got To Get Better In A Little While / Have You Ever Loved A Woman / Badge / Wonderful Tonight / Layla / Cocaine / Sunshine Of Your Love[1] / Got My Mojo Working[1]

[1]with Robert Randolph on pedal steel guitar

JUNE 2004

FILM SESSION FOR SESSIONS FOR ROBERT J 2004

2 June 2004, The Studios at Las Colinas, 6301 Riverside Drive, Irving, Texas

This session was recorded at studios at Las Colinas

in Irving, Texas, on 2 June 2004, with Eric and his band rehearsing for the huge Crossroads Festival.

SESSION II (for *Sessions For Robert J* CD/DVD, a companion project to the *Me And Mr. Johnson* album)

SETLIST: Milkcow Calf Blues / Judgment Day / Stop Breakin' Down Blues / Little Queen Of Spades / Traveling Riverside Blues

FILM SESSION FOR SESSIONS FOR ROBERT J. 2004

3 June 2004, 508 Park Avenue, Dallas, Texas (this address is supposedly where Robert Johnson originally recorded his songs)

SESSION III (for *Sessions For Robert J* CD/DVD, a companion project to the *Me And Mr. Johnson* album)

SETLIST: Terraplane Blues / Hellhound On My Trail / Me And The Devil Blues / From Four Until Late / Love In Vain

CROSSROADS GUITAR FESTIVAL 2004

Although Eric had played a star-studded benefit for Crossroads at New York's Madison Square Garden back in 1999, this was the first large-scale event organized for the charity. The other major difference was the huge number of guitarists invited to play at the three-day concert that tied in with a huge auction of some of Eric's iconic guitars.

Guest guitarists included Jeff Beck, Doyle Bramhall II, JJ Cale, Larry Carlton, Robert Cray, Buddy Guy, David Hidalgo, Eric Johnson, Sonny Landreth, John McLaughlin, Robert Randolph, Hubert Sumlin, Dan Tyminski, and Steve Vai among many others.

Over the three days, the Crossroads Guitar Festival featured exhibits and clinics sponsored by the Guitar Center. The second day featured performances on three stages, one of which was sponsored by Sirius Satellite Radio. People unable to attend the show could tune in to the radio and listen to most of it. The whole event was filmed and recorded and edited highlights were released on DVD.

JJ CALE SET

5 June 2004, Guitar Center Village, Outdoor Main Stage, Dallas, Texas

Eric joins JJ Cale and his band for six songs.

BAND LINEUP:
JJ Cale: guitar, vocals
Eric Clapton: guitar
Christine Lakeland: guitar, vocals
Rocky Frisco: keyboards
Jim Karstein: drums
Bill Raffensperger: bass

SETLIST:

Reality unreleased

Ride Me High unreleased

Call Me The Breeze *Crossroads Guitar Festival 2004* DVD Warner Bros. released November 2004

Cocaine unreleased

After Midnight *Crossroads Guitar Festival 2004* DVD Warner Bros. released November 2004

Travelin' Light unreleased

BLUES JAM SET

5 June 2004, Guitar Center Village, Outdoor Main Stage, Dallas, Texas

The Saturday evening highlight was a blues guitar jam with Eric Clapton, Robert Cray, Jimmie Vaughan, Buddy Guy, Robert Randolph, and Hubert Sumlin.

BAND LINEUP:
Eric Clapton: guitar, vocals
Robert Cray: guitar, vocals

Buddy Guy: guitar, vocals
Robert Randolph: pedal steel guitar
Hubert Sumlin: guitar
Jimmie Vaughan: guitar
George Rains: drums
Bill Willis: Hammond B3 organ
Billy Pitman: guitar

SETLIST:

The Dirty Girl unreleased

Jimmie Vaughan: guitar
George Rains: drums
Bill Willis: Hammond B3 organ
Blly Pitman: guitar

Five Long Years (Eric Clapton) unreleased

Eric Clapton: guitar, vocals
Jimmie Vaughan: guitar
George Rains: drums
Bill Willis: Hammond B3 organ
Blly Pitman: guitar

The 12 Year Old Boy (Robert Cray) unreleased

Eric Clapton: guitar
Robert Cray: guitar, vocals
Jimmie Vaughan: guitar
George Rains: drums
Bill Willis: Hammond B3 organ
Blly Pitman: guitar

Killing Floor (Hubert Sumlin with Robert Cray vocals) *Crossroads Guitar Festival 2004* DVD Warner Bros. released 2004

Eric Clapton: guitar
Robert Cray: guitar, vocals
Hubert Sumlin: guitar
Jimmie Vaughan: guitar
George Rains: drums
Bill Willis: Hammond B3 organ
Blly Pitman: guitar

Going Down Slow (Eric Clapton) unreleased

Eric Clapton: guitar, vocals
Robert Cray: guitar
Hubert Sumlin: guitar
Jimmie Vaughan: guitar
George Rains: drums
Bill Willis: Hammond B3 organ
Blly Pitman: guitar

Sweet Home Chicago (Buddy Guy) *Crossroads Guitar Festival 2004* DVD Warner Bros. released 2004

Eric Clapton: guitar

Robert Cray: guitar
Buddy Guy: guitar, vocals
Hubert Sumlin: guitar
Jimmie Vaughan: guitar
George Rains: drums
Bill Willis: Hammond B3 organ
Blly Pitman: guitar

My Time After A While (Buddy Guy) unreleased

Eric Clapton: guitar
Robert Cray: guitar
Buddy Guy: guitar, vocals
Hubert Sumlin: guitar
Jimmie Vaughan: guitar
George Rains: drums
Bill Willis: Hammond B3 organ
Billy Pitman: guitar

Six Strings Down (Jimmie Vaughan) *Crossroads Guitar Festival 2004* DVD Warner Bros. released 2004

Eric Clapton: guitar
Robert Cray: guitar
Robert Randolph: pedal steel guitar
Hubert Sumlin: guitar
Jimmie Vaughan: guitar, vocals
George Rains: drums
Bill Willis: Hammond B3 organ
Billy Pitman: guitar

Early In The Morning (Eric Clapton) unreleased

Eric Clapton: guitar, vocals
Robert Cray: guitar, vocals
Buddy Guy: guitar, vocals
Robert Randolph: pedal steel guitar
Hubert Sumlin: guitar
Jimmie Vaughan: guitar
George Rains: drums
Bill Willis: Hammond B3 organ
Billy Pitman: guitar

Hoochie Coochie Man (Buddy Guy) unreleased

Eric Clapton: guitar, vocals
Robert Cray: guitar, vocals
Buddy Guy: guitar, vocals
Robert Randolph: pedal steel guitar
Hubert Sumlin: guitar
Jimmie Vaughan: guitar
George Rains: drums
Bill Willis: Hammond B3 organ
Billy Pitman: guitar

B.B. KING SET

6 June 2004, Cotton Bowl Stadium, Dallas, Texas

The festival moved to the huge Cotton Bowl Stadium for Sunday. Halfway through the afternoon, Eric joined B.B. King for his sit-down set.

BAND LINEUP:
Eric Clapton: guitar
B.B. King: guitar
Buddy Guy: guitar
Jimmie Vaughan: guitar
George Rains: drums
Bill Willis: Hammond B3 organ, bass
Billy Pitman: rhythm guitar

SETLIST:

Rock Me Baby (Jimmie Vaughan, Eric Clapton, and Buddy Guy) *Crossroads Guitar Festival 2004* DVD Warner Bros. released November 2004

Eric Clapton: guitar
B.B. King: guitar
Buddy Guy: guitar
Jimmie Vaughan: guitar
George Rains: drums
Bill Willis: Hammond B-3 organ, bass
Billy Pitman: rhythm guitar

Jam session (with Jimmie Vaughan, Eric Clapton, and Buddy Guy) unreleased

Eric Clapton: guitar
B.B. King: guitar
Buddy Guy: guitar
Jimmie Vaughan: guitar
George Rains: drums
Bill Willis: Hammond B-3 organ, bass
Billy Pitman: rhythm guitar

Everyday I Have The Blues (with Jimmie Vaughan, Eric Clapton, Buddy Guy, and John Mayer) unreleased

Eric Clapton: guitar
B.B. King: guitar
Buddy Guy: guitar
John Mayer: guitar
Jimmie Vaughan: guitar
George Rains: drums
Bill Willis: Hammond B-3 organ, bass
Billy Pitman: rhythm guitar

SANTANA WITH ERIC CLAPTON SET

6 June 2004, Cotton Bowl Stadium, Dallas, Texas

Eric joined Carlos Santana and his band for one song in their set. Eric tears it up with some answer and call guitar runs with Carlos Santana.

BAND LINEUP:
Carlos Santana: guitar
Eric Clapton: guitar
Dennis Chambers: drums
Chester Thompson: keyboards
Benny Rietveld: bass
Karl Perazzo: timbales, percussion

SETLIST:

Jingo *Crossroads Guitar Festival 2004* DVD Warner Bros. released November 2004

ERIC CLAPTON SET

BAND LINEUP:
Eric Clapton: guitar, vocals
Nathan East: bass, vocals
Chris Stainton: keyboards
Steve Gadd: drums
Doyle Bramhall II: guitar, vocals
Billy Preston: keyboards, vocals
Sharon White: backing vocals
Michelle John: backing vocals

SETLIST:

Me And The Devil Blues unreleased

They're Red Hot unreleased

Milkcow's Calf Blues unreleased

If I Had Possession Over Judgement Day *Crossroads Guitar Festival 2004* DVD Warner Bros. released November 2004

Kind Hearted Woman Blues unreleased

I Shot The Sheriff *Crossroads Guitar Festival 2004* DVD Warner Bros. released November 2004

Have You Ever Loved A Woman *Crossroads Guitar Festival 2004* DVD Warner Bros. released November 2004

Badge unreleased

Wonderful Tonight unreleased

Layla unreleased

Cocaine *Crossroads Guitar Festival 2004* DVD Warner Bros. released November 2004

Cause We've Ended As Lovers[1] (with Jeff Beck) unreleased

[1]with Jeff Beck on guitar

ME AND MR. JOHNSON
U.S. TOUR 2004

9 June 2004, Ford Center, Oklahoma City, Oklahoma (with Robert Randolph and the Family Band)

SETLIST: Let It Rain / Hoochie Coochie Man / Walk Out In The Rain / I Want A Little Girl / I Shot The Sheriff / Me And The Devil Blues / They're Red Hot / Milkcow's Calf Blues / If I Had Possession Over Judgment Day / Kind Hearted Woman / Got To Get Better In A Little While / Have You Ever Loved A Woman / Badge / Wonderful Tonight / Layla / Cocaine / Sunshine Of Your Love[1] / Got My Mojo Working[1]

[1]with Robert Randolph on pedal steel guitar

11 June 2004, Alltel Arena, North Little Rock, Arkansas (with Robert Randolph and the Family Band)

SETLIST: Let It Rain / Hoochie Coochie Man / Walk Out In The Rain / I Want A Little Girl / I Shot The Sheriff / Me And The Devil Blues / They're Red Hot / Milkcow's Calf Blues / If I Had Possession Over Judgment Day / Kind Hearted Woman / Got To Get Better In A Little While / Have You Ever Loved A Woman / Badge / Wonderful Tonight / Layla / Cocaine / Sunshine Of Your Love[1] / Got My Mojo Working[1]

[1]with Robert Randolph on pedal steel guitar

12 June 2004, New Orleans Arena, New Orleans, Louisiana (with Jimmie Vaughan and the Tilt-A-Whirl Band with Lou Anne Barton)

SETLIST: Let It Rain / Hoochie Coochie Man / Walk Out In The Rain / I Want A Little Girl / I Shot The Sheriff / Me And The Devil Blues / They're Red Hot / Milkcow's Calf Blues / If I Had Possession Over Judgment Day / Kind Hearted Woman / Got To Get Better In A Little While / Have You Ever Loved A Woman / Badge / Wonderful Tonight / Layla / Cocaine / Sunshine Of Your Love / Sweet Home Chicago[1]

[1]with Jimmie Vaughan on guitar

Billy Preston did not play at this show due to illness.

Jimmie Vaughan and the Tilt-A-Whirl Band replaced Robert Randolph and the Family Band as the opening act tonight as Robert Randolph and the Family Band were playing at the Bonaroo Music Festival in Manchester, Tennessee.

14 June 2004, St. Pete Times Forum, Tampa, Florida (with Robert Randolph and the Family Band)

SETLIST: Let It Rain / Hoochie Coochie Man / Walk Out In The Rain / I Want A Little Girl / I Shot The Sheriff / Me And The Devil Blues / They're Red Hot / Milkcow's Calf Blues / If I Had Possession Over Judgment Day / Kind Hearted Woman / Got To Get Better In A Little While / Have You Ever Loved A Woman / Badge / Wonderful Tonight / Layla / Cocaine / Sunshine Of Your Love[1] / Got My Mojo Working[1]

[1]with Robert Randolph on pedal steel guitar

Billy Preston did not play at this show due to illness. Tim Carmon is brought in to play keyboards in Billy's absence.

15 June 2004, Office Depot Center, Sunrise, Florida (with Robert Randolph and the Family Band)

SETLIST: Let It Rain / Hoochie Coochie Man / Walk Out In The Rain / I Want A Little Girl / I Shot The Sheriff / Me And The Devil Blues / They're Red Hot / Milkcow's Calf Blues / If I Had Possession Over Judgment Day / Kind Hearted Woman / Got To Get Better In A Little While / Have You Ever Loved A Woman / Badge / Wonderful Tonight / Layla / Cocaine / Sunshine Of Your Love[1] / Got My Mojo Working[1]

[1]with Robert Randolph on pedal steel guitar

Tim Carmon is still in the band due to Billy Preston's illness.

16 June 2004, Jacksonville Veterans Memorial Arena, Jacksonville, Florida (with Robert Randolph and the Family Band)

SETLIST: Let It Rain / Hoochie Coochie Man / Walk Out In The Rain / I Want A Little Girl / I Shot The Sheriff / Me And The Devil Blues / They're Red Hot / Milkcow's Calf Blues / If I Had Possession Over Judgment Day / Kind Hearted Woman / Got To Get Better In A Little While / Have You Ever Loved A Woman / Badge / Wonderful Tonight / Layla / Cocaine / Sunshine Of Your Love[1] / Got My Mojo Working[1]

[1]with Robert Randolph on pedal steel guitar

Tim Carmon is still in the band due to Billy Preston's illness.

18 June 2004, Philips Arena, Atlanta, Georgia (with Jimmie Vaughan and the Tilt-A-Whirl Band)

SETLIST: Let It Rain / Hoochie Coochie Man / Walk Out In The Rain / I Want A Little Girl / I Shot The Sheriff / Me And The Devil Blues / They're Red Hot / Milkcow's Calf Blues / If I Had Possession Over Judgment Day / Kind Hearted Woman / Got To Get Better In A Little While / Have You Ever Loved A Woman / Badge / Wonderful Tonight / Layla / Cocaine / Sunshine Of Your Love / Sweet Home Chicago[1]

[1]with Jimmie Vaughan on guitar

Tim Carmon is still in the band due to Billy Preston's illness. Jimmie Vaughan replaced Robert Randolph and the Family Band as the opening act tonight as Robert Randolph and the Family Band were playing at the Wakarusa Festival in Kansas.

19 June 2004, BI-LO Center, Greenville, South Carolina

SETLIST: Let It Rain / Hoochie Coochie Man / Walk Out In The Rain / I Want A Little Girl / I Shot The Sheriff / Me And The Devil Blues / They're Red Hot / Milkcow's Calf Blues / If I Had Possession Over Judgment Day / Kind Hearted Woman / Got To Get Better In A Little While / Have You Ever Loved A Woman / Badge / Wonderful Tonight / Layla / Cocaine / Sunshine Of Your Love / Sweet Home Chicago[1]

[1]with Jimmie Vaughan on guitar

Tim Carmon is still in the band due to Billy Preston's illness. Jimmie Vaughan replaced Robert Randolph and the Family Band as the opening act tonight as Robert Randolph and the Family Band were playing

at the Playboy Jazz Festival in Los Angeles.

21 June 2004, MCI Center, Washington, D.C. (with Robert Randolph and the Family Band)

SETLIST: Let It Rain / Hoochie Coochie Man / Walk Out In The Rain / I Want A Little Girl / I Shot The Sheriff / Me And The Devil Blues / They're Red Hot / Milkcow's Calf Blues / If I Had Possession Over Judgment Day / Kind Hearted Woman / Got To Get Better In A Little While / Have You Ever Loved A Woman / Badge / Wonderful Tonight / Layla / Cocaine / Sunshine Of Your Love[1] / Got My Mojo Working[1]

[1]with Robert Randolph on pedal steel guitar

Tim Carmon is still in the band due to Billy Preston's illness.

23 June 2004, Pepsi Arena, Albany, New York (with Robert Randolph and the Family Band)

SETLIST: Let It Rain / Hoochie Coochie Man / Walk Out In The Rain / I Want A Little Girl / I Shot The Sheriff / Me And The Devil Blues / They're Red Hot / Milkcow's Calf Blues / If I Had Possession Over Judgment Day / Kind Hearted Woman / Got To Get Better In A Little While / Have You Ever Loved A Woman / Badge / Wonderful Tonight / Layla / Cocaine / Sunshine Of Your Love[1] / Got My Mojo Working[1]

[1]with Robert Randolph on pedal steel guitar

Tim Carmon is still in the band due to Billy Preston's illness.

26 June 2004, Wachovia Center, Philadelphia, Pennsylvania (with Robert Randolph and the Family Band)

SETLIST: Let It Rain / Hoochie Coochie Man / Walk Out In The Rain / I Want A Little Girl / I Shot The Sheriff / Me And The Devil Blues / They're Red Hot / Milkcow's Calf Blues / If I Had Possession Over Judgment Day / Kind Hearted Woman / Got To Get Better In A Little While / Have You Ever Loved A Woman / Badge / Wonderful Tonight / Layla / Cocaine / Sunshine Of Your Love[1] / Got My Mojo Working[1]

[1]with Robert Randolph on pedal steel guitar

Tim Carmon is still in the band due to Billy Preston's illness.

28 June 2004 Madison Square Garden, New York City (with Robert Randolph and the Family Band)

SETLIST: Let It Rain / Hoochie Coochie Man / Walk Out In The Rain / I Want A Little Girl / I Shot The Sheriff / Me And The Devil Blues / They're Red Hot / Milkcow's Calf Blues / If I Had Possession Over Judgment Day / Kind Hearted Woman / Got To Get Better In A Little While / Have You Ever Loved A Woman / Badge / Wonderful Tonight / Layla / Cocaine / Sunshine Of Your Love[1] / Got My Mojo Working[1]

[1]with Robert Randolph on pedal steel guitar

Tim Carmon is replacing Billy Preston due to illness.

29 June 2004, Madison Square Garden, New York City (with Robert Randolph and the Family Band)

SETLIST: Let It Rain / Hoochie Coochie Man / Walk Out In The Rain / I Want A Little Girl / I Shot The Sheriff / Me And The Devil Blues / They're Red Hot / Milkcow's Calf Blues / If I Had Possession Over Judgment Day / Kind Hearted Woman / Got To Get Better In A Little While / Have You Ever Loved A Woman / Badge / Wonderful Tonight / Layla / Cocaine / Sunshine Of Your Love[1] / Got My Mojo Working[1]

[1]with Robert Randolph on pedal steel guitar

Tim Carmon is replacing Billy Preston due to illness.

30 June 2004, Madison Square Garden, New York City (with Robert Randolph and the Family Band)

SETLIST: Let It Rain / Hoochie Coochie Man / Walk Out In The Rain / I Want A Little Girl / I Shot The Sheriff / Me And The Devil Blues / They're Red Hot / Milkcow's Calf Blues / If I Had Possession Over Judgment Day / Kind Hearted Woman / Got To Get Better In A Little While / Have You Ever Loved A Woman / Badge / Wonderful Tonight / Layla / Cocaine / Sunshine Of Your Love[1] / Got My Mojo Working[1]

[1]with Robert Randolph on pedal steel guitar

Tim Carmon is replacing Billy Preston due to illness.

JULY 2004

3 July 2004, Tweeter Center for the Performing Arts, Mansfield, Massachusetts (with Robert Randolph and the Family Band)

SETLIST: Let It Rain / Hoochie Coochie Man / Walk Out In The Rain / I Want A Little Girl / I Shot The Sheriff / Me And The Devil Blues / They're Red Hot / Milkcow's Calf Blues / If I Had Possession Over Judgment Day / Kind Hearted Woman / Got To Get Better In A Little While / Have You Ever Loved A Woman / Badge / Wonderful Tonight / Layla / Cocaine / Sunshine Of Your Love[1] / Got My Mojo Working[1]

[1]with Robert Randolph on pedal steel guitar

Billy Preston is back beginning with tonight's performance.

4 July 2004, Tweeter Center for the Performing Arts, Mansfield, Massachusetts (with Robert Randolph and the Family Band)

SETLIST: Let It Rain / Hoochie Coochie Man / Walk Out In The Rain / I Want A Little Girl / I Shot The Sheriff / Me And The Devil Blues / They're Red Hot / Milkcow's Calf Blues / If I Had Possession Over Judgment Day / Kind Hearted Woman / Got To Get Better In A Little While / Have You Ever Loved A Woman / Badge / Wonderful Tonight / Layla / Cocaine / Sunshine Of Your Love[1] / Got My Mojo Working[1]

[1]with Robert Randolph on pedal steel guitar

7 July 2004, Air Canada Centre, Toronto, Ontario, Canada (with Robert Randolph and the Family Band)

SETLIST: Let It Rain / Hoochie Coochie Man / Walk Out In The Rain / I Want A Little Girl / I Shot The Sheriff / Me And The Devil Blues / They're Red Hot / Milkcow's Calf Blues / If I Had Possession Over Judgment Day / Kind Hearted Woman / Got To Get Better In A Little While / Have You Ever Loved A Woman / Badge / Wonderful Tonight / Layla / Cocaine / Sunshine Of Your Love[1] / Got My Mojo Working[1]

[1]with Robert Randolph on pedal steel guitar

9 July 2004, HSBC Arena, Buffalo, New York (with Robert Randolph and the Family Band)

SETLIST: Let It Rain / Hoochie Coochie Man / Walk Out In The Rain / I Want A Little Girl / I Shot The Sheriff / Me And The Devil Blues / They're Red Hot / Milkcow's Calf Blues / If I Had Possession Over Judgment Day / Kind Hearted Woman / Got To Get Better In A Little While / Have You Ever Loved A Woman / Badge / Wonderful Tonight / Layla / Cocaine / Sunshine Of Your Love[1] / Got My Mojo Working[1]

[1]with Robert Randolph on pedal steel guitar

10 July 2004, Gund Arena, Cleveland, Ohio (with Robert Randolph and the Family Band)

SETLIST: Let It Rain / Hoochie Coochie Man / Walk Out In The Rain / I Want A Little Girl / I Shot The Sheriff / Me And The Devil Blues / They're Red Hot / Milkcow's Calf Blues / If I Had Possession Over Judgment Day / Kind Hearted Woman / Got To Get Better In A Little While / Have You Ever Loved A Woman / Badge / Wonderful Tonight / Layla / Cocaine / Sunshine Of Your Love[1] / Got My Mojo Working[1]

[1]with Robert Randolph on pedal steel guitar

12 July 2004, Nationwide Arena, Columbus, Ohio (with Robert Randolph and the Family Band)

SETLIST: Let It Rain / Hoochie Coochie Man / Walk Out In The Rain / I Want A Little Girl / I Shot The Sheriff / Me And The Devil Blues / They're Red Hot / Milkcow's Calf Blues / If I Had Possession Over Judgment Day / Kind Hearted Woman / Got To Get Better In A Little While / Have You Ever Loved A Woman / Badge / Wonderful Tonight / Layla / Cocaine / Sunshine Of Your Love[1] / Got My Mojo Working[1]

[1]with Robert Randolph on pedal steel guitar

13 July 2004, Palace of Auburn Hills, Auburn Hills, Michigan (with Robert Randolph and the Family Band)

SETLIST: Let It Rain / Hoochie Coochie Man / Walk Out In The Rain / I Want A Little Girl / I Shot The Sheriff / Me And The Devil Blues / They're Red Hot / Milkcow's Calf Blues / If I Had Possession Over Judgment Day / Kind Hearted Woman / Got To Get Better In A Little While / Have You Ever Loved A

Woman / Badge / Wonderful Tonight / Layla / Cocaine / Sunshine Of Your Love[1] / Got My Mojo Working[1]

[1]with Robert Randolph on pedal steel guitar

15 July 2004, Conseco Fieldhouse, Indianapolis, Indiana (with Robert Randolph and the Family Band)

SETLIST: Let It Rain / Hoochie Coochie Man / Walk Out In The Rain / I Want A Little Girl / I Shot The Sheriff / Me And The Devil Blues / They're Red Hot / Milkcow's Calf Blues / If I Had Possession Over Judgment Day / Kind Hearted Woman / Got To Get Better In A Little While / Have You Ever Loved A Woman / Badge / Wonderful Tonight / Layla / Cocaine / Sunshine Of Your Love[1] / Got My Mojo Working[1]

[1]with Robert Randolph on pedal steel guitar

17 July 2004, United Center, Chicago, Illinois (with Robert Randolph and the Family Band)

SETLIST: Let It Rain / Hoochie Coochie Man / Walk Out In The Rain / I Want A Little Girl / I Shot The Sheriff / Me And The Devil Blues / They're Red Hot / Milkcow's Calf Blues / If I Had Possession Over Judgment Day / Kind Hearted Woman / Got To Get Better In A Little While / Have You Ever Loved A Woman / Badge / Wonderful Tonight / Layla / Cocaine / Sunshine Of Your Love[1] / Got My Mojo Working[1]

[1]with Robert Randolph on pedal steel guitar

18 July 2004, Xcel Energy Center, St. Paul, Minnesota (with Robert Randolph and the Family Band)

SETLIST: Let It Rain / Hoochie Coochie Man / Walk Out In The Rain / I Want A Little Girl / I Shot The Sheriff / Me And The Devil Blues / They're Red Hot / Milkcow's Calf Blues / If I Had Possession Over Judgment Day / Kind Hearted Woman / Got To Get Better In A Little While / Have You Ever Loved A Woman / Badge / Wonderful Tonight / Layla / Cocaine / Sunshine Of Your Love[1] / Got My Mojo Working[1]

[1]with Robert Randolph on pedal steel guitar

20 July 2004, Bradley Center, Milwaukee, Wisconsin (with Robert Randolph and the Family Band)

SETLIST: Let It Rain / Hoochie Coochie Man / Walk Out In The Rain / I Want A Little Girl / I Shot The Sheriff / Me And The Devil Blues / They're Red Hot / Milkcow's Calf Blues / If I Had Possession Over Judgment Day / Kind Hearted Woman / Got To Get Better In A Little While / Have You Ever Loved A Woman / Badge / Wonderful Tonight / Layla / Cocaine / Sunshine Of Your Love[1] / Got My Mojo Working[1]

[1]with Robert Randolph on pedal steel guitar

22 July 2004, Qwest Center Omaha, Omaha, Nebraska (with Robert Randolph and the Family Band)

SETLIST: Let It Rain / Hoochie Coochie Man / Walk Out In The Rain / I Want A Little Girl / I Shot The Sheriff / Me And The Devil Blues / They're Red Hot / Milkcow's Calf Blues / If I Had Possession Over Judgment Day / Kind Hearted Woman / Got To Get Better In A Little While / Have You Ever Loved A Woman / Badge / Wonderful Tonight / Layla / Cocaine / Sunshine Of Your Love[1] / Got My Mojo Working[1]

[1]with Robert Randolph on pedal steel guitar

24 July 2004, Pepsi Center, Denver, Colorado (with Robert Randolph and the Family Band)

SETLIST: Let It Rain / Hoochie Coochie Man / Walk Out In The Rain / I Want A Little Girl / I Shot The Sheriff / Me And The Devil Blues / They're Red Hot / Milkcow's Calf Blues / If I Had Possession Over Judgment Day / Kind Hearted Woman / Got To Get Better In A Little While / Have You Ever Loved A Woman / Badge / Wonderful Tonight / Layla / Cocaine / Sunshine Of Your Love[1] / Got My Mojo Working[1]

[1]with Robert Randolph on pedal steel guitar

27 July 2004, Key Arena, Seattle, Washington (with Robert Randolph and the Family Band)

SETLIST: Let It Rain / Hoochie Coochie Man / Walk Out In The Rain / I Want A Little Girl / I Shot The Sheriff / Me And The Devil Blues / They're Red Hot / Milkcow's Calf Blues / If I Had Possession Over Judgment Day / Kind Hearted Woman / Got To Get Better In A Little While / Have You Ever Loved A Woman / Badge / Wonderful Tonight / Layla / Cocaine / Sunshine Of Your Love[1] / Got My Mojo Working[1]

[1]with Robert Randolph on pedal steel guitar

28 July 2004, Rose Garden Arena, Portland, Oregon (with Robert Randolph and the Family Band)

SETLIST: Let It Rain / Hoochie Coochie Man / Walk Out In The Rain / I Want A Little Girl / I Shot The Sheriff / Me And The Devil Blues / They're Red Hot / Milkcow's Calf Blues / If I Had Possession Over Judgment Day / Kind Hearted Woman / Got To Get Better In A Little While / Have You Ever Loved A Woman / Badge / Wonderful Tonight / Layla / Cocaine / Sunshine Of Your Love[1] / Got My Mojo Working[1]

[1]with Robert Randolph on pedal steel guitar

30 July 2004, HP Pavilion, San Jose, California (with Robert Randolph and the Family Band)

SETLIST: Let It Rain / Hoochie Coochie Man / Walk Out In The Rain / I Want A Little Girl / I Shot The Sheriff / Me And The Devil Blues / They're Red Hot / Milkcow's Calf Blues / If I Had Possession Over Judgment Day / Kind Hearted Woman / Got To Get Better In A Little While / Have You Ever Loved A Woman / Badge / Wonderful Tonight / Layla / Cocaine / Sunshine Of Your Love[1] / Got My Mojo Working[1]

[1]with Robert Randolph on pedal steel guitar

31 July 2004, HP Pavilion, San Jose, California (with Robert Randolph and the Family Band)

SETLIST: Let It Rain / Hoochie Coochie Man / Walk Out In The Rain / I Want A Little Girl / I Shot The Sheriff / Me And The Devil Blues / They're Red Hot / Milkcow's Calf Blues / If I Had Possession Over Judgment Day / Kind Hearted Woman / Got To Get Better In A Little While / Have You Ever Loved A Woman / Badge / Wonderful Tonight / Layla / Cocaine / Sunshine Of Your Love[1] / Got My Mojo Working[1]

[1]with Robert Randolph on pedal steel guitar

AUGUST 2004

2 August 2004, Hollywood Bowl, Los Angeles, California (with Robert Randolph and the Family Band)

SETLIST: Let It Rain / Hoochie Coochie Man / Walk Out In The Rain / I Want A Little Girl / I Shot The Sheriff / Me And The Devil Blues / They're Red Hot / Milkcow's Calf Blues / If I Had Possession Over Judgment Day / Kind Hearted Woman / Got To Get Better In A Little While / Have You Ever Loved A Woman / Badge / Wonderful Tonight / Layla / Cocaine / Sunshine Of Your Love[1] / Got My Mojo Working[1]

[1] with Robert Randolph on pedal steel guitar

THE CRICKETS AND THEIR BUDDIES 2004

4 August 2004, House Of Blues, Sunset Strip, West Hollywood, California

Billed as "The Crickets and Their Buddies" Eric plays on three numbers with members of Buddy Holly's orginal band.

BAND LINEUP:
Sonny Curtis: vocals, guitar
Jerry Allison: drums
Joe B. Mauldin: bass
Albert Lee: guitar
Eric Clapton: guitar, vocals
Bobby Keys: saxophone on "Fool's Paradise"

SETLIST: Someone, Someone / Fool's Paradise / Think It Over

FILM SESSION FOR *SESSIONS FOR ROBERT J.* 2004

14 August 2004, Hotel Casa Del Mar, Santa Monica, California

SESSION IV (for *Sessions For Robert J* CD/DVD, a companion project to the *Me And Mr. Johnson* album)

SETLIST: Ramblin' On My Mind / Stones In My Passway / Love In Vain

Eric with an acoustic at his raw best in a stripped-down fashion in a big hotel room at the Hotel Casa Del Mar in Santa Monica, California.

DECEMBER 2004

2 December 2004, Abbey Road Studios, London

Eric takes part in the filming of a tribute to Scotty Moore. Eric had first met Scotty during the Rock and Roll Hall Of Fame awards ceremony in New York when Scotty was inducted in 2000. He mentioned that he hoped to record with him at some point in the future. Eric could only attend the first two days of the sessions at Abbey Road and performed three songs with Scotty: "That's All Right," "Money Honey," and "Mystery Train." He sang and performed Elvis's guitar parts on his Signature Martin accompanied by Scotty's leads and backing by Pete Pritchard on bass, Graham Broad on drums, and Scotty's friend Steve Shepherd who filled in on keyboards.

OFFICIAL PRESS RELEASE FOR THE EVENT:
December 2004 and London's famous Abbey Road Studios plays host to a stellar lineup of legendary guitar gods, for a very special one-off tribute concert in honour of The King, with musical direction from his first guitarist, first manager and life-long friend, Scotty Moore. Universal Music is proud to announce the October 3rd 2005 DVD premiere of *A Tribute To The King,* featuring the songs made famous by Elvis Presley, performed by Scotty Moore and friends.

Following on from the re-release of Presley's first single, "That's All Right Mama," it seemed only fitting that during a year which will see more celebrations to mark the 50th Anniversary of Rock 'n' Roll, distinguished guitarist Scotty Moore should lead an exclusive tribute concert, showcasing the music made famous by The King. Moore was joined at Abbey Road by a roster of international guitar heroes including Eric Clapton, Pink Floyd's David Gilmour, Mark Knopfler of Dire Straits, Rolling Stones past and present Bill Wyman and Ronnie Wood, Steve Gibbons, Mike Sanchez, and many more.

Over two dozen Presley classics including "Heartbreak Hotel," "Shake, Rattle And Roll," "All Shook Up," and "Blue Suede Shoes" are captured for DVD in stunning 5.1 dts, 5.1 Dolby Digital Surround Sound, and 2.0 Dolby Stereo. The producer also conducted extensive interviews with Moore,

Jerry Schilling, and the musicians who gathered at Abbey Road, in order to present a collection of bonus feature interviews exclusive to the DVD *A Tribute To The King*.

While fans of Elvis hold a warm place in their hearts for his original guitar player, Scotty Moore is cited as a genuine rock pioneer by guitarists worldwide. A musical role model, respected and admired by professional and amateur guitarists alike, *A Tribute To The King* is a chance for those fans to enjoy again the songs made famous by Elvis Presley and the music founded by Scotty Moore.

Eric plays on the following three numbers:

That's All Right Mama *Tribute To The King* DVD Universal 987294-9 released October 2005

Money Honey *Tribute To The King* DVD Universal 987294-9 released October 2005

Mystery Train *Tribute To The King* DVD Universal 987294-9 released October 2005

Scotty Moore: guitar
Eric Clapton: guitar, vocals
Steve Shepherd: keyboards
Pete Pritchard: bass
Graham Broad: drums

JOOLS HOLLAND'S *HOOTENANNY 2004*

16 December 2004, BBC Television Centre Studios, Wood Lane, London (Jools Holland 12th annual *Hootenanny* rehearsals and filming. Eric joins Jools Holland and His Rhythm & Blues Orchestra to play a couple of numbers. The show is broadcast on 31 December 2004)

BAND LINEUP:
Eric Clapton: guitar, vocals
Mark Flanagan: guitar
Jools Holland: piano
Christopher Holland: organ
Dave Swift: bass
Gilson Lavis: drums
Phil Veacock: saxophone
Lisa Grahame: saxophone
Michael Rose: saxophone
Derek Nash: saxophone

Nick Lunt: baritone saxophone
Rico Rodriguez: trombone
Roger Goslyn: trombone
Fayyaz Virji: trombone
Winston Rollins: trombone
Jason McDermid: trumpet
Jon Scott: trumpet
Chris Storr: trumpet

SETLIST: Stop Breakin' Down Blues / Little Queen Of Spades
Director: Janet Fraser-Crook
Producer: Alison Howe

GARY BROOKER CHRISTMAS CHARITY SHOW 2004

18 December 2004, Chiddingfold Club, Chiddingfold, Surrey (Eric plays with Gary Brooker's No Stiletto Shoes for a thirty-minute guest spot. Eric sang lead on "Kansas City" and "Love Her With A Feeling." The concert raised money for local charities)

GARY BROOKER'S NO STILETTO SHOES LINEUP:
Gary Brooker: keyboards, vocals
Andy Fairweather Low: guitar, vocals
Henry Spinetti: drums
Dave Bronze: bass, vocals
Frank Mead: saxophone, harmonica
Eric Clapton: guitar, vocals

SETLIST: Kansas City / Love Her With A Feeling / Come Together / My Babe / The Weight / Natural Sinner

NEW YEAR'S EVE DANCE 2004

31 December 2004, Woking Leisure Centre, Woking, Surrey

Eric and his band are called Trusted Servants.

BAND LINEUP:
Eric Clapton: guitar, vocals
Gary Brooker: keyboards, vocals
Andy Fairweather Low: guitar, vocals

Chris Stainton: keyboards
Henry Spinetti: drums
Dave Bronze: bass
Ringo Starr: drums and vocals on selected songs

SETLIST 1: Knock On Wood / Reconsider Baby / Home Lovin' / Blueberry Hill / Love Her With A Feeling / Sweet Little Rock And Roller / If Paradise Is Half As Nice / Got My Mojo Working / Hoochie Coochie Man / Sticks And Stones / Lay My Burden Down / Will The Circle Be Unbroken / Whole Lotta Shakin'

SETLIST 2: With A Little Help From My Friends[1] / Honey Don't[1] / Boys[1] / Stormy Monday[2] / I Hear You Knocking[1,2] / Come Together / Old Black Joe / Gin House / Willie And The Hand Jive / Five Long Years / A Whiter Shade Of Pale / Cocaine / Little Queenie

[1] with Ringo Starr on vocals
[2] with Ringo Starr on drums

RECORDING SESSIONS 2004

ERIC CLAPTON GUEST SESSION

OLYMPIC STUDIOS
117 Church Road,
Barnes, London
Guitar overdub session
for Toots and the
Maytals

JANUARY 2004

PRESSURE DROP *True Love* CD V2 released April 2004

Eric overdubs his guitar part for the above number.

ERIC CLAPTON GUEST SESSION

OLYMPIC STUDIOS

117 Church Road, Barnes, London
Guitar and vocal overdub
session for Bruce
Hornsby

JANUARY 2004

GONNA BE SOME CHANGES MADE (Bruce Hornsby) *Halcyon Days* CD Columbia 517400 2 released 2004

Bruce Hornsby: keyboards, vocals
Sting: vocals
Eric Clapton: guitar
J. V. Collier: bass
Sonny Emory: drums

CANDY MOUNTAIN RUN (Bruce Hornsby) *Halcyon Days* CD Columbia 517400 2 released 2004

Bruce Hornsby: keyboards, vocals
Eric Clapton: guitar, vocals
J. V. Collier: bass
Sonny Emory: drums

HALCYON DAYS (Bruce Hornsby) *Halcyon Days* CD Columbia 517400 2 released 2004

Bruce Hornsby: keyboards, vocals
Sting: vocals
Eric Clapton: guitar
J. V. Collier: bass
Sonny Emory: drums
Wayne Pooley: guitar

SPACE IS THE PLACE ((Sonny Emory / J. V. Collier / Bruce Hornsby) *Levitate* CD Verve Records B0013115-02 released September 2009

Bruce Hornsby: piano, vocals
Eric Clapton: guitar
J. V. Collier: bass
Sonny Emory: drums
John "J.T." Thomas: keyboards

Producers: Wayne Pooley / Bruce Hornsby
Engineer: Alan Douglas

ERIC CLAPTON GUEST SESSION

OLYMPIC STUDIOS
117 Church Road,
Barnes, London
Guitar overdub session
for Joe Cocker

MARCH 2004

I PUT A SPELL ON YOU *Heart And Soul* CD released September 2004

Joe Cocker: vocals

Eric Clapton: guitar solo
Ray Brinker: drums
Lee Sklar: bass
Dean Parks: nylon guitar
Mike Landau: guitar
Shane Fontayne: guitar
Rafael Padilla: percussion

ERIC CLAPTON GUEST SESSION

OLYMPIC STUDIOS
117 Church Road,
Barnes, London
Guitar overdub session
for Rod Stewart

MAY 2004

BLUE MOON (Richard Rogers / Lorenz Hart) *Stardust: The Great American Songbook, Volume III* CD J Records released October 2004

Rod Stewart: vocals
Eric Clapton: guitar solo
Joe Sample: piano
Bob Cranshaw: bass
Bob Mann: guitar
Alan Schwatzberg: drums

Producers: Steve Tyrell / Clive Davis
Eric's guitar solo recorded by: Simon Climie

ERIC CLAPTON GUEST SESSION

OLYMPIC STUDIOS
117 Church Road,
Barnes, London
Guitar overdub for Tony
Joe White

OCTOBER 2004

DID SOMEBODY MAKE A FOOL OUT OF YOU (Tony Joe White)
Uncovered CD Swamp 7707243 released September 2006

2005

In terms of musical events, 2005 was without a doubt most notable for the unthinkable reunion of Cream. I say unthinkable because for several decades all the rumors of a reformation came to nothing. Even a three-song set in 1993 at the Rock and Roll Hall of Fame concert led to nothing. It's no surprise that by 2005 people pretty much accepted that it would never happen. So when the announcement was made, it created a huge worldwide buzz. The impact that Cream had made in the musical world was such that the idea of them playing together again was simply incredible. These were the hottest tickets in town.

The first concerts would be at the venue at which they played their last shows back in November 1968, the Royal Albert Hall in London. Anyone in attendance at the first show, and I include the band in this, will never forget the moment they stepped onto the stage. The whole of the Albert Hall stood on their feet and gave them a standing ovation that seemed to go on forever.

The Albert Hall shows were a triumph and the original plan was to head off to New York and play a further three shows at Madison Square Garden. Frustratingly, due to visa complications for Ginger Baker, they were not able to carry on the good vibes over to America and had to wait six months for the matter to be resolved. By the time they made it over to New York, Jack and Ginger started up their aguments again, this time on stage. Eric's anger was obvious for all to see and in his mind at least, they wouldn't be playing together again anytime soon, if at all.

TSUNAMI RELIEF BENEFIT 2005

14 January 2005, BBC Television Centre Studios, Wood Lane, London.

Eric and Roger Waters record an acoustic version of the Pink Floyd classic "Wish You Were Here" that would be transmitted the next day as part of a Tsunami Benefit Relief. They ran through a few takes and nailed it on Take 5. Roger and Eric both sat on stools playing acoustic guitars, Roger singing the lead vocals and playing rhythm, and Eric playing lead. They were backed by vocalists Katie Kissoon, Carol Kenyon, and PP Arnold.

The Tsunami Aid: A Concert of Hope was a high-profile music-and-celebrity-driven benefit that was broadcast from Universal Studios in Universal City, Los Angeles, Rockefeller Center in New York, and the BBC Studios in London. The two-hour concert event was held on 15 January to benefit the victims of the South Asian tsunami disaster that occurred on 26 December 2004. It was broadcast on numerous American television channels and all proceeds raised by the telethon were donated to the American Red Cross International Response Fund.

As well as Eric Clapton and Roger Waters, the show featured performances by artists such as Madonna, Sheryl Crow, Diana Ross, Stevie Wonder, Maroon 5, Norah Jones, Sarah McLachlan, Mary J. Blige, Lenny Kravitz, John Mayer, Kenny Chesney, India Arie, Tom Jones, Brian Wilson, Elton John, Nelly, and

Gloria Estefan. Each artist performed one number in between running documentary and commentary about the tsunami disaster. All performances were recorded in television studios, both in Los Angeles and New York, without an audience present.

BAND LINEUP:
Roger Waters: guitar, vocals
Eric Clapton: guitar
P. P. Arnold: backing vocals
Katie Kissoon: backing vocals
Carol Kenyon: backing vocals

SETLIST: Wish You Were Here

22 January 2005, Tsunami Relief Benefit, Cardiff Millenium Stadium, Cardiff, Wales

Eric at the Tsunami Relief Benefit, Cardiff Millenium Stadium, Cardiff, Wales.

Several of the UK's best-known bands came together at Cardiff's Millennium Stadium on Saturday 22 January to perform in a special fund-raising concert for the victims of the 2004 Indian Ocean tsunami disaster. The seven-hour concert attracted over 60,000 fans who were treated to performances from twenty British bands and solo artists with heavy emphasis on Welsh representatives. The concert was headlined by Eric Clapton and 60,000 tickets sold out within three days. All the musicians performed for free, with all the money raised going toward relief efforts in the tsunami-affected regions. On the day, quite naturally, the atmosphere was emotionally charged, and while the thousands of people gathered at the stadium enjoyed the music, they didn't forget the real reason they were there—to raise as much money as possible for the victims of the Indian Ocean tsunami disaster. The whole concert was broadcast on BBC Radio Wales and on BBC Red Button television.

BAND LINEUP:
Eric Clapton: guitar, vocals
Mark Flanagan: guitar
Jools Holland: piano
Christopher Holland: organ
Pino Palladino: bass
Gilson Lavis: drums
Phil Veacock: saxophone
Lisa Grahame: saxophone
Michael Rose: saxophone
Derek Nash: saxophone

SETLIST: Reconsider Baby / Little Queen Of Spades / Willie And The Hand Jive / Everyday I Have The Blues / Love Her With A Feeling / Shake, Rattle And Roll (all-star finale)

MARCH 2005

COUNTRYSIDE ALLIANCE CONCERT 2005

8 March 2005, Annabel's, London

Eric Clapton plays a concert in support of the Countryside Alliance. Although tickets were £500, the whole place was packed. He played a special thirty-minute performance with Jools Holland accompanied by a full band.

RED NOSE DAY 2005

11 March 2005, Red Nose Day, BBC Television Centre Studios, Wood Lane, London

This was *Comic Relief's 10th Annual Red Nose Day* benefit telethon on the BBC. Eric Clapton joined Jools Holland and His Rhythm & Blues Orchestra for "Reconsider Baby" which was broadcast live. This event supported the Make Poverty History Campaign and was hosted by Chris Evans, Lenny Henry, Jonathon Ross, Davina McCall, Graham Norton, and Dermot O'Leary.

BAND LINEUP:
Eric Clapton: guitar, vocals
Mark Flanagan: guitar
Jools Holland: piano
Christopher Holland: organ
Dave Swift: bass
Gilson Lavis: drums
Phil Veacock: saxophone
Lisa Grahame: saxophone
Michael Rose: saxophone
Derek Nash: saxophone
Nick Lunt: baritone saxophone
Rico Rodriguez: trombone
Roger Goslyn: trombone
Fayyaz Virji: trombone
Winston Rollins: trombone
Jason McDermid: trumpet
Jon Scott: trumpet
Chris Storr: trumpet

SETLIST: Reconsider Baby

ROCK AND ROLL HALL OF FAME 2005

14 March 2005, Waldorf Astoria, Grand Ballroom, New York City

Eric Clapton and B.B. King shared the honor of inducting Buddy Guy into the Rock and Roll Hall Of Fame. Other inductees that evening were U2, the Pretenders, and the O'Jays.

BAND LINEUP:
Eric Clapton: guitar, vocals
Buddy Guy: guitar, vocals
B.B. King: guitar, vocals
Robbie Robertson: guitar, vocals
Jerry Lee Lewis: guitar, vocals
Bo Diddley: guitar, vocals
Rock & Roll Hall Of Fame Band

SETLIST:

Let Me Love You Baby (Buddy Guy, Eric Clapton, B.B. King, and house band) available on Time Life's *Rock and Roll Hall Of Fame* DVD box set and audio from iTunes)

Hey Bo Diddley (Bo Diddley, Eric Clapton, Robbie Robertson, and house band) available on Time Life's *Rock and Roll Hall Of Fame* DVD box set and audio from iTunes)

Whole Lotta Shakin' Goin' On (Jerry Lee Lewis, Eric Clapton, and Robbie Robertson, house band) available on Time Life's *Rock and Roll Hall Of Fame* DVD box set and audio from iTunes

APRIL 2005

TEENAGE CANCER TRUST CONCERT 2005

8 April 2005, Royal Albert Hall, London (Teenage Cancer Trust Concert headlined by UB40 who were also celebrating their 25th anniversary. Eric Clapton was listed among the special guests on adverts for the show. He brought along John Mayer to play as well and Eric shared lead vocals with UB40's Ali Campbell on the Bob Marley classic "I Shot The Sheriff." Eric and John Mayer stayed on stage and played on "Kiss And Say Goodbye" and "Food For Thought")

BAND LINEUP:
Ali Campbell: guitar, vocals
Robin Campbell: guitar, vocals
Earl Falconer: bass
Jimmy Brown: drums
Norman Hassan: percussion, trombone, vocals
Astro: percussion, trumpet, toasting vocals

Brian Travers: saxophone, wind synth, lyricon
Mickey Virtue: keyboards
Eric Clapton: guitar, vocals on "I Shot The Sheriff"
John Mayer: guitar

SETLIST: I Shot The Sheriff / Kiss And Say Goodbye / Food For Thought

Rehearsals for the Cream reunion shows.

MAY 2005

Eric's setup for these concerts were four Fender Stratocasters, all black with two set up for slide, a Fender Custom Shop Tweed twin amp (1957 Tweed reissue), Leslie speaker, Samson wireless pack, Jimi Hendrix Wah Wah Pedal, and a box to switch from the amp to the Leslie or to select both.

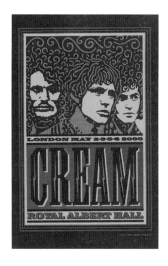

Poster for Cream reunion shows at London's Royal Albert Hall in May 2005.

CREAM REUNION CONCERTS 2005

BAND LINEUP:
Eric Clapton: guitar, vocals
Jack Bruce: bass, vocals, harmonica
Ginger Baker: drums

2 May 2005, Royal Albert Hall, London

SETLIST: I'm So Glad / Spoonful / Outside Woman Blues / Pressed Rat And Wart Hog / Sleepy Time / N.S.U. / Badge / Politician / Sweet Wine / Rollin' And Tumblin' / Stormy Monday / Deserted Cities Of The Heart / Born

Under A Bad Sign / We're Going Wrong / Crossroads / Sitting On Top Of The World / White Room / Toad / Sunshine Of Your Love

3 May 2005, Royal Albert Hall, London

Ginger Baker and Eric Clapton reunite for four special nights as Cream at London's Royal Albert Hall in May 2005.

SETLIST: I'm So Glad / Spoonful / Outside Woman Blues / Pressed Rat And Wart Hog / Sleepy Time / N.S.U. / Badge / Politician / Sweet Wine / Rollin' And Tumblin' / Stormy Monday / Deserted Cities Of The Heart / Born Under A Bad Sign / We're Going Wrong / Crossroads / Sitting On Top Of The World / White Room / Toad / Sunshine Of Your Love

Cream reunited at London's Royal Albert Hall on 3 May 2005.

5 May 2005, Royal Albert Hall, London

SETLIST: I'm So Glad / Spoonful / Outside Woman Blues / Pressed Rat And Wart Hog / Sleepy Time / N.S.U. / Badge / Politician / Sweet Wine / Rollin' And Tumblin' / Stormy Monday / Deserted Cities Of The Heart / Born Under A Bad Sign / We're Going Wrong / Crossroads

/ Sitting On Top Of The World / White Room / Toad / Sunshine Of Your Love

Eric Clapton and Ginger Baker at London's Royal Albert Hall in May 2005.

6 May 2005, Royal Albert Hall, London

SETLIST: I'm So Glad / Spoonful / Outside Woman Blues / Pressed Rat And Wart Hog / Sleepy Time, Time / N.S.U. / Badge / Politician / Sweet Wine / Rollin' And Tumblin' / Stormy Monday / Deserted Cities Of The Heart / Born Under A Bad Sign / We're Going Wrong / Crossroads / Sitting On Top Of The World / White Room / Toad / Sunshine Of Your Love

View from the back: Cream reunited at London's Royal Albert Hall on 3 May 2005.

RECORDING DATES FOR OFFICIAL CD AND DVD RELEASES

DVD TRACK LIST

DISC 1:

I'm So Glad Friday 6 May
Spoonful Friday 6 May
Outside Woman Blues Friday 6 May

Pressed Rat And Warthog Friday 6 May

Sleepy Time Time Tuesday 3 May

N.S.U. Friday 6 May

Badge Tuesday 3 May

Politician Friday 6 May

Sweet Wine Friday 6 May

Rollin' And Tumblin' Friday 6 May

Stormy Monday Tuesday 5 May

Deserted Cities Of The Heart Tuesday 3 May

Born Under A Bad Sign Friday 6 May

We're Going Wrong Friday 6 May

ALTERNATE VERSIONS

Sleepy Time Time Friday 6 May

We're Going Wrong Tuesday 3 May

DISC 2:

Crossroads Friday 6 May

Sitting On Top Of The World Friday 6 May

White Room Tuesday 3 May

Toad Tuesday 5 May

Sunshine Of Your Love Tuesday 3 May

ALTERNATE VERSIONS

Sunshine Of Your Love Friday 6 May

Interviews: Ginger Baker, Jack Bruce, Eric Clapton

Directed by: Martyn Atkins
Executive producer: John Beug
Producer: James Pluta
Co-producer: Scooter Weintraub
Concert producers: Mick Double / Peter Jackson
Audio produced by: Simon Climie

CD TRACK LIST

DISC 1:

I'm So Glad Friday 6 May

Spoonful Friday 6 May

Outside Woman Blues Friday 6 May

Pressed Rat And Warthog Friday 6 May

Sleepy Time Time Tuesday 3 May

N.S.U. Friday 6 May

Badge Tuesday 3 May

Politician Friday 6 May

Sweet Wine Friday 6 May

Rollin' And Tumblin' Friday 6 May

Stormy Monday Thursday 5 May

Deserted Cities Of The Heart Tuesday 3 May

DISC 2:

Born Under A Bad Sign Friday 6 May

We're Going Wrong Friday 6 May

Crossroads Friday 6 May

White room Tuesday 3 May

Toad Thursday 5 May

Sunshine of your love 5

DISC 1: BONUS TRACK

Sleepy Time Time Friday 6 May

Recorded by: Sanctuary Mobile
Audio produced by: Simon Climie
Recording engineer: Alan Douglas

JUNE 2005

THE PICNIC CONCERT BY THE CHAPEL ON THE LAKE 2005

11 June 2005, Wintershall Estate, Bramley, Surrey (the Picnic Concert by the Chapel on the Lake is a charity show in aid of HASTE [Heart And Stroke Trust Endeavour])

BAND DU LAC LINEUP:
Gary Booker: keyboards, vocals
Mike Rutherford: guitar
Andy Fairweather Low: guitar, vocals
Dave Bronze: bass, vocals
Henry Spinetti: drums
Paul Carrack: keyboards, vocals
Graham Broad: percussion
Frank Mead: saxophone, tambourine, maracas
Nick Pentelow: saxophone
Maggie Ryder: backing vocals
Tracy Graham: backing vocals
Tara McDonald: backing vocals

Eric at Wintershall, 11 June 2005.

SETLIST:

Reconsider Baby *Band Du Lac One Night Only Live* DVD Eagle Rock EREDV560 released May 2006

Eric Clapton: guitar, vocals
Gary Brooker: keyboards
Mike Rutherford: guitar
Andy Fairweather Low: guitar
Dave Bronze: bass
Henry Spinetti: drums
Paul Carrack: Hammond B3 organ
Graham Broad: drums
Frank Mead: saxophone
Nick Pentelow: saxophone

Lay Down Sally *Band Du Lac One Night Only Live* DVD Eagle Rock EREDV560 released May 2006

Eric Clapton: guitar, vocals
Gary Brooker: keyboards
Mike Rutherford: guitar
Andy Fairweather Low: guitar, backing vocals
Dave Bronze: bass
Henry Spinetti: drums
Paul Carrack: Hammond B3 organ
Graham Broad: drums
Frank Mead: tambourine
Maggie Ryder: backing vocals
Tracy Graham: backing vocals
Tara McDonald: backing vocals

How Long Blues *Band Du Lac One Night Only Live* DVD Eagle Rock EREDV560 released May 2006

Eric Clapton: guitar
Gary Brooker: keyboards
Mike Rutherford: guitar
Andy Fairweather Low: guitar, backing vocals
Dave Bronze: bass, backing vocals
Henry Spinetti: drums
Paul Carrack: Hammond B3 organ
Graham Broad: drums
Frank Mead: saxophone
Nick Pentelow: saxophone
Maggie Ryder: backing vocals
Tracy Graham: backing vocals
Tara McDonald: backing vocals

Willie And The Hand Jive *Band Du Lac One Night Only Live* DVD Eagle Rock EREDV560 released May 2006

Eric Clapton: guitar, vocals
Gary Brooker: keyboards, vocals
Mike Rutherford: guitar
Andy Fairweather Low: guitar, vocals
Dave Bronze: bass
Henry Spinetti: drums
Paul Carrack: Hammond B3 organ
Graham Broad: drums
Frank Mead: maracas
Nick Pentelow: saxophone
Maggie Ryder: backing vocals
Tracy Graham: backing vocals
Tara McDonald: backing vocals

Stormy Monday *Band Du Lac One Night Only Live* DVD Eagle Rock EREDV560 released May 2006

Eric Clapton: guitar, vocals
Gary Brooker: keyboards
Mike Rutherford: guitar
Andy Fairweather Low: guitar
Dave Bronze: bass
Henry Spinetti: drums
Paul Carrack: Hammond B3 organ
Graham Broad: drums
Frank Mead: saxophone
Nick Pentelow: saxophone
Chris Barber: trombone

Under The Boardwalk (with the Drifters) *Band Du Lac One Night Only Live* DVD Eagle Rock EREDV560 released May 2006

Patrick Alan: vocals
Rohan Delano Turney: vocals
Victor Bynoe: vocals
Peter Lamarr: vocals
Eric Clapton: guitar

Gary Brooker: keyboards
Mike Rutherford: guitar
Andy Fairweather Low: guitar
Dave Bronze: bass
Henry Spinetti: drums
Paul Carrack: Hammond B3 organ
Graham Broad: percussion
Frank Mead: saxophone
Nick Pentelow: saxophone

Stand By Me (with the Drifters) *Band Du Lac One Night Only Live* DVD Eagle Rock EREDV560 released May 2006

Patrick Alan: vocals
Rohan Delano Turney: vocals
Victor Bynoe: vocals
Peter Lamarr: vocals
Eric Clapton: guitar
Gary Brooker: keyboards
Mike Rutherford: guitar
Andy Fairweather Low: guitar
Dave Bronze: bass
Henry Spinetti: drums
Paul Carrack: Hammond B3 organ
Graham Broad: percussion
Frank Mead: saxophone
Nick Pentelow: saxophone

Cocaine *Band Du Lac One Night Only Live* DVD Eagle Rock EREDV560 released May 2006

Eric Clapton: guitar, vocals
Gary Brooker: keyboards
Mike Rutherford: guitar
Andy Fairweather Low: guitar
Dave Bronze: bass
Henry Spinetti: drums
Paul Carrack: Hammond B3 organ
Graham Broad: drums
Frank Mead: saxophone
Nick Pentelow: saxophone
Maggie Ryder: backing vocals
Tracy Graham: backing vocals
Tara McDonald: backing vocals

I Can't Dance *Band Du Lac One Night Only Live* DVD Eagle Rock EREDV560 released May 2006

Eric Clapton: guitar
Gary Brooker: keyboards, vocals
Mike Rutherford: guitar
Andy Fairweather Low: guitar
Dave Bronze: bass

Henry Spinetti: drums
Paul Carrack: Hammond B3 organ
Graham Broad: percussion
Frank Mead: saxophone
Nick Pentelow: saxophone
Maggie Ryder: backing vocals
Tracy Graham: backing vocals
Tara McDonald: backing vocals
Roger Taylor: drums
Patrick Alan: vocals
Rohan Delano Turney: vocals
Victor Bynoe: vocals
Peter Lamarr: vocals

Producer / Director: Perry Joseph
Filmed and recorded by: Outside Broadcast Mobile Unit

AUGUST 2005

PACIFICO JAM 2005

10 August 2005, Largo, Los Angeles, California (Eric jams with Pacifico, a band put together by Wendy Melvoin, Lisa Coleman, and Doyle Bramhall II. Eric joined them to play an epic fifteen-minute version of "Compared To What" with some incendiary guitar work. Both Eric and Doyle were on top of their game this evening. The band consisted of Wendy and Lisa, Doyle Bramhall II, Mike Elizando, Abe Laboriel, Jr., and Susannah Melvoin. Guests at this show were Nikka Costa and Eric Clapton. Prince was in the audience but declined to jam)

Part of the jam is included in the DVD *Before The Music Dies.*

SEPTEMBER 2005

LARRY KING LIVE 2005

3 September 2005, *Larry King Live,* "How You Can Help," CNN Television Studios, New York City

A live fundraising telethon to aid the victims of Hurricane Katrina in New Orleans hosted by Larry King which was broadcast live throughout the U.S. Musical performances were interspersed throughout the show which also included interviews and live reports from New Orleans. Eric and John Mayer played an acoustic version of "Broken Hearted" from Eric's *Pilgrim* album. On the show, Eric (acoustic guitar and vocals) played a 000-28 Martin Acoustic Signature model which was autographed by both him and John Mayer (acoustic guitar and guitar solos) before being auctioned to raise further money for the cause.

OCTOBER 2005

CREAM REUNION CONCERTS NEW YORK 2005

24 October 2005, Madison Square Garden, New York City

SETLIST: I'm So Glad / Spoonful / Outside Woman Blues / Pressed Rat And Warthog / Sleepy Time Time / Tales Of Brave Ulysses / N.S.U. / Badge / Politician / Sweet Wine / Rollin' And Tumblin' / Stormy Monday / Deserted Cities Of The Heart / Born Under A Bad Sign / We're Going Wrong / Crossroads / Sitting On The Top Of The World / White Room / Toad / Sunshine Of Your Love

25 October 2005, Madison Square Garden, New York City

SETLIST: I'm So Glad / Spoonful / Outside Woman Blues / Pressed Rat And Warthog / Sleepy Time Time / Tales Of Brave Ulysses / N.S.U. / Badge / Politician / Sweet Wine / Rollin' And Tumblin' / Stormy Monday / Deserted Cities Of The Heart / Born Under A Bad Sign / We're Going Wrong / Crossroads / Sitting On The Top Of The World / White Room / Toad / Sunshine Of Your Love

26 October 2005, Madison Square Garden, New York City

SETLIST: I'm So Glad / Spoonful / Outside Woman Blues / Pressed Rat And Warthog / Sleepy Time Time / Tales Of Brave Ulysses / N.S.U. / Badge / Politician / Sweet Wine / Rollin' And Tumblin' / Stormy Monday / Deserted Cities Of The Heart / Born Under A Bad Sign / We're Going

Wrong / Crossroads / Sitting On The Top Of The World / White Room / Toad / Sunshine Of Your Love

NOVEMBER 2005

TODAY SHOW

18 November 2005, *Today Show,* NBC Television Studios, New York City (Eric plays "Back Home" on a Martin 000-ECHF Bellezza Bianca acoustic guitar)

DECEMBER 2005

NEW YEAR'S EVE DANCE 2005

31 December 2005, Woking Leisure Centre, Woking, Surrey.

Eric and his band were called Self Denial.

BAND LINEUP:
Eric Clapton: guitar, vocals
Gary Brooker: keyboards, vocals
Chris Stainton: keyboards
Henry Spinetti: drums
Dave Bronze: bass

SETLIST 1: Knock On Wood / Reconsider Baby / Ooh Poo Pa Doo / You Can't Judge A Book / Hoochie Coochie Man / Knockin' On Heaven's Door / Sweet Little Rock And Roller / Not Fade Away / Black Jack / Willie And The Hand Jive / Old Black Joe

SETLIST 2: In the Midnight Hour / Stormy Monday / Poison Ivy / Goodnight Irene / Got My Mojo Working / Blueberry Hill / Five Long Years / A Whiter Shade Of Pale / Cocaine / Little Queenie / Kansas City

RECORDING SESSIONS 2005

ERIC CLAPTON GUEST SESSSION

OLYMPIC STUDIOS
117 Church Road, London
Guitar overdub for
Les Paul

JANUARY 2005

SOMEBODY EASE MY TROUBLIN' MIND *Les Paul & Friends: American Made World Played* CD Capitol 34064 released August 2005

Guitar recorded by: Simon Climie

OLYMPIC STUDIOS
117 Church Road,
Barnes, London
Sessions for *Back Home*

SEPTEMBER 2003, JANUARY 2005–APRIL 2005

Sessions had started back in September 2003 but were abandoned in favor of recording a tribute to Robert Johnson. Eric spent most of 2004 touring in support of the *Me And Mr. Johnson* album and sessions for his new album resumed on and off during January and April 2005.

Eric was joined by numerous guests on this album, including his friend Steve Winwood. Eric had asked him if he would contribute some synth to a cover of George Harrison's "Love Comes To Everyone." Winwood was happy to oblige and suggested he do the overdub at his own home studio in Gloucestershire, Wincraft, and send the results back to Eric as a soundfile via email. Eric was fascinated by this process and had no idea that it could be done that way.

Eric recording Back Home *at Olympic Studios in April 2005.*

SO TIRED (Eric Clapton / Simon Climie) *Back Home* CD Reprise Records US 49395-2 / UK 9362-49395-2 released August 2005

SAY WHAT YOU WILL (Eric Clapton / Simon Climie) *Back Home* CD Reprise Records US 49395-2 / UK 9362-49395-2 released August 2005

I'M GOING LEFT (Stevie Wonder / Syreeta Wright) *Back Home* CD Reprise Records US 49395-2 / UK 9362-49395-2 released August 2005

LOVE DON'T LOVE NOBODY (Charles Simmons / Joseph Jefferson) *Back Home* CD Reprise Records US 49395-2 / UK 9362-49395-2 released August 2005

REVOLUTION (Eric Clapton / Simon Climie) *Back Home* CD Reprise Records US 49395-2 / UK 9362-49395-2 released August 2005

LOVE COMES TO EVERYONE (George Harrison) *Back Home* CD Reprise Records US 49395-2 / UK 9362-49395-2 released August 2005

LOST AND FOUND (Doyle Bramhall II / Jeremy Stacey) *Back Home* CD Reprise Records US 49395-2 / UK 9362-49395-2 released August 2005

PIECE OF MY HEART (Doyle Bramhall II / Mike Elizondo / Susannah Melvoin) *Back Home* CD Reprise Records US 49395-2 / UK 9362-49395-2 released August 2005

ONE DAY (Beverly Darnall / Vince Gill) *Back Home* CD Reprise Records US 49395-2 / UK 9362-49395-2 released August 2005

ONE TRACK MIND (Eric Clapton / Simon Climie) *Back Home* CD Reprise Records US 49395-2 / UK 9362-49395-2 released August 2005

RUN HOME TO ME (Eric Clapton / Simon Climie) *Back Home* CD Reprise Records US 49395-2 / UK 9362-49395-2 released August 2005

BACK HOME (Eric Clapton) *Back Home* CD Reprise Records US 49395-2 / UK 9362-49395-2 released August 2005

IF THAT'S WHAT IT TAKES (Michael MCDonald / Jackie De Shannon) unreleased

FURTHER ON DOWN THE ROAD (Jesse Davis / Taj Mahal) *Old Sock* CD released March 2013

HAPPY HERE unreleased

JOURNEY unreleased

MOCKINGBIRD unreleased

TAKE MY LOVE unreleased

THOUSAND TIMES unreleased

HERE WITHOUT YOU unreleased

Eric Clapton: guitar, vocals
Andy Fairweather Low: guitar
Doyle Bramhall II: guitar

Nathan East: bass
Abraham Laboriel, Jr.: drums
Steve Gadd: drums
Billy Preston: Hammond B3 organ, piano
Simon Climie: programmed keyboards
Lawrence Johnson: backing vocals
Michelle John: backing vocals
Sharon White: backing vocals
Pino Paladino: bass
Chris Stainton: keyboards
Roddy Lorimer: trumpet
Tim Sanders: tenor saxophone
Simon Clarke: baritone saxophone
John Mayer: guitar
Robert Randolph: pedai steel
Paul Fakhourie: bass
Stephen Marley: vocals
Toby Baker: keyboards
Vince Gill: guitar on "One Day"
Steve Winwood: synth on "Love Comes To Everyone"
Gavin Wright: strings
Isobelle Griffiths: strings
Nick Ingman: strings

Producers: Eric Clapton / Simon Climie
Recorded by: Alan Douglas

ERIC CLAPTON GUEST SESSION
OLYMPIC STUDIOS 117 Church Road, Barnes, London Guitar overdub for Marcus Miller

JANUARY 2005

SILVER RAIN (Eric Clapton / Kem / Joey Kibble / Marcus Miller / Bill Withers) *Silver Rain* CD Koch Records 5779 released April 2005

Marcus Miller: bass, piano, keyboards, backing vocals
Eric Clapton: guitar, vocals
Poogie Bell: drums
Bruce Flowers: electric piano
Dean Brown: guitar
Roger Byam: tenor saxophone
Patches Stewart: trumpet
Kenny Garrett: alto saxophone
Jessica Celious: backing vocals
Mark Kibble: backing vocals
Joey Kibble: backing vocals

Producer: Marcus Miller

ERIC CLAPTON GUEST SESSION

OLYMPIC STUDIOS
117 Church Road, Barnes, London
Sessions for B.B. King

14 APRIL 2005

THE THRILL IS GONE (Roy Hawkins / Rick Darnell) *B.B. King 80* CD Geffen Records B0005263-02 released September 2005

B.B. King: guitar, vocals
Eric Clapton: guitar
Clem Clemson: guitar
Chris Stainton: keyboards
Yolander Charles: bass
Ian Thomas: drums
Luke "The Duke" Smith: Hammond B3 organ

Producers: Gary Ashley / Andy McKaie / Floyd Liebermann
Engineers: Phillipe Rose / George Renwick

ERIC CLAPTON GUEST SESSION

OLYMPIC STUDIOS
117 Church Road, London
Guitar overdub for Bob Marley and the Wailers single

APRIL 2005

SLOGAN (Bob Marley) *Africa Unite: The Singles Collection* CD Tuff Gong B0005723-02 released November 2005

Producers: David Marley / Stephen Marley
Engineers: James "Bonzai" Caruso / Marc Lee

ERIC CLAPTON GUEST SESSION

OLYMPIC STUDIOS
117 Church Road, London
Guitar overdub for Robert Randolph and the Family Band

APRIL 2005

JESUS IS JUST ALRIGHT (Arthur S. Reynolds) *Colorblind* CD Warner Bros. 44393-2 released September 2006

Robert Randolph: guitar, vocals
Eric Clapton: guitar
Marcus Randolph: drums
Danyel Morgan: bass
Jason Crosby: Hammond B3 organ

Producer: Tom Whalley
Eric's guitar recorded by: Simon Climie

ERIC CLAPTON AND JJ CALE RECORDING SESSION

CAPITOL STUDIOS
Studio B, 1750 North Vine Street, Hollywood, California
Sessions for *Road To Escondido*

AUGUST 2005

For this session Eric used a Gibson L5 and a black custom shop Fender Stratocaster. These were played through a reissue "low-powered" Fender Tweed twin amp.

DANGER (JJ Cale) *The Road To Escondido* CD Reprise US 44418-2 / UK 9362-44418-2 released November 2006

HEADS IN GEORGIA (JJ Cale) *The Road To Escondido* CD Reprise US 44418-2 / UK 9362-44418-2 released November 2006

MISSING PERSON (JJ Cale) *The Road To Escondido* CD Reprise US 44418-2 / UK 9362-44418-2 released November 2006

WHEN THIS WAR IS OVER (JJ Cale) *The Road To Escondido* CD Reprise US 44418-2 / UK 9362-44418-2 released November 2006

SPORTING LIFE BLUES (Brownie McGhee) *The Road To Escondido* CD Reprise US 44418-2 / UK 9362-44418-2 released November 2006

DEAD END ROAD (JJ Cale) *The Road To Escondido* CD Reprise US 44418-2 / UK 9362-44418-2 released November 2006

IT'S EASY (JJ Cale) *The Road To Escondido* CD Reprise US 44418-2 / UK 9362-44418-2 released November 2006

HARD TO THRILL (Eric Clapton / John Mayer) *The Road To Escondido* CD Reprise US 44418-2 / UK 9362-44418-2 released November 2006

ANYWAY THE WIND BLOWS (JJ Cale) *The Road To Escondido* CD Reprise US 44418-2 / UK 9362-44418-2 released November 2006

THREE LITTLE GIRLS (Eric Clapton) *The Road To Escondido* CD Reprise US 44418-2 / UK 9362-44418-2 released November 2006

DON'T CRY SISTER (JJ Cale) *The Road To Escondido* CD Reprise US 44418-2 / UK 9362-44418-2 released November 2006

LAST WILL AND TESTAMENT (JJ Cale) *The Road To Escondido* CD Reprise US 44418-2 / UK 9362-44418-2 released November 2006

WHO AM I TELLING YOU (JJ Cale) *The Road To Escondido* CD Reprise US 44418-2 / UK 9362-44418-2 released November 2006

RIDE THE RIVER (JJ Cale) *The Road To Escondido* CD Reprise US 44418-2 / UK 9362-44418-2 released November 2006

ANGEL (JJ Cale) *Old Sock* CD Surfdog released March 2013

Eric Clapton: guitars, vocals
JJ Cale: guitars, keyboards, vocals
Christine Lakeland: acoustic guitar, backing vocals
Gary Gilmore: bass
Nathan East: bass
Pino Palladino: bass
Willie Weeks: bass
Abraham Laboriel, Jr.: drums

James Cruce: drums, percussion
Jim Karstein: drums, percussion
Steve Jordan: drums
Dennis Caplinger: fiddle
Albert Lee: guitar
Derek Trucks: guitar
Doyle Bramhall II: guitar
John Mayer: guitar
Taj Mahal: harmonica
Bruce Fowler: horns
Jerry Peterson: horns
Marty Grebb: horns
Steve Madaio: horns
Billy Preston: Hammond B3 organ, Fender Rhodes, Wurlitzer
Walt Richmond: acoustic piano, elecric piano

Producers: Eric Clapton / JJ Cale
Recorded by: Alan Douglas
Co-producer: Simon Climie

24

2006

Eric's touring band for 2006 was quite a treat for anyone who witnessed the shows. The addition of Derek Trucks gave the band the Duane Allman touch and gave several songs a Derek and the Dominos vibe. Eric, Doyle, and Derek worked beautifully together weaving in and out of intricate solos. This lineup was certainly one of the greatest bands Eric had ever put together. Surprisingly, no live recordings were released despite a show in 2007 being filmed and recorded.

Eric's equipment for 2006 consisted of Eric Clapton Signature Fender Stratocasters, some of which were set up for slide work, Martin Acoustics EC Signature models, including the Bellezza Nera, Fender Custom Shop Tweed twin amp (1957 Tweed Reissue), Leslie speaker, Samson wireless pack, Vox Wah Wah Pedal, Boss TR-2 Tremelo Pedal, box to switch from the amp to the Leslie or to select both.

BACK HOME EUROPEAN / UK TOUR 2006

BAND LINEUP:
Eric Clapton: guitar, vocals
Doyle Bramhall II: guitar, vocals
Derek Trucks: guitar
Chris Stainton: keyboards
Tim Carmon: keyboards
Willie Weeks: bass
Steve Jordan: drums
Michelle John: backing vocals
Sharon White: backing vocals
Simon Clarke: baritone saxophone
Roddy Lorimer: tenor saxophone
Tim Sanders: tenor saxophone

MAY 2006

5 May 2006, La Palestre, Le Cannet, Côte d'Azur, France

SETLIST: Pretending / So Tired / Got To Get Better In A Little While / Lost And Found / I Shot The Sheriff / Anyday / Back Home / I Am Yours / Nobody Knows You When You're Down And Out / Milkcow's Calf Blues / Running On Faith / After Midnight / Little Queen Of Spades / Everybody Oughta Make A Change / Motherless Childre / Wonderful Tonight / Cocaine / Layla / Crossroads

8 May 2006, SECC, Glasgow, Scotland (with Robert Cray)

SETLIST: Pretending / So Tired / Got To Get Better In A Little While / Run Home To Me / Revolution / Let It Rain / Back Home / I Am Yours / Nobody Knows You When You're Down And Out / Milkcow's Calf Blues / Running On Faith / After Midnight / Little Queen Of Spades / Everybody Oughta Make A Change / Motherless Children / Wonderful Tonight / Cocaine / Layla / Crossroads[1]

[1]with Robert Cray

9 May 2006, MEN Arena, Manchester (with Robert Cray)

SETLIST: Pretending / So Tired / Got To Get Better In A Little While / Lost And Found / I Shot The Sheriff / Anyday / Back Home / I Am Yours / Nobody Knows You When

You're Down And Out / Milkcow's Calf Blues / Running On Faith / After Midnight / Little Queen Of Spades / Everybody Oughta Make A Change / Motherless Children / Wonderful Tonight / Layla / Cocaine / Crossroads

11 May 2006, NEC, Birmingham (with Robert Cray)

SETLIST: Pretending / So Tired / Got To Get Better In A Little While / Lost And Found / I Shot The Sheriff / Let It Rain / Back Home / I Am Yours / Nobody Knows You When You're Down And Out / Milkcow's Calf Blues / Running On Faith / After Midnight / Little Queen Of Spades / Everybody Oughta Make A Change / Motherless Children / Wonderful Tonight / Layla / Cocaine / Crossroads

12 May 2006, Hallam FM, Sheffield (with Robert Cray)

SETLIST: Pretending / So Tired / Got To Get Better In A Little While / Lost And Found / I Shot The Sheriff / Anyday / Back Home / I Am Yours / Nobody Knows You When You're Down And Out / Milkcow's Calf Blues / Running On Faith / After Midnight / Little Queen Of Spades / Everybody Oughta Make A Change / Motherless Children / Wonderful Tonight / Layla / Cocaine / Crossroads

14 May 2006, Nottingham Arena, Nottingham (with Robert Cray)

SETLIST: Pretending / So Tired / Got To Get Better In A Little While / Bell Bottom Blues / Anyday / I Shot The Sheriff / Back Home / I Am Yours / Nobody Knows You When You're Down And Out / Milkcow's Calf Blues / Running On Faith / After Midnight / Little Queen Of Spades / Everybody Oughta Make A Change / Motherless Children / Wonderful Tonight / Layla / Cocaine / Crossroads[1]

[1]with Robert Cray

16 May 2006, Royal Albert Hall, London (with Robert Cray)

SETLIST: Pretending / So Tired / Got To Get Better In A Little While / Lost And Found / I Shot The Sheriff / Anyday / Back Home / I Am Yours / Nobody Knows You When You're Down And Out / Milkcow's Calf Blues / Running On Faith / After Midnight / Little Queen Of Spades / Everybody Oughta Make A Change / Motherless Children / Wonderful Tonight / Layla / Cocaine / Crossroads[1]

[1]with Robert Cray

The full Band Du Lac lineup including Gary Brooker, Mike Rutherford, Dave Bronze, Henry Spinetti, Paul Carrack, Roger Waters, and Eric Clapton amongst others on stage at Highclere Castle, Hampshire.

17 May 2006, Royal Albert Hall, London (with Robert Cray)

SETLIST: Pretending / So Tired / Got To Get Better In A Little While / Lost And Found / I Shot The Sheriff / Let It Rain / Back Home / I Am Yours / Nobody Knows You When You're Down And Out / Milkcow's Calf Blues / Running On Faith / After Midnight / Little Queen Of Spades / Everybody Oughta Make A Change / Motherless Children / Wonderful Tonight / Layla / Cocaine / Crossroads[1]

[1]with Robert Cray

19 May 2006, Royal Albert Hall, London (with Robert Cray)

SETLIST: Pretending / So Tired / Got To Get Better In A Little While / Lost And Found / I Shot The Sheriff / Anyday / Back Home / I Am Yours / Nobody Knows You When You're Down And Out / Milkcow's Calf Blues / Running On Faith / After Midnight / Little Queen Of Spades / Everybody Oughta Make A Change / Motherless Children / Wonderful Tonight / Layla / Cocaine / Crossroads[1]

[1]with Robert Cray

COUNTRYSIDE ALLIANCE CONCERT 2006

20 May, Highclere Castle, Hampshire

BAND DU LAC LINEUP:
Gary Brooker: keyboards, vocals
Mike Rutherford: guitar
Andy Fairweather Low: guitar
Dave Bronze: bass
Henry Spinetti: dru ms
Paul Carrack: keyboards, vocals
Graham Broad: drums
Frank Mead: saxophone

GUEST APPEARANCES BY:
Eric Clapton: guitar, vocals
Roger Waters: bass, vocals

On a night off from his Albert Hall residency, Eric plays with some mates at the Highclere Rocks Picnic Concert. Appearing with the Band du Lac, he plays "Knock On Wood," "Reconsider Baby," "Stormy Monday," and "Wonderful Tonight." Roger Waters joined the band for the classic Pink Floyd numbers "Wish You Were Here" and "Comfortably Numb" with Eric playing lead guitar.

Mike Rutherford, Roger Waters, and Eric Clapton on stage at Highclere Castle, Hampshire.

SETLIST: Knock On Wood / Reconsider Baby / Stormy Monday / Wonderful Tonight / Wish You Were Here / Comfortably Numb / Whiter Shade Of Pale / Cocaine / Get Up Stand Up / Rainy Day Women

Eric Clapton on stage at Highclere Castle, Hampshire.

22 May 2006, Royal Albert Hall, London (with Robert Cray)

SETLIST: Pretending / So Tired / Got To Get Better In A Little While / Lost And Found / I Shot The Sheriff / Let It Rain / Back Home / I Am Yours / Nobody Knows You When You're Down And Out / Milkcow's Calf Blues / Running On Faith / After Midnight / Little Queen Of Spades / Everybody Oughta Make A Change / Motherless Children / Wonderful Tonight / Layla / Cocaine / Crossroads[1]

[1]with Robert Cray

23 May 2006, Royal Albert Hall, London (with Robert Cray)

Eric Clapton at Royal Albert Hall, May 2006.

SETLIST: Pretending / So Tired / Got To Get Better In A Little While / Old Love / I Shot The Sheriff / Why Does Love Got To Be So Sad / Back Home / I Am Yours / Nobody Knows You When You're Down And Out / Running On Faith / Milkcow's Calf Blues / After Midnight / Little Queen Of Spades / Everybody Oughta Make A Change / Motherless Children / Wonderful Tonight / Layla / Cocaine / Crossroads[1]

[1]with Robert Cray

25 May 2006, Royal Albert Hall, London (with Robert Cray)

SETLIST: Pretending / So Tired / Got To Get Better In A Little While / Old Love / I Shot The Sheriff / Why Does Love Got To Be So Sad / Back Home / I Am Yours / Nobody Knows You When You're Down And Out / Running On Faith / Milkcow's Calf Blues / After Midnight / Little Queen Of Spades / Everybody Oughta Make A Change / Motherless Children / Wonderful Tonight / Layla / Cocaine / Crossroads[1]

[1]with Robert Cray

26 May 2006, Royal Albert Hall, London (with Robert Cray)

SETLIST: Pretending / So Tired / Got To Get Better In A Little While / Old Love[1] / I Shot The Sheriff / Let It Rain / Back Home / I Am Yours / Nobody Knows You When You're Down And Out / Running On Faith / Milkcow's Calf Blues / After Midnight / Little Queen Of Spades / Everybody Oughta Make A Change / Motherless Children / Wonderful Tonight / Layla / Cocaine / Crossroads[1]

[1]with Robert Cray

28 May 2006, Bercy, Paris, France (with Robert Cray)

SETLIST: Pretending / So Tired / Got To Get Better In A Little While / Old Love[1] / I Shot The Sheriff / Anyday / Back Home / I Am Yours / Nobody Knows You When You're Down And Out / Running On Faith / Milkcow's Calf Blues / After Midnight / Little Queen Of Spades / Motherless Children / Wonderful Tonight / Layla / Cocaine / Crossroads[1]

[1]with Robert Cray

29 May 2006, Zenith Arena, Lille, France (with Robert Cray)

SETLIST: Pretending / So Tired / Got To Get Better In A Little While / Old Love[1] / I Shot The Sheriff / Anyday / Back Home / I Am Yours / Nobody Knows You When You're Down And Out / Running On Faith / Milkcow's Calf Blues / After Midnight / Little Queen Of Spades / Everybody Oughta Make A Change / Motherless Children / Wonderful Tonight / Layla / Cocaine / Crossroads[1]

[1]with Robert Cray

31 May 2006, Sports Paleis, Antwerp, Belgium (with Robert Cray)

SETLIST: Pretending / So Tired / Got To Get Better In A Little While / Bell Bottom Blues / After Midnight / Little Queen Of Spades / Let It Rain / Back Home / I Am Yours / Nobody Knows You When You're Down And Out / Running On Faith / Why Does Love Got To Be So Sad / Everybody Oughta Make A Change / Motherless Children / Wonderful Tonight / Layla / Cocaine / Crossroads[1]

[1]with Robert Cray

JUNE 2006

1 June 2006, Ahoy Halle, Rotterdam, Netherlands (with Robert Cray)

SETLIST: Pretending / So Tired / Got To Get Better In A Little While / Bell Bottom Blues / After Midnight / Little Queen Of Spades / Let It Rain / Back Home / I Am Yours / Nobody Knows You When You're Down And Out / Running On Faith / Why Does Love Got To Be So Sad / Everybody Oughta Make A Change / Motherless Children / Wonderful Tonight / Layla / Cocaine / Crossroads[1]

[1]with Robert Cray

3 June 2006, Festhalle, Frankfurt, Germany (with Robert Cray)

SETLIST: Pretending / So Tired / Got To Get Better In A Little While / Bell Bottom Blues / Why Does Love Got To Be So Sad / Everybody Oughta Make A Change / Motherless Children / Back Home / I Am Yours / Nobody Knows You When You're Down And Out / Running On Faith / After Midnight / Little Queen Of Spades / Let It Rain / Wonderful Tonight / Layla / Cocaine / Crossroads[1]

[1]with Robert Cray

4 June 2006, Schleyerhalle, Stuttgart, Germany (with Robert Cray)

SETLIST: Pretending / So Tired / Got To Get Better In A Little While / Old Love[1] / Why Does Love Got To Be So Sad / Everybody Oughta Make A Change / Motherless Children / Back Home / I Am Yours / Nobody Knows You When You're Down And Out / Running On Faith / After Midnight / Little Queen Of Spades / Let It Rain / Wonderful Tonight / Layla / Cocaine / Crossroads[1]

[1]with Robert Cray

6 June 2006, Leipzig Arena, Leipzig (with Robert Cray)

SETLIST: Pretending / So Tired / Got To Get Better In A Little While / Old Love[1] / Everybody Oughta Make A Change / Motherless Children / Back Home / I Am Yours / Nobody Knows You When You're Down And Out / Running On Faith / After Midnight / Little Queen Of Spades / Let It Rain / Wonderful Tonight / Layla / Cocaine / Crossroads[1]

[1]with Robert Cray

7 June 2006, Wuhlheide, Berlin, Germany (with Robert Cray)

SETLIST: Pretending / So Tired / Got To Get Better In A Little While / Old Love[1] / Everybody Oughta Make A Change / Motherle ss Children / Back Home / I Am Yours / Nobody Knows You When You're Down And Out / Running On Faith / After Midnight / Little Queen Of Spades / Let It Rain / Wonderful Tonight / Layla / Cocaine / Crossroads[1]

[1]with Robert Cray

9 June 2006, Hampton Court Festival, Hampton Court Palace, Surrey

Eric Clapton tears into a solo during his show at Hampton Court on 9 June 2006.

SETLIST: Pretending / So Tired / Got To Get Better In A Little While / Old Love / Everybody Oughta Make A Change / Motherless Children / Back Home / I Am Yours / Nobody Knows You When You're Down And Out / Running On Faith / After Midnight / Little Queen Of Spades / Let It Rain / Wonderful Tonight / Layla / Cocaine / Crossroads

10 June 2006, Hampton Court Festival, Hampton Court Palace, Surrey

SETLIST: Pretending / So Tired / Got To Get Better In A Little While / Old Love / Everybody Oughta Make A Change / Motherless Children / Back Home / I Am Yours / Nobody Knows You When You're Down And Out / Running On Faith / After Midnight / Little Queen Of Spades / Let It Rain / Wonderful Tonight / Layla / Cocaine / Crossroads

JULY 2006

7 July 2006, Piazza Napoleone, Lucca, Italy (with Robert Cray)

SETLIST: Pretending / So Tired / Got To Get Better In A Little While / Old Love[1] / Everybody Oughta Make A Change / Motherless Children / Back Home / I Am Yours / Nobody Knows You When You're Down And Out / Running On Faith / After Midnight / Little Queen Of Spades / Let It Rain / Wonderful Tonight / Layla / Crossroads[1]

[1]with Robert Cray

8 July 2006, Umbria Jazz Festival, Perugia, Italy (with Robert Cray)

SETLIST: Pretending / So Tired / Got To Get Better In A Little While / Old Love / Everybody Oughta Make A Change / Motherless Children / Back Home / I Am Yours / Nobody Knows You When You're Down And Out / Running On Faith / After Midnight / Little Queen Of Spades / Let It Rain / Wonderful Tonight / Layla / Cocaine / Crossroads[1]

[1]with Robert Cray

10 July 2006, Verona Arena, Verona, Italy (with Robert Cray)

SETLIST: Pretending / So Tired / Got To Get Better In A Little While / Old Love[1] / Everybody Oughta Make A Change / Motherless Children / Back Home / I Am Yours / Nobody Knows You When You're Down And Out / Running On Faith / After Midnight / Little Queen Of Spades[1] / Let It Rain / Wonderful Tonight / Layla / Cocaine / Crossroads[1]

[1]with Robert Cray

11 July 2006, Piazza Grande, Locarno, Italy (with Robert Cray)

SETLIST: Pretending / So Tired / Got To Get Better In A Little While / Old Love[1] / Everybody Oughta Make A Change / Motherless Children / Back Home / I Am Yours / Nobody Knows You When You're Down And Out / Running On Faith / After Midnight / Little Queen Of Spades / Let It Rain / Wonderful Tonight / Layla / Cocaine / Crossroads[1]

[1]with Robert Cray

13 July 2006, Cologne Arena, Cologne, Germany (with Robert Cray)

SETLIST: Pretending / So Tired / Got To Get Better In A Little While / Old Love[1] / Everybody Oughta Make A Change / Motherless Children / Back Home / I Am Yours / Nobody Knows You When You're Down And Out / Running On Faith / After Midnight / Little Queen Of Spades / Let It Rain / Wonderful Tonight / Layla / Cocaine / Crossroads[1]

[1]with Robert Cray

14 July 2006, Westfalenhalle, Dortmund, Germany (with Robert Cray)

SETLIST: Pretending / So Tired / Got To Get Better In A Little While / Old Love[1] / Everybody Oughta Make A Change / Motherless Children / Back Home / I Am Yours / Nobody Knows You When You're Down And Out / Running On Faith / After Midnight / Little Queen Of Spades / Let It Rain / Wonderful Tonight / Layla / Cocaine / Crossroads[1]

[1]with Robert Cray

16 July 2006, Stadthalle, Vienna, Austria (with Robert Cray)

SETLIST: Pretending / So Tired / Got To Get Better In A Little While / Old Love[1] / Everybody Oughta Make A Change / Motherless Children / Back Home / I Am Yours / Nobody Knows You When You're Down And Out / Running On Faith / After Midnight / Little Queen Of Spades / Let It Rain / Wonderful Tonight / Layla / Cocaine / Crossroads[1]

[1]with Robert Cray

18 July 2006, László Arena, Budapest, Hungary (with Robert Cray)

SETLIST: Pretending / Got To Get Better In A Little While / I Shot The Sheriff / Old Love[1] / Everybody Oughta Make A Change / Motherless Children / Back Home / I Am Yours / Nobody Knows You When You're Down And Out / Running On Faith / After Midnight / Little Queen Of Spades / Further On Up The Road / Wonderful Tonight / Layla / Cocaine / Crossroads[1]

[1]with Robert Cray

20 July 2006, Sazka Arena, Prague, Czech Republic (with Robert Cray)

SETLIST: Pretending / I Shot The Sheriff / Got To Get Better In A Little While / Old Love[1] / Everybody Oughta Make A Change / Motherless Children / Back Home / I Am Yours / Nobody Knows You When You're Down And Out / Running On Faith / After Midnight / Little Queen Of Spades / Further On Up The Road / Wonderful Tonight / Layla / Cocaine / Crossroads[1]

[1]with Robert Cray

22 July 2006, Olympiahalle, Munich, Germany (with Robert Cray)

SETLIST: Pretending / I Shot The Sheriff / Got To Get Better In A Little While / Old Love[1] / Everybody Oughta Make A Change / Motherless Children / Back Home / I Am Yours / Nobody Knows You When You're Down And Out / Running On Faith / After Midnight / Little Queen Of Spades / Further On Up The Road / Wonderful Tonight / Layla / Cocaine / Crossroads[1]

[1]with Robert Cray

23 July 2006, SAP Arena, Mannheim, Germany (with Robert Cray)

SETLIST: Pretending / I Shot The Sheriff / Got To Get Better In A Little While / Old Love[1] / Everybody Oughta Make A Change / Motherless Children / Back Home / I Am Yours / Nobody Knows You When You're Down And Out / Running On Faith / After Midnight / Little Queen Of Spades / Further On Up The Road / Wonderful Tonight / Layla / Cocaine / Crossroads[1]

[1]with Robert Cray

25 July 2006, Color Line Arena, Hamburg, Germany (with Robert Cray)

SETLIST: Pretending / I Shot The Sheriff / Got To Get Better In A Little While / Old Love[1] / Everybody Oughta Make A Change / Motherless Children / Back Home / I Am Yours / Nobody Knows You When You're Down And Out / Running On Faith / After Midnight / Little Queen Of Spades / Further On Up The Road / Wonderful Tonight / Layla / Cocaine / Crossroads[1]

[1]with Robert Cray

26 July 2006, Augustenborg Castle, Denmark (with Robert Cray)

SETLIST: Pretending / I Shot The Sheriff / Got To Get Better In A Little While / Old Love[1] / Everybody Oughta Make A Change / Motherless Children / Back Home / I Am Yours / Nobody Knows You When You're Down And Out / Running On Faith / After Midnight / Little Queen Of Spades / Further On Up The Road / Wonderful Tonight / Layla / Cocaine / Crossroads[1]

[1]with Robert Cray

28 July 2006, Spektrum, Oslo, Norway (with Robert Cray)

SETLIST: Pretending / I Shot The Sheriff / Got To Get Better In A Little While / Old Love[1] / Everybody Oughta Make A Change / Motherless Children / Back Home / I Am Yours / Nobody Knows You When You're Down And Out / Running On Faith / After Midnight / Little Queen Of Spades / Further On Up The Road / Wonderful Tonight / Layla / Cocaine / Crossroads[1]

[1]with Robert Cray

29 July 2006, Globen, Stockholm, Sweden (with Robert Cray)

SETLIST: Pretending / I Shot The Sheriff / Got To Get Better In A Little While / Old Love[1] / Everybody Oughta Make A Change / Motherless Children / Back Home / I Am Yours / Nobody Knows You When You're Down And Out / Running On Faith / After Midnight / Little Queen Of Spades / Further On Up The Road / Wonderful Tonight / Layla / Cocaine / Crossroads[1]

[1]with Robert Cray

31 July 2006, Hartwall Arena, Helsinki, Finland (with Robert Cray)

SETLIST: Pretending / I Shot The Sheriff / Got To Get Better In A Little While / Old Love[1] / Everybody Oughta Make A Change / Motherless Children / Back Home / I Am Yours / Nobody Knows You When You're Down And Out / Running On Faith / After Midnight

/ Little Queen Of Spades / Further On Up The Road / Wonderful Tonight / Layla / Cocaine / Crossroads[1]

[1]with Robert Cray

AUGUST 2006

3 August 2006, Red Square, Moscow (canceled)

JAM WITH JIMMIE VAUGHAN 2006

13 August 2006, Cooper Stadium, Columbus, Ohio (Eric Clapton joins Jimmie Vaughan and the Tilt-A-Whirl Band for three numbers. Vaughan was opening for Bob Dylan)

BAND LINEUP:
Jimmie Vaughan: guitar, vocals
Lou Ann Barton: vocals
Eric Clapton: guitar, vocals on "Reconsider Baby"
George Rains: drummer
Bill Willis: Hammond B3 organ, bass foot pedal
Billy Pitman: guitar

SETLIST: Reconsider Baby / Boom-Bapa-Boom / Extra Jimmies

SEPTEMBER 2006

BACK HOME U.S. TOUR 2006

BAND LINEUP:
Eric Clapton: guitar, vocals
Doyle Bramhall II: guitar, vocals
Derek Trucks: guitar
Chris Stainton: keyboards
Tim Carmon: keyboards
Willie Weeks: bass
Steve Jordan: drums
Michelle John: backing vocals
Sharon White: backing vocals

16 September 2006, Xcel Energy Center, Minneapolis, St. Paul, Minnesota (with Robert Cray)

SETLIST: Pretending / I Shot The Sheriff / Got To Get Better In A Little While / Old Love[1] / Everybody Oughta Make A Change / Motherless Children / Back Home / I Am Yours / Nobody Knows You When You're Down And Out / Running On Faith / After Midnight / Little Queen Of Spades / Further On Up The Road / Wonderful Tonight / Layla / Cocaine / Crossroads[1]

[1]with Robert Cray

18 September 2006, Scottrade Center, St. Louis, Missouri (with Robert Cray)

SETLIST: Pretending / I Shot The Sheriff / Got To Get Better In A Little While / Old Love[1] / Everybody Oughta Make A Change / Motherless Children / Back Home / I Am Yours / Nobody Knows You When You're Down And Out / Running On Faith / After Midnight / Little Queen Of Spades / Further On Up The Road / Wonderful Tonight / Layla / Cocaine / Crossroads[1]

[1]with Robert Cray

20 September 2006, United Center, Chicago, Illinois (with Robert Cray)

SETLIST: Pretending / I Shot The Sheriff / Got To Get Better In A Little While / Old Love[1] / Everybody Oughta Make A Change / Motherless Children / Back Home / I Am Yours / Nobody Knows You When You're Down And Out / Running On Faith / After Midnight / Little Queen Of Spades / Further On Up The Road / Wonderful Tonight / Layla / Cocaine / Crossroads[1]

[1]with Robert Cray

21 September 2006, Van Andel Arena, Grand Rapids, Michigan (with Robert Cray)

SETLIST: Pretending / I Shot The Sheriff / Got To Get Better In A Little While / Old Love[1] / Everybody Oughta Make A Change / Motherless Children / Back Home / I Am Yours / Nobody Knows You When You're Down And Out / Running On Faith / After Midnight

/ Little Queen Of Spades / Further On Up The Road / Wonderful Tonight / Layla / Cocaine / Crossroads[1]

[1]with Robert Cray

24 September 2006, Air Canada Center, Toronto, Ontario (with Robert Cray)

SETLIST: Pretending / I Shot The Sheriff / Got To Get Better In A Little While / Old Love[1] / Everybody Oughta Make A Change / Motherless Children / Back Home / I Am Yours / Nobody Knows You When You're Down And Out / Running On Faith / After Midnight / Little Queen Of Spades / Further On Up The Road / Wonderful Tonight / Layla / Cocaine / Crossroads[1]

[1]with Robert Cray

26 September 2006, Scotiabank Place, Ottawa, Ontario, Canada (with Robert Cray)

SETLIST: Pretending / I Shot The Sheriff / Got To Get Better In A Little While / Old Love[1] / Everybody Oughta Make A Change / Motherless Children / Back Home / I Am Yours / Nobody Knows You When You're Down And Out / Running On Faith / After Midnight / Little Queen Of Spades / Further On Up The Road / Wonderful Tonight / Layla / Cocaine / Crossroads[1]

[1]with Robert Cray

28 September 2006, Madison Square Garden, New York City (with Robert Cray)

Beautiful three-poster set for Eric Clapton's concerts at Madison Square Garden on 28, 29, 30 September 2006.

SETLIST: Pretending / I Shot The Sheriff / Got To Get Better In A Little While / Old Love[1] / Everybody Oughta Make A Change / Motherless Children / Back Home / I Am Yours / Nobody Knows You When You're Down And Out / Running On Faith / After Midnight / Little Queen Of Spades / Further On Up The Road / Wonderful Tonight / Layla / Cocaine / Crossroads[1]

[1]with Robert Cray

29 September 2006, Madison Square Garden, New York City (with Robert Cray)

SETLIST: Pretending / I Shot The Sheriff / Got To Get Better In A Little While / Old Love[1] / Everybody Oughta Make A Change / Motherless Children / Back Home / I Am Yours / Nobody Knows You When You're Down And Out / Running On Faith / After Midnight / Little Queen Of Spades / Further On Up The Road / Wonderful Tonight / Layla / Cocaine / Crossroads[1]

[1]with Robert Cray

30 September 2006, Madison Square Garden, New York City (with Robert Cray)

SETLIST: Pretending / I Shot The Sheriff / Got To Get Better In A Little While / Old Love[1] / Everybody Oughta Make A Change / Motherless Children / Back Home / I Am Yours / Nobody Knows You When You're Down And Out / Running On Faith / After Midnight / Little Queen Of Spades / Further On Up The Road / Wonderful Tonight / Layla / Cocaine / Crossroads[1]

[1]with Robert Cray

OCTOBER 2006

3 October 2006, Bank North Garden, Boston, Massachusetts (with Robert Cray)

SETLIST: Pretending / I Shot The Sheriff / Got To Get Better In A Little While / Old Love[1] / Everybody Oughta Make A Change / Motherless Children / Back Home / I Am Yours / Nobody Knows You When You're Down And Out / Running On Faith / After Midnight / Little Queen Of Spades / Further On Up The Road / Wonderful Tonight / Layla / Cocaine / Crossroads[1]
[1]with Robert Cray

4 October 2006, Bank North Garden, Boston, Massachusetts (with Robert Cray)

SETLIST: Pretending / I Shot The Sheriff / Got To Get Better In A Little While / Old Love[1] / Anyday / Motherless Children / Back Home / I Am Yours / Nobody

Knows You When You're Down And Out / Running On Faith / After Midnight / Little Queen Of Spades / Let It Rain / Wonderful Tonight / Layla / Cocaine / Crossroads[1]

[1]with Robert Cray

6 October 2006, Mohegan Sun Casino, Uncasville, Connecticut (with Robert Cray)

SETLIST: Pretending / I Shot The Sheriff / Got To Get Better In A Little While / Old Love[1] / Anyday / Motherless Children / Back Home / I Am Yours / Nobody Knows You When You're Down And Out / Running On Faith / After Midnight / Little Queen Of Spades / Further On Up The Road / Wonderful Tonight / Layla / Crossroads[1]

[1]with Robert Cray

7 October 2006, Mohegan Sun Casino, Uncasville, Connecticut (with Robert Cray)

SETLIST: Pretending / I Shot The Sheriff / Got To Get Better In A Little While / Old Love[1] / Anyday / Motherless Children / Back Home / I Am Yours / Nobody Knows You When You're Down And Out / Running On Faith / After Midnight / Little Queen Of Spades / Let It Rain / Wonderful Tonight / Layla / Cocaine / Crossroads[1]

[1]with Robert Cray

9 October 2006, Wachovia Center, Philadelphia, Pennsylvania (with Robert Cray)

SETLIST: Pretending / I Shot The Sheriff / Got To Get Better In A Little While / Old Love[1] / Anyday / Motherless Children / Back Home / I Am Yours / Nobody Knows You When You're Down And Out / Running On Faith / After Midnight / Little Queen Of Spades / Further On Up The Road / Wonderful Tonight / Layla / Cocaine / Crossroads[1]

[1]with Robert Cray

10 October 2006, Verizon Center, Washington, D.C. (with Robert Cray)

SETLIST: Pretending / I Shot The Sheriff / Got To Get Better In A Little While / Old Love[1] / Anyday / Motherless Children / Back Home / I Am Yours / Nobody Knows You When You're Down And Out / Running On Faith / After

Midnight / Little Queen Of Spades / Further On Up The Road / Wonderful Tonight / Layla / Cocaine / Crossroads[1]

[1]with Robert Cray

12 October 2006, John Paul Jones Arena, Charlottesville, Virginia (with Robert Cray)

SETLIST: Pretending / I Shot The Sheriff / Got To Get Better In A Little While / Old Love[1] / Anyday / Motherless Children / Back Home / I Am Yours / Nobody Knows You When You're Down And Out / Running On Faith / After Midnight / Little Queen Of Spades / Further On Up The Road / Wonderful Tonight / Layla / Cocaine / Crossroads[1]

[1]with Robert Cray

14 October 2006, Gwinnet Civic Center, Duluth, Georgia (with Robert Cray)

SETLIST: Pretending / I Shot The Sheriff / Got To Get Better In A Little While / Old Love[1] / Anyday / Motherless Children / Back Home / I Am Yours / Nobody Knows You When You're Down And Out / Running On Faith / After Midnight / Little Queen Of Spades / Further On Up The Road / Wonderful Tonight / Layla / Cocaine / Crossroads[1]

[1]with Robert Cray

15 October 2006, RBC Center, Raleigh, North Carolina (with Robert Cray)

SETLIST: Pretending / I Shot The Sheriff / Got To Get Better In A Little While / Old Love[1] / Anyday / Motherless Children / Back Home / I Am Yours / Nobody Knows You When You're Down And Out / Running On Faith / After Midnight / Little Queen Of Spades / Further On Up The Road / Wonderful Tonight / Layla / Cocaine / Crossroads[1]

[1]with Robert Cray

17 October 2006, Charlotte Bobcats Arena, Charlotte, North Carolina (with Robert Cray)

SETLIST: Pretending / I Shot The Sheriff / Got To Get Better In A Little While / Old Love[1] / Anyday / Motherless Children / Back Home / I Am Yours / Nobody Knows You When You're Down And Out / Running On Faith / After Midnight / Little Queen Of Spades / Further On Up The Road / Wonderful Tonight / Layla / Cocaine / Crossroads[1]

¹with Robert Cray

18 October 2006, Jefferson Arena, Birmingham, Alabama (with Robert Cray)

SETLIST: Pretending / I Shot The Sheriff / Got To Get Better In A Little While / Old Love¹ / Anyday / Motherless Children / Key To The Highway / San Francisco Bay Blues / Nobody Knows You When You're Down And Out / Running On Faith / After Midnight / Little Queen Of Spades / Further On Up The Road / Wonderful Tonight / Layla / Cocaine / Crossroads¹

¹with Robert Cray

“'Got to Get Better in a Little While' was written after the *Layla* sessions or it would have for sure been on the record. When we did the Johnny Cash show we had nothing to do with what they aired or didn't air. We left the next morning to continue on our road trip. The reason that song hasn't worked yet for Eric since we were together is that it has to do with the guitar and the piano working off of each other. It's not that I consider myself a great piano player because I'm not! Chuck Leavell is, though. But having said that, I do play a mighty fine rhythm keyboard no matter if it's an organ or a piano. That's just the way I approach my instrument. Like it was a kit of drums. That song plays off of the piano rhythm and the guitar rhythm. It's Eric and me feeding off each other. Check it out! Now it will make sense to you I'm sure. Everything gets it's queue from the guitar rhythm, then the piano rhythm. And the deal is that I never played it the same way twice. Ever! Even when we played it every night it was always different. That's because it is infinite! Always changing. Always evolving. We went to see Eric and his band in Birmingham, Alabama. They knew that we were going to be there. That night Eric dedicated 'Anyday' to me and he kept looking our way. . . . That is until they did 'Got to Get Better in a Little While.' Chris was playing some real straight part and they were trying to make it happen with the drums and clever little moves and rhythms but it wasn't happening. The keyboard player ain't got it right! And he never will get it right because he would have to be me to do it!”

—BOBBY WHITLOCK

20 October 2006, TD Waterhouse Center, Orlando, Florida (with Robert Cray)

SETLIST: Pretending / I Shot The Sheriff / Got To Get Better In A Little While / Old Love¹ / Anyday / Motherless Children / Key To The Highway / San Francisco Bay Blues / Nobody Knows You When You're Down And Out / Running On Faith / After Midnight / Little Queen Of Spades / Further On Up The Road / Wonderful Tonight / Layla / Cocaine / Crossroads¹

¹with Robert Cray

21 October 2006, Veterans Memorial Arena, Jacksonville, Florida (with Robert Cray)

SETLIST: Pretending / I Shot The Sheriff / Got To Get Better In A Little While / Old Love¹ / Anyday / Motherless Children / Key To The Highway / San Francisco Bay Blues / Nobody Knows You When You're Down And Out / Running On Faith / After Midnight / Little Queen Of Spades / Further On Up The Road / Wonderful Tonight / Layla / Cocaine / Crossroads¹

¹with Robert Cray

23 October 2006, American Airlines Arena, Miami, Florida (with Robert Cray)

SETLIST: Pretending / I Shot The Sheriff / Got To Get Better In A Little While / Old Love¹ / Anyday / Motherless Children / Key To The Highway / San Francisco Bay Blues / Nobody Knows You When You're Down And Out / Running On Faith / After Midnight / Little Queen Of Spades / Further On Up The Road / Wonderful Tonight / Layla / Cocaine / Crossroads¹

¹with Robert Cray

NOVEMBER 2006

JAPAN TOUR 2006

BAND LINEUP:
Eric Clapton: guitar, vocals
Doyle Bramhall II: guitar
Derek Trucks: guitar
Chris Stainton: keyboards
Tim Carmon: keyboards
Willie Weeks: bass

Steve Jordan: drums
Michelle John: backing vocals
Sharon White: backing vocals

11 November 2006, Castle Hall, Osaka, Japan

Eric and his band on stage at the Osaka-Jo Hall, Castle Hall, Osaka, Japan, on 11 November 2006.

SETLIST: Pretending / I Shot The Sheriff / Got To Get Better In A Little While / Old Love / Tell The Truth / Motherless Children / Key To The Highway / Outside Woman Blues / San Francisco Bay Blues / Nobody Knows You When You're Down And Out / Running On Faith / After Midnight / Little Queen Of Spades / Further On Up The Road / Wonderful Tonight / Layla / Cocaine / Crossroads

12 November 2006, Castle Hall, Osaka, Japan

SETLIST: Pretending / I Shot The Sheriff / Got To Get Better In A Little While / Old Love / Tell The Truth / Motherless Children / Key To The Highway / Outside Woman Blues / San Francisco Bay Blues / Nobody Knows You When You're Down And Out / Running On Faith / After Midnight / Little Queen Of Spades / Further On Up The Road / Wonderful Tonight / Layla / Cocaine / Crossroads

14 November 2006, Castle Hall, Osaka, Japan

SETLIST: Pretending / Got To Get Better in A Little While / Old Love / Tell The Truth / Anyday / Motherless Children / Drifting Blues / Key To The Highway / Outside Woman Blues / Nobody Knows You When You're Down And Out / Running On Faith / After Midnight / Little

Queen Of Spades / Further On Up The Road / Wonderful Tonight / Layla / Cocaine / Crossroads

15 November 2006, Castle Hall, Osaka, Japan

SETLIST: Pretending / Got To Get Better In A Little While / Old Love / Anyday / Motherless Children / Drifting Blues / Key To The Highway / Outside Woman Blues / Nobody Knows You When You're Down And Out / Running On Faith / After Midnight / Little Queen Of Spades / Tell The Truth / Wonderful Tonight / Layla / Cocaine / Crossroads

17 November 2006, Rainbow Hall, Nagoya, Japan

Eric Clapton in Nagoya, Japan, 17 November 2006.

SETLIST: Tell The Truth / Got To Get Better In A Little While / Old Love / Anyday / Motherless Children / Drifting Blues / Key To The Highway / Outside Woman Blues / Nobody Knows You When You're Down And Out / Running On Faith / After Midnight / Little Queen Of Spades / Pretending / Wonderful Tonight / Layla / Cocaine / Crossroads

18 November 2006, Rainbow Hall, Nagoya, Japan

SETLIST: Tell The Truth / Pretending / Got To Get Better In A Little While / Old Love / Motherless Children / Drifting Blues / Key To The Highway / Outside Woman Blues / Nobody Knows You When You're Down And Out / Running On Faith / After Midnight / Little Queen Of Spades / Before You Accuse Me / Wonderful Tonight / Layla / Cocaine / Crossroads

20 November 2006, Budokan, Tokyo, Japan

SETLIST: Tell The Truth / Five Long Years / Got To Get Better In A Little While / Old Love / Motherless Children / Drifting Blues / Key To The Highway / Outside Woman Blues / Nobody Knows You When You're Down And Out / Running On Faith / After Midnight / Little Queen Of Spades / Before You Accuse Me / Wonderful Tonight / Layla / Cocaine / Crossroads

21 November 2006, Budokan, Tokyo, Japan

SETLIST: Tell The Truth / Five Long Years / Got To Get Better In A Little While / Old Love / Motherless Children / Drifting Blues / Key To The Highway / Outside Woman Blues / Nobody Knows You When You're Down And Out / Running On Faith / After Midnight / Little Queen Of Spades / Before You Accuse Me / Wonderful Tonight / Layla / Cocaine / Crossroads

23 November 2006, Budokan, Tokyo, Japan

SETLIST: Tell The Truth / Five Long Years / Got To Get Better In A Little While / Old Love / Motherless Children / Drifting Blues / Key To The Highway / Outside Woman Blues / Nobody Knows You When You're Down And Out / Running On Faith / After Midnight / Little Queen Of Spades / Anyday / Wonderful Tonight / Layla / Cocaine / Crossroads

24 November 2006, Budokan, Tokyo, Japan

SETLIST: Tell The Truth / Five Long Years / Got To Get Better In A Little While / Old Love / Motherless Children / Drifting Blues / Key To The Highway / Outside Woman Blues / Nobody Knows You When You're Down And Out / Running On Faith / After Midnight / Little Queen Of Spades / Anyday / Wonderful Tonight / Layla / Cocaine / Crossroads

26 November 2006, Sapporo Dome, Sapporo, Japan

SETLIST: Tell The Truth / Got To Get Better In A Little While / Old Love / Motherless Children / When You Got A Good Friend / Key To The Highway / Outside Woman Blues / Nobody Knows You When You're Down And Out / Running On Faith / After Midnight / Little Queen Of Spades / Anyday / Wonderful Tonight / Layla / Cocaine / Crossroads

29 November 2006, Budokan, Tokyo, Japan

SETLIST: Tell The Truth / Got To Get Better In A Little While / Old Love / Motherless Children / Ramblin' On My Mind / Key To The Highway / Outside Woman Blues / Nobody Knows You When You're Down And Out / Running On Faith / After Midnight / Little Queen Of Spades / Anyday / Wonderful Tonight / Layla / Cocaine / Crossroads

30 November 2006, Budokan, Tokyo, Japan

SETLIST: Tell The Truth / Key To The Highway / Got To Get Better In A Little While / Old Love / Motherless Children / Ramblin' On My Mind / Outside Woman Blues / Nobody Knows You When You're Down And Out / Running On Faith / After Midnight / Little Queen Of Spades / Anyday / Wonderful Tonight / Layla / Cocaine / Crossroads

DECEMBER 2006

2 December 2006, Saitama Super Arena, Saitama, Japan

SETLIST: Tell The Truth / Key To The Highway / Got To Get Better In A Little While / Old Love / Motherless Children / Ramblin' On My Mind / Outside Woman Blues / Nobody Knows You When You're Down And Out / Running On Faith / After Midnight / Little Queen Of Spades / Anyday / Wonderful Tonight / Layla / Cocaine / Crossroads

4 December 2006, Saitama Super Arena, Saitama, Japan (Eric attends U2 show. U2 were in Japan playing at the Saitama Super Arena and were staying in the same hotel as Eric. They spent some time together and they invited Eric to their 4 December show. Eric attended and chatted with The Edge and Larry Mullen before they went on stage. As a little tribute to Eric, at the end of "Beautiful Day," Bono sang, "I have finally found a way to live in the presence of the Lord . . . Eric Clapton!")

5 December 2006, Budokan, Tokyo, Japan

SETLIST: Tell The Truth / Key To The Highway / Got To Get Better In A Little While / Old Love / Motherless Children / Drifting Blues / Outside Woman Blues / Nobody

Final bow during Japan tour 2006.

Knows You When You're Down And Out / Running On Faith / After Midnight / Little Queen Of Spades / Anyday / Wonderful Tonight / Layla / Cocaine / Crossroads

6 December 2006, Budokan, Tokyo, Japan

SETLIST: Tell The Truth / Key To The Highway / Got To Get Better In A Little While / Little Wing / Motherless Children / Ramblin' On My Mind / Outside Woman Blues / Nobody Knows You When You're Down And Out / Running On Faith / After Midnight / Little Queen Of Spades / Further On Up The Road / Wonderful Tonight / Layla / Cocaine / Crossroads

8 December 2006, Budokan, Tokyo, Japan

SETLIST: Tell The Truth / Key To The Highway / Got To Get Better In A Little While / Little Wing / Motherless Children / Drifting Blues / Outside Woman Blues / Nobody Knows You When You're Down And Out / Running On Faith / Why Does Love Got To Be So Sad / Little Queen Of Spades / Further On Up The Road / Wonderful Tonight / Layla / Cocaine / Crossroads

Eric solos at the Budokan, Tokyo, on 8 December 2006.

9 December 2006, Budokan, Tokyo, Japan

Derek Trucks on slide and Eric Clapton on lead in Japan 2006.

SETLIST: Tell The Truth / Key To The Highway / Got To Get Better In A Little While / Little Wing / Why Does Love Got To Be So Sad / Ramblin' On My Mind / Outside Woman Blues / Nobody Knows You When You're Down And Out / Running On Faith / Motherless Children / Little Queen Of Spades / Anyday / Wonderful Tonight / Layla / Cocaine / Crossroads

GARY BROOKER CHRISTMAS SHOW 2006

15 December 2006, Chiddingfold Club, Woodside Road, Chiddingfold, Surrey (Eric Clapton sits in with Gary Brooker's No Stiletto Shoes and plays on four numbers)

NO STILETTO SHOES LINEUP:
Gary Brooker: vocals, keyboards
Andy Fairweather Low: guitar, vocals
Dave Bronze: bass, vocals
Frank Mead: saxophone, harmonica, percussion
Eric Clapton: guitar, vocals

SETLIST: Little Wheel / Drifting Blues / Reconsider Baby / Stand By Me

NEW YEAR'S EVE DANCE 2006

31 December 2006, Woking Leisure Centre, Woking, Surrey

Eric and the band are called the Hampshire Grenadiers.

BAND LINEUP:
Eric Clapton: guitar, vocals
Andy Fairweather Low: guitar, vocals
Gary Brooker: keyboards, vocals
Chris Stainton: keyboards
Dave Bronze: bass
Henry Spinetti: drums
Michelle John: backing vocals
Sharon White: backing vocals

SETLIST 1: Knock On Wood / Reconsider Baby / Poison Ivy / Shake, Rattle And Roll / Hoochie Coochie Man / Got My Mojo Working / It Takes A Worried Man / Willie And The Hand Jive / Whole Lotta Shakin'

SETLIST 2: Midnight Hour / Stormy Monday / You Can't Judge A Book / Blueberry Hill / Lay My Burden Down / Will The Circle Be Unbroken / Five Long Years / A Whiter Shade Of Pale / Cocaine / Little Queenie / Cigarettes, Whiskey And Wild, Wild Women

RECORDING SESSIONS 2006
ERIC CLAPTON GUEST SESSION
OLYMPIC STUDIOS 117 Church Road, Barnes, London Session for Sam Moore

MAY 2006

YOU ARE SO BEAUTIFUL (Bruce Fisher / Billy Preston) *Overnight Sensational* CD Rhino Kode1009 released August 2006

Sam Moore: vocals
Eric Clapton: guitar solo
Billy Preston: piano
Zucchero Fornaciari: vocals
Robert Randolph: pedal steel guitar
Robert Bacon: guitar
Mike Finnigan: Hammond B3 organ
Kenneth Crouch: keyboards
Cornelius Mims: bass
Michael Bland: drums
Sherree Ford Brown: backing vocals
Tabitha Fair: backing vocals

Siedah Garrett: backing vocals
Sharlotte Gibson: backing vocals
Joel Derouin: concert master
Charles Bisharat: violin
Susan Chapman: violin
Mario Deleon: violin
Armen Garabedian: violin
Gerry Hilera: violin
Alyssa Park: violin
Michelle Richards: violin
Josefiina Vergara: violin
Karen Bakunin: viola
Andrew Dickles: viola
David Stenske: viola
Larry Corbett: cello
Steve Richards: cello
Dan Smith: cello
Rudy Stein: cello

Producer: Randy Jackson
Engineer: Alan Douglas

ERIC CLAPTON GUEST SESSION

CAPITOL STUDIOS
Studio B, 1750 North Vine Street, Hollywood, California
Sessions for Stephen Bishop

4 NOVEMBER 2006

> **"**Eric's been on tour for almost a year . . . he's still on tour. But he took off time from his really busy schedule here. He zoomed in to L.A. and was doing all these interviews for his new album, and then he just came over and we wound up trying him on three different guitars. Electric guitars, Spanish guitar, and we borrowed this acoustic steel string 'cause we didn't have one—I have a million at home, but we didn't have one in the studio.**"**
>
> **—STEPHEN BISHOP**

SAVE IT FOR A RAINY DAY (Stephen Bishop) *Saudade* CD OEM-00035-5 released February 2007 / *Romance In Rio* CD 180 Music 17796 released September 2009

Stephen Bishop: vocals
Eric Clapton: acoustic steel guitar
Oscar Castro-Neves: keyboards, guitar
Alex Acuna: drums
Brian Bromberg: bass
Kevin Ricard: percussion
Charlotte Gibson: backing vocals

Producer: Oscar Castro-Neves
Engineer: Charlie Paakkari

25

2007

JANUARY 2007

FAR EAST TOUR 2007

13 January 2007, Singapore Indoor Stadium, Singapore (due to strict drug laws Eric is banned from playing "Cocaine")

SETLIST: Tell The Truth / Key To The Highway / Got To Get Better In A Little While / Little Wing / Why Does Love Got To Be So Sad / Drifting Blues / Outside Woman Blues / Nobody Knows You When You're Down and Out / Running On Faith / Motherless Children / Little Queen Of Spades / Further On Up The Road / Wonderful Tonight / Layla / Crossroads

15 January 2007, Impact Arena, Bangkok, Thailand

SETLIST: Tell The Truth / Key To The Highway / Got To Get Better In A Little While / Little Wing / Why Does Love Got To Be So Sad / Drifting Blues / Outside Woman Blues / Nobody Knows You When You're Down and Out / Running On Faith / Motherless Children / Little Queen Of Spades / Further On Up The Road / Wonderful Tonight / Layla / Crossroads

17 January 2007, Asia World Arena, Hong Kong, China

SETLIST: Tell The Truth / Key To The Highway / Got To Get Better In A Little While / Little Wing / Why Does Love Got To Be So Sad / Drifting Blues / Outside Woman Blues / Nobody Knows You When You're Down And Out / Running On Faith / Motherless Children / Little Queen Of Spades / Anyday / Wonderful Tonight / Layla / Cocaine / Crossroads

20 January 2007, Grand Stage, Shanghai, China (once again, Eric was banned from playing "Cocaine")

SETLIST: Tell The Truth / Key To The Highway / Got To Get Better In A Little While / Little Wing / Why Does Love Got To Be So Sad / Drifting Blues / Outside Woman Blues / Nobody Knows You When You're Down and Out / Running On Faith / Motherless Children / Little Queen Of Spades / Further On Up The Road / Wonderful Tonight / Layla / Crossroads

23 January 2007, Olympic Gymnasium No.1, Seoul, Korea

SETLIST: Tell The Truth / Key To The Highway / Got To Get Better In A Little While / Little Wing / Why Does Love Got To Be So Sad / Drifting Blues / Outside Woman Blues / Nobody Knows You When You're Down And Out / Running On Faith / Motherless Children / Little Queen Of Spades / Anyday / Wonderful Tonight / Layla / Cocaine / Crossroads

Poster for Eric Clapton 2007 tour in Australia.

AUSTRALIA / NEW ZEALAND TOUR 2007

BAND LINEUP:
Eric Clapton: guitar, vocals
Doyle Bramhall II: guitar
Derek Trucks: guitar
Chris Stainton: keyboards
Tim Carmon: keyboards
Willie Weeks: bass
Steve Jordan: drums
Michelle John: backing vocals
Sharon White: backing vocals

27 January 2007, Mission Estate Winery Concert, Hawkes Bay, New Zealand

SETLIST: Tell The Truth / Key To The Highway / Got To Get Better In A Little While / Little Wing / Why Does Love Got To Be So Sad / Drifting Blues / Outside Woman Blues / Nobody Knows You When You're Down And Out / Running On Faith / Motherless Children / Little Queen Of Spades / Further On Up The Road / Wonderful Tonight / Layla / Cocaine / Crossroads

29 January 2007, Entertainment Arena, Sydney, Australia

SETLIST: Tell The Truth / Key To The Highway / Got To Get Better In A Little While / Little Wing / Why Does Love Got To Be So Sad / Drifting Blues / Outside Woman Blues / Nobody Knows You When You're Down and Out / Running On Faith / Motherless Children / Little Queen Of Spades / Further On Up The Road / Wonderful Tonight / Layla / Cocaine / Crossroads

30 January 2007, Entertainment Arena, Sydney, Australia

SETLIST: Tell The Truth / Key To The Highway / Got To Get Better In A Little While / Little Wing / Why Does Love Got To Be So Sad / Drifting Blues / Outside Woman Blues / Nobody Knows You When You're Down And Out / Running On Faith / Motherless Children / Little Queen Of Spades / Further On Up The Road / Wonderful Tonight / Layla / Cocaine / Crossroads

FEBRUARY 2007

1 February 2007, Entertainment Arena, Sydney, Australia

SETLIST: Tell The Truth / Key To The Highway / Got To Get Better In A Little While / Little Wing / Why Does Love Got To Be So Sad / Drifting Blues / Outside Woman Blues / Nobody Knows You When You're Down And Out / Running On Faith / Motherless Children / Little Queen Of Spades / Further On Up The Road / Wonderful Tonight / Layla / Cocaine / Crossroads

3 February 2007, Rod Laver Arena, Melbourne, Australia

SETLIST: Tell The Truth / Key To The Highway / Got To Get Better In A Little While / Little Wing / Why Does Love Got To Be So Sad / Drifting Blues / Outside Woman Blues / Nobody Knows You When You're Down And Out / Running On Faith / Motherless Children / Little Queen Of Spades / Further On Up The Road / Wonderful Tonight / Layla / Cocaine / Crossroads

4 February 2007, Rod Laver Arena, Melbourne, Australia

SETLIST: Tell The Truth / Key To The Highway / Got To Get Better In A Little While / Little Wing / Why Does Love Got To Be So Sad / Drifting Blues / Outside Woman Blues / Nobody Knows You When You're Down And Out / Running On Faith / Motherless Children / Little Queen Of Spades / Further On Up The Road / Wonderful Tonight / Layla / Cocaine / Crossroads

6 February 2007, Entertainment Centre, Brisbane, Australia

SETLIST: Tell The Truth / Key To The Highway / Got To Get Better In A Little While / Little Wing / Anyday / Drifting Blues / Outside Woman Blues / Nobody Knows You When You're Down and Out / Running On Faith / Motherless Children / Little Queen Of Spades / Further On Up The Road / Wonderful Tonight / Layla / Cocaine / Crossroads

7 February 2007, Entertainment Centre, Brisbane, Australia

SETLIST: Pretending / Key To The Highway / Got To Get Better In A Little While / Little Wing / Motherless Children / Ramblin' On My Mind / Outside Woman Blues / Nobody Knows You When You're Down And Out / Running On Faith / After Midnight / Little Queen Of Spades / Further On Up The Road / Wonderful Tonight / Layla / Cocaine / Crossroads

9 February 2007, Entertainment Centre, Adelaide, Australia

SETLIST: Tell The Truth / Key To The Highway / Got To Get Better In A Little While / Little Wing / Anyday / Drifting Blues / Outside Woman Blues / Nobody Knows You When You're Down And Out / Running On Faith / Motherless Children / Little Queen Of Spades / Further On Up The Road / Wonderful Tonight / Layla / Cocaine / Crossroads

11 February 2007, Members Equity Stadium, Perth, Australia

SETLIST: Tell The Truth / Key To The Highway / Got To Get Better In A Little While / Little Wing / Why Does Love Got To Be So Sad / Drifting Blues / Outside Woman Blues / Nobody Knows You When You're Down And Out / Running On Faith / Motherless Children / Little Queen Of Spades / Further On Up The Road / Wonderful Tonight / Layla / Cocaine / Crossroads

U.S./CANADIAN TOUR 2007

28 February 2007 American Airlines Arena, Dallas, Texas (with Robert Cray)

SETLIST: Tell The Truth / Key To The Highway / Got To Get Better In A Little While / Little Wing / Anyday / Drifting Blues / Outside Woman Blues / Nobody Knows You When You're Down And Out / Running On Faith / Motherless Children / Little Queen Of Spades / Further On Up The Road / Wonderful Tonight / Layla / Cocaine / Crossroads[1]

[1]with Robert Cray

MARCH 2007

2 March 2007, Toyota Center, Houston, Texas (with Robert Cray)

SETLIST: Tell The Truth / Key To The Highway / Got To Get Better In A Little While / Little Wing / Why Does Love Got To Be So Sad / Drifting Blues / Outside Woman Blues / Nobody Knows You When You're Down And Out / Running On Faith / Motherless Children / Little Queen Of Spades / Further On Up The Road / Wonderful Tonight / Layla / Cocaine / Crossroads[1]

[1]with Robert Cray

3 March 2007, SBC Center, San Antonio, Texas (with Robert Cray)

SETLIST: Tell The Truth / Key To The Highway / Got To Get Better In A Little While / Little Wing / Why Does Love Got To Be So Sad / Drifting Blues / Outside Woman Blues / Nobody Knows You When You're Down And Out / Running On Faith / Motherless Children / Little Queen Of Spades / Further On Up The Road / Wonderful Tonight / Layla / Cocaine[1] / Crossroads[1, 2]

[1]with Jimmie Vaughan
[2]with Robert Cray

5 March 2007, Ford Center, Oklahoma City, Oklahoma (with Robert Cray)

SETLIST: Tell The Truth / Key To The Highway / Got To Get Better In A Little While / Little Wing / Why Does Love Got To Be So Sad / Drifting Blues / Outside Woman Blues / Nobody Knows You When You're Down And Out / Running On Faith / Motherless Children / Little Queen Of Spades / Further On Up The Road / Wonderful Tonight / Layla / Cocaine / Crossroads[1]

[1]with Robert Cray

7 March 2007, Pepsi Center, Denver, Colorado (with Robert Cray)

SETLIST: Tell The Truth / Key To The Highway / Got To Get Better In A Little While / Little Wing / Anyday / Drifting Blues / Outside Woman Blues / Nobody Knows You When

You're Down And Out / Running On Faith / Motherless Children / Little Queen Of Spades / Further On Up The Road / Wonderful Tonight / Layla / Cocaine / Crossroads[1]

[1]with Robert Cray

8 March 2007, Delta Center, Salt Lake City, Utah (with Robert Cray)

SETLIST: Tell The Truth / Key To The Highway / Got To Get Better In A Little While / Little Wing / Anyday / Drifting Blues / Outside Woman Blues / Nobody Knows You When You're Down And Out / Running On Faith / Motherless Children / Little Queen Of Spades / Further On Up The Road / Wonderful Tonight / Layla / Cocaine / Crossroads[1]

[1]with Robert Cray

10 March 2007, MGM, Las Vegas, Nevada (with Robert Cray)

SETLIST: Tell The Truth / Key To The Highway / Got To Get Better In A Little While / Little Wing / Why Does Love Got To Be So Sad / Drifting Blues / Outside Woman Blues / Nobody Knows You When You're Down and Out / Running On Faith / Motherless Children / Little Queen Of Spades / Further On Up The Road / Wonderful Tonight / Layla / Cocaine / Crossroads[1]

[1]with Robert Cray

11 March 2007, US Airways Center, Phoenix, Arizona (with Robert Cray)

SETLIST: Tell The Truth / Key To The Highway / Got To Get Better In A Little While / Little Wing / Why Does Love Got To Be So Sad / Drifting Blues / Outside Woman Blues / Nobody Knows You When You're Down And Out / Running On Faith / Motherless Children / Little Queen Of Spades / Further On Up The Road / Wonderful Tonight / Layla / Cocaine / Crossroads[1]

[1]with Robert Cray

14 March 2007, Staples Center, Los Angeles, California (with Robert Cray)

SETLIST: Tell The Truth / Key To The Highway / Got To Get Better In A Little While / Little Wing / Anyday / Drifting Blues / Outside Woman Blues / Nobody Knows You When

You're Down and Out / Running On Faith / Motherless Children / Little Queen Of Spades / Further On Up The Road / Wonderful Tonight / Layla / Cocaine / Crossroads[1]

[1]with Robert Cray

15 March 2007, Ipay One Center, San Diego, California (with Robert Cray)

SETLIST: Tell The Truth / Key To The Highway / Got To Get Better In A Little While / Little Wing / Anyday / Anyway The Wind Blows[1] / After Midnight[1] / Who Am I Telling You[1] / Don't Cry Sister[1] / Cocaine[1] / Motherless Children / Little Queen Of Spades / Further On Up The Road / Wonderful Tonight / Layla / Crossroads[2]

[1]with JJ Cale
[2]with Robert Cray

The whole show is filmed and recorded for potential release. Sadly it remains unreleased.

17 March 2007, Pond, Anaheim, California (with Robert Cray)

SETLIST: Tell The Truth / Key To The Highway / Got To Get Better In A Little While / Little Wing / Why Does Love Got To Be So Sad / Drifting Blues / Outside Woman Blues / Nobody Knows You When You're Down And Out / Running On Faith / Motherless Children / Little Queen Of Spades / Further On Up The Road / Wonderful Tonight / Layla / Cocaine / Crossroads[1]

[1]with Robert Cray

18 March 2007, HP Pavilion, San Jose, California (with Robert Cray)

This is Derek Trucks's last show with Eric as he is committed to rejoin the Allman Brothers.

SETLIST: Tell The Truth / Key To The Highway / Got To Get Better In A Little While / Little Wing / Why Does Love Got To Be So Sad / Drifting Blues / Outside Woman Blues / Nobody Knows You When You're Down And Out / Running On Faith / Motherless Children / Little Queen Of Spades / Further On Up The Road / Wonderful Tonight / Layla / Cocaine / Crossroads[1]

[1]with Robert Cray

BAND LINEUP FOR REMAINDER OF TOUR:
Eric Clapton: guitar, vocals
Doyle Bramhall II: guitar
Chris Stainton: keyboards
Tim Carmon: keyboards
Willie Weeks: bass
Steve Jordan: drums
Michelle John: backing vocals
Sharon White: backing vocals

20 March 2007, Arco Arena, Sacramento, California
(with Robert Cray)

SETLIST: Tell The Truth / Key To The Highway / Got To Get Better In A Little While / Little Wing / Why Does Love Got To Be So Sad / Drifting Blues / Outside Woman Blues / Nobody Knows You When You're Down And Out / Running On Faith / Motherless Children / Little Queen Of Spades / Further On Up The Road / Wonderful Tonight / Layla / Cocaine / Crossroads[1]

[1] with Robert Cray

22 March 2007, Key Arena, Seattle, Washington (with Robert Cray)

SETLIST: Tell The Truth / Key To The Highway / Got To Get Better In A Little While / Little Wing / Why Does Love Got To Be So Sad / Drifting Blues / Outside Woman Blues / Nobody Knows You When You're Down And Out / Running On Faith / Motherless Children / Little Queen Of Spades / Further On Up The Road / Wonderful Tonight / Layla / Cocaine / Crossroads[1]

[1] with Robert Cray

23 March 2007, General Motors Place, Vancouver, British Columbia, Canada (with Robert Cray)

SETLIST: Tell The Truth / Key To The Highway / Got To Get Better In A Little While / Little Wing / I Shot The Sheriff / Drifting Blues / Outside Woman Blues / Nobody Knows You When You're Down And Out / Running On Faith / Motherless Children / Little Queen Of Spades / Further On Up The Road / Wonderful Tonight / Layla / Cocaine / Crossroads[1]

[1] with Robert Cray

25 March 2007, Rexall Place, Edmonton, Alberta, Canada (with Robert Cray)

SETLIST: Tell The Truth / Key To The Highway / Got To Get Better In A Little While / Little Wing / Why Does Love Got To Be So Sad / Drifting Blues / Outside Woman Blues / Nobody Knows You When You're Down And Out / Running On Faith / Motherless Children / Little Queen Of Spades / Further On Up The Road / Wonderful Tonight / Layla / Cocaine / Crossroads[1]

[1] with Robert Cray

26 March 2007, Pengrowth Saddledome, Calgary, Alberta, Canada (with Robert Cray)

SETLIST: Tell The Truth / Key To The Highway / Got To Get Better In A Little While / Little Wing / Let It Rain / Drifting Blues / Outside Woman Blues / Nobody Knows You When You're Down And Out / Running On Faith / Motherless Children / Little Queen Of Spades / Further On Up The Road / Wonderful Tonight / Layla / Cocaine / Crossroads[1]

[1] with Robert Cray

28 March 2007, MTS Centre, Winnipeg, Manitoba, Canada (with Robert Cray)

SETLIST: Tell The Truth / Key To The Highway / Got To Get Better In A Little While / Little Wing / Why Does Love Got To Be So Sad / Drifting Blues / Outside Woman Blues / Nobody Knows You When You're Down And Out / Running On Faith / Motherless Children / Little Queen Of Spades / Further On Up The Road / Wonderful Tonight / Layla / Cocaine / Crossroads[1]

[1] with Robert Cray

30 March 2007, Fargodome, Fargo, North Dakota (with Robert Cray)

SETLIST: Tell The Truth / Key To The Highway / Got To Get Better In A Little While / Little Wing / Why Does Love Got To Be So Sad / Drifting Blues / Outside Woman Blues / Nobody Knows You When You're Down And Out / Running On Faith / Motherless Children / Little Queen Of Spades / Further On Up The Road / Wonderful Tonight / Layla / Cocaine / Crossroads[1]

[1] with Robert Cray

31 March 2007 Qwest Center, Omaha, Nebraska (with Robert Cray)

SETLIST: Tell The Truth / Key To The Highway / Got To Get Better In A Little While / Little Wing / Why Does Love Got To Be So Sad / Drifting Blues / Outside Woman Blues / Nobody Knows You When You're Down And Out / Running On Faith / Motherless Children / Little Queen Of Spades / Further On Up The Road / Wonderful Tonight / Layla / Cocaine / Crossroads[1]

[1]with Robert Cray

APRIL 2007

2 April 2007, Kemper Arena, Kansas City, Missouri (with Robert Cray)

SETLIST: Tell The Truth / Key To The Highway / Got To Get Better In A Little While / Little Wing / Why Does Love Got To Be So Sad / Drifting Blues / Outside Woman Blues / Nobody Knows You When You're Down And Out / Running On Faith / Motherless Children / Little Queen Of Spades / Further On Up The Road / Wonderful Tonight / Layla / Cocaine / Crossroads[1]

[1]with Robert Cray

3 April 2007, Mark of the Quad Cities, Moline, Illinois (with Robert Cray)

SETLIST: Tell The Truth / Key To The Highway / Got To Get Better In A Little While / Little Wing / Why Does Love Got To Be So Sad / Drifting Blues / Outside Woman Blues / Nobody Knows You When You're Down And Out / Running On Faith / Motherless Children / Little Queen Of Spades / Further On Up The Road / Wonderful Tonight / Layla / Cocaine / Crossroads[1]

[1]with Robert Cray

5 April 2007, Palace of Auburn Hills, Detroit, Michigan (with Robert Cray)

SETLIST: Tell The Truth / Key To The Highway / Got To Get Better In A Little While / Little Wing / Why Does Love Got To Be So Sad / Drifting Blues / Outside Woman Blues / Nobody Knows You When You're Down And Out / Running On Faith / Motherless Children / Little Queen Of Spades / Further On Up The Road / Wonderful Tonight / Layla / Cocaine / Crossroads[1]

[1]with Robert Cray

6 April 2007, Schotenstein Center, Columbus, Ohio (with Robert Cray)

SETLIST: Tell The Truth / Key To The Highway / Got To Get Better In A Little While / Little Wing / Why Does Love Got To Be So Sad / Drifting Blues / Outside Woman Blues / Nobody Knows You When You're Down And Out / Running On Faith / Motherless Children / Little Queen Of Spades / Further On Up The Road / Wonderful Tonight / Layla / Cocaine / Crossroads[1]

[1]with Robert Cray

AHMET ERTEGUN TRIBUTE CONCERT 2007

17 April 2007, Ahmet Ertegun Tribute, Rose Theater, Jazz at Lincoln Center, New York City (Eric appears at an amazing tribute concert for Ahmet Ertegun who had died in 2006. Eric Clapton, along with Dr. John, play "Drinking Wine Spo-Dee-O-Dee" and "Please Send Me Someone to Love." Eric also backed Solomon Burke on "Just Out Of Reach." The whole event is filmed and recorded)

MAY 2007

19 May 2007, Countryside Rocks, Highclere Castle, Hampshire

Eric and Steve Winwood reunite for a charity concert. This leads to a more formal reunion at Madison Square Garden in New York.

Eric mid-solo during his set at Highclere Castle on 19 May 2007.

Stevie Winwood and Eric Clapton at Highclere Castle on 19 May 2007.

BAND LINEUP:

Steve Winwood: organ, guitar, vocals
Jose Neto: guitar
Paul Booth: organ, saxophone
Richard Bailey: drums
Karl Vanden Bossche: percussion
Eric Clapton: guitar, vocals

Eric embraces Steve Winwood.

SETLIST: Watch Your Step / Presence Of The Lord / Crossroads / Little Queen Of Spades / Can't Find My Way Home / Had To Cry Today / Gimme Some Lovin

The concert was broadcast on the Countryside Alliance's website.

JULY 2007

GOOD MORNING AMERICA CONCERT SERIES 2007

20 July 2007, *Good Morning America* Concert Series, Bryant Park, New York City (Eric plays a version of "Crossroads" with John Mayer which is broadcast live on television. Eric played his 2007 Fender Stratocaster Signature Crossroads guitar)

Eric Clapton and John Mayer performing on ABC's Good Morning America *Concert Series in New York, 20 July 2007.*

Finale of Crossroads Guitar Festival, 28 July 2007. L to R: John Mayer, Robert Cray, Johnny Winter, Hubert Sumlin, Buddy Guy, Eric Clapton.

PRIVATE CONCERT 2007

21 July 2007, Belle Haven Club, Greenwich, Connecticut (private concert)

CROSSROADS GUITAR FESTIVAL 2007

28 July 2007, Crossroads Guitar Festival, Toyota Park, Bridgeview, Chicago, Illinois

Eric Clapton and Robbie Robertson at the Crossroads Guitar Festival, 28 July 2007.

ERIC CLAPTON WITH BILL MURRAY SET

Gloria unreleased

ERIC CLAPTON WITH SONNY LANDRETH SET

Hell At Home *Crossroads Guitar Festival 2007* DVD Warner Bros. released 2007

ERIC CLAPTON WITH SHERYL CROW, VINCE GILL, AND ALBERT LEE SET

Tulsa Time *Crossroads Guitar Festival 2007* DVD Warner Bros. released November 2007

ERIC CLAPTON AND HIS BAND SET

Tell The Truth *Crossroads Guitar Festival 2007* DVD Warner Bros. released November 2007

Key To The Highway unreleased

Got To Get Better In A Little While unreleased

Isn't It A Pity (dedicated to George Harrison) *Crossroads Guitar Festival 2007* DVD Warner Bros. released November 2007

Why Does Love Got To Be So Sad unreleased

Little Queen Of Spades *Crossroads Guitar Festival 2007* DVD Warner Bros. released November 2007

ERIC CLAPTON AND HIS BAND WITH ROBBIE ROBERTSON SET

Who Do You Love *Crossroads Guitar Festival 2007* DVD Warner Bros. released November 2007

Further On Up The Road unreleased

ERIC CLAPTON AND HIS BAND WITH STEVE WINWOOD SET

Pearly Queen unreleased

Presence Of The Lord *Crossroads Guitar Festival 2007* DVD Warner Bros. released November 2007

Can't Find My Way Home *Crossroads Guitar Festival 2007* DVD Warner Bros. released November 2007

Had To Cry Today *Crossroads Guitar Festival 2007* DVD Warner Bros. released November 2007

Dear Mr. Fantasy (Steve Winwood solo; Eric left the stage for this number)

Cocaine unreleased

Crossroads *Crossroads Guitar Festival 2007* DVD Warner Bros. released November 2007

ERIC CLAPTON AND HIS BAND WITH BUDDY GUY SET

Hoochie Coochie Man unreleased

ENCORES WITH ERIC CLAPTON AND HIS BAND AND GUESTS SET

Sweet Home Chicago (with Buddy Guy, Johnny Winter, John Mayer, Robert Cray, Jimmie Vaughan, Hubert Sumlin) *Crossroads Guitar Festival 2007* DVD Warner Bros. released November 2007

Stone Crazy (with Buddy Guy, Johnny Winter, John Mayer, Robert Cray, Jimmie Vaughan, Hubert Sumlin) unreleased

She's 19 Years Old (with Buddy Guy, Johnny Winter, John Mayer, Robert Cray, Jimmie Vaughan, Hubert Sumlin) unreleased

NOVEMBER 2007

JEFF BECK AT RONNIE SCOTT'S 2007

29 November 2007, Ronnie Scott's Club, Soho, London (Eric joins Jeff Beck for his encores. In the audience were Brian May, Tony Iommi, Jon Bon Jovi, and Jimmy Page)

BAND LINEUP:
Jeff Beck: guitar
Tal Wilkenfeld: bass
Vinnie Colaiuta: drums
Jason Rebello: keyboards
Eric Clapton: guitar, vocals

Little Brown Bird (Muddy Waters) *Jeff Beck Performing This Week . . . Live At Ronnie Scott's* DVD Eagle Vision EREDV723 released 2008

You Need Love (Willie Dixon) *Jeff Beck Performing This Week . . . Live At Ronnie Scott's* DVD Eagle Vision EREDV723 released 2008

DECEMBER 2007

GARY BROOKER'S CHRISTMAS SHOW 2007

21 December 2007, Chiddingfold Club, Woodside Road, Chiddingfold, Surrey (Eric joined Gary Brooker's No Stiletto Shoes on stage for an hour)

BAND LINEUP:
Gary Brooker: keyboards, vocals
Dave Bronze: bass, vocals
Graham Broad: drums
Andy Fairweather Low: guitar, vocals
Frank Mead: saxophone, percussion
Eric Clapton: guitar, vocals

SETLIST: Santa Claus Is Back In Town / Shotgun / Get Up Stand Up / Route 66 / Gin House / Willie And The Hand Jive / Old Black Joe / High School Confidential / Bright Lights Big City / Blueberry Hill / Lucille / You Can't Judge A Book / Goodnight Irene

NEW YEAR'S EVE DANCE 2007

31 December 2007, Woking Leisure Centre, Woking, Surrey

Eric's band is called Complete Abandon.

BAND LINEUP:
Eric Clapton: guitar, vocals
Andy Fairweather Low: guitar, vocals
Paul Wassif: guitar
Gary Brooker: keyboards, vocals
Chris Stainton: keyboards
Dave Bronze: bass
Henry Spinetti: drums
Sharon White: backing vocals
Michelle John: backing vocals
Joe Walsh: guitar [1]
Ringo Starr: drums [2]
Pete Townshend: guitar [3]

SETLIST 1: Knock On Wood / Reconsider Baby / You Can't Judge A Book / Sea Cruise / Gin House / Rockin' Robin [1] / Rocky Mountain Way [1] / Boys [2] / Honey Don't [2] / Old Black Joe

SETLIST 2: In The Midnight Hour / Hoochie Coochie Man / Lucille / Blueberry Hill / We Shall Not Be Moved / Goodnight Irene / Three Steps To Heaven [3] / Cocaine [3] / A Whiter Shade Of Pale / Shake, Rattle And Roll / Little Queenie

RECORDING SESSIONS 2007

ERIC CLAPTON GUEST SESSION

LEGACY RECORDING STUDIOS 168 West 48th Street, New York City Session for David Sanborn

JULY 2007

I'M GONNA MOVE TO THE OUTSKIRTS OF TOWN (Roy Jordan / William Weldon) *Here & Gone* CD Decca released June 2008

David Sanborn: saxophone
Eric Clapton: guitar
Steve Gadd: drums
Christian McBride: bass
Russell Malone: guitar
Gil Goldstein: Hammond B3 organ
Keyon Harrold: trumpet
Mike Davis: tenor trombone
Lou Marini: tenor saxophone
Howard Johnson: baritone saxophone
Charles Pillow: bass clarinet

Producer: Phil Ramone
Engineer: Joe Ferla

ERIC CLAPTON GUEST SESSION

LEGACY RECORDING STUDIOS
168 West 48th Street, New York City
Guitar overdub for Dr. John and the Lower 911

JULY 2007

TIME FOR A CHANGE (Mac Rebennack / Bobby Charles) *City That Care Forgot* CD Cooking Vinyl COOKCD468

Dr. John: piano, organ, vocals
Eric Clapton: guitar
Herman Ernest III: drums
David Barard: bass
John Fohl: guitar
Charlie Miller: trumpet
Alonzo Bowens: tenor saxophone
Jason Mingledorff: baritone saxophone
Kenneth "Afro" Williams: percussion

STRIPPED AWAY (Mac Rebennack / Chris Rose) *City That Care Forgot* CD Cooking Vinyl COOKCD468

Dr. John: piano, organ, vocals
Eric Clapton: guitar
Herman Ernest III: drums
David Barard: bass
John Fohl: guitar

CITY THAT CARE FORGOT (Mac Rebennack / Rev. Goat Carson) *City That Care Forgot* CD Cooking Vinyl COOKCD468

Dr. John: piano, organ, vocals
Eric Clapton: guitar
Herman Ernest III: drums
David Barard: bass
John Fohl: guitar
Ani DiFranco: background vocals, guitar

Producers: Dr. John / Herman "Roscoe" Ernest / The Jedi Master
Eric's guitar recorded by: Jerry Rothmans

ERIC CLAPTON GUEST SESSION

WINCRAFT STUDIOS
Northleach, Gloucestershire
Session for Steve Winwood

NOVEMBER 2007

DIRTY CITY (Steve Winwood / Peter Douglas Godwin) *Nine Lives* CD Columbia 88697222502 released April 2008

Steve Winwood: guitar, organ, Hammond B3 organ, vocals
Eric Clapton: guitar
Richard Bailey: drums
Paul Booth: flute, saxophone, human whistle
Tim Cansfield: guitar
Jose Pires de Almeida Neto: guitar
Karl Van Den Bossche: percussion

Producer: Steve Winwood
Engineer: James Towler

ERIC CLAPTON GUEST SESSION

117 Church Road, London
Guitar overdub for Sonny Landreth

NOVEMBER 2007

WHEN I STILL HAD YOU (Sonny Landreth) *From The Reach* CD Landfall LF-0001 released May 2008

STORM OF WORRY (Sonny Landreth) *From The Reach* CD Landfall LF-0001 released May 2008

Sonny Landreth: guitar, vocals
Eric Clapton: guitar
Sam Broussard: acoustic guitar
David Ranson: bass
Michael Burch: drums
Steve Conn: keyboards
Brian Brignac: percussion
Tony Daigle: percussion

Producer: Sonny Landreth
Eric's guitar recorded by: Alan Douglas

26

2008

A little while after the Chicago Crossroads Festival in 2007 Eric was quoted as saying, "I don't want to do anything for a while. Robbie [Robertson] and I will probably kick some things around. And that probably won't even start till next year. I really want to be with my family for a couple of years. And if I've got something left to say . . . I'll probably go on the road again. But I don't want to make any plans now." Clearly, he decided he did have something to say and a summer tour was announced for 2008.

The early part of the year was spent at Olympic Studios in Barnes recording a new album with Robbie Robertson. The two guitarists had often spoken about doing a studio project together. They had made some tentative recordings in the nineties, but these were abandoned due to time constraints.

Eric also spent several weeks rehearsing with Steve Winwood for their shows at New York's Madison Square Garden.

ERIC CLAPTON AND STEVE WINWOOD NEW YORK 2008

FEBRUARY 2008

BAND LINEUP:
Eric Clapton: guitar, vocals
Steve Winwood: Hammond B3 organ, guitar, vocals
Ian Thomas: drums
Chris Stainton: keyboards
Willie Weeks: bass

25 February 2008, Madison Square Garden, New York City

Advert for the Eric Clapton/Steve Winwood shows at New York's Madison Square Garden in February 2008.

SETLIST:

Had To Cry Today (Steve Winwood) unreleased

Low Down (JJ Cale) unreleased

Forever Man (Jerry Lynn Williams) unreleased

Them Changes (Buddy Miles) unreleased

Sleeping In The Ground (Sam Myers) unreleased

Presence Of The Lord (Eric Clapton) unreleased

Glad (Steve Winwood) unreleased

Well Alright (Jerry Allison / Buddy Holly / Joe B. Mauldin / Norman Petty) unreleased

Double Trouble (Otish Rush) unreleased

Pearly Queen (Jim Capaldi / Steve Winwood) unreleased

Tell The Truth (Eric Clapton / Bobby Whitlock) unreleased

No Face, No Name, No Number (Jim Capaldi / Steve Winwood) unreleased

After Midnight (JJ Cale) unreleased

Split Decision (Joe Walsh / Steve Winwood) unreleased

Ramblin' On My Mind (Robert Johnson) (Eric Clapton acoustic) *Eric Clapton And Steve Winwood Live from Madison Square Garden* 2CD Reprise 9362-49798-8 released May 2009

Georgia On My Mind (Hoagy Carmichael / Stuart Gorrell) (Steve Winwood on Hammond B3 organ) unreleased

Little Wing (Jimi Hendrix) unreleased

Voodoo Child (Jimi Hendrix) unreleased

Can't Find My Way Home (Steve Winwood) unreleased

Dear Mr. Fantasy (Jim Capaldi / Steve Winwood)

Crossroads (Robert Johnson) bonus track on *Eric Clapton And Steve Winwood Live From Madison Square Garden* DVD Reprise 7599-39992-5 released May 2009

26 February 2008, Madison Square Garden, New York City

Eric Clapton and Steve Winwood poster for their three shows at Madison Square Garden, 2008.

SETLIST:

Had To Cry Today (Steve Winwood) *Eric Clapton And Steve Winwood Live From Madison Square Garden* 2CD Reprise 9362-49798-8 released May 2009

Low Down (JJ Cale) unreleased

Forever Man (Jerry Lynn Williams) *Eric Clapton And Steve Winwood Live From Madison Square Garden* 2CD Reprise 9362-49798-8 released May 2009

Them Changes (Buddy Miles) *Eric Clapton And Steve Winwood Live From Madison Square Garden* 2CD Reprise 9362-49798-8 released May 2009

Sleeping In The Ground (Sam Meyers) *Eric Clapton And Steve Winwood Live From Madison Square Garden* 2CD Reprise 9362-49798-8 released May 2009

Presence Of The Lord (Eric Clapton) *Eric Clapton And Steve Winwood Live from Madison Square Garden* 2CD Reprise 9362-49798-8 released May 2009

Glad (Steve Winwood) *Eric Clapton And Steve Winwood Live From Madison Square Garden* 2CD Reprise 9362-49798-8 released May 2009

Well Alright (Jerry Allison / Buddy Holly / Joe B. Mauldin / Norman Petty) unreleased

Double Trouble (Otis Rush) unreleased

Pearly Queen (Jim Capaldi / Steve Winwood) *Eric Clapton And Steve Winwood Live From Madison Square Garden* 2CD Reprise 9362-49798-8 released May 2009

Tell The Truth (Eric Clapton / Bobby Whitlock) *Eric Clapton And Steve Winwood Live From Madison Square Garden* 2CD Reprise 9362-49798-8 released May 2009

No Face, No Name, No Number (Jim Capaldi / Steve Winwood) *Eric Clapton And Steve Winwood Live From Madison Square Garden* 2CD Reprise 9362-49798-8 released May 2009

After Midnight (JJ Cale) unreleased

Split Decision (Joe Walsh / Steve Winwood) *Eric Clapton And Steve Winwood Live From Madison Square Garden* 2CD Reprise 9362-49798-8 released May 2009

Ramblin' On My Mind (Robert Johnson) (Eric Clapton acoustic) unreleased

Georgia On My Mind (Hoagy Carmichael / Stuart Gorrell) (Steve Winwood on Hammond B3 organ) *Eric Clapton And Steve Winwood Live From Madison Square Garden* 2CD Reprise 9362-49798-8 released May 2009

Little Wing (Jimi Hendrix) unreleased

Voodoo Child *Eric Clapton And Steve Winwood Live From Madison Square Garden* 2CD Reprise 9362-49798-8 released May 2009

Can't Find My Way Home (Steve Winwood) unreleased

Cocaine (JJ Cale) *Eric Clapton And Steve Winwood Live From Madison Square Garden* 2CD Reprise 9362-49798-8 released May 2009

Dear Mr. Fantasy (Jim Capaldi / Steve Winwood) *Eric Clapton And Steve Winwood Live From Madison Square Garden* 2CD Reprise 9362-49798-8 released May 2009

28 February 2008, Madison Square Garden, New York City

SETLIST:

Had To Cry Today (Steve Winwood) unreleased

Low Down (JJ Cale) *Eric Clapton And Steve Winwood Live From Madison Square Garden* 2CD Reprise 9362-49798-8 released May 2009

Forever Man (Jerry Lynn Williams) unreleased

Them Changes (Buddy Miles) unreleased

Sleeping In The Ground (Sam Meyers) unreleased

Presence Of The Lord (Eric Clapton) unreleased

Glad (Steve Winwood) unreleased

Well Alright (Jerry Allison / Buddy Holly / Joe B. Mauldin / Norman Petty) unreleased

Double Trouble (Otis Rush) *Eric Clapton And Steve Winwood Live From Madison Square Garden* 2CD Reprise 9362-49798-8 released May 2009

Pearly Queen (Jim Capaldi / Steve Winwood) unreleased

Tell The Truth (Eric Clapton / Bobby Whitlock) unreleased

No Face, No Name, No Number (Jim Capaldi / Steve Winwood) unreleased

After Midnight (JJ Cale) unreleased

Split Decision (Joe Walsh / Steve Winwood) unreleased

Kind Hearted Woman (Robert Johnson) (Eric Clapton acoustic) bonus track on *Eric Clapton And Steve Winwood Live From Madison Square Garden* DVD Reprise 7599-39992-5 released May 2009

Georgia On My Mind (Hoagy Carmichael / Stuart Gorrell) (Steve Winwood on Hammond B3 organ) unreleased

Little Wing (Jimi Hendrix) unreleased

Voodoo Child (Jimi Hendrix) unreleased

Can't Find My Way Home (Steve Winwood) *Eric Clapton And Steve Winwood Live From Madison Square Garden* 2CD Reprise 9362-49798-8 released May 2009

Cocaine (JJ Cale) unreleased

Dear Mr. Fantasy (Jim Capaldi / Steve Winwood) unreleased

APRIL 2008

Eric flew to Florida in April to start rehearsing with his band for the upcoming tour as well as hanging out with Roger Waters and doing some recording with him. He also found time to jam with Sheryl Crow at the West Palm Beach Sunfest.

SUNFEST JAM 2008

30 April 2008, Sunfest, West Palm Beach, Florida (Eric joined Sheryl Crow on stage for a version of Stevie Wonder's "Higher Ground." Eric plays a great solo and receives rapturous applause from the crowd)

Eric joins Sheryl Crow on stage for a version of Stevie Wonder's "Higher Ground" on 30 April 2008 at Sunfest, West Palm Beach, Florida.

MAY 2008

U.S. / EUROPEAN TOUR 2008

BAND LINEUP:
Eric Clapton: guitar, vocals
Doyle Bramhall II: guitar, vocals
Chris Stainton: keyboards
Pino Palladino: bass
Ian Thomas: drums
Sharon White: backing vocals
Michelle John: vocals

3 May 2008, Ford Amphitheatre, Tampa, Florida (with Robert Randolph and the Family Band)

SETLIST: Tell The Truth / Key To The Highway / Hoochie Coochie Man / Little Wing / Double Trouble / Don't Knock My Love / Outside Woman Blues / Nobody Knows You When You're Down And Out / Rocking Chair / Motherless Child / Travelling Riverside Blues / Running On Faith / Motherless Children /

Little Queen Of Spades / Before You Accuse Me / Wonderful Tonight / Layla / Cocaine / Crossroads[1]

[1]with Robert Randolph on pedal steel guitar

5 May 2008, Hard Rock Live, Hollywood, Florida (with Robert Randolph and the Family Band)

SETLIST: Tell The Truth / Key To The Highway / Hoochie Coochie Man / Little Wing / Outside Woman Blues / Double Trouble / Don't Knock My Love / Drifting Blues / Rocking Chair / Motherless Child / Travelling Riverside Blues / Running On Faith / Motherless Children / Little Queen Of Spades / Before You Accuse Me / Wonderful Tonight / Layla / Cocaine / Got My Mojo Working[1]

[1]with Robert Randolph on pedal steel guitar

6 May 2008, Amway Arena, Orlando, Florida (private concert sponsored by SAP and Deloitte Consulting for attendees of SAP's annual SAPPHIRE User Convention)

SETLIST: Tell The Truth / Key To The Highway / Hoochie Coochie Man / Little Wing / Outside Woman Blues / Double Trouble / Don't Knock My Love / Drifting Blues / Rocking Chair / Motherless Child / Travelling Riverside Blues / Running On Faith / Motherless Children / Little Queen Of Spades / Before You Accuse Me / Wonderful Tonight / Layla / Cocaine / Crossroads

BUNBURY CHARITY EVENT 2008

8 May 2008, Grosvenor House Hotel, London (during a short break in the tour, Eric flies home to play at a special Bunbury's party at the Grosvenor House Hotel. The evening was a tribute to Sir Ian Botham and all money raised went to Leukemia Research, of which Ian Botham is president, and Eric Clapton's Crossroads drug and alcohol treatment centre)

BAND LINEUP:
Eric Clapton: guitar, vocals
Chris Stainton: keyboards
Pino Palladino: bass
Ian Thomas: drums
Sharon White: backing vocals
Michelle John: backing vocals

SETLIST: Rocking Chair (acoustic) / Nobody Knows You When You're Down And Out (acoustic) / Motherless Child (12-string acoustic) / Running On Faith / Key To The Highway / Hoochie Coochie Man / Don't Knock My Love / Little Queen Of Spades / Before You Accuse Me / Wonderful Tonight / Cocaine / Crossroads

U.S. / EUROPEAN 2008 TOUR RESUMES

22 May 2008, PNC Bank Arts Center, Holmdel, New Jersey (with Robert Randolph and the Family Band)

SETLIST: Tell The Truth / Key To The Highway / Hoochie Coochie Man / Little Wing / Outside Woman Blues / Double Trouble / Don't Knock My Love / Drifting Blues / Rocking Chair / Motherless Child / Travelling Riverside Blues / Running On Faith / Motherless Children / Little Queen Of Spades / Before You Accuse Me / Wonderful Tonight / Layla / Cocaine / Got My Mojo Working[1]

[1]with Robert Randolph on pedal steel guitar

Ian Thomas on drums and Eric Clapton at PNC Bank Arts Center, Holmdel, New Jersey, on 22 May 2008.

24 May 2008 Borgata Hotel, Atlantic City, New Jersey (private concert)

SETLIST: Tell The Truth / Key To The Highway / Hoochie Coochie Man / Little Wing / Outside Woman Blues / Double Trouble / Don't Knock My Love / Drifting Blues / Rocking Chair / Motherless Child / Travelling Riverside Blues / Running On Faith / Motherless Children / Little Queen Of Spades / Before You Accuse Me / Wonderful Tonight / Layla / Cocaine / Crossroads

25 May 2008 Borgata Hotel, Atlantic City, New Jersey (with Robert Randolph and the Family Band)

SETLIST: Motherless Children / Key To The Highway / Hoochie Coochie Man / Little Wing / Outside Woman Blues / Double Trouble / Don't Knock My Love / Drifting Blues / Rocking Chair / Motherless Child / Travelling Riverside Blues / Running On Faith / Tell The Truth / Little Queen Of Spades / Before You Accuse Me / Wonderful Tonight / Layla / Cocaine / Got My Mojo Working[1]

[1]with Robert Randolph on pedal steel guitar

27 May 2008, Molson Amphitheatre, Toronto, Canada (with Robert Randolph and the Family Band)

SETLIST: Motherless Children / Key To The Highway / Hoochie Coochie Man / Little Wing / Outside Woman Blues / Double Trouble / Don't Knock My Love / Drifting Blues / Rocking Chair / Motherless Child / Travelling Riverside Blues / Running On Faith / Tell The Truth / Little Queen Of Spades / Before You Accuse Me / Wonderful Tonight / Layla / Cocaine / Got My Mojo Working[1]

[1]with Robert Randolph on pedal steel guitar

28 May 2008, Bell Centre, Montreal, Quebec, Canada (with Robert Randolph and the Family Band)

SETLIST: Motherless Children / Key To The Highway / Hoochie Coochie Man / Little Wing / Outside Woman Blues / Double Trouble / Don't Knock My Love / Drifting Blues / Rocking Chair / Motherless Child / Travelling Riverside Blues / Running On Faith / Tell The Truth / Little Queen Of Spades / Before You Accuse Me / Wonderful Tonight / Layla / Cocaine / Got My Mojo Working[1]

[1]with Robert Randolph on pedal steel guitar

30 May 2008, Verizon Wireless Center, Noblesville, Indiana (with Robert Randolph and the Family Band)

SETLIST: Tell The Truth / Key To The Highway / Hoochie Coochie Man / Little Wing / Outside Woman Blues / Double Trouble / Don't Knock My Love / Come Back Baby / Rocking Chair / Motherless Child / Travelling Riverside Blues / Running On Faith / Motherless Children / Little Queen Of Spades / Wonderful Tonight / Layla / Got My Mojo Working

Tonight's concert was cut short by a couple of numbers due to incoming storms and tornado warnings. "Cocaine" was one of the numbers dropped and Eric played a rare version of "Come Back Baby" instead of the usual "Drifting Blues." Eric had covered this Ray Charles song on his *Reptile* album.

> **"**There were as many flashes of light outside the pavilion of Verizon Wireless Music Center as there was under the roof, but Eric Clapton played on, losing himself in the familiar blues riffs of his music. Clapton played to a sellout crowd Friday night despite nearby tornado warnings and storms that drenched other areas. The rain held off until just before his encore. Clapton didn't say much, preferring to sing instead. 'What a lovely night,' he said.**"**
> **—NOBLESVILLE NEWS DAILY**

31 May 2008, Blossom Music Center, Cuyahoga Falls, Ohio (with Robert Randolph and the Family Band)

SETLIST: Motherless Children / Key To The Highway / Hoochie Coochie Man / Little Wing / Outside Woman Blues / Double Trouble / Don't Knock My Love / Drifting Blues / Rocking Chair / Motherless Child / Travelling Riverside Blues / Running On Faith / Tell The Truth / Little Queen Of Spades / Before You Accuse Me / Wonderful Tonight / Layla / Cocaine / Got My Mojo Working[1]

[1]with Robert Randolph on pedal steel guitar

JUNE 2008

2 June 2008, Mohegan Sun Arena, Uncasville Connecticut (with Robert Randolph and the Family Band)

SETLIST: Tell The Truth / Key To The Highway / Hoochie Coochie Man / Little Wing / Outside Woman Blues / Double Trouble / Don't Knock My Love / Drifting Blues / Rocking Chair / Motherless Child / Travelling Riverside Blues / Running On Faith / Motherless Children / Little Queen Of Spades / Before You Accuse Me / Wonderful Tonight / Layla / Cocaine / Got My Mojo Working[1]

[1]with Robert Randolph on pedal steel guitar

4 June 2008, Comcast Center, Mansfield, Massachusetts (with Robert Randolph and the Family Band)

SETLIST: Motherless Children / Key To The Highway / Hoochie Coochie Man / Little Wing / Outside Woman Blues / Double Trouble / Don't Knock My Love / Drifting Blues / Rocking Chair / Motherless Child / Travelling Riverside Blues / Running On Faith / Tell The Truth / Little Queen Of Spades / Before You Accuse Me / Wonderful Tonight / Layla / Cocaine / Got My Mojo Working[1]

[1]with Robert Randolph on pedal steel guitar

5 June 2008, Nikon at Jones Beach Theater, Wantagh, New York (with Robert Randolph and the Family Band)

SETLIST: Tell The Truth / Key To The Highway / Hoochie Coochie Man / Little Wing / Outside Woman Blues / Double Trouble / Don't Knock My Love / Ramblin' On My Mind / Rocking Chair / Motherless Child / Travelling Riverside Blues / Running On Faith / Motherless Children / Little Queen Of Spades / Before You Accuse Me / Wonderful Tonight / Layla / Cocaine / Got My Mojo Working[1]

[1]with Robert Randolph on pedal steel guitar

OLLIE G BIG TOP BALL 2008

14 June 2008, Whithorn Farm, Brook, near Hasslemere, Surrey

Eric Clapton joined Gary Brooker and friends as guest guitarist at the Ollie G Big Top Ball, which was a benefit for the Society for Mucopolysaccharide Diseases, which is a support group for children and adults in the UK who suffer from mucopolysaccharide and related lysosomal storage diseases. Eric sat in for about an hour. The full setlist is not known.

Poster for the Ollie G Big Top Ball, 14 June 2008.

BAND LINEUP:
Gary Brooker: keyboards, vocals
Murray Gould: guitar

Dave Bronze: bass
Graham Broad: drums
Frank Mead: saxophone
Nick Pentalow: saxophone
Tara McDonald: backing vocals
Tracey Graham: backing vocals
Nikki Lambourne: vocals
Andy Fairweather Low: guitar, vocals
Eric Clapton: guitar

EUROPEAN TOUR 2008

BAND LINEUP:
Eric Clapton: guitar, vocals
Doyle Bramhall II: guitar, vocals
Chris Stainton: keyboards
Willie Weeks: bass
Abe Laboriel, Jr.: drums
Sharon White: backing vocals
Michelle John: backing vocals

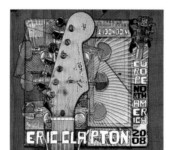

Tour poster for U.S. and European Tour 2008.

20 June 2008, Marquee, Cork, Ireland (with Robert Randolph and the Family Band)

SETLIST: Tell The Truth / Key To The Highway / Hoochie Coochie Man / Little Wing / Outside Woman Blues / Double Trouble / Why Does Love Got To Be So Sad / When You Got A Good Friend / Rocking Chair / Motherless Child / Travelling Riverside Blues / Running On Faith / Motherless Children / Little Queen Of Spades / Before You Accuse Me / Wonderful Tonight / Layla / Cocaine / I've Got My Mojo Working[1]

[1]with Robert Randolph on pedal steel guitar

21 June 2008, Malahide Castle, Dublin, Ireland (with Robert Randolph and the Family Band)

SETLIST: Tell The Truth / Key To The Highway / Hoochie Coochie Man / Isn't It A Pity / Outside Woman Blues / Double Trouble / Why Does Love Got To Be So Sad / Drifting Blues / Rocking Chair / Motherless Child / Travelling Riverside Blues / Running On Faith / Motherless Children / Little Queen Of Spades / Before You Accuse Me / Wonderful Tonight / Layla / Cocaine / I've Got My Mojo Working[1]

[1]with Robert Randolph on pedal steel guitar

23 June 2008, Trent FM Nottingham Arena, Nottingham (with Robert Randolph and the Family Band)

SETLIST: Tell The Truth / Key To The Highway / Hoochie Coochie Man / Here But I'm Gone / Outside Woman Blues / Double Trouble / Why Does Love Got To Be So Sad / Midnight Hour Blues / Rocking Chair / Motherless Child / Travelling Riverside Blues / Running On Faith / Motherless Children / Little Queen Of Spades / Before You Accuse Me / Wonderful Tonight / Layla / Cocaine / I've Got My Mojo Working[1]

[1]with Robert Randolph on pedal steel guitar

Eric Clapton at the huge Hard Rock Calling show on 28 June 2008.

28 June 2008, Hard Rock Calling, Hyde Park, London (with Sheryl Crow, John Mayer, Robert Randolph and the Family Band, Steve Boyce Band, and Jason Mraz)

SETLIST: Tell The Truth / Key To The Highway / Hoochie Coochie Man / Outside Woman Blues / Here But I'm Gone / Why Does Love Got To Be So Sad / Drifting Blues / Rocking Chair / Motherless Child / Travelling Riverside Blues / Running On Faith / Motherless Children / Little Queen Of Spades / Before You Accuse Me / Wonderful Tonight / Layla / Cocaine / Crossroads[1]

[1]with Sheryl Crow on vocals, John Mayer on guitar and vocals, and Robert Randolph on pedal steel guitar

The whole show is filmed and recorded but only the following were broadcast by VH1: "Tell The Truth," "Drifting Blues," "Motherless Child," "Layla," "Cocaine," and "Crossroads."

29 June 2008, Harewood House, Leeds (with Robert Randolph and the Family Band)

SETLIST: Tell The Truth / Key To The Highway / Hoochie Coochie Man / Isn't It A Pity / Outside Woman Blues / Here But I'm Gone / Why Does Love Got To Be So Sad / Drifting Blues / Rocking Chair / Motherless Child / Travelling Riverside Blues / Running On Faith / Motherless Children / Little Queen Of Spades / Before You Accuse Me / Wonderful Tonight / Layla / Cocaine / I've Got My Mojo Working[1]

[1]with Robert Randolph on pedal steel guitar

AUGUST 2008

6 August 2008, Koengen, Bergen, Norway (with Grande)

SETLIST: Tell The Truth / Key To The Highway / Hoochie Coochie Man / Isn't It A Pity / Outside Woman Blues / Here But I'm Gone / Why Does Love Got To Be So Sad / Drifting Blues / Nobody Knows You When You're Down And Out / Motherless Child / Travelling Riverside Blues / Running On Faith / Motherless Children / Little Queen Of Spades / Before You Accuse Me / Wonderful Tonight / Layla / Cocaine / Crossroads

8 August 2008, Egilsholl Arena, Reykjavic, Iceland (with Ellen Kristjansdottir)

SETLIST: Tell The Truth / Key To The Highway / Hoochie Coochie Man / Here But I'm Gone / Outside Woman Blues / Isn't It A Pity / Why Does Love Got To Be So Sad / Drifting Blues / Nobody Knows You When You're Down And Out / Motherless Child / Travelling Riverside Blues / Running On Faith / Motherless Children / Little Queen Of Spades / Before You Accuse Me / Wonderful Tonight / Cocaine / Crossroads

10 August 2008, Skanderborg Festival, Skanderborg, Denmark

SETLIST: Tell The Truth / Key To The Highway / Hoochie Coochie Man / Here But I'm Gone / Outside Woman

Blues / Drifting Blues / Nobody Knows You When You're Down And Out / Motherless Child / Running On Faith / Why Does Love Got To Be So Sad / Little Queen Of Spades / Before You Accuse Me / Wonderful Tonight / Layla / Cocaine

12 August 2008, Leipzig Arena, Leipzig, Germany (with Jakob Dylan)

SETLIST: Tell the Truth / Key To The Highway / Hoochie Coochie Man / Here But I'm Gone / Outside Woman Blues / Isn't It A Pity / Why Does Love Got To Be So Sad / Drifting Blues / Nobody Knows You When You're Down And Out / Motherless Child / Travelling Riverside Blues / Running On Faith / Motherless Children / Little Queen Of Spades / Before You Accuse Me / Wonderful Tonight / Layla / Cocaine / Crossroads

14 August 2008, Skwer Kosciuszki, Gdynia, Poland (with Dzem)

SETLIST: Tell The Truth / Key To The Highway / Hoochie Coochie Man / Here But I'm Gone / Outside Woman Blues / Isn't It A Pity / Why Does Love Got To Be So Sad / Drifting Blues / Nobody Knows You When You're Down And Out / Motherless Child / Travelling Riverside Blues / Running On Faith / Motherless Children / Little Queen Of Spades / Before You Accuse Me / Wonderful Tonight / Layla / Cocaine / Crossroads

15 August 2008, Waldbühne, Berlin, Germany (with Jakob Dylan)

SETLIST: Tell The Truth / Key To The Highway / Hoochie Coochie Man / Here But I´m Gone / Outside Woman Blues / Isn´t It A Pity / Why Does Love Got To Be So Sad / Rock Me Baby / Nobody Knows You When You're Down And Out / Motherless Child / Travelling Riverside Blues / Running On Faith / Motherless Children / Little Queen Of Spades / Before You Accuse Me / Wonderful Tonight / Layla / Cocaine / Crossroads

17 August 2008, Königsplatz, München, Germany (with Jakob Dylan)

SETLIST: Tell The Truth / Key To The Highway / Hoochie Coochie Man / Here But I´m Gone / Outside Woman Blues / Isn´t It A Pity / Why Does Love Got To Be So Sad / Drifting Blues / Nobody Knows You When You're Down

And Out / Motherless Child / Travelling Riverside Blues / Running On Faith / Motherless Children / Little Queen Of Spades / Before You Accuse Me / Wonderful Tonight / Layla / Cocaine / Crossroads

19 August 2008, Kurhaus-Bowling Green, Wiesbaden, Germany (with Jakob Dylan)

SETLIST: Tell The Truth / Key To The Highway / Hoochie Coochie Man / Here But I´m Gone / Outside Woman Blues / Little Wing / Why Does Love Got To Be So Sad / Drifting Blues / Nobody Knows You When You're Down And Out / Motherless Child / Travelling Riverside Blues / Running On Faith / Got To Get Better In A Little While / Little Queen Of Spades / Before You Accuse Me / Wonderful Tonight / Layla / Cocaine / Crossroads

20 August 2008, Hallenstadion, Zurich, Switzerland (with Jakob Dylan)

SETLIST: Tell The Truth / Key To The Highway / Hoochie Coochie Man / Here But I´m Gone / Outside Woman Blues / Isn't It A Pity / Why Does Love Got To Be So Sad / Help Me / Nobody Knows You When You're Down And Out / Motherless Child / Travelling Riverside Blues / Running On Faith / Got To Get Better In A Little While / Little Queen Of Spades / Before You Accuse Me / Wonderful Tonight / Layla / Cocaine / Crossroads[1]

[1] with Jakob Dylan on vocals and guitar

22 August 2008, Monte Carlo Sporting Summer Festival, Salle Des Etoiles, Monte Carlo (with the Sporting Orchestra featuring Ty Stephens)

SETLIST: Layla / Hoochie Coochie Man / Here But I'm Gone / Outside Woman Blues / Drifting Blues / Nobody Knows You When You're Down And Out / Motherless Child / Travelling Riverside Blues / Running On Faith / Got To Get Better In A Little While / Little Queen Of Spades / Before You Accuse Me / Wonderful Tonight / Cocaine / Crossroads

23 August 2008, Monte Carlo Sporting Summer Festival, Salle Des Etoiles, Monte Carlo (with the Sporting Orchestra featuring Ty Stephens)

SETLIST: Hoochie Coochie Man / Tell The Truth / Little Wing / Outside Woman Blues / Drifting Blues / Nobody Knows You When You're Down And Out / Motherless

Child / Travelling Riverside Blues / Running On Faith / Got To Get Better In A Little While / Little Queen Of Spades / Before You Accuse Me / Wonderful Tonight / Layla / Cocaine / Crossroads

SEPTEMBER 2008

9 September 2008, Floridita, London (Eric plays a concert in aid of the Countryside Alliance at this Soho restaurant which occupies the space where the Marquee Club once stood)

DECEMBER 2008

22 December 2008, Cranleigh Arts Center, Cranleigh, Surrey (local charity concert. Eric Clapton joined the Guy Tortora Band and Paul Jones)

SETLIST: All Your Loving / Can't Judge Nobody / Christmas Tears / Everything's Gonna Be Alright

NEW YEAR'S EVE DANCE, 2008

31 December 2008, Woking Leisure Centre, Woking, Surrey

Eric and the band are called the Fourth Edition.

BAND LINEUP:
Eric Clapton: guitar, vocals
Andy Fairweather Low: guitar, vocals
Gary Brooker: keyboards, vocals
Chris Stainton: keyboards
Dave Bronze: bass
Henry Spinetti: drums
Sharon White: backing vocals
Michelle John: backing vocals

SETLIST 1: Knock On Wood / Reconsider Baby / Can't Judge A Book / Santa Claus Is Back In Town / Route 66 / Will The Circle Be Unbroken / Five Long Years / Wonderful Tonight / Shake, Rattle And Roll

SETLIST 2: In The Midnight Hour / Hoochie Coochie Man / Blueberry Hill / Sweet Soul Music / Putting On The

Style / Gin House / Willie And The Hand Jive / Whiter Shade Of Pale / Cocaine / Old Black Joe

RECORDING SESSIONS 2008
ERIC CLAPTON SONGS FOR SOLOMON BURKE
JANUARY 2008

Solomon Burke was recording his new album at the Village Recorder in Los Angeles. He and Eric were friends and had played together on a session for a Jools Holland album. Eric offered a couple of songs for the project although he was unable to attend and play at the session. It's a great album and a worthy addition to any respectable music collection.

LIKE A FIRE (Eric Clapton) *Like A Fire* CD Shout Factory released June 2008

THANK YOU (Eric Cllapton / Solomon Burke) *Like A Fire* CD Shout Factory released June 2008

> "Eric Clapton—he is the man! He's not only a songwriter and a musician, he's a friend. When someone like Eric Clapton says, 'I got a song for you,' sends it to you and then turns around and says 'You know what, I've got another one in my heart, but all I've got is music and an idea—you finish it'!—that was a mind-blower, and that song was 'Thank You.'"
> —SOLOMON BURKE

ERIC CLAPTON GUEST SESSION
OLYMPIC STUDIOS 117 Church Road, London Guitar overdub for Pinetop Perkins
JANUARY 2008

HOW LONG BLUES / COME BACK BABY (Leroy Carr, J. Williams, Ray Charles) *Pinetop Perkins and Friends* CD Telrac CD-83680 released June 2008

Pinetop Perkins: piano, vocals

Eric Clapton: guitar
Nora Jean Brusco: vocals
Paul Diethelm: rhythm guitar
Bob Stoger: bass
Kenny Smith: drums

Producer: Simon Climie
Engineer: Alan Douglas

ERIC CLAPTON GUEST SESSION

OLYMPIC STUDIOS
117 Church Road, London
Guitar overdub for Buddy Guy

18 JANUARY 2008

EVERY TIME I SING THE BLUES (Tom Hambridge / Gary Nicholson) *Skin Deep* CD Silvertone 88697-34316-2 released July 2008

Buddy Guy: guitar, vocals
Eric Clapton: guitar, vocals
Tom Hambridge: drums, percussion, background vocals
Willie Weeks: bass
Reese Wynans: keyboards
David Grissom: guitar

Producer: Tom Hambrige
Eric's guitar recorded by: Alan Douglas

> "It was tracked on 28 November 2007, at Blackbird Studio, Nashville, Tennessee. Eric's guitar was recorded at Olympic Studios on 18 January 2008. It was mixed by Tom Hambridge and Ryan Hewitt at Alchemy Sound in Venice Beach, California, 14 April 2008."
>
> —TOM HAMBRIDGE

OLYMPIC STUDIOS
117 Church Road, London
Session with Robbie Robertson

MARCH 2008

Eric was hooked on The Band from the moment he heard the *Music From Big Pink* album. He even went to see them at their Woodstock house for some informal jams in the late sixties. He later recorded his *No*

Reason To Cry album at their studio in California and joined them for their farewell show at the Winterland in 1976. Eric and Robbie had collaborated in 1986 on some songs for the soundtrack for a film called *The Color Of Money*. Then in 1993 in Los Angeles they played around with some demos but never went back to them due to other commitments. Finally, in early 2008 the time came to revisit those and possibly record some new material as a joint album.

Olympic Studios was booked for March after Eric's return from playing three historic shows with Steve Winwood in New York. By the end of March, the album was still not completed and Eric had other commitments. Eric suggested that the album should be a Robbie Robertson solo album with Eric guesting. Eric revisited the project in September 2009 in Los Angeles when the album was finally finished. Full details can be found under the September 2009 entry.

Guitars used by Eric included a Martin 000-42, a Robbie Robertson Signature 00-size Martin made of koa, a black Fender CS Stratocaster with noiseless pickups, a custom Stratocaster with two slanted pickups at the bridge, a sunburst 1960 Gibson ES-335TD with dot markers, a '57 Gibson Byrdland, two Fender Stratocasters for slide work, one black Graffiti with noiseless single-coils, and another black one with Lace Sensors.

ERIC CLAPTON GUEST SESSION

PALM BEACH SOUND
3885 Investment Lane, Riviera Beach, West Palm Beach, Florida

18 APRIL 2008

THE CHILD WILL FLY (Roger Waters)

Producer: Roger Waters
Engineer: Gustavo Celis

Seven-time Grammy Award winning mix engineer Gustavo Celis engineered sessions with Roger Waters and Eric Clapton in Florida in April 2008. The

Eric Clapton recording a solo at Palm Beach Studios, 18 April 2008. Gustavo Celis is at the controls and Roger Waters sits listening to the take.

recording was to help the ALAS (America Latina en Accion Solidaria—Latin America in Solidary Action) foundation, which helps improve health and education for children in Latin America. The number recorded, "The Child Will Fly," is an epic "We Are The World" type song that is around fifteen minutes long and features great Latin American artists such as Gustavo Cerati and Pedro Aznar. It is reminiscent of the Pink Floyd classic "Comfortably Numb."

❝The session occurred on 18 April 2008 at Palm Beach Sound in West Palm Beach, Florida. Eric walked in very casually wearing Bermuda shorts and said to me, 'I just borrowed this Fender amp and Strat from a friend.' I was like WOW, I never thought Eric Clapton was going to carry his own amp. I thought he would have a guitar tech and a crew of people around him, but I was totally wrong because the only thing he really needed was his fingers. This guy can play even the worst instrument on a bad day and it would still sound incredible.

The whole session was really friendly and casual, and by the end Roger brought out some coffees and they started chatting and having fun. We recorded about five takes, and every single one of them could be used without a problem. I think Eric was trying to find out what Roger was looking for because each take had quite distinct personalities. One would sound a bit like Gilmour, another like B.B. King, and so on.

After Take 4 Roger asked for more but he didn't really articulate what he was expecting, so Eric got a little pissed and ultimately I think Roger was just messing with him because the previous takes were amazing. He graciously played another take but we all knew the session was over. Then they looked at each other and smiled.

I stayed for another hour and put together a comp of the tracks and sent Roger a rough mix. He called me shortly after, telling me he was very pleased and that everything sounded great.

As far as other artists in the song I remember the great Argentinian rocker Gustavo Cerati was in it as well as Pedro Aznar, but the song was about thirteen minutes long and the production was ongoing. So I am sure they added a lot more singers.**❞**

—GUSTAVO CELIS

ERIC CLAPTON GUEST SESSION
OLYMPIC STUDIOS
117 Church Road, London
Session for Paul Jones

OCTOBER 2008

CHOOSE OR COP OUT (Paul Jones) *Starting All Over Again* CD Continental Blue Heaven CD 2015 released March 2009

Paul Jones: lead vocals, harmonica
Jale Andrews: guitars
Eric Clapton: guitar
Tony Marsico: bass
Alvino Bennett: drums
Mike Thompson: Hammond B3 organ

STARTING ALL OVER AGAIN (Phillip Mitchell) *Starting All Over Again* CD Continental Blue Heaven CD 2015 released March 2009

Paul Jones: lead vocals, harmonica
Jake Andrews: guitars
Eric Clapton: guitar
Tony Marsico: bass
Alvino Bennett: drums
Mike Thompson: Hammond B3 organ

Producer: Carla Olsen
Engineer: Alan Douglas

2009

The year started with a Japanese tour. The big news was the announcement of two shows with Jeff Beck at the huge Saitama Super Arena. Although fans were expecting the two guitarists to be on stage the whole time, it was actually an opening set by Jeff, followed by an Eric set. The two then came back on stage together and played a forty-five-minute set to the delight of Japanese fans. Although their styles and tone are very different, it worked well. Having Doyle with them as well was a bonus, especially on the gorgeous version of Curtis Mayfield's "Here But I'm Gone."

FEBRUARY 2009

JAPAN TOUR 2009

BAND LINEUP:
Eric Clapton: guitar, vocals
Doyle Bramhall II: guitar, vocals
Chris Stainton: keyboards
Willie Weeks: bass
Abe Laboriel, Jr.: drums
Michelle John: backing vocals
Sharon White: backing vocals

12 February 2009, Osaka-Jo Hall, Osaka, Japan

SETLIST: Hoochie Coochie Man / Key To The Highway / I Shot The Sheriff / Isn't It A Pity / Tell The Truth / Why Does Love Got To Be So Sad / Drifting Blues / Travelin' Alone / That's All Right / Motherless Child / Running On Faith / Motherless Children / Little Queen Of Spades / Everything's Gonna Be Alright / Wonderful Tonight / Layla / Cocaine / Crossroads

13 February 2009, Osaka-Jo Hall, Osaka, Japan

SETLIST: Hoochie Coochie Man / Key To The Highway / Tell The Truth / I Shot The Sheriff / Here But I'm Gone / Why Does Love Got To Be So Sad / Drifting Blues / Travelin' Alone / That's All Right / Nobody Knows You When You're Down And Out / Running On Faith / Motherless Children / Little Queen Of Spades / Before You Accuse Me / Wonderful Tonight / Layla / Cocaine / Crossroads

15 February 2009, Budokan, Tokyo, Japan

SETLIST: Tell The Truth / Key To The Highway / Hoochie Coochie Man / I Shot The Sheriff / Isn't It A Pity / Why Does Love Got To Be So Sad / Drifting Blues / Travelin' Alone / That's All Right / Motherless Child / Running On Faith / Motherless Children / Little Queen Of Spades / Before You Accuse Me / Wonderful Tonight / Layla / Cocaine / Crossroads

18 February 2009, Budokan, Tokyo, Japan

SETLIST: Tell The Truth / Key To The Highway / Hoochie Coochie Man / I Shot The Sheriff / Isn't It A Pity / Why Does Love Got To Be So Sad / Drifting Blues / Travelin'

Alone / I Can't Judge Nobody / Motherless Child / Running On Faith / Motherless Children / Little Queen Of Spades / Before You Accuse Me / Wonderful Tonight / Layla / Cocaine / Crossroads

19 February 2009, Budokan, Tokyo, Japan

SETLIST: Tell The Truth / Key To The Highway / Hoochie Coochie Man / I Shot The Sheriff / Here But I'm Gone / Why Does Love Got To Be So Sad / Drifting Blues / Travelin' Alone / That's All Right / Motherless Child / Running On Faith / Motherless Children / Little Queen Of Spades / Before You Accuse Me / Wonderful Tonight / Layla / Cocaine / Crossroads

Poster for Eric's shows at Tokyo's Budokan in February 2009.

21 February 2009, Saitama Super Arena, Saitama, Japan

JEFF BECK LINEUP:
Jeff Beck: guitar
Tal Wikenfeld: bass
David Sancious: keyboards
Vinnie Colaiuta: drums

JEFF BECK SETLIST: The Pump / You Never Know / Cause We've Ended As Lovers / Stratus / Angel / Led Boots / Goodbye Pork Pie Hat / Brush With The Blues / Solo Instrumental / Blue Wind / A Day In The Life / Peter Gunn Theme

ERIC CLAPTON SETLIST: Drifting Blues / Layla / Motherless Child / Running On Faith / Tell The Truth / Little Queen Of Spades / Before You Accuse Me / Cocaine / Crossroads

ERIC CLAPTON AND JEFF BECK SETLIST: You Need Love / Listen Here–Compared To What / Here But

I'm Gone / Outside Woman Blues / Little Brown Bird / Wee Wee Baby / Want To Take You Higher

22 February 2009, Saitama Super Arena, Saitama, Japan

JEFF BECK LINEUP:
Jeff Beck: guitar
Tal Wikenfeld: bass
David Sancious: keyboards
Vinnie Colaiuta: drums

JEFF BECK SETLIST: The Pump / You Never Know / Cause We've Ended As Lovers / Stratus / Angel / Led Boots / Goodbye Pork Pie Hat / Brush With The Blues / Solo Instrumental / A Day In The Life / Big Block / Where Were You / Peter Gunn Theme

ERIC CLAPTON SETLIST: Drifting Blues / Layla / Motherless Child / Running On Faith / Tell The Truth / Key To The Highway / I Shot The Sheriff / Wonderful Tonight / Cocaine / Crossroads

ERIC CLAPTON AND JEFF BECK SETLIST: You Need Love / Listen Here–Compared To What / Here But I'm Gone / Outside Woman Blues / Little Brown Bird / Wee Wee Baby / I Want To Take You Higher

24 February 2009, Budokan, Tokyo, Japan

SETLIST: Tell The Truth / Key To The Highway / Hoochie Coochie Man / I Shot The Sheriff / Here But I'm Gone / Why Does Love Got To Be So Sad / Drifting Blues / Travelin' Alone / That's All Right / Motherless Child / Running On Faith / Motherless Children / Little Queen Of Spades / Before You Accuse Me / Wonderful Tonight / Layla / Cocaine / Crossroads

25 February 2009, Budokan, Tokyo, Japan (complete show broadcast on Japanese television)

SETLIST: Tell The Truth / Key To The Highway / Hoochie Coochie Man / I Shot The Sheriff / Isn't It A Pity / Why Does Love Got To Be So Sad / Drifting Blues / Travelin' Alone / That's All Right / Motherless Child / Running On Faith / Motherless Children / Little Queen Of Spades /

Everything's Gonna Be Alright / Wonderful Tonight / Layla / Cocaine / Crossroads

27 February 2009, Budokan, Tokyo, Japan

SETLIST: Tell The Truth / Key To The Highway / Hoochie Coochie Man / I Shot The Sheriff / Isn't It A Pity / Why Does Love Got To Be So Sad / Drifting Blues / Travelin' Alone / That's All Right / Motherless Child / Running On Faith / Motherless Children / Little Queen Of Spades / Everything's Gonna Be Alright / Wonderful Tonight / Layla / Cocaine / Crossroads

28 February 2009, Budokan, Tokyo, Japan

SETLIST: Tell The Truth / Key To The Highway / Hoochie Coochie Man / I Shot The Sheriff / Here But I'm Gone / Why Does Love Got To Be So Sad / Drifting Blues / Travelin' Alone / That's All Right / Motherless Child / Running On Faith / Motherless Children / Little Queen Of Spades / Before You Accuse Me / Wonderful Tonight / Layla / Cocaine / Crossroads

MARCH 2009

NEW ZEALAND / AUSTRALIA TOUR 2009

4   March 2009, Vector Arena, Auckland, New Zealand (with David McCrum Band)

Tour poster for Eric's Australia tour in March 2009.

SETLIST: Tell The Truth / Key To The Highway / Hoochie Coochie Man / I Shot The Sheriff / Here But I'm Gone /

Eric in New Zealand, 2009. L to R: Doyle Bramhall II, Abe Laboriel, Jr., Eric Clapton, and Willie Weeks at the Vector Arena, Auckland, New Zealand, 4 March 2009.

Why Does Love Got To Be So Sad / Drifting Blues / Travelin' Alone / That's All Right / Motherless Child / Running On Faith / Motherless Children / Little Queen Of Spades / Before You Accuse Me / Wonderful Tonight / Layla / Cocaine / Crossroads

7 March 2009, Hope Estate Winery, Hunter Valley, Australia (with Jeff Lang)

SETLIST: Tell The Truth / Key To The Highway / Hoochie Coochie Man / I Shot The Sheriff / Isn't It A Pity / Why Does Love Got To Be So Sad / Drifting Blues / Travelin' Alone / That's All Right / Motherless Child / Running On Faith / Motherless Children / Little Queen Of Spades / Everything's Gonna Be Alright / Wonderful Tonight / Layla / Cocaine / Crossroads

8 March 2009, Entertainment Centre, Sydney, Australia (with Jeff Lang)

SETLIST: Tell The Truth / Key To The Highway / Hoochie Coochie Man / Here But I'm Gone / I Shot The Sheriff / Little Wing / Drifting Blues / Travelin' Alone / Nobody Knows You When You're Down And Out / Motherless Child / Running On Faith / Motherless Children / Little Queen Of Spades / Before You Accuse Me / Wonderful Tonight / Layla / Cocaine / Crossroads

10 March 2009, Rod Laver Arena, Melbourne, Australia

SETLIST: Tell The Truth / Key To The Highway / Hoochie Coochie Man / I Shot The Sheriff / Little Wing / Why Does Love Got To Be So Sad / Drifting Blues / Travelin' Alone / Nobody Knows You When You're Down And Out / Motherless Child / Running On Faith / Motherless Children / Little Queen Of Spades / Everything's Gonna Be Alright / Wonderful Tonight / Layla / Cocaine / Crossroads

ALLMAN BROTHERS 40th ANNIVERSARY SHOWS 2009

19 March 2009, Beacon Theater, New York City

The year 2009 was a double celebration for the Allman Brothers Band. They were marking the 20th anniversary of performances at New York's Beacon Theater as well as celebrating the 40th anniversary of their founding. The band celebrated in style by playing a series of very special concerts at the Beacon Theater with musicians they have been associated with over that forty-year period. To celebrate Duane Allman's presence on Derek and the Dominos' *Layla* album, Eric Clapton was invited to two shows.

Eric seemed a little out of his comfort zone during the first night. These guys jam every night and Eric comes from a different background and pretty much stepped back and observed on the first night. However, on the second night he was inspired and played some of his best guitar work in years. In fact, after a particularly devastating solo on "Dreams," which left the band and audience open-mouthed, Eric leaned into Derek Trucks and told him, "I haven't played like that since 1968!"

BAND LINEUP:
Gregg Allman: Hammond B3 organ, piano, vocals
Butch Trucks: drums
Jaimoe: drums
Warren Haynes: guitar, vocals
Derek Trucks: guitar
Oteil Burbridge: bass
Marc Quinones: percussion
Eric Clapton: guitar, vocals
Susan Tedeschi: vocals on "Anyday"
Danny Louis: piano on "Layla"

SETLIST:

Key To The Highway *The Allman Brothers Band Live Beacon Theater* 3CD Hittin' The Note

Dreams *The Allman Brothers Band Live Beacon Theater* 3CD Hittin' The Note

Why Does Love Got To Be So Sad *The Allman Brothers Band Live Beacon Theater* 3CD Hittin' The Note

Little Wing *The Allman Brothers Band Live Beacon Theater* 3CD Hittin' The Note

Anyday *The Allman Brothers Band Live Beacon Theater* 3CD Hittin' The Note

Layla *The Allman Brothers Band Live Beacon Theater* 3CD Hittin' The Note

20 March 2009, Beacon Theater, New York City

Eric plays for a second night with the Allman Brothers Band. Eric is in top form tonight delivering some truly spectacular playing.

BAND LINEUP:
Gregg Allman: Hammond B3 organ, piano, vocals
Butch Trucks: drums
Jaimoe: drums
Warren Haynes: guitar, vocals
Derek Trucks: guitar
Oteil Burbridge: bass
Marc Quinones: percussion
Eric Clapton: guitar, vocals
Danny Louis: piano on "Layla"

SETLIST:

Key To The Highway *The Allman Brothers Band Live Beacon Theater* 3CD Hittin' The Note

Stormy Monday *The Allman Brothers Band Live Beacon Theater* 3CD Hittin' The Note

Dreams *The Allman Brothers Band Live Beacon Theater* 3CD Hittin' The Note

Why Does Love Got To Be So Sad *The Allman Brothers Band Live Beacon Theater* 3CD Hittin' The Note

Little Wing *The Allman Brothers Band Live Beacon Theater* 3CD Hittin' The Note

In Memory Of Elizabeth Reed *The Allman Brothers Band Live Beacon Theater* 3CD Hittin' The Note

Layla *The Allman Brothers Band Live Beacon Theater* 3CD Hittin' The Note

MAY 2009

APPEARANCE WITH JOE BONAMASSA 2009

4 May 2009, Royal Albert Hall, London

Eric joins Joe Bonamassa and his band.

SETLIST:

Further On Up The Road *Joe Bonamassa Live From The Royal Albert Hall* DVD / CD released October 2009

BUNBURY DINNER AUCTION 2009

9 May 2009, Grosvenor House Hotel, London (Eric and his band performed at a gala dinner and auction in aid of the Bunbury Cricket Club)

BAND LINEUP:
Eric Clapton: guitar, vocals
Andy Fairweather Low: guitar
Steve Gadd: drums
Chris Stainton: keyboards
Tim Carmon: keyboards
Willie Weeks: bass
Michelle John: backing vocals
Sharon White: backing vocals

SETLIST: Lay Down Sally / Nobody Knows You When You're Down And Out / Somewhere Over The Rainbow / Badge / Old Love / Before You Accuse Me / Wonderful Tonight / Layla / Cocaine

Advert for short UK tour in May 2009.

UK / IRELAND TOUR 2009

BAND LINEUP:
Eric Clapton: guitar, vocals
Andy Fairweather Low: guitar
Steve Gadd: drums

Chris Stainton: keyboards
Tim Carmon: keyboards
Willie Weeks: bass
Michelle John: backing vocals
Sharon White: backing vocals

11 May 2009, O2, Dublin, Ireland

SETLIST: Going Down Slow / Anything For Your Love / Key To The Highway / Old Love / Hoochie Coochie Man / I Shot The Sheriff / Drifting Blues / Lay Down Sally / Not Dark Yet / Anytime For You / Somewhere Over The Rainbow / Badge / Little Queen Of Spades / Before You Accuse Me / Wonderful Tonight / Layla / Cocaine / Crossroads

13 May 2009, Liverpool Echo Arena, Liverpool (with the Arc Angels)

SETLIST: Going Down Slow / Anything For Your Love / Key To The Highway / Old Love / I Shot The Sheriff / Layla / Lay Down Sally / Not Dark Yet / Anytime For You / Somewhere Over The Rainbow / Badge / Little Queen Of Spades / Before You Accuse Me / Wonderful Tonight / Cocaine / Crossroads

14 May 2009, MEN Arena, Manchester (with the Arc Angels)

SETLIST: Going Down Slow / Anything For Your Love / Key To The Highway / Old Love / I Shot The Sheriff / Layla / Lay Down Sally / Not Dark Yet / Anytime For You / Somewhere Over The Rainbow / Badge / Little Queen Of Spades / Before You Accuse Me / Wonderful Tonight / Cocaine / Crossroads

16 May 2009, Royal Albert Hall, London (with the Arc Angels)

Tour poster for Eric Clapton's run of shows at the Royal Albert Hall, May 2009.

SETLIST: Going Down Slow / Anything For Your Love / Key To The Highway / Old Love / I Shot The Sheriff / Layla / Lay Down Sally / Not Dark Yet / Anytime For You

/ Somewhere Over The Rainbow / Badge / Little Queen Of Spades / Before You Accuse Me / Wonderful Tonight / Cocaine / Crossroads

17 May 2009, Royal Albert Hall, London (with the Arc Angels)

SETLIST: Going Down Slow / Anything For Your Love / Key To The Highway / Old Love / I Shot The Sheriff / Layla / Lay Down Sally / Not Dark Yet / Anytime For You / Somewhere Over The Rainbow / Badge / Little Queen Of Spades / Before You Accuse Me / Wonderful Tonight / Cocaine / Crossroads

19 May 2009, Royal Albert Hall, London (with the Arc Angels)

SETLIST: Going Down Slow / Key To The Highway / Old Love / Anything For Your Love / I Shot The Sheriff / Layla / Lay Down Sally / Not Dark Yet / Anytime For You / Somewhere Over The Rainbow / Badge / Little Queen Of Spades / Everything's Gonna Be Alright / Wonderful Tonight / Cocaine / Crossroads

20 May 2009, Royal Albert Hall, London (with the Arc Angels)

SETLIST: Going Down Slow / Key To The Highway / Old Love / Anything For Your Love / I Shot The Sheriff / Layla / Nobody Knows You When You're Down And Out / Not Dark Yet / Anytime For You / Somewhere Over The Rainbow / Badge / Little Queen Of Spades / Everything's Gonna Be Alright / Wonderful Tonight / Cocaine / Crossroads

22 May 2009, Royal Albert Hall, London (with the Arc Angels)

SETLIST: Going Down Slow / Key To The Highway / Old Love / Anything For Your Love / I Shot The Sheriff / Three Little Girls / Layla / Nobody Knows You When You're Down And Out / Not Dark Yet / Anytime For You / Somewhere Over The Rainbow / Badge / Little Queen Of Spades / Before You Accuse Me / Wonderful Tonight / Cocaine / Crossroads

23 May 2009, Royal Albert Hall, London (with the Arc Angels)

SETLIST: Going Down Slow / Key To The Highway / Old Love / Anything For Your Love / I Shot The Sheriff / Layla / Nobody Knows You When You're Down And Out / Not Dark Yet / Anytime For You / Somewhere Over The Rainbow / Badge / Little Queen Of Spades / Before You Accuse Me / Wonderful Tonight / Cocaine / Crossroads

25 May 2009, Royal Albert Hall, London (with the Arc Angels)

SETLIST: Going Down Slow / Key To The Highway / Old Love / Anything For Your Love / I Shot The Sheriff / Drifting Blues / Layla / Nobody Knows You When You're Down And Out / Anytime For You / Somewhere Over The Rainbow / Badge / Little Queen Of Spades / Before You Accuse Me / Wonderful Tonight / Cocaine / Crossroads

26 May 2009, Royal Albert Hall, London (with the Arc Angels)

SETLIST: Going Down Slow / Key To The Highway / Got To Got Better In A Little While / Old Love / I Shot The Sheriff / Drifting Blues / Nobody Knows You When You're Down And Out / Lay Down Sally / Anytime For You / Somewhere Over The Rainbow / Badge / Little Queen Of Spades / Before You Accuse Me / Wonderful Tonight / Layla[1] / Cocaine[1] / Crossroads[1]

[1]with Doyle Bramhall II on guitar

Eric Clapton at the Royal Albert Hall, May 2009.

28 May 2009, Royal Albert Hall, London (with the Arc Angels)

SETLIST: Going Down Slow / Key To The Highway / Anything For Your Love / Old Love / Got To Got Better In A Little While / Drifting Blues / Nobody Knows You When You're Down And Out / Lay Down Sally / Somewhere Over The Rainbow / Badge / Little Queen Of Spades / Before You Accuse Me / Wonderful Tonight / Layla[1] / Cocaine[1] / Crossroads[1]

[1]with Doyle Bramhall II on guitar

29 May 2009, Royal Albert Hall, London (with the Arc Angels)

SETLIST: Going Down Slow / Key To The Highway / Anything For Your Love / Old Love / Got To Get Better In A Little While / Drifting Blues / Three Little Girls / Nobody Knows You When You're Down And Out / Lay Down Sally / Somewhere Over The Rainbow / Badge / Little Queen Of Spades / Before You Accuse Me / Wonderful Tonight / Layla[1] / Cocaine[1] / Crossroads[1]

[1]with Doyle Bramhall II on guitar

Eric and band at the Royal Albert Hall in May 2009. L to R: Doyle Bramhall II, Andy Fairweather Low, Willie Weeks, Chris Stainton, Eric Clapton.

Andy Fairweather Low and Eric Clapton at the Royal Albert Hall in May 2009.

31 May 2009, Royal Albert Hall, London (with the Arc Angels)

SETLIST: Going Down Slow / Key To The Highway / Anything For Your Love / Old Love / I Shot The Sheriff / Drifting Blues / Nobody Knows You When You're Down And Out / Lay Down Sally / Somewhere Over

The Rainbow / Badge / Little Queen Of Spades / Before You Accuse Me / Wonderful Tonight / Layla[1] / Cocaine[1] / Crossroads[1]

[1]with Doyle Bramhall II on guitar

JUNE 2009

ERIC CLAPTON AND STEVE WINWOOD U.S. TOUR 2009

BAND LINEUP:
Steve Winwood: keyboards, guitar, vocals
Eric Clapton: guitar, vocals
Chris Stainton: keyboards
Willie Weeks: bass
Abe Laboriel, Jr.: drums
Michelle John: backing vocals
Sharon White: backing vocals

10 June 2009, Izod Center, East Rutherford, New Jersey

SETLIST: Had To Cry Today / Low Down / After Midnight / Sleeping In The Ground / Presence Of The Lord / Glad / Well Alright / Tough Luck Blues / Tell The Truth / Pearly Queen / No Face, No Name, No Number / Forever Man / Georgia On My Mind / Drifting Blues / Nobody Knows You When You're Down And Out / Layla / Can't Find My Way Home / Split Decision / Little Wing / Voodoo Chile / Cocaine / Dear Mr. Fantasy

12 June 2009, Wachovia Center, Philadelphia, Pennsylvania

SETLIST: Had To Cry Today / Low Down / After Midnight / Sleeping In The Ground / Presence Of The Lord / Glad / Well Alright / Tough Luck Blues / Pearly Queen / Tell The Truth / No Face, No Name, No Number / Forever Man / Georgia On My Mind / Drifting Blues / Nobody Knows You When You're Down And Out / Layla / Can't Find My Way Home / Split Decision / Little Wing / Voodoo Chile / Cocaine / Dear Mr. Fantasy

13 June 2009, Verizon Center, Washington, D.C.

SETLIST: Had To Cry Today / Low Down / After Midnight / Presence Of The Lord / Sleeping In The Ground / Glad / Well Alright / Tough Luck Blues / Pearly Queen / No Face, No Name, No Number / Forever Man / Little Wing / Georgia On My Mind / Drifting Blues / Nobody Knows You When You're Down And Out / Layla / Can't Find My Way Home / Crossroads / Voodoo Chile / Cocaine / Dear Mr. Fantasy

15 June 2009, Schottenstein Center, Columbus, Ohio

SETLIST: Had To Cry Today / Low Down / After Midnight / Presence Of The Lord / Sleeping In The Ground / Glad / Well Alright / Tough Luck Blues / Pearly Queen / There's A River / Little Wing / Forever Man / Georgia On My Mind / Drifting Blues / How Long Blues / Layla / Can't Find My Way Home / Split Decision / Voodoo Chile / Cocaine / Dear Mr. Fantasy

"Crossroads" is dropped in favor of "Split Decision" tonight. Steve Winwood performed "There's A River" instead of "No Face, No Name, No Number" and Eric performed "How Long Blues" instead of "Nobody Knows You When You're Down And Out."

> **"**Opening with Blind Faith's 'Had To Cry Today' set the stage perfectly. Winwood's pleading vocals and Clapton's energetic guitar work did not stray far from the recorded version. From there, the two traded center stage, performing their signature songs and then returning to Blind Faith material. Clapton offered a perfectly phrased and smartly built solo in 'After Midnight.' Later, Winwood delivered a memorable version of Traffic's 'Pearly Queen,' a song with his trademark take on the blues and that last night was swung mightily by Clapton's copacetic guitar solo.**"**
> —COLUMBUS DISPATCH

17 June 2009, United Center, Chicago, Illinois

SETLIST: Had To Cry Today / Low Down / After Midnight / Presence Of The Lord / Sleeping In The Ground / Glad / Well Alright / Tough Luck Blues / Pearly Queen / Crossroads / There's A River / Forever Man / Georgia On My Mind / Drifting Blues / How Long Blues / Layla

/ Can't Find My Way Home / Split Decision / Voodoo Chile / Sweet Home Chicago[1] / Drowning On Dry Land[1]

[1] Buddy Guy on guitar and vocals

> The headlining duo opened by looking back forty years to 'Had To Cry Today,' the first song on the first and only Blind Faith album, released in 1969. That was to be the only album-length studio collaboration between Clapton and Winwood in their long, much-acclaimed careers. Upon returning to it, they clung to every note with tenacity. Clapton took the first solo, then went toe-to-toe with Winwood on the second, and things were off to fly ing start.
> —CHICAGO TRIBUNE

18 June 2009, Xcel Energy Center, St. Paul, Minnesota

SETLIST: Had To Cry Today / Low Down / After Midnight / Presence Of The Lord / Sleeping In The Ground / Glad / Well Alright / Tough Luck Blues / Pearly Queen / Crossroads / No Face, No Name, No Number / Forever Man / Georgia On My Mind / Drifting Blues / How Long Blues / Layla / Can't Find My Way Home / Split Decision / Voodoo Chile / Cocaine / Dear Mr. Fantasy

"Crossroads" is back in the set and "Cocaine" is now part of the encore with "Dear Mr. Fantasy."

> Forty years after they made a forty-two-minute album together, Rock and Roll Hall of Famers Eric Clapton, sixty-four, and Steve Winwood, sixty-one, have teamed up again for a fourteen-show U.S. tour. Their 130-minute reunion concert Thursday night at Xcel Energy Center was nostalgic fun, with some magical moments, but not enough to live up to the fantasies of the two musicians or the 14,000 fans.
> —STAR TRIBUNE

20 June 2009, Qwest Center, Omaha, Nebraska

SETLIST: Had To Cry Today / Low Down / After Midnight / Presence Of The Lord / Sleeping In The Ground / Glad / Well Alright / Tough Luck Blues / Pearly Queen / No Face, No Name, No Number / Forever Man / Georgia On My Mind / Drifting Blues / How Long Blues / Layla / Can't Find My Way Home / Split Decision / Voodoo Chile / Cocaine / Dear Mr. Fantasy

21 June 2009, Pepsi Center, Denver, Colorado

SETLIST: Had To Cry Today / Low Down / After Midnight / Presence Of The Lord / Sleeping In The Ground / Glad / Well Alright / Tough Luck Blues / Pearly Queen / No Face, No Name, No Number / Forever Man / Georgia On My Mind / Drifting Blues / How Long Blues / Layla / Can't Find My Way Home / Split Decision / Voodoo Chile / Cocaine / Dear Mr. Fantasy

23 June 2009, American Airlines Arena, Dallas, Texas

SETLIST: Had To Cry Today / Low Down / After Midnight / Presence Of The Lord / Sleeping In The Ground / Glad / Well Alright / Tough Luck Blues / Pearly Queen / No Face, No Name, No Number / Forever Man / Georgia On My Mind / Drifting Blues / How Long Blues / Layla / Can't Find My Way Home / Split Decision / Voodoo Chile / Cocaine / Dear Mr. Fantasy

24 June 2009, Toyota Center, Houston, Texas

SETLIST: Had To Cry Today / Low Down / After Midnight / Presence Of The Lord / Sleeping In The Ground / Glad / Well Alright / Tough Luck Blues / Pearly Queen / There's A River / Forever Man / The Low Spark Of High Heeled Boys / Drifting Blues / How Long Blues / Layla / Can't Find My Way Home / Split Decision / Voodoo Chile / Cocaine / Dear Mr. Fantasy

Steve Winwood performed "Low Spark Of High Heeled Boys" tonight instead of "Georgia."

> The former Blind Faith bandmates could have filled their two-hour show with a rote rendition of greatest hits but dug into the book of basic blues for numbers like 'How Long Blues' from Leroy Carr and 'Tough Luck Blues' from Big Maceo alongside the expected hits like Clapton's 'Layla' and Winwood's 'Glad' from his days with Traffic.
> —HOUSTON CHRONICLE

26 June 2009, AZ Jobing.com Arena, Glendale, Arizona

SETLIST: Had To Cry Today / Low Down / After Midnight / Presence Of The Lord / Sleeping In The Ground / Glad / Well Alright / Tough Luck Blues / Pearly

Queen / There's A River / Forever Man / Georgia On My Mind / Drifting Blues / How Long Blues / Layla / Can't Find My Way Home / Split Decision / Voodoo Chile / Cocaine / Dear Mr. Fantasy

27 June 2009, MGM Grand Garden Arena, Las Vegas, Nevada

SETLIST: Had To Cry Today / Low Down / After Midnight / Presence Of The Lord / Sleeping In The Ground / Glad / Well Alright / Tough Luck Blues / Pearly Queen / There's A River / Forever Man / The Low Spark Of High Heeled Boys / Drifting Blues / How Long Blues / Layla / Can't Find My Way Home / Split Decision / Voodoo Chile / Cocaine / Dear Mr. Fantasy

> **"**Some things do get better with age. Eric Clapton and Steve Winwood had a ball Saturday night—and they took 18,000 fans at the MGM Grand Garden Arena along for the ride.**"**
> —*LAS VEGAS SUN*

29 June 2009, Oracle Arena, Oakland, California

SETLIST: Had To Cry Today / Low Down / After Midnight / Presence Of The Lord / Sleeping In The Ground / Glad / Well Alright / Tough Luck Blues / Pearly Queen / There's A River / Forever Man / The Low Spark Of High Heeled Boys / Drifting Blues / How Long Blues / Layla / Can't Find My Way Home / Split Decision / Voodoo Chile / Cocaine / Dear Mr. Fantasy

30 June 2009, Hollywood Bowl, Los Angeles, California

SETLIST: Had To Cry Today / Low Down / After Midnight / Presence Of The Lord / Sleeping In The Ground / Glad / Well Alright / Tough Luck Blues / Pearly Queen / There's A River / Forever Man / Low Spark Of High Heeled Boys / Drifting Blues / How Long Blues Blues / Layla / Can't Find My Way Home / Split Decision / Voodoo Chile / Cocaine / Dear Mr. Fantasy

SEPTEMBER 2009

17 September 2009, *Tonight Show* with Jay Leno, NBC Studios, Burbank, California

Eric joins Bruce Hornsby and the Noisemakers for a performance of "Space Is The Place" on the Jay Leno *Tonight Show.*

OCTOBER 2009

LATER WITH JOOLS HOLLAND 2009

20 October 2009, *Later With Jools Holland,* BBC Television Center Studios, London

Eric Clapton makes a special guest appearance on tonight's *Later With Jools Holland* show backing Smokey Robinson. Broadcast live on BBC 2 on Tuesday 20 October 2009, with an extended version with prerecorded segments on Friday 23 October 2009. Eric was a last-minute surprise guest when Jools's regular guitarist fell ill. Eric and the band put in a great performance as did Smokey Robinson, who was promoting his new album.

BAND LINEUP:
Smokey Robinson: vocals
Eric Clapton: guitar
Jools Holland: piano
Dave Swift: bass
Gilson Lavis: drum
Demetrious Pappas: keyboards

SETLIST: Don't Know Why / You've Really Got A Hold On Me

> **"**Our regular guitarist was due to do those recordings but couldn't make it for one reason or another and Jools got Eric Clapton in to do the show. We had worked with Eric on numerous occasions, so it was great to see him again at the BBC studios. Normally when we back artists on *Later* I usually stand up, whether I'm playing double bass or bass guitar, but Eric said he would prefer to sit down, so two chairs were brought in for us both.

Eric and I spent the whole day chatting and having a laugh as this was the longest period we'd ever spent together. We had a great time running through the song and just having fun. The next thing we knew, the recording of the TV show began. Eventually we saw Smokey enter the studio, Jools introduced him, and we were off! Once the songs were over, another band began to play and we were all off camera. Smokey walked over to Eric and myself and gave us both a hug, and simply said, 'beautiful guys, thank you.' Personally, I was on Cloud Nine! Even now, after many years of backing countless artists on Jools's TV show, the performances I did with Eric and Smokey on that episode of *Later* are among the proudest moments of my career. If you watch the footage, you will notice I have the biggest grin on my face the whole time, and rightly so!**

—DAVE SWIFT
(bassist with Jools Holland)

30 October 2009, Madison Square Garden, New York City

Eric Clapton and his band were due to perform on the second night of the 25th Anniversary Rock & Roll Hall of Fame Concert along with Aretha Franklin, Metallica, Ozzy Osborne, U2, and others. On 23 October 2009, it was announced that Eric canceled his appearance as he needed a minor medical procedure for gallstones. On 27 October, the Rock & Roll Hall Of Fame announced that Jeff Beck along with special guests would perform in Eric's place. Van Morrison also canceled; both he and Eric were due to do something together at the show.

NOVEMBER 2009

4 November 2009, Jazz Cafe, Camden, London

Ginger Baker celebrates his birthday with a concert at the Jazz Café. Eric was due to appear with Ginger and Steve Winwood for a mini Blind Faith reunion. Sadly, although Eric turned up to wish Ginger well, he was not fit enough to play as he was recuperating from his gallstone operation. Steve Winwood sat in for several numbers.

CHILDREN ACTION 15th ANNIVERSARY FUND RAISER 2009

23 November 2009, Children Action's 15th anniversary fund raiser, Geneva, Switzerland (Arthur, Mira Awad, Dany Boon, Michel Boujenah, Eric Clapton, Catherine Deneuve, Gad Elmaleh, Nikos, Noa, Elie Semoun, all provided an unforgettable evening of laughter, music, and emotion. Eric played three acoustic numbers for the charity event. The evening's auction raised approximately $5 million for Children Action, including $150,000 for an Eric Clapton autographed Martin 000-28 acoustic guitar)

DECEMBER 2009

NEW YEAR'S EVE DANCE 2009

31 December 2009, Woking Leisure Centre, Woking, Surrey

Eric Clapton and his band are called Any Lengths.

BAND LINEUP:
Eric Clapton: guitar, vocals
Andy Fairweather Low: guitar, vocals
Gary Brooker: keyboards, vocals
Chris Stainton: keyboards
Dave Bronze: bass
Henry Spinetti: drums
Sharon White: backing vocals
Michelle John: backing vocals

SETLIST 1: Knock On Wood / Reconsider Baby / You Can't Judge A Book / Unchain My Heart / Route 66 / Will The Circle Be Unbroken / Let The Good Times Roll / Knockin' On Heaven's Door / Five Long Years / Shake, Rattle And Roll

SETLIST 2: In The Midnight Hour / Hoochie Coochie Man / Blueberry Hill / Stagger Lee / Got Love If You Want It / Gin House / Willie And The Hand Jive / A Whiter Shade Of Pale / Cocaine / Old Black Joe

RECORDING SESSIONS 2009

ERIC CLAPTON GUEST SESSION

METROPOLIS STUDIOS
The Power House, 70 Chiswick High Road, London
Session for Paul Wassif

25 MAY 2009

PLEASE DON'T LEAVE (Paul Wassif) *Looking Up Feeling Down* CD Black Brown and White BBWCD-001 released 2011

Paul Wassif: acoustic guitar, vocals
Eric Clapton: acoustic guitar
Bert Jansch: acoustic guitar
Evan Jenkins: drums
Robin Clayton: double bass
David Watson: harmony vocals
James Watson: grand piano

SOUTHBOUND TRAIN (William Broonzy) *Looking Up Feeling Down* CD Black Brown and White BBWCD-001 released 2011

Paul Wassif: acoustic guitar, vocals
Eric Clapton: Dobro
Bert Jansch: acoustic guitar
Evan Jenkins: drums
Robin Clayton: double bass
David Watson: harmony vocals

Producers: Paul Wassif / David Watson

> **“**We set up the band and we had a drummer to the left of me, bass player to the right, me in the middle, and then Eric and Bert facing me. We wanted it to be live and audible to everyone. Eric brought along his lovely old Dobro he bought in 1970 at the insistence of Duane Allman, and one of his 000-28 signature Martin guitars.**”**
>
> **—PAUL WASSIF**
> (*Guitar Magazine*, Summer 2011)

ERIC CLAPTON GUEST SESSION

BRITISH GROVE STUDIO
20 British Grove, Chiswick, London
Session for Paul Stewart

29 MAY 2009

FLY FREE (Paul Stewart) available as a downlowd and rare pressed promo CD single

Paul Stewart: vocals, acoustic guitar
Eric Clapton: solo guitar
Matt Prior: guitars
Lee Pomeroy: bass
Adam Wakeman: piano, mellotron
Don Airey: Hammond B3 organ
Alex Toff: drums
Paul Wassif: backing vocals
Victoria: backing vocals
Dylan: backing vocals
Lucas: backing vocals
Zac and Ashton Mark: backing vocals
Anne: backing vocals
Leona: backing vocals
Marcus: backing vocals
Andreas: backing vocals
Johan: backing vocals

Drums and keyboards recorded at: Konk Studios
Engineer: Ben Mason

Backing vocals recorded at: Echo Studios
Engineer: Jamie Masters

Lead vocal, solo guitar, and additional guitars recorded at: British Grove Studios
Engineer: Richard Cooper
Assistant: Joe Kearns
Mixed by: Richard Cooper at British Grove Studios
Mastered by: Mazen Murad at Metropolis
Produced, recorded, mixed by: Paul Stewart / Matt Prior
British Grove Studio manager: David Stewart
Technical engineer: Graham Meek

This song was a gift to Sir Jackie Stewart for his birthday by his son, Paul. Eric is a family friend and was delighted to have been able to contribute.

Steve Winwood: organ
Marius de Vries: keyboard
Pino Palladino: bass
Ian Thomas: drums
Bill Dillon: guitorgan, guitar
Sharon White: backing vocals
Michelle John: backing vocals
Angelyna Boyd: backing vocals

THIS IS WHERE I GET OFF (Robbie Robertson) *How To Become Clairvoyant* CD 429 Records released April 2011

Robbie Robertson: vocal, guitar, keyboard
Eric Clapton: guitar
Marius de Vries: piano
Pino Palladino: bass
Ian Thomas: drums
Rocco Deluca: backing vocals
Daryl Johnson: backing vocals
Sharon White: backing vocals
Michelle John: backing vocals
Angelyna Boyd: backing vocals

FEAR OF FALLING (Eric Clapton / Robbie Robertson) *How To Become Clairvoyant* CD 429 Records released April 2011

Robbie Robertson: vocal, electric guitar
Eric Clapton: vocal, acoustic guitar, electric guitar
Steve Winwood: organ
Pino Palladino: bass
Ian Thomas: drums
Taylor Goldsmith: backing vocals
Sharon White: backing vocals
Michelle John: backing vocals

SHE'S NOT MINE (Robbie Robertson) *How To Become Clairvoyant* CD 429 Records released April 2011

Robbie Robertson: vocal, guitar
Eric Clapton: guitar solo, harmony vocal
Steve Winwood: organ
Pino Palladino: bass
Ian Thomas: drums
Jim Keltner: drums
Rocco Deluca: Dobro, backing vocals
Taylor Goldsmith: backing vocals

MADAME X (Eric Clapton) *How To Become Clairvoyant* CD 429 Records released April 2011

Robbie Robertson: electric guitar, keyboard
Eric Clapton: guitar
Trent Reznor: additional textures
Pino Palladino: bass
Ian Thomas: drums

WON'T BE BACK (Eric Clapton / Robbie Robertson) *How To Become Clairvoyant* CD 429 Records released April 2011

Robbie Robertson: vocal, guitar, keyboard
Eric Clapton: guitar, harmony vocal
Pino Palladino: bass
Ian Thomas: drums
Marius de Vries: keyboard
Eldad Guetta: horns

FEAR OF FALLING (Robbie Robertson) (an alternate version of Robbie's "Fear Of Falling" which features Robbie singing lead on all the verses

---

> **❝**I cannot think of a more wonderful gift to receive for my birthday. I did not know that my son Paul could sing or write music, or lyrics for such music. What a surprise and delight. Our younger son Mark created the pictures to go with the music so well, representing the wonderful and exciting life that I have enjoyed with my wife Helen and both of my sons and their families.
>
> To have Eric Clapton play on this CD and DVD is another enormous thrill and privilege for somebody who enjoys Eric's music as much as I do. Eric is a good friend and one of the great musicians of the world. I am so proud and honored that they created all of this for me.**❞**
>
> —SIR JACKIE STEWART

ERIC CLAPTON GUEST SESSION

OLYMPIC STUDIOS
117 Church Road, London

BEGUN IN MARCH 2008

and

THE VILLAGE RECORDER
1616 Butler Avenue, Los Angeles, California Session for Robbie Robertson

SEPTEMBER 2009

HE DON'T LIVE HERE NO MORE (Robbie Robertson) *How To Become Clairvoyant* CD 429 Records released April 2011

Robbie Robertson: vocal, guitar, keyboard
Eric Clapton: electric guitar, slide guitar, harmony vocal
Marius de Vries: keyboard
Pino Palladino: bass
Ian Thomas: drums
Rocco Deluca: backing vocals
Daryl Johnson: backing vocals
Taylor Goldsmith: backing vocals

THE RIGHT MISTAKE (Robbie Robertson) *How To Become Clairvoyant* CD 429 Records released April 2011

Robbie Robertson: vocal, guitar solo, keyboard
Eric Clapton: guitar solo

accompanied by Eric Clapton on the choruses. This is an early mix of the song that was done by Robbie. The track was exclusive to Robbie's online community through his website)

Producers: Marius de Vries / Robbie Robertson
Engineer: Alan Douglas

OCEAN WAY RECORDING
6050 Sunset Boulevard, Hollywood, California
Session for *Clapton*

SEPTEMBER 2009

Details in 2010 recording sessions.

ERIC CLAPTON GUEST SESSION
EAST WEST (CELLO) STUDIOS
6000 Sunset Boulevard, Hollywood, California
Session for Jerry Lee Lewis

26 SEPTEMBER 2009

YOU CAN HAVE HER (Bill Cook) *Mean Old Man* CD Verve 001467402 released September 2010

Jerry Lee Lewis: piano, vocals
Eric Clapton: guitar, vocals
Jim Keltner: drums
James Burton: guitar

Producers: Jim Keltner / Steve Bing

2010

ERIC CLAPTON & JEFF BECK *TOGETHER & APART* TOUR 2010

13 February 2010, The O2, London

BAND LINEUP:
Jeff Beck: guitar
Jason Rebello: keyboards
Rhonda Smith: bass
Narada Michael Walden: drums

JEFF BECK SETLIST: Eternity's Breath / Stratus / Led Boots / Corpus Christi Carol[1] / Bass Solo (by Rhonda Smith) / Hammerhead[1] / Mna Na Heireann[1, 2] / People Get Ready / Big Block / There's No Other Me[3] / I Put A Spell On You[3] / A Day In The Life[1]

[1]with 12-piece orchestra
[2]with Sharon Corr on violin
[3]with Joss Stone on vocals

BAND LINEUP:
Eric Clapton: guitar, vocals
Walt Richmond: keyboards
Chris Stainton: keyboards
Willie Weeks: bass
Steve Gadd: drums
Michelle John: backing vocals
Sharon White: backing vocals

ERIC CLAPTON SETLIST: Drifting Blues / Layla / Nobody Knows You When You're Down And Out / Running On Faith / When Somebody Thinks You're Wonderful / Tell The Truth / Key To The Highway / I Shot The Sheriff / Wonderful Tonight / Cocaine / Crossroads

BAND LINEUP:
Eric Clapton: guitar, vocals
Jeff Beck: guitar, vocals on "Hi Ho Silver Lining"
Walt Richmond: keyboards
Chris Stainton: keyboards
Willie Weeks: bass
Steve Gadd: drums
Michelle John: backing vocals
Sharon White: backing vocals

ERIC CLAPTON AND JEFF BECK SETLIST: Shake Your Moneymaker / Moon River / You Need Love / Outside Woman Blues / Little Brown Bird / Wee Wee Baby / (I Want To Take You) Higher / Hi Ho Silver Lining

14 February 2010, The O2, London

BAND LINEUP:
Jeff Beck: guitar
Jason Rebello: keyboards
Rhonda Smith: bass
Narada Michael Walden: drums

Jeff Beck and Eric Clapton "Together And Apart" at the O2 in London on 14 February 2010.

JEFF BECK SETLIST: Eternity's Breath / Stratus / Led Boots / Corpus Christi Carol[1] / Bass Solo (by Rhonda Smith) / Hammerhead[1] / Mna Na Heireann[1,2] / People Get Ready / Big Block / Lilac Wine[3] / A Day In The Life[1] / Nessun Dorma

[1]with 12-piece orchestra
[2]with Sharon Corr on violin
[3]with Imelda May on vocals

BAND LINEUP:
Eric Clapton: guitar, vocals
Walt Richmond: keyboards
Chris Stainton: keyboards
Willie Weeks: bass
Steve Gadd: drums
Michelle John: backing vocals
Sharon White: backing vocals

ERIC CLAPTON SETLIST: Drifting Blues / Nobody Knows You When You're Down And Out / Running

On Faith / When Somebody Thinks You're Wonderful / Tell The Truth / Key To The Highway / I Shot The Sheriff / Little Queen Of Spades / Cocaine

BAND LINEUP:
Eric Clapton: guitar, vocals
Jeff Beck: guitar, vocals on "Hi Ho Silver Lining"
Walt Richmond: keyboards
Chris Stainton: keyboards
Willie Weeks: bass
Steve Gadd: drums
Michelle John: backing vocals
Sharon White: backing vocals

ERIC CLAPTON AND JEFF BECK SETLIST: Shake Your Moneymaker / Moon River / You Need Love / Outside Woman Blues / Little Brown Bird / Wee Wee Baby / (I Want To Take You) Higher / Hi Ho Silver Lining

PLASTIC ONO BAND REUNION 2010

16 February 2010, BAM Howard Gilman Opera House, Brooklyn, New York (guest appearance with the Plastic Ono Band)

Poster for the Plastic Ono Band.

SETLIST: Yer Blues / Death Of Samatha / Don't Worry Kyoko

BAND LINEUP:
Yoko Ono: vocals
Eric Clapton: guitar, slide guitar on "Don't Worry Kyoto"
Jim Keltner: drums
Klaus Voorman: bass
Sean Lennon: guitar, vocals

The concert was filmed and recorded but remains unreleased.

JEFF BECK & ERIC CLAPTON TOGETHER & APART U.S. / CANADA TOUR 2010

18 February 2010, Madison Square Garden, New York City

JEFF BECK BAND LINEUP:
Jeff Beck: guitar
Jason Rebello: keyboards
Rhonda Smith: bass
Narada Michael Walden: drums

JEFF BECK SETLIST: Eternity's Breath / Stratus / Led Boots / Corpus Christi Carol[1] / Bass Solo (by Rhonda Smith) / Hammerhead[1] / Mna Na Heireann[1] / Brush With The Blues / Big Block / A Day In The Life[1] / Nessun Dorma[1]

[1]with 30-piece orchestra

ERIC CLAPTON BAND LINEUP:
Eric Clapton: guitar, vocals
Walt Richmond: keyboards
Chris Stainton: keyboards
Willie Weeks: bass
Steve Gadd: drums
Michelle John: backing vocals
Sharon White: backing vocals

ERIC CLAPTON SETLIST: Drifting Blues / Nobody Knows You When You're Down And Out / Running On Faith / Tell The Truth / Key To The Highway / I Shot The Sheriff / Little Queen Of Spades / Cocaine

JEFF BECK AND ERIC CLAPTON BAND LINEUP:
Eric Clapton: guitar, vocals
Jeff Beck; guitar
Walt Richmond: keyboards
Chris Stainton: keyboards
Willie Weeks: bass
Steve Gadd: drums
Michelle John: backing vocals
Sharon White: backing vocals

JEFF BECK AND ERIC CLAPTON SETLIST: Shake Your Moneymaker / Moon River / You Need Love / Outside Woman Blues / Little Brown Bird / Wee Wee Baby / (I Want To Take You) Higher / Crossroads

19 February 2010, Madison Square Garden, New York City

JEFF BECK BAND LINEUP:
Jeff Beck: guitar
Jason Rebello: keyboards
Rhonda Smith: bass
Narada Michael Walden: drums

JEFF BECK SETLIST: Eternity's Breath / Stratus / Led Boots / Corpus Christi Carol[1] / Bass Solo (by Rhonda Smith) / Hammerhead[1] / Mna Na Heireann[1] / Brush With The Blues / Big Block / A Day In The Life[1] / Nessun Dorma[1]

[1]with 30-piece orchestra

ERIC CLAPTON BAND LINEUP:
Eric Clapton: guitar, vocals
Walt Richmond: keyboards
Chris Stainton: keyboards
Willie Weeks: bass
Steve Gadd: drums
Michelle John: backing vocals
Sharon White: backing vocals

ERIC CLAPTON SETLIST: Drifting Blues / Nobody Knows You When You're Down And Out / Running On Faith / Tell The Truth / Key To The Highway / I Shot The Sheriff / Little Queen Of Spades / Cocaine

JEFF BECK AND ERIC CLAPTON BAND LINEUP:
Eric Clapton: guitar, vocals
Jeff Beck: guitar
Walt Richmond: keyboards
Chris Stainton: keyboards
Willie Weeks: bass
Steve Gadd: drums
Michelle John: backing vocals
Sharon White: backing vocals

JEFF BECK AND ERIC CLAPTON SETLIST: Shake Your Moneymaker / Moon River / You Need Love /

Outside Woman Blues / Little Brown Bird / Wee Wee Baby / (I Want To Take You) Higher / Crossroads

21 February 2010, Air Canada Centre, Toronto, Ontario, Canada

JEFF BECK BAND LINEUP:
Jeff Beck: guitar
Jason Rebello: keyboards
Rhonda Smith: bass
Narada Michael Walden: drums

JEFF BECK SETLIST: Eternity's Breath / Stratus / Led Boots / Corpus Christi Carol[1] / Bass Solo (by Rhonda Smith) / Hammerhead[1] / Mna Na Heireann[1] / Brush With The Blues / Big Block / A Day In The Life[1] / Nessun Dorma[1]

[1]with 30-piece orchestra

ERIC CLAPTON BAND LINEUP:
Eric Clapton: guitar, vocals
Walt Richmond: keyboards
Chris Stainton: keyboards
Willie Weeks: bass
Steve Gadd: drums
Michelle John: backing vocals
Sharon White: backing vocals

ERIC CLAPTON SETLIST: Drifting Blues / Layla / Running On Faith / I've Got A Rock 'N' Roll Heart / Tell The Truth / Key To The Highway / I Shot The Sheriff / Little Queen Of Spades / Cocaine

JEFF BECK AND ERIC CLAPTON BAND LINEUP:
Eric Clapton: guitar, vocals
Jeff Beck: guitar
Walt Richmond: keyboards
Chris Stainton: keyboards
Willie Weeks: bass
Steve Gadd: drums
Michelle John: backing vocals
Sharon White: backing vocals

JEFF BECK AND ERIC CLAPTON SETLIST: Shake Your Moneymaker / Moon River / You Need Love / Outside Woman Blues / Little Brown Bird / Wee Wee Baby / (I Want To Take You) Higher / Crossroads

22 February 2010, Bell Centre, Montreal, Canada

JEFF BECK BAND LINEUP:
Jeff Beck: guitar
Jason Rebello: keyboards
Rhonda Smith: bass
Narada Michael Walden: drums

JEFF BECK SETLIST: Eternity's Breath / Stratus / Led Boots / Corpus Christi Carol[1] / Bass Solo (by Rhonda Smith) / Hammerhead[1] / Mna Na Heireann[1] / Brush With The Blues / Big Block / A Day In The Life[1] / Nessun Dorma[1]

[1]with 30-piece orchestra

ERIC CLAPTON BAND LINEUP:
Eric Clapton: guitar, vocals
Walt Richmond: keyboards
Chris Stainton: keyboards
Willie Weeks: bass
Steve Gadd: drums
Michelle John: backing vocals
Sharon White: backing vocals

ERIC CLAPTON SETLIST: Drifting Blues / Layla / Running On Faith / I've Got A Rock 'N' Roll Heart / Tell The Truth / Key To The Highway / I Shot The Sheriff / Little Queen Of Spades / Cocaine

JEFF BECK AND ERIC CLAPTON BAND LINEUP:
Eric Clapton: guitar, vocals
Jeff Beck: guitar
Walt Richmond: keyboards
Chris Stainton: keyboards
Willie Weeks: bass
Steve Gadd: drums
Michelle John: backing vocals
Sharon White: backing vocals

JEFF BECK AND ERIC CLAPTON SETLIST: Shake Your Moneymaker / Moon River / You Need Love / Outside Woman Blues / Little Brown Bird / Wee Wee Baby / (I Want To Take You) Higher / Crossroads

ERIC CLAPTON U.S. TOUR 2010 (First leg)

BAND LINEUP:
Eric Clapton: guitar, vocals
Walt Richmond: keyboards
Chris Stainton: keyboards
Willie Weeks: bass
Steve Gadd: drums
Michelle John: backing vocals
Sharon White: backing vocals

25 February 2010, Mellon Arena, Pittsburgh, Pennslvania (with Roger Daltrey)

SETLIST: Going Down Slow / Key To The Highway / Tell The Truth / Old Love / I Shot The Sheriff / Drifting Blues / Nobody Knows You When You're Down And Out / Running On Faith / I've Got A Rock 'N' Roll Heart / Badge / Little Queen Of Spades / Before You Accuse Me / Wonderful Tonight / Cocaine / Crossroads

27 February 2010, Sommet Center, Nashville, Tenessee (with Roger Daltrey)

SETLIST: Going Down Slow / Key To The Highway / Tell The Truth / Old Love / I Shot The Sheriff / Drifting Blues / Nobody Knows You When You're Down And Out[1] / Running On Faith[1] / Layla[1] / I've Got A Rock 'N' Roll Heart[1] / Badge / Little Queen Of Spades / Before You Accuse Me / Wonderful Tonight / Cocaine / Crossroads[1]

[1]with Vince Gill on guitar

Vince Gill joined Eric and his band for most of the acoustic sit-down set and came back on for the encore of "Crossroads." He played rhythm parts and a few brief solos.

28 February 2010, Birmingham Jefferson Civic Center, Birmingham, Alabama (with Roger Daltrey)

SETLIST: Going Down Slow / Key To The Highway / Tell The Truth / Old Love / I Shot The Sheriff / Drifting Blues / Nobody Knows You When You're Down And Out / Running On Faith / Layla / I've Got A Rock 'N' Roll Heart / Badge / Little Queen Of Spades / Before You Accuse Me / Wonderful Tonight / Cocaine / Crossroads

MARCH 2010

2 March 2010, BOK Center, Tulsa, Oklahoma (with Roger Daltrey)

SETLIST: Going Down Slow / Key To The Highway / Tell The Truth / Old Love / I Shot The Sheriff / Drifting Blues / Nobody Knows You When You're Down And Out / Running On Faith / Layla / Badge / Little Queen Of Spades / Before You Accuse Me / Wonderful Tonight / Cocaine / Crossroads

3 March 2010, Sprint Center, Kansas City, Missouri (with Roger Daltrey)

SETLIST: Going Down Slow / Key To The Highway / Tell The Truth / Old Love / I Shot The Sheriff / Drifting Blues / Nobody Knows You When You're Down And Out / Running On Faith / Layla / I've Got A Rock 'N' Roll Heart / Badge / Little Queen Of Spades / Before You Accuse Me / Wonderful Tonight / Cocaine / Crossroads

5 March 2010, FedEx Forum, Memphis, Tenessee (with Roger Daltrey)

SETLIST: Going Down Slow / Key To The Highway / Tell The Truth / Old Love / I Shot The Sheriff / Drifting Blues / Nobody Knows You When You're Down And Out / Running On Faith / Layla / I've Got A Rock 'N' Roll Heart / Badge / Little Queen Of Spades / Before You Accuse Me / Wonderful Tonight / Cocaine / Crossroads

6 March 2010, New Orleans Arena, New Orleans, Louisiana (with Roger Daltrey)

SETLIST: Going Down Slow / Key To The Highway / Tell The Truth / Old Love / I Shot The Sheriff / Drifting Blues / Nobody Knows You When You're Down And Out / Running On Faith / Layla / I've Got A Rock 'N' Roll Heart / Badge / Wonderful Tonight / Before You Accuse Me / Little Queen Of Spades / Cocaine / Crossroads

8 March 2010, RBC Center, Raleigh, North Carolina (with Roger Daltrey)

SETLIST: Going Down Slow / Key To The Highway / Tell The Truth / Old Love / I Shot The Sheriff / Drifting

Blues / Nobody Knows You When You're Down And Out / Running On Faith / Layla / I've Got A Rock 'N' Roll Heart / Badge / Wonderful Tonight / Before You Accuse Me / Little Queen Of Spades / Cocaine / Crossroads

9 March 2010, Arena at Gwinnett Center, Atlanta, Georgia (with Roger Daltrey)

SETLIST: Going Down Slow / Key To The Highway / Tell The Truth / Old Love / I Shot The Sheriff / Drifting Blues / Nobody Knows You When You're Down And Out / Running On Faith / I've Got A Rock 'N' Roll Heart / Badge / Wonderful Tonight / Before You Accuse Me / Little Queen Of Spades / Cocaine / Crossroads

11 March 2010, Bank Atlantic Center, Sunrise, Florida (with Roger Daltrey)

SETLIST: Going Down Slow / Key To The Highway / Tell The Truth / Old Love / I Shot The Sheriff / Drifting Blues / Nobody Knows You When You're Down And Out / Running On Faith / Layla / I've Got A Rock 'N' Roll Heart / Badge / Wonderful Tonight / Before You Accuse Me / Little Queen Of Spades / Cocaine / Crossroads

13 March 2010, Amway Arena, Orlando, Florida (with Roger Daltrey)

SETLIST: Going Down Slow / Key To The Highway / Tell The Truth / Old Love / I Shot The Sheriff / Drifting Blues / Nobody Knows You When You're Down And Out / Running On Faith / Layla / I've Got A Rock 'N' Roll Heart / Badge / Wonderful Tonight / Before You Accuse Me / Little Queen Of Spades / Cocaine / Crossroads

MAY 2010

ERIC CLAPTON AND STEVE WINWOOD UK / EUROPEAN TOUR 2010

Eric Clapton's gear on this tour consists of an Eric Clapton Signature Model Fender Stratocaster in daphne blue; Eric Clapton Signature Model Fender Stratocaster in Ferrari Grigio silvertone; 6-string Martin acoustic guitars—EC Signature Model 000-28EC; Fender Custom Shop Tweed twin amp (1957 Tweed reissue); Leslie speaker; Samson wireless pack; Vox V847 wah wah pedal; box to switch from the amp to the Leslie or to select both.

BAND LINEUP:
Eric Clapton: guitar, vocals
Steve Winwood: Hammond B3 organ, piano, guitar, vocals
Chris Stainton: keyboards
Willie Weeks: bass
Steve Gadd: drums
Michelle John: backing vocals
Sharon White: backing vocals

18 May 2010, LG Arena at the National Exhibition Centre, Birmingham

SETLIST: Had To Cry Today / Low Down / After Midnight / Presence Of The Lord / The Shape You're In / Glad / Well Alright / Tuff Luck / Pearly Queen / Forever Man / Midland Maniac / Going Down / Georgia / Drifting Blues / How Long Blues / Layla / Can't Find My Way Home / Split Decision / Voodoo Chile / Cocaine / Dear Mr. Fantasy

20 May 2010, Wembley Arena, London

Steve Winwood and Eric Clapton at Wembley Arena, London, 20 May 2010.

SETLIST: Had To Cry Today / Low Down / After Midnight / Presence Of The Lord / The Shape You're In / Glad / Well Alright / Tuff Luck / Pearly Queen / Forever Man / Midland Maniac / Going Down Slow / Georgia / Drifting Blues / How Long Blues / Layla / Can't Find My Way Home / Split Decision / Voodoo Chile / Cocaine / Dear Mr. Fantasy

21 May 2010, Wembley Arena, London

SETLIST: Had To Cry Today / Low Down / After Midnight / Presence Of The Lord / The Shape You're In / Glad / Well Alright / Tuff Luck / Pearly Queen / Forever Man / Midland Maniac / Going Down Slow / Georgia / Drifting Blues / How Long Blues / Layla / Can't Find My Way Home / Split Decision / Voodoo Chile / Cocaine / Dear Mr. Fantasy

23 May 2010, Sportpaleis, Antwerp, Belgium

SETLIST: Had To Cry Today / Low Down / After Midnight / Presence Of The Lord / The Shape I'm In / Glad / Well Alright / Tuff Luck / While You See A Chance / Going Down Slow / Midland Maniac / Slide Song (A) / Georgia / Drifting Blues / How Long Blues / Layla / Can't Find My Way Home / Split Decision / Voodoo Chile / Cocaine / Dear Mr. Fantasy

First appearance of "Slide Song (A)" in the set as written on the setlist. The song is actually "Run Back To Your Side" from the forthcoming *Clapton* album. "Forever Man" and "Pearly Queen" are dropped from the setlist tonight.

25 May 2010, Palais Omnisports de Bercy, Paris, France

SETLIST: Had To Cry Today / Low Down / After Midnight / Presence Of The Lord / The Shape I'm In / Glad / Well Alright / Tuff Luck / While You See A Chance / Key To The Highway / Midland Maniac / Slide Song (A) / Georgia / Drifting Blues / How Long Blues / Layla / Can't Find My Way Home / Gimme Some Lovin' / Voodoo Chile / Cocaine / Dear Mr. Fantasy

"Going Down Slow" is replaced with "Key To The Highway" and "Split Decision" is replaced with "Gimme Some Lovin'."

26 May 2010 St. Jakobshalle, Basel, Switzerland

SETLIST: Had To Cry Today / Low Down / After Midnight / Presence Of The Lord / The Shape I'm In / Glad / Well Alright / Tuff Luck / While You See A Chance / Key To The Highway / Midland Maniac / Crossroads / Georgia / Drifting Blues / How Long Blues / Layla / Can't Find My Way Home / Gimme Some Lovin' / Voodoo Chile / Cocaine / Dear Mr. Fantasy

"Crossroads" replaces "Slide Song (A)" at this show.

28 May 2010, ISS Dome, Dusseldorf, Germany

SETLIST: Had To Cry Today / Low Down / After Midnight / Presence Of The Lord / The Shape I'm In / Glad / Well Alright / Tuff Luck / While You See A Chance / Key To The Highway / Midland Maniac / Crossroads / Georgia / Drifting Blues / How Long Blues / Layla / Can't Find My Way Home / Gimme Some Lovin' / Voodoo Chile / Cocaine / Dear Mr. Fantasy

29 May 2010, GelreDome Stadium, Arnhem, Netherlands

SETLIST: Had To Cry Today / Low Down / After Midnight / Presence Of The Lord / The Shape I'm In / Glad / Well Alright / Tuff Luck / While You See A Chance / Key To The Highway / Midland Maniac / Crossroads / Georgia / Drifting Blues / How Long Blues / Layla / Can't Find My Way Home / Gimme Some Lovin' / Voodoo Chile / Cocaine / Dear Mr. Fantasy

31 May 2010, Malmo Arena, Malmo, Sweden

SETLIST: Had To Cry Today / Low Down / After Midnight / Presence Of The Lord / Glad / Well Alright / Tuff Luck / While You See A Chance / Key To The Highway / Midland Maniac / Crossroads / Georgia / Drifting Blues / How Long Blues / Layla / Can't Find My Way Home / Gimme Some Lovin' / Voodoo Chile / Cocaine / Dear Mr. Fantasy

"The Shape I'm In" is dropped from this show onwards.

JUNE 2010

2 June 2010, O2 World, Berlin, Germany

SETLIST: Had To Cry Today / Low Down / After Midnight / Presence Of The Lord / Glad / Well Alright / Tuff Luck / While You See A Chance / Key To The Highway / Pearly Queen / Crossroads / Georgia / Drifting Blues / How Long Blues / Layla / Can't Find My Way Home / Gimme Some Lovin' / Voodoo Chile / Cocaine / Dear Mr. Fantasy

"Pearly Queen" replaces "Midland Maniac" tonight.

3 June 2010, Color Line Arena, Hamburg, Germany

SETLIST: Had To Cry Today / Low Down / After Midnight / Presence Of The Lord / Glad / Well Alright / Tuff Luck / While You See A Chance / Key To The Highway / Pearly Queen / Crossroads / Georgia / Drifting Blues / How Long Blues / Layla / Can't Find My Way Home / Gimme Some Lovin' / Voodoo Chile / Cocaine / Dear Mr. Fantasy

5 June 2010, Konigsplatz, Munich, Germany

SETLIST: Had To Cry Today / Low Down / After Midnight / Presence Of The Lord / Glad / Well Alright / Tuff Luck / While You See A Chance / Key To The Highway / Midland Maniac / Crossroads / Georgia / Drifting Blues / How Long Blues / Layla / Can't Find My Way Home / Gimme Some Lovin' / Voodoo Chile / Cocaine / Dear Mr. Fantasy

7 June 2010, Stadthalle, Vienna, Austria

SETLIST: Had To Cry Today / Low Down / After Midnight / Presence Of The Lord / Glad / Well Alright / Tuff Luck / While You See A Chance / Key To The Highway / Midland Maniac / Crossroads / Georgia / Drifting Blues / How Long Blues / Layla / Can't Find My Way Home / Gimme Some Lovin' / Voodoo Chile / Cocaine / Dear Mr. Fantasy

9 June 2010, Belgrade Arena, Belgrade, Serbia

SETLIST: Had To Cry Today / Low Down / After Midnight / Presence Of The Lord / Glad / Well Alright / Tuff Luck / While You See A Chance / Key To The Highway / Midland Maniac / Crossroads / Georgia / Drifting Blues / How Long Blues / Layla / Can't Find My Way Home / Gimme Some Lovin' / Voodoo Chile / Cocaine / Dear Mr. Fantasy

11 June 2010, Rugby Park, Bucharest, Romania

SETLIST: Had To Cry Today / Low Down / After Midnight / Presence Of The Lord / Glad / Well Alright / Tuff Luck / While You See A Chance / Key To The Highway / Midland Maniac / Crossroads / Georgia / Drifting Blues / How Long Blues / Layla / Can't Find My Way Home / Gimme Some Lovin' / Voodoo Chile / Cocaine / Dear Mr. Fantasy

13 June 2010, Turkcell Kurucesme Arena, Istanbul, Turkey

SETLIST: Had To Cry Today / Low Down / After Midnight / Presence Of The Lord / Glad / Well Alright / Tuff Luck / While You See A Chance / Key To The Highway / Midland Maniac / Crossroads / Georgia / Drifting Blues / How Long Blues / Layla / Can't Find My Way Home / Gimme Some Lovin' / Voodoo Chile / Cocaine / Dear Mr. Fantasy

Final show of Eric Clapton and Steve Winwood's 2010 European tour. During "Midland Maniac" a huge fireworks display took place over the nearby Bosphorus Strait and carried on right through to "Crossroads." The sound of the display was so loud that the band were forced to turn up the volume.

CROSSROADS GUITAR FESTIVAL 2010

26 June 2010, Crossroads Guitar Festival, Toyota Park, Bridgeview, Illinois

Single-day event which like previous concerts is a fundraiser for the Crossroads Centre in Antigua, a

Crossroads 2010 all-star finale jam featuring Eric Clapton, B.B. King, Johnny Winter, Joe Bonamassa, Pino Daniele, Robert Cray, Jimmie Vaughan, Buddy Guy, Jonny Lang, Derek Trucks, Warren Hayes, Susan Tedeschi, Keb Mo, and others at Toyota Park in Bridgeview, Illinois, 26 June 2010.

drug and alcohol rehabilitation clinic founded by Eric Clapton. The show started shortly before noon and finished more than eleven hours later.

ARTISTS APPEARING:
Albert Lee
B.B. King
Bert Jansch
Buddy Guy
Citizen Cope
David Hidalgo and Cesar Rosas of Los Lobos
Derek Trucks & Susan Tedeschi Band
Warren Haynes
Doyle Bramhall II
Earl Klugh
Eric Clapton
Gary Clark, Jr.
Hubert Sumlin
James Burton

Jeff Beck
Jimmie Vaughan
Joe Bonamassa
John Mayer
Johnny Winter
Jonny Lang
Keb Mo
Pino Daniele
Robert Cray
Robert Randolph
Sheryl Crow
Sonny Landreth
Stefan Grossman
Steve Winwood
Vince Gill
ZZ Top

Only the numbers featuring Eric are shown here.

BILL MURRAY INTRODUCTION

Not Fade Away (with Eric Clapton)

SONNY LANDRETH SET

Promised Land (with Eric Clapton) *Crossroads Guitar Festival 2010* DVD/Blu-Ray Warner Bros. released November 2010

DOYLE BRAMHALL II WITH SHERYL CROW, GARY CLARK, DEREK TRUCKS & SUSAN TEDESCHI SET

Doyle Bramhall II: guitar
Eric Clapton: guitar
Gary Brooker: keyboards, vocals
Sheryl Crow: guitar, keyboards, vocals
Gary Clark, Jr.: guitar
Derek Trucks: guitar
Susan Tedeschi: guitar, vocals
Tommy Sims: bass
Justin Stanley: drums

Our Love Is Fading (with Eric Clapton) *Crossroads Guitar Festival 2010* DVD/Blu-Ray Warner Bros. released November 2010

ERIC CLAPTON AND HIS BAND WITH JEFF BECK, CITIZEN COPE, AND STEVE WINWOOD SET

Eric Clapton: guitar, vocals
Chris Stainton: keyboards
Walt Richmond: keyboards
Willie Weeks: guitar
Steve Gadd: drums
Michelle John: backing vocals

Sharon White: backing vocals
Jeff Beck: guitar
Citizen Cope: guitar vocals
Steve Winwood: guitar, keyboards, vocals

Crossroads *Crossroads Guitar Festival 2010* DVD/Blu-Ray Warner Bros. released November 2010

Key To The Highway unreleased

Hands Of The Saints (with Citizen Cope) *Crossroads Guitar Festival 2010* DVD/Blu-Ray released November 2010

Tough Luck Blues unreleased

I Shot The Sheriff *Crossroads Guitar Festival 2010* DVD/Blu-Ray Warner Bros. released November 2010

Shake Your Money Maker (with Jeff Beck) *Crossroads Guitar Festival 2010* DVD/Blu-Ray Warner Bros. released November 2010

Had To Cry Today (with Steve Winwood) *Crossroads Guitar Festival 2010* DVD/Blu-Ray Warner Bros. released November 2010

Low Down (with Steve Winwood) unreleased

Glad (with Steve Winwood) unreleased

Well Alright (with Steve Winwood) unreleased

Voodoo Chile (with Steve Winwood) *Crossroads Guitar Festival 2010* DVD/Blu-Ray Warner Bros. released November 2010

Cocaine (with Steve Winwood) unreleased

Dear Mr. Fantasy (with Steve Winwood) *Crossroads Guitar Festival 2010* DVD/Blu-Ray Warner Bros. released November 2010

B.B. KING WITH ROBERT CRAY BAND, ERIC CLAPTON, JIMMIE VAUGHAN SET

B.B. King: guitar, vocals
Eric Clapton: guitar
Jimmie Vaughan: guitar
Robert Cray: guitar
Tony Braunagel: drums
Jim Pugh: keyboards
Richard Cousins: bass

Blues Jam (while B.B. walks on stage) unreleased

Rock Me Baby unreleased

Key to the Highway unreleased

The Thrill Is Gone *Crossroads Guitar Festival 2010* DVD/ Blu-Ray Warner Bros. released November 2010

ALL-STAR FINALE SET

Eric Clapton: guitar
B.B. King: guitar
Buddy Guy: guitar
James Burton: guitar
Ron Wood: guitar
Vince Gill: guitar
Derek Trucks: guitar
Warren Haynes: guitar
Jimmie Vaughan: guitar
Susan Tedeschi: guitar
Robert Cray: guitar
Johnny Winter: guitar
Jonny Lang: guitar
Hubert Sumlin: guitar
Sonny Landreth: guitar
Cesar Rojas: guitar
David Hidalgo: guitar
Joe Bonamassa: guitar
Gary Clark, Jr.: guitar
Pino Daniele: guitar
Robert Randolph: pedal steel guitar
Steve Winwood: keyboards
Jim Pugh: guitar
Richard Cousins: bass
Tony Braunagel: drums

Just about everyone sang, but the verses were mostly sung by Buddy Guy, with one verse by Keb Mo who did not bring out a guitar.

SETLIST:

Sweet Home Chicago unreleased

CLAPTON U.S. TOUR 2010 (Second leg)

BAND LINEUP:
Eric Clapton: guitar, vocals
Walt Richmond: keyboards

Chris Stainton: keyboards
Willie Weeks: bass
Steve Gadd: drums
Michelle John: backing vocals
Sharon White: backing vocals

28 June 2010, Marcus Ampitheater, Milwaukee, Wisconsin (with Roger Daltrey)

SETLIST: Tell The Truth / Key To The Highway / After Midnight / Tuff Luck Blues / I Shot The Sheriff / Drifting Blues / Nobody Knows You When You're Down and Out / I've Got A Rock 'N' Roll Heart / Layla / When Somebody Thinks You're Wonderful / Badge / Wonderful Tonight / Before You Accuse Me / Little Queen Of Spades / Cocaine / Crossroads

30 June 2010, Riverbend Music Center, Cincinnati, Ohio (with Roger Daltrey)

SETLIST: Going Down Slow / Key To The Highway / Tell The Truth / Tuff Luck Blues / I Shot The Sheriff / Drifting Blues / Nobody Knows You When You're Down And Out / I've Got A Rock 'N' Roll Heart / Layla / When Somebody Thinks You're Wonderful / Badge / Wonderful Tonight / Before You Accuse Me / Little Queen Of Spades / Cocaine / Crossroads

JULY 2010

2 July 2010, Verizon Wireless Music Center, Indianapolis, Indiana (with Roger Daltrey)

SETLIST: Going Down Slow / Key To The Highway / Tell The Truth / Tuff Luck Blues / I Shot The Sheriff / Drifting Blues / Nobody Knows You When You're Down And Out / I've Got A Rock 'N' Roll Heart / Layla / When Somebody Thinks You're Wonderful / Badge / Wonderful Tonight / Before You Accuse Me / Little Queen Of Spades / Cocaine / Crossroads

3 July 2010, DTE Energy Music Theatre, Clarkston, Michigan (with Roger Daltrey)

SETLIST: Going Down Slow / Key To The Highway / Tell The Truth / Tuff Luck Blues / I Shot The Sheriff / Drifting Blues / Nobody Knows You When You're Down And Out / Layla / When Somebody Thinks You're Wonderful / Badge / Wonderful Tonight / Before You Accuse Me / Little Queen Of Spades / Cocaine / Crossroads

OCTOBER 2010

WILLIAM J. CLINTON FOUNDATION 2010

23 October 2010, Cathedral Church of Saint John The Divine, New York City (annual fundraiser for the William J. Clinton Foundation which was founded in 2001 by former U.S. President Bill Clinton. Jon Bon Jovi and Angelique Kidjo also performed. Eric and his Band performed "Happy Birthday" in honor of U.S. Secretary of State Hilary Clinton, with the former President joining in on the vocals with Eric)

BAND LINEUP:
Eric Clapton: guitar, vocals
Steve Gadd: drums
Chris Stainton: keyboards
Willie Weeks: bass

SETLIST: Going Down Slow / Nobody Knows You When You're Down And Out / Key To The Highway / Hoochie Coochie Man / Wonderful Tonight / Cocaine / Crossroads

NOVEMBER 2010

LATER WITH JOOLS HOLLAND 2010

2 November 2010, *Later With Jools Holland,* BBC Television Centre Studios, Shepherds Bush, London (today's show was broadcast live. An extended recorded version of the show is broadcast on Friday 5 November)

Eric Clapton playing a Gibson Les Paul on Later With Jools Holland *show, 2 November 2010.*

SETLIST:

Travelin' Alone, Version 1 (broadcast on 2 November)

Travelin' Alone, Version 2 (broadcast on 5 November)

When Somebody Thinks You're Wonderful (broadcast on 2 and 5 November)

Rocking Chair (broadcast on 5 November)

Crossroads (broadcast on 5 November)

BAND LINEUP:
Eric Clapton: guitar, vocals
Chris Stainton: keyboards
Dave Bronze: bass
Henry Spinetti: drums
Jools Holland: keyboards on "Rocking Chair" and "When Somebody Thinks You're Wonderful"

PRINCE'S TRUST ROCK GALA 2010

17 November 2010, Royal Albert Hall, London (Prince's Trust Rock Gala with Eric Clapton and others)

THE PRINCE'S TRUST ALL-STARS (HOUSE BAND) WITH ERIC CLAPTON LINEUP:

Midge Ure: musical director, vocals, guitar
Mark Brzezicki: drums
Jamie Cullum: vocals, keyboards
Snake Davis: saxophone
Guy Fletcher: keyboards, backing vocals
Simon Gardner: trumpet
Mark King: bass
Eric Clapton: guitar, vocals
Neil Sidwell: trombone
Johnny Thirkell: trumpet
Eric Clapton: guitar, vocals

SETLIST:

Rocking Chair broadcast on television

Same Old Blues broadcast on television

Little Queen Of Spades broadcast on television

Crossroads broadcast on television

DECEMBER 2010

NEW YEAR'S EVE DANCE 2010

31 December 2010, Woking Leisure Centre, Woking, Surrey

Eric and his band are called We Are Not Saints.

BAND LINEUP

Eric Clapton: guitar, vocals
Andy Fairweather Low: guitar, vocals
Gary Brooker: keyboards, vocals
Chris Stainton: keyboards
Dave Bronze: bass
Henry Spinetti: drums

Sharon White: backing vocals
Michelle John: backing vocals

SETLIST 1: Knock On Wood / Reconsider Baby / Unchain My Heart / Too Much Monkey Business / Traveling Light[1] / Route 66 / Don't You Just Know It / When Somebody Thinks You're Wonderful[2] / Five Long Years / Shake, Rattle And Roll

[1]This was the Cliff Richard song, not the JJ Cale song of the same title.
[2]Eric plays electric guitar

SETLIST 2: In The Midnight Hour / Hoochie / Coochie Man / Young Blood / Blueberry Hill / Will The Circle Be Unbroken / Gin House / Willie And The Hand Jive / Whiter Shade Of Pale / Cocaine / Cigarettes, Whiskey And Wild, Wild Women

RECORDING SESSIONS 2010

OCEAN WAY RECORDING 6050 Sunset Boulevard, Hollywood, California Sessions for *Clapton*

SEPTEMBER 2009

Initial sessions for Eric's new album begun in 2009.

GERMANO STUDIOS Studio 1, 676 Broadway, New York City

FEBRUARY 2010

Eric records guitars and vocals in Germano's Studio 1 in New York with producer Doyle Bramhall and engineer Justin Stanley. More sessions will take place in New Orleans in March and in Los Angeles in June 2010.

PIETY STREET STUDIO
3240 Dauphine Street,
New Orleans, Louisiana
and

OCEAN WAY STUDIOS
6050 Sunset Boulevard,
Hollywood, California

JUNE 2010

Eric had enjoyed the *Road To Escondido* sessions so much that he wanted to do another album with JJ Cale. There is a lot of love and mutual respect there. Unfortunately, JJ had to leave the sessions early and the album became a solo album by Eric. Originally planned as a double CD, Warner Bros. decided that with the current economic climate it would be too expensive. As a result, Eric's original concept of one CD of covers and the other of blues and original material was scrapped.

TRAVELIN' ALONE (Melvin Jackson) *Clapton* CD Duck released 2010
Eric Clapton: guitar, vocals
Willie Weeks: bass
Jim Keltner: drums, percussion
Doyle Bramhall II: guitar
Walt Richmond: Hammond B3 organ

ROCKING CHAIR (Hoagy Carmichael) *Clapton* CD Duck released 2010

Eric Clapton: guitar, vocals
Nikka Costa: backing vocals
Willie Weeks: upright bass
Abe Laboriel, Jr.: drums
Walt Richmond: piano
Derek Trucks: slide guitar

RIVER RUNS DEEP (John Cale) *Clapton* CD Duck released 2010

Eric Clapton: guitar, vocals
JJ Cale: guitar, vocals
Willie Weeks: upright bass
Jeremy Stacey: drums
Justin Stanley: echo drums
Walt Richmond: Wurlitzer
Thomas Brenneck: Menahan horns
James Poyser: Hammond B3 organ
Greg Leisz: pedal steel guitar
Neal Sugarman: tenor saxophone
Leon Michels: trumpet
London Session Orchestra: strings

JUDGMENT DAY (Snooky Pryor) *Clapton* CD Duck released 2010

Eric Clapton: guitar, vocals
Willie Weeks: bass
Jim Keltner: drums

Kim Wilson: harmonica
Doyle Bramhall II: guitar, vocal arrangements
Walt Richmond: piano
Arnold McCuller: backing vocals
Terry Evans: backing vocals
Willie Green, Jr.: backing vocals

HOW DEEP IS THE OCEAN (Irving Berlin) *Clapton* CD Duck released 2010

Willie Weeks: upright bass
Jim Keltner: drums
Walt Richmond: piano
Wynton Marsalis: trumpet
London Session Orchestra: strings

MY VERY GOOD FRIEND THE MILKMAN (Harold Spina, Johnny Burke) *Clapton* CD Duck released 2010

Eric Clapton: guitar, vocals
Dr. Michael White: clarinet
Chris Severan: upright bass
Herman Labeaux: drums
Cayetano "Tanio" Hingle: bass drum, cymbal
Allen Toussaint: piano
Walt Richmond: piano
Troy "Trombone Shorty" Andrews: trombone, trumpet
Wynton Marsalis: trumpet
Matt Pyreem: tuba

CAN'T HOLD OUT MUCH LONGER (Walter Jacobs) *Clapton* CD Duck released 2010

Eric Clapton: guitar, vocals
Willie Weeks: upright bass
Jim Keltner: drums
Doyle Bramhall II: guitar, hi-hat
Kim Wilson: harmonica
Walt Richmond: piano

THAT'S NO WAY TO GET ALONG (Robert Wilkins) *Clapton* CD Duck released 2010

Eric Clapton: guitar, vocals
JJ Cale: guitar, vocals
Steve Riley: accordion
Clarence Slaughter: baritone saxophone
Willie Weeks: bass
Cayetano "Tanio" Hingle: clarinet
Troy "Trombone Shorty" Andrews: bass drum, trombone, trumpet, snare
Jim Keltner: drums, percussion
Doyle Bramhall II: guitar solos, percussion
Dan Ostreicher: baritone saxophone
James Poyser: Hammond B3 organ
Justin Stanley: percussion
Walt Richmond: piano
Bruce Brackman: sousaphone
Edward Lee: tenor saxophone
Sherelle Chenier Mouton: rugboard
Arnold McCuller: backing vocals
Terry Evans: backing vocals
Willie Green, Jr.: backing vocals

EVERYTHING WILL BE ALRIGHT (John Cale) *Clapton* CD Duck released 2010

Eric Clapton: guitar, vocals
JJ Cale: vocals
Willie Weeks: bass

Paul Carrack: Hammond B3 organ
Walt Richmond: piano
Tim Izo Orindgreff: saxophone
Elizabeth Lea: trombone
Printz Board: trumpet
London Session Orchestra: strings

DIAMONDS MADE FROM RAIN (Doyle Bramhall II / Justin Stanley / Nikka Costa) *Clapton* CD Duck released 2010

Eric Clapton: guitar, vocals
Doyle Bramhall II: guitar, vocals
Sheryl Crow: vocals
Willie Weeks: bass
Jeremy Stacey: drums
Jim Keltner: drums
Doyle Bramhall II: guitar
Sereca Henderson: organ
Walt Richmond: piano
Tim Izo Orindgreff: saxophone
Elizabeth Lea: trombone
Printz Board: trumpet
Debra Parsons: backing vocals
Lynn Mabry: backing vocals
Nikka Costa: backing vocals
London Session Orchestra: strings

WHEN SOMEBODY THINKS YOU'RE WONDERFUL (Harry Woods) *Clapton* CD Duck released 2010

Eric Clapton: guitar
Dr. Michael White: clarinet
Chris Severan: upright bass
Herman Labeaux: drums
Cayetano "Tanio" Hingle: drums, cymbal
Allen Toussaint: piano
Walt Richmond: piano
Wynton Marsalis: trumpet
Troy Andrews: trumpet, trombone
Mat Pyreem: tuba

HARD TIMES BLUES (Lane Hardin) *Clapton* CD Duck released 2010

Eric Clapton: guitar, mandolin, vocals
Willie Weeks: upright bass
Jim Keltner: drums, percussion
Doyle Bramhall II: guitar solo
Walt Richmond: piano

RUN BACK TO YOUR SIDE (Doyle Bramhall II, Eric Clapton) *Clapton* CD Duck released 2010

Eric Clapton: guitar, vocals
Willie Weeks: bass
Jim Keltner: drums, percussion
Derek Trucks: guitar
Doyle Bramhall II: guitar
Walt Richmond: piano
Debra Parsons: backing vocals
Lynn Mabry: backing vocals
Nikka Costa: backing vocals

AUTUMN LEAVES (Andre Prevert / Johnny Mercer / Joseph Kosma) *Clapton* CD Duck released 2010

Eric Clapton: guitar, vocals
Willie Weeks: upright bass
Abe Laboriel, Jr.: drums

Walt Richmond: keyboards
London Session Orchestra: strings

YOU BETTER WATCH YOURSELF (Walter Jacobs) ericclapton.com deluxe limited edition bonus track

Eric Clapton: guitar, vocals
Doyle Bramhall II: guitar
Jason Moeller: drums
Willi Weeks: bass
Kim Wilson: harmonica

TAKE A LITTLE WALK WITH ME (Robert Lockwood, Jr.) Barnes & Noble and Best Buy bonus track

Eric Clapton: guitar, vocals
Doyle Bramhall II: guitar
Jason Moeller: drums
Willi Weeks: bass
Kim Wilson: harmonica

I WAS FOOLED (Billy Boy Arnold) iTunes bonus track

Eric Clapton: guitar, vocals
Doyle Bramhall II: guitar
Jason Moeller: drums
Willi Weeks: bass
Kim Wilson: harmonica

MIDNIGHT HOUR BLUES (Leroy Carr) Amazon.com bonus track

Eric Clapton: guitar, vocals
Doyle Bramhall II: guitar
Jason Moeller: drums
Willi Weeks: bass
Kim Wilson: harmonica

Producers: Doyle Bramhall II / Eric Clapton
Engineer: Justin Stanley

ERIC CLAPTON GUEST SESSION
UNKNOWN STUDIO
Hampton Court, Surrey
Session for Chris Barber

APRIL 2010

WEEPING WILLOW *Memories Of My Trip* CD Proper Records released April 2011

Chris Barber: trombone
Eric Clapton: guitar, vocals
Dave Bronze: bass
Chris Stainton: keyboards
Henry Spinetti: drums

Producer: not known
Engineer: not known

"I knew Eric as a real blues enthusiast way back, and indeed when he walked out of the Yardbirds, they were signed to our management office, and my partner Harold Pendleton had to go to Eric's flat to get back a guitar when he left, because it belonged to the group. I've listened to him over the years, and I noticed that whenever he worked with a brass section it was all just backing riffs, not instruments actually interacting with the blues, which the trombone in particular is capable of doing. The first time I did this with Eric, I went along and played at a charity concert that Mike Rutherford [of Genesis] runs, and when Eric brought me up we did 'Stormy Monday,' and as he finished singing the first phrase, I played something similar on the trombone to the fill he did on the guitar. And it surprised him, because I don't think that happens very much in his world. I made contact with him again when the late Andrew Sheehan, my partner on the *Blues Legacy* record project, was able to give Eric a lot of video clips of him playing to be used in Martin Scorsese's film biography of Eric. When he got the clips, Eric said to Andrew, 'If there's anything I can do for you or Chris, let me know.' And so in due course I suggested we record together. I was thinking of asking members of my band, but Eric immediately suggested Chris Stainton, Dave Bronze, and Henry Spinetti, all of whom he works with regularly. So we did it while Eric was at home between tours, in a little homey studio near Hampton Court. We didn't have any elaborate separation for the drums, and just played together as if it was a small concert. I love Eric's playing because he's the only blues musician I've heard apart from B.B. King who can play an opening phrase on the guitar that catches you immediately. An audience can have tears in their eyes before he's even sung a note because of the strength of his playing."

—CHRIS BARBER
(from the liner notes)

2011

CRANLEIGH ARTS CENTRE 2011

13 January 2011, Cranleigh Arts Centre, Cranleigh, Surrey

Benefit concert postponed from 21 December due to snow. The concert raised funds for the Cranleigh Arts Centre, National Deaf Children's Society, Evelina Children's Heart Organisation, and Crossroads Centre in Antigua. Eric plays with an adhoc band called the Bad Apples.

BAD APPLES LINEUP:
Paul Jones: vocals
Roger Hart: vocals
Mick Rogers: guitar
Micky Moody: guitar
Matt Empson: keyboards
Ian Jennings: bass
Jimmy Copley: drums

SETLIST: Blues With A Feeling / Same Old Blues / Before You Accuse Me

CLAPTON MIDDLE EAST/ FAR EAST TOUR 2011

BAND LINEUP:
Eric Clapton: guitar, vocals
Chris Stainton: keyboards
Tim Carmon: keyboards
Steve Gadd: drums
Willie Weeks: bass
Sharon White: backing vocals
Michelle John: backing vocals

11 February 2011, Yas Arena, Abu Dhabi, United Arab Emirates

SETLIST: Key To The Highway / Going Down Slow / Hoochie Coochie Man / Old Love / I Shot The Sheriff / Drifting Blues / Nobody Knows You When You're Down And Out / River Runs Deep / Rocking Chair / Same Old Blues / When Somebody Thinks You're Wonderful / Layla / Badge / Wonderful Tonight / Before You Accuse Me / Little Queen Of Spades / Crossroads / Further On Up The Road

14 February 2011, Singapore Indoor Stadium, Singapore

SETLIST: Key To The Highway / Going Down Slow / Hoochie Coochie Man / Old Love / I Shot The Sheriff / Drifting Blues / Nobody Knows You When You're Down And Out / River Runs Deep / Rocking Chair / Same Old

Blues / When Somebody Thinks You're Wonderful / Layla / Badge / Wonderful Tonight / Before You Accuse Me / Little Queen Of Spades / Crossroads / Further On Up The Road

16 February 2011, Impact Arena, Bangkok, Thailand

SETLIST: Key To The Highway / Going Down Slow / Hoochie Coochie Man / Old Love / I Shot The Sheriff / Drifting Blues / Nobody Knows You When You're Down And Out / River Runs Deep / Rocking Chair / Same Old Blues / When Somebody Thinks You're Wonderful / Layla / Badge / Little Queen Of Spades / Before You Accuse Me / Wonderful Tonight / Cocaine / Further On Up The Road

18 February 2011, Asia World Arena, Hong Kong, China

SETLIST: Key To The Highway / Going Down Slow / Hoochie Coochie Man / Old Love / I Shot The Sheriff / Drifting Blues / Nobody Knows You When You're Down And Out / River Runs Deep / Rocking Chair / Same Old Blues / When Somebody Thinks You're Wonderful / Layla / Badge / Wonderful Tonight / Before You Accuse Me / Little Queen Of Spades / Cocaine / Further On Up The Road

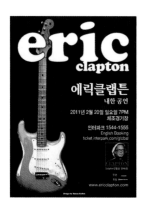

World Tour 2011 poster for Eric Clapton.

20 February 2011, Olympic Gym #1, Seoul, South Korea

SETLIST: Key To The Highway / Going Down Slow / Hoochie Coochie Man / Old Love / I Shot The Sheriff / Drifting Blues / Nobody Knows You When You're Down And Out / River Runs Deep / Rocking Chair / Same Old Blues / When Somebody Thinks You're Wonderful / Layla / Badge / Wonderful Tonight / Before You Accuse Me / Little Queen Of Spades / Cocaine / Crossroads

CLAPTON CANADA/U.S.A. TOUR 2011

25 February 2011, Rogers Arena, Vancouver, British Columbia, Canada (with Los Lobos)

SETLIST: Key To The Highway / Going Down Slow / Hoochie Coochie Man / Old Love / I Shot The Sheriff / Drifting Blues / Nobody Knows You When You're Down And Out / River Runs Deep / Rocking Chair / Same Old Blues / When Somebody Thinks You're Wonderful / Layla / Badge / Wonderful Tonight / Before You Accuse Me / Little Queen Of Spades / Cocaine / Further On Up The Road

26 February 2011, Key Arena, Seattle, Washington (with Los Lobos)

SETLIST: Key To The Highway / Going Down Slow / Hoochie Coochie Man / Old Love / I Shot The Sheriff / Drifting Blues / Nobody Knows You When You're Down And Out / River Runs Deep / When Somebody Thinks You're Wonderful / Same Old Blues / Layla / Badge / Wonderful Tonight / Before You Accuse Me / Little Queen Of Spades / Cocaine / Crossroads

28 February 2011, Rose Garden Arena, Portland, Oregon (with Los Lobos)

SETLIST: Key To The Highway / Going Down Slow / Hoochie Coochie Man / Old Love / I Shot The Sheriff / Drifting Blues / Nobody Knows You When You're Down And Out / River Runs Deep / When Somebody Thinks You're Wonderful / Same Old Blues / Layla / Badge / Wonderful Tonight / Before You Accuse Me / Little Queen Of Spades / Cocaine / Crossroads

MARCH 2011

2 March 2011, HP Pavilion, San Jose, California (with Los Lobos)

SETLIST: Key To The Highway / Going Down Slow / Hoochie Coochie Man / Old Love / I Shot The Sheriff / Drifting Blues / Nobody Knows You When You're Down And Out / River Runs Deep / When Somebody Thinks You're Wonderful / Same Old Blues / Layla / Badge /

Wonderful Tonight / Before You Accuse Me / Little Queen Of Spades / Cocaine / Further On Up The Road

3 March 2011, ARCO Arena, Sacramento, California (with Los Lobos)

SETLIST: Key To The Highway / Going Down Slow / Hoochie Coochie Man / Old Love / I Shot The Sheriff / Drifting Blues / Nobody Knows You When You're Down And Out / River Runs Deep / When Somebody Thinks You're Wonderful / Same Old Blues / Layla / Badge / Wonderful Tonight / Before You Accuse Me / Little Queen Of Spades / Cocaine / Crossroads

5 March 2011, MGM Grand Garden Arena, Las Vegas, Nevada (with Los Lobos)

SETLIST: Key To The Highway / Going Down Slow / Hoochie Coochie Man / Old Love / I Shot The Sheriff / Drifting Blues / Nobody Knows You When You're Down And Out / River Runs Deep / When Somebody Thinks You're Wonderful / Same Old Blues / Layla / Badge / Wonderful Tonight / Before You Accuse Me / Little Queen Of Spades / Cocaine / Crossroads

6 March 2011, Valley View Casino Center, San Diego, California (with Los Lobos)

SETLIST: Key To The Highway / Going Down Slow / Hoochie Coochie Man / Old Love / I Shot The Sheriff / Drifting Blues / Nobody Knows You When You're Down And Out / River Runs Deep / When Somebody Thinks You're Wonderful / Same Old Blues / Layla / Badge / Wonderful Tonight / Before You Accuse Me / Little Queen Of Spades / Cocaine / Crossroads

8 March 2011, Gibson Amphitheater at Universal CityWalk, Universal City, California (with Los Lobos)

SETLIST: Key To The Highway / Going Down Slow / Hoochie Coochie Man / Old Love / I Shot The Sheriff / Drifting Blues / Nobody Knows You When You're Down And Out / River Runs Deep / When Somebody Thinks You're Wonderful / Same Old Blues / Layla / Tell The Truth / Little Queen Of Spades / Badge / Wonderful Tonight / Cocaine / Further On Up The Road

9 March 2011, Gibson Amphitheater at Universal CityWalk, Universal City, California (with Los Lobos)

SETLIST: Key To The Highway / Going Down Slow / Hoochie Coochie Man / Old Love / I Shot The Sheriff / Drifting Blues / Nobody Knows You When You're Down And Out / River Runs Deep / When Somebody Thinks You're Wonderful / Same Old Blues / Layla / Badge / Wonderful Tonight / Before You Accuse Me / Little Queen Of Spades / Cocaine / Crossroads

Eric and the band stayed on in Los Angeles after their shows to record some numbers for the album that will eventually be released as *Old Sock*.

JIMMIE VAUGHAN'S 60th BIRTHDAY PARTY 2011

21 March 2011, Hill Top Café, 10661 North Highway 87, Fredericksburg, Texas

Eric joins Jimmie Vaughan and friends for a jam at Austin's celebrated Hill Top Café.

APRIL 2011

WYNTON MARSALIS & ERIC CLAPTON PLAY THE BLUES 2011

BAND LINEUP:
Wynton Marsalis: trumpet
Eric Clapton: guitar, vocals
Marcus Printup: trumpet
Chris Crenshaw: trombone
Victor Goines: clarinet
Jonathan Batiste: piano
Carlos Henriquez: bass
Ali Jackson: drums
Don Vapple: banjo

The show on 7 April was a black-tie gala concert in support of Jazz at Lincoln Center. The two public performances on 8 and 9 April were filmed and recorded for later edited release as *Wynton Marsalis & Eric Clapton Play The Blues: Live From Jazz At Lincoln Center*. The setlist, with the exception of "Layla," was drawn from songs selected by Eric Clapton and arranged by Wynton Marsalis. "Layla" was added during rehearsals at the suggestion of Carlos Henriquez.

Jazz Gala at Lincoln Center, New York, 7 April 2011, with Wynton Marsalis and Eric Clapton. The shows were recorded and a subsequent live album and DVD were released to critical acclaim.

7 April 2011, Rose Theater / JALC, New York City (black-tie fundraising gala for Jazz at Lincoln Center)

SETLIST: Ice Cream / Forty Four Blues / Joe Turner's Blues / The Last Time / Careless Love / Kidman Blues / Layla / Joliet Bound / Just A Closer Walk With Thee / Corrine Corrina[1]

[1]with Taj Mahal

8 April 2011, Rose Theater / JALC, New York City (with Taj Mahal)

SETLIST: Ice Cream / Forty Four Blues / Joe Turner's Blues / The Last Time / Careless Love / Kidman Blues / Layla / Joliet Bound / Just A Closer Walk With Thee / Corrine Corrina[1]

[1]with Taj Mahal

9 April 2011, Rose Theater / JALC, New York (with Taj Mahal)

SETLIST: Ice Cream / Forty Four Blues / Joe Turner's Blues / The Last Time / Careless Love / Kidman Blues / Layla / Joliet Bound / Just A Closer Walk With Thee / Corrine Corrina [1]

[1]with Taj Mahal

BUNBURY GALA 2011

7 May 2011, Grosvernor House Hotel, London (celebrating the 25th anniversary of the Bunbury Celebrity Cricket Team)

SETLIST: Key To The Highway / Hoochie Coochie Man / Tell The Truth / Wonderful Tonight / Crossroads / Little Queen Of Spades / Cocaine

"Eric Clapton and band were seemingly in their element in the run-up to Clapton's UK and Royal Albert Hall dates of spring / summer 2011. EC delivered primarily a blues orientated show, comprising seven songs with a veteran band lineup featuring Steve Gadd on drums, Willie Weeks on bass, Chris Stainton and Tim Carmon on keys, and the wonderful Michelle John and Sharon White on vocals. EC began with 'Key To The Highway' and the unmistakable 'Hoochie Coochie Man.' Undoubtedly, Eric's assured presence on Fender was pleasing to see as his concerts have now provided a rare treat at several Bunbury balls. 'Who says this one need be the last?' declared Eric. (With any luck this Bunbury 25th Ball will be like a quintessential Frank Sinatra style farewell!) Clapton's set progressed toward some of his most revered hits including 'Wonderful Tonight' and Cream's version of Robert Johnson's 'Crossroads.' Johnson made a further appearance on the setlist with 'Little Queen Of Spades' and Eric subsequently closed the night with a rousing rendition of 'Cocaine.'"

—STEPHANIE LYNNE THORBURN
(author)

CLAPTON IRELAND / UK / SCANDINAVIA TOUR 2011

BAND LINEUP:
Eric Clapton: guitar, vocals
Chris Stainton: keyboards
Tim Carmon: keyboards
Steve Gadd: drums

Willie Weeks: bass
Sharon White: backing vocals
Michelle John: backing vocals

9 May 2011, O2, Dublin, Ireland (with Andy Fairweather Low and the Low Riders)

SETLIST: Key To The Highway / Going Down Slow / Hoochie Coochie Man / Old Love / I Shot The Sheriff / Drifting Blues / Nobody Knows You When You're Down And Out / Still Got The Blues / Same Old Blues / When Somebody Thinks You're Wonderful / Layla / Badge / Wonderful Tonight / Before You Accuse Me / Little Queen Of Spades / Cocaine / Crossroads

10 May 2011, Odyssey Arena, Belfast, Northern Ireland (with Andy Fairweather Low and the Low Riders)

SETLIST: Key To The Highway / Going Down Slow / Hoochie Coochie Man / Old Love / I Shot The Sheriff / Drifting Blues / Nobody Knows You When You're Down And Out / Still Got The Blues / Same Old Blues / When Somebody Thinks You're Wonderful / Layla / Badge / Wonderful Tonight / Before You Accuse Me / Little Queen Of Spades / Cocaine / Crossroads

12 May 2011, SECC, Glasgow, Scotland (with Andy Fairweather Low and the Low Riders)

SETLIST: Key To The Highway / Going Down Slow / Hoochie Coochie Man / Old Love / I Shot The Sheriff / Drifting Blues / Nobody Knows You When You're Down And Out / Still Got The Blues / Same Old Blues / When Somebody Thinks You're Wonderful / Layla / Badge / Wonderful Tonight / Before You Accuse Me / Little Queen Of Spades / Cocaine / Crossroads

14 May 2011, Cardiff International Arena, Cardiff, Wales (with Andy Fairweather Low and the Low Riders)

SETLIST: Key To The Highway / Going Down Slow / Hoochie Coochie Man / Old Love / I Shot The Sheriff / Drifting Blues / Nobody Knows You When You're Down And Out / Still Got The Blues / Same Old Blues / When Somebody Thinks You're Wonderful / Layla / Badge / Wonderful Tonight / Before You Accuse Me / Little Queen Of Spades / Cocaine / Crossroads

15 May 2011, Cardiff International Arena, Cardiff, Wales (with Andy Fairweather Low and the Low Riders)

SETLIST: Key To The Highway / Going Down Slow / Hoochie Coochie Man / Old Love / I Shot The Sheriff / Drifting Blues / Nobody Knows You When You're Down And Out / Still Got The Blues / Same Old Blues / When Somebody Thinks You're Wonderful / Layla / Badge / Wonderful Tonight / Before You Accuse Me / Little Queen Of Spades / Cocaine / Crossroads

17 May 2011, Royal Albert Hall, London (with Andy Fairweather Low and the Low Riders)

SETLIST: Key To The Highway / Going Down Slow / Hoochie Coochie Man / Old Love / I Shot The Sheriff / Drifting Blues / Nobody Knows You When You're Down And Out / Still Got The Blues / Same Old Blues / When Somebody Thinks You're Wonderful / Layla / Badge / Wonderful Tonight / Tearing Us Apart / Little Queen Of Spades / Cocaine / Crossroads

18 May 2011, Royal Albert Hall, London (with Andy Fairweather Low and the Low Riders)

SETLIST: Key To The Highway / Tell The Truth / Hoochie Coochie Man / Old Love / Tearing Us Apart / Drifting Blues / Nobody Knows You When You're Down And Out / Still Got The Blues / Same Old Blues / When Somebody Thinks You're Wonderful / Layla / Badge / Wonderful Tonight / Before You Accuse Me / Little Queen Of Spades / Cocaine / Crossroads

20 May 2011, Royal Albert Hall, London (with Andy Fairweather Low and the Low Riders)

SETLIST: Key To The Highway / Tell The Truth / Hoochie Coochie Man / Old Love / Tearing Us Apart / Drifting Blues / Nobody Knows You When You're Down And Out / Still Got The Blues / Same Old Blues / When Somebody Thinks You're Wonderful / Layla / Badge / Wonderful Tonight / Before You Accuse Me / Little Queen Of Spades / Cocaine / Crossroads

21 May 2011, Royal Albert Hall, London (with Andy Fairweather Low and the Low Riders)

SETLIST: Key To The Highway / Going Down Slow / Hoochie Coochie Man / Old Love / I Shot The Sheriff / Drifting / Nobody Knows You When You're Down And Out / Still Got The Blues / Same Old Blues / When Somebody Thinks You're Wonderful / Layla / Badge / Wonderful Tonight / Tearing Us Apart / Little Queen Of Spades / Cocaine / Crossroads

23 May 2011, Royal Albert Hall, London (with Andy Fairweather Low and the Low Riders)

Eric Clapton at the Royal Albert Hall, May 2011.

SETLIST: Key To The Highway / Tell The Truth / Hoochie Coochie Man / Old Love / Tearing Us Apart / Drifting Blues / Nobody Knows You When You're Down And Out / Still Got The Blues / Same Old Blues / When Somebody Thinks You're Wonderful / Layla / Badge / Wonderful Tonight / Before You Accuse Me / Little Queen Of Spades / Cocaine / Crossroads

24 May 2011, Royal Albert Hall, London (with Andy Fairweather Low and the Low Riders)

SETLIST: Key To The Highway / Going Down Slow / Hoochie Coochie Man / Old Love / I Shot The Sheriff / Drifting Blues / Nobody Knows You When You're Down And Out / Still Got The Blues / Same Old Blues / When Somebody Thinks You're Wonderful / Layla / Badge / Wonderful Tonight / Tearing Us Apart / Little Queen Of Spades / Cocaine / Crossroads

ERIC CLAPTON AND STEVE WINWOOD 2011

BAND LINEUP:
Eric Clapton: guitar, vocals
Chris Stainton: keyboards
Steve Winwood: piano, Hammond B3 organ, guitar, vocals
Steve Gadd: drums
Willie Weeks: bass
Sharon White: backing vocals
Michelle John: backing vocals

Poster for Eric Clapton/Steve Winwood Royal Albert Hall, 26 May 2011 to 1 June 2011.

26 May 2011, Royal Albert Hall, London (with Andy Fairweather Low and the Low Riders)

Steve Winwood and Eric Clapton during their concert at London's Royal Albert Hall, 26 May 2011.

Eric Clapton at London's Royal Albert Hall, May 2011.

At London's Royal Albert Hall, May 2011.

Eric Clapton on his Martin acoustic at the Royal Albert Hall, May 2011.

SETLIST: Had To Cry Today / Low Down / After Midnight / Presence Of The Lord / Glad / Well Alright / Hoochie Coochie Man / While You See A Chance / Key To The Highway / Midland Maniac / Crossroads / Georgia / That's No Way To Get Along / Can't Find My Way Home / Gimme Some Lovin' / Voodoo Chile / Cocaine / Dear Mr. Fantasy

27 May 2011, Royal Albert Hall, London (with Andy Fairweather Low and the Low Riders)

SETLIST: Had To Cry Today / Low Down / After Midnight / Presence Of The Lord / Glad / Well Alright / Hoochie Coochie Man / While You See A Chance / Key To The Highway / Midland Maniac / Crossroads / Georgia Drifting Blues / That's No Way To Get Along / Layla / Can't Find My Way Home / Gimme Some Lovin' / Voodoo Chile / Cocaine / Dear Mr. Fantasy

29 May 2011, Royal Albert Hall, London (with Andy Fairweather Low and the Low Riders)

SETLIST: Had To Cry Today / Low Down / After Midnight / Presence Of The Lord / Glad / Well Alright / Hoochie Coochie Man / While You See A Chance / Key To The Highway / Pearly Queen / Crossroads / Georgia / Still Got The Blues / That's No Way To Get Along / Layla / Can't Find My Way Home / Gimme Some Lovin' / Voodoo Chile / Cocaine / Dear Mr. Fantasy

30 May 2011, Royal Albert Hall, London (with Andy Fairweather Low and the Low Riders)

SETLIST: Had To Cry Today / Low Down / After Midnight / Presence Of The Lord / Glad / Well Alright / Hoochie Coochie Man / While You See A Chance / Key To The Highway / Pearly Queen / Crossroads / Georgia / Drifting Blues / That's No Way To Get Along / Layla / Can't Find My Way Home / Gimme Some Lovin' / Voodoo Chile / Cocaine / Dear Mr. Fantasy

JUNE 2011

1 June 2011, Royal Albert Hall, London (with Andy Fairweather Low and the Low Riders)

SETLIST: Had To Cry Today / Low Down / After Midnight / Presence Of The Lord / Glad / Well Alright / Hoochie Coochie Man / While You See A Chance / Key To The Highway / Pearly Queen / Crossroads / Georgia / Drifting Blues / That's No Way To Get Along / Layla / Can't Find My Way Home / Gimme Some Lovin' / Voodoo Chile / Cocaine / Dear Mr. Fantasy

Eric and band's final bow at Royal Albert Hall, 24 May 2011.

WINTERSHALL 2011

4 June 2011, Wintershall Estate, Bramley, Surrey (charity concert)

BAND DU LAC LINEUP:
Eric Clapton: guitar, vocals
Lulu: vocals
Gary Brooker: keyboards, vocals
Georgie Fame: keyboards, vocals
Andy Fairweather Low: guitar, vocals
Paul Carrack: keyboards, vocals
Dave Bronze: bass
Paul Bevis: drums
Jody Linscott: percussion
Nick Pentalow: horns
Frank Mead: horns
Matt Wynch: horns
Tracy Graham: backing vocals
Anna McDonald: backing vocals
Roger Taylor: drums

SETLIST: Money Honey / That's No Way To Get Along / You Don't Know Like I Know / Nobody Knows You When You're Down And Out / After Midnight / How Long Blues / Uptight / Whiter Shade Of Pale / Shout / Cocaine

CLAPTON SCANDINAVIAN TOUR 2011

BAND LINEUP:
Eric Clapton: guitar, vocals
Chris Stainton: keyboards
Tim Carmon: keyboards
Steve Gadd: drums
Willie Weeks: bass
Sharon White: backing vocals
Michelle John: backing vocals

6 June 2011, Hartwall Arena, Helsinki, Finland (with Anssi Kela)

SETLIST: Key To The Highway / Going Down Slow / Hoochie Coochie Man / Old Love / Tearing Us Apart / Drifting Blues / Nobody Knows You When You're Down And Out / Same Old Blues / Layla / Badge / Wonderful Tonight / Before You Accuse Me / Little Queen Of Spades / Cocaine / Crossroads

8 June 2011, Ericsson Globe, Stockholm, Sweden

SETLIST: Key To The Highway / Going Down Slow / Hoochie Coochie Man / Old Love / Tearing Us Apart / Drifting Blues / Nobody Knows You When You're Down And Out / Same Old Blues / Layla / Badge / Wonderful Tonight / Before You Accuse Me / Little Queen Of Spades / Cocaine / Crossroads

9 June 2011, Norwegian Wood Festival, Oslo, Norway (with the Real Ones)

SETLIST: Key To The Highway / Tell The Truth / Hoochie Coochie Man / Old Love / Tearing Us Apart / Drifting Blues / Nobody Knows You When You're Down And Out / Same Old Blues / When Somebody Thinks You're Wonderful / Layla / Badge / Wonderful Tonight / Before You Accuse Me / Little Queen Of Spades / Cocaine / Crossroads

11 June 2011, Jyske Bank Boxen, Herning, Denmark (with the Monks)

SETLIST: Key To The Highway / Going Down Slow / Hoochie Coochie Man / Old Love / I Shot The Sheriff / Drifting Blues / Nobody Knows You When You're Down

And Out / Lay Down Sally / When Somebody Thinks You're Wonderful / Layla / Badge / Wonderful Tonight / Before You Accuse Me / Little Queen Of Spades / Cocaine / Crossroads

CHARITY CONCERT ITALY 2011

BAND LINEUP:
Eric Clapton: guitar, vocals
Pino Daniele: guitar, vocals
Chris Stainton: keyboards
Gianluca Podio: keyboards
Mel Collins: saxophone
Willie Weeks: bass
Steve Gadd: drums

24 June 2011, Stadio di Cava De' Tirreni, Cava De' Tirreni, Italy (Eric Clapton and Pino Daniele play a benefit concert to help fund a CT scanner for the Pediatric Oncology Hospital Pausilipon in Naples as well as the work of the charitable foundation Open Onlus, which is committed to fighting childhood tumors and cancers. Pino Daniele is a successful Italian guitarist and singer who Eric had asked to play at the 2010 Crossroads Guitar Festival in Chicago. In return, Pino asked if Eric would come to Italy to play this benefit concert. Eric's contribution was a set full of electrifying solos. Unfortunately poor old Pino struggled with the chords for "Layla" on the day of the show)

SETLIST: Boogie Boogie Man[1] / Napule è[1] / Per Te[2] / Key To The Highway[2] / Hoochie Coochie Man[3] / Crossroads[3] / Wonderful Tonight[2] / Cocaine[4] / Layla[4]

[1]Pino Daniele and Eric Clapton
[2]Pino Daniele and Eric Clapton band
[3]Eric Clapton and band
[4]Eric Clapton, Pino Daniele, and band

AUGUST 2011

27 August 2011, Odescalchi Casle, Bracciano, Italy (Eric plays at the wedding reception of Bernie Ecclestone's daughter providing the music for the couple's first dance)

CLAPTON SOUTH AMERICAN TOUR 2011

BAND LINEUP:
Eric Clapton: guitar, vocals
Chris Stainton: keyboards
Tim Carmon: keyboards
Willie Weeks: bass
Steve Gadd: drums
Michelle John: backing vocals
Sharon White: backing vocals

OCTOBER 2011

6 October 2011, Centro de Eventos Fiergs, Porto Alegre, Brazil (with Cartolas)

Eric in concert at Centro de Eventos Fiergs, Porto Alegre, Brazil, on 6 October 2011.

SETLIST: Going Down Slow / Key To The Highway / Hoochie Coochie Man / Old Love / Tearing Us Apart / Drifting Blues / Nobody Knows You When You're Down And Out / Lay Down Sally / When Somebody Thinks You're Wonderful / Layla / Badge / Wonderful Tonight / Before You Accuse Me / Little Queen Of Spades / Cocaine / Crossroads

9 October 2011, HSBC Arena, Rio De Janeiro, Brazil (with Gary Clark, Jr.)

Eric Clapton, Day by Day

SETLIST: Going Down Slow / Key To The Highway / Hoochie Coochie Man / Old Love / I Shot The Sheriff / Drifting Blues / Nobody Knows You When You're Down And Out / Lay Down Sally / When Somebody Thinks You're Wonderful / Layla / Badge / Wonderful Tonight / Before You Accuse Me / Little Queen Of Spades / Cocaine / Crossroads

10 October 2011, HSBC Arena, Rio De Janeiro, Brazil (with Gary Clark, Jr.)

SETLIST: Key To The Highway / Tell The Truth / Hoochie Coochie Man / Old Love / Tearing Us Apart / Drifting Blues / Nobody Knows You When You're Down And Out / Lay Down Sally / When Somebody Thinks You're Wonderful / Layla / Badge / Wonderful Tonight / Before You Accuse Me / Little Queen Of Spades / Cocaine / Crossroads[1]

[1]with Gary Clark, Jr. on guitar

12 October 2011, Morumbi Stadium, São Paulo, Brazil (with Gary Clark, Jr.)

SETLIST: Key To The Highway / Tell The Truth / Hoochie Coochie Man / Old Love / Tearing Us Apart / Drifting Blues / Nobody Knows You When You're Down And Out / Lay Down Sally / When Somebody Thinks You're Wonderful / Layla / Badge / Wonderful Tonight / Before You Accuse Me / Little Queen Of Spades / Cocaine / Crossroads[1]

[1]with Gary Clark, Jr. on guitar

Eric dedicated tonight's show to Felipe Massa, the Formula One driver who races for the Scuderia Ferrari team. During the concert Eric used the Port Authority of New York–New Jersey Stratocaster, which is one of three guitars created by the Fender custom shop to commemorate the events and heroes of 9/11 at the World Trade Center.

14 October 2011, River Plate Stadium, Buenos Aires, Argentina

SETLIST: Key To The Highway / Going Down Slow / Hoochie Coochie Man / Old Love / I Shot The Sheriff / Drifting Blues / Nobody Knows You When You're Down And Out / Lay Down Sally / When Somebody Thinks You're Wonderful / Layla / Badge / Wonderful Tonight /

Before You Accuse Me / Little Queen Of Spades / Cocaine / Crossroads

16 October 2011, Movistar Arena, Santiago, Chile

SETLIST: Key To The Highway / Tell The Truth / Hoochie Coochie Man / Old Love / Tearing Us Apart / Drifting Blues / Nobody Knows You When You're Down And Out / Lay Down Sally / When Somebody Thinks You're Wonderful / Layla / Badge / Wonderful Tonight / Before You Accuse Me / Little Queen Of Spades / Cocaine / Crossroads

26 October 2011, Bush Hall, Shepherds Bush, London (Eric was due to play with Gary Clark, Jr. tonight but was unable due to a flu bug)

ERIC CLAPTON AND STEVE WINWOOD JAPAN TOUR 2011

BAND LINEUP:
Eric Clapton: guitar, vocals
Steve Winwood: Hammond B3 organ, piano, guitar, vocals
Chris Stainton: keyboards
Willie Weeks: bass
Steve Gadd: drums
Michelle John: backing vocals
Sharon White: backing vocals

Eric Clapton and Steve Winwood had not toured Japan together before and a tour to promote their live album was organized for November 2011. When Eric arrived in Japan, he found he could not get to sleep and was suffering badly from jetlag. He could not shake it off and according to reviews his fatigue was reflected in his playing which meant he made quite a few mistakes. Luckily he was given some herbal medication, which enabled him to sleep, and he was able to finish the tour in better shape.

NOVEMBER 2011

17 November 2011, Hokkaido Prefectural Sports Center, Sapporo, Japan

SETLIST: Had To Cry Today / Low Down / After Midnight / Presence Of The Lord / Glad / Well Alright / Hoochie Coochie Man / While You See A Chance / Key To The Highway / Midland Maniac / Crossroads / Georgia On My Mind / Drifting Blues / That's No Way To Get Along / Layla / Can't Find My Way Home / Gimme Some Lovin' / Voodoo Chile / Cocaine / Dear Mr. Fantasy

19 November 2011, Yokohama Arena, Yokohama, Japan

SETLIST: Had To Cry Today / Low Down / After Midnight / Presence Of The Lord / Glad / Well Alright / Hoochie Coochie Man / While You See A Chance / Key To The Highway / Pearly Queen / Crossroads / Georgia On My Mind / Drifting Blues / That's No Way To Get Along / Wonderful Tonight / Can't Find My Way Home / Gimme Some Lovin' / Voodoo Chile / Cocaine / Dear Mr.Fantasy

Handbill for Eric Clapton/Steve Winwood Japan Tour, November 2011.

Eric plays an "unplugged" version of "Wonderful Tonight" for the first time since its release in 1977.

21 November 2011, Osaka Jo-Hall, Osaka, Japan

SETLIST: Had To Cry Today / Low Down / After Midnight / Presence Of The Lord / Glad / Well Alright / Hoochie Coochie Man / While You See A Chance / Key To The Highway / Midland Maniac / Crossroads / Georgia On My Mind / Drifting Blues / That's No Way To Get Along / Wonderful Tonight / Can't Find My Way Home / Gimme Some Lovin' / Voodoo Chile / Cocaine / Dear Mr.Fantasy

22 November 2011, Osaka Jo-Hall, Osaka, Japan

SETLIST: Had To Cry Today / Low Down / After Midnight / Presence Of The Lord / Glad / Well Alright / Hoochie Coochie Man / While You See A Chance / Key To The Highway / Midland Maniac / Crossroads / Georgia On My Mind / Drifting Blues / That's No Way To Get Along / Wonderful Tonight / Can't Find My Way Home / Gimme Some Lovin' / Voodoo Chile / Dear Mr. Fantasy / Cocaine

24 November 2011, Marine Messe, Fukuoka

SETLIST: Had To Cry Today / Low Down / After Midnight / Presence Of The Lord / Glad / Well Alright / Hoochie Coochie Man / While You See A Chance / Key To The Highway / Midland Maniac / Crossroads / Georgia On My Mind / Drifting Blues / That's No Way To Get Along / Wonderful Tonight / Can't Find My Way Home / Gimme Some Lovin' / Voodoo Chile / Cocaine / Dear Mr. Fantasy

26 November 2011, Green Arena, Hiroshima, Japan

SETLIST: Had To Cry Today / Low Down / After Midnight / Presence Of The Lord / Glad / Well Alright / Hoochie Coochie Man / While You See A Chance / Key To The Highway / Midland Maniac / Crossroads / Georgia On My Mind / Drifting Blues / That's No Way To Get Along / Wonderful Tonight / Can't Find My Way Home / Gimme Some Lovin' / Voodoo Chile / Cocaine / Dear Mr. Fantasy

28 November 2011, Ishikawa Sports Center, Kanazawa, Japan

SETLIST: Had To Cry Today / Low Down / After Midnight / Presence Of The Lord / Glad / Well Alright / Hoochie Coochie Man / While You See A Chance / Key

To The Highway / Pearly Queen / Crossroads / Georgia On My Mind / Drifting Blues / That's No Way To Get Along / Wonderful Tonight / Can't Find My Way Home / Gimme Some Lovin' / Voodoo Chile / Dear Mr. Fantasy / Cocaine

30 November 2011, Nippon Gaishi Hall, Nagoya, Japan

SETLIST: Had To Cry Today / Low Down / After Midnight / Presence Of The Lord / Glad / Well Alright / Hoochie Coochie Man / While You See A Chance / Key To The Highway / Pearly Queen / Crossroads / Georgia / Drifting Blues / That's No Way To Get Along / Wonderful Tonight / Can't Find My Way Home / Gimme Some Lovin' / Voodoo Chile / Dear Mr. Fantasy / Cocaine

DECEMBER 2011

2 December 2011, Budokan, Tokyo, Japan

SETLIST: Had To Cry Today / Low Down / After Midnight / Presence Of The Lord / Glad / Well Alright / Hoochie Coochie Man / While You See A Chance / Key To The Highway / Midland Maniac / Crossroads / Georgia / Drifting Blues / That's No Way To Get Along / Wonderful Tonight / Can't Find My Way Home / Gimme Some Lovin' / Voodoo Chile / Dear Mr. Fantasy / Cocaine

3 December 2011, Budokan, Tokyo, Japan

SETLIST: Had To Cry Today / Low Down / After Midnight / Presence Of The Lord / Glad / Well Alright / Hoochie Coochie Man / While You See A Chance / Key To The Highway / Pearly Queen / Crossroads / Georgia / Drifting Blues / That's No Way To Get Along / Wonderful Tonight / Can't Find My Way Home / Gimme Some Lovin' / Voodoo Chile / Dear Mr. Fantasy / Cocaine

6 December 2011, Budokan, Tokyo, Japan

SETLIST: Had To Cry Today / Low Down / After Midnight / Presence Of The Lord / Glad / Well Alright / Hoochie Coochie Man / While You See A Chance / Key To The Highway / Pearly Queen / Crossroads / Georgia / Drifting Blues / That's No Way To Get Along / Wonderful Tonight / Can't Find My Way Home / Gimme Some Lovin' / Voodoo Chile / Dear Mr. Fantasy / Cocaine

This show is dedicated to blues guitarist Hubert Sumlin who died on 4 December 2011.

7 December 2011, Budokan, Tokyo, Japan

SETLIST: Had To Cry Today / Low Down / After Midnight / Presence Of The Lord / Glad / Well Alright / Hoochie Coochie Man / While You See A Chance / Key To The Highway / Pearly Queen / Crossroads / Georgia / Drifting Blues / That's No Way To Get Along / Wonderful Tonight / Can't Find My Way Home / Gimme Some Lovin' / Voodoo Chile / Dear Mr. Fantasy / Cocaine

10 December 2011, Budokan, Tokyo, Japan

SETLIST: Had To Cry Today / Low Down / After Midnight / Presence Of The Lord / Glad / Well Alright / Hoochie Coochie Man / While You See A Chance / Key To The Highway / Pearly Queen / Crossroads / Georgia / Drifting Blues / That's No Way To Get Along / Wonderful Tonight / Can't Find My Way Home / Gimme Some Lovin' / Voodoo Chile / Dear Mr. Fantasy / Cocaine

This show was dedicated to the memory of Dick Sims who died on 8 December. Dick played keyboards in Eric's band from 1974 to 1979.

BUCKINGHAM PALACE CHARITY EVENT 2011

15 December 2011, Buckingham Palace, London (Eric, along with Andy Fairweather Low, Chris Stainton, Dave Bronze, and Henry Spinetti play an unplugged set at Prince Phillip's 90th birthday gala dinner in aid of two youth charities, the Outward Bound Trust and the Duke Of Edinburgh's Award)

NEW YEAR'S EVE DANCE 2011

31 December 2011, Woking Leisure Centre, Woking, Surrey

Eric and his band are called Half Measures.

BAND LINEUP:
Eric Clapton: guitar, vocals

Andy Fairweather Low: guitar, vocals
Chris Stainton: keyboards
Gary Brooker: keyboards, vocals
Dave Bronze: bass
Henry Spinetti: drums
Judy Blair: keyboards

SETLIST 1: Knock On Wood / Reconsider Baby / Unchain My Heart / Hey Bo Diddley / Travelin' Light[1] / Route 66 / Cryin' Time Again / Rock Me Baby / Willie And The Hand Jive / Shake, Rattle And Roll

[1]from Andy Fairweather Low's *Be Bop 'N' Holla* album

SETLIST 2: In The Midnight Hour / Hoochie Coochie Man / Jambalaya (On The Bayou) / Blueberry Hill / Lay My Burden Down / Gin House / Five Long Years / Whiter Shade Of Pale / Cocaine / Old Black Joe

RECORDING SESSIONS 2011

HENSON RECORDING STUDIOS
1416 North La Brea, Hollywood, California
Sessions for *Old Sock*

10 MARCH 2011–17 MARCH 2011

THE FOLKS WHO LIVE ON THE HILL (Oscar Hammerstein II, Jerome Kern) *Old Sock* CD US Surfdog 2-18015 / UK Polydor 3733098 released March 2013

GOTTA GET OVER (Doyle Bramhall II / Justin Stanley / Nikka Costa) (featuring Chaka Khan) *Old Sock* CD US Surfdog 2-18015 / UK Polydor 3733098 released March 2013

TILL YOUR WELL RUNS DRY (Peter Tosh) *Old Sock* CD US Surfdog 2-18015 / UK Polydor 3733098 released March 2013

ALL OF ME (Gerald Marks, Seymour Simons) (featuring Paul McCartney) *Old Sock* CD US Surfdog 2-18015 / UK Polydor 3733098 released March 2013

BORN TO LOSE (Ted Daffan) *Old Sock* CD US Surfdog 2-18015 / UK Polydor 3733098 released March 2013

STILL GOT THE BLUES (Gary Moore) (featuring Steve Winwood) *Old Sock* CD US Surfdog 2-18015 / UK Polydor 3733098 released March 2013

GOODNIGHT IRENE (Huddie Ledbetter / John A. Lomax, Sr.) *Old Sock* CD US Surfdog 2-18015 / UK Polydor 3733098 released March 2013

YOUR ONE AND ONLY MAN (Otis Redding) *Old Sock* CD US Surfdog 2-18015 / UK Polydor 3733098 released March 2013

EVERY LITTLE THING (Doyle Bramhall II / Justin Stanley, Nikki Costa) *Old Sock* CD US Surfdog 2-18015 / UK Poly dor 3733098 released March 2013

OUR LOVE IS HERE TO STAY (George Gershwin / Ira Gershwin) *Old Sock* CD US Surfdog 2-18015 / UK Polydor 3733098 released March 2013

NO SYMPATHY (Peter Tosh) bonus track on iTunes and deluxe version of "Old Sock" on a USB card

Eric Clapton: vocals, electric guitar, acoustic guitar, 12-string guitar, Dobro, mandolin
Doyle Bramhall II: electric guitar, acoustic guitar, slide guitar, mandolin, backing vocals
Willie Weeks: bass guitar, upright bass
Steve Gadd: drums
Walt Richmond: upright piano, keyboards
Greg Leisz: pedal steel guitar, mandolin
Chris Stainton: clavinet, Fender Rhodes, Wurlitzer, Hammond B3 organ
Taj Mahal: harmonica, banjo
Jim Keltner: drums
Steve Winwood: Hammond B3 organ
Paul McCartney: upright bass, vocals
Abe Laboriel, Jr.: drums
Tim Carmon: Hammond B3 organ, chord organ
Henry Spinetti: drums
Justin Stanley: clavinet, mellotron, drums
Matt Chamberlain: drums
Matt Rollings: keyboards
Simon Climie: percussion, piano
Frank Marocco: accordion
Gabe Witcher: fiddle
Stephen "Doc" Kupka: baritone saxophone
Joseph Sublett: tenor saxophone
Nicholas Lane: trombone
Sal Cracchiolo: trumpet
Sharon White: backing vocals
Michelle John: backing vocals
Chaka Khan: vocals
Julie Clapton: guest vocals
Ella Clapton: guest vocals
Sophie Clapton: guest vocals
Nikka Costa: guest vocals
Wendy Moten: guest vocals
Lisa Vaughan: guest vocals
Nick Ingman: string arrangements

ERIC CLAPTON GUEST SESSION

AVATAR STUDIOS
441 West 53rd Street, New York City
Session for Paul McCartney

APRIL 2011

MY VALENTINE (Paul McCartney) *Kisses On The Bottom* CD Hear Music HRM-33671-02 released February 2012

Paul McCartney: vocals
Eric Clapton: guitar

Diana Krall: piano, rhythm arrangement
Karriem Riggins: drums
Robert Hurst: bass
John Pizzarelli: guitar
Alan Broadbent: conductor, London Symphony Orchestra

GET YOURSELF ANOTHER FOOL (Ernest Monroe Tucker / Frank Haywood) *Kisses On The Bottom* CD Hear Music HRM-33671-02 released February 2012

Paul McCartney: vocals, acoustic guitar
Eric Clapton: guitar
Diana Krall: piano, rhythm arrangement
Karriem Riggins: drums
Christian McBride: bass
Anthony Wilson: rhythm guitar
Alan Broadbent: conductor, London Symphony Orchestra

Producer: Tommy LiPuma
Engineer: Fernando Lodeiro

ERIC CLAPTON GUEST SESSION
ELECTRIC LADY STUDIOS
52 West 8th Street, New York City
Session for Jerry Douglas

AUGUST 2011

SOMETHING YOU GOT (Chris Kenner) *Traveler* CD One Music EOM-CD2128 released June 2012

Jerry Douglas: lap steel guitar, harmony vocals
Eric Clapton: guitar, vocals
Dr. John: piano
Matt Perrine: bass
Shannon Powell: drums
Wendell Brunious: trumpet
Rex Leary: saxophone
Aron Fletcher: saxophone
Sam Bush: harmony vocals

Producer: Russ Titelman
Engineer: Justin Stanley

> "Eric put his bit on at Electric Lady in August of 2011 while he was working on his own album. He gave me an hour or so and we did the vocal first, then the solo. It went very quickly. We hadn't done anything together since *From the Cradle* so it was like old times . . . fun and great. I love what he did on this recording and so did he."
>
> —**RUSS TITELMAN**

2012

HOWLIN' FOR HUBERT 2012

24 February 2012, Apollo Theater, New York City

Benefit show for the Jazz Foundation of America, which helps impoverished musicians pay the bills for their basic necessities. It was to have been a celebration of blues great Hubert's 80th birthday, but since he passed away on 4 December 2011, it became a memorial show instead. A multitude of special guests turned up to play including Eric, Billy Gibbons, Gary Clark, Jr., Keith Richards, and many more as listed below. A great evening in honor of a great man.

The show is not recorded.

HOUSE BAND:
Willie Weeks: bass
Larry Taylor: standup bass
Billy Flynn: guitar
Eddie Taylor, Jr.: guitar
Danny "Kootch" Kortchmar: guitar
Chuck Goering: upright piano
Ivan Neville: organ, electric piano
Jim Keltner: drums
Steve Jordan: drums, musical director

Kim Wilson: harp, vocals

SPECIAL GUESTS:
Eric Clapton: guitar, vocals
Keith Richards: guitar, vocals
Jimmie Vaughan: guitar, vocals
Warren Haynes: guitar, vocals
Lonnie Brooks: guitar, vocals
Ronnie Baker Brooks: guitar, vocals
Keb Mo: guitar, vocals
Susan Tedeschi: guitar, vocals
Todd Park Mohr: guitar, vocals
Buddy Guy: guitar, vocals
Gary Clark, Jr.: guitar, vocals
Doyle Bramhall II: guitar
Derek Trucks: guitar
Jody Williams: guitar
Kenny Wayne Shepherd: guitar
Billy Gibbons: guitar
Jimmy Vivino: guitar
Quinn Sullivan: guitar
Eddy Shaw: upright piano
Henry Gray: saxophone
James Cotton: harmonica
Robert Randolph: pedal steel guitar, vocals
Shemekia Copeland: vocals
David Johansen: vocals

SETLIST:

Key To The Highway (Eric Clapton, James Cotton)
Roll Where You Want (Todd Mohr)
Six Strings Down (Jimmie Vaughan)

Lucky Lou (Jody Williams, Kenny Wayne Shepherd)

Evil (Jody Williams, Kenny Wayne Shepherd, Jimmy Vivino, David Johansen, Kim Wilson)

Born In Chicago / Sweet Home Chicago (Ronnie Baker Brooks, Lonnie Brooks)

Sitting On Top Of The World (Eddy Shaw, Henry Gray)

Hidden Charms (Elvis Costello, Eddy Shaw, Henry Gray)

You'll Be Mine (Warren Haynes)

I Asked For Water (Warren Haynes, Billy Gibbons)

Mister Highway Man (Warren Haynes, Billy Gibbons)

Who's Been Talking (Kim Wilson)

Howlin' For My Baby (Keb Mo, Eddy Shaw)

Commit A Crime (Doyle Bramhall II, Jimmie Vaughan, Keb Mo)

Meet Me At The Bottom (Derek Trucks, Doyle Bramhall II, Jimmie Vaughan)

How Many More Years (Susan Tedeschi, Derek Trucks)

Three Hundred Pounds Of Joy (Susan Tedeschi, Derek Trucks)

Who Do You Love (Robert Randolph, Jody Williams)

Goin' Down (Buddy Guy, Robert Randolph, Quinn Sullivan)

Hoochie Koochie Man (Buddy Guy, Robert Randolph)

Beggin' You Please (Buddy Guy, Shemekia Copeland)

Catfish Blues (Gary Clark, Jr.)

Shake For Me (Eric Clapton, Gary Clark, Jr.)

Little Baby (Eric Clapton, Gary Clark, Jr.)

Forty Four Blues (Eric Clapton, Gary Clark, Jr., Jody Williams)

Going Down Slow (Eric Clapton, Keith Richards, Gary Clark, Jr.)

Little Red Rooster (Keith Richards, James Cotton)

Spoonful (Keith Richards, Eric Clapton, James Cotton)

Wang Dang Doodle (all except Elvis Costello)

Smokestack Lightning (all except Elvis Costello)

28 February 2012, Village Vanguard, New York City (Eric and Russ Titelman attended the opening night of Kurt Rosenwinkel's week-long residency at New York's Village Vanguard. Eric called Kurt an inspiration. Kurt was invited to play at the Crossroads shows in 2013)

ROLLING STONES O2 2012

29 November 2012, O2 Arena, London

Eric joins the Rolling Stones for a version of Muddy Waters's "Champagne And Reefer." The show is recorded.

Eric Clapton and Keith Richards on stage at the O2 in London on 29 November 2012. Eric joined them for "Champagne and Reefer."

Eric Clapton, Ronnie Wood, and Keith Richards on stage at the O2 in London on 29 November 2012.

Chuck Leavell, Eric Clapton, and Mick Jagger on stage at the O2 in London on 29 November 2013.

DECEMBER 2012

CONCERT FOR SANDY 2012

12 December 2012, Concert For Sandy, Madison Square Garden, New York City

A special concert to raise funds for the victims of the hurricane that devasated the New Jersey/New York area. Other artists who appeared were Paul McCartney, Bruce Springsteen and the E Street Band, Kanye West, Billy Joel, the Who, Alicia Keys, and Jon Bon Jovi.

BAND LINEUP:
Eric Clapton: guitar, vocals
Steve Jordan: drums
Willie Weeks: bass

SETLIST:

Nobody Knows You When You're Down And Out (Jimmy Cox) *Concert For Sandy* CD Columbia 88765448893 released 2013

Got To Get Better In A Little While (Eric Clapton) *Concert For Sandy* CD Columbia 88765448893 released 2013

Crossroads (Robert Johnson) *Concert For Sandy* CD Columbia 88765448893 released 2013

Producers: Jim Dolan / John Sykes / Harvey Weinstein
Recorded by: Music Mix Mobile

NEW YEAR'S EVE DANCE 2012

31 December 2012, Woking Leisure Centre, Woking, Surrey)

Eric and his band are called Happy Destiny.

BAND LINEUP:
Eric Clapton: guitar, vocals
Steve Winwood: keyboards, guitar, vocals
Andy Fairweather Low: guitar, vocals
Chris Stainton: keyboards
Gary Brooker: keyboards, vocals
Dave Bronze: bass
Henry Spinetti: drums
Michelle John: backing vocals
Sharon White: backing vocals
Sylvia Clapp: vocals on "I Will Walk Beside You"
Judy Blair: keyboards on "Kansas City"

SETLIST 1: I'll Walk Beside You / Knock On Wood / Reconsider Baby / Unchain My Heart / Can't Judge A Book / Lay My Burden Down / Will The Circle Be Unbroken / Fannie May / Willie And The Hand Jive / Shake, Rattle And Roll / Gimme Some Lovin'

SETLIST 2: Midnight Hour / Hoochie Coochie Man / Poison Ivy / Kansas City / Gin House / Can't Find My Way Home / Five Long Years / Whiter Shade Of Pale / Cocaine / Mr Fantasy / Little Queenie

A bittersweet evening. After twenty years of playing on New Year's Eve at the Woking Leisure Centre, Eric announced that this would be his last one. He certainly ended it on a high note with a great performance, and special guest Steve Winwood was clearly thrilled to be part of this special evening.

RECORDING SESSIONS 2012

BRITISH GROVE STUDIOS
20 British Grove, Chiswick, London
Session for *Old Sock*

30 APRIL 2012

Paul McCartney overdubs bass and vocals.

ALL OF ME (Gerald Marks / Seymour Simons) *Old Sock* CD US Surfdog 2-18015 / UK Polydor 3733098 released March 2013

Eric Clapton: guitar, vocals
Paul McCartney: double bass, vocals

ERIC CLAPTON GUEST SESSION

UNKNOWN STUDIO
Session for Sonny Emory

APRIL 2012

TRUTH'LL SET U FREE (Borden / Keck / Kennedy) *Rock Hard Cachet* CD Moosicus Records released March 2013

Eric Clapton: solo guitar
Sonny Emory: drums
Kipper Jones: lead and background vocals
Isaac West: bass
Dick Smith: guitar
Stanyos Young: organ
Morris Pleasure: clavinet
Darian Emory: saxophone
Chris Burns: trombone
Jerry Freeman: trumpet

Producer: Sonny Emory

2013

After a relatively calm 2012, Eric released his latest album, *Old Sock*, in March 2013 which was followed with a U.S., UK, and European tour. Eric's album title came indirectly via David Bowie who had affectionately referred to him as an old sock. Eric loved that and asked Bowie if he minded if he used it as the name of his new album. The setlists were a joy to longtime fans with Eric revisiting his past mixed with some new material with a top-notch band. There was something for everyone, some Cream, some hits, some blues, and some pop. It was great to have Doyle Bramhall II back in the fold. Surely the best foil Eric has ever had? Paul Carrack added his perfect vocal talents as well as keyboards. Greg Leisz on pedal steel also added a new dimension to the sound.

Eric admitted that he was finding the road quite hard, not the playing gigs part, but the travel element of it. He said he would retire from touring when he reaches seventy and would just play local gigs after that. He also suggested that a planned tour of Japan and the Far East in 2014 would be his last as he found the jetlag too difficult to deal with. It really felt like he was slowly winding down—and why not? The man has left us with quite a musical legacy over the last fifty years. And I have no doubt there may be one or more surprises left before he does retire.

At the time of this writing the only other plans Eric has is a farewell tour of some major cities in 2015.

MARCH 2013

OLD SOCK U.S. TOUR 2013

BAND LINEUP:

Eric Clapton: guitar, vocals
Doyle Bramhall II: guitar
Greg Leisz: pedal steel guitar
Chris Stainton: piano, keyboards
Paul Carrack: organ, keyboards
Willie Weeks: bass
Steve Jordan: drums
Michelle John: backing vocals
Sharon White: backing vocals

14 March 2013, US Airways Center, Phoenix, Arizona (with the Wallflowers)

SETLIST: Hello Old Friend / My Father's Eyes / Tell The Truth / Gotta Get Over / Black Cat Bone / Got To Get Better / Tempted / I Shot The Sheriff / Drifting Blues / Nobody Knows You When You're Down And Out/ Tears In Heaven / Goodnight Irene / Wonderful Tonight / How Long Blues / Stones In My Passway / Love In Vain / Crossroads / Little Queen Of Spades / Cocaine / Layla / Sunshine Of Your Love / High Time We Went

“Early highlights included a slinkier reading of 'I Shot The Sheriff,' which featured an epic Clapton solo that ended with him mirroring the melody on his way to restating the opening riff really high on the neck of his guitar, and a wah-guitar-driven rendition of 'Got To Get Better In A Little While,' a funky, gospel-flavored gem by Derek and the Dominos.”

—AZCENTRAL.COM

16 March 2013, Toyota Center, Houston, Texas (with the Wallflowers)

No "Layla" this evening.

SETLIST: Hello Old Friend / My Father's Eyes / Tell The Truth / Gotta Get Over / Black Cat Bone / Got To Get Better In A Little While / Tempted / I Shot The Sheriff / Drifting Blues / Nobody Knows You When You're Down And Out / Tears In Heaven / Goodnight Irene / Wonderful Tonight / How Long Blues / Stones In My Passway / Love In Vain / Crossroads / Little Queen Of Spades / Cocaine / Sunshine Of Your Love / High Time We Went

17 March 2013, Frank Erwin Center, Austin, Texas (with the Wallflowers)

Jimmie Vaughan joins in for "Black Cat Bone." "Layla" is back in the setlist albeit in unplugged mode. Also, "Lay Down Sally" replaces "Nobody Knows You."

SETLIST: Hello Old Friend / My Father's Eyes / Tell The Truth / Gotta Get Over / Black Cat Bone[1] / Got To Get Better In A Little While / Tempted / I Shot The Sheriff / Drifting Blues / Lay Down Sally / Tears In Heaven / Wonderful Tonight / Layla / How Long Blues / Stones In My Passway / Love In Vain / Crossroads / Little Queen Of Spades / Cocaine / Sunshine Of Your Love / High Time We Went

[1] with Jimmie Vaughan on guitar

19 March 2013, American Airlines Center, Dallas, Texas (with the Wallflowers)

"Layla" remains unplugged while "Badge" replaces "I Shot The Sheriff."

SETLIST: Hello Old Friend / My Father's Eyes / Tell The Truth / Gotta Get Over / Black Cat Bone / Got To Get Better In A Little While / Tempted / Badge / Drifting Blues / Tears In Heaven / Lay Down Sally / Wonderful Tonight / Layla / How Long Blues / Stones In My Passway / Love In Vain / Crossroads / Little Queen Of Spades / Cocaine / Sunshine Of Your Love / High Time We Went

"Restless hands working acoustic and electric guitars with equal fervor, his fingers setting off fretboard firew orks at regular intervals. Even his legs—occasionally bracing the sixty-seven-year-old singer-songwriter against a squall of notes—appeared animated."

—DFW.COM

20 March 2013, Chesapeake Energy Arena, Oklahoma City, Oklahoma (with the Wallflowers)

"Tempted," "I Shot The Sheriff," and "Badge" are dropped in favor of "Going Down Slow" and "Singin' The Blues." Jamie Oldaker was backstage with Eric.

SETLIST: Hello Old Friend / My Father's Eyes / Tell The Truth / Gotta Get Over / Black Cat Bone / Got To Get Better In A Little While / Going Down Slow / Singin' The Blues / Drifting Blues / Tears In Heaven / Lay Down Sally / Wonderful Tonight / Layla / How Long Blues / Stones In My Passway / Love In Vain / Crossroads / Little Queen Of Spades / Cocaine / Sunshine Of Your Love / High Time We Went

"Eric Clapton's *Fifty Years Further On Up The Road* Tour stopped at the Chesapeake Energy Center Wednesday, bringing blistering blues to an appreciative near-sellout crowd."

—LOOK AT OKC WEBSITE

22 March 2013, Bridgestone Arena, Nashville, Tennessee (with the Wallflowers)

"Layla" is MIA.

SETLIST: Hello Old Friend / My Father's Eyes / Tell The Truth / Gotta Get Over / Black Cat Bone / Got To Get Better In A Little While / Tempted / I Shot The Sheriff / Drifting Blues / Nobody Knows You When You're Down And Out / Tears In Heaven / Goodnight Irene / Wonderful Tonight / How Long Blues / Stones In My Passway / Love In Vain / Crossroads / Little Queen Of Spades / Cocaine / Sunshine Of Your Love / High Time We Went

23 March 2013, New Orleans Arena, New Orleans, Louisiana (with the Wallflowers)

"Layla" remains MIA.

SETLIST: Hello Old Friend / My Father's Eyes / Tell The Truth / Gotta Get Over / Black Cat Bone / Got To Get Better In A Little While / Tempted / I Shot The Sheriff / Drifting Blues / Nobody Knows You When You're Down And Out / Tears In Heaven / Goodnight Irene / Wonderful Tonight / How Long Blues / Stones In My Passway / Love In Vain / Crossroads / Little Queen Of Spades / Cocaine / Sunshine Of Your Love / High Time We Went

> "Bookending a show that began with 'Hello Old Friend,' Joe Cocker's 'High Time We Went,' sung by Carrack, closed this overwhelmingly splendid Clapton concert."
> —*THE ADVOCATE*

26 March 2013, Jacksonville Veterans Memorial Arena, Jacksonville, Florida (with the Wallflowers)

"Layla" is back tonight.

SETLIST: Hello Old Friend / My Father's Eyes / Tell The Truth / Gotta Get Over / Black Cat Bone / Got To Get Better In A Little While / Tempted / Badge / Drifting Blues / Tears In Heaven / Lay Down Sally / Wonderful Tonight / Layla / How Long Blues / Stones In My Passway / Love In Vain / Crossroads / Little Queen Of Spades / Cocaine / Sunshine Of Your Love / High Time We Went

27 March 2013, Gwinnett Arena, Duluth, Georgia (with the Wallflowers)

SETLIST: Hello Old Friend / My Father's Eyes / Tell The Truth / Gotta Get Over / Black Cat Bone / Got To Get Better In A Little While / Tempted / Badge / Drifting Blues / Lay Down Sally / Tears In Heaven / Layla / Wonderful Tonight / How Long Blues / Stones In My Passway / Love In Vain / Crossroads / Little Queen Of Spades / Cocaine / Sunshine Of Your Love / High Time We Went

29 March 2013, Seminole Hard Rock Live, Hollywood, Florida (with the Wallflowers)

"I Shot The Sheriff" replaces "Badge."

SETLIST: Hello Old Friend / My Father's Eyes / Tell The Truth / Gotta Get Over / Black Cat Bone / Got To Get Better In A Little While / Tempted / I Shot The Sheriff / Drifting Blues / Nobody Knows You When You're Down And Out / Tears In Heaven / Goodnight Irene / Wonderful Tonight / How Long Blues / Stones In My Passway / Love In Vain / Crossroads / Little Queen Of Spades / Cocaine / Sunshine Of Your Love / High Time We Went

30 March 2013, Seminole Hard Rock Live, Hollywood, Florida (with the Wallflowers)

Eric's 68th birthday and the poor guy is having to work!

SETLIST: Hello Old Friend / My Father's Eyes / Tell The Truth / Gotta Get Over / Black Cat Bone / Got To Get Better In A Little While / Tempted / Badge / Drifting Blues / Lay Down Sally / Tears In Heaven / Layla / Wonderful Tonight / How Long Blues / Stones In My Passway / Love In Vain / Crossroads / Little Queen Of Spades / Cocaine / Sunshine Of Your Love / High Time We Went

APRIL 2013

2 April 2013, Time Warner Cable Arena, Charlotte, North Carolina (with the Wallflowers)

SETLIST: Hello Old Friend / My Father's Eyes / Tell The Truth / Gotta Get Over / Black Cat Bone / Got To Get Better In A Little While / Tempted[1] / I Shot The Sheriff / Drifting Blues / Nobody Knows You When You're Down And Out / Tears In Heaven / Goodnight Irene / Wonderful Tonight / How Long Blues / Stones In My Passway / Love In Vain / Crossroads / Little Queen Of Spades / Cocaine / Sunshine Of Your Love / High Time We Went

3 April 2013, PNC Arena, Raleigh, North Carolina (with the Wallflowers)

SETLIST: Hello Old Friend / My Father's Eyes / Tell The Truth / Gotta Get Over / Black Cat Bone / Got To Get Better In A Little While / Tempted / I Shot The Sheriff / Drifting Blues / Lay Down Sally / Tears In Heaven / Layla / Wonderful Tonight / How Long Blues / Stones In My

Eric Clapton and Keith Richards during the Crossroads Guitar Festival, 13 April 2013.

L to R: Robert Cray, Eric Clapton, Jimmie Vaughan, and B.B. King at the Crossroads Festival at Madison Square Garden, 12 April 2013.

Passway / Love In Vain / Crossroads / Little Queen Of Spades / Cocaine / Sunshine Of Your Love / High Time We Went

5 April 2013, Mohegan Sun Arena, Uncasville, Connecticut (with the Wallflowers)

SETLIST: Hello Old Friend / My Father's Eyes / Tell The Truth / Gotta Get Over / Black Cat Bone / Got To Get Better In A Little While / Tempted / Badge / I Shot The Sheriff / Drifting Blues / Nobody Knows You When You're Down And Out / Tears In Heaven / Goodnight Irene / Wonderful Tonight / How Long Blues / Stones In My Passway / Love In Vain / Crossroads / Little Queen Of Spades / Cocaine / Sunshine Of Your Love / High Time We Went

6 April 2013, Consol Energy Center, Pittsburgh, Pennsylvania (with the Wallflowers)

As it is the last show of the U.S. tour, Eric makes a special appearance with support act the Wallflowers for a version of The Band's "The Weight."

SETLIST: Hello Old Friend / My Father's Eyes / Tell The Truth / Gotta Get Over / Black Cat Bone / Got To Get Better In A Little While / Tempted / Badge / Drifting Blues / Lay Down Sally / Tears In Heaven / Layla / Wonderful Tonight / How Long Blues / Stones In My Passway / Love In Vain / Crossroads / Little Queen Of Spades / Cocaine / Sunshine Of Your Love / High Time We Went

"On Saturday, they packed into Consol Energy Center for the full immersion of his talents. We got some Cream, some Derek and the Dominos, the songs your wife likes, one *Old Sock,* and a scorching tribute to his muse. We also got an unassuming bandleader more than willing to share the spotlight."
—*PITTSBURGH POST GAZETTE*

CROSSROADS GUITAR FESTIVAL 2013

12 April 2013, Madison Square Garden, New York City (Crossroads Guitar Festival Day 1)

Eric Clapton joins the Allman Brothers at Madison Square Garden for a version of the Dominos classic "Why Does Love Got To Be So Sad" during the Crossroads Guitar Festival, 12 April 2013. Derek Trucks is playing Duane Allman's original Gibson Gold Top Les Paul guitar.

ERIC CLAPTON SET

Drifting Blues (with Steve Jordan and Willie Weeks)
Spider Jiving (with Andy Fairweather Low, Steve Jordan, and Willie Weeks)
Tears In Heaven (with Andy Fairweather Low, Doyle Bramhall II, Greg Leisz, Chris Stainton, Steve Jordan, and Willie Weeks)
Lay Down Sally (with Vince Gill, Andy Fairweather Low, Doyle Bramhall II, Greg Leisz, Chris Stainton, Steve Jordan, and Willie Weeks)
Wonderful Tonight (with Vince Gill, Andy Fairweather Low, Doyle Bramhall II, Greg Leisz, Chris Stainton, Steve Jordan, and Willie Weeks)

ROBERT CRAY, B.B. KING, JIMMIE VAUGHN, ERIC CLAPTON SET

Everyday I Have the Blues

KURT ROSENWINKEL SET

If I Should Lose You (with Eric Clapton)
Way Down That Lonesome Road (with Eric Clapton)

ALLMAN BROTHERS BAND SET

Why Does Love Got to Be So Sad (with Eric Clapton)

13 April 2013, Madison Square Garden, New York City (Crossroads Guitar Festival Day 2)

LOS LOBOS SET

Tin Can Trust (with Eric Clapton)

Eric Clapton and Cesar Rosas during the Crossroads Guitar Festival, 13 April 2013.

ERIC CLAPTON AND HIS BAND SET

Key To The Highway (with Keith Richards, Doyle Bramhall II, Greg Leisz, Chris Stainton, Steve Jordan, and Willie Weeks)

Sweet Little Rock & Roller (with Keith Richards, Doyle Bramhall II, Greg Leisz, Chris Stainton, Steve Jordan, and Willie Weeks)

He Don't Live Here No More (with Robbie Robertson, Doyle Bramhall II, Greg Leisz, Chris Stainton, Steve Jordan, and Willie Weeks)

I Shall Be Released (with Robbie Robertson, Doyle Bramhall II, Greg Leisz, Chris Stainton, Steve Jordan, and Willie Weeks)

Gin House (with Andy Fairweather Low, Doyle Bramhall

II, Greg Leisz, Chris Stainton, Steve Jordan, and Willie Weeks)

Got To Get Better In A Little While (Doyle Bramhall II, Greg Leisz, Chris Stainton, Steve Jordan, and Willie Weeks)

Crossroads (Doyle Bramhall II, Greg Leisz, Chris Stainton, Steve Jordan, and Willie Weeks)

Little Queen Of Spades (Doyle Bramhall II, Greg Leisz, Chris Stainton, Steve Jordan, and Willie Weeks)

Sunshine Of Your Love (Doyle Bramhall II, Greg Leisz, Chris Stainton, Steve Jordan, and Willie Weeks)

High Time We Went (with Doyle Bramhall II, Greg Leisz, Chris Stainton, Steve Jordan and Willie Weeks, Vince Gill, Warren Haynes, Derek Trucks, Sonny Landreth, Robert Cray, Gary Clark Jr., Kurt Rosenwinkel, Buddy Guy, Taj Mahal, David Hidalgo, Cesar Rosas, Robbie Robertson, Quinn Sullivan)

The two days are filmed and recorded and edited highlights are released on DVD and Blu-Ray.

OLD SOCK UK TOUR 2013

BAND LINEUP:
Eric Clapton: guitar, vocals
Doyle Bramhall II: guitar
Greg Leisz: pedal steel guitar
Chris Stainton: piano, keyboards
Paul Carrack: organ, keyboards
Willie Weeks: bass
Steve Jordan: drums
Michelle John: backing vocals
Sharon White: backing vocals

MAY 2013

9 May 2013, The O2, Dublin, Ireland (with Andy Fairweather Low and the Low Riders)

Welcome return of "Blues Power," first time since the eighties.

Eric Clapton and Doyle Bramhall II during the sit-down set Royal Albert Hall, May 2013.

Eric Clapton with Martin acoustic at the Royal Albert Hall, May 2013.

SETLIST: Hello Old Friend / My Father's Eyes / Tell The Truth / Gotta Get Over / Black Cat Bone / Got To Get Better / Come Rain Or Come Shine / Badge / Drifting Blues / Further On Down The Road / Layla / Stones In My Passway / It Ain't Easy / Lay Down Sally / Wonderful Tonight / Blues Power / Love In Vain / Crossroads / Little Queen Of Spades / Cocaine / Sunshine Of Your Love / High Time We Went

10 May 2013, Odyssey Arena, Belfast, Ireland (with Andy Fairweather Low and the Low Riders)

SETLIST: Hello Old Friend / My Father's Eyes / Tell The Truth / Gotta Get Over / Black Cat Bone / Got To Get Better In A Little While / Come Rain Or Come Shine / Help Me1 / Drifting Blues / Further On Down The Road / Layla / Stones In My Passway / It Ain't Easy / Lay Down Sally / Wonderful Tonight / Blues Power / Love In Vain / Crossroads / Little Queen Of Spades / Cocaine / Sunshine Of Your Love / High Time We Went

¹with Van Morrison on harmonica and lead vocals on a cover of Sonny Boy Williamson's "Help Me."

13 May 2013, LG Arena, Birmingham (with Gary Clark, Jr.)

SETLIST: Hello Old Friend / My Father's Eyes / Tell The Truth / Black Cat Bone / Got To Get Better In A Little While / Come Rain Or Come Shine / I Shot The Sheriff / Drifting Blues / Further On Down The Road / Layla / Stones In My Passway / Wonderful Tonight / Lay Down Sally / Badge / Love In Vain / Crossroads / Little Queen Of Spades / Cocaine / High Time We Went

14 May 2013, Manchester Arena, Manchester (with Gary Clark, Jr.)

SETLIST: Hello Old Friend / My Father's Eyes / Tell The Truth / Black Cat Bone / Gotta Get Over / Come Rain Or Come Shine / Got To Get Better In A Little While / Badge / Drifting Blues / Goodnight Irene / It Ain't Easy / Layla / Tears In Heaven / Nobody Knows You When You're Down And Out / Lay Down Sally / Blues Power / Love In Vain / Crossroads / Little Queen Of Spades / Cocaine / Sunshine Of Your Love[1] / High Time We Went

1with comedian Peter Kay holding a hilarious doubled-necked shovel and miming along on stage

17 May 2013, Royal Albert Hall, London (with Gary Clark, Jr.)

L to R: Doyle Bramhall II, Eric Clapton, and Gary Clark, Jr. during "Sunshine Of Your Love" at London's Royal Albert Hall, May 2013.

SETLIST: Hello Old Friend / My Father's Eyes / Tell The Truth / Gotta Get Over / Black Cat Bone / Got To Get Better In A Little While / Come Rain Or Come Shine / Badge / Drifting Blues / Goodnight Irene / Layla / It Ain't Easy / Nobody Knows You When You're Down And Out / Lay Down Sally / Wonderful Tonight / Blues Power / Love In Vain / Crossroads / Little Queen Of Spades / Cocaine / Sunshine Of Your Love / High Time We Went

18 May 2013, Royal Albert Hall, London (with Gary Clark, Jr.)

SETLIST: Hello Old Friend / My Father's Eyes / Tell The Truth / Gotta Get Over / Black Cat Bone / Got To Get Better In A Little While / Come Rain Or Come Shine / I Shot The Sheriff / Drifting Blues / Further On Down The Road / Nobody Knows You When You're Down And Out / It Ain't Easy / Layla / Stones In My Passway / Tears In Heaven / Blues Power / Love In Vain / Crossroads / Little Queen Of Spades / Cocaine / Sunshine Of Your Love / High Time We Went

20 May 2013, Royal Albert Hall, London (with Gary Clark, Jr.)

SETLIST: Hello Old Friend / My Father's Eyes / Tell The Truth / Gotta Get Over / Black Cat Bone / Got To Get Better In A Little While / Come Rain Or Come Shine / I Shot The Sheriff / Drifting Blues / Nobody Knows You When You're Down And Out / It Ain't Easy / Layla / Wonderful Tonight / Lay Down Sally / Tears In Heaven / Blues Power / Love In Vain / Crossroads / Little Queen Of Spades / Cocaine / Sunshine Of Your Love[1] / High Time We Went[1]

1with Gary Clark, Jr. on guitar

21 May 2013, Royal Albert Hall, London (with Gary Clark, Jr.)

Eric Clapton on acoustic at Royal Albert Hall, May 2013.

SETLIST: Hello Old Friend / My Father's Eyes / Tell The Truth / Gotta Get Over / Black Cat Bone / Got To Get Better In A Little While / Come Rain Or Come Shine / Badge / Drifting Blues / Nobody Knows You When You're Down And Out / It Ain't Easy / Layla / Wonderful Tonight / Blues Power / Love In Vain / Crossroads / Little Queen Of Spades / Cocaine / Sunshine Of Your Love[1] / High Time We Went[1]

[1]with Gary Clark, Jr. on guitar

23 May 2013, Royal Albert Hall, London (with Gary Clark, Jr.)

SETLIST: Hello Old Friend / My Father's Eyes / Tell The Truth / Gotta Get Over / Black Cat Bone / Got To Get Better In A Little While / Come Rain Or Come Shine / I Shot The Sheriff / Drifting Blues / Further On Down The Road / Layla / It Ain't Easy / Wonderful Tonight / Blues Power / Love In Vain / Crossroads / Little Queen Of Spades / Cocaine / Sunshine Of Your Love[1] / High Time We Went[1]

[1]with Gary Clark, Jr. on guitar

24 May 2013, Royal Albert Hall, London (with Gary Clark, Jr.)

SETLIST: Hello Old Friend / My Father's Eyes / Tell The Truth / Gotta Get Over It / Black Cat Bone / Got To Get Better In A Little While / Come Rain Or Come Shine / Badge / Drifting Blues / Nobody Know You When You're Down And Out / It Ain't Easy / Layla / Tears In Heaven / Stones In My Passway / Wonderful Tonight / Blues Power / Love In Vain / Crossroads / Little Queen Of Spades / Cocaine / Sunshine Of You're Love[1] / High Time We Went[1]

[1]with Gary Clark, Jr. on guitar

26 May 2013, Royal Albert Hall, London (with Gary Clark, Jr.)

SETLIST: Hello Old Friend / My Father's Eyes / Tell The Truth / Gotta Get Over / Black Cat Bone / Got To Get Better In A Little While / Come Rain Or Come Shine / I Shot The Sheriff / Drifting Blues / Nobody Knows You When You're Down And Out / It Ain't Easy / Layla / Tears In Heaven / Lay Down Sally / Wonderful Tonight / Blues Power / Love In Vain / Crossroads / Little Queen Of Spades / Cocaine / Sunshine Of Your Love[1] / High Time We Went[1]

[1]with Gary Clark, Jr. on guitar

OLD SOCK EUROPEAN TOUR 2013

29 May 2013, Festhalle, Frankfurt, Germany (with Andy Fairweather Low and the Low Riders)

SETLIST: Hello Old Friend / My Father's Eyes / Tell The Truth / Gotta Get Over / Black Cat Bone / Got To Get Better In A Little While / Come Rain Or Come Shine / Badge / Driftin g Blues / Nobody Knows You When You're Down And Out / It Ain't Easy / Layla / Wonderful Tonight / Blues Power / Love In Vain / Crossroads / Little Queen Of Spades / Cocaine / Sunshine Of Your Love[1] / High Time We Went[1]

[1]with Andy Fairweather Low on guitar

30 May 2013, O2 World, Berlin, Germany (with Andy Fairweather Low and the Low Riders)

SETLIST: Hello Old Friend / My Father's Eyes / Tell The Truth / Gotta Get Over / Black Cat Bone / Got To Get Better In A Little While / Come Rain Or Come Shine / Badge / Drifting Blues / Goodnight Irene / Layla / It Ain't Easy / Tears In Heaven / Blues Power / Love In Vain / Crossroads / Little Queen Of Spades / Cocaine / Sunshine Of Your Love / High Time We Went[1]

[1]with Kurt Rosenwinkel on second lead guitar

Advert for 2013 UK Tour.

JUNE 2013

1 June 2013, 02 World, Hamburg, Germany (with Andy Fairweather Low and the Low Riders)

SETLIST: Hello Old Friend / My Father's Eyes / Tell The Truth / Gotta Get Over / Black Cat Bone / Got To Get Better In A Little While / Come Rain Or Come Shine / Badge / Drifting Blues / Layla / It Ain't Easy / Nobody Knows You When You're Down And Out / Tears In Heaven / Blues Power / Love In Vain / Crossroads / Little

Queen Of Spades / Cocaine / Sunshine Of Your Love[1] / High Time We Went[1]

[1]with Andy Fairweather Low on guitar

2 June 2013, Leipzig Arena, Leipzig, Germany (with Andy Fairweather Low and the Low Riders)

SETLIST: Hello Old Friend / My Father's Eyes / Tell The Truth / Gotta Get Over / Black Cat Bone / Got To Get Better In A Little While / Come Rain Or Come Shine / I Shot The Sheriff / Drifting Blues / Tears In Heaven / Layla / It Ain't Easy / Wonderful Tonight / Blues Power / Love In Vain / Crossroads / Little Queen Of Spades / Cocaine / Sunshine Of Your Love[1] / High Time We Went[1]

[1]with Andy Fairweather Low on guitar

4 June 2013, Zalgirlo Arena, Kaunas, Lithuania (with Andy Fairweather Low and the Low Riders)

SETLIST: Hello Old Friend / My Father's Eyes / Tell The Truth / Gotta Get Over / Black Cat Bone / Got To Get Better In A Little While / Come Rain Or Come Shine / Badge / Drifting Blues / Tears In Heaven / Layla / It Ain't Easy / Wonderful Tonight / Blues Power / Love In Vain / Crossroads / Little Queen Of Spades / Cocaine / Sunshine Of Your Love / High Time We Went

5 June 2013, Riga Arena, Riga, Latvia (with Andy Fairweather Low and the Low Riders)

SETLIST: Hello Old Friend / My Father's Eyes / Tell The Truth / Gotta Get Over / Black Cat Bone / Got To Get Better In A Little While / Come Rain Or Come Shine / I Shot The Sheriff / Drifting Blues / Tears In Heaven / Layla / It Ain't Easy / Nobody Knows You When You're Down And Out / Blues Power / Love In Vain / Crossroads / Little Queen Of Spades / Cocaine / Sunshine Of Your Love[1] / High Time We Went[1]

[1]with Andy Fairweather Low on guitar

7 June 2013, Atlas Arena, Lodz, Poland (with Andy Fairweather Low and the Low Riders)

SETLIST: Hello Old Friend / My Father's Eyes / Tell The Truth / Gotta Get Over / Black Cat Bone / Got To Get Better In A Little While / Come Rain Or Come Shine / Badge / Drifting Blues / Layla / It Ain't Easy / Wonderful

Tonight / Lay Down Sally / Blues Power / Love In Vain / Crossroads / Little Queen Of Spades / Cocaine / Sunshine Of Your Love[1] / High Time We Went[1]

[1]with Andy Fairweather Low on guitar

9 June 2013, Olympiahalle, Munich, Germany (with Andy Fairweather Low and the Low Riders)

SETLIST: Hello Old Friend / My Father's Eyes / Tell The Truth / Gotta Get Over / Black Cat Bone / Got To Get Better In A Little While / Come Rain Or Come Shine / I Shot The Sheriff / Drifting Blues / Layla / It Ain't Easy / Nobody Knows You When You're Down And Out / Tears In Heaven / Blues Power / Love In Vain / Crossroads / Little Queen Of Spades / Cocaine / Sunshine Of Your Love[1] / High Time We Went[1]

[1]with Andy Fairweather Low on guitar

11 June 2013, Stadthalle, Vienna, Austria (with Andy Fairweather Low and the Low Riders)

Canceled. The official statement: "Unfortunately Eric Clapton has had to cancel his concerts in Vienna, Austria, and Stuttgart, Germany, on his current tour due to severe back pain. He is currently with specialists who will be able to better determine the course of treatment. He was looking forward to these concerts and regrets that he is not to be able to perform for the fans. He would like to apologize for any inconveniences these cancellations may cause and would like to thank the fans for their understanding. All tickets can be returned to the Box Offices for refund."

12 June 2013, Schleyerhalle, Stuttgart, Germany (with Andy Fairweather Low and the Low Riders)

Canceled.

14 June 2013, Koenig-Pilsener Arena, Oberhausen, Germany (with Andy Fairweather Low and the Low Riders)

SETLIST: Hello Old Friend / My Father's Eyes / Tell The Truth / Gotta Get Over / Black Cat Bone / Got To Get Better In A Little While / Come Rain Or Come Shine / Badge / Drifting Blues / Layla / It Ain't Easy / Nobody Knows You When You're Down And Out / Wonderful Tonight / Blues Power / Love In Vain / Crossroads / Little Queen Of Spades / Cocaine / Sunshine Of Your Love / High Time We Went

15 June 2013, Lanxess Arena, Cologne, Germany (with Andy Fairweather Low and the Low Riders)

SETLIST: Hello Old Friend / My Father's Eyes / Tell The Truth / Gotta Get Over / Black Cat Bone / Got To Get Better In A Little While / Come Rain Or Come Shine / I Shot The Sheriff / Drifting Blues / Layla / It Ain't Easy / Wonderful Tonight / Lay Down Sally / Blues Power / Love In Vain / Crossroads / Little Queen Of Spades / Cocaine / Sunshine Of Your Love / High Time We Went[1]

[1]with Andy Fairweather Low on guitar

18 June 2013, Arena Nuernberger Versicherung, Nuernberg, Germany (with Andy Fairweather Low and the Low Riders)

SETLIST: Hello Old Friend / My Father's Eyes / Tell The Truth / Gotta Get Over / Black Cat Bone / Got To Get Better In A Little While / Come Rain Or Come Shine / Badge / Drifting Blues / Layla / It Ain't Easy / Nobody Knows You When You're Down And Out / Tears In Heaven / Blues Power / Love In Vain / Crossroads / Little Queen Of Spades / Cocaine / Sunshine Of Your Love / High Time We Went[1]

[1]with Andy Fairweather Low on guitar

19 June 2013, O2 Arena, Prague, Czech Republic (with Andy Fairweather Low and the Low Riders)

SETLIST: Hello Old Friend / My Father's Eyes / Tell The Truth / Gotta Get Over / Black Cat Bone / Got To Get Better In A Little While / Come Rain Or Come Shine / I Shot The Sheriff / Drifting Blues / Layla / It Ain't Easy / Nobody Knows You When You're Down And Out / Wonderful Tonight / Blues Power / Love In Vain / Crossroads / Little Queen Of Spades / Cocaine / Sunshine Of Your Love / High Time We Went[1]

[1]with Andy Fairweather Low on guitar

Everyone in the band help Eric try and find his car keys for a quick getaway from the Royal Albert Hall, May 2013.

Eric Clapton at Hammersmith Odeon, pg. 9, Mark Knopfler and Eric Clapton, pg. 70, Eric Clapton and Elton John, pg. 85, Eric Clapton at Orchestra Nights, pg. 131, Eric Clapton at Brighton Centre, pg. 140, Eric Clapton at Royal Albert Hall, pg. 154, Eric Clapton in Birmingham, pg. 158: John Peck. Prince's Trust concert at Royal Albert Hall, pg. 15, Eric Clapton in Stockholm, pg. 25, Eric Clapton and Roger Waters, pg. 26, Eric Clapton and Lionel Richie, pg. 74, Eric Clapton and Tina Turner, pg. 76, George Harrison and Eric Clapton, pg. 225: Richard Young/Rex Features. Jimmy Page, Eric Clapton, and Jeff Beck, pg. 17, Jimmy Page, Eric Clapton, and Jeff Beck, pg. 18: Roger Ressmeyer/Corbis. Eric Clapton on Roland G-505, pg. 39, Eric Clapton and Chuck Berry, pg. 59: C Corbis. Eric Clapton and Lionel Richie, pg. 51: Joe Hadlock. Mick Jagger, Keith Richards, and Eric Clapton, pg. 54, Eric Clapton in Antibes, pg. 57, Eric Clapton at Dingwalls, pg. 78: Simon Bell. Eric Clapton and Buddy Guy, pg. 73: Linda Matlow/Rex Features. Jack Bruce and Eric Clapton, pg. 77, Elton John, Eric Clapton, and Phil Palmer, pg. 118, Paul McCartney, Sting, Mark Knopfler, and Eric Clapton, pg. 201: Rex Features. Buddy Guy and Eric Clapton, pg. 77, Phil Collins, Mark Rutherford, and Eric Clapton, pg. 87, Eric Clapton at Royal Albert Hall, pg. 98 (4 images), Mark Knopfler, pg. 99, Eric Clapton and Band Du Lac, pg. 101: Mark Roberty. Mark Knopfler and Eric Clapton, pg. 84: Neal Preston/Corbis. Event for Celia Hammond, pg. 91 (2 images): Linda Vollmer. Eric Clapton at Royal Albert Hall, pg. 155, Eric Clapton with Dobro, pg. 164, Eric Clapton at Royal Albert Hall, pg. 245 (top), Cream at Royal Albert Hall, pg. 304, Eric Clapton at Hard Rock Calling, pg. 347, Steve Winwood and Eric Clapton, pg. 372 (top), Eric Clapton and Keith Richards, pg. 398, Eric Clapton, Ronnie Wood, and Keith Richards, pg. 399, Chuck Leavell, Eric Clapton, and Mick Jagger, pg. 399: Brian Rasic/Rex Features. Eric Clapton with Gibson L5, pg. 176, Eric Clapton and band at Nynex Centre, pg. 189, Jerry Portnoy and Eric Clapton, pg. 190, Eric Clapton at Royal Albert Hall, pg. 245, Eric Clapton at Royal Albert Hall, pg. 272, B.B. King and Eric Clapton, pg. 273, Eric Clapton and John Mayall, pg. 273, Eric Clapton at Civic Hall, pg. 281, Doyle Bramhall II, pg. 287, Eric Clapton on custom Strat, pg. 287, Cream at Royal Albert Hall, pg. 305, Band Du Lac, pg. 314, Eric Clapton at Highclere Castle, pg. 315, Eric Clapton at Hampton Court, pg. 317, band in final bow, pg. 326, Derek Trucks and Eric Clapton, pg. 327, Steve Winwood and Eric Clapton, pg. 372 (bottom): Paul Cook. Joe Cocker and Eric Clapton, pg. 158: Isopress Senepart/Rex Features. B.B. King and Eric Clapton, pg. 273, Eric Clapton and John Mayer, pg. 335, Crossroads Festival finale, pg. 336: Startracks Photo/Rex Features. Eric Clapton on wah wah, pg. 286, Eric Clapton and Zucchero Fornaciari, pg. 287, Eric Clapton with band, pg. 287, Eric Clapton at Royal Albert Hall, pg. 288, Eric Clapton and Doyle Bramhall II, pg. 288, Ginger Baker and Eric Clapton, pg. 304, Eric Clapton and Ginger Baker, pg. 305, Eric Clapton at Wintershall, pg. 306, Mark Rutherford, Roger Waters, and Eric Clapton, pg. 315, Eric Clapton at Royal Albert Hall, pg. 316, Eric Clapton and band at Osaka-Jo Hall, pg. 324, Eric Clapton in Nagoya, pg. 324, Eric Clapton at Budokan, pg. 326, Eric Clapton at Highclere Castle, pg. 335, Steve Winwood and Eric Clapton, pg. 335, Eric Clapton embraces Steve Winwood, pg. 335: Chikahiko Inden. Eric Clapton in Modena, pg. 193, Eric Clapton and Luciano Pavarotti, pg. 193, Eric Clapton on UK Pilgrim Tour, pg. 217: Ilpo Musto/Rex Features. Eric Clapton and Sheryl Crow, pg. 228: Mike Segar C Reuters/Corbis. Eric Clapton at Tsunami Relief benefit, pg. 302: Huw John/Rex Features. Eric Clapton recording Back Home, pg. 310: Gemma Booth/Corbis Outline. Eric Clapton and Robbie Robertson, pg. 336: Alexandra Buxbaum/Rex Features. Eric Clapton and Sheryl Crow, pg. 343: C Gary Coronado/Palm Beach Post/ZUMA Press. Ian Thomas and Eric Clapton, pg. 344: C Mark Dye/Star Ledger/Corbis. Eric Clapton at Palm Beach Studios, pg. 351: Gustavo Celis. Eric Clapton and band in New Zealand, pg. 355: David Rowland/Rex Features. Eric Clapton at Royal Albert Hall, pg.